Brazilian History

Brazilian History:

Culture, Society, Politics 1500-2010

By

Roberto Pinheiro Machado

**Cambridge
Scholars**
Publishing

Brazilian History: Culture, Society, Politics 1500-2010

By Roberto Pinheiro Machado

This book first published 2018

Cambridge Scholars Publishing

Lady Stephenson Library, Newcastle upon Tyne, NE6 2PA, UK

British Library Cataloguing in Publication Data
A catalogue record for this book is available from the British Library

Copyright © 2018 by Roberto Pinheiro Machado

All rights for this book reserved. No part of this book may be reproduced, stored in a retrieval system, or transmitted, in any form or by any means, electronic, mechanical, photocopying, recording or otherwise, without the prior permission of the copyright owner.

ISBN (10): 1-5275-0349-6
ISBN (13): 978-1-5275-0349-6

To Cláudia Mendonça Scheeren

Contents

Introduction 1

Chapter One 9
The Colonial Period (1500–1822)
    1.1 From the Discovery to the Colonization
    1.2 The French Invasions (1555–1560 and 1594–1615)
    1.3 The Dutch Invasions (1624–1625 and 1630–1654)
    1.4 The Iberian Union and the Portuguese Territorial Expansion
    1.5 The Discovery of Gold and the Minas Gerais
    1.6 The Conspiracy of Minas Gerais and Brazilian Neoclassicism
    1.7 The Conspiracy of Bahia and the Emergence of the Notion of Citizenship
    1.8 A European Monarchy in the Tropics and the End of Colonial Rule

Chapter Two 49
The Brazilian Empire (1822–1889)
    2.1 The Costly Independence
    2.2 The First Empire (1822–1831)
    2.3 The Regency (1831–1840)
    2.4 The Second Empire (1840–1889)
    2.5 Culture and Society in the Brazilian Empire

Chapter Three 111
The First Republic (1889–1930)
    3.1 The Initial Instability (1889–1894)
    3.2 Prudente de Morais (1894–1898)
    3.3 Campos Sales (1898–1902)
    3.4 Rodrigues Alves (1902–1906)
    3.5 Afonso Pena (1906–1909)
    3.6 Hermes da Fonseca (1910–1914)
    3.7 Venceslau Brás (1914–1918)
    3.8 Epitácio Pessoa (1918–1922)
    3.9 Artur Bernardes (1922–1926)
    3.10 Washington Luís (1926–1930)
    3.11 Culture and Society in the First Brazilian Republic

Chapter Four 186
Getúlio Vargas and the Estado Novo (1930–1945)
    4.1 The Rise of Getúlio Vargas and the 1930 Revolution
    4.2 The Provisory Government (1930–1934)
    4.3 The Constitutional Period (1934–1937)
    4.4 The Estado Novo (1937–1945)
    4.5 Culture and Society in the First Vargas Government

Chapter Five 229
The Liberal Republic (1946–1964)
    5.1 Eurico Gaspar Dutra and Economic Liberalism (1946–1951)
    5.2 The Second Vargas Government and Nationalism (1951–1954)
    5.3 Café Filho and the Return of Liberalism (1954–1955)
    5.4 Juscelino Kubitschek and Liberal Development (1956–1961)
    5.5 Jânio Quadros and High Populism (January–August 1961)
    5.6 João Goulart: Parliamentarism and the Left (1961–1964)
    5.7 Culture and Society in the Liberal Republic

Chapter Six 295
The Military Dictatorship (1964–1985)
    6.1 Marshal Castelo Branco and the PAEG (1964–1967)
    6.2 Marshal Artur da Costa e Silva and the Hardline (1967–1969)
    6.3 General Emílio Garrastazu Médici and the *Brasil Potência* (1969–1974)
    6.4 General Ernesto Geisel and the Castelista Group (1974–1979)
    6.5 General João Figueiredo and the End of Military Rule (1979–1985)
    6.6 Culture and Society in the Dictatorial Period

Chapter Seven 365
The New Republic (1985–2010)
    7.1 José Sarney and the Cruzado Economic Plan (1985–1990)
    7.2 Fernando Collor de Mello and the Impeachment (1990–1992)
    7.3 Itamar Franco and the Plano Real (1992–1994)
    7.4 Fernando Henrique Cardoso and the New Price Stability (1995–2002)
    7.5 Luiz Inácio Lula da Silva: Finally the Left (2003–2010)
    7.6 Culture and Society in the New Republic

Conclusion 418
Brazil after 2010

Notes 429

Index 468

INTRODUCTION

Brazil is the largest nation in Latin America and the fifth largest in the world. It occupies 3,265,059 square miles in an area extending from about 120 miles above the Equator to approximately 700 miles below the Tropic of Capricorn. The country's northernmost point is found in the city of Uiramutã, in Roraima State, and the southernmost in that of Chuí, in Rio Grande do Sul State. Despite the long distance extending between these points, the country is larger from East to West than it is from North to South. The precise distances are 2,689 miles East–West and 2,684 miles North–South. Brazil's large territory is a legacy from the Portuguese colonial system. Throughout several centuries of colonial rule, Portuguese officials controlled the land with a tight grip in order to keep the colonial revenue flowing into Lisbon. The exploitative nature of the colony worked to preserve its political unity, creating a strong centralized administration that was kept in place even after the end of Portuguese rule. Until 1808, it was primarily a closed territory, with commercial lines limited to those established by the Portuguese administration. Prior to its independence in 1822, all those living in Brazil were either Portuguese, African, or South American aboriginal.

This book provides an introduction to Brazilian history. Its approach is critical and interdisciplinary. Analyses of several aspects of the country's development, such as the economy, the arts, foreign policy, and society appear intermingled in each chapter. The presentation is organized chronologically around the nation's political history, following the successive governments that controlled each of the three major historical periods: the Colony (1500–1822), the Empire (1822–1889), and the Republic (1889–present). The political-chronological presentation follows the most common pattern found in Brazilian books of similar scope, offering thus a perspective akin to that employed by Brazilians in learning their own history. The choice of format aims to facilitate the use of this book as a reference for further research, providing a sequential storyline from which data can be selected, analyzed, and further developed from a clear temporal perspective.

The chronological account is divided into seven chapters that emerge as subdivisions of the three major periods mentioned above. Chapter one examines the Colonial Period, which extends from the arrival of the

Portuguese in South America in the year 1500 until the Brazilian proclamation of independence in 1822. The Colonial Period comprises a long historical phase in which an exploitation colony was gradually established in the newly discovered territory as the result of a capitalist enterprise commanded by the Portuguese Crown. The new land would experience several transformations throughout these three hundred years of fierce Portuguese rule. It would face several foreign invasions, which would alter the territory's material and cultural landscape; it would suffer the effects of the various wars between Portugal and Spain in Europe; and it would finally fall prey to the effects of the Napoleonic Wars, which would cause the transfer of the Portuguese court from Lisbon to Rio de Janeiro, thus creating a new aristocratic society in the tropical territory. This first chapter also discusses how an incipient sentiment of national belonging gradually emerged in the colony, aiding the Portuguese in maintaining their control over that vast territory, which from the beginning was fiercely disputed with other European nations also interested in taking hold of its profitable, fertile land.

Chapter two describes the period of what is called the Brazilian Empire. It begins with the events of 1822, when Brazil became independent from Portugal, and ends in 1889, when a republic was proclaimed. As the chapter unfolds, we will see that Brazilian independence did not ensue from an all-encompassing revolutionary rupture with Portugal. Although clashes between Brazilian and Portuguese troops did occur in specific areas, the transition to autonomy resulted primarily from an agreement between the two contending parties. This allowed for the continuation of several colonial institutions into the newly emerging nation. Such institutional endurance strengthened the grip on power of the same ruling class that had controlled the colony under the Portuguese administration: in spite of becoming free from the direct rule of the Portuguese king, a Portuguese prince took power.

The rule of Pedro I, the heir apparent to the Braganza dynasty, established a monarchical continuity that linked Europe and America politically. This, as the chapter will show, provoked considerable suspicion from Brazil's neighbors. While the former Spanish colonies severed their ties with monarchical Europe more thoroughly, adopting republican systems almost immediately, Brazil remained connected to the European monarchies by ties of blood, that is, by those existing between its Braganza ruler and his European family. The presence of a European monarch ruling a large portion of South America thus became a source of fear among Spanish Americans, who suspected that Brazil might serve as a transatlantic bridge for European imperialism and for the recolonization of South America immediately after the end of Spanish rule. Besides the contradictions and disputes between Brazil and its neighbors, the chapter will also discuss how, during this period, the new country's ruling class worked to forge a Brazilian nationality, that is, a general sense of national belonging and of a distinctive national culture. Towards the end of the chapter, we will observe the economic and social factors that led to the Empire's demise. We will see that the country's ruling class, which supported the maintenance of the monarchical system throughout the period, was comprised of a landed aristocracy based on slave labor and on a fierce patriarchal mentality. When slave labor crumbled, so crumbled the monarchy. The way was then open for a new historical period, the First Republic.

Chapter three narrates the events that marked the first Brazilian republican experience. From 1889 to 1930, the country adopted a republican presidential system that was sustained through the offices of ten presidents. The fall of the monarchy had resulted in part from political and ideological disputes between those who, on one side, argued for administrative centralization as the ideal formula for the nation's governance and those who, on the other, defended decentralization and provincial autonomy as a necessity for the maintenance of the nation. The provinces demanded more political and economic freedom than they had theretofore been granted under the monarchic system, which tended to centralize authority in Rio de Janeiro. As the provincial landlords achieved their goal of greater autonomy, the Republic was established in the American federalist model, with presidents being elected every four years. As the chapter will demonstrate, elections, however, were seldom fair, and the rise of a president was primarily a matter of pre-established political arrangements between members of the ruling classes, rather than a result of democratic electoral competition. The republican system was kept on course through the maintenance of a series of economic and political pacts between the central government and the provincial administrations, an arrangement known as the Oligarchical Pact. The arrangement worked well while the country managed to sustain the handsome revenue generated from its foremost export product, coffee. The apparent political stability would come to an end, however, when the world crisis of 1929 prevented coffee returns from satisfying the demands of both the central government and the provincial landlords. The collapse of the American economy in 1929 had profound effects on the Brazilian Republic: as the United States was Brazil's foremost coffee client, and given the monolithic nature of the Brazilian economy, U.S. economic retraction provoked a severe financial crisis in the Latin American country, giving rise to a political revolution. The ensuing civil war, as we shall see, provoked the end of the period known as the First Republic.

Chapter four examines the revolutionary undertaking that caused the First Republic's demise and proceeds to discuss the main characteristics of the dictatorial period that ensued. It covers the years from 1930 to 1945, with special attention on the rise of nationalism and state-led developmental policies after 1937. As we shall see, this will be a time when the contenders for administrative centralization will win the long-standing struggle for power between the provinces and the central government. We will note that this struggle had assumed clear regional contours during the former period, the First Republic, when the oligarchy ruling the southern province of Rio Grande do Sul became the main proponent of political centralization, vying against the rulers of São Paulo, who profited from the economic freedom allowed by the decentralized federative system. As the chapter will show, the revolution which started in 1930 represented the victory of the southern landlords, who possessed superior military power in relation to the northern provinces. The South's military clout resulted from the historical militarization of the southernmost state, Rio Grande do Sul, which had for centuries been the theater of fierce territorial disputes between Portugal and Spain. The chapter will discuss the fact that Brazil's southern frontiers are the only ones in the nation to have been settled by means of war, a condition that in turn reflects the pugnacious character of the southern landowners who, in 1930, assumed control of the nation. The chapter will also discuss how the political history of Brazil in the twentieth century is in great part the history of the clash between Rio Grande do Sul's military power and São Paulo's economic might. The chapter will end with a depiction of Rio Grande do Sul's dictatorship over the entire nation in the context of anti-communism, nationalism, and the Second World War.

Chapter five starts at the end of the Second World War, when the fall of the dictatorship established in 1937 opened the way to a new period: the Liberal Democracy. The liberal-democratic period extends from 1946 to 1964. It begins with the rise of democracy in 1946 and ends with its fall less than twenty years later. We will see the emergence of a new era in Brazilian political and economic history, with presidential elections resuming after a twenty-year hiatus and with measures for economic liberalization being adopted according to the rules of the Bretton Woods Agreement, which was co-signed by Brazil in 1944. During the liberal-democratic period, Brazilians attempted to do away with the former nationalism of the previous era, and sought political rapprochement with both the United States and Western Europe. An attempt to open Brazil to the world economy was pursued through the adoption of bold political and economic measures aimed at attracting foreign investments to the country. This was a golden age of mounting economic prosperity and an increased belief in the nation's bright future: the time of the construction of the new capital, Brasilia; the rise of *bossa nova*, the new musical style born in the city of Rio de Janeiro; the building of roads, airports, and the implantation of a national automobile industry. The general popular expectation at the time was that Brazil would finally become a modern nation. The democratic and liberal economic endeavor, however, came to an end with a military *coup d'état* that threw the nation into a new period of extreme authoritarianism, ravaging political persecution, increased social inequality, mounting foreign debt, and a series of army generals, most of them from Rio Grande do Sul, succeeding one another in the presidency.

Chapter six narrates this new period of fierce authoritarianism: the Military Dictatorship (1964–1985). This was probably the darkest period in Brazilian history. Historians usually compare it, and mostly unfavorably, to the previous dictatorial experience in the country's republican history, the one that lasted from 1937 to 1945. We will see how the new military rulers managed to remain in power for more than 20 years by forging a series of tacit agreements with the ruling classes, as well as by imposing several forms of control over society. The chapter will show how the fiercely anti-communist dictators used political propaganda to boost Brazil's victory in the 1970 Soccer World Cup in Mexico while state agents committed human rights violations throughout the country in the name of freedom and social order. The chapter will show how an annual double-digit GDP growth rate was achieved by means of compressing salaries and imposing harsh labor conditions on the population; how attempts to colonize the Amazon forest with impoverished inhabitants from the Northeast ended in failure; how the international oil crisis of 1973 put an end to state-driven stellar economic growth; and how the period came to an end in 1985, when the country was on the verge of an economic collapse. Inflation, poverty, foreign debt, corruption, and violence were some of the results of this long period of military dictatorship.

Our seventh chapter covers the years from 1985 to 2010, which fall under what is called the New Republic. Also called the Sixth Republic, this is an extended period that comes up to the present. It starts with the end of the military dictatorship and with the rise of another era of popular high hopes and expectations regarding the country's future and its capacity to achieve economic well-being. We will see how such expectations were soon thwarted when it became clear that the severe financial crisis inherited from the military period would not end quickly. Starting in 1986, inflation became Brazilians' most feared enemy; and when the Brazilians gathered in a national popular effort to beat the wave of inflation, it just turned into hyperinflation. In 1992, a series of failed economic plans, corruption scandals, and the impeachment of a president made Brazilians question whether the dictatorship had not, after all, been a better political system. Disillusionment became the norm in Brazilian society at large. As the struggle against inflation continued, however, a series of well-planned economic measures achieved what everyone had already given up hoping for. In 1994, the rising inflation rates were finally subdued and the prospects of economic stability opened the way to a new period in which Brazilian rulers attempted to portray the country as an important member of the international community of nations. Foreign policy started being conducted almost directly by the president, and the search for international prestige became an integral part of state policy. The chapter will show how the attraction of foreign investment became a *sine qua non* for the maintenance of low inflation rates, which were in turn sustained through a fixed exchange rate directly dependent on a high level of foreign reserves. In spite of the low inflation, however, the economy failed to grow and the spread of bankruptcies throughout the country, together with high unemployment rates, caused significant popular discontent. In the first years of the twentieth-first century, the low inflation rates were no longer capable of satisfying popular wishes and expectations. Popular dissatisfaction opened the way to surprising political developments that resulted in the electoral victory of the left in the presidential elections of 2002, and the subsequent rise of a new government in 2003. The chapter will finish by relating the successes and shortcomings of the leftist government in office from 2003 to 2010.

This book will end with an analysis of some relevant aspects of Brazilian society after 2010. The aim is to offer a realistic portrayal of some of the major problems the country still faced after the first 510 years of its history. Widespread corruption, a deficient educational system, massive popular protests, general popular dissatisfaction, poverty, hunger, urban violence, and mounting political unrest form a sinister picture of Brazil after 2010.

Before we proceed to the story of the first European encounter with the Brazilian territory during the Age of Discovery, however, we should make one last remark regarding the structure of this book. Together with the presentation of Brazil's political history, the reader will find at the end of each chapter a subdivision dedicated to an analysis of the literature and art of the period. Brazil is a country that enjoys a unique cultural heritage, and the nation's artistic achievements have been informed by centuries of ethnic mixture. This mixture paved the way for the emergence of interesting forms of cultural syncretism and for a general openness to new ideas, trends, and styles. As Brazilian popular creativity and aesthetic sensibility went on to reflect the country's ethnic diversity, it produced expressions marked by a tendency toward the effacement of the frontiers between popular and classical art, and also favored the development of styles and forms that challenge European aesthetic and ideological dominance. In this sense, Brazilian artists produced works that tend to be almost naturally post-modern in disposition. Brazilian art's syncretic temperament, however, did not prevent it from being embedded with strong nationalist sentiments. Throughout the country's history, nationalism has been an ever-present feature of Brazilian artistic expression. As we will discuss in detail at the end of chapter three, the Brazilian avant-garde movement of the early twentieth century, called *Modernismo*, provides us with a case in point regarding nationalism in the arts. In contrast with the great majority of the international avant-garde movements that spread throughout the world in the first decades of the twentieth century, the Brazilian avant-garde did not adopt all the basic tenets of new European styles and programs, among which figure a tendency towards internationalism and universalism. Brazilian artists of the period attempted to create novelty in art through the discovery of a true national expression. Unlike the cases of Spanish-America, Eastern Europe, and Asia, no consistent Brazilian version of Futurism, Dadaism, or Surrealism is to be found in the country's twentieth-century movements of renovation in the arts. Instead, Brazilian artists promoted a strangely self-centered rupture with the traditional forms found in the previous Brazilian tradition, which they found too foreign and Europeanized. They thus went in search of an anti-European national aesthetic, which became their primary avant-garde intent in the 1920s. As this book will discuss in considerable detail, this would produce lasting effects in the country's artistic output. We will see that twentieth-century Brazilian music, literature, and cinema became marked by a strong nationalist aesthetic, which involved a very peculiar and original expression, but which also tended to come up short in terms of approaching more universalizing and internationally oriented themes through art.

 Finally, the author would like to state his hope that this book will be read as a general introduction to Brazilian society and culture. The narrative presented in the following pages is broad in temporal scope, and most of the events recounted could not be approached in sufficient depth. For this reason, the reader should approach the book as an entry into subjects and events that might then be considered for further study. The history of Brazil fully reflects the country's many complexities, contradictions, and idiosyncrasies. My hope is that the reader will enjoy exploring some of them in these pages.

Chapter One

The Colonial Period (1500–1822)

From the Discovery to the Colonization

Brazil's official history begins in the year 1500, when Portuguese nobleman and navigator Pedro Álvares Cabral (1467–1520) reached a tract of land in the West Atlantic that he initially thought was an island. The tract of land was immediately named *Ilha de Vera Cruz*, or True Cross Island. Several weeks went by before Cabral understood that what he had found was in fact not an island, but an entire continent. When he realized that the place where he had landed was not completely surrounded by water, Cabral quickly changed its name to *Terra de Santa Cruz*, or Land of the Holy Cross.

After disembarking on the luxuriant tropical shore, Cabral's first task was to make contact with the locals. Natives of fairly amiable disposition inhabited the areas surrounding the Portuguese landing. Some of them were taken onto the Portuguese fleet's main ship, where Cabral offered them gifts. These natives were members of the Tupiniquim, a large tribe of hunter-gatherers of which some 2,500 descendants survive today, inhabiting a reserved area demarcated by the Brazilian federal government in the southeast of the country, close to where this first encounter took place in 1500. This first exchange between the Portuguese and the natives in the new land forms one of the major symbolic events in Brazilian history, one that would assume considerable ideological importance in the future. The encounter is generally construed as the emblematic starting point of the nation, suggesting the idiosyncratic development of interracial exceptionality, as well as the intentional building of a multi-ethnic national identity. This first encounter would thus become a recurrent theme in the Brazilian imagination. A few centuries later, the word *tupiniquim* would enter the popular vocabulary and would start to be employed humorously, or more precisely self-mockingly, by Brazilians when they attempted to describe themselves in their most genuine characteristics. This witty use of the word would traverse several centuries of usage to be popularized by the early twentieth-century Brazilian avant-garde movement, when artists attempted to define the national identity as the product of a mixture of indigenous and European elements. The word *tupiniquim* would then come to mean anything originally Brazilian, that is, anything genuinely simple, endearingly naïve, somewhat unrefined, and above all blatantly funny.

Back in 1500, after that first contact was made, Cabral's next task was to take care of religious matters. Four days after his arrival on the South American coast, he ordered his crew to build an altar near the shore and the first Catholic mass celebrated on Brazilian soil took place on April 26, 1500. This religious service is also of great historical and symbolic significance. In its inclusiveness, the Mass engaged the indigenous population in a religious celebration that marked the beginning of a long process of acculturation conducted by the Catholic Church. The indigenous population inhabiting the tropics lived in communal semi-nomadic societies that were naturally integrated within the forested geography of the continent. In contrast with the Europeans, the natives wore no clothes and many tribes were characterized by matriarchal societal arrangements. So the Catholic Church immediately established a process of dressing the natives, attempting to bring them into the sphere of what the Christians conceived as "civilization."

This First Mass thus became the symbolical landmark of the acculturation process that was enacted throughout the construction of the Brazilian nation. It established a myth of peaceful integration and mutual acceptance between the Europeans and the American natives. In doing so, however, it helped mask the truly genocidal aspects of the European conquest of the territory. The mass itself, it should be noted, would feature as a major theme in the future history of Brazilian art and literature. The very celebratory scene would be immortalized 360 years later by one of Brazil's most prestigious nineteenth-century painters, Victor Meirelles (1832–1903). In the 1860s, during the Imperial Period, Meirelles would be officially employed by the monarchy to depict the great historical scenes that forged Brazilian nationality. His *The First Mass in Brazil* (1860) would become one of his most celebrated works.[1]

Together with Meirelles' painting, the First Mass also figures prominently in what is considered to be the foundational work of Brazilian literary history, namely the famous *Carta de Pero Vaz de Caminha*, an account written by one of Cabral's officials, Pero Vaz de Caminha (1450–1500), to the Portuguese king, Manuel I, reporting the discovery of the new land—or island, as it was initially believed. The account is dated May 1, 1500, and it describes the land's beauty in ornamented language. The elegant quality of Caminha's writing may justify the classification of his letter as a literary work of art. His account's inclusion in the Brazilian literary canon parallels that of the *Crónicas de Conquista* in Spanish America, where the reports and descriptions by the first Spaniards in the new world have pride of place in the Hispanic-American canon.[2] Caminha's enthusiastic description of the land's beauty would serve the purposes of those who in the future would attempt to build a sense of national unity and identity in the territory. The work's rendering of the new land as a magnificent and mythic island would also produce important effects in the future nation's foreign relations. Caminha's idealization of the "Brazilian Island" would have remarkable psychological influence on the Portuguese conquerors, and would thus indirectly boost what we will see as the unrelenting Portuguese obsession for territorial expansion, an expansion that would take place in contention with the neighboring Spanish settlers in the new world. In the centuries following the discovery of the land, the Portuguese rulers would make a series of attempts to delineate the colonial territory on the basis of what historians came to call the "Myth of the Brazilian Island," that is, the idea that the La Plata River, which crossed the southern part of the territory, had somewhere a meeting point with the Amazon River, which ran in the North. The imaginary meeting of the two rivers, much in accord with Caminha's initial account, supported the Portuguese belief that its colonial territory should contain all the land found encased by the two rivers, much as if the territory were in fact an island. If this were the case, however, the Portuguese territory would necessarily include a substantial portion of what is today Argentina. As we shall see, from the contradictions between the Portuguese myth of the Brazilian Island and the reality of the Spanish Viceroyalty of the River Plate, many a war would ensue.[3]

Cabral and his crew left the newly discovered land at the beginning of May 1500, a few days after the holding of the First Mass. Some thirty years would pass before the Portuguese reached a decision on what to do with their new possession. Around 1530, the Portuguese Crown started sending exploratory expeditions to America. These soon found a lucrative economic activity in which to engage in the new territory, namely the extraction of Brazilwood, a species that was abundant all along the coast as well as in part of the hinterland. The wood had significant economic interest in Europe, where it was valued for the red dye it produced and which was used in the manufacture of luxury textiles. The tree would thus give the future colony, as well as the future country, its name.

Intense felling and shipping ensued in the decades after the finding of Brazilwood. The Portuguese attempted to establish a monopoly on the commerce of the wood throughout the entire territory, which they now considered their own. The product's high profitability, however, soon encouraged other nations to enter the market, creating fierce competition. The first to vie for Brazilian natural resources were the French, whose fearsome corsairs conducted several attacks on Portuguese ships. the resulting disputes between the Portuguese and the French over the new land and its Brazilwood immediately escalated into something close to all-out war. The French king, Francis I (1494–1547), openly defied the Portuguese and the Spanish in their attempts to secure dominance over the South Atlantic region. The two Iberian nations had signed a controversial treaty in 1494, the famous Treaty of Tordesillas, by which all newly discovered lands in the new world would be divided between Portugal and Spain along a meridian that crossed the Cape Verde islands, a Portuguese territory, and the island of Cuba, which had been discovered by Christopher Columbus on his first voyage to the region and claimed for Spain. Learning of the exclusivist treaty between the Iberians, Francis I uttered the famous phrase: "Show me Adam's will!"

The Portuguese were thus obliged to arrange a military defense of what they considered to be their rightfully owned territory. During the first decades of the sixteenth century, the growing commerce of Brazilwood led the Portuguese to establish a series of trading posts along the coast. These included warehouses for the wood that was shipped to Europe, and functioned as operational bases for the capturing and enslavement of native inhabitants. The natives were employed directly in the extractive process, the communal experience of the First Mass having given way to the enslavement of the indigenous populations under the guise of capitalist enterprise.

Unlike the Portuguese, however, the French adopted a less violent strategy in their pursuit of Brazilwood. They established alliances with the native Brazilians, just as they would do with the native inhabitants of the northern hemisphere. These alliances strengthened the French conquerors to a point where, in 1528, the Portuguese chief commander for the region, Cristóvão Jacques (1480–c.1530), had to report to the Portuguese king the unfeasibility of defending such a large coast from the subjects of the French king, Francis I. Cristóvão Jacques then suggested a policy of colonization.

By the sixteenth century, the Portuguese had already established a functioning centralized bureaucratic state in Europe. Starting in the year 1385, when a succession dispute resulted in the overthrow of the House of Burgundy by the House of Aviz, the new ruling dynasty had begun to form a centralized bureaucracy that would be responsible for conducting the affairs of the state. Portugal had moved away from the typically decentralized feudal administrative arrangements of medieval Europe towards a centralized organization in which the ruling classes were directly employed under the king's orders. The nobility thus shared in the government's power and authority, transcending the limits of their individual estates or feuds. This form of political arrangement resulted in the emergence of an administrative structure known as the patrimonial state. The concept comes from German sociologist Max Weber (1864–1920), who described the patrimonial state as the expression of the amalgamation between the public and private realms in a given political entity. In the case of Portugal, the analysis of its emerging patrimonial arrangement, initiated in 1385, comes from Brazilian historian Raymundo Faoro (1925–2003), who argued that the structure of the Portuguese state since the Revolution of Aviz allowed the nobility employed in the governmental bureaucracy to merge its private interests with those of the kingdom. The merging of the personal and the public spheres allowed for the self-interested use of the state; soon the administrative structure, or the state itself, would become the bureaucrat's patrimony, whence the concept of *patrimonialism*.[4]

This was the administrative structure that would be transferred to the new American territory when the Portuguese king realized that his overseas possessions could not be defended without an active colonization policy. When encouraged by Cristóvão Jacques to start occupation, John III employed a scheme to maintain the Crown's ownership over the land while at the same time engaging private investments in it. The king divided the territory into fifteen hereditary captaincies, that is, administrative divisions that were entrusted to the management of men of confidence. The captaincies were awarded to businessmen by means of two specific legal instruments, the *Carta de doação* (Donation Letter) and the *Foral* (Register). These documents gave entrepreneurs the right to explore their allotted captaincy, but the ownership of the land remained with the Crown. Prospects of the existence of gold and silver in the American territory made the captaincy system especially attractive to Portuguese entrepreneurs, who started arriving in Brazil in 1530.[5]

The Portuguese had already employed the captaincy system in the colonization of the island of Madeira. Located in the Atlantic Ocean, around 540 miles southwest of the Portuguese coast, the island had been under Portuguese rule since 1425. A successful captaincy system had operated there since 1440. The remoteness and peculiarities of the Brazilian territory, however, sealed the fate of the captaincy arrangement in the Americas. Of the fifteen administrative units initially devised, only two, those of Pernambuco and São Vicente, prospered. Pernambuco, a captaincy located in the Northeast, thrived from the production of sugar cane and São Vicente, in the Southeast, prospered mostly from dealing in indigenous slaves. São Vicente would be established as one of the first urban administrative units, or villages, in 1532, during an expedition led by nobleman and military commander Martim Afonso de Sousa (1500–1571). King John III had sent de Souza to Brazil with orders to patrol the coast, get rid of the French, and found the first colonial settlement on the new land. São Vicente prospered to become what is today a portion of the metropolitan area of Santos, a major port city in the state of São Paulo.

In spite of its general failure, the captaincy system lasted for more than two centuries until it was finally abolished in 1754. The system left a lasting impression on the Brazilian territorial arrangement, becoming the basis for the country's future oligopolistic structure of land tenure and distribution. The captaincies allowed for the implementation of a policy of agricultural land partition called *sesmaria*, which was based on practices customary in Portugal. The Sesmaria Act of 1375 was promulgated in Lisbon to counter a food crisis that was plaguing the country at the time. The Act consisted of several dispositions designed to maintain agricultural output, such as the expropriation of unproductive land and the employment of forced labor in sowing and harvesting. When it came to the colonization of Brazil, however, the sesmaria was turned into a political instrument whereby the designated administrator of a captaincy transferred the right to cultivate land to private entrepreneurs. Under this disposition, land was distributed in the form of gigantic plots to only a few beneficiaries. In time, this situation gave rise to conflict, as large areas were left unproductive and subject to unlawful occupation. The system generated conditions of unfairness and miscommunication in rural areas. The sesmaria system survived until 1822, when the newly independent country, self-denominated as the Brazilian Empire, attempted a series of structural reforms. These notwithstanding, after the official termination of the system in 1822, the ownership of the traditional estates acquired under the legal provisions of the sesmaria was recognized by a law of 1850, meaning that in practice the old sesmaria arrangement would be sustained.[6]

In any case, at the time of the establishment of the captaincy system, the Portuguese king took measures to consolidate the general control of the colony in the hands of the state. This was done with considerable haste, following the sudden realization of the lack of economic dynamism in the captaincies. In 1549, John III sent another nobleman and military commander, a man called Tomé de Sousa (1503–1579), to Brazil with the task of establishing a centralized local government that would answer directly to Lisbon. From then on, the Portuguese bureaucratic state apparatus would be directly transplanted to the colony. The *Governo Geral* (General Government) was established at the entrance of a large inlet opening to the Atlantic Ocean some 300 miles north of where Pedro Álvares Cabral had first disembarked on the American continent in 1500. Called Baía de Todos os Santos (All Saints' Bay), the inlet's surrounding areas offered favorable agricultural conditions, with a hot climate and fertile soil. Its geography also facilitated territorial defense. The area had been made into a captaincy entrusted to nobleman Francisco Pereira Coutinho (d. 1547), from whose descendants the land had to be expropriated (Pereira died in 1547, eaten by the members of the Tupinambá tribe, a group of aboriginals who practiced cannibalism against their enemies). The Governor General was entrusted with the task of bringing political and judicial order to the colony. The bureaucratic structure then established comprised three instances of regulation and control that were run directly by Portuguese officials. These were the Ouvidor-mor, who managed the affairs of justice; the Provedor-mor, who conducted the economic affairs of the colony; and the Capitão-mor, who was in charge of defense. The office of General Governor was entrusted to Tomé de Sousa. The administrative unit called *Estado do Brasil* was thus officially created as a Portuguese colonial institution.

The implementation of a bureaucratic state apparatus in the colony meant above all the immediate transference of Portuguese political culture to the new territory. This culture was naturally aristocratic and highly hierarchical. In the absence of the usual feudal system where the aristocracy tended primarily to its agricultural estates, the Portuguese nobility developed distinctive urban habits, which seemed appropriate to their bureaucratic positions. Over time, they acquired a great distaste for any form of manual labor, which was generally considered demeaning to their status. This meant that the appropriate occupation for an aristocrat was primarily that of giving orders. Coupled with the tradition of a patrimonial state, where, as mentioned above, bureaucrats tended to misperceive the public sphere as their own private property, the aristocratic Portuguese political culture transplanted to the colony provided for the spread of fierce authoritarianism and individualism in the local administration. This was enhanced by a logic in which colonial bureaucrats, as the lawful representatives of a power whose center was located overseas, could assume a posture of factual ownership of their offices.

The Portuguese aristocratic bureaucracy would impose severe limitations on the political participation of the general colonial population in the administrative affairs of the settlements. As it developed into a number of evolving urban centers that gradually emerged throughout the territory, the colony's provincial administration would be carried out in city councils called *Câmaras dos homens bons*, or "City Councils of Good Men." The "good men" in question were those who by law were eligible to assume administrative positions in the government, namely Catholic white men over twenty-five years of age who could prove they owned a significant portion of land. Any Jewish ancestry was considered a just cause to prevent individuals to participate in governmental affairs. The first colonial city council was established in the village of São Vicente in 1532. From then on, those who did not own land, such as merchants and liberal professionals, would be prevented from taking part in politics. This would give rise to a series of civil conflicts, the most remarkable of which broke out in the state of Pernambuco in the early eighteenth century, when the traders of the city of Recife took up arms against the landowners of the village of Olinda in what came to be known as the War of the Mascates (1710). The war reflected an incipient native sentiment that pitted the Brazilians against the Portuguese in matters of colonial administration.[7]

The primary goals of Tomé de Sousa's first General Government in the 1550s were: 1) subduing rebellious indigenous tribes; 2) enhancing agricultural output; 3) defending the territory from foreign invasions; and 4) prospecting deposits of gold and silver in the land. The Portuguese official arrived in the colony with a group of Jesuit missionaries, who immediately went about converting the natives to Roman Catholicism. The Jesuit enterprise was enmeshed in the intellectual debate set in motion in Europe regarding what it meant to be human in a broader international context. This was a time of intense theoretical discussion among Christian theorists and theologians regarding the nature of the soul and its participation in the higher spheres of being. Thinkers such as the Spanish renaissance philosophers Francisco de Vitoria (1483–1546), Domingo de Soto (1494–1560), Francisco Suárez (1548–1617), Bartolomé de las Casas (1474–1566), and the Dutch humanists Erasmus of Rotterdam (1466–1536) and Hugo Grotius (1583–1645) were in the process of developing the principles of what today forms the historical-theoretical basis of international and human rights law. Francisco de Vitoria was especially interested in the moral and legal status of indigenous populations in the new world. In his *De Indis* (1532), the Spaniard, actually the leader of the so-called Salamanca school of philosophy, defended the existence of a soul in the American natives. Such an acknowledgment automatically conferred upon the indigenous individuals the status of creatures of God.

The Portuguese rulers accepted Francisco de Vitoria's ideas and in 1575 the Crown issued an edict prohibiting the enslavement of the indigenous inhabitants of the colony, except in the case of a 'just war,' that is, one started by the natives against the Portuguese. The Jesuits thus had legal support in their efforts to pacify hostile indigenous tribes and integrate them into the emerging colonial society. They would, however, find great opposition from several, very powerful, groups of entrepreneurs and explorers, who preferred to keep the natives as slaves. The most resilient of these groups was that of the *Bandeirantes*, men who lived off activities such as gold prospecting and trading in slaves. As we shall see in more detail in the next chapter, the Bandeirantes played an important role in advancing the Portuguese territorial expansion in America. Such advancement, however, took place primarily at the cost of disrupting the traditional forms of life previously established in the original colonial territory.

Aided by the Bandeirantes, the General Government established in 1549 would succeed in founding and sustaining Portuguese control over the vast territory discovered by Cabral in 1500. The administrative system of the General Government would only be abolished in 1808, when the Portuguese court was transferred from Lisbon to Rio de Janeiro as a result of the Napoleonic wars. From 1549 to 1808, sixty-one General Governors assumed the function of controlling the colony. Starting in 1640, after a period called the Iberian Union, when Portugal came virtually under Spanish rule, the General Governors would have their status raised to that of Viceroys, and their power would grow accordingly.

Before moving on to a discussion of the territorial invasions experienced during the first two centuries of Brazilian colonial history, we should note that Tomé de Sousa's first central government became the starting point for fierce metropolitan domination over the new land. The General Government itself functioned as a textbook application of mercantile capitalism, in which all riches found or produced in the colony were immediately embarked to Lisbon. Local reinvestment would be kept to a minimum; the new territory existed to be exploited and the General Government was created with the aim of maintaining the flow of capital to Portugal at all costs. Soon the fiscal burden would become unbearable for the local inhabitants, and important fiscal revolts would ensue. Before those took place, however, and in fact even before the Portuguese General Government had finally secured its grip on the colonial territory, one major obstacle had to be cleared away: the French.

The French Invasions (1555–1560 and 1594–1615)

In 1555, French commander, Nicolas Durand de Villegagnon (1510–1571) led an expedition sponsored by the French Crown to start a colonial enterprise in the tropics. Villegagnon chose one of the best spots on the South American coast to start his venture. The Guanabara Bay, the site of present-day Rio de Janeiro, was a stunning area with geographical features quite favorable for building a settlement. After crossing the Atlantic, the French fleet reached the calm and dark-blue waters that stretch from the Sugarloaf Mountain towards the hilly land bordering what today is the Botafogo beach. Villegagnon had in mind a well-devised plan: with the help of allies in the tribe of the Tamoios he would lure the Portuguese into an ambush near a small island just off the coast. The modest Portuguese defenses would be easy prey for the superior French naval forces.

Much to Villegagnon's disappointment, however, an unexpected explosion in one of the Portuguese defense ships, which would soon be ascribed to divine intervention, scared his men off, and the French fleet retreated. The initial ambush resulted in failure, but Villegagnon succeeded in maintaining control over the island where the French had been hiding to trap the Portuguese. As a result of the commander's obstinate intention to stay and fight the Portuguese, his island became the hub of what was named *La France Antarctique*, the first French colony in Brazil.[8]

This first French invasion of the Portuguese colonial territory echoed important developments taking place in Europe in the sixteenth century, most notably the Protestant Reforms. Villegagnon was a distinguished nobleman and knight of the Catholic Military Order of Malta who, during a previous secret expedition to the Brazilian coast in 1554, had learned of the fierce opposition the Portuguese were encountering from two powerful indigenous tribes, the Tamoios and the Tupinambás. Villegagnon then decided to employ all his political prestige to convince the Catholic king Henry II, Francis I's son, that Brazil would be the right place to build a French colony to which the Protestants could be invited to emigrate. The commander's claim was that, by setting the native inhabitants against the Portuguese, the French Crown would be able rescue the land from the Iberians and create a realm of religious freedom under French rule, thus earning an opportunity to cast aside the Protestants.

Besides this social and religious objective, Villegagnon's project also aimed at transforming the Portuguese colony into a powerful naval base from which the French Crown would control the world's main commercial routes to India. This was the heyday of state monopoly capitalism, an economic model that would not be challenged in the Atlantic until at least 1621, when Flemish Calvinists launched the private Dutch West India Company, which would be granted the monopoly over the slave trade and other commerce from the Dutch Crown. Villegagnon thus immediately started the construction of a fortification in the French controlled Serigipe Island, which he had occupied on November 10, 1555. Curiously, the island is known in Brazil today as *Ilha de Villegagnon* (Villegagnon Island), a name that is used in place of its original denomination given by the Portuguese settlers, that is, Ilha de Serigipe. Be that as it may, Fort Coligny, the French headquarters, soon towered over the area. The Fort was named in honor of one of Villegagnon's commanders, the French Huguenot Gaspard de Coligny (1519–1572). The French enterprise, however, soon began to fail. General discontent arose among Villegagnon's men and a mutiny occurred in 1556, caused by the insubordination of a few soldiers outraged at their leader's conservative rules determining that any man who took an indigenous woman should be obliged marry her.

The Portuguese would only defeat the French in 1560, when the third succeeding Portuguese General Governor, Mem de Sá (1500–1572), marched on Fort Coligny, conquering it in the absence of Villegagnon, who had returned to France. Even after that, however, the French were not willing to give up their South American colonial ambition. Together with their allies, the Tamoios, they reorganized their forces and, in 1565, Estácio de Sá (1520–1567), Mem de Sá's nephew, was obliged to establish a local settlement in the area with the aim of blocking the French. The settlement would become the present-day city of Rio de Janeiro. The French forces attacked Estácio de Sá's defense in 1567, provoking a confrontation known as the Uruçu-mirim battle. During the skirmishes, Estácio de Sá was wounded in the eye by a Tamoio spear and died a few days later. The French were finally defeated after this battle and their colony, the France Antarctique, foundered. Estácio de Sá would go down in Brazilian history as a national hero. Today various sites in Rio de Janeiro bear his name: a university, an avenue, and a samba school that parades every year in the city's carnival.

But the French were tenacious. Unsuccessful in the South, in 1594 they came back to the Portuguese colony and now invaded the North. This time their presence would last a little longer: the *France Équinoxiale* (Equinoctial France) was formally established in 1612 on the island of Upaon-Açu, a large landmass just off the coast of present-day Maranhão State. The French turned the Upaon-Açu island into a trading post and renamed it after their king, Louis XIII (1610–1643). The trading post grew into an urban settlement and its French name remained in place even after the French were defeated. Today the Upaon-Açu island, which harbors the capital city of the Brazilian state of Maranhão, is called São Luís, the Portuguese version of the French king's name.

The French came to control a considerable expanse of territory in the northern part of the colony during the years immediately following 1612, but were defeated again by the Portuguese in 1615. At that time, Portugal was under the rule of Philip III of Spain. The French defeat, however, did not result in the Portuguese achieving final and complete control over the land. Before colonial control could be decisively settled for the Portuguese, one more group of invaders had to be ousted: the Dutch.

The Dutch Invasions (1624–1625 and 1630–1654)

The Low Countries were under the rule of the Spanish Empire until 1581, when a war of independence broke out. Just one year before, in 1580, Portugal and Spain had come under a single ruler, the Habsburg Spanish king, Phillip II (1527–1598). The union of the Portuguese and the Spanish Crowns under a single king was the result of a dynastic crisis that had begun in 1578, when the young Portuguese ruler, Sebastian I (1554–1578), was killed fighting the Moors in the Battle of Alcácer Quibir, in present-day Morocco. With Portugal and Spain united, the Low Countries, in war with latter, turned against the former, vying for what were now Spain's colonial possessions. Among the Spanish territories in America, the Brazilian colony was of special interest, for, by then, it had become one of the world's largest producers of sugar cane. Cane cultivation had been brought to the colony together with the captaincy system, thriving, as we have seen, in the North, especially in the captaincy of Pernambuco.

So, once freed from Spanish rule, the Low Countries, or more properly the Dutch, began their own colonial enterprises in the Atlantic. The first Dutch invasion of the Iberian colonial territory occurred in 1624. The city of Salvador, then the seat of the General Government and the capital of the State of Brazil, was the chosen target for the Dutch West India Company's attack. The Company was a militarized private enterprise run by Dutch merchants. It had been granted a trade monopoly with the Caribbean, as well as control over the slave trade in the region, from the recently founded Republic of the Seven United Netherlands. The occupation of the city of Salvador lasted almost one year; the city was recaptured in 1625 by a combination of Portuguese and Spanish forces.

Unwilling to surrender, the Dutch continued their fierce opposition to the Spanish. In 1628, engaging in a juggling act of piracy and deception, they seized a Spanish silver convoy, taking possession of the precious metal. The newly seized financial resource provided the Dutch West India Company with enough funds for another South American attempt, in 1630. The cities to be targeted were the sugar cane-rich Recife and Olinda, two villages located in the captaincy of Pernambuco. After meeting with fierce resistance from the Portuguese, the Dutch finally managed to gain control of a considerable tract of land, which they named New Holland. The Dutch West India Company assigned control of the newly seized territory to Prince John Maurice of Nassau (1604–1679), who was appointed governor of the new Dutch colonial possession.

Brazilian history records Nassau as a prince who had a genuine liking for the country. The Prince appears to have been enthralled by the beauty of the tropical landscape and of its native dwellers. With the assistance of several renowned Dutch architects, he modeled the city of Recife on Amsterdam, adorning the urban landscape with splendid canals and public gardens. The city was renamed Mauritsstad, *Cidade Maurícia* in Portuguese, after the Prince. The name, however, was maintained only until 1654, when the Portuguese recaptured the city from the Dutch. By then, however, Nassau had long left the colony. He was dismissed in 1644 for spending too much of the Dutch West India Company's profits on the development of his colonial city's infrastructure.

The ousting of the Dutch figures prominently, and rather abstrusely, in the official history of Brazil. According to the national narrative, the Portuguese local landowners would have become dissatisfied with the new state of affairs after Nassau's dismissal, that is, with the new economic impositions issued from the Dutch West India Company, and organized a victorious revolt. This version, based on the idea of a local and heroic anti-Dutch rebellion, would be the one sanctioned by the independent Brazilian State in 1854, when the historian and nobleman Francisco Adolfo de Varnhagen (1816–1878) would publish his *História Geral do Brasil* (General History of Brazil). The work was commissioned by the Brazilian Historic and Geographic Institute (IHGB), a governmental foundation established in 1838 to promote the research and preservation of the national culture. Conceived along official lines devised to build the country's national identity, Varnhagen's work transformed the Battle of Guararapes (1649), the final skirmish that allegedly sealed the fate of the Dutch in the Brazilian territory, into a national founding myth. According to Varnhagen, the military union between three heroes, the black man Henrique Dias (d. 1662), the ethnically indigenous Filipe Camarão (1580–1648), and the white man André Vidal de Negreiros (1606–1680) in the battle secured the nation's victory over the invaders. Following this narrative, the coming together of the three races to fight a common enemy would give rise to the Brazilian myth of racial democracy, with the Battle of Guararapes appearing as the official starting point of Brazilian nationality. Together with the previously mentioned *The First Mass in Brazil* (1860), the battle's final combat scene would figure prominently in a series of heroic canvases from the above mentioned official painter of the Brazilian Empire, Victor Meirelles (1832–1903).

In his *História Geral do Brasil*, however, Varnhagen ingeniously overlooked the fact that the Dutch only surrendered in 1654, five years after the Battle of Guararapes. This supports the interpretation that the battle itself was not as decisive in the Portuguese recovery of the territory as Varnhagen attempted to demonstrate. The Brazilian historian also omitted the fact that, following the Dutch withdrawal, the Treaty of The Hague, signed in 1661, ordered the Portuguese Crown to pay an onerous sum in indemnities to the Dutch for their loss of the Brazilian colony. The sum was paid in gold and the truth is that, by 1654, the date of the Dutch retreat, the former citizens of the Low Countries were already producing sugar cane elsewhere. In other words, by 1654 the Brazilian colony had become economically irrelevant, if not actually onerous, to the Dutch. In any case, the concocted heroic Portuguese victory and subsequent recovery of the land provides a good example of what would be necessary for an independent Brazil to build a sense of nationality in the former Portuguese colony.[9]

The Dutch colonial experience in the Brazilian territory also suggests that the maintenance of that large expanse of land under Portuguese control was rooted more on the lack of economic interest in the colony from some countries than on Portuguese bravery alone. By the mid-seventeenth century, the Dutch, just as the English, were finding more profitable colonies elsewhere. Soon, the industrial revolution would lead these nations into a different sort of colonial enterprise, one that would require new markets for their manufactured goods. All the while, and in great contrast, Portugal, as we shall see in more detail below, would remain dependent on a colony that was not sufficiently interesting in economic terms to more advanced nations.

The Iberian Union and the Portuguese Territorial Expansion

The French and Dutch invasions occurred in great part during the period described above as the Iberian Union, which lasted from 1580 to 1640. During that time, the 1494 Treaty of Tordesillas, which had established an imaginary dividing line between Portuguese and Spanish possessions in

South America, became mostly inoperative, for now, united under a common ruling dynasty, the former fierce colonial division between the two nations had perforce to be relaxed. It was in this context that the Portuguese colonizers began to expand their settlements inland from the coast, crossing that imaginary line of 1494. In order to secure the Amazon region from the French, the Portuguese and the Spanish established a fortification, the Forte do Presépio, in 1616 at the mouth of the Amazon River. The fortification would become an urban settlement, giving birth to present-day Belém, the capital city of the state of Pará.[10]

While the city of Belém began to prosper in the North, in the South a series of expeditions, or *Bandeiras*, emerged as another factor promoting Portuguese territorial expansion. The Bandeiras were the missions organized by the aforementioned Bandeirantes with the aim of capturing slaves and prospecting for gold and silver in the hinterland. These expeditions were usually violent and involved the pillage of indigenous villages in the forests, with acts of rape, murder, and genocide becoming commonplace.

The intrepid and violent Bandeirantes gathered in the captaincy of São Vicente to start their expeditions into the wild western lands. Together they moved resolutely towards the Spanish territorial possessions. Extending their reach close to the border of what is today Paraguayan territory, the Bandeirantes became responsible for the actual colonization of the region of present-day São Paulo State. Over the centuries, they have come to be seen as a symbol of the economic leadership of that state, and today the *Rodovia dos Bandeirantes*, a large highway running inland from São Paulo's coastal area, stands as a monument to what local history construed as their colonial bravery.

Throughout the construction of the nation's history, the Bandeirantes' terrible deeds in the cause of Portuguese territorial expansion have been manipulated to represent the values of heroism and entrepreneurship. The most famous of the Bandeirantes explorers was a man named Domingos Jorge Velho (1641–1705), now recognized as the most aggressive and merciless of all slave traders and gold prospectors of old São Vicente. Velho's fame is due above all to his annihilation of the Quilombo dos Palmares, a community of runaway slaves built in the interior of the captaincy of Alagoas, in the Northeast, sometime around 1604. Palmares appears to have been home to as many as 15,000 inhabitants, with a political structure that many historians claim was similar to that of a republic.[11] Through the figure of its destroyer, Domingos Jorge Velho, the history of Palmares and of Brazilian slavery is intertwined with that of São Paulo and its Bandeirantes. Palmares was destroyed in 1694 at the hands of Jorge Velho after six Portuguese expeditions sent to the region between 1680 and 1686 had failed to dismantle the settlement. The Quilombo dos Palmares became a symbol of African Brazilian culture and its struggle for freedom; Domingos Jorge Velho and the Bandeirantes became a symbol of São Paulo and its (white) economic prowess. Brazilian historians today tend to accommodate the difference, rather than emphasize it.[12]

Back in the first and second centuries of Portuguese colonization, the Bandeiras were usually financed either by private entrepreneurs who wanted their runaway slaves recaptured, or organized by the Bandeirantes themselves, who promoted expeditions to search for gold and silver. In both cases, however, the Bandeiras would be encouraged by the colonial administration, which saw the expeditions' potential for advancing its desired territorial expansion. Although not a state-led enterprise, the Bandeiras thus served the Portuguese Crown's interests in America.

The Portuguese colonial administration's craving for land conquest and territorial expansion must be understood in terms of the political and economic restrictions suffered by Portugal in Europe at the time. Portugal was a very small country on the western fringe of Spanish territory. Hemmed in by the Atlantic Ocean to the West, and by powerful Spain to the North, East, and South, the country suffered from a territorial confinement that provoked in its ruling classes a constant fear of annexation and disintegration. The potential for territorial expansion provided by the South American colony appeared to the Portuguese as the solution to their most fundamental problem, namely lack of space. From the early eighteenth century onwards, Portugal progressively lost economic dynamism, becoming, as we will see in more detail below, a virtual satellite state of Great Britain. The Brazilian colony thus began to appear more and more as an essential source of income and as a guarantee of survival.

Starting in the decades immediately following the end of the Iberian Union in 1640, territorial expansion in the southern part of the colony became particularly important to the Portuguese colonizers. No longer under the rule of a single king, the Portuguese and the Spanish settlers in the new world now found themselves again on opposite sides of the rush for conquest. This opposition would provoke a series of bloody disputes between Portuguese and Spanish colononists that would proliferate throughout the following centuries. In 1680, in order to establish Portuguese possession over the southern part of the continent, the governor of the captaincy of Rio de Janeiro, Manuel Lobo (1635–1683), founded the Colônia do Santíssimo Sacramento, a small settlement built at the southernmost point of the colonial territory. The colony was built on the banks of the River Plate, right across from the city of Buenos Aires, which stood on the opposite bank. The Portuguese aim in establishing Colônia do Sacramento was not only to extend its possessions to the South, gaining lawful ownership over the land expanse that is the present-day Uruguay, but also to eventually acquire control over the flow of silver that was transported from the Spanish mines of Potosí, in Peru, to Europe along the River Plate.

Outraged by such an overt threat, the Spanish settlers of Buenos Aires attacked the Sacramento Colony in 1681, starting a series of gruesome battles that would continue and multiply for the next two hundred years, turning the southern part of the South American continent into what was probably one of the most violent areas of the new world. From 1680 to 1828, the Sacramento Colony would change hands between the Spanish and the Portuguese as many as eleven times before the independent Republic of Uruguay was established in the region as a means of settling the furious disputes between the contending Iberians. As we shall see in more detail in the next chapter, the extended conflict in this southern portion of the Portuguese colony would forge a local culture of violence and disagreement, which emerges as one of the possible causes of the various civil wars in the region during the nineteenth and twentieth centuries.

A chronological list of the historical carnage in the area, which corresponds roughly to the territory of present-day Rio Grande do Sul State, starts with the bloody disputes over the Sacramento Colony initiated in 1681 and follows with the Spanish linked invasions and conquest of the southern Portuguese territory in 1703, 1714, and 1735; the Guarani War, which began in 1752, lasted four years and resulted in the virtual extermination of the indigenous population of the region; the new Spanish invasion of 1777, which reached the island of Desterro, the present-day city of Florianópolis, with accompanying violence, rape, and murder; the Portuguese invasions of Montevideo in 1811 and 1817, which lead to the annexation of the territory of present-day Uruguay by the Portuguese Crown; the Cisplatine War of 1825–28, which saw severe bloodshed between Brazilians and Argentines, resulting in the establishment of Uruguay as an independent country; the Farroupilha Revolution of 1835–45, which started seven years after the Cisplatine War and lasted other ten years with the unrealistic aim of establishing an independent republic in the state of Rio Grande do Sul; the Paraguayan War of 1864–70, which started nine years after the end of the Farroupilha Revolution when Paraguayan dictator Francisco Solano López (1827–1870) invaded Rio Grande do Sul State and ended up provoking the virtual extermination of the entire Paraguayan male adult population; the Federalist Riograndense Revolution of 1893, also known as the *Revolução das Degolas* (Revolution of Beheadings), where unrestrained savagery led the contenders to kill their rivals in the same way that they sacrificed sheep, that is, by cutting their throat from ear to ear; the Libertadora Revolution of 1923, caused by internal political disputes in the state of Rio Grande Sul; and the 1930 Revolution, which was somewhat less violent but which led to a fierce fifteen-year dictatorship by a Rio Grande do Sul landlord, Getúlio Dornelles Vargas (1882–1954).

These conflicts can be regarded as upshots of the Portuguese territorial expansion in the southernmost portion of its American colony. There, the proximity to Spanish forces required enhanced warfare capability, translating territorial expansion into fierce regional militarization. As we shall see, this militarization would result in a surplus of fighting power emerging in the southernmost Brazilian province, a situation that in the future would stimulate that province's attempts at controlling the entire nation. One interesting fact to keep in mind is that of the one hundred years of the twentieth century, independent Brazil would spend thirty-five under some form of dictatorial government; and of those thirty-five, twenty-seven would be under a dictator born in Rio Grande do Sul.

Up to this point we have seen the Portuguese advancing towards the heartland of the South American continent as the result of three primary elements: the Bandeiras, in the central part of the colony; the defense of the Amazon against the French, in the North; and the disputes with the Spanish, in the South. At the beginning of the eighteenth century, another important event would further stimulate the occupation of the interior: the discovery of gold.

The Discovery of Gold and the Minas Gerais

The eighteenth century in Brazil was marked by important social and economic transformations brought about by the discovery of gold in the southeastern part of the colony. In the closing years of the seventeenth century, large mineral reserves were found in the outskirts of Vila Rica (present-day city of Ouro Preto), a village founded in 1652 about 170 miles north of Rio de Janeiro. The discoverers of the precious metal were the aforementioned Bandeirantes from São Paulo, and the ensuing gold rush, more than real prosperity, would produce great tension and instability in the area.

The number of gold diggers heading for Vila Rica in the late seventeenth century was so great that in 1703 a terrible famine broke out in the village. In 1708, invaders from the captaincies of Bahia and Pernambuco, the so-called *emboabas*, attempted to take control of the mines. In order to do so, they had to overcome the resistance of the Bandeirantes, or *Paulistas*, as they were called in the area. After a violent clash known as the War of the Emboabas, the invaders from the Northeast managed to expel the Paulistas and assume control over the entire mining area. The Bandeirantes were thus forced out and deprived of the lucrative gold-mining activities

The discovery of gold in the colony brought about a sudden increase in Portuguese bureaucratic control over the lives of colonial Brazilians. Heavy taxation soon became a matter of discontent, and the colonial administration began to be seen as merciless and greedy. Initially, the chief instrument the metropolitan authorities used to extract money from the mining activity was the so-called *capitação*, a system in which a heavy duty was charged for each slave employed by a given mining entrepreneur in the processes of mineral prospecting and extraction (hence the term "capitation," that is, *per head*).[13] In 1719, a new metropolitan directive prohibited the circulation of any form of gold that was not properly smelted into bars and sealed with a royal stamp in one of the recently established foundry houses maintained by the Crown. In such houses, one fifth of the gold smelted would be retained by the colonial administration and sent to Portugal. This form of taxation, coupled with the official monopoly of commerce in the region granted exclusively to Portuguese-born merchants, brought the local colonials into conflict with the administration. The situation in Vila Rica became increasingly tense when a man named Filipe dos Santos (1680–1720) decided to raise his voice against fiscal abuse and metropolitan privilege.

Filipe dos Santos seemed to have little personal interest in the taxation system itself, for he suffered no direct financial damage from it. He was, however, a great orator, and his oratorical talents were employed by a group of local chieftains to promote a riot against the fiscal administrators. The proficient speaker was thus coopted into a conspiracy against the Portuguese forces that controlled the extraction and commerce of gold in the colony. Unaware of the actual limit of his power, however, dos Santos brought the Crown's rage down upon himself rather more than he had expected. After repeatedly rising in public protest against the Crown, he was arrested and executed in a way intended to set an exemple: he was brought to the center of the village, his limbs were tightly fastened to four horses, and these were made to run in opposite directions. Filipe dos Santos's cruel punishment was meant as a warning not only for the local people of the Minas Gerais, but also for all colonials who dared oppose the Crown.

Historians have noted that the Brazilians who then witnessed the execution would probably not have been so shocked if the body that exploded in front of their eyes had been that of a black man or an indigenous slave. Seeing a white male Christian bursting into pieces, however, appears to have had a strong psychological effect on the miners, such that, after Filipe dos Santos's execution, almost six decades would pass before a new revolt would break out in the region. In any case, the plight of the skillful orator, together with the conspiracy it entailed, is generally regarded in Brazilian historiography as an important, albeit incipient, movement of native aspiration and self-affirmation in colonial times. It became known as the Vila Rica Revolt.[14]

As the eighteenth century proceeded under the influence of a gold rush that was rapidly transforming the colony's economic and political outlook, the Portuguese administration remained unswerving in its strict policies of mercantile capitalism. Local industrial development was strongly discouraged, and the monopoly of commerce was maintained in the hands of Portuguese merchants with the aim of facilitating the sale in the colony of goods produced in Portugal. Such restraints notwithstanding, the general colonial shift from an economy based on large sugar cane plantations extending throughout the vast rural areas into a more geographically restricted mining activity gave rise to an incipient urban culture and to the flourishing of small businesses and crafts in the areas adjacent to the mining region. Soon the availability of new products, artifacts, and services would extend to the surrounding provinces. Important social and political transformations ensued, resulting in new territorial arrangements and cultural manifestations. In order to better control the flow of gold extracted from the mines, the Crown transferred the administrative capital of the colony 750 miles to the south, from the city of Salvador, in Bahia, to that of Rio de Janeiro. The new capital would be formally established in 1763. On the Atlantic coast, its proximity to the mining region allowed the Crown enhanced control over the riches that were shipped to Lisbon. Rio de Janeiro would remain Brazil's capital until 1960, when the city of Brasilia was inaugurated.

Still around the mid-eighteenth century, new political developments in Portugal resulted in important reforms in the colonial administration. The year 1750 marked a turning point in relations between Portugal and its colony with the beginning of the reign of King Joseph I, which lasted from 1750 to 1777. Joseph I appointed as Prime Minister the nobleman and diplomat Sebastião José de Carvalho e Melo (1699–1782), who was known by the title of Marquis of Pombal. Joseph I and Pombal embodied the Portuguese version of enlightened absolutism, with its emphasis on religious freedom, the right to hold private property, and the advancement of the arts, sciences, and education. The Marquis of Pombal was a polemic and charismatic figure who gained many enemies by promoting sweeping economic and social reforms in the Portuguese government. In 1761, he abolished slavery in the European part of the kingdom and suppressed religious persecution. In 1755, he rebuilt the city of Lisbon after the devastating earthquake of that year and attempted new economic policies aimed at turning Portugal into an economically self-sufficient and commercially strong nation.

Pombal had high hopes for his country, but his task of injecting dynamism into the Portuguese economy was not an easy one. Portugal's economic development had been stymied in the preceeding decades by a dreadful treaty signed with England in 1703 in the context of the War of the Spanish Succession, which lasted from 1701 to 1714. The war pitted two competing dynasties, the French Bourbons and the Austrian Habsburgs, against each other in a fight for the throne of Spain. Austria, Prussia, England, and the Dutch Republic lined up on the side of the Habsburgs; Spain and Portugal supported the Bourbons. With the use of military coercion, the English managed to make the Portuguese swap sides, forcing them into an unequal treaty, which came to be known as the Treaty of Methuen (1703).

The pact established that the English would not tax Portuguese wines higher than they would French ones. In return, English textiles would be able to enter Portugal free of any taxation. The treaty could be described as an "I give you ten, you give me twenty" sort of arrangement. The result was the emergence of Portugal's historical trade deficit with England, a continuous debt that the Iberian nation had to pay with Brazilian gold. After the signing of the treaty, Portugal entered a long period of severe economic dependence and productive sluggishness, which echoed its ruling class's satisfaction with the consumption of luxury goods imported from England, paid for with the wine produced by the lower classes, as well as with the gold brought from Brazil.

It is interesting to note that if the well-being of its dominant class led to the maintenance throughout the eighteenth century of a monochrome economy based on wine production in Portugal, something similar would occur in the case of an independent Brazil in the following century, where an equally monochrome economy based on coffee production would satisfy the ruling class to an extent similar to that previously experienced in Portugal, that is, to the point of generating economic sluggishness and dependence.

Any possible atavisms running between the Portuguese and the Brazilians notwithstanding, the trade situation between Portugal and England represented a heavy load on the Brazilian colony. The arrangement would be famously employed as a case study in the economic model produced by nineteenth-century British theorist David Ricardo (1772–1823) who, in his description of the situation, painted a picture in which both parties, Great Britain (formed by the union of England and Scotland in 1707) and Portugal, gained from the exchange. Following Ricardo's argument, modern theorists of free exchange avow that trade deficits are not necessarily bad, for they tend to correct naturally over time. That is not the case, however, when structural constraints are generated in one of the parts, as was the case with Portugal in its dealings with Great Britain. The Treaty of Methuen worked to prevent industrial development in Portugal. This was a fact that Pombal understood with considerable clarity, and which his ensuing Pombaline Reforms would attempt to redress starting in 1750.

Pombal's reforms, however, could not miraculously turn Portugal into a productive nation, especially in light of the apathy of the Portuguese aristocracy. The reforms were, however, successful in many ways, especially with regard to the development of the Portuguese colony. Under Pombal's rule, colonial territorial expansion was again instigated. The geographical enlargement of the colony figured prominently among the Prime Minister's directives as something that should be achieved at any cost. This takes us back to the tensions in the southern part of the colonial territory, where, by then, clashes between the Portuguese and Spanish had become almost customary.

A few months before the enthronement of Joseph I, which took place on July 31, 1750, a treaty was signed between Joseph's father, John V of Portugal, and Ferdinand VI of Spain with the aim of settling new frontiers between the two nations' colonial territories. The settlement was needed since the sixty-year period of the Iberian Union (1580–1640) had seen multiple transgressions of the dividing lines established in the Treaty of Tordesillas of 1494, with the encroachment of Portuguese settlements on Spanish territory. The treaty was signed under the name of the Treaty of Madrid, a document drafted by the Brazilian-born diplomat Alexandre de Gusmão (1695–1753). During the Treaty's negotiations, Gusmão claimed that the alleged Portuguese usurpation of Spanish possessions in America mirrored the Spanish usurpation of Portuguese ones in Asia, and as such, Gusmão argued, matters should be settled by the principle of the Roman law *uti possidetis*, that is, the principle that a nation should continue to possess the territory that it has lawfully taken possession of.

The argument seemed sound to Ferdinand VI and his diplomats, and the agreement was signed in Madrid in 1750. The Treaty's dispositions, however, would generate a terrible humanitarian crisis in the southern part of the Portuguese American colony. During the Treaty's negotiations, Gusmão had conceded the transfer of the aforementioned Sacramento Colony to the Spanish; the Portuguese, in turn, would retain the Jesuit missions located some 450 miles north of Sacramento in what was clearly Spanish territory. The Jesuit missions encompassed a large and economically prosperous area, amounting to what today is the western portion of Rio Grande do Sul State. Efforts on both sides to enforce the Treaty's main clauses were initiated in 1750. They included the displacement of the large indigenous population that inhabited the missionary settlements from what had become Portuguese territory into the neighboring Spanish lands, that is, into what is the northeastern part of present-day Argentina. This soon turned into a bloody affair, where both the Jesuit missions' indigenous residents and the Spanish priests who directed them were removed by force from their dwellings, having to leave their possessions and walk away from what would thereafter become Portuguese territory. The bloodshed began in 1752 when the native South American leader Sepé Tiaraju (d. 1756) organized a defense against the Portuguese and the Spanish troops that had been put in charge of the region's ethnic cleansing. The confrontation came to be known as the Guarani War, and it ended with the massacre of a large group of extremely vulnerable, and otherwise peaceful, indigenous individuals.

The war occurred during the rule of the Marquis of Pombal, who criticized Gusmão's Treaty of Madrid, arguing that the Sacramento Colony should never have been handed to the Spanish. Pombal needed to obtain enormous revenue from the Brazilian colony in order to cover Portugal's recurrent trade deficits with Great Britain, and this depended on maximum colonial territorial expansion. That expansion would be helped more by control of the Sacramento Colony than by the occupation of the Jesuit missions.

In the 1750s, Portugal's ultimate aim with the Sacramento Colony continued to be that of 1680, the date of its founding, that is, to eventually take control of the silver trade that flowed down the River Plate on its way to Europe. The Treaty of Madrid was canceled in 1761, when another agreement, the Treaty of el Pardo, was signed between the two Iberian nations. Two other treaties, the Treaty of Santo Ildefonso (1777) and the Treaty of Badajoz (1801), would follow, with the end result being the re-establishment of the frontiers formerly agreed under Gusmão's Treaty of Madrid. In any event, the region would not enjoy peace for a long time to come.[15]

Besides maximum territorial expansion, Pombal attempted several economic and social reforms in the colony. Among these, perhaps the most socially pervasive was the establishment of a government policy for the active assimilation of the indigenous populations into Portuguese society and culture. Pombal banished all Jesuit missionaries from the colonial territory, eradicating the practice of religious conversion of the natives. Religious education was replaced with a system based upon the ideas of the Enlightenment, with regular schools built in each indigenous village. The Prime Minister's directives were summarized in his 1757 *Diretório dos Índios*, a law dictating the new social rules regarding the natives in the colony. The directory created an administrative cabinet in charge of the former Jesuit missions, which were now emancipated from religious control. The Tupi language, a colonial vernacular consisting of a mixture of Portuguese and several indigenous dialects, was prohibited by the same government decree. The language had developed during 250 years of contact between the Portuguese and the natives; its use, however, was now proscribed, with severe penalties imposed on anyone using it in public.[16] Prohibited also were any acts of discrimination towards indigenous individuals. The law provided incentives for marriage between Portuguese and natives. By favoring the assimilation of the indigenous population as Portuguese subjects, Pombal hoped to increase the population of the colony and, by extension, promote its territorial expansion.

Joseph I's Prime Minister established two governmental enterprises that were given a monopoly over the commerce with the colony, the *Companhia Geral de Comércio do Grão-Pará e Maranhão* (1755) and the *Companhia Geral de Comércio de Pernambuco e Paraíba* (1759). Both companies attempted to increase economic activity in the North, which had begun to stagnate after the discovery of gold and the consequent shift of the economic center towards the South. The two enterprises promoted the production of commodities such as sugar, coffee, and cotton. Cotton received particular incentives in light of growing demand from the English textile industry. The Portuguese Crown thus worked to combine the profitable product with colonial gold in order to cover its trade deficit with England.

In 1759, the Marquis of Pombal executed another important part of his administrative reform: the reincorporation of all hereditary captaincies back into the Crown. The goal was to give the Portuguese rulers a firmer grip on the colonial economy, allowing for greater control over its productive output. The measure caused considerable discontent among colonial residents. Together with enhanced fiscal control, the policy resulted in further administrative centralization and boosted the government's authority. Pombal's more liberal ideas, however, did result in policies that were better received by the colonials. For the first time, the production of manufactured goods was allowed in Brazilian territory, with the caveat that such goods should not have Portuguese equivalents. This meant the opening of an important route to autonomy.[17]

The death of King Joseph I in 1777 would bring an end to Pombal's administration. The next monarch to assume the throne would be Mary I (1734–1816), Joseph I's daughter, a woman who had always disliked Sebastião José de Carvalho e Melo and his reforms. Once crowned, the Queen immediately turned against the Prime Minister with accusations of corruption and dismissed him from his governmental functions. The Queen would then proceed to an even more oppressive fiscal treatment of the colony than the one theretofore imposed by her father's Prime Minister. The thorough prohibition of industrial manufacturing in colonial territory would be reinstated by Mary I in 1785, resulting in a firmer harnessing of the local economy and its incipient internal market in favor of Portuguese metropolitan interests.

During Mary I's reign, a second attempt at revolt in the mining region would take place. The attempt, which consisted of a conspiracy against metropolitan fiscal tyranny and political despotism, would again be violently suppressed. In spite of its failure, however, this second revolt would set an important precedent in the emerging efforts towards Brazilian independence.

The Conspiracy of Minas Gerais and Brazilian Neoclassicism

In 1789, an important attempt at sedition known as the *Inconfidência Mineira* broke out in the mining region. This movement brought together several distinct groups and interests in a common effort against the abuses of the Portuguese colonial administration. As authoritarianism and misappropriation of individual property by the Crown and its officials became increasingly evident, monarchists and republicans, slave owners and abolitionists, intellectuals and military men started conspiring against what they perceived as the actions of a rogue state. The general fear promoted by the Crown and its bureaucracy's acts of terror, such as the 1720 execution of Filipe dos Santos in a public square, had reached boiling point, and popular tolerance of metropolitan malfeasance was coming to an end.

The foremost cause of discontent was the introduction of a tax called *derrama*. The tax law established that the captaincy of Minas Gerais should provide the Portuguese Crown with 3,000 pounds of gold annually, and that in case this amount was not collected through the yearly mining output, it would be exacted by means of the confiscation of private possessions from the aforementioned "good men," that is, those who owned land and were not of immediate Jewish ancestry.

The derrama had been officially established in 1751, at the beginning of Pombal's administration, but by 1789 it had been enforced only once, in 1763. Thereafter, the "good men" had managed to negotiate postponements on several occasions. As the region's natural reserves of gold declined over the years, however, the confiscation seemed to be drawing closer and closer. Influenced by the ideals of the French Revolution and of the American War of Independence, the Minas Gerais regional elite began to rise up against the oppressive Portuguese rule. Joaquim José da Silva Xavier (1746–1792), a low-ranking military officer, whose abilities with dental medicine had earned him the pejorative nickname *Tiradentes* (tooth-puller), emerged as an important and charismatic figure in the movement. Aware of the severity of the exploitation to which colonial Brazilians were being subjected, with their gold being pillaged and sent to Portugal, Tiradentes aligned with members of the local political elite to devise the means of resistance. The group that was then formed had a clear understanding of the relationship between Brazilian colonial poverty and British industrial prosperity, Portugal being the missing link.

Tiradentes's lack of an aristocratic background had prevented his rise in the military hierarchy, but his peculiar intellectual capacity, bolstered by readings of Rousseau, allowed him to assume the leadership of the revolutionary movement. Among the *Inconfidentes*, as they would later be called, were poets and artists whose ideals of freedom and independence were expressed in literary form. To a considerable extent, the movement's call to liberty was inspired by the native sentiments expressed in the words of men such as Cláudio Manuel da Costa (1729–1789), a poet and musician who introduced neoclassicism to Brazil; Tomás António Gonzaga (1744–1810), a Portuguese-born bucolic poet who sang love ballads in the tone of Horace's *aura mediocritas* and let the conspirators hold meetings at his house; and Alvarenga Peixoto (1744–1793), a Brazilian-born poet who would end his life in Angola after being banished from Brazil by Mary I.

The revolutionaries' motto, *Libertas Quae Sera Tamen* (Freedom, Even If It Be Late), was taken from Virgil's first *Eclogue* and was inscribed on a white flag with a red triangle. Instead of calling for the total independence of Brazil from Portugal, however, the general aim of the conspiracy was primarily republican and secessionist, that is, it was mostly limited to Minas Gerais and the vicinity. Given the great isolation between the different regions of the colony at the time, a national sentiment encompassing the entire colonial territory did not yet figure in the thinking of the *Inconfidência* leaders. Futhermore, the movement also lacked a clear policy against slavery: the desire for freedom expressed in the motto was only meant for the white elites.

Tiradentes's plan was to take to the streets of Vila Rica and proclaim a Brazilian republic in Minas Gerais on the day they expected the derrama, when tensions would be highest. He did not expect, however, that Joaquim Silvério dos Reis (1756–1792), one of the conspiracy's members, would inform on the revolution before it started. The rebels were imprisoned and most of them were subsequently banished from the colony. Tiradentes alone, after a three-year trial, was hanged in Rio de Janeiro on April 21, 1792. His body was then quartered and sent to Vila Rica to be displayed to the populace as a warning against new attempts at independence.[18]

Tiradentes's fate was similar to that of Filipe dos Santos some sixty years earlier. The story of the two men suggests that in colonial Brazil severe punishment was imposed solely upon individuals of low social rank, a trend that would be confirmed in the nation's future history. Unlike Filipe dos Santos, however, Tiradentes would assume the place of a national hero in the popular imagination. The date of his execution would be marked as a national holiday, and the story of the aborted insurrection would feature in literature and the arts of nationalistic inclination throughout the following centuries.

Before we proceed to observe one last insurrection that marks the end of the Brazilian eighteenth century, we should note the important cultural dimension of the conspiracy of Minas Gerais, as it brought about a revolution in not only politics, but also in colonial aesthetics and artistic creation. The main aesthetic trend characterizing the colonial period of Brazilian history was undoubtedly the baroque. And the gold rush, together with the flourishing of Minas Gerais around 1700, represented the baroque's high point in Brazilian art history. The Inconfidência conspiracy of 1789, however, reflected the baroque's initial demise, and the introduction of neoclassicism as the new aesthetic that would prevail in the first decades of the nineteenth century. The conspiracy of Minas Gerais can thus be regarded as entailing a turning point in Brazilian aesthetic sensibility, one that was visible above all in the emergence of the neoclassical poetry of the Inconfidentes.

A brief discussion of the distinction between the baroque and neoclassicism can help clarify the aesthetic turn taking place in eighteenth-century colonial Brazil. The baroque style had its roots in late sixteenth-century Rome, where the Catholic Church favored its exuberant splendor and high emotion as a form of psychological support for its Counter-Reformation. The Church's stylistic directive in Europe soon reached the Spanish and Portuguese American colonies. While baroque literature developed in Europe in the works of authors such as Luis de Góngora (1561–1627), Francisco de Quevedo (1580–1645), Molière (1622–1673), and Racine (1639–1699), in the Americas it emerged in the chronicles of conquest of Frei Bartolomé de las Casas (1484–1566) and El Inca Garcilaso de la Vega (1539–1616), as well in the Brazilian poetry of Gregório de Matos e Guerra (1636–1696) and in the sermons of the priest Antônio Vieira (1608–1697).

Gregório de Matos provides us with what is presumably the best example of the Brazilian literary baroque. The poet was born in the then colonial capital, Salvador, in Bahia, and his lyricism reflected his passion as a rebel who criticized everything and everyone. He was given the sobriquet of *Boca do Inferno* (Hell's Mouth), especially for his disparaging lines against the Catholic Church. Matos's severe criticism of established power came in verses such as the following:

> A nossa Sé da Bahia,
> com ser um mapa de festas,
> é um presépio de bestas,
> se não for estrebaria.

> Our Cathedral of Bahia
> in being a map of celebration,
> is a coterie of beasts,
> if not in fact a stable.

Besides poetry, the Brazilian baroque flourished especially in sculpture and architecture, a tendency that followed the economic boom of the gold cycle. Minas Gerais and its capital, Vila Rica, became home to a rich late-baroque architecture. Baroque buildings spread through Vila Rica's hilly landscape especially in the mode of highly ornamented Catholic churches. Instead of using the term "baroque," some art historians prefer to call the style Rococo. The name designates an upshot of the original baroque emerging in early eighteenth-century Paris. The florid and graceful architectural patterns of Portuguese Rococo, however, displayed considerable originality and resulted in works that are quite different from the original French version.

Sculpture was probably the art form in which Brazilian baroque artists became most accomplished. Among Brazilian colonial sculptors, Antônio Francisco Lisboa (1738–1814) achieved the highest artistic standards, giving material form to religious sentiment through his simple and honest wood-carved religious images. Known as *Aleijadinho* (Little Cripple), Lisboa's somewhat obscure life story is shrouded in legend. The artist seemed to suffer from a degenerative illness, probably leprosy, from which he received the above sobriquet. Very little is known with certainty about his life, some scholars even question whether he existed at all. The works attributed to him, however, are of truly remarkable quality. Lisboa's *Twelve Prophets*, that is, twelve sculptures that stand around the main building of the church of Bom Jesus, in the city of Congonhas, a small town located about 25 miles southwest of Vila Rica, prove the worth of the sculptor's fame. Aleijadinho was also a master of architecture, and several of the baroque churches that today color the highlands of Minas Gerais State are attributed to him.

As we have seen, the days of the republican conspiracy of Minas Gerais, the *Inconfidência*, brought a new literary aesthetic to the colony. Classicism emerged in the late seventeenth century in opposition to the previous, and overtly effusive, baroque style. The works of the aforementioned poets Cláudio Manuel da Costa (1729–1789), Tomás António Gonzaga (1744–1810), and Alvarenga Peixoto (1744–1793) are often cited as the height of Brazilian colonial neoclassicism.[19] However, in spite of the revolutionary breeding ground from which neoclassical poetry emerged in the colony, we should note that a truly revolutionary poetry never actually emerged in the works of colonial neoclassicists. The authors associated with the style appear to have lacked concrete ideas or motivation for real political change. The bucolic aesthetic of their neoclassicism, with its peculiar esteem for the natural landscape, gave a new perspective on the land, promoting the emergence of a positive sentiment towards the native soil. Brazilian neoclassical poets, however, never truly thought of themselves as Brazilian as opposed to Portuguese, nor did they strive for independence from the European metropolis. The new native sentiment they set in motion, nevertheless, would soon develop into a truly nationalistic consciousness that would reverberate for many years to come. As we will see in the next chapter, the neoclassical aesthetic would become a powerful ideological weapon for the construction of the Brazilian nationality in the nineteenth century.

Before we finish our overview of the Brazilian eighteenth century, we must look at one last insurrection that contributed to the gradual emergence of a feeling of national belonging in the colony. The *Conjuração Baiana* (Conspiracy of Bahia) was a much less elitist movement than the one previously attempted in Minas Gerais. As we will see next, it involved individuals of a considerably larger social spectrum, and it strove for a freedom of larger scope. It started in 1798.

The Conspiracy of Bahia and the Emergence of the Notion of Citizenship

As we have seen, the advent of a gold rush in the central part of the colony produced a radical shift in the colonial economy. The regional distribution of wealth and power was geographically shaken, and the transfer of the capital from Salvador to Rio de Janeiro in 1763 marked the beginning of prolonged economic stagnation in the North. By 1798, the former colonial capital, which, during the previous two centuries of Portuguese rule, had prospered from the revenues of sugar production and the slave trade, was now thrown into turmoil with the poor and dissatisfied populace protesting over numerous social issues. For the first time in the colony's history, the horrors of slavery became a subject of open debate, and a new discourse on liberty and universal rights arose together with ideas of republicanism and revolution. Being the major colonial center of African heritage, the city of Salvador became a hotbed of ideas influenced by international developments, such as the French Revolution and the Haitian struggle for independence.[20] Enlightenment ideals were now directly adopted and spread over a much broader social basis than in the previous case of the Minas Gerais's conspiracy.

It was in such a context of political and ideological turbulence that a man called Cipriano Barata (1762–1838), a medical doctor educated in Portugal at the University of Coimbra, rose to the leadership of a popular movement that took to the streets of Salvador in 1798. Barata was a freemason who overtly criticized the institution of slavery and the evil policies of Portuguese mercantile capitalism. The commercial monopoly exercised by the official Portuguese trading companies over the years had had a devastating impact on the local economy. Mary I's proscription of industrial manufacturing in colonial territory had enhanced the need for imported goods, and local products had seen their prices forced down as a result of the monopsony established by the Crown. The deflationary effect on the prices of local goods created a shortage of currency and an ensuing inflation in the price of the highly demanded imports.

Barata mobilized a large group of followers and began a process of pamphleteering—an activity prohibited by the Crown—in order to engage popular support. Among Barata's demands were the abolition of slavery, the proclamation of a republic, the establishment of free international trade, the end of racial discrimination, and the lowering of taxes. Salvador was then a city of approximately 50,000 residents, with more or less 250 sugar cane plantations established on its outskirts. The movement soon gained support from the lower echelons of the military class. This notwithstanding, Barata's undertaking was almost immediately stalled when the Portuguese authorities began adopting repressive measures in August 1798.

Hundreds of people were arrested and five were executed on charges of high treason, receiving the same fate as Tiradentes. Since the present revolt had a more popular following than the elitist conspiracy of Minas Gerais, punishment was distributed accordingly. The previous trend seen throughout colonial history was maintained: penalties were applied with severity to the poor, while upper class partisans were mostly exculpated. Cipriano Barata himself, the conspiracy's leader, was incarcerated for less than two years. After being freed, he went back into politics and became one of the leading figures of another major revolt, the Pernambucan Revolution of 1817.

In spite of being thoroughly put down, the Conjuração Baiana gave a significant boost to the Brazilian social conscience. For the first time revolutionary action had been undertaken by common people, and for the first time the abominable institution of slavery had been called into question. The movement was also the first overt attempt at overthrowing the old regime, as well as the first instance of a consciousness of citizenship and an awareness of human rights. Like a sudden epiphany, the Conjuração Baiana opened the possibility of a new discourse on what it meant to be human in the Portuguese colonial domains.[21]

The revolt in Bahia brings us to the end of the Brazilian eighteenth century. The first years of the following century would be marked by major political transformations in Europe, which would have direct effects in the Portuguese colony. Under the social and political disruptions caused by the Napoleonic wars, the monarchs of Portugal would flee their country and seek refuge in their tropical colony. To that story, which closes the Brazilian colonial period, we will now turn.

A European Monarchy in the Tropics and the End of Colonial Rule

The period from 1808 to 1821 is known in Brazilian history as *Período Joanino*, a time of significant transformation as a result of the transfer of the Portuguese court from Lisbon to Rio de Janeiro. The term "Joanino" refers to the rule of John VI in Brazil, first as Prince Regent of Portugal, his official title from 1792 to 1816, and then as King of Portugal from 1816 until Brazil's independence in 1822. The period starts with the episode of the Portuguese court's flight from the Iberian Peninsula and subsequent arrival on the coast of Bahia after a three-month transatlantic voyage. The court's transfer from Europe to America can claim to be the most significant political event in Brazilian colonial history.

In spite of its great historical importance, namely that of entailing a thorough about-face in the colony's relationship with its metropolis, the Portuguese court's transmigration is often viewed as an amusing event and described humorously in Brazilian popular culture. The occurrence of a storm during the transatlantic crossing, which separated the royal vessel from the original convoy so that it arrived at Bahia, instead of Rio de Janeiro as initially planned, is frequently greeted with laughter. Incidents such as the Portuguese nobility's hygiene problems during the crossing, as well as John VI's act of supposed bravery in declaring war on Napoleonic France only after having arrived safely in colonial territory, are depicted as pathetic and ludicrous.[22]

The precise number of Portuguese émigrés attempting to escape Napoleon's army as part of the court's migration to America is a moot point, still debated by scholars. Estimates vary from 5,000 to 10,000, amounting to what would be a good part of Lisbon's aristocracy at the time.[23] Be that as it may, the story abounds with lurid details. A few months before departing Lisbon, Queen Mary I had been declared mentally insane, and she had to be dragged into the main royal vessel while screaming the words "Jesus, please save me!" As the royal convoy was about to leave the shore, many of those who were left behind started jumping desperately into the water to try and board the ship, apparently fearing the approaching Napoleonic troops. During the voyage, an infestation of lice attacked the royal family and its accompanying nobility, which caused the members of the purportedly refined European court to disembark in American soil with their heads shaved. A few days later, the bald Portuguese aristocracy would start dislodging the Brazilian locals from their homes. Since all that existed in the colony belonged primarily to the Crown, private buildings were "requested" to accommodate the

Portuguese nobility. The Brazilians were thus obliged to leave their houses and find new accommodation wherever they could.

Underneath all the petty details, the transfer of the Portuguese court from Europe to South America was put into effect under the protection of the British naval forces. In specific political terms, it resulted from the dispositions of the Treaty of Tilsit, agreed secretly between France and Russia in July 1807, establishing that the Bourbon and Bragança dynasties should cease to exist in Spain and Portugal, where a prince chosen from Napoleon's family would be enthroned as monarch. Before a direct military invasion was initiated, however, the French gave the Portuguese an ultimatum to comply with Napoleon's continental blockade and close all ports to the British, declare war upon the United Kingdom (formed in 1801 by the union of Great Britain and Ireland), and then arrest all British citizens in Portuguese territory. However, none of these demands could be met, partly because, since the previously mentioned Treaty of Methuen of 1703, Portugal had been little more than a satellite state of Great Britain. As a result, a few months later, a new pact was signed, this time between the French and the Spanish, who, unaware of Napoleon's arrangements with the Russians, would allow the French army to cross Spanish territory and invade Portugal. This latter arrangement was contracted in the so-called Treaty of Fontainebleau, which was also signed secretly, this time between Napoleon and the Spanish Minister, Manuel de Godoy, in October 1807.

The only option left to the Portuguese royal family, then, was to run away. And their only chance of doing so successfully without being caught by Napoleon's naval forces was if the escape were carried out under the auspices of the British. The British, for their part, were ready and eager to offer their transatlantic escort services; the charge, however, would be extremely high. Adding to the general Portuguese desperation was the fact that their nation's financial situation at the time was as foreboding as ever. Since the end of the eighteenth century, Portugal had been a very weak and impoverished state. The colossal amount of gold and diamonds extracted from Brazil during the colonial period, which some historians estimate as reaching the astronomical amounts of 2,500 tons of gold and 1.5 million carats of diamonds, had been used up in the reconstruction of Lisbon after the earthquake of 1755, and also in paying Portugal's chronic trade debts to Great Britain. Thus Portuguese payment for British protection had to be negotiated on, again, unequal terms: all the Portuguese could offer in return at this time was the colony itself.

The British compensation for the protection of the Portuguese royal family was thus formalized through another unequal treaty. This one included a package of small agreements, which came to be known in Brazil as the Treaties of 1810. They were negotiated in Rio de Janeiro with Britain's Ambassador to Portugal, Percy Sydney Smythe, 6th Viscount Strangford (1780–1855). The package included provisos such as: 1) that British citizens would not be subject to Portuguese law in the colony, answering solely to a specially designated British judge; 2) that British naval forces would have unlimited access to Brazilian waters and would be maintained by the Portuguese state; and 3) that the import tax on British products would be kept at 15% *ad valorem*, while the rate imposed on Portuguese goods would be 16%.

By means of the Treaties of 1810 Britain gained almost complete control over Brazilian trade. Portugal's dependence on the British economy was thus transferred to its colony, and later to the independent Brazilian nation, as we will see in more detail in the next chapter.

It is worth noting that the idea of transferring the Portuguese court from Lisbon to Rio de Janeiro was not new. The move had been proposed by at least two prestigious individuals on two separate occasions: the priest Antônio Vieira (1608–1697), an influential councilor of the kingdom from 1641 to 1656; and Rodrigo de Sousa Coutinho (1755–1812), a nobleman who in the eighteenth century argued that Brazil had become much richer than Portugal, and that as such it made more sense to administer it *in situ*. In 1798, under the title of Count of Linhares, Coutinho would note that the European domain no longer comprised the center of the Portuguese Empire.[24]

The way in which the transfer of the Portuguese court was realized, however, was not how any Portuguese officials had planned it. Under the pressure of Napoleon on one side and the British on the other, John VI was obliged to make concessions regarding Portuguese control over its American territory. One of his first acts upon arriving in Brazil was to declare the end of the Portuguese monopoly over colonial trade. Since, by housing the Portuguese court, Brazil would henceforth become the de facto center of the Portuguese Empire, it became impossible to maintain the former colony's commerce with Portugal's European territory. In other words, Brazilian trade would no longer pass through Portugal, which hitherto had functioned as an intermediary in the commerce of all colonial production.

This had significant implications for the colony's growing economic emancipation. Brazil no longer needed Portugal, and Portugal was weak and impoverished. After the Portuguese court fled Lisbon, French commander Jean-Andoche Junot (1771–1813) took the defenseless capital on November 30, 1807. From then on, Portugal would be an occupied nation, falling first into the hands of the French, and then into those of the British.

John VI had thus no other option than to regard the uncultured colony as his new home. Mostly against his will, there he would spend the next thirteen years of his life. Forced to recognized the growing economic centrality of Brazil in regard to now peripheral Portugal, and under great pressure from the European powers eager to rearrange the continent's political map after Napoleon's defeat, in December 1815 the Prince Regent formally elevated his colony to the rank of a kingdom, establishing the United Kingdom of Portugal, Brazil, and the Algarves. From then on, John would be obliged to regard his American territory as more than a mere source of income for the maintenance of his royal lifestyle.

The year 1815 thus marks the formal end of the Brazilian colonial era. The former colony had gained pre-eminence over its former ruling kingdom; its internal market had grown to surpass that of Portugal; its territory had expanded into what in a few years would be given the name, albeit somewhat farcically, of *Empire*. The large Portuguese American domain had been extended in all directions. Seven years earlier, in 1808, upon arriving in his colony, John VI had felt the Portuguese innate craving for territorial expansion. Seeing the possibility of new portions of land added to his domain, he raised his scepter and declared war against the French and the Spanish, whom he saw as evil for having obliged him to relocate. The Prince Regent's vow was for territorial conquest, a yearning that had always stirred the blood of his ancestors.

Pitiful as John's declaration of war may have seemed to Napoleon and his generals, it succeeded in transferring the European war to America. Ordering the invasion of French and Spanish territories adjacent to his American colony, the Portuguese Prince took the French Guyana in 1809, expanding his colonial territory to the north. The area of present-day Uruguay was invaded in 1811, enlarging the colony to the south. This latter incursion gave continuity to the old quarrel over the Sacramento Colony and resumed the historical violence that, as we have seen, characterized the southernmost part of the colony. The dispute over the southern territory, which the Portuguese called *Banda Oriental*, would not be settled until 1828, when, as we shall see in detail below, the Republic of Uruguay was established as a means of ending a gruesome war over the disputed area between the newly independent Brazil and the United Provinces of the River Plate, that is, the political unit that amounts roughly to present-day Argentina.[25]

Besides inducing new attempts at territorial expansion, the migration of the monarchy and the installation of the Portuguese court in Rio de

Janeiro led to remarkable cultural developments in the colony. Intellectual repression and censorship had been fierce throughout the three hundred years of Portuguese rule, all the more so during Queen Mary I's reign, started in 1777. With the court now in Rio de Janeiro, however, the situation of intellectual restraint was bound to be altered. From the start, the Prince Regent understood the need to lay the foundations for normal court life in the colony. He created the Royal Press in 1808, allowing for the first time the publication of newspapers in his American territory. Unlike the situation found in the Spanish colonial domains, which had enjoyed considerable freedom of press since the sixteenth century, Portuguese America had not seen anything printed lawfully until 1808. Before that year, any attempts at propagating ideas through print would have been severely repressed, as was the case in the revolt in Bahia described earlier.

John VI also established the Royal Military Academy in 1810, which trained military officials as well as engineers, geographers, and topographers. The Botanical Garden was created the following year. It brought the first Chinese immigrants to Brazil to work in the development of a tea plantation built in the royal tropical orchard. The Royal Library was also established in 1810, and the Royal Museum in 1818.

Now that the court was firmly established in Rio de Janeiro, it was necessary to provide it with a cultural life able to meet European standards and to maintain the nobility's traditions. In order to support the lifestyle that his coutiers believed befitted them, John VI invited a group of French artists and architects to reside in his new palace. They formed what went down in history as the French Artistic Mission of 1816, which included the painters Jean-Baptiste Debret (1768–1848) and Nicolas Antoine Taunay (1755–1830), the sculptors Auguste Marie Taunay (1768–1824) and Marc Ferrez (1788–1850), and the renowned architect Grandjean de Montigny (1776–1850). Joachim Lebreton (1760–1819), the French official who was designated as curator of fine arts in France during Napoleon's rule, acted as the mission's director.

After Napoleon's fall and the start of the process of restoration in France in 1815, most of these artists, who had received Napoleon's official patronage, fell into political disfavor in their home country. John VI's invitation thus came as a timely offer for most of them. Lebreton proposed the creation of an educational institute for the arts, which would be established as the Imperial Academy of Fine Arts in 1826. The school promoted a style that later came to be known as Brazilian academicism.

The French Artistic Mission is especially remembered for having introduced neoclassicism into Brazilian painting and architecture. The style, as we have seen, had made its initial incursion into poetry, influencing the conspirators of Minas Gerais. Now it would start supplanting the baroque in other art forms as well. While the baroque served to express more popular and individual religious sentiments, neoclassicism tended to portray grandiose feelings and events. It thus served the monarchy's purpose of establishing a nationalistic aesthetic. Given the syncretic tendencies of Brazilian colonial culture, however, neoclassicism was soon combined with elements of romanticism and realism to give birth to an eclectic original style.

John VI also promoted long overdue reforms in the colony's educational system. Given the oppressive nature of Portuguese colonial rule, popular education had been virtually suppressed in the colony. Higher education was only available to those who could move to Portugal or France and study at the Universities of Coimbra or Paris.

The appalling situation of Brazilian colonial education contrasted sharply with that in Spanish America. The first Brazilian university would be established only in 1912, in the city of Curitiba in Paraná State, while the National University of San Marcos, in Peru, and the National Autonomous University of Mexico both date from 1551. It would not be a mistake to suggest that the very deficient educational system with which Brazilians struggle today is in great part a cultural inheritance from the fierce educational restrictions imposed by Portuguese rule during colonial times.

In his educational reforms, John VI established two schools of medicine, one in Bahia and another in Rio de Janeiro. The Royal Military Academy was established in Rio de Janeiro in 1810, offering for the first time in the colony courses in engineering. A chemistry course was instituted in Bahia in 1817, with professors being called from the University of Coimbra to teach in the tropics.[26]

Besides a virtually non-existent system of higher education, industrial development, as we have seen, had also been mostly proscribed, especially after Maria I's edict of 1785. John VI now allowed the building of a gunpowder factory, together with an iron foundry, in the region of the Minas Gerais. The former governor of Rio de Janeiro, Artur de Sá Menezes (d. 1702), had identified geological layers of iron in the village's vicinities as early as 1701. After arriving in Brazil, John decided that now was the time to start mining. He hired the German geologist, architect, and metallurgist Baron Wilhelm Ludwig von Eschwege (1777–1855) for the task. In 1812, the German Baron started setting the structural foundations for iron ore extraction in Minas Gerais, thus launching an economic activity that would turn the future independent nation into one of the world's leading producers of the metal.

The colonial economy was also boosted with John VI's establishment of the first bank in Portuguese colonial territory. The Bank of Brazil was created in 1808 with the main objective of funding the royal family's expenses, that is, of financing the maintenance of court life. The Bank issued fiduciary money without backing it with real reserves, meaning there was always the possibility of insolvency. In spite of attracting considerable deposits from Brazilian residents, the Bank tended to spend much more than it earned, quickly becoming highly indebted.

The new financial system, in any case, contributed to surprising economic growth during the last decade of Portuguese rule in Brazil. The indebted Portuguese state, which now had to cope without the commercial advantages it had ceded to Britain in the colony, promoted local growth through unplanned expansionary fiscal and monetary policy. The building of the infrastructure required to accommodate the newly arrived aristocracy required the adoption of bold fiscal measures, and the Bank of Brazil's liberal attitude to issuing money generated enough currency to cover such costs by means of its multiplier effect. The capacity for industrialization, however, was restrained by the open access to the internal marked given to British industrial products.

In the political sphere, as mentioned above, Brazil was raised to the status of a kingdom in union with Portugal in 1815. This came as a result of the rules established by the major European powers convening at the Congress of Vienna that year. After the fall of Napoleon, Austria, the United Kingdom, Russia, Prussia, and France gathered to discuss the redrawing of Europe's political map, which had been disrupted by Napoleon's imperial warfare. The French representative to the Congress, Charles Maurice de Talleyrand (1754–1838), espoused the principle of legitimacy, which held that former monarchs who had had their thrones usurped by Napoleon and his cohorts should be reinstated as monarchs of their respective kingdoms. The case of John VI, however, was complicated by the fact that the powers gathering in Vienna also agreed that monarchs who had left their kingdoms should not be entitled to regain their former positions. Having fled Lisbon in 1808, John VI was thus set to lose his rights over Portugal. However, his ingenious change to Brazil's status, making it a united kingdom with Portugal and the Algarves, satisfied the requirements of the Congress of Vienna and he was able to maintain his Braganza dynasty's rule over its former territories.

The Portuguese aristocracy that had remained in Lisbon, however, felt that the Prince Regent's scheme of elevating his colony's status should be considered little more than a formality. The Brazilians, on the other hand, preferred to regard it as the official end of colonial rule. This disagreement intensified when the Brazilians began to fear the real possibility of a political reversal and of a return to the previous state of affairs, that is, a reinstatement of their territory's colonial status.

This was a time when the ghost of re-colonization loomed over the entire Latin American continent, where the former Spanish colonies were in the processes of acquiring their independence primarily by means of republican enterprises. Following the Congress of Vienna of 1815, a coalition was formed by Russia, Austria, and Prussia—termed the Holy Alliance—with the goal of defending the divine right of kings and promoting Christian values in Europe and its colonial domains. The militarily and politically powerful Holy Alliance was a source of discouragement for attempts at independence, especially those tinged with republican ideals.[27]

Matters were further complicated by a series of political uprisings breaking out in Europe at the time, generally known as the Revolutions of 1820. This revolutionary wave started in peripheral nations, and included turbulence in Spain, Portugal, Russia, Italy, and Greece. Liberal movements demanded the establishment of constitutional monarchies in their respective countries. In the case of Portugal, unrest started in the city of Porto and soon spread to the rest of the country. The Portuguese revolutionaries demanded the immediate return of King John VI and his court to Portugal, and the establishment of a constitution.

The peninsular elite was suffering great economic distress from having its main source of revenue, trade with Brazil, cut off. One of the Porto Revolution's primary goals was to re-establish colonial rule over what was still considered Portuguese territory. It was thus that in 1821 John VI, yielding to his countrymen's demands, decided to return to Portugal. He assumed that the wealth of his kingdom was his personal wealth. So, with Brazil and Portugal being equally part of his domain, he made sure, before leaving his American territory, to withdraw all the money that was deposited in the Bank of Brazil and carry it in his convoy directly to Portugal. This left the Brazilian financial institution virtually bankrupt (the Bank would be declared bankrupt in 1829). Obviously, the King withdrew not only his own deposits, but also those of the Bank's other clients, perpetrating what our modern sensibility generally refers to as larceny.

Thus, in 1821, the King of Portugal left Brazil for good. Despite having lived in the tropical part of his kingdom for thirteen years of his life, he left it behind and showed little concern for its future. After boarding his royal vessel with a heavy load of Brazilian money, John VI would never again return to his American colony.

The episode of the King's return to Portugal confirms what Brazilian historians have regarded as the Braganza's tendency to favor their own dynastic interests above those of the nations they ruled.[28] The Brazilian territory, however, would not be left without a Braganza to rule over it. Although John VI had left for Portugal, his son, Pedro, would remain in Brazil and tend to his father's affairs. To the story of Prince Pedro, and to that of the Brazilian independence, we will turn next.

Chapter Two

The Brazilian Empire (1822–1889)

The years between 1822 and 1889 saw the gradual emergence of a stable independent nation in the former Portuguese colonial territory in America. The rupture with metropolitan European rule proved arduous and the establishment of an internal legal order was a source of conflict. The building of the new nation was heavily influenced by the emerging economic necessities. Immigration enlarged and enriched the country's ethnic and cultural landscape. Politically, the years were marked by the continuity of the Braganza dynasty in power. The monarchy maintained its firm grip on the nation's administration throughout the period. Political factions materialized, though their role would be subordinated to the Emperor's commands. Monarchical favor determined the fate of ambitious political careers. Toward the end of the period, however, abolitionism and republicanism emerged and coalesced, playing a decisive role in the fall of the monarchy in 1889.

In 1822, however, the future of the independent nation still seemed uncertain. Brazilians were hesitant, unsure of how to manage their own political affairs in what was their first experience with self-government. They conceived a constitution that would favor local interests and foster national sentiment, but their intentions were thwarted by the impositions of a foreign-born monarch. In the rush to fill the vacuum of power left by the deserting king in 1821, the Prince Regent had emerged as a liberator; less than two years later, he appeared ready to reinstate colonial rule. As suspicions deepened, the newly acquired autonomy would experience both advances and setbacks. The Portuguese would have to be confronted until the territory was fully seized. During the brief period from 1821 to 1825, nothing seemed certain, and the final rupture with metropolitan rule had yet to happen.

Brazilians responded to their new political freedom with a combination of anxiety and enthusiasm. Self-government entailed responsibility and self-assurance. Above all, it called for the assumption of a new perspective on the land, which was no longer tied to foreign ownership and control. The new independence would prompt the emergence of a national sentiment and heighten the need for better integration between the various regions that had formerly belonged to the Portuguese Empire in America. In 1822, what was being inherited from that empire was a geographically fragmented political entity, divided into different areas dispersed throughout the former colonial territory. During the centuries of dependent existence, only limited communication had been possible between the distant provinces. Surprisingly, these provinces had remained mostly faithful to the Portuguese Crown since the beginning of colonization in 1530. Now the sharing of a common autonomous destiny called for the enhancement of mutual ties and the recognition of mutual dependence among the dissimilar and mostly isolated polities. The large territory, which for centuries had been subjected to the whims of Portuguese expansionism, could no longer maintain cohesion by means of external, colonial forces; a natural immanent power to maintain the integrity of the nation was needed, and for that, the establishment of interprovincial consensus had to be achieved.

In the decades immediately following 1822, the newly acquired autonomy would face severe threats. Difficulties arose from both internal and external factors. Popular discontent with the economic situation and foreign impositions coming from Europe compounded to form a wide range of varied problems. Separatist movements would break out soon after the severing of ties with Portugal, lasting well into the late 1840s. These revolts had to be controlled at the expense of the country's already meager financial resources, and measures to tackle the printing of money and other inflationary policies would have to be taken in order to subdue what appeared to be a potential repetition of the political fragmentation experienced in the Spanish colonial empire after 1810.

Foreign influences were also important factors restricting the new nation's effective autonomy. These came in the guise of unfavorable commercial agreements imposed as conditions for the international recognition of Brazil's independence. On top of that, the freedom from Portuguese rule had to be bought and paid for in cash. Autonomy was thus not wrested from the oppressors in a fight for rightful self-determination: it was financially arranged through compensatory measures that would satisfy the already deserting colonizers. As we will see below, a high sum had to be borrowed and paid to the Portuguese in exchange for the right to self-government. Brazil would thus be born as a nation already heavily in debt.

The new financial constraints caused by foreign debt would add to the old ones resulting from the country's previous history of exploitative administration. Centuries of colonial rule had left a record of backwardness and a lack of economic dynamism throughout the vast territory covetously disputed and steadfastly maintained by the Portuguese monarchs. Brazil's old contradictions were those common to agrarian societies economically dependent on the export of a few products of low aggregate value. The disadvantages and vulnerabilities generated by widespread monoculture and the consequential financial reliance on the trade of a limited number of products would deepen with the rise of coffee to the position of Brazil's largest export in the late 1830s. The product would take hold of the national economy, producing a deleterious lethargic effect on the nation's industry and general entrepreneurship. Added to this situation was the social backwardness that plagued the country as an offshoot of widespread slave labor. The exclusion of a large proportion of the nation's workforce from participation in a monetary national economy produced a condition of continuous bartering and hence sustained economic stagnation.

Thus, the independence achieved in 1822 would prove to be limited, the product of only a partial break with the metropolis. The ruling colonial dynasty would maintain its grip on all its former possessions. Its ownership and control of all there was in the land, and of the land itself, would, in the end, simply have passed from father to son.

The Costly Independence

Pedro de Alcântara was born in Portugal in 1798. He was the fourth child of John VI and his ambitious and unfaithful wife, the Queen Carlota Joaquina (1775–1830), daughter of King Charles IV of Spain. Having assumed the position of heir apparent to the throne of Portugal on the death of his older brother, Dom Francisco Antônio, the Prince of Beira (1795–1801), Pedro became Brazil's liberator when John VI returned to Lisbon at the request of the Portuguese Liberal Revolution of 1820. Finding themselves without a king after the Napoleonic wars, the Portuguese revolted and called their monarch back home. Although summoned to Europe to join his father, the Prince insisted on staying in Brazil, defying the orders of the Portuguese court, which hoped to reinstate the former colonial status of the Brazilian territory. The intrepid Prince proclaimed Brazilian independence on September 7, 1822, assuming the title of Brazilian Emperor with the name Pedro I.

The decision to break definitively from Portugal was made during a voyage to the province of São Paulo, where Pedro hoped to gather support for the Brazilian cause of autonomy. The break came easily and emphatically with the Prince crying out the words "Independence or death!" on the banks of the Ipiranga brook, a small rivulet that runs through the outskirts of what is today the city of São Paulo. The process of turning Pedro's formal proclamation of September 7 into political reality, however, was laborious and complex. A long and difficult negotiation with the former rulers had to be undertaken. The Braganza King, John VI, insisted on the new nation's formal international recognition as an independent state. This implied a series of financial and diplomatic negotiations, which above all meant it needed recognition from Portugal itself, as well as from the United Kingdom. Such recognition, as we will see in more detail below, would not be granted free of charge. It would, rather, have to be paid for with a very large financial sum, involving a complex business transaction, which, in turn, would plunge the nation into severe economic dependence on the United Kingdom, just as had been the case with Portugal itself since at least 1703.

Brazilian historians have remarked that the indemnities paid to Portugal in exchange for its recognition of Brazilian independence were mostly irrelevant to the actual process of independence.[1] The reparations were arranged well after the last Portuguese troops had been driven out of Brazilian territory, and the Portuguese had no military power to regain control over the land. The request for payment in exchange for official recognition appears thus to have been inspired by little more than a desire for financial gain.

Here, a note on the ousting of the Portuguese troops from Brazilian territory during the early years of the 1820s is in order. Pedro's declaration of Brazilian independence in September 1822 had reflected the demands for freedom and self-government spreading throughout the former colonial territory after the king's return to Portugal a year earlier, in April 1821. As we have seen, the Lisbon revolutionaries had made it clear that they would not accept the maintenance of equal status between Brazil and Portugal established under the united kingdom arrangement of 1815. Enraged with the attempt at re-colonization, Brazilians began to arm themselves. In November 1821, a war of independence between Brazilian and Portuguese troops broke out in the state of Bahia. The fighting was concentrated in the city of Salvador when the Portuguese officer Inácio Luís Madeira de Melo (1775–1833) was appointed commander-in-chief of the forces deployed to subdue the Brazilian separatists. Popular resistance against Madeira de Melo's forces was fierce, but the Portuguese managed to bring the city under control in February 1822. Celebrating their initial success, the Portuguese soldiers marched through the city perpetrating acts of pillage and violence. After occupying the southern part of the city, they proceeded to take the Catholic Convent of Lapa, threatening its nuns with rape and murder. The convent's Mother Superior, Sor Joana Angélica (1761–1822), took on the Portuguese soldiers herself in an attempt to protect the nuns, but was murdered mercilessly as the soldiers dashed into the convent. Angered by the Sor's death, the Brazilians moved fast to hire English mercenaries as commanders for their naval forces being deployed against the Portuguese. The ensuing naval battles spread to the land and into the city, the bloodshed leaving thousands of dead bodies lying on the streets. The siege of Salvador would only end in 1823, when the Brazilians, under the leadership of Admiral Thomas Cochrane (1775–1860), crushed Madeira de Melo's army. Sor Joana Angélica's bravery saw her become the first national martyr and the heroine of Brazilian independence, thus strengthening the emerging national sentiment.[2]

Together with the war in Bahia, clashes between Portuguese and Brazilian forces also occurred in the provinces of Piauí, Maranhão, Grão-Pará, and Cisplatina, with repeated Brazilian victories. Cochrane's fleet crushed the Portuguese at Bahia and Maranhão on July 2 and July 28, 1823, respectively. In the province of Piauí, after a series of bloody clashes, the forces of local chieftain Manuel de Sousa Martins (1767–1856) finally ousted the Portuguese on July 31. In Grão-Pará, Cochrane's subordinate officer John Pascoe Grenfell (1800–1869) secured an easy victory for the Brazilians by taking the capital, Belém, on October 12. The last province to be wrested from the Portuguese was the southern Cisplatine Province, which, as we have seen, comprised the area of present-day Uruguay, that is, the land extending from the southern frontier of present-day Rio Grande do Sul State southward to the Sacramento Colony. There the troops of General Carlos Frederico Lecor (1764–1836), governor of the Cisplatine Province since its annexation by John VI in 1817, finally evicted the Portuguese on March 8, 1824.

By mid-1824, the entire Brazilian territory had been put under Brazilian national control. Pedro de Alcântara, however, chose to accept his father's aforementioned requirement of international (i.e. mostly Portuguese and British) recognition as a condition for accepting the partition. This, as we have seen, would entail the payment of burdensome indemnities to Portugal. The process of procuring such financial resources is described below.

The British Foreign Secretary, George Canning (1770–1827), assumed the role of mediator between Brazil and Portugal, that is, between Pedro and his father. Canning had been the British ambassador to Lisbon from 1814 to 1816 and became Foreign Secretary in 1822, after the former Secretary, Lord Castlereagh, had committed suicide. The new Foreign Secretary was thus well acquainted with the peculiarities of the Braganzas, and knew of their tendency to promote their dynastic interests at the expense of their nation's needs. During the negotiation process, Canning made a point of not confirming the United Kingdom's recognition of Brazilian independence before Portugal had done so. This, of course, was not done because of any chivalric consideration for the old ally; Canning's strategy was to maneuver between the two sides of the dispute in order to guarantee the maintenance of British commercial privileges in Brazil, as accorded in the treaties of 1810.

The international status of Brazilian independence in the years immediately following Pedro I's declaration was as follows. The first states to express their recognition were Benin and Onin, two African nations involved in the slave trade with Brazil at the time. They were followed by the United States in 1824. Brazil's Latin American neighbors had adopted a republican system of government and were not inclined to immediately acknowledge the rule of a monarchy on their doorstep. As mentioned above, the new Latin American republics feared that a monarchist Brazil could serve as a springboard for European recolonization at a time when the Holy Alliance continued its stern political campaign in Europe, touting the divine rights of kings with support from conservative aristocrats such as Prince Klemens von Metternich (1773–1859), Austria's chancellor. U.S. President James Monroe's recognition of Brazilian independence in 1824 can in fact be interpreted as a response to the Alliance's threats. The recognition followed the principles expounded in Monroe's famous State of the Union Address of 1823, which presented the doctrine that any attempt by European nations to interfere with countries in the Americas would be regarded as an act of aggression requiring U.S. intervention. The doctrine was, however, something of an empty threat, for in 1823, the United States did not possess enough military force to take on the European powers of the Holy Alliance. Monroe's words were, nevertheless, met with enthusiasm by the militarily weak Latin American nations.

The United Kingdom, on the other hand, as of 1823, still had enough military clout to keep the Holy Alliance out of Latin America. With such bargaining power, Canning could maneuver the Brazilians into accepting the Portuguese and British conditions for their recognition of independence. The negotiations for the final deal were carried out in London between July and August 1824, when the Brazilian representative, the nobleman Felisberto Caldeira Brant Pontes de Oliveira Horta (1772–1842), was instructed to accept the Portuguese-British, or the Canning-Braganza, arrangement. The deal involved a hefty loan contracted by the newborn country with the British banker Nathan Mayer Rothschild (1777–1836). The loan would be issued in two parts, one in 1824 and another in 1825, and would be used to compensate the Portuguese for the loss of their former colony. The loan would mark the beginning of Brazil's long relationship of debt with the house of Rothschild, or with the United Kingdom, more generally.

In reality, however, the deal meant that Brazil was paying reparations for a war it had won. The country had been deprived of the financial reserves of its only bank, the Bank of Brazil, and still had to contract a large loan to pay indemnities to the Portuguese, the actual swindlers. No matter what angle one looks at it from, the deal appears 'circular' in that all the payments and repayments were being made between the members of a single family, making the whole thing little more than a private, family affair. Brazilian independence was thus the result of some squalid horse-trading.

In the horse-trading for Brazilian independence, the British were perhaps the greatest winners. They profited, firstly by extending a high interest loan that would be repaid at a 5% annual rate of interest, providing a remarkable profit for their banker. (As we will see in the next chapter, the loan would actually have to be refinanced in 1898 as a "Funding Loan," that is, a loan to repay a loan.) Secondly, they also profited by including in the deal the continuation of all the privileges acquired in the aftermath of the Portuguese court's transfer to Brazil in 1808. The treaties of 1810 would thus remain in force until 1844, enslaving the Brazilian economy by not allowing it to implement any form of protectionist tariffs in foreign trade, such tariffs being a vital source of revenue for an agricultural exporting economy characterized by the virtual absence of a domestic industry. Furthermore, the United Kingdom profited by getting rid of the Portuguese as intermediaries in Brazilian commerce. And they also profited by including an anti-slave traffic clause in the agreement. The clause determined that the Brazilian Empire would proscribe the slave trade within three years of 1827. Since slave labor lowered the price of Brazilian tropical products in relation to similar ones produced in British colonies, this British insistence on the end of slavery served its commercial interests well. Finally, and to make matters worse for the Brazilians even in terms of the symbolic dimensions of their independence, after all the wheeling and dealing, John VI would still maintain the Brazilian Crown, which he would hand on to his son only when it suited him.

The loan contracted with the British and then swapped between the Braganza father and son placed a heavy burden on the new nation, which would suffer a series of financial crises starting as early as 1825. Having these new financial liabilities contracted with a foreign nation represented a loss of sovereignty and a weakened capacity for domestic investment and growth. Added to this was a costly war sustained by the new nation, the so-called Brazilian Empire, in the south of its territory against the United Provinces of the River Plate. The most immediate results of this combination of foreign debt and war would be high inflation, popular discontent, and social unrest. Together, these phenomena would contribute to the fall of Pedro I six years after his signing of the independence loan in London.

Before we finish this account of Brazil's mostly unheroic achievement of independence in the hands of the Braganza dynasty, we must mention one man who emerged as a beacon of Brazilian national sentiment, offering a stark contrast to the monarchy's financial self-indulgence. This man was José Bonifácio de Andrada e Silva (1763–1838), a statesman, biologist, historian, academic, and poet who would be granted the title of Brazil's Patriarch of Independence. Bonifácio played an important role in Pedro de Alcântara's decision to defy the Lisbon court's summons in 1821. He urged the Prince to stay and to lead the new nation to autonomy.

José Bonifácio was a man of superior intelligence who emerged as one of the first opponents of slavery and the general racial prejudice that prevailed in the fiercely aristocratic and hierarchical Brazilian society of the early nineteenth century. In early 1823, he presented a detailed project to the recently established Constituent Assembly proposing measures for the integration of the indigenous peoples into the new nation's society. An unyielding abolitionist, Bonifácio declared slavery to be contrary to natural law, and proposed the end of slavery in favor of reason, honor, Christian faith, and national dignity. He did not own slaves and did not employ slave labor on his estates. The "Patriarch of Independence" also defended environmental causes, proposing the establishment of national preservation areas in the country as early as 1819. His most advanced ideas, however, were those related to land reform and to the revision of the property rights applicable to the owners of the enormous age-old sesmaria estates. Bonifácio's progressive inclinations, however, would meet robust resistance from the aristocratic and authoritarian rule of Pedro I. In 1823, the politician's democratic and egalitarian ideas led to his arrest and banishment from the country by the Emperor. Authoritarianism and dictatorship were thus emerging as defining traits of Brazilian government in the first days of its independence.[3]

Having thus briefly examined the way in which Brazil acquired political autonomy from Portugal, we are now ready to observe what historians usually refer to as *Primeiro Reinado*, the period between Pedro I's coronation as Brazilian Emperor on October 12, 1822, and his abdication on April 7, 1831. As we will see in the following pages, this was a period of conflict and instability, when wars (internal and external), economic uncertainty, inflation, and the arrogance and voracity of a Portuguese-born monarch resulted in the fall of the nation's first autonomous government.

The First Empire (1822–1831)

As we have seen, when Pedro de Alcântara proclaimed Brazilian independence in 1822 what he had on his hands was a number of geographically disconnected provinces that had little in common with each other. The immense territory amassed by the Portuguese colonizers since the days of the Iberian Union was distributed among a small class of landowners, and the ingrained culture of land and income concentration, expressed very early in the sesmaria system, generated vast, empty spaces that enhanced the isolation of the distant provincial capitals from one another. One of the few connecting factors between these primarily unrelated political units was their ruling elites, which were interrelated by means of speaking a common language, Portuguese, and by having a similar educational background, that is, they had studied at the same university, the University of Coimbra, in Portugal.

The total population of Portuguese America in 1822 is estimated at 4.5 million residents, in an area of more than 8 million square kilometers. About 47% of the population lived in the northeastern part of the country, and the capital, Rio de Janeiro, had around 100,000 residents.[4] The underdeveloped system of transportation and communication further isolated the growing urban centers of São Paulo, Rio de Janeiro, Salvador, and Recife. The central part of the territory would not begin to be populated until 1960, with the construction of Brasilia during the government of President Juscelino Kubitschek.

The notion Brazilians adopted to describe what Pedro was acquiring through his proclamation of independence was that of *empire*. The concept expressed the grandiosity, the diversity, and also the alleged political unity of the Portuguese-inherited domain. In that year, 1822, the Portuguese monarchy's sustained control over a vast expanse of land contrasted sharply with the breaking off of the Spanish colonies into various small and weak republics. For Brazilians, the call for unity and the wish to avoid the same fate as their neighbors justified the maintenance of the monarchic system. They thus sanctioned the notion of empire as a way to suggest the superiority and the stateliness of the new independent political entity.

The notion of empire also suggested that some degree of provincial autonomy would be allowed within the new political arrangement. Self-administrative leeway would be granted to the various localized centers of power, however, only as long as the prevailing central authority of the emperor went unchallenged. In the end, and as we will see in more detail below, such political centralization did in fact succeed in maintaining the territorial unity of Portuguese America, even if repeated attempts at autonomy kept breaking out in some of the provinces.

The fundamental element underpinning the maintenance of the new nation's territorial unity was the small and homogenous dominant class that ruled the various regions of the country. As we have mentioned, this class had important points of contact in spite of its geographical disconnection. Above all, it shared the same basic aristocratic values that had been hegemonic throughout the previous centuries of Portuguese rule. Among a general population marked by a 99% rate of illiteracy, these powerful local aristocrats comprised what Brazilian historian José Murilo de Carvalho (b. 1939) famously called "an island of literates, in an ocean of illiterates."[5] To a great extent, they were the ones responsible for preventing the dissolution of the country's territorial unity after the end of Portuguese rule in Brazil.

These ruling aristocrats were also the same individuals who convened at the Constituent Assembly gathered in Rio de Janeiro on May 3, 1823 to draft the nation's first legal charter. In those times of crisis in the *ancien régime*, Pedro I was called to swear to a constitution, just like his father had pledged to respect and obey the one hastily devised by the Lisbon revolutionaries in Portugal in 1821. While John VI was presented with a ready-made text that reproduced the main directives of the Spanish constitution of 1812, however, Pedro I had enough leeway to impose his own views and interests on what he insisted had to be a document "worthy of himself." The Braganza Prince made it clear that he would swear the text drafted by the Brazilians only if it reflected his own views, which were primarily conservative and authoritarian.

During the Assembly's procedures, dissent arose among the deputies. They soon split into two factions, the Brazilian and the Portuguese. The former defended the drafting of a liberal constitution that limited the powers of the monarch and expanded provincial autonomy; the latter sought almost unlimited power for the emperor, calling for a centralized system founded on the very figure of Pedro I. The anti-absolutist proposal of the Brazilian faction was tinted with anti-lusitanism: for the Brazilians, the centralizing preferences of the Portuguese party appeared to be a disguise to promote Portuguese views and interests, and thus to open the way for a future re-colonization of the now independent nation. The logic behind the Brazilian faction's fears was that since Pedro was in fact

Portuguese, his personal sentiments should include an innate sense of loyalty towards his motherland. This being the case, he could not be fully trusted to sustain Brazilian independence.

Faced with such mounting dissent, Pedro I was quick in asserting his power against the rebelling deputies who dared defy his authority. On November 12, 1823, the Emperor ordered his army to invade the Constituent Assembly's plenary session. Several deputies attempted to resist and were immediately arrested and banished from the country. Among them was José Bonifácio de Andrada e Silva, the man who had, from the beginning, supported the idea of Pedro as leader of the new independent nation.

The episode of 1823 became known as the "Night of Agony." The term suggests the sense of political crisis and the general anxiety Brazilians experienced at the event, understanding the frailty of the newly acquired autonomy and facing the threat of a re-establishment of Portuguese rule. The constitution drafted at the event was rejected, and the Constituent Assembly was immediately terminated.[6]

After closing the Constituent Assembly, and still in an atmosphere of authoritarianism, Pedro de Alcântara gathered ten of his closest followers and ordered the drafting of a new constitution. The resulting charter would be imposed upon the nation on March 25, 1824. It established a centralized administrative form of government, one in which the emperor appointed a governor for each province. Regional autonomy was thus curtailed in favor of a primarily absolutist arrangement. The Charter established four state powers: the Executive, the Legislature, the Judiciary, and the reserve power called "Moderator." The latter allowed for imperial arbitration over all administrative affairs, giving the Emperor the last word on political decisions. The reserve power would become a subject of great political disagreement throughout the following sixty-seven years of monarchical rule. It would be seen as a means of legitimizing despotism and arbitrariness.[7]

Dissent regarding the politically centralizing disposition of the Charter soon gave rise to unrest in the provinces. A secessionist movement broke out on July 2, 1824 in the Northeast, with the province of Pernambuco leading what came to be known as the *Confederation of the Equator*. The province had already staged a major uprising a few years earlier in 1817, when a group of liberal politicians and intellectuals, influenced by the ideas of the French Revolution and supported by the various local lodges of the masonry, claimed local independence from Portuguese rule. Espousing liberal and republican ideals, the revolutionaries of 1817 attempted to curry favor from foreign nations such as the United States and Argentina in support of the founding of a republic in the northeastern part of Brazil. Though eventually unsuccessful in their attempts, the revolutionaries did win from the monarchy the promise that enhanced autonomy would be granted to their province.[8]

After the 1824 Constitution was promulgated, however, republican ideals again emerged in Pernambuco. The province was divided into two factions, with monarchists and republicans vying for control over the local government. Pernambuco had long been the colony's administrative unit where feelings of hostility towards the Portuguese and their Crown were most intense. The roots of anti-Portuguese sentiment could be traced back to the aforementioned War of the Mascates, the conflict staged in 1710 when Portuguese merchants from Recife and Brazilian landowners from Olinda fought each other in an armed conflict. The dispute's name was borrowed from a pejorative denomination of the Portuguese merchants, *mascates*. The conflict's most immediate causes had been the restrictions imposed on the merchants' political participation in the colonial administration, as well as the high price for commodities imposed by these same merchants in the area. At the time, Portuguese merchants were granted commercial monopoly in the colony, which earned them the hatred of the Brazilians whenever food shortages or monetary inflation came into play. The War of the Mascates was one of the first instances of conflict between Brazilians and Portuguese in the colonial territory, and it remained in the minds of people in Pernambuco as a mark of local pride and defiance.

In 1824, the situation became even more fraught than it had been in 1710. Peace in the province became unsustainable when the same revolutionaries who had surrendered in 1817 on the promise that the monarchy would cede them enhanced political autonomy found themselves faced with a constitution that allowed the Emperor to impose an unwanted governor in the region. The ensuing rebellion was led by the freemason Manuel de Carvalho Paes de Andrade (1774–1855) and by the Carmelite monk Joaquim da Silva Rabelo (1779–1825), known as Frei Caneca. Caneca was an important religious and intellectual figure, who used the local press to propagate liberal ideas in the country. His journal, the *Typhis Pernambucano* (est. 1823), was a breeding ground for anti-monarchism and for the fight for freedom of the press. Backed by the Carmelite monk, Paes de Andrade seized the provincial government and proclaimed a republic in Pernambuco on July 2, 1824. The central government's coffers were still empty as a result of John VI's 1821 flight to Lisbon, so the crushing of the rebellion had to be paid for with the financial resources obtained from the same loan that was being negotiated with the British bankers in London and which was supposed to be used to pay for independence. Pedro I once again hired the naval commander Thomas Cochrane to subdue the rebels. Together with the Brazilian general Francisco de Lima e Silva (1786–1853), Cochrane suppressed the revolt in late October 1824.[9] The Carmelite monk, Frei Caneca, was hanged on January 13, 1825.[10]

Although the northeastern rebellion was rapidly extinguished, it left a lasting impression in people's minds. It showed that freedom and autonomy, if achieved at all, would be only limited. In any case, peace was certainly not evident with Pedro I's figure occupying the imperial chair in Rio de Janeiro. In the historically violent and unsettled South, where it had never been clear whether the rightful owners of the territory were the Spanish or the Portuguese, the Brazilian emperor faced a double threat: both his former Portuguese countrymen and his traditional Spanish enemies were quick to question his authority. In 1817, the army of Pedro's father had occupied the city of Montevideo and defeated the forces of José Gervasio Artigas (1764–1850), the Uruguayan national hero who, in 1811, had wrested the city from Spain and attached it to the United Provinces of the River Plate, present-day Argentina. After the final defeat of Artigas by the Portuguese forces in the Battle of Tacuarembó, in 1820, the region that had historically been called by the Portuguese *Banda Oriental*, that is, the portion of land spreading from the eastern bank of the River Plate, was annexed to the Portuguese Crown under the name of *Província Cisplatina*.

In that year, 1820, the Portuguese king entrusted the region's administration to the abovementioned nobleman and military commander, Carlos Frederico Lecor (1764–1836) who, in 1817, had led John VI's troops against Artigas. The King's plans for the region involved the potential dowry of his wife, Queen Carlota Joaquina of Bourbon (1775–1830). As we have seen, the Queen was the daughter of King Carlos IV, who had recently been ousted from his throne in Spain. John VI had learned from the three hundred-year history of conflict in the region that the Spanish would never stop fighting for the territory of what was his recently acquired Cisplatine Province. That notwithstanding, he surmised that his Spanish wife being the rightful heir to that very land he now disputed, a solution might be arranged in a way agreeable to both the Portuguese and the Spanish. If Carlota Joaquina managed to rule the Cisplatine Province, and perhaps along with it also the United Provinces of the River Plate, then their children would inherit a powerful Portuguese-Spanish empire extending through the greater part of South America. Carlota Joaquina readily accepted this idea, which she appears to have shared with her lover, the British naval officer Sir William Sidney Smith (1764–1840).[11]

The plan seemed perfect, but was soon vetoed by the British. Through its Ambassador to Rio de Janeiro, Lord Strangford (1780–1855), the United Kingdom rapidly dissuaded the Spanish Queen from her imperialistic intentions; British interests would be better served by a weak and fragmented Latin America.

Be that as it may, soon after Pedro I's proclamation of Brazilian independence the situation in the Cisplatine region became convoluted. Part of the forces occupying the area since John VI's invasion in 1817 remained loyal to Portugal, and conflict with the partisans of the Brazilian faction involved another episode of the so-called Brazilian War of Independence. One of the Portuguese regional military officers, D. Álvaro da Costa (1789–1835), rose against Carlos Lecor, the region's administrative commander who opted to offer his loyalty to Pedro I and to the Brazilian Empire. Following a first battle, Lecor was obliged to retreat north with his troops towards Rio Grande do Sul. After a later confrontation fought on March 2, 1824, however, Lecor managed to subdue the insurgents and the last bastion of Portuguese resistance in America was finally overpowered.

The Portuguese-Brazilian dispute's resolution notwithstanding, a few months later new instability would arise in the region. Juan Antonio Lavalleja (1784–1853) and Fructuoso Rivera (1784–1854), two local warlords dissatisfied with the unfulfilled Brazilian promises of granting autonomy to the region after the Portuguese had been defeated, initiated a military campaign for Uruguayan independence. Lavalleja and Rivera received support from the governor of the province of Buenos Aires, the powerful Bernardino Rivadavia (1780–1845). Their concerted plan was to incorporate the Brazilian Cisplatine Province into the Argentine United Provinces of the River Plate. Lavalleja led a group of *caudillos* (warlords) self-denominated the *Treinta y Tres Orientales*—a name derived from the masonic lodge to which Lavalleja belonged—and invaded the Cisplatine Province on April 19, 1825.

The Treinta y Tres Orientales' conflict with the Brazilians, as well as their insistence on gaining autonomy from the Empire, had mostly economic causes. As we have seen, the disputes in the region were long-standing. The violence had begun with the Portuguese obsession with territorial expansion and the resulting foundation of the Sacramento Colony in 1680. The Colony, once again, was meant to advance the Portuguese ambition of controlling the silver that was transported along the River Plate and shipped to Europe from the port at Buenos Aires. Over time, however, new actors and new interests came into play in the area, enhancing the fierce opposition between the Spanish and the Portuguese. Cattle farming emerged as a common economic activity that again set the two Iberian peoples against each other in economic and territorial competition. The common climate and general geography of the territories of southern Brazil, northeastern Argentina, and Uruguay, which share the same landscape of vast plains covered with pastures and pampas grass, encouraged a single economic activity that crossed the imaginary lines drawn as national borders between these political units.

The Portuguese annexation of the Cisplatine strengthened the cattle industry of Rio Grande do Sul, destabilizing that of the United Provinces of the River Plate. Colonization in the area had historically been made through the granting of large estates to military commanders who would move to the region and establish themselves as local chieftains, maintaining control over the territory in constant conflict with their neighbors. The emergence of the cattle economy entailed the emergence of local types that came to characterize the region's human landscape: on one side, the *caudilho*, that is, the powerful landowner and military commander; on the other, the *gaúcho*, that is, the caudilho's cowboy and militia man. These were the rustic individuals whose livelihood was tied to the hardships of cattle farming, and whose interests now diverged from those of their neighbors as the result of economic competition. This rivalry now pitted the Uruguayan Treinta y Tres Orientales against the Brazilian chieftains from Rio Grande do Sul.

The ensuing Uruguayan War of Independence thus resulted from the age-old mutual dislikes that roiled the Brazilian southern landlords, the Riograndenses, as well as the Uruguayan-Argentines. The war began when Juan Antonio Lavalleja proclaimed Uruguayan independence on August 25, 1825. Since Lavalleja's interests were closely connected to those of the Argentine leader, Bernardino Rivadavia, the resulting war would not be fought simply between the Brazilian Empire and its secessionist Province, the Cisplatine, but between Brazil and the United Provinces of the River Plate, the powerful political entity that would adopt the name of Argentine Confederation in 1826.

Over the next three years, the war raged through the historically bloody region. From the start of the conflict, the Brazilian forces were at a significant disadvantage. Their decision-makers were far to the north in the Empire's capital, Rio de Janeiro, and the southern Riograndenses were left almost alone with the responsibility of handling the battles. Moreover, part of what had become the local Brazilian army had vanished when Lecor superseded Álvaro da Costa a year earlier, in 1824. In other words, the army's Portuguese faction had fled after being defeated by the Brazilian Empire's forces.

The Argentines had their first major victory in 1826, in what they called "Battle of Ituzaingó," which is known in Brazil as the "Battle of Passo do Rosário." The Brazilian army was led by Felisberto Caldeira Brant (1772–1842), the Marquis of Barbacena, the same man who a few years earlier had received a generous commission for contracting the notorious "Loan of the Independence" with the Rothschild House in London.[12]

As the war progressed, Pedro I sent a fleet to block the port of Buenos Aires, while the Argentines attacked the coast of Rio Grande do Sul. Aided by German, British, and American mercenaries, the Brazilians won the Battle of Monte Santiago in 1827. European mercenaries led both contending forces: British captain James Norton commanded the Brazilian fleet, while the Irish commander William Brown steered the Argentines.[13] In a reversal of the developments of 1826, when the Argentines had won at Passo do Rosário, in 1827 Pedro I's naval forces resisted and took the conflict to a stalemate. As the prolonged war was causing important financial losses for European merchants, the British pushed for a diplomatic solution. Peace was agreed on August 27, 1828, when, through the mediation of British diplomat, Lord John Ponsonby (1770–1855), the Cisplatine Province was recognized as an independent state under the name of the Oriental Republic of Uruguay. The outcome, again, favored British interests, for the newly achieved peace allowed them to enhance their economic and political influence in the region. Lord Ponsonby became famous for saying that, with the independence of Uruguay, a piece of cotton was being placed between two crystal vessels, that is, Brazil and Argentina, which were likely to destroy each other upon contact. The Oriental Republic of Uruguay was thus established as a buffer state.[14]

The Cisplatine War was the first of four international armed conflicts breaking out in the South between Brazil and its neighbors. The other three are the Platine War (1851–1852), which again saw Brazil and Argentina at war; the Uruguayan War (1864–1865), fought between the Uruguayan Blanco Party on one side, and an alliance between Brazil and the Uruguayan Colorado Party on the other; and the Paraguayan War (1865–1870), in which Brazil, Argentina and Uruguay allied against Paraguay. Together these four conflicts are known in Brazilian diplomatic history as the "Platine Questions."

The Cisplatine War had significant consequences for the future development of Brazilian independence, as well as for the construction of Brazilian nationality. The loss of the province added to the growing popular dissatisfaction with Pedro I's policies. As we have seen, following independence, the Brazilian political scene was divided among supporters of a centralized administrative structure on one side, and of a decentralized system with enhanced provincial autonomy on the other. In general terms, the former constituted what was called the Portuguese party, while the latter formed its Brazilian counterpart. Portuguese-born Pedro was regarded as biased towards the Portuguese faction. His continual favoring of the Portuguese side, together with complaints about his licentiousness in sexual matters, were provoking a serious decline in his popularity. The war with Argentina resulted in a great financial burden for the newly independent nation, and its unsatisfactory outcome was blamed in part on the Emperor.

The Emperor and his imperial court tried to find a scapegoat to blame for the defeat by the Argentines in the Cisplatine War. Since the war had been fought primarily in the province of Rio Grande do Sul, and since the confrontation's main purpose had in fact been to defend the interests of the southern landowning cattle raisers and beef curers, the blame was finally placed on the Riograndenses themselves. Commander Lecor was summoned to Rio de Janeiro and submitted to a war council, which investigated the lack of bravery among Rio Grande do Sul's troops as the possible cause for the embarrassing fiasco experienced at the hands of Argentina.

After a long trial, Lecor was finally absolved from the charges of treason, but the humiliation suffered by the Riograndense *caudilhos*, who had seen their honor and bravery questioned, would not be easily forgotten.[15] They started a process of regional self-assertion that would soon foster delusions of nationalism. As we will see in more detail below, the situation in the South would become further convoluted after a series of liberal reforms imposed by the central government in the early 1830s, which allowed for the levying of tariffs at provincial borders. The new tariffs increased the price of Rio Grande do Sul's beef for out-of-state consumers, adding dissatisfaction to the humiliation the southern landlords had suffered in the war.[16] Together with the rampant indignation at accusations of cowardice in fighting the Argentines, these new economic disadvantages would inspire the Riograndenses to take up arms and proclaim a republic of their own. Through what they called the Farroupilha Revolution, the Riograndenses would establish the "Republic of Piratini," a failed republican attempt that lasted from 1835 to 1845, being finally crushed by the imperial government after almost ten years of bloodshed in the area.

The Cisplatine War entailed a severe loss of territory for the new nation. The Province, inherited from the Portuguese Crown as part of the Brazilian domain, was lost forever. And to make matters worse, the struggle against Argentina had emptied the Empire's coffers right after a colossal foreign loan had been contracted. The country's ability to repay the loan was thus limited and inflation rose to astronomical levels after the war began, fueled by recurrent waves of new money issued from a squashed and hollowed-out Bank of Brazil. After the war ended, the bank was declared insolvent, closing its doors on September 23, 1829. The shutting down of the nation's only bank was the result of an intractable ministerial debate on public finance, probably the first one to be carried out on Brazilian soil. The powerful liberal deputy Bernardo Pereira de Vasconcelos (1795–1850), who would later perform a u-turn and leave the Liberal Party to become one of the country's fiercest conservatives, was the first politician to note what he called the "swelling" of currency, and to propose the Bank's closure in 1828.[17]

Pedro I's political position weakened further when his opponents began to criticize his recurrent sex scandals. The Emperor had married the Austrian princess, Maria Leopoldina (1797–1826) in 1818. His sexual voracity, however, gave him a roving eye for the various court ladies that vied for his favor. Pedro enjoyed all sorts of female companionship, including the less courtly variety. In 1822, he met Domitila de Castro do Canto e Melo (1797–1867) during a trip to the province of São Paulo. Domitila was a married woman, one year Pedro's senior. She had three children and a history of being abused by her husband who, to judge by the scars on her body, appeared to have stabbed her on more then one occasion.

Pedro fell deeply in love with Domitila and brought her to Rio de Janeiro, offering her a position at the court as the Empress's lady-in-waiting and giving her the title of Marchioness of Santos. The Empress, Maria Leopoldina, was of very delicate nature and had a gentle physical disposition. She was greatly loved by her subjects. The humiliation of having Domitila at her side appears to have been unbearable to the young Empress. She died in 1826 following a miscarriage, and public opinion was swift to lay the blame on Domitila. Soon after the Empress's death, the Emperor's lover was banished from the court.[18]

While Pedro's sexual dalliances accounted for part of his growing unpopularity, a looming economic crisis and a series of bad political decisions brought about the final decay of his government. The incident of the death of a journalist, the Italian-born Giovanni Battista Libero Badaró (1798–1830), inflamed public opinion against the foreign (that is,

Portuguese) emperor. Badaró was an avid defender of liberal principles and of the freedom of the press. In 1829, he founded the newspaper *O observador constitucional* in São Paulo, from where his liberal ideals were publicized in a moderate way, not far removed from other journals such as Evaristo da Veiga's *Aurora Fluminense*. Despite his generally moderate tone, Badaró's enthusiasm for the European Revolution of 1830, touted openly in the pages of his *O observador constitucional*, made him an object of hatred among several conservative politicians who supported the Emperor's authoritarian ways, as well as the idea of a centralized administration, as the best political option for the country. Badaró's urging Brazilians to follow the example of the French, who had just deposed Charles X in the July Revolution, stirred the conservatives into action and he was murdered on November 20, 1830, on the way home from his office in São Paulo. The Emperor's lenience toward the murderers at their trial shocked the population. Some began to think that the Emperor himself had ordered the crime. In response, liberals began to plot his downfall.

Pedro I was aware of his waning prestige. At the end of 1830, he traveled to Minas Gerais, a province of strong liberal inclination controlled by the powerful Bernardo Pereira de Vasconcelos. The imperial visit was part of Pedro I's attempt at reconciliation with the liberals. In Minas Gerais, however, the Emperor was received with popular indifference. Seeing his efforts at a rapprochement with the liberals frustrated, Pedro I started back to Rio de Janeiro. Knowing of his return, the Emperor's conservative supporters, most of them Portuguese-born, started preparing a feast to mark his arrival. They planned to greet Pedro in exuberant style, with an impressive public welcoming celebration arranged in the center of the imperial capital. Before the Emperor's convoy appeared on Rio de Janeiro's mountainous horizon, however, a fight between activists from both parties, Brazilian and Portuguese, broke out. The two sides began throwing bottles at each other and the large-scale riot that ensued continued into the night, becoming known as the *Noite das garrafadas* (Evening of Bottlefights). The incident brought into sharp relief the reality of mounting chaos and political instability in the country. The next morning, the brawl continued with each side demanding punishment for the other.[19]

Pedro I's political situation had been further complicated by the death of his father in 1826. The King's death in Portugal had made the Brazilian Emperor the rightful heir to the Portuguese Crown. In spite of his abdication of the European throne in favor of his daughter, Maria da Glória de Bragança (1819–1853), Brazilians still feared Pedro's possible intention of reuniting the two crowns, the Brazilian and the Portuguese. As long as Pedro I stayed in power, the Brazilians' age-old dread of renewed Portuguese rule persisted.

Trying to appease the mutual dislike left on both sides by the pathetic spectacle of the bottle-throwing confrontation, the Emperor decided to appoint a new ministerial cabinet comprised solely of Brazilian officials. However, soon afterwards, Pedro I, in a display of his characteristic impulsiveness, decided to substitute the recently formed Brazilian cabinet with a Portuguese one. This second ministerial cabinet came to be known as *Ministério dos Marqueses*. Formed by the fiercest conservatives, historically referred to as *corcundas* (hunchbacks), the appointment of the cabinet was seen as an outright attack on the Brazilian faction. A series of public protests ensued, with widespread criticism of Pedro's almost whimsical irregularities and indecisiveness. Faced with the people's opposition to his unstable policies, Pedro I abdicated on April 7, 1831, bringing to an end the *Primeiro Reinado*.

In the aftermath of the period from 1822 to 1831, Brazil was still politically unstable, constrained by foreign debt, hampered by a weak sense of nationality, and inept when it came to devising and controlling its own destiny. Some historians have attempted to restore Pedro I's reputation by pointing to the positive aspects of his administration as Brazil's first monarch. Charges of absolutism are thus dismissed on the grounds that Pedro I kept his vow to respect the Constitution of 1824, did not interfere with elections, and protected freedom of speech. In his defense, his anti-slavery position is also cited, which was real and attested to his good sense, but which in the end was not actually effective in bringing about an end to slavery in a backward nation that was controlled by slave-owning landowners. After the abdication, 34-year-old Pedro would head immediately for Europe, where, heroically, he would fight his treacherous brother who had usurped the throne of his daughter.[20]

In what follows we will see what happened to the Brazilian Empire after the fall of its first ruler. Civil war, chaos, internal strife, economic and political meltdown, disputes among liberals and conservatives, and the final ascension of another Braganza to the Brazilian throne are some of the events described next.

The Regency (1831–1840)

On April 7, 1831, the Brazilian Emperor, Pedro I, abdicated in favor of his five-year-old son who, like his father, was named Pedro de Alcântara. Because of his age, the new Emperor was prevented from being crowned and was placed under the protection of three tutors. José Bonifácio, who had been pardoned by Pedro I and allowed to return to Brazil in 1829, was appointed as one of the young Pedro's mentors. The new political administration of the Empire was entrusted to executive councils. This allowed a new form of competition to emerge between liberals and conservatives, who vied for pre-eminence in the Rio de Janeiro court.

Following Pedro I's abdication, the Empire's deputies and senators convened to elect a provisional regency, in accordance with the procedure established in the 1824 Imperial Constitution. Senators Francisco de Lima e Silva (1785–1853), the military commander responsible for suppressing the Pernambucan rebellion of 1824, Nicolau Pereira de Campos Vergueiro (1778–1859), a Portuguese-born landowner and slave dealer who defended the idea of Brazil's annexation of Angola to facilitate the transfer of African slaves to his coffee plantations, and José Joaquim Carneiro de Campos (1768–1836), the man responsible for drafting the Imperial Constitution of 1824, were elected as regents, taking office on the day of Pedro I's abdication, April 7, 1831. The provisional triumvirate reinstated the Brazilian ministers deposed by Pedro I a few days before his abdication and restricted the executive reserve power established in the constitution. The triumvirate resigned on May 3, 1831, when a permanent tripartite regency was elected.

The nine years that followed would see the rise and decline of both liberals and conservatives in power during what came to be known as the Regency Period. The permanent triumvirate remained in office from 1831 to 1835. It was composed of moderate liberals who found themselves faced with the task of extinguishing a series of rebellions that broke out in the provinces as a result of the vacuum of power left by Pedro I's abdication.

As the abdication had resulted from the liberal faction's maneuvering, a range of liberal reforms ensued under the cabinet installed in 1831. The first political innovation introduced by the permanent triumvirate was the establishment of the National Guard in 1831. The imperial army had become a source of suspicion for the liberals, for it was composed mostly of officers born in Portugal, or at least of men potentially loyal to Pedro I. The National Guard was thus created as a paramilitary force aimed at countering the army's tendency to favor absolutist restoration.[21]

A larger legal reform was also put into effect. It was instituted through the so-called 1834 Additional Act, a constitutional amendment aimed at enhancing provincial autonomy in the Empire. The Act resulted from the presence of a liberal majority in the House of Representatives. Drafted by Bernardo Pereira de Vasconcelos, it established important democratizing reforms, of which the foremost was a new election process whereby a single regent would be selected as head of state, thus filling the administrative void left by Pedro I until his son reached adulthood. The 1834 Additional Act also extinguished the Council of State, a body with an auxiliary function in the emperor's exercise of his reserve power. The Council tended to reproduce conservative values, being responsible for the formulation of the Empire's foreign policy.

Increased provincial autonomy was accompanied by the establishment of interprovincial tariffs. Such tariffs represented the triumph of the federalist model, as each province would be granted autonomy to procure public revenue from interprovincial trade.[22] The implementation of such tariffs, however, was not welcomed in all the provinces. As already mentioned, they became an important source of discontent in the traditionally unsettled Rio Grande do Sul, where they would emerge as one of the causes of a revolutionary secessionist uprising.

As liberals and conservatives alternated in power, the legal framework of the Empire fluctuated, creating a sense of general instability and political indecision. In all a total of fifteen civil revolts broke out during the nine-year period of the Regency. In the province of Maranhão, an armed rebellion called *Setembrada* started on December 13, 1831, when a man named Antônio João Damasceno led a violent mob against the Portuguese residents. Maranhão had been the stage of one of the first anti-Portuguese revolts in the colony, the Beckman Brothers uprising which, in 1685, rose up against the monopolistic practices of the Commercial Company of Maranhão, one of the aforementioned exploitative enterprises owned by the Portuguese Crown.

Anti-Portuguese sentiment also flared up again in Pernambuco, where attempts to drive Portuguese-born officials and businessmen out of the province continued from 1831 to 1834. This unrest would ultimately result in the larger uprising of 1848 called the *Revolução Praieira*. While anti-Portuguese feelings spread though the coastal areas, in the interior a distinct uprising called the War of the Cabanos broke out in 1832, lasting until 1835. In contrast with the anti-Portuguese sentiment driving unrest elsewhere, this revolt reflected dissatisfaction with economic stagnation and the privileges enjoyed by British subjects in national territory. It also demanded the return of Pedro I.

In 1835, in compliance with the dispositions of the 1834 Additional Act, an individual regent was elected to replace the triumvirate. The moderate liberal Diogo Antônio Feijó (1784–1843) took office on October 12, 1835. A Catholic priest from São Paulo, Feijó was hampered by opposition from powerful politicians such as Bernardo Pereira de Vasconcelos, Honório Hermeto Carneiro Leão (1801–1856), and Maciel

Monteiro (1780–1847). Feijó's administration faced two violent uprisings that threatened the territorial integrity of the Empire, one in the province of Pará, called *Cabanagem*, and another in Rio Grande do Sul, the aforementioned Farroupilha. The Cabanagem was caused by the extreme poverty and political negligence experienced in the province of Pará after independence in 1822. The movement started among the lower classes, including members of the indigenous population, black slaves, and poor mestizo peasants who took control of the provincial government. The rebellion ended only in 1840, when the central authorities perpetrated a massacre that exterminated about 40% of the province's population. The Cabanagem counts as one of the many instances in Brazilian history where revolts started by the lower classes ended in severe repression and massacre.[23]

The Farroupilha Revolt sits at the opposite end of the class spectrum that marked the civil uprisings of the period. The southern conflict sprang from the dissatisfaction of the provincial elite of cattle raisers and warlords in Rio Grande do Sul. The humiliating charge of treason during the Cisplatine War, together with the economically harmful provisions of the 1834 Additional Act, led the southern landowners to take up arms on September 20, 1835. The Riograndenses began entertaining the idea of annexing Rio Grande do Sul's territory to Argentina, which at the time was ruled by Juan Manuel de Rosas (1793–1877), a shrewd politician who for many years managed to prevent Brazilian hegemony in the Platine region. The negotiations with Rosas gave the southern warlords enhanced clout to defy the Brazilian Empire. They pursued a prolonged military campaign, engaging a group of Italian adventurers and mercenaries such as Giuseppe Garibaldi (1807–1882), Tito Lívio Zambeccari (1802–1862), and Luigi Rossetti (1800–1840), most of them refugees from the Carbonaria, the secret society that had attempted the unification of Italy in the 1810s.[24] The Riograndenses also offered freedom to slaves, provided they were willing to swell the ranks of their armies. On September 11, 1836, a short-lived and mostly unrealistic republic was proclaimed in the area.

The destiny of the black slaves engaged in the Farroupilha Revolution is still a point of great controversy among historians. The revolt ended in 1845 with an agreement between Rio Grande do Sul's provincial leaders and the central government, but the promises of freedom for the slave soldiers who were employed in the rebellious Riograndense army were never honored. In the aftermath of the conflict, the Empire feared that granting freedom to the slaves involved in the southern conflict could set off a national uprising among slaves. The example of Haiti, where in 1804 a rebellion led to the massacre of the white population and to the subsequent establishment of the first independent country in Latin America, loomed in the minds of the Brazilian imperial elite. The only option left to the Riograndense leaders was thus to do away with the black soldiers who had fought for them throughout ten years of continuous rebellion. Men such as Bento Gonçalves (1788–1847) and David Canabarro (1796–1867), who would later achieve the status of local heroes in Rio Grande do Sul's ill-fated nationalism, seem to have devised an efficient plan to rid the army of the slave soldiers. In a deal with the imperial army, they allowed their black soldiers to die at the Battle of Porongos, which took place on the night of November 14, 1844. The few black soldiers who survived the battle were imprisoned in ship holds and made to disappear on their way to Rio de Janeiro. Some historians suggest that they may have been buried alive in quicklime in the dark storage rooms of the Empire's ships.[25]

Since the Farroupilha Revolution sprang from an economically and militarily powerful elite, it could not be put down violently, as the Cabanagem Revolt had been in Pará. A solution had to be negotiated. Following the Brazilian tradition of showing considerable judicial leniency toward the upper classes, the leaders of the revolt were never punished. On the contrary, they were celebrated by Rio Grande do Sul's provincial historians, who soon began to promote the legend of Riograndense greatness. Even if the *caudilhos* of southern Brazil could not win the civil conflict or regain some of the pride they had lost in 1828, a lurid local historiography performed the function of creating a sense of local greatness that would satisfy their vanity.[26]

Unable to suppress the multiple provincial revolts that were emerging throughout the national territory, such as the ongoing Riograndense Farroupilha, on September 19, 1837 the nation's leader, Diogo Feijó, resigned from his position of imperial regent. The conservative Pedro de Araújo Lima (1793–1870) assumed temporary charge of the ministerial cabinet until new elections could be convened the following year. The same Pedro de Araújo Lima won the poll held in 1838, remaining in office until the crowning of Pedro II on July 23, 1840.

The short two-year period of Araújo Lima's regency (1838–1840) was marked by important developments in the Empire's social and political structure. The Brazilian Historic and Geographic Institute, known by the acronym IHGB, was founded in October 1838 with the objective of promoting national culture. As such, it contributed to the conservative agenda of building a strong and centralized state. Conservative administrative reforms were now enacted, producing rampant dissatisfaction among the liberals and a new round of revolts in the provinces.

In Bahia, a revolt called Sabinada (1837–1838) emerged from the dissatisfaction with Feijó's resignation from the regency, which in political terms meant an overall shift towards conservatism and the consequent lessening of provincial autonomy. The central government's practice of forced military recruitment was also a point of discord. Men from Bahia were obliged to enlist and move to the south to put down the disturbances instigated by the Riograndenses. The imperial government thus found itself with the quandary of having to deal both with the call for liberalism in Bahia, and with its rejection in Rio Grande do Sul. The contrasting economies of the two regions made their interests collide. While in Bahia liberalism meant economic freedom and the disentanglement from the war that was being fought in the south, in Rio Grande do Sul it meant economic collapse. The southern province depended on the national market as the place to sell its beef, and the interprovincial tariffs introduced by the liberal reforms of 1834 produced an astronomical rise in the price of their product. The tariffs favored Argentine and Uruguayan curers. Finding itself divided between the demands of Bahia and Rio Grande do Sul, the imperial government was unable to satisfy either side.[27]

Another major revolt broke out in the province of Maranhão. The Balaiada (1838–1841) was caused by the severe economic meltdown produced by a crisis in the local cotton industry. The revolt involved a large number of slaves and was violently crushed by the imperial commander Luís Alves de Lima e Silva, a heavy-handed military officer who, a few years later, would put down the Riograndense revolution, suppress liberal uprisings in Minas Gerais and São Paulo, and, under the title of Duke of Caxias, defeat the armies of Francisco Solano López, Paraguay's dictator, in the Paraguayan War.

Several other smaller revolts broke out during the violent decade of the Regency. Perhaps the most remarkable were those that involved slave uprisings. The Carrancas Rebellion (1833) in Minas Gerais, the Malês Revolt (1835) in Bahia, and the Manuel Congo Revolt (1838) in Rio de Janeiro encouraged the national elites' fear of Haitianism, that is, of a potentially disastrous uprising of slaves like the one that had occurred in Haiti.[28] Adding to the liberals' general discontent was the suppression of the 1834 Additional Act on May 12, 1840, which would emerge as one of the causes of revolt in 1842 in the provinces of São Paulo and Minas Gerais, two liberal bastions.

Pedro de Araújo Lima now took his turn to attempt to control the multiple uprisings that were again leading the country to the verge of political fragmentation. Faced with sheer chaos and aware of the threat of national dissolution, he decided to anticipate Pedro II's ascension to the throne as a means to consolidate central authority. The event came to be known in Brazilian history as the *Golpe da Maioridade* (Legal Age Coup), a kind of agreed *coup d'état* based on the anticipation of the young Emperor's age of consent. Just as the liberals demanded Pedro's coronation, the conservative Senate convened on July 18, 1840, to declare the Braganza heir ready to accede to the throne. Liberals and conservatives thus agreed that only the restoration of legitimate imperial authority in the central government could bring back unity to the divided nation.[29]

On July 23, 1840, Pedro de Alcântara was crowned Brazilian Emperor, assuming the title of Pedro II. For the first time a Brazilian-born monarch would extend his rule over the vast territory of the Empire. As we will see in the following pages, under Pedro II's reign Brazilian nationality began to be forged under a fierce state-oriented program. Only then would the shadow of Portugal begin to fade into the vagueness of a distant memory.

The Second Empire (1840–1889)

Upon assuming the throne in 1840, fifteen-year-old Pedro de Alcântara found himself having to face a nation full of contradictions. Although internally the political situation was catastrophic, as indicated in the proliferation of armed upheavals north and south, on the external front the Empire's export economy was progressing steadily. Between 1840 and 1889, the timespan historians define as the "Second Empire," foreign trade grew at an annual rate of almost 4%. By 1850, the absolute value of Brazil's exports was the highest in Latin America. The exporting economy was achieving remarkable prosperity, and the trade balance would remain positive until the end of the Imperial Era.

Industrial production, however, was still very limited. The low tariffs applied to British products as a result of the old treaties of 1810 continued to prevent the emergence of a national industry until at least 1844, when the abrogation of the trade agreements with the United Kingdom allowed for the implementation of the Alves Branco tariff, a set of regulations named after the new Finance Minister, Manuel Alves Branco (1797–1855). Branco would adopt measures to stimulate the national industry, something that was contingent on the implementation of the protectionist tariffs that took his name. There were many complicated entanglements between foreign trade and national revenue. Above all, until 1844 Brazilian cities housed a great number of British commercial establishments, and only a few small factories of non-durable goods, such as food, beverages, and textiles, could survive the fierce foreign competition.

Adding to the difficulties of galvanizing the internal market was the fact that interprovincial communication was seriously underdeveloped. The province of Mato Grosso, for instance, was virtually unreachable by land; the rivers that ran along the Empire's borders with Paraguay and Argentina served as the only means of transportation to the western part of the territory. When Pedro II assumed the throne, there were as yet no railroads in the country, and transportation was extremely limited. The first Brazilian railroad would not be inaugurated until 1854. This first railway line, which connected the Guanabara Bay in Rio de Janeiro to the low mountain range near the adjacent city of Petropolis, was the product of the rare entrepreneurial verve of a man called Irineu Evangelista de Sousa (1813–1889), who had the title Baron of Mauá. In 1854, the Baron proudly presented the nation with a track of 14.5 km, which was in fact a very small achievement when compared to the 14,000 km of railroad lines built in the United States by 1850.

The example of the railroad provides a good picture of how the revenue from growing international trade was not being invested in national infrastructure, a situation which was mirrored in other Latin American countries. Argentina, for instance, did not see its first railroad finished until 1857.[30]

The nation inherited by Pedro II was, in any case, much more complex and structurally developed than the one inherited by his father eighteen years earlier. In spite of the various provincial revolts, internal political organization had developed steadily during the Regency Period. From 1837 onwards, the rivalry between liberals and conservatives began to settle down into a recognizable two-party system. The conservative and the liberal parties would continue their quest for political pre-eminence in a manner which was more or less organized, if not always fair, throughout Pedro II's reign. Until the final demise of the Empire in 1889, conservatives and liberals would manage to maintain their political agendas within the boundaries of the established constitutional arrangement, refraining from questioning the monarchical system. Any serious questioning of the monarchy's rule would not appear until 1870, with the emergence of the Republican Party.

During the Second Empire, the conservatives tended to do better in moments of greater political instability, such as in 1848, when the revolution in Pernambuco threatened to undo the nation's territorial integrity, and in 1868, when winning the Paraguayan War demanded a firmer hand than the one provided by the liberals. Since their agenda was based on political centralization, the conservatives favored the authority of the monarchy as a matter of principle. For a long time, they called themselves the *Party of Order*, in opposition to the liberals, whom they termed *Party of Disorder*.

The liberals, on the other hand, were interested above all in provincial autonomy and in the maintenance of the slave labor system. As long as the monarchy maintained these two basic fundamentals, it would have their support. During a liberal rebellion that broke out in Minas Gerais in 1842, the liberals began to be called *luzias*, a name taken from the village where they first rose against the central government. Conservatives, on the other hand, were called *saquaremas* after the region where they had their coffee plantations, an area not too far from the capital, Rio de Janeiro.

In spite of their distinct political agendas, however, whenever they assumed control of the government both parties differed little in terms of the actual application of their policies. This fact was expressed in the famous saying of freemason, landowner, military commander, and Senator Antônio Francisco de Paula de Holanda Cavalcanti (1797–1863): "There is nothing more like a *saquarema* than a *luzia* in power."[31]

The differences between the two political parties would become more noticeable towards the end of the Imperial Period. For some years, the conservatives had been gradually acquiring a more urban profile, while the liberals remained mostly as provincial landowners. The central government's bureaucracy began to be populated primarily by conservatives, and its highest posts were almost invariably occupied by conservative coffee producers who had their plantations not far from the imperial capital.

The period of the Regency had seen the rise of coffee to become Brazil's largest export in 1838. The conservative *saquaremas*, who extended their coffee plantations throughout the Paraíba River valley, a vast forested region between Rio de Janeiro and São Paulo, celebrated the prosperity of their businesses. The rise of coffee gave them renewed political clout, and they soon became known as the "coffee barons." The barons, and their coffee, would dominate the Brazilian economy for the next 120 years. The product would become the source both of the country's economic prosperity and of its backwardness, like a drug with a dose of lethargy in every shot of excitement.

Pedro II thus rose to power in an empire where power was gradually starting to slip through the fingers of the emperor. Over the years, he would have to learn to balance his policies between the competing whims of the *luzias* and the *saquaremas*. In other words, the absolutist attitude of Pedro I would be for Pedro II simply impossible.

Soon after assuming the throne, fifteen-year-old Pedro de Alcântara understood the intricacies of the liberal-conservative rivalry. General elections were held in 1840, and the prevailing atmosphere of violence and fraud at the polls provided Pedro with a glimpse of what awaited him over the next fifty years of his life. Fraud and physical violence were openly employed by the liberals to win the poll of 1840 and secure the majority of the seats in the House of Representatives. Since, from the start of his reign, the Emperor had convened a ministerial cabinet comprised of liberal politicians, these had control over the electoral system. They bribed officials, substituted provincial governors, threatened with death those who did not vote for the Liberal Party, and also counted the votes themselves. The elections of 1840 became known as the *Eleições do Cacete*, or "Billy Club Elections."[32] They were not an isolated case in Brazilian history. On the contrary, they represent an enduring trend in the country's political culture, that is, a trend towards almost farcical abuse of power and corruption in political and electoral affairs.

The 1840 general elections were so biased that Pedro II decided to dissolve the liberal cabinet that was formed in their aftermath, replacing it with a conservative one. The conservatives, however, proved to be just as corrupt as their liberal counterparts. When new elections were arranged, they employed the same illegitimate methods used by the liberals to win. The liberals then decided to take up arms in 1842.

Fierce liberal revolts broke out in Minas Gerais and São Paulo. They were a response both to the return of the conservatives to power, as well as to the suppression of the 1834 Additional Act, which was carried out through the so-called *Lei Interpretativa do Ato Adicional de 1834*, a new regulation that returned to the central government the prerogative of appointing public officials in the provinces.

To complicate matters further, the bloody Farroupilha Revolt continued to ravage the lowlands of Rio Grande do Sul. The Gaúcho rebels had taken part of the northern state of Santa Catarina in 1839, and the revolts in São Paulo and Minas Gerais now gave them new impetus to defy the Empire. No matter where Pedro II turned, all he could see was discontent and confusion.

Another disagreeable element emerged when the unequal treaties signed with the United Kingdom in 1810, and which had been renewed in 1827 as a condition for the recognition of the independence, had to be extended until 1844 as the result of British military coercion. The treaties should have expired in 1842, but the weak Brazilian Empire could not enforce their termination clauses in the face of the United Kingdom's greater power. The extension of the treaties meant the continuation of the difficult financial situation in which the politically unstable Empire found itself.

After less than three years on the throne, the young Emperor had acquired the taciturn countenance of a much older man. The role of arbiter in so many irreconcilable disputes had turned distress into outward bitterness. Pedro was of a disposition quite distinct from that of his father. He was a quiet man, a lover of art and science, better suited to be a scholar than a king. As his inwardness began to preoccupy his former tutors, they decided to arrange a marriage with the beautiful Italian princess, Teresa Cristina of Bourbon (1822–1889). Upon seeing the princess's picture, Pedro immediately accepted the idea. A marriage by proxy took place in 1843, and the princess arrived in Brazil the same year.[33]

Although Pedro seemed to thrive after his marriage, the nation remained in a parlous state. In 1844, the Emperor dismissed the conservative cabinet formed in 1841, replacing it with a liberal one. The expiry of the treaties of 1810 allowed the new Minister of Finance, the aforementioned Manuel Alves Branco, to raise import tariffs to 30%, a decision that provoked rage from the British diplomats in Rio de Janeiro. The United Kingdom would not be lenient with what they saw as Brazilian misconduct: in the following year, the Parliament of the United Kingdom passed the Aberdeen Act, a law that authorized the Royal Navy to stop and search any Brazilian vessel suspected of engagement in the slave trade, as well as to arrest and prosecute the crew as criminals.[34]

Brazilians regarded the Act as a humiliation and as a violation of the Empire's sovereignty. The British threat added to the turmoil experienced in a nation already rife with insecurity. And as foreign predicaments increased, domestically the liberal-conservative rivalry continued. Attempting to preserve an image of impartiality, in 1847 the Emperor created the office of President of the Council of Ministers, appointing to the position his former Minister of Finance, Manuel Alves Branco. The new post would protect the Emperor from direct involvement in everyday political affairs and thus safeguard his popularity.

The decree creating the office of President of the Council of Ministers officially established a parliamentary system in the Empire, with the President of the Council acting as Prime Minister. The Brazilian arrangement, however, would be severely criticized on various grounds. The reserve power given to the Emperor by the 1824 Constitution granted him the right to appoint and dismiss the Council's president at will. This produced what came to be called the Brazilian "inverted parliamentarism," that is, a system in which the right to appoint a Prime Minister lied not with the National Assembly, but with the Emperor.

The general dissatisfaction with the new system suggested that Pedro II's attempts at reaching consensus between liberals and conservatives would simply continue to be futile. His next major headache came with a new revolt in the province of Pernambuco. This time the European Revolutions of 1848 provided the model for the latest recourse to arms. The uprisings in Europe were aimed at overthrowing absolutism in France, Prussia, and the Austrian Empire. In Brazil, unrest started in the city of Olinda on November 7, 1848, when Pedro II dismissed the liberal provincial governor, Chichorro da Gama (1800–1887), whose egalitarian ideas defied the most powerful clan in the local landed aristocracy, the conservative Cavalcanti family.

The revolt was named *Revolução Praieira* after the locality where the revolutionaries had established a revisionist newspaper. There they published a manifesto based on utopian socialism and took up arms to defend freedom of speech and federalism, and fight for an end to the constitutional reserve power. Faced with the opposition of the liberals, Pedro II now dissolved the liberal cabinet established in 1844 and nominated a group of heavy-handed conservatives, establishing a new governmental administration. The new 1848 cabinet was composed of what Brazilian historians call the *Saquarema Trinity*, the three most powerful coffee barons of the Paraíba River Valley: Paulino José Soares de Sousa (1807–1866), who assumed the Ministry of Foreign Affairs; Eusébio de Queirós (1812–1868), the new Minister of Justice; and Joaquim José Rodrigues Torres (1802–1872), who took the office of Minister of Finance. The three ministers reported to the new Prime Minister, the ultra-conservative former regent Pedro de Araújo Lima (1793–1870).

Pedro II needed the conservatives' firm hand not only to suppress the rebellion in Pernambuco, but also to establish a new position for the Brazilian Empire in the South. The so-called "Platine Questions" remained a source of distress for the descendants of the Portuguese who now controlled the free Brazilian nation. Just like their ancestors, they sensed a threat from the Spanish conquerors looming across their southern frontier. If in the past their forefathers had fought for the Platine region in the hope of getting their hands on Spanish silver, they now returned to the struggle, greedy to achieve pre-eminence in the very competitive, and extremely lucrative, cattle industry. The atavistic tenedency to suppress their neighbor was alive and well in the Empire's lust for control over the Platine sub-system of intra-American relations. The Brazilian conservatives now fought for the interests of those very men whom their forefathers had sent to the South in order to conquer territory for the

Portuguese Crown. Until 1848, these conservatives had been held back, their hands tied by the weak liberal administration that had allowed the money-draining provincial revolts to continue uninterrupted since 1844. Even while foreign trade was progressing steadily, providing national income and some sense of prosperity, the regional unrest increased the Empire's vulnerability and ruled out governmental action in the Platine region.

The long period of internal instability following the end of the Cisplatine War in 1828 had resulted in Brazil's loss of its former influence in the River Plate region. It produced what Brazilian historian Amado Luiz Cervo called the country's prolonged "Platine Immobility."[35] With the stronger conservatives now in power, the Emperor expected to put down the uprising in Pernambuco and then turn to the quest for political hegemony in the South. The plan was not simply the reflection of a whimsical desire for power, but was vital to the maintenance of the Empire's territorial integrity. The Farroupilha rebellion had been silenced by the forces of conservative commander, the Duke of Caxias in 1845, but the Riograndense *caudilhos* had not been completely suppressed. It was necessary to gain their support for the Empire, lest they turned again towards the shrewd Argentine leader, Juan Manuel de Rosas, who had embarked on his quest for a large Argentine state that would include his present Argentine Confederation together with the territories of Uruguay, Rio Grande do Sul, Bolivia, and Paraguay. Rosas embodied the fact that Paraguay's independence in 1811 had never been fully accepted by the Argentines, who considered the neighboring country's territory to be part of the old colonial Spanish Viceroyalty of the Río de la Plata, that is, part of what they considered the rightful domain of a large Argentina.

The French-born Brazilian Foreign Minister, Paulino José Soares de Sousa, understood that in order to regain hegemony in the Platine region the Empire would have to put an end to its potentially disastrous differences with the United Kingdom regarding the slave trade. The conservative politician, who was later given the title Viscount of Uruguay for his successful intervention in the southern neighbor's internal affairs, knew that only after the British threat had disappeared, would the imperial forces again be able to take action against the Argentines, if need be. The problem of the revolt in Pernambuco would also have to be solved: if another war broke out in the South, the empire would not be able to fight the secessionists in the North, a war on two fronts being something the conservatives dreaded and sought to avoid.

Soares de Sousa was thus confronted with a complex and pressing situation. The Argentine Confederation was unstable and plagued by several regional rebellions, while Uruguay itself was wracked by a civil war. Rosas, the Argentine dictator, started threatening the Empire with the annexation of part of Rio Grande do Sul. The Riograndense landlords themselves were already growing restless with the constant invasions of their territory by Uruguayan leader Manuel Oribe, a fierce opponent of the Empire. They thus demanded immediate action from Rio de Janeiro. The Uruguayan civil war was being fought between the two main political parties, the Blancos, who had the support of Rosas and were led by Oribe, and the Colorados, who were backed by the Brazilian Empire together with the anti-Rosas Argentine provinces of Entre Ríos y Corrientes. Such a potentially catastrophic geopolitical situation demanded immediate action from the Empire.

The Brazilian Foreign Minister was an experienced and able man, an important theoretician of Law and of military organization, as well as a respected figure in the field of political philosophy.[36] He concentrated his efforts first on solving the Pernambucan question, where he decided to employ direct military force. After a series of violent clashes between the imperial army and the liberal revolutionaries of Recife, the Pernambucan rebellion was finally suppressed on January 26, 1850, in what came to be known as the Battle of Água Preta. This opened the way for dealing with the British question, which had, by then, become the Minister's most immediate preoccupation. His solution was to comply with the United Kingdom's requirements and pass a law prohibiting trade in slaves. British demands for the end of the slave trade were long-standing. An abolitionist clause was included in the Portuguese Treaties of 1810, and their renewal in 1827 included a Brazilian vow to end the trade in three years. Attempting to comply with the agreement, the Empire promulgated a law on November 7, 1831 declaring all Africans that arrived in the country after that date to be free. The bill, however was never enforced, and became known as the *lei para inglês ver* (the law to fool the British).[37]

In 1850, however, things would have to be done differently. The Aberdeen Act of 1845 and the political instability in the South did not leave room for any maneuvering. Soares de Sousa drafted the law under the name of the Minister of Justice, Eusébio de Queirós. The British representative to Rio de Janeiro, James Hudson (1810–1885), in an attempt to humble the South American nation wrote in a secret communication to his country's Foreign Office that the law had been dictated by himself to the Brazilian Foreign Minister, who played the role of a mere copyist. The diplomatic communication was made public by the British government, creating an incident that forced Eusébio de Queirós to present a formal explanation to the Brazilian Congress.[38]

Regardless of the diplomatic incident, the law came into effect on September 4, 1850, seven months after the suppression of the Pernambucan Praieira Revolt. This allowed for the Brazilians' desired intervention in the South. On May 29, 1851, the Brazilian Empire formed an alliance with the Uruguayan Colorados and the Argentine provinces of Entre Ríos and Corrientes to launch an offensive against Rosas and the Uruguayan Blancos. On September 4, 1851, responding to Rosas's declaration of war, the Brazilian army crossed the southern frontier of Rio Grande do Sul and entered Uruguayan territory to begin what was called the Platine War.

After a series of confrontations, Uruguayan president Manuel Oribe surrendered on October 19, 1851. Rosas was defeated on February 3, 1852. The allied victory was pivotal in establishing a new Brazilian hegemony in the Platine region. The independence of Paraguay and Uruguay were secured, and the threat of an Argentine invasion of Rio Grande do Sul was dissipated.[39]

Brazilian and Argentine historians tend to diverge on the role of the imperial forces in Rosas's fall. The Brazilians tend to emphasize it, while the Argentines prefer to downplay it. The latter usually portray the dictator's demise as caused almost solely by the Argentine forces of anti-Rosas commander Justo José de Urquiza (1801–1870), who would have enjoyed only marginal Brazilian support. This divergence suggests the obviously politicized nature of the debate, and presumably also of history itself as a speculative discipline.[40]

In any case, after the Platine War the Brazilian Empire entered a new period of internal stability. Economic independence was finally achieved after the expiry of the Treaties of 1810, and, for the first time, reconciliation between liberals and conservatives seemed possible. In 1853, a new ministerial cabinet was formed under the leadership of Prime Minister Honório Hermeto Carneiro Leão (1801–1856). The cabinet brought together members of the two opposing parties and was appropriately called the *Ministério da Conciliação* (Cabinet of Conciliation). From then on, Foreign Minister Paulino José Soares de Sousa would concentrate on his new task of maintaining the Platine region's geopolitical stability in favor of the Brazilian Empire. The Minister's strategy was to secure a stable government in Uruguay and neutralize Rosas's supporters by means of what came to be known as *Diplomacia dos Patacões*, effectively financial diplomacy based on a series of loans issued to the region's most powerful warlords. This form of interventionist foreign policy was used freely as a means of advancing Brazilian interests in the region until at least 1858.[41]

The new political stability in the River Plate basin allowed for the establishment of new commercial relations among the Southern Cone nations, much to the profit of Brazilian exporters. Regional development ensued in the southern areas of the Empire, which started to move ahead of the North economically. A good example of economic benefit produced by the new political stability in the region appears in the case of *erva-mate*, an herbal leaf traditionally used as infusion and widely consumed in the area. The exceptional growth in the export of the product to the neighboring countries started after the end of the Platine War and promoted the economic emancipation of part of the province of São Paulo, leading to the establishment of the Paraná Province in December 1853. The new administrative unit, with its handsome highlands extending through the Brazilian southern plateau, emerged as one of the most prosperous areas in the country.

The absolute value of Brazilian exports in 1850 was the highest in Latin America, a trend that would continue until the end of the Imperial Period. Between 1850 and 1889, the country's GDP grew at an annual rate of almost 5%, paralleling the similar rate in the growth of gross exports. Technological innovations began to appear and boost economic expansion. The first railroad, as we have seen, was built in 1854, and new factories sprung up as a result of capital being diverted from the slave trade into productive activities. The textile industry, in particular, benefited from this process. It expanded significantly, especially during the American Civil War (1861–1865), which brought about an increase in Brazil's cotton exports. 1866 saw the first signs of the Amazon rubber boom, which would produce positive economic developments in the forested areas of the North. Furthermore, the development of infrastructure for the cultivation of coffee beans brought considerable economic growth to the province of São Paulo.

The 1850s thus saw the beginning of Brazil's gradual transformation from a strictly agrarian society into a more economically diversified nation. The country's inherited mercantile capitalistic structures started to become more versatile, incorporating new and more varied economic activities. A well-developed internal market would still take several decades to emerge, but an enhanced social and economic make-up was already noticeable.

Relative economic prosperity and political stability had positive effects on the Emperor's mood. After the initial excitement produced by his engagement to the beautiful Princess Teresa Cristina in 1843, Pedro had reverted back into his austere and introspective ways. From 1850 onwards, however, new interests came into his life and he began having discreet romantic affairs with various women, the most remarkable being the lovely Luísa Margarida de Barros Portugal (1816–1891), the Countess of Barral. It is true that Pedro II was not as prodigious or skillful a womanizer as his father, but he managed to maintain a lasting entanglement with the Countess which did much to lift his spirits.

Pedro's nascent romantic flare, together with the sudden improvement in his overall well-being, mirrored the Empire's own sense of optimistic confidence. Amid the placid self-satisfaction of regional hegemony and internal harmony, an intellectual revolution began to stir. The first signs of the positivist philosophy that would impact the Empire began to appear in 1850 and 1851. The new intellectual trend was brought in from Europe with the elite's younger members who customarily received their formal education in France before returning to their motherland and resuming their lives as landowners with occasional periods in the military. The general make-up of the Brazilian elite tended to be a mixture of landed aristocracy, freemasonry, and military command. This proved to be a fertile breeding ground for the philosophies of Auguste Comte (1798–1857), the prestigious French thinker who proposed a new social doctrine based on the procedures of the sciences.

Comte's new philosophical trend found its Brazilian form in the works of pioneering intellectuals such as Dionísia Gonçalves Pinto (1810–1885) and Benjamin Constant Botelho de Magalhães (1833–1891). Pinto was an early Brazilian feminist who published her groundbreaking *Opúsculo Humanitário* in 1853, a collection of essays on female emancipation that was praised by none other than Comte himself. Benjamin Constant was a military officer, engineer, professor, and statesman who is credited with having founded the Brazilian Positivist Church. Positivism's characteristic scientificist perspectives had the advantage of providing ideological support for the general desire for modernization, to be carried out by the nation's elite. Inevitably, however, it would clash with the religious beliefs most firmly defended by the Catholic Church, an ever-present influence in the country.

Positivist ideology also had the benefit of being compatible with abolitionism. It favored liberalism and republicanism, going against monarchical and aristocratic values. During the 1850s, the new philosophy became the battleground for an unprecedented conflict between the generations that emerged in the still-conservative former Portuguese colony. Young aristocrats would prefer Comte's ideas to the stern and conservative beliefs of their fathers. Comte's philosophy also began to be seen in the rivalry between liberals and conservatives. While the former called for modernization and science, the latter tended to hold fast to Catholic ethics and religious worldviews.

Pedro II himself favored the liberal positivist outlook. The Emperor's inclination towards Positivism may have been contrary to his political interests as monarch, but in many ways Pedro was a man to whom the Crown was more a burden than a blessing. He was more at ease with his books, in the company of artists and scientists, and in the discreet and intimate company of the most charming ladies of the court, than giving orders or making use of his reserve constitutional power. The Emperor was an important patron of the arts and favored a simple life marked by introspection and moderation.

On the opposite side of the growing engagement between Positivism, Abolitionism, Liberalism, and Republicanism, the conservatives held firm to their own ideology. Men such as the French thinker and diplomat Joseph Arthur de Gobineau (1816–1882) exerted remarkable influence on the Empire's conservative elite. Gobineau presented his theory of the Aryan master race in the work *An Essay on the Inequality of the Human Races* (1853). He attempted to accommodate Christian mythology within a racist worldview by arguing, absurdly, that although the biblical notion that all human beings share common ancestors, namely Adam and Eve, was correct, it did not apply to Africans and Asians, for at the time of the writing of the bible these were not yet counted as part of the human species, and hence should not be considered fully human.

Gobineau arrived in Brazil in 1869 with a diplomatic mission at the behest of Napoleon III. His animosity towards the South American nation, which he considered doomed to eternal chaos on account of its manifest racial miscegenation, made him abhor his mission and leave the following year. The diplomat and social theoretician's flawed theories and ideas, however, took firm root among the Empire's conservatives, influencing the country's future policies on immigration and citizenship. The contrast between Comte and Gobineau's philosophies reflected the ideological gap between liberals and conservatives in mid-nineteenth-century Brazil. The two Frenchmen represent opposite poles around which Brazilian intellectuals would gravitate for several decades starting in the 1850s.[42]

In terms of domestic and foreign politics, the 1860s saw the emergence of new internal and external constraints on the Empire. Contrasting with the previous decade, complications began to arise on various and unexpected fronts. The rise of a weak liberal cabinet in 1862, the rupture of diplomatic relations with the United Kingdom in 1863, the vicious Paraguayan War which started in 1864, the avidity of the United States for the Amazon in 1866, and the final fall of the liberals from government in

1868, formed a complex web of political developments that demanded careful, and at the same time, energetic action from the nation's ruler.

The rise of the so-called *Liga Progressista*, a version of the Liberal Party augmented by some conservative dissidents, occurred as a result of the conciliatory policies initiated by Prime Minister Honório Hermeto Carneiro Leão in 1853. The fierce political polarization between liberals and conservatives seen in the 1830s and 1840s had now dissolved into a much more stable and interactive arrangement. Although ideological differences survived, such as those that opposed Positivism and racist Gobineausianism, liberals and conservatives were no longer in overt conflict with each other. A few decades before, former liberals, such as the powerful Bernardo Pereira de Vasconcelos, had been severely criticized for changing sides and suddenly becoming conservatives. Now, men such as the equally powerful deputy from Bahia, Nabuco de Araújo (1813–1878), could switch sides from conservative to liberal, without causing any commotion.

Zacarias de Góis e Vasconcelos (1815–1877), a liberal politician famous for campaigning against the constitutional reserve power enjoyed by the Emperor, assumed the post of Prime Minister on May 24, 1862. This provided for the initial rise of the *Liga Progressista*, which would only be officially constituted two years later. On taking office, one of the first problems Zacarias was faced with was a series of incidents involving British citizens in Brazilian territory. The problems had started in 1861 when a British commercial vessel that was on its way to Argentina became stranded in the dangerous waters off the coast of Rio Grande do Sul. The vessel was ransacked and members of its crew murdered. The incident infuriated the British Ambassador William Dougal Christie (1816–1874). This was a time of strong anti-British sentiment in the Empire, an animosity that had grown steadily since the humiliation suffered with the Aberdeen Act of 1845. The incident in Rio Grande do Sul was indicative of the popular dissatisfaction with the privileges British citizens still enjoyed in the country. Christie demanded an apology and financial compensation from the Emperor, who refused to heed the diplomat's claims.

Relations deteriorated further the following year, when a group of sailors from the British Royal Navy got into a fight in Rio de Janeiro with some Brazilian mariners. The British sailors, dressed in civilian clolthes, were arrested and jailed overnight, an incident that, again, enraged Christie. At the time, British subjects were still not subject to Brazilian law. Recalling the previous incident with the vessel in Rio Grande do Sul, Christie threatened military intervention if financial compensation was not offered. Pedro II again refused the Ambassador's demands and, in April 1862, the British navy blockaded the port of Rio de Janeiro, threatening to move south and attack the coast of Rio Grande do Sul. Popular sentiment was outraged by the British action, and threats of violence against British citizens arose throughout the country.

It was amid such tension that Zacarias de Góis e Vasconcelos assumed the ministerial cabinet in May 1862, a few weeks after the beginning of the British blockade of the capital. The new Prime Minister opted to sever diplomatic relations with the United Kingdom and to submit the dispute to the arbitration of King Leopold I of Belgium. The King's judgment was favorable to Brazil, but diplomatic relations with the British did not resume until 1865. The event is known in Brazilian history as the *Questão Christie*. It was an unprecedented instance of national self-assertion against a strong European nation.

Resolute in the face of the British threat, the Brazilian Empire was soon forced to show its mettle in another problematic incident in its foreign policy, this time in connection to one of its Hispanic-American neighbors. The Platine region once again became a source of instability when Francisco Solano López (1827–1870), Paraguay's dictator since 1862, declared war on Brazil on December 13, 1864. López had assumed control of his country after his father's death. Carlos Antonio López (1792–1862) had been a strong dictator, as well as Paraguay's first president; Francisco Solano, his son, followed the same path of dictatorship. He promoted his country's militarization and embarked on a frenetic quest for dominance over the South American Platine sub-system. His formal declaration of war against the Brazilian Empire marked the start of the vicious Paraguayan War.

In December 1864, the Paraguayan dictator ordered his army to invade Brazilian territory and occupy the provinces of Mato Grosso and Rio Grande do Sul. The Empire's defenses met the challenge, bringing about a protracted war that would only end six years later at the site of one of the greatest massacres in human history. Each battle would be fought as if the last, with great displays of savagery on both sides spreading beyond the battle fields into the surrounding farms and villages, consuming the lives of the descendants of those age-old rivals, the Spanish and the Portuguese, who for centuries had disputed the territory. The mercilessness of the Brazilian Empire vis-à-vis the Paraguayan civilian population would result in a human catastrophe, unprecedented in the history of the Americas, and one of the most infamous acts of man's inhumanity to man seen anywhere in the world.

A little more than five decades before that dreadful year of 1864, the Portuguese king had been quick to recognize Paraguayan independence. Fearing the emergence of a large and powerful Hispanic-American state at the southern border of his colonial territory, in 1811 John VI had defended the separation of Paraguay from the emerging state that forty-nine years later would take the name of the Argentine Republic. From then on, Brazil and Paraguay had maintained good relations, especially when they started sharing a strong suspicion of what they saw as a common enemy, namely the *caudillo* Juan Manuel de Rosas, who controlled the Argentine Confederation with a firm hand from 1829 to 1852. After the fall of Rosas, however, the region's geopolitics altered drastically. Uruguay remained a focus of great tension. Since independence in 1828, its two political parties had waged continuous war against each other. They vied for pre-eminence internally, and while doing so, sought external support from different camps, fueling the rivalry between their two powerful neighbors.

The foreign preferences of the two Uruguayan rival parties were very clear: the Blancos were allied to Rosas, while the Colorados were allied to the Brazilian Empire. The Blancos rose to power in 1860, first under the rule of Bernardo Berro (1803–1868), who remained in office until 1864, and then under that of Atanasio Aguirre (1801–1875), who ruled Uruguay until early 1865, being deposed by the Colorado leader Venancio Flores (1808–1868) with military support from the Brazilian Empire. The Empire's pretext for supporting the Colorados was the recurrent clashes between Aguirre and the Riograndense warlords over territory and cattle.

The region's geopolitics were further complicated by the association of the Uruguayan Blancos with the Argentine Federalists, who were led by Justo José de Urquiza (1801–1870), the former Brazilian ally in the overthrow of Juan Manuel de Rosas. Urquiza and the Federalists had assumed control of the Argentine Confederation after Rosas's fall, but then faced opposition from the governor of the Province of Buenos Aires, the Unitarian Bartolomé Mitre (1821–1906). Urquiza and his Federalists defeated Mitre's Unitarians in 1859 in the Battle of Cepeda. But Mitre exacted revenge in September 1861 at the Battle of Pavón, when he defeated Urquiza and unified the country.

In 1864, besides their continued association with Urquiza, the Uruguayan Blancos were also establishing an alliance with the Paraguayan dictator, Solano López. Such was the complex political situation in the Platine region when the Brazilian Empire and the Uruguayan Colorados sent an ultimatum to Uruguay's President, the Blanco Atanasio Aguirre. The Empire's meddling in its neighbors' affairs added to the already pronounced regional instability.

Solano López, who rather irrationally overestimated Paraguay's military clout, threatened to declare war on Brazil if the latter invaded Uruguay to depose Paraguay's Blanco ally. Since the Blancos were still on good terms with Urquiza and the Argentine Federalists, López expected to form an alliance with the latter and defeat the Brazilian Empire, as well as the Colorados. The Paraguayan dictator's expected alliance, however, never came into effect. After defeat in battle at the hands of Mitre in 1861, Urquiza had adopted a more peaceful form of opposition to the new Argentine president. Faced with Urquiza's hesitation, López found himself alone. The refusal of military support from Urquiza, coupled with López's thirst for war, would result in nothing short of Paraguay's total demise.

On May 1, 1865, Brazil, Argentina, and Uruguay signed in Buenos Aires the Treaty of the Triple Alliance, vowing to defeat the Republic of Paraguay. Once again, the Platine region and its emaciated inhabitants saw the outbreak of war, a prospect to which they had no doubt grown accustomed, being as they were the heirs of Iberian rivalry and resentment in America. The war would last until 1870, and from it many a national hero would emerge on each side. It would be a war of extermination, one that once again would drench in blood the already grim history of the Spanish and Portuguese dispute over the River Plate basin's territory.

In the Brazilian Empire, the protracted war soon became unpopular. A few months after the conflict started, the liberal government of Zacarias de Góis e Vasconcelos began to appear incapable of handling the implications of the all-out war. The confrontation reached stalemate after the Paraguayan victory in the Battle of Curupayty, fought in September 1866.[43] The allied debacle led to severe disagreements between the Brazilian commander, Marshal Manuel Luís Osório (1808–1879), known by the title of Marquis of Herval, and the Argentine President, Bartolomé Mitre. While the former, backed by Pedro II's steadfast attitude in calling for the total destruction of Paraguay, wished to continue the war until Paraguay's final annihilation, the latter preferred to wait and perhaps end the war through diplomatic negotiation. The Argentines had a strong interest in the Paraguayan Chaco region, which they considered their own, as it had been part of the Spanish Viceroyalty of the River Plate, the historical political unit that, as we have seen, the Argentines hoped to re-establish under the government of Buenos Aires. A destroyed Paraguay, subjugated to Brazilian military forces, however, would mean the possible permanent loss of the Chaco region for Argentina.

The differing interests of Brazil and Argentina regarding the Paraguayan territory thus contributed to the impasse in the war. After Curupayty, the Paraguayan forces retreated to the Fortress of Humaitá, a stronghold on the

Paraguay River that cut off the advance of the allied forces into Paraguayan territory. Humaitá was surrounded by land in November 1867, and by water in February 1868. It remained, however, unassailable in the face of political indecision and lack of military motivation by the allies.

In the Brazilian Empire, the deadlock experienced in the war after the defeat at Curupayty was seen as the product of liberal weakness. The ruling *Liga Progressista* was replaced by a conservative cabinet under the leadership of Joaquim José Rodrigues Torres (1802–1872), the Viscount of Itaboraí, who took office on July 16, 1868. Pedro II's aim in using his constitutional reserve power to dismiss Zacaria's cabinet was to get a firmer grip on the war against Solano López. The Emperor would accept nothing other than the complete defeat of the Paraguayan forces, and to that end he would not refrain from using his constitutional powers.

The fiery conservatives were thus once again summoned to replace the lenient liberals at a time of violence and distress. With the conservatives now in office, Brazilian commander Luís Alves de Lima e Silva, the Duke of Caxias, who had assumed command of the imperial forces in October 1866, could fight on to the total destruction of Paraguay. Six days after the establishment of Itaboraí's ministerial cabinet, the siege of Humaitá came to an end with the Paraguayan surrender on July 25, 1868. On January 1, 1869, Caxias marched through the Paraguayan capital, Asunción, which had been completely abandoned by its residents. Inside the ghost city only the Paraguayan dictator himself remained with what was left of his army. At the site of the approaching Brazilians, López escaped with a small force of some 500 men to the mountains in the north of his country.

Historians debate whether Lopez's flight was facilitated by Caxias's leniency.[44] By 1869, the Brazilian commander had seen enough bloodshed and despair in this endless conflict, perhaps more than any human being was capable of standing. Caxias had shown that same sort of mercy in the past, when he commanded the Empire's forces against the rebelling Riograndense warlords during the Farroupilha Revolution. Instead of simply ravaging the entire southern province, bringing down its rebellious people and leaders all at once, Caxias let the Farroupilha Revolution drag on for years in order to avoid an outright massacre.[45]

With Paraguay, however, the situation was somewhat different. The population was foreign, and mercy appeared to be less advisable. Nevertheless, on that day of January 1, 1869, entering the city of Asunción and facing the emptiness and desolation left by five years of incessant carnage, the old commander seems to have concluded that the war was, in fact, over. He probably believed that Paraguay and its people had been completely destroyed, that the bloodshed and inhumanity had surpassed the Empire's initial aims and expectations. His final decision was based on the understanding that it would be meaningless to pursue and kill the fleeing dictator.

However, unhappy with Caxias's display of mercy, Pedro II reiterated the order to pursue and annihilate López and his remaining men. To this end, he transferred the imperial army's command to his son-in-law, the French nobleman Luís Filipe Gastão de Orléans (1842–1922), known by the title of Count d'Eu. The unpopular Count, generally disliked for being a foreigner and frequently ridiculed for his French accent, ordered the Empire's troops into the northern mountains of the Paraguayan territory. On March 1, 1870, the 4,500 soldiers who comprised the Brazilian army annihilated the 450 men that still remained faithful to López. The final massacre became known as the Battle of Cerro Corá. After the dictator was executed, the Brazilian troops undertook furious raids around the country, murdering civilians, setting fire to refugee camps, and pillaging villages.

In the aftermath of the destruction of Paraguay a new balance of power emerged in the River Plate basin. Brazil had borne the cost of the long war and its financial position was now desperate. Argentina, by contrast, had profited economically and politically from the conflict. By 1870, the former center of the Spanish Viceroyalty of the River Plate had become a stable nation, enjoying considerable economic and military strength, ready to face the Brazilian Empire in another war if need be.

And such a war began to appear inevitable. After the annihilation of Paraguay, the way was open for Argentina to reclaim its former historical territory. Freed from the rule of López, Paraguay now became the focus of a new dispute between Brazil and Argentina. Pedro II thus had to bear the cost of an unpopular occupation and maintain the Empire's troops on Paraguayan soil in order to avoid its annexation by Argentina. Tensions between the two countries built up during the government of Argentine president Domingos Faustino Sarmiento (1811–1888), which lasted from 1868 to 1874. During those six years, the competition with Argentina proved to be extremely burdensome to the Brazilians. Their country was lagging behind on several fronts. While, in Argentina, the progressive policies of Domingos Sarmiento were enhancing the living standards of the population, with the near eradication of illiteracy and the gradual building of a modern nation, in Brazil, under the archaic economic system based on slave labor, the old forms of social injustice and immorality continued to thrive, making the country appear more and more a monstrous, sluggish, and sick giant. The comparison was stark: Argentina was rising; Brazil was declining.

Pedro II maintained Brazilian troops in Asunción until 1876, that is, until Argentina signed a peace treaty recognizing Paraguay's independence. The pact was signed during the government of Argentine president Nicolás Avellaneda (1837–1885) who, at the time, had to tend to his country's momentary economic downturn. Argentina's recurrent fiscal deficits had led to a financial crisis in 1875, which was compounded by what is known in Argentine history as The Conquest of the Desert, a military campaign against the indigenous population of Patagonia led by Commander Julio Roca (1843–1914), one of the country's future heroes and presidents. In the face of the financial crisis and the cost of the Conquest, a war with Brazil was out of the question. Nevertheless, the successors to Rivadavia, Rosas, and Mitre would not regard the territorial question with Paraguay as simply settled. Argentina would remain adamant in coveting Paraguay's territory. As we will see later, that craving would resurface with particular strength during the War of the Chaco, a fierce military confrontation between Bolivia and Paraguay from 1932 to 1935.

In the Brazilian Empire, the end of the war coincided with the rise of two new political forces: the military and the republican. The 1870s saw the growing intermingling of these two groups, which shared common ground in Positivism.[46] The army gained prestige after the Empire's victory in the Paraguayan War. Their new political clout was strengthened by the rise of Luís Alves de Lima e Silva, the Brazilian commander in the War, to the post of Prime Minister on July 25, 1875. In the following decade, disagreements between the army and the monarchy would emerge as a great threat to the Empire's stability.

The Empire's most fierce opponents gathered in the Republican Movement, which was formally established in 1870 with the publication of the Republican Manifesto, a document drafted by Quintino Bocaiuva (1836–1912), a journalist from Rio de Janeiro who would become the future Brazilian Republic's first Foreign Minister. Identifying Republicanism with America on one side, and Monarchism with Europe on the other, the Manifesto expressed the republicans' desire to be American. In spite of forming a cohesive group, the republicans of Rio de Janeiro did not establish a formal party; that task was left to those of São Paulo, who convened in 1873 to form the Republican Party of São Paulo, the first party of its type in Brazilian history.

The imperial government granted official recognition to the Paulista Republican Party, which would remain lawful until 1937, when the Rio Grande do Sul-born dictator, Getúlio Vargas, would close down all political parties in the country. It should be noted that until 1945 there would be no national parties in Brazil, only regional ones. Political organizations would represent specific provinces or states, having thus a regional character and scope. The Republican Party of São Paulo was no different. It accommodated liberals and conservatives alike who were dissatisfied with the monarchy. The conservatives were mostly members of the landed aristocracy who abhorred the new abolitionist law promulgated by Prime Minister Visconde do Rio Branco (1819–1880). Paradoxically, the Viscount was also a conservative. The law was promulgated on September 28, 1871, establishing the freedom of all children born of slaves after that date.[47] The adoption of the legal document meant the irreversibility of the abolitionist process, a fact that provoked great fear and discontent among the conservative slave owners, who began to oppose the monarchy. At the same time, these same landowners started to promote European immigration to the Empire with the aim of reducing the labor shortage that would inevitably result from the end of the now doomed compulsory labor system.

In the case of the liberals, those who joined the Republican Party of São Paulo were mostly urban professionals who formed a nascent middle class: lawyers, doctors, engineers, journalists. They reflected the Empire's, and especially São Paulo's, new urban social make-up. By 1870, Brazil had around 10 million inhabitants, of whom some 800,000 lived in the province of São Paulo. Rio de Janeiro had a slightly higher number, 900,000 residents. São Paulo was growing at a fast pace as a result of the proliferation of coffee plantations in the province. Starting in the 1860s, the cultivation of coffee had begun to run its course in the Paraiba River Valley, the original plantation site that runs from the coast of Rio de Janeiro State towards the hinterland. With deterioration of the valley's soil due to overuse, plantations began to advance westward in search of fertile land. They soon started entering the province of São Paulo and new centers of productivity were established in cities such as Campinas and Sorocaba. Coffee plantations would subsequently extend southwest, advancing into the northern portion of the province of Paraná.

It was thus that in the 1870s the province of São Paulo would see the emergence of its own coffee barons who would soon start to join forces in the Paulista Republican Party. These new coffee magnates differed substantially from those of the 1850s, of whom the most powerful were those who formed the aforementioned Saquarema Trinity, the conservative triumvirate that put down the Praieira Rebellion in Pernambuco in 1848 and ousted Juan Manuel de Rosas from the government in Buenos Aires in 1852. While the fiercely monarchist conservatives of 1850 had defended the central authority of Pedro II's government from their coffee plantations in the province of Rio de Janeiro, the new republican conservatives of

1870 demanded provincial autonomy from theirs in São Paulo. The new center of coffee production would soon become the nation's economic engineroom and start demanding federalism and enhanced autonomy. From their still slave-operated farms, capital would spread into parallel economic activities that supported coffee farming. Railways began to be built for the transportation of crops from the interior to the port of Santos: the São Paulo Railway connected the city of Jundiaí to Santos in 1868; the Ituana Railroad connected Itu to Campinas in 1873; the Mogiana and Sorocabana, two railways interconnected with the previous ones, began to be built in 1875.

Together with the rise of republicanism and the new political clout of São Paulo's coffee barons, historians point to three other important factors that contributed to the weakening of the monarchy in the 1870s and 1880s: the so-called Religious Question, the Military Question, and the Servile Question. The Religious Question refers to a protracted conflict between the Catholic Church and the imperial government lasting from 1872 to 1874. During those years, several of Pedro II's ministers of state entered the Freemasonry, a fraternal organization that had emerged in Europe during the Middle Ages and spread through various parts of the world in the modern era, acquiring considerable political clout in several countries. The Catholic Church had been in open conflict with Freemasonry since at least 1738, when Pope Clement XII had issued the papal bull *In Eminenti Apostolatus*, banning Freemasons from the Church. It was widely believed that a Jewish influence was at work in Freemasonry, and Clement XII's bull had a significant anti-Semitic component. In any case, in the 1870s, a conservative Catholic movement called *Ultramontanism* swelled the ranks of those opposed to Freemasonry. Their doctrine, also initiated in the Middle Ages, defended the superiority of popes over kings. Ultramontanism was strengthened in 1864 by Pope Pious IX's bull *Syllabus Errorum*, which outlawed secret societies, and then again by the First Vatican Council, which decreed papal infallibility. The council reiterated the ban on Freemasonry, reminding the faithful that joining the organization would entail immediate excommunication.

In Brazil, a major dispute arose between the Ultramontanes and Freemasons. Since many Freemasons had government positions, the dispute soon turned into a conflict between the government and the Catholic Church. It started in 1872 when the Ultramontane Bishop of Rio de Janeiro, Dom Pedro Maria de Lacerda (1830–1890), reprimanded a priest, Almeida Martins, for a panegyric delivered in honor of the Viscount of Rio Branco, then President of the Council of Ministers, who had drafted the aforementioned abolitionist law of 1871. Rio Branco was a

Freemason, and that alone was sufficient to provoke Bishop Lacerda's anger. Similar incidents took place in the provinces of Pará and Pernambuco, where local Bishops proceeded to the excommunication of priests involved with freemasonry. The reprimanded priests took their cases to respective Provincial Courts, which, in defiance of the Bishops, concluded that only the Emperor was in a position to punish the clerics in question. The Court's decision was based on the legal status of Catholicism in Brazil. The Constitution of 1824 had adopted two traditional Portuguese statutes that regulated the relationship between the Church and the State: the *padroado* and the *beneplácito*. These statutes established that in the Kingdom of Portugal, Catholic priests would be appointed by Rome but would take office only after being approved by the King. The kingdom would also pay the priests' salaries, which in practice conferred upon them the status of public servants. Based on these traditional Portuguese dispositions, the Brazilian Court judged that the Emperor had the last word on the priests' punishment.

Enraged and unwilling to yield, the Bishops of Pará and Pernambuco defied the Emperor, upholding the priests' excommunication. The government's Council of Ministers then decided to present a formal complaint in court. The Bishops were arrested, prosecuted, and sentenced to four years in prison in 1874.

This incident was a serious blow to Pedro II's popularity. The Emperor had to walk a tightrope between the powerful aristocrats who ran his government and the common people who had strong religious sentiments. In the end, he leaned towards the former, provoking considerable dissatisfaction among the latter. Historians agree that the crisis contributed to Pedro II's subsequent fall in 1889 in that it removed one of the pillars that sustained the monarchy in power, namely the Catholic Church. After 1874, the Empire's powerful Catholic Bishops became eager for the ascension of the Emperor's eldest daughter, Isabel, to the throne. The Princess was known as a firm supporter of Ultramontane views.[48]

The second factor that contributed to the fall of the monarchy in 1889 was the so-called Military Question. The term refers to a series of conflicts between the Monarchy and the Empire's high military commanders lasting approximately from 1884 to 1887. During these years, the armed forces had many grievances. After the victory in the Paraguayan War, army officers had gained considerable prestige and begun demanding, as recognition, a higher social and political standing within the Empire. One demand was that the army's role be limited to that of protecting the nation; since colonial times, soldiers had customarily been called upon to perform policing roles such as patrolling, something they saw as beneath their position. One such task was to seize runaway slaves, an obligation that became increasingly incompatible with the growing influence of Positivism and Abolitionism in the army.

Another source of dissatisfaction was the government's constant delays in paying war veterans' pensions. This issue became a point of conflict between liberal and conservative officers, generating an intra-army dispute. Problems escalated when some officers began taking their quarrels to the press, especially in Rio Grande do Sul, which by then had become a hotbed of Positivism and Republicanism. Júlio Prates de Castilhos (1860–1903), a future provincial dictator, published an article in his republican newspaper, *The Federation*, criticizing the monarchy for the way it treated the army, which he claimed was the only institution still left in the country that was free of corruption. The government then banned the army from speaking to the media, creating a row that further weakened the already fragile central administration.

The army's relations with the monarchy deteriorated further when these demands became entangled in the process of the abolition of slavery. In the province of Ceará, severe droughts experienced during the 1870s led to the death of a great part of the slave population. The difficulty of keeping slaves alive on farms led to the abolition of slavery in the Province in 1884. Four years later, in 1888, the hideous system of compulsory labor would be abolished in the entire nation by a decree signed by Isabel Cristina Leopoldina de Bragança (1846–1921), Pedro II's daughter. Back in the year of 1884, however, attempting to avoid the financial losses involved in the recently instated compulsory manumission, several local landlords in Ceará began to send their slaves to be sold in other provinces. Tensions emerged when a man named Francisco Nascimento, one of the sailors responsible for the transportation of Ceará's former slaves who were now being sold abroad, sparked a riot and refused to perform the task of taking the black men to provinces where they could be sold. Learning of this, an abolitionist army officer called Sena Madureira invited Nascimento to Rio de Janeiro, where the brave sailor was honored in the military academy.[49]

Sena Madureira's attitude mirrored the army's strong inclination towards abolitionism. The military's sympathy for the slaves had its roots in the Paraguayan War, where members of the landed aristocracy had been exempt from serving in the army as long as they sent their slaves to fight in their place. The Brazilian forces thus contained a large number of black slaves, who entered the corps in place of their masters. The proximity with slaves in combat worked to establish a bond between the white soldiers and these black men who were giving their lives for a nation that had always mistreated them.

Madureira's tribute to Nascimento enraged the conservatives in the central government. The Minister of War, a civilian named Alfredo Chaves, attempted to punish Madureira. But the powerful military commander and war hero, Marshal Deodoro da Fonseca (1827–1892) came to his defense. Fonseca was in charge of the army stationed in Rio Grande Sul, a province where the military had been historically strong, controlling the local administration while waging war against the Spanish neighbors. After allowing his Riograndense troops to come to Madureira's defense, Fonseca was severely chastised by the central government. He was summoned to Rio de Janeiro in order to offer an explanation to the President of the Council of Ministers, the fierce conservative João Maurício Wanderley, known as Baron of Cotegipe (1815–1889). The call, however, backfired. Fonseca was received in the capital with a boisterous demonstration of praise organized by a group of his fellow officers. Together, these army commanders claimed the army's right to participate in national politics and founded the *Military Club*, an organization that would play an important role in the future, asserting the interests of the military class in Brazilian society.

The episode involving abolitionists and the army weakened the imperial government, bringing to light its lack of support. The crisis between the government and the military reached its peak when Afonso Celso de Assis Figueiredo (1836–1912), the Viscount of Ouro Preto, was appointed Prime Minister on July 7, 1889. Ouro Preto attempted to solve the Military Question by weakening the army. Among measures to that end were a purge of dissatisfied commanders, who were forced to transfer to distant provinces, and the strengthening of the National Guard, which had been created in 1831 with the aim of downplaying the influence of Portuguese commanders in national politics after the abdication of Pedro I. Watching the rising tension between the army and the imperial government, the republicans began to spread the rumor that Ouro Preto intended to arrest Deodoro da Fonseca and disband the army. By 1889, the Republican Movement had grown with the advent of the so-called Republicans of May 14, a group of powerful landowners who had withdrawn their support for the monarchy after Princess Isabel had decreed the abolition of slavery on May 13, 1888, that is, the previous day.

On November 14, 1889, the republicans finally convinced Deodoro to stage a coup and oust Ouro Preto. The military commander was a personal friend of Pedro II, and had no intention of provoking the Emperor's fall.

For Deodoro, the coup was intended only to bring about a change in the ministerial cabinet: Ouro Preto would go, but the monarchy would stay.

One of the main reasons for Deodoro's wish to maintain Pedro II in power was that the Emperor was already an old man, and one who had been faithful to his nation his entire life. Hence Deodoro's position was that the fall of the monarchy, though necessary and unavoidable, should come only after the Emperor's death. Events, however, took an unexpected turn.

Enticed by the republican rumormongers who publicized his potential arrest, Deodoro gathered a few troops and proceeded to the administrative center of the capital. There he ordered the fall of Ouro Preto, while at the same time shouting "God Save the Emperor!" The republicans, however, managed to act fast, plotting a scheme to convince Deodoro that the simple ousting of Ouro Preto would not do. They informed Deodoro that the Emperor was about to appoint as Prime Minister a man named Gaspar da Silveira Martins (1835–1901), a *caudilho* from Rio Grande do Sul who happened to be Deodoro's foremost political enemy. The conflict between Deodoro and Martins was in fact rooted in more than mere political disagreements. Both men had competed for the favor of the same Riograndense lady during the time Deodoro had acted as Rio Grande do Sul's provincial governor.[50] The dispute had ended to the Commander's disadvantage, leaving him bitter and resentful. It was thus that, learning of the possible appointment of his rival to the ministerial position, Deodoro accepted the republicans' request and proclaimed the Brazilian Republic on November 15, 1889.

A concatenation of several elements had led to the fall of Pedro II: the discontent of the landed aristocracy with the end of slavery in 1888; the religious and military entanglements of imperial politics; the general dread of having a woman on the throne after the death of the Emperor, namely the latter's daughter, Isabel. From a wider perspective, and as we will see in more detail below, the fall of the monarchy entailed above all a cultural and political estrangement from Europe. Over the next several decades, the Brazilian Republic would make a rapid turn to the Americas. The United States would become a new model, and its influence would be at the same time welcomed and resisted, creating a long-lasting dialectic through which the relationship with the powerful northern nation would be negotiated. Furthermore, disputes with Argentina would persist, the coffee barons would seize political power over the entire nation, and a wave of immigration would produce lasting transformations in culture and society.

Culture and Society in the Brazilian Empire

The period between 1822 and 1889 was marked by a strong governmental effort to establish a national culture in the former Portuguese colony. Such a culture would be modeled on that of Europe, but would comprise an important degree of originality and, hopefully, indigenous creativity. A national aesthetic was thus constructed on top of the initial impulse provided by Portuguese court life and its importation of European art and culture into the colony started in 1808. During the years of John VI's reign, European artists would be financed by the Crown to come to the colony and reproduce in the tropics the aesthetic elements required for satisfactory court life. The French Artistic Mission of Debret and Montigny, as we have seen, left its mark in the colony's imagery, painting with local colors the glorious images of the Portuguese Empire. In architecture, the gracious and colorful eighteenth-century baroque of Minas Gerais gradually gave way to the sumptuous and linear neoclassical style of the capital, Rio de Janeiro, which became the official site of the new aesthetic. The visual arts began to assume stronger traces of local sensibility, prompting what would be recognized as the new national style.

The literary arts also showed a marked development from the prevailing aesthetic of Minas Gerais towards a new stance proper to Rio de Janeiro's court life. More precisely, they moved from the neoclassical poetry that inspired the revolutionaries of the mining region into a romantic nationalist aesthetic that reproduced Napoleonic grandiosity in a tropical style. Romanticism emerged in the works of poets such as Domingos Gonçalves de Magalhães (1811–1882), Antônio Teixeira de Sousa (1812–1861), Manuel de Araújo Porto Alegre (1806–1879), and Antônio Gonçalves Dias (1823–1864). These form what literary critics term the first generation of romantic poets, a group of artists highly influenced by the nation's process of independence, and whose works show strong traits of nationalism and sentimentalism. The portrayal of the indigenous individual as a national hero is often cited as one of the main features of the first romantic generation.[51]

A second generation of romantic poets appeared with Manuel Álvares de Azevedo (1831–1852), Casimiro de Abreu (1839–1860), Luís José Junqueira Freire (1832–1855), and Fagundes Varella (1841–1875). These were men who for the most part lived very short lives, and whose existence was marked by entrenched despair, deep-rooted angst, and bohemian decadence. With the establishment of the Brazilian Empire in 1822, the former aristocratic habit of sending one's sons to study in Coimbra shifted to France and England. With this opening up to new

European venues, Baudelaire and Lord Byron became strong influences in this second generation of Brazilian romantic poets.

A third generation appeared with Antônio Frederico de Castro Alves (1847–1871), Joaquim de Sousa Andrade (1832–1902), and João da Cruz e Sousa (1861–1898). These poets are identified with the new themes of Abolitionism and the Republic. Since they praised freedom above all things, they came to be known as *Condoreiros*, a name derived from the condor, the Andean vulture that symbolizes liberty. In Brazilian literary history, these poets are generally portrayed according to their basic formal and thematic peculiarities. Castro Alves is known as the fiercest abolitionist, a characteristic that bestowed on him the title of *Poeta dos Escravos* (Poet of the Slaves). Sousa Andrade was educated in Paris and in the United States, and his poetry is usually seen as transitional from Romanticism to Realism. Known as the *Dante Negro* (the Black Dante), Cruz e Sousa was a mulatto of humble origins who succeeded in the world of letters by means of uncommon talent and extreme hardship. He is considered to be Brazil's first symbolist poet.[52]

While in poetry Romanticism started with Gonçalves de Magalhães' 1836 collection *Suspiros poéticos e saudades*, in narrative the first romantic work was Antônio Gonçalves Teixeira e Sousa's (1812–1861) *O filho do pescador* (1843). Teixeira e Sousa's work was followed by Joaquim Manuel de Macedo's (1820–1882) *A moreninha* (1844). Besides Teixeira e Sousa and Macedo, some of the most noted Brazilian romantic novelists are José de Alencar (1829–1877), Bernardo Guimarães (1825–1884), Franklin Távora (1842–1888), and Alfredo d'Escragnolle Taunay (1843–1899). Alongside such a substantial romantic canon, one unique and remarkable example of a Picaresque novel appeared in Manuel Antônio de Almeida's (1831–1861) *Memórias de um Sargento de Milícias* (1852).

From the early 1870s Brazilian poetry began to mirror the European decline of Romanticism, which started to find opposition in a new generation of poets who adhered to Parnassianism. The Parnassian style originated in France in the 1850s, and was strongly influenced by Positivism. Standing between Romanticism and Symbolism, Parnassians adopted the strong formalist aesthetic found in the doctrine of art for art's sake proposed by French poet Théophile Gautier (1811–1872). Unlike the French version, however, Brazilian Parnassianism maintained a more subjective perspective on reality, using the objectivity and scientific jargon prescribed by Positivism more sparingly. A remarkable number of poets embraced the movement, among them Gonçalves Crespo (1846–1883), Alberto de Oliveira (1857–1937), Teófilo Dias (1854–1889), Raimundo

Correia (1859–1911), and many others. The most remembered of them all is probably Olavo Bilac (1865–1918), who is regarded as the most nationalistic of all Brazilian poets. From 1890 onwards, Symbolism began to surpass Parnassianism in Brazilian poetry.[53]

In the novel, the last decade of the Empire saw the rise of various trends imported from Europe. Realism is thought to have emerged in Brazil in 1881 with the publication of Machado de Assis's (1839–1908) *Memórias Póstumas de Brás Cubas*. The same year saw the publication of Aluísio Azevedo's (1857–1913) *O Mulato* (1881), a monumental work that is generally considered to be the starting point of Brazilian Naturalism. Naturalism is arguably the genre of novels that produced the best narrative in Brazil. Aluísio Azevedo's *O Cortiço* (1890) is unsurpassed in descriptive force and emotional intensity. Azevedo can in fact be regarded as perhaps the best Brazilian novelist of all time.[54]

Besides Aluísio Azevedo, several other Brazilian novelists adopted the tenets of Naturalism as a basic aesthetic, producing a consistent body of naturalist novels. Among these are Horácio de Carvalho's (1857–1933) *O Cromo* (1888); Júlio Ribeiro's (1845–1890) *A Carne* (1888); Adolfo Caminha's (1867–1897) *A Normalista* (1893) and *Bom Criolo* (1895), and Inglês de Sousa's (1853–1918) *O Missionário* (1888). Together with these authors and works, a movement from Realism to Impressionism can be perceived in Raul Pompeia (1863–1895) and his *O Ateneu* (1888). Pompeia produced a narrative remarkably similar to Proust many years before Proust himself. In any case, in the closing years of the Empire Naturalism emerged as the prevailing aesthetic, and a rich corpus of naturalist works contributed to the country's exceling in the genre.[55]

Brazilian theater also developed significantly during the Imperial Period. The history of national drama dates back to 1549, when Tomé de Sousa (1503–1579), the first governor general of the colony, arrived on the coast of Bahia bringing a group of Jesuit missionaries. Among them was a priest named Manuel da Nóbrega (1517–1570), who would put his religious plays and dialogues to the service of catechizing the indigenous population. Following Tomé de Sousa's expedition, another colonial administrator, Duarte da Costa (d. 1560), arrived in Brazil in 1553 bringing the priest and playwright José de Anchieta (1534–1597), who would become known as the father of Brazilian theater.

During the Colonial Period, theater flourished, especially after 1750 with the rise of the Marquis of Pombal, who fostered the arts and culture. The first opera houses appeared in the colony during the 1760s, bringing theater groups to Vila Rica, Salvador, Recife, and Rio de Janeiro. Cláudio Manuel da Costa (1729–1789), one of the classicist poets from Minas

Gerais, staged his *O Parnaso Obsequioso* in 1768, one of the first plays in the history of Brazilian theater.

In the Imperial Era, Romanticism made its appearance in the plays of Gonçalves de Magalhães (1811–1882), the same man who, as we have seen, established Brazilian Romanticism in poetry through works such as *Suspiros poéticos e saudades* (1836) and the epic *A Confederação dos Tamoios* (1857). Magalhães's *Antônio José, ou O poeta e a Inquisição* (1838) is considered to be another foundational work in the history of Brazilian drama. The play went on stage on March 13, 1838. João Caetano (1808–1863), a pioneer actor and dramaturge, directed the performance.

In the same year, the play *O juiz de paz da roça* (The Countryside Judge), by Martins Pena (1815–1848), established the comedy of manners in Brazil. Pena wrote about thirty plays and became the master of the genre in Brazil. The theater of Molière had been very popular in the country since the eighteenth century, with plays usually staged in the original French. Following Molière's popularity, Pena's oeuvre soon gained a wide audience. His reworking of the French playwright's themes and techniques with Brazilian society as the backdrop became very popular at Rio de Janeiro's imperial court.

Realism appeared in drama through the works of Artur Azevedo (1855–1908), the older brother of Naturalism's master novelist, Aluísio Azevedo. More than Aluísio's, however, Artur's works suffered from the ineptitude of the public, who preferred comedies and vaudeville instead of plays that contained realist portrayals of society. Azevedo wrote more than one hundred plays and is considered the most important Brazilian playwright of the nineteenth century.[56]

Music also flourished during the Imperial Era. As in the case of theater, records of early musical activity also date back to the Jesuit missions established in various parts of the territory, starting in 1549. Sacred music was written and performed as part of the catechization, and the most vigorous examples of musical culture from the sixteenth and seventeenth centuries are found in the former Jesuit Spanish reductions of the South.

During the eighteenth century, the captaincy of Minas Gerais became an important musical center in the colony. With the gold rush, music flourished in the cathedrals of Ouro Preto, where the black priest João de Deus de Castro Lobo (1794–1832) stood out as an early prodigy who would become a great composer and music master. Since the Portuguese banned non-European music from the official sacred repertory, a rule that was relaxed in the Spanish colonies, Castro Lobo's musical production was of a purely European essence, developing mostly without African or indigenous influence.[57]

Following the same current as seen in the development of the other art forms, the transfer of the Lisbon Court to Rio de Janeiro in 1808 inspired a revolution in colonial music. With the presence of the Portuguese nobility, for the first time the coastal colonial capital superseded Minas Gerais's Ouro Preto in artistic matters. At the court, the works of mulatto musician José Maurício Nunes Garcia (1767–1830) flourished. He, together with Castro Lobo, is generally regarded as the founder of Brazilian classical music. John VI brought from Portugal his entire musical library, which was considered one of the best in Europe, and the arrival in 1811 of Marcos Portugal (1762–1830), the official Portuguese court composer, injected further vigor into Brazilian colonial music, both in composition and in performance.

Romanticism emerged during the reign of Pedro II with the works of Antônio Carlos Gomes (1836–1896). Born into a musical family, Carlos Gomes's talent was noticed at a very early age. His prodigious musical abilities were highly favored by Rio de Janeiro's nobility, and the Emperor himself decided to finance his studies. Imperial support warranted the composer's lifelong gratitude to the monarchy, one that continued even after 1889. Carlos Gomes's first opera, *A noite do castelo* (1861), was very successful in the Empire. His *O Guarani* (1870), based on romantic novelist José de Alencar's homonymous novel of 1857, premiered in the La Scala Theater in Milan to critical acclaim. Carlos Gomes is generally regarded as the first composer in the new world to be fully accepted in Europe. His story is a good example of how the Brazilian Empire maintained strong cultural ties with Europe through the monarchy, while the same did not happen, or at least not with such intensity, in the case of the American republics.[58]

The final years of the Imperial Period also saw the rise of nationalism in Brazilian classical music. While Carlos Gomes had infused his music with *Indianism*, a style that brought Rousseau's myth of the noble savage to artistic representation, the works of Alberto Nepomuceno (1864–1920) marked the final incorporation of nationalistic aesthetic elements into music. One year before the abolition of slavery, in 1887, Nepomuceno composed his *Dança de Negros*, a work that is regarded as the first classical composition based on national ethnic motifs. Tellingly, the composition had its premier in Ceará, the only province where slavery had already been abolished.

Among the art forms flourishing in the Brazilian Empire, painting is perhaps the one that received stronger financial support from the State, and also the one more deliberately infused with ideology. Painting served the State's aim of forging a distinctive sense of nationality in what, at least until 1808, was generally seen as little more than a distant colony to be exploited. The most significant visual works of the period sprang from artists related to the aforementioned Royal Academy of Fine Arts, which was established by John VI in 1816 under the name of *Escola Real de Ciências, Artes e Ofícios*. There, nationalistic themes and scenes were constantly favored: the Battle of Guararapes, the Paraguayan War, the enthronement of emperors. Artists such as Victor Meirelles (1832–1903), Pedro Américo (1843–1905), and Almeida Júnior (1850–1899) established a strong and official Romantic tradition, although the last of these painters already showed a strong influence of Realism.

As we can see, the canon of Brazilian art and literature of the Imperial Period reflects the State's pressing need for the establishment of a national identity. Be it in poetry, music, or the visual arts, the styles and trends were imported from Europe but assimilated to the local experience so as to create a national aesthetic. As internal and external political stability was gradually achieved, however, a more critical form of art began to appear. That art began to reflect upon the very nationality that had been under construction. It started questioning established views, as well as the established power structure. The naturalist novel of Aluísio Azevedo presents a case in point, with its denunciation of slavery and social stigmatization. One could say that Alberto Nepomuceno's music proceeded along a similar path.

By the beginning of the 1880s, Brazilian society had developed from a collection of various disconnected provinces and villages into a more coherent national entity. A national culture had emerged, and the country that had experienced continuous regional uprisings during the 1830s and 1840s was now more stable and integrated. That same integration, however, allowed for the emergence of revolution at a higher level. With the establishment of national unity, for the first time an emerging revolt might no longer be limited to the overthrowing of this or that provincial governor, but could have truly national scope, as was the case in 1889.

In economic and social terms, the Empire reproduced most of the traditional structures inherited from Portugal. A dominant class continued to prevail through the intermingling of landownership and state-bureaucratic membership, restating the colonial mentality prevailing in the aforementioned *Câmara dos Homens Bons*, or "City Council of the Good Men." The Portuguese ethos thus lingered as part of a collective unconscious that favored hierarchy and patrimonialism as the widely accepted forms of political and social culture.

Enmeshed in that culture, a new oligarchy emerged in 1838, when coffee became the nation's foremost export commodity. The province of São Paulo began a process of accelerated growth, turning gradually into a magnet for foreign migrants. Immigration soon appeared as one of the main elements characterizing Brazilian culture and society in its development from the nineteenth to the twentieth centuries. In tandem with the dreadful institute of slavery, it produced the interplay of economic forces that resulted in the dialectic of lethargy and vitality characteristic of the Brazilian ethos.[59]

Looking at Brazilian history from the second half of the nineteenth century onwards, one finds immigration and slavery as two deeply interconnected elements. As we have seen, throughout the nineteenth century abolition laws presaged a shortage in the supply of labor, and immigrants began to be seen as a means to offset that problem.[60] Immigration thus became entangled with the idea of introducing individuals into the country in order to cope with the reality of an end to slave labor. Immigrants of European origin were favored since they could fulfill the elite's desire to "whiten" the country. Gobineau's aforementioned racist ideas, together with the widespread belief in the benefits of eugenics, became very influential in the Empire's policymaking on immigration.[61]

Prior to 1808 immigration was virtually non-existent in Brazil. In order to maintain a firm and exclusive grip on the colonial economy, the Portuguese Crown virtually proscribed the entry of foreigners into its American territory. The first immigrants to arrive in Brazil were, as we have seen, a group of 300 Chinese citizens brought by John VI from Macau in 1808 with the aim of introducing tea cultivation into the colony. Ten years later, in 1818, a Royal Decree authorized the settling of 260 Swiss families in the highlands of the province of Rio de Janeiro. This was the first organized movement of immigration into Brazil. Swiss immigrants came from the Canton of Fribourg, located in the West of their country, not far from the border with France. In order to accommodate the group, John VI founded what today is the city of Nova Friburgo in Rio de Janeiro State.

A similar undertaking was carried out with German immigrants, who were allowed to occupy part of the southern province of Rio Grande do Sul. In 1824, the first group was settled in the Sinos River Valley region, founding what is today the city of São Leopoldo. This region was much less hospitable than the one found by the Swiss immigrants in the highlands of Rio de Janeiro State. In spite of its southern, sub-tropical climate, the low altitude of the greater part of Rio Grande do Sul State means long hot summers with generally high humidity, which suggests a harder life for the German immigrants than that enjoyed by their Swiss counterparts. Germans were especially welcome because the Empress, Maria Leopoldina (1797–1826), was an Austrian archduchess, which facilitated the transfer. The Germans came from various different places including Holstein, Hamburg, Hanover, Hunsrück, Pomerania, Westphalia, Württemberg. By 1874, about 30,000 German immigrants had settled in the region. They moved into other provinces as well and, as a result, several Brazilian cities today have German as an official language. Pomeranian, German, and Riograndenser Hunsrückisch German are official languages in cities such as Pomerode and Blumenau, in the state of Santa Catarita; São Lourenço do Sul and Nova Petrópolis, in Rio Grande do Sul; and Domingos Martins and Pancas, in Espírito Santo.

German immigration to Brazil, however, was not without its setbacks. In 1852 a German uprising occurred in what came to be known as the Ibicaba Farm Revolt. The incident occurred on the estate of powerful landlord and imperial senator, Nicolau Pereira de Campos Vergueiro (1778–1859). Vergueiro's attempt at employing German labor in his coffee plantations followed the issuing of the aforementioned Law of 1850, or the Eusébio de Queirós Law, as it was named in honor to the Minister of Justice who outlawed the slave trade, fearing the threat contained in the Aberdeen Act of 1845. After the issuing of the Law, the imperial government created two systems of employment meant to attract European immigrants to the country, the *parceria* and the *colonato*. The first, which was employed by Vergueiro on his Ibicaba Farm, established that landowners would offer part of their land to immigrants, who would in turn cultivate it and share their profits with the landowner. Immigrants, however, were generally bound to purchase essential goods from the same landowner, thus establishing a debt that was higher than the shareable profit produced by their labor. This inevitably created a system of debt bondage, against which the Germans rebelled in 1852. The uprising on Vergueiro's farm resulted in the Prussian government's proscription of immigration to Brazil in 1859. The ban, however, was for the most part unsuccessful, for German immigrants continued to reach the Brazilian Empire, mostly fleeing Bismarck's wars against Denmark, Austria, and France.

Italian immigrants started to arrive in the Empire around 1875, settling in the northeast of Rio Grande do Sul, as well as in the neighboring state of Santa Catarina. In geographical terms, they had better luck than the Germans, settling in a region with a more temperate climate and better natural resources. Italians came mostly from the region of the Veneto, in

Northern Italy, and spoke a mix of Venetian dialects, which came to form the language called Brazilian Veneto, also known as the Talian language. Today Talian is the official language in the city of Serafina Corrêa, in Rio Grande do Sul State. As we shall see later, present-day Brazil would probably have a much larger population of Italian and German speakers if it were not for the attempts to suppress these languages during the dictatorship of Rio Grande do Sul's canny landlord Getulio Dornelles Vargas, which started in 1937.

As the nineteenth century proceeded, European immigration expanded and became more diversified. Polish and Ukrainian immigrants arrived in the second half of the century. Asian settlers would also become part of the web of peoples and languages that would forge the diverse and rich ethnic landscape of twentieth-century Brazil. From the beginning of the Imperial Era, these peoples started intermingling with the natives, who shared a mixed culture of Portuguese, African, and indigenous elements. In spite of such mixing, however, Portuguese culture remained hegemonic, and immigrants had to adapt to its dominance. The Portuguese language had to be mastered, and while religious freedom was enforced, the traditional Catholic religion remained dominant.[62]

The new country's most shocking feature for these European newcomers would have been the hideous Brazilian practice of slavery. The complexities involving the history of African slavery in Brazil must be understood in connection to slavery's existence in Africa itself. The Portuguese started dealing in slaves from Mauritania in the first half of the fifteenth century. The practice existed traditionally in the African country, which was the world's last jurisdiction to officially outlaw slavery, in 1981. The difference between traditional forms of slavery found in Africa and those employed in the Portuguese colonies, however, seem to reside in the latter's extensive use of chattel slavery. Chattel slavery denied the captive the recognition of his or her humanity, and it seems to have been less common in Africa than in the European versions of compulsory servitude.[63]

The level of brutality involved in Portuguese-Brazilian chattel slavery displays aspects of extreme perversion and psychological deformity on the part of traders and proprietors. Details of the treatment meted out to slaves in Brazil tend to be too horrifying for our modern sensibilities. Forms of abuse ranged from psychological intimidation to physical mutilation. Economically, however, the mistreatment produced the doubly unfavorable result of making the mortality rate of Brazilian slaves extremely high, and their rate of reproduction in captivity very low. Cruelty thus backfired upon the proprietors, who faced the high costs of buying new slaves to replace their ever-shrinking labor force.

This explains the necessity for the continued and growing trade in slaves. During the relatively short period from 1450 to 1500, hundreds of thousands of African slaves were bought and sold by Portuguese traders. The human slave proved to be a very cost effective product, and soon the Dutch entered the market, outdoing the Portuguese around the middle of the eighteenth century. The Portuguese took the system of compulsory labor to its American colony in the first decades after the discovery. The number of slaves entering Brazil between 1500 and 1850 is estimated at 3.5 million. The first statistical survey on the Brazilian population, carried out in 1872, pointed to 9,930,478 residents, of whom 1,510,806, that is, roughly 15%, were still captives in spite of the slave trade having ended in 1850.[64]

The situation of the captive became even more pitiful with the advent of urbanization and the emergence of slave ownership among middle-class Brazilians living in urban centers. As the emerging bourgeoisie started employing slaves as a way of obtaining regular income, a new type of captive emerged, the so-called *escravo de ganho*. This was a slave who would work as a cleaner, carrier, or even beggar or prostitute, and at the end of the day turn his or her earnings over to the owner.[65] Around the middle of the nineteenth century, urban dwellers began engaging more and more frequently in this outrageously inhuman form of exploitation, buying slaves in order to avoid doing any work at all, as the captive's income would provide for the household's financial needs. Needless to say, this system fostered general idleness and lethargy in the country's middle class, echoing the traditional Portuguese aristocratic perception of labor as intrinsically demeaning. The historical record of the systematic employment of the *escravo de ganho* in the country's emerging urban centers suggests the existence of profound scars left in the Brazilian social psyche as well as one of the possible causes for some of the country's persistent social maladies.[66]

In the early 1880s, important sectors of Brazilian society began to demand reform of the old structure of domination and exploitation. The Abolitionist Movement emerged, raising its voice against the evil of slavery when the situation in urban centers had become unbearable. The Movement's roots can be traced back to the days of the dawning of the Brazilian Empire when, in his report to the Constituent Assembly of 1824, José Bonifácio identified the practice as a lethal cancer threatening the foundations of the nation. Bonifácio's socially progressive ideas notwithstanding, the Abolitionist Movement only gathered momentum in the early 1880s, when two prestigious individuals, Joaquim Nabuco (1849–1910) and José do Patrocínio (1853–1905), established the Brazilian Society Against Slavery. The Society was formed on September 7, 1880, gaining the immediate support of some of the country's leading political and intellectual figures. Rui Barbosa (1849–1923), Tavares Bastos (1839–1875), Sousa Dantas (1831–1894), André Rebouças (1838–1898), and Luís Gama (1830–1882) were some of the intellectuals who fought against the prevailing interests of slave owners. Raising their voices against the hegemonic classes and their dishonorable practices, these men wrote articles, books, and laws against the savagery, cruelty, and abuse involved in compulsory labor and captivity. Together, their works form an impressive corpus of anti-slavery literature and, as outright denunciations of servitude and its horrors, they can be regarded as foreshadowing human rights thinking and activism in Latin America.

The literary arts also entered the fray in lyric and novelistic form. Poet Castro Alves (1847–1871) and the aforementioned novelist Aluísio Azevedo (1857–1913) presented anti-slavery demands in distinguished artistic form. Castro Alves's poems *O Navio Negreiro* (1869) and *Os Escravos* (1883), together with Aluísio Azevedo's *O Mulato* (1881), provided Brazilian literature with an epistemological aspect, conferring upon it valuable moral and political significance.[67] Joaquim Nabuco's *O Abolicionismo* (1883) set forth in strong argumentative form the ideas espoused by his Brazilian Society Against Slavery. Rui Barbosa's discourses in the House of Representatives exposed the urgency of abolition in high and passionate rhetorical form. The newspaper *O Abolicionista* and the revue *Revista Ilustrada* adopted the end of slavery as central themes.[68]

While Abolitionism helped elevate Brazilian literature to a socially constructive textual tool, anti-slavery sentiments reached the powerful sphere of the armed forces. The high point of the abolitionist campaign came in 1887, when commander Deodoro da Fonseca petitioned the Crown for the army's exemption from the work of capturing runaway slaves, as mentioned above. From Deodoro's missive, Princess Isabel, Pedro II's daughter, understood that the army would no longer accept the practice of slavery in the country. On May 13, 1888, the Princess signed the law known as *Lei Áurea*. Slavery was abolished and, for the first time, those human beings who had known no other life than one of exploitation, cruelty, and humiliation could experience freedom.

The law of 1888, however, did not provide for building a sense of citizenship among the newly free population. Ex-slaves were mostly left to their own devices, without any support from the State. With no means of forging a new direction in their lives, many of them remained bound to their former owners.

Dissatisfied with the government's new law, many conservative landowners turned to republicanism. They became the "Republicans of May 14" who, as we have mentioned above, contributed to the fall of the monarchy in 1889. Now, the task was to build a Republic, a task that would also see many barriers placed in its path.

CHAPTER THREE

THE FIRST REPUBLIC (1889–1930)

The Initial Instability (1889–1894)

The period from 1889 to 1930 saw the appearance of a new type of society in the large territory inherited from Braganza dynastic rule. The ongoing process of immigration and urbanization, together with the new mass of free individuals now becoming economically active after the end of compulsory labor, produced profound changes in the nation's social and cultural landscape. The regional distribution of power and wealth began to converge towards the South, focused in particular on the city of São Paulo.

In 1872, São Paulo had a population of 32,000. By 1890, that number had doubled to 64,934. By 1900, ten years later, it had reached 239,820. Rio de Janeiro, the nation's capital, was still a bigger city, but with a much lower growth rate. Between 1872 and 1890 its population had gone from 274,000 to 522,000, and by 1900 it had reached 811,443.

The coffee economy was the main factor contributing to São Paulo's spectacular growth, which occurred both at the state and the city levels. Expansion had started during the second half of the nineteenth century, when railways built to connect the countryside with the port of Santos, from where coffee was exported, promoted the emergence of new business and services, turning the state's capital city into an economic and financial center whose dynamism would soon surpass that of any other municipality in the country. São Paulo city's mild climate, which resulted from its altitude of approximately 800 meters above sea level, was attractive to the country's financial elite, and it fostered urban development, facilitating the emergence of city life and culture.

The years from 1889 to 1930 also saw the rise and fall of a new system of government. Once the centralizing disposition of the monarchy and its reserve power were out of the way, a new decentralized administrative model was adopted. Enhanced provincial autonomy, however, did not necessarily entail a change in political practices. The new decentralized model would further intensify the traditional schemes of patronage and back-scratching between the central administration and the provincial elites. At the national level, presidents would be elected with the support of landowners who represented regional interests, and regional administrators would be approved by a discreet system of reciprocal approvals. This quid pro quo shows that the country enjoyed democracy in name only; elections were, as always, conducted under a cloak of violence, corruption, and repression.

While at the national level the most powerful provinces struggled against each other for supremacy in the central administration (turning presidential elections into regional confrontations), at the provincial level local landlords vied against each another for political pre-eminence. Arrangements were made for mutual support between the central government and the ruling provincial landlords, establishing an oligarchical system of government where powerful elites dominated all aspects of political life. The old liberal-versus-conservative dispute that had prevailed during the Imperial Era was now diluted into regional political parties that agreed upon the maintenance of provincial autonomy, but which at the same time attempted to achieve pre-eminence in the broader context of the nation.

The period of the First Brazilian Republic is known as *República Velha* (Old Republic). The name covers the time from the fall of the monarchy in 1889 to the Revolution of 1930, when a new political arrangement emerged in the context of the world financial crisis that started in 1929. Historians tend to divide the *República Velha* period into two sub-periods: the *República da Espada* (Republic of the Sword) and the *República Oligárquica* (Oligarchical Republic). The first is a shorter, initial period from 1889 to 1894, characterized by political instability and by the settling of the old dispute between the conservative claim for administrative centralization and the liberal demand for provincial autonomy. The second period runs from 1894 to 1930, being the one when the dispute between centralization and decentralization was resolved by a series of tacit agreements between the federal government and the provincial administrators.

Following the Republic's proclamation in 1889, the army assumed control of the central government. Soon, however, the military class in power started to meet resistance from the various political forces that could now vie for pre-eminence within the new system. In the absence of the authoritative figure of the Emperor, distinct groups with diverging interests entered the dispute. There were the monarchists, who wished to reinstate Pedro II, the federalists, who claimed greater provincial autonomy, and the defenders of a Comtean version of republican dictatorship, who wanted an even harsher form of authoritarianism. The latter were comprised primarily of the higher hierarchical echelons of Rio Grande do Sul's army. More and more the Riograndense warlords gained power and momentum, adopting concurrently a narrow, fundamentalist version of ideological Positivism.[1]

Three regional leaderships emerged with distinct political, economic, and cultural characteristics: Minas Gerais, Rio Grande do Sul, and São Paulo. The first represented the old economic and political influence of the mining region, which had risen to prominence during the gold cycle. The second embodied the conservative military clout derived from centuries of territorial disputes in the South. The third symbolized the new wealth derived from slave-labor-based coffee production.

On November 15, 1889, Marshal Deodoro da Fonseca assumed the leadership of the Republic. The National Congress would be founded one year later, on November 15, 1890. Its most immediate aim was that of drafting a Constitution. In spite of having issued directly from the new republican mores sustained by Deodoro, however, the Congress would soon become a focus of resistance against the President's centralizing efforts. The army commander had been given dictatorial powers on December 19, 1889, when the newly installed Provisory Government had been placed under his rule. He had formed a cabinet solely of freemasons, he himself being one of the most prestigious members of the fraternity. Eager to impose order, and following the logic of Comtean republican dictatorship, the Marshal suppressed the freedom of the press, promoted the naturalization of foreigners residing in national territory, and established the separation between the Church and the State. Deodoro's rule came to be the first truly dictatorial period in Brazilian history since independence.[2]

Staring in 1890, the divergent interests of the various regional leaderships provoked mounting disagreement among federal deputies, leading to an overt dispute within the National Constituent Assembly. Two approaches immediately clashed, generating a division in the Provisory Government: those of the liberal-democrats on one side, and those of the conservative-authoritarians on the other. The first group strove for the establishment of a federal republic with a clear separation between executive and legislative powers, thus proposing a constitutional arrangement similar to that of the United States. This was the view held in São Paulo and Minas Gerais. The second remained steadfast in adherence to the principles of Positivism, demanding a centralized national administration in the form of a dictatorial republic. This was the line defended by Rio Grande do Sul. The liberal-democratic group prevailed in the drafting of the constitution, which was promulgated on February 24,

1891. In the long run, however, the dispute between Rio Grandenses on one side, and São Paulo and Minas Gerais on the other, would resurface and intensify still further.

The Constitution of 1891 established presidential elections every four years, proscribing the president's re-election for the immediately subsequent term. The first presidential election would be carried out by the Constituent Assembly itself; the following ones would be based on universal suffrage. As such, censitary voting was abolished. In general terms, the Charter was modeled on the Constitution of the United States, establishing a decentralized form of government under a federalist system. Each state would draft its own constitution and elect its own president. The Constitution of Rio Grande do Sul, for instance, would follow the preference for authoritarianism prevailing in the region, allowing multiple re-elections of the State's president. This, as we shall see in more detail below, would soon give the southernmost state a local dictatorial government.

Deodoro da Fonseca was elected president on February 25, 1891. Commander Floriano Peixoto, an army officer enlisted in the party that opposed Deodoro, was elected vice-president. Deodoro's victory augmented the general fear that the old military leader could stage a *coup d'état* and reinstate the monarchy. Unlike the majority of the landed military aristocracy in Rio Grande do Sul, Deodoro's republican convictions were feeble. His feelings of respect and friendship for Pedro II were well known, as was the fact that he never intended to overthrow the monarchy. His personal intention in 1889, as we have seen, was nothing more than to oust Ouro Preto from the post of Prime Minister. In sum, in spite of being in tune with the Riograndenses in defending the implementation of a centralized form of government, Deodoro appeared more inclined to have that centralization in monarchical than republican form.

Deodoro's centralizing views soon provided the battleground for a fierce dispute between military and civilian politicians. This new dispute absorbed the old rivalry between liberals and conservatives. While the military defended political centralization and the concept of a unitary state, civilians advocated decentralization and federalism. This new development revisited that other point of fracture, that is, the one between Rio Grande do Sul on one side, and São Paulo and Minas Gerais on the other.

With such mounting discord among powerful contenders, the powder keg was ready to be ignited. Since the Congress was constituted mostly of civilian politicians, notably the members of São Paulo's landed aristocracy of coffee producers, a clash with the military executive was almost inevitable. To make matters worse, being a man of strong personality,

Deodoro would not budge from his centralizing position. He went into a head-on confrontation with the Legislative Assembly that had elected him president but that had also produced a federalist constitution against his wishes.

The President's Ministerial Cabinet soon emerged as another point of discord between the Congress and the Head of the Executive. Deodoro's government was composed mostly of monarchist ministers, the most obvious example being perhaps that of the Minister of Justice, Henrique Pereira de Lucena (1835–1913), who under the title of Baron of Lucena had been a respected member of the imperial nobility. Such a heavily monarchist cabinet, added to the nation's deplorable economic situation, made the President's position very difficult. In the face of so much conflict, on February 3, 1891, the Congress attempted to approve a bill limiting the powers of the Executive. Deodoro then mounted a fresh *coup d'état*, closing the National Legislative Assembly and bringing about the end of his constitutional government, which now became a dictatorship.

Even with dictatorial powers, however, things did not move according to the Commander's wishes. Disagreements with the powerful coffee oligarchy of São Paulo deepened as the central government insisted on economic policies that favored industrialization. Such policies were the product of a plan devised by the Minister of Finance, Rui Barbosa de Oliveira (1849–1923). Rui Barbosa was a renowned republican and abolitionist from the state of Bahia who had drafted the Constitution of 1891. His expertise in the field of Law was widely recognized, and he was respected in the army as one of the most reliable civilian leaders. His expertise in Law, however, did not extend to the field of Economics, and his support for the adoption of fiat money as opposed to the gold standard as a means of providing liquidity for the nation's economy resulted in political failure and economic breakdown.

The ensuing financial crisis became known as the *Encilhamento*. The word describes the act of people saddling their horses and rushing to the Rio de Janeiro Stock Exchange in order to sell their stocks and bonds after finding out that they were the product of a scam. Finance Minister Rui Barbosa's vigorous expansionist monetary policy was coupled with intensive industrial incentives based on new forms of credit. Credit lines were open for hundreds of firms that sold their stock in the financial market without having any real intention of establishing production. In other words, a stock market was created with firms that existed only on paper. The get-rich-quick scheme soon brought the entire economy down.[3]

The inflationary tendency of Rui Barbosa's policies was further enhanced by his efforts to establish an adequate monetary economy, much needed after the abolition of slavery. After 1888, former slaves now needed to be paid for their work. Currency was also necessary to pay for the labor of immigrants who continued to settle in Brazil as a workforce destined to replace slave labor, that is, the labor of the large number of ex-slaves who would not be willing to continue working even in exchange for regular wages. In order to meet the new demand for currency, Rui Barbosa simply printed more and more notes.

The bubble thus created was soon to burst and the economy quickly experienced hyperinflation. Rui Barbosa stepped down from office on January 20, 1891 and focused his attention on a private enterprise he had created during the *Encilhamento* period, and which appeared to be involved in the stock exchange. The Minister's controversial attitudes would lead him to exile in London during the following government. Rui Barbosa would be allowed to return to Brazil only after the landlords of São Paulo had seized the government in 1894. After that, he would become an important civilian politician and lawmaker, and stand for the presidency on two occasions.

The *Encilhamento*'s dismal economic effects lasted throughout the decade of 1890. They were an important factor in the fall of President Deodoro da Fonseca at the end of 1891. Deodoro's political situation deteriorated when anti-authoritarian voices were raised in Rio Grande do Sul, leading to the ousting of local governor, Júlio de Castilhos (1860–1903), a positivist sentinel who acted as dictator among the Riograndense warlords. While Castilhos was being ousted in the South on November 12, 1891, the first major strike in the country's history was taking place in the capital, Rio de Janeiro. The stoppage occurred in the Central Brazilian Railway Company when workers decided to protest against Deodoro's closing of the National Legislative Assembly. The popular protests were joined by the armed forces, and the situation escalated into a *coup d'état*. For the first time popular protests were seen near the capital, heralding a new social arrangement in which politicians would now have to worry about more than just their own connections, deals, and intra-negotiations.

As the political situation became more unstable, on November 23, the first of two connected naval revolts broke out in Rio de Janeiro. Prompted by the vice president, Marshal Floriano Peixoto, who, as we have seen, belonged to Deodoro's opposing party, Navy Admiral Custódio José de Melo (1840–1902) mutinied and threatened to bombard Rio de Janeiro. The mutiny assumed monarchist overtones in its overt defiance of the republican government. Deodoro da Fonseca, then 64 and in very poor health, had little power to resist. Faced with a political crisis compounded by economic breakdown, he soon understood that his presidency's fate was sealed. In order to avoid a civil war, the President resigned on that very day, November 23, 1891.

Deodoro's overthrow occurred under circumstances of great tension. Besides displeasing the powerful coffee barons of São Paulo with his industrialist and politically centralizing policies, Deodoro had started to face strong popular discontent because of the high inflation generated by his Finance Minister's policies. Beset by much turmoil, the young Brazilian Republic seemed no different from its South American neighbors, most of them politically unstable and rife with corruption and insecurity.[4]

Vice-President Floriano Vieira Peixoto (1839–1895) assumed the head of the Executive immediately after Deodoro da Fonseca's resignation. The nation's new leader took office in an atmosphere of great social and political unrest: the country he now had to govern faced an unprecedented financial crisis and, at the same time, was being governed by inexperienced republican politicians. The revisionary monarchist threat was also a constant headache for the new President.

President Floriano Peixoto's enigmatic and solitary character soon assumed mythical overtones in the eyes of the general population. He was a strongly nationalist military man who would remain steadfast in adherence to his firm moral principles. After assuming the presidency, he refused to occupy the official presidential palace and continued to live in his humble middle-class suburban house. Even in the hardest moments of his government, he would dismiss his bodyguards and take the streetcar back to his home, always moving by himself and mingling with the common people in Rio de Janeiro without being noticed.

Owing to his heavy-handed centralizing policies, Floriano Peixoto would come to be known as *Marechal de Ferro* (Iron Marshal). Like his predecessor, Deodoro da Fonseca, he also confronted the landlords of São Paulo, who vied for greater autonomy from the central government. Unlike Deodoro, however, Floriano managed the country with more skill and succeeded in staying in office until the end of his term on November 15, 1894. Among some of his most defiant political acts was the overthrow of all provincial governors who had supported Deodoro da Fonseca. Facing the outbreak of riots promoted by his opponents in April 1892, the Iron Marshal responded by declaring a state of emergency and carrying out a series of arrests and banishments. He was also keen on repressing two new revolts that threatened to sweep the country: the so-called Second Naval Revolt, which restated the claims of the naval uprising that took place during Deodoro's government, and the Federalist Revolution, a bloody uprising started in Rio Grande do Sul in 1893 and leaving a trail of murder and destruction throughout the southern part of the country.[5]

Technically, President Floriano Peixoto's government was also the product of a *coup d'état*. Deodoro da Fonseca had been in power for only nine months on November 23, 1891, and the Constitution established that if the president left office after less than two years, new presidential elections should be called. On March 13, 1892, thirteen military commanders signed a petition requesting the new poll. On the following day, however, Floriano Peixoto arrested most of the commanders. Dissatisfied with the unconstitutionality of the current political situation, the navy started bombarding Rio de Janeiro on September 13, 1893, thus starting what became known as the Second Naval Revolt. Floriano refused to leave office, taking firm control of the army and setting it against the navy. Convinced of the impossibility of ousting the President from Rio de Janeiro, the members of the naval revolt sailed South, trying to join forces with the Federalist Revolt mentioned above that had started in Rio Grande do Sul.[6]

The Riograndense rebellion had started as a provincial dispute between the two local political parties. In line with a tendency for factionalism that resulted from centuries of conflict and war in the region, the political arena was clearly divided between two cliques that upheld divergent political agendas: the Federalist Party and the Republican Party. While the former advocated the establishment of a parliamentary system in local administration, a demand that required the revision of the provincial Constitution promulgated in 1891, the latter defended a centralized, positivist presidential system. The federalists were led by Gaspar da Silveira Martins, the man whose rivalry with Deodoro da Fonseca had contributed to the *coup d'état* that brought about the Republic in 1889; the republicans were headed by Júlio de Castilhos, Rio Grande do Sul's governor. Castilhos had drafted the state's Constitution himself and had been elected governor (or "president," under the new decentralized arrangement now in force) on July 15, 1891. Facing fierce opposition from the local federalist faction, however, he was ousted in that same year. Nonetheless, on January 25, 1893, Castilhos was once again elected governor.

The federalists then resumed their opposition to the local government and moved quickly to overthrow Castilhos for a second time. By mid-1893 they had resorted to violence and turned the regional political dispute into a bloody civil war. President Floriano Peixoto sent troops from Rio de Janeiro in defense of Castilhos. Among Floriano's commanders was Rio Grande do Sul's powerful Senator José Gomes Pinheiro Machado (1851–

1915), who left his seat in the Congress to command Floriano's northern division against the federalists. Pinheiro Machado represented Rio Grande do Sul's positivism and centralizing authoritarianism at the national level. His political aim was to extend Rio Grande do Sul's clout into Rio de Janeiro and control the central government, an aim that, as we shall see, would be achieved in 1910 with the election of a Riograndense military commander to the presidency, Marshal Hermes da Fonseca (1855–1923). For the time being, however, Pinheiro Machado would lead his troops only in defense of Castillos, his fellow countryman from Cruz Alta, a traditional breeding ground for warlords and freemasons located in the northwestern part of Rio Grande do Sul State.

The war in the South thus became entangled with the naval uprising taking place in the capital. The federalist forces gained the support of the naval officers of the Second Naval Revolt, who, as we have seen, moved southwards after meeting Floriano's fierce resistance in Rio de Janeiro. Aided by Rio de Janeiro's rebellious navy, the federalists gained strength and marched northwards to the capital, entering the territory of the state of Santa Catarina. On October 14, 1893, they took the island of Desterro, the present-day city of Florianópolis, proclaiming it the capital of their newly created republic. During January and February 1894, the federalist troops moved further north, entering the state of Paraná. There they encountered strong resistance in the city of Lapa, located 30 miles south of Curitiba, the state's capital. The heroic resistance of commander Antônio Ernesto Gomes Carneiro (1846–1894) who, with 639 men, resisted 3,000 Riograndense federalist troops for 26 days, provided the central government with enough time to relocate and ambush de federalists. On April 16, 1894, the island of Desterro was retaken by Floriano's troops who, under the command of the ferocious captain Moreira César (1850–1897), ransacked and virtually destroyed the city. The municipality's name was changed to Florianópolis, in tribute to President Floriano. Two months later, on June 27, 1894, the troops of José Gomes Pinheiro Machado, aided by a cavalry division under the command of his younger brother, Salvador Pinheiro Machado, defeated the federalists in the Battle of Passo Fundo.

The reports of murder and maltreatment of prisoners on both sides led the war between the federalists and the republicans to be dubbed the *Revolução das Degolas* (Cut Throat Revolution). The traditional beef-curing economy of Rio Grande do Sul created a rough local culture marked by animal slaughtering and general ruthlessness. Throughout the many wars fought in the region, it became common practice for humans to be butchered in the same way as cattle were in meat production. In the case of the Federalist Revolution, besides the traditional forms of animal slaughtering, one of the most common means of punishment applied to prisoners was their emasculation in captivity. The massacre of 300 soldiers from Pinheiro Machado's contingent, all of whom were kept in a cattle enclosure and then beheaded, gave the present-day city of Hulha Negra, located in the Southwest of Rio Grande do Sul State, the sobriquet of *Potreiro das Almas* (Enclosure of the Dead). The cruelty applied in the slaughter of prisoners seems to have had roots also in the state's economic decadence. Suffering from the local situation of sheer penury, Rio Grande do Sul's rebelling forces could not afford to look after prisoners, and the solution found was to kill them.[7]

After the defeat of the southern federalists, the naval officers that had revolted in Rio de Janeiro a year earlier resumed their attacks on the capital until Floriano's troops finally put down the uprising in September 1894. The federalists would still attempt a recovery at the Battle of Campo Osório, in 1895, but by then they had lost momentum and the country could finally be pacified. The so-called Republic of the Sword had played its role in producing the transition from the monarchy to the republic. A new period was about to begin with the rise of the first of a series of presidents originating from São Paulo's coffee oligarchy.

Prudente de Morais (1841–1902) assumed command of the nation on November 15, 1894. In the following year, he signed a peace agreement with the Riograndense leaders, who were pardoned and returned to their large southern estates. Morais's government would deepen the polarization between the economically strong states of São Paulo and Minas Gerais on one side, and militarily strong Rio Grande do Sul on the other.

As we shall see below, the government of Prudente de Morais would be tainted by popular dissatisfaction regarding the nation's terrible financial situation. Floriano Peixoto had been a very popular president. He had faced the *Encilhamento* crisis with economic policies that had earned his government considerable sympathy from the middle classes. The use of price controls over rent and food favored the middle classes, who were most affected by high inflation. Floriano Peixoto's deflationary policies were very similar to those adopted during the French revolution, and his followers became know by the humorous title of "Jacobins." Peixoto's followers would continue to hold considerable political influence throughout the first decade of the republic. They demanded the establishment of a national identity, reviving signs of anti-Portuguese sentiment. As we will see in more detail below, Floriano Peixoto's Jacobins would be fierce opponents of Prudente de Morais's administration.[8]

In the domain of foreign relations, the Republic of the Sword was marked by the flagrant inexperience of its republican officials. In itself, the recognition of the new government was not particularly problematic. Argentina was the first country to recognize the new Brazilian Republic, doing so in 1890. Considerable embarrassment, however, arose in connection with that same neighbor as a result of the Brazilian republicans' shortcomings regarding the protocols of diplomacy. The first republican Foreign Minister, Quintino Bocaiuva (1836–1912), the same man who in 1870 had drafted the Republican Manifesto, would be the protagonist in a great misunderstanding regarding an important territorial dispute with the neighboring country.

Brazil and Argentina had long been involved in a contest over the territory of the former Portuguese and Spanish reductions, which extended through the frontier separating the two countries. At the end of the 1880s, Argentina claimed a large portion of land equivalent to approximately half of the present-day states of Paraná and Santa Catarina. Upon the establishment of the Brazilian Republic, the newly appointed members of Brazil's Foreign Office were eager to shake off the pervasive influence of Europe, which had prevailed during the monarchical regime, and establish closer relations with the neighboring republics. Rather impetuously, Quintino Bocaiuva signed with Argentina the Treaty of Montevideo (1890), by means of which the disputed territory would be divided between the two nations. The agreement was greatly disadvantageous to Brazil, and the Brazilian National Congress refused to ratify the pact. The question was sent for arbitration to the President of the United States, Grover Cleveland, who, in 1895, decided in favor of the Brazilian claim. The inexperience of their representatives had almost cost the Brazilians a large portion of territory that was fundamental to communications between the central and southern parts of the country.[9]

The transition from the monarchy to the republic required important adjustments in foreign policy and this proved to be difficult from the very start of the new regime. The fall of the monarchy came during the meeting of the Pan-American Conference of 1889 in Washington. With the change in regime, the new government replaced the nation's representative, the nobleman Lafayette Rodrigues Pereira (1834–1917), with the republican Salvador de Mendonça (1841–1913). This change brought with it a radical shift in political orientation. While Rodrigues had been cautious about some of the policies proposed by the United States during the conference, Mendonça aligned himself with the powerful North American republic. The new representative accepted the U.S. proposal for the establishment of a system of arbitration that was likely to enhance U.S. influence in the region. However, Argentina remained defiant and prevented the establishment of the system. This confrontation marked the beginning of a historical antagonism between the United States and Argentina on one side, and of a closeness between Brazil and the United States on the other. In the end, the outcome of the New Republic's turn towards the United States would result in Brazil substituting its economic dependence on Great Britain with a new one centered on the North American nation. The first sign of this new dependence would come with the Blaine-Mendonça Treaty of 1891, a trade agreement involving sugar and coffee that was flagrantly unfavorable to Brazil.[10]

It is to this new Brazilian Republic, marked now by the strong influence of the United States, that we will turn in the following pages. We will see how the first civilian president in Brazilian history ruled a country with an economy based on the export of a single product. We will see how this product's foremost buyer was the United States, and how international dependence resurfaced under a new guise as the interests of the landed aristocracy of coffee producers worked to stymie economic diversification. The enhancement of oligarchical power, the deepening of social divisions, the massacre of civilian populations, and the continued opposition between Rio Grande do Sul and São Paulo were some of key fetures of the First Brazilian Republic that we will observe below.

Prudente de Morais (1894–1898)

On March 1, 1894, São Paulo's candidate Prudente José de Morais e Barros (1841–1902) won the first presidential election in Brazilian history based on direct voting. The new President defeated his main rival, Afonso Augusto Moreira Pena (1847–1909), a politician from Minas Gerais who would become the nation's president twelve years later, in 1906. The contest of 1894 would be one of the rare instances during the First Republic where São Paulo and Minas Gerais would not be allied against Rio Grande do Sul. As we will see, it would not be until 1929 that the alliance would break down, and this would result in a long dictatorial period at the hands of the Riograndenses.

It is difficult to assess the real strength of Prudente de Morais's victory in 1894, for almost all elections during the first republican period were fraudulent. The Constitution of 1891 conferred the right to vote solely on male citizens over the age of 21 who were literate and not involved in military or religious service. The ballot method adopted did not involve secret voting, and voter coercion was common throughout the process. Fraud was the norm and violence ruled, carrying on the trend established in that first poll of 1840, which, as we have mentioned, became known as "Elections of the Stick." As we will see in more detail below, electoral corruption became more and more a source of discontent among important sections of the army, turning into one of the foremost concerns of the revolutionary movement that would end the First Republic in 1930.

Upon assuming the presidency in 1894, Prudente de Morais had to face a series of complex political issues. Opposition from the Jacobins, that is, the supporters of the Iron Marshal, Floriano Peixoto, was fierce, and the federalists threatened to resume fighting in the South. Monarchist voices were still being raised, and harsh financial difficulties roiled at the President's doorstep. The United States, Brazil's chief market for coffee exports, was experiencing the effects of the Panic of 1893, a serious economic depression caused by the overbuilding of railroads with funds from the bank Baring Brothers. The consequence was a drastic fall in coffee imports, with devastating consequences for Brazil.[11]

In terms of domestic politics, the new President attempted to pacify the contending factions that rioted throughout the nation. In a display of rare political ability, Morais invited important Jacobin leaders to take part in his government and at the same time tried to favor the economic interests of coffee producers. Given the impending economic meltdown that the new republic was facing, the President was obliged to undo most of Floriano Peixoto's economic measures that had benefited the middle classes. Inflation became increasingly problematic in an economy dependent on imported goods. As a countermeasure, a policy of industrialization was attempted in spite of resistance from São Paulo's landowners, who wanted all national resources to be channeled to the maintenance of their coffee crops.

Jacobins and coffee producers soon emerged as the two new political forces vying with each other in the nascent Brazilian Republic. Both the military and the coffee oligarchy had been responsible for the establishment of that republic, but these groups diverged in their political ideals. The military inherited the conservative agenda of building a centralized national state, while the oligarchies defended the liberal project of provincial autonomy, favoring the fulfillment of their local interests. The old imperial dichotomy between liberals and conservatives was now being re-enacted in a new republican guise.

Prudente de Morais, as well as the presidents that followed him, had to walk a tightrope between these two political conterweights, much as Pedro II had done during his 49-year imperial rule. Problems now, however, were compounded by the limitations of Brazil's export economy in the context of a much more complex nation than the one found during the Imperial Era. The country was no longer one in which power was concentrated solely in the hands of a landed aristocracy of slave owners.

Distinct forces now began to emerge, and the favoring of one class over the others provoked anger and rightful discontent.

Adding to these new difficulties, the downside of an economy based on a single export product soon became noticeable. Problems arising from overproduction of coffee began to be experienced with the aforementioned North American crisis of 1893. The product had become Brazil's most significant export in 1838, and by 1845 the country was producing around 45% of the world's coffee. In 1857, international prices rose substantially as a result of factors such as the end of the slave trade, the sudden boom in the European economy, and a bad crop caused by pests that decimated Brazilian production. To make matters worse, the rise in coffee's international price set off a cycle of significant expansion in production during the 1860s. While the national production kept growing, however, the price rise was suddenly reversed with the fall in demand caused by the American Civil War. By 1893 the symptoms of what would be one of the major problems in the Brazilian economy in the decades to come were already visible, namely coffee overproduction.

Besides the financial downturns of an economy lacking diversification, President Prudente de Morais had to face a new provincial uprising which started in the semi-arid and poverty-stricken lands of the state of Bahia. There, some 30,000 settlers had founded a community called Canudos. Poverty-stricken and cut off from the rapidly modernizing society of the Southeast, Canudos' population survived on subsistence agriculture and some cattle farming. Ethnically, it was comprised of poor white Brazilians and mestizos. Social unrest started when a mystic preacher named Antônio Vicente Mendes Maciel (1830–1897) began predicting the return of the monarchy and with it the establishment of a better world where the poor would be rescued from their hunger and deprivation.

Mendes Maciel was known by the nickname Antônio Conselheiro, or *Counselor* which, to the common, illiterate people he sought to guide suggested visionary capabilities. As the number of his followers grew, the authorities in the neighboring city of Juazeiro accused him of monarchist sedition. The provincial government sent an initial force of approximately 30 men to disband the potentially revolutionary settlers of Canudos. Against all expectations, however, the outcome of the expedition was the massacre of the government's forces. Learning of the local population's resistance, President Prudente de Morais sent a military expedition from Rio de Janeiro to arrest Antônio Conselheiro and his followers. This second expedition, however, was also unsuccessful. It was violently repelled by the poor villagers of Canudos, who fought bravely against the modern military equipment of the federal forces.

Sensationalist reports circulated in the capital recounting the ferocity and fanaticism of the Canudos inhabitants. Under the pressure of what became a national uproar, the army was once again sent to rout the village, but, again, the expedition was met with the fierceness of the population and was forced to retreat. A fourth expedition was arranged. The prestige of the armed forces and of the republican government was at stake. This new powerful regiment would be under the command of Captain Moreira César, the same man who had defeated the federalist rebels on the island of Desterro in 1894, terrorizing its population in the processs. In spite of Moreira César's ferocity and experience, however, on March 6, 1897, he was slain by the fanatical, poverty-stricken residents of Canudos.

The next military expedition would have to be sent in fully armed with the aim of thoroughly suppressing the local population. An epidemic of hunger had befallen the inhabitants of Canudos and this time they were easy prey for the large army with modern military equipment that was sent from the capital. The massacre was carried out with no mercy. Antonio Conselheiro was killed on September 22, 1897, but atrocities against the civilian population continued until October 2, when the last villagers were murdered after all the women had been raped.

Canudos' brutal demise in October 1897 left another taint of blood on Brazilian history. It showed once again the elitist nature of Brazilian society. The President adopted very different approaches to the two conflicts that emerged during his government. While the high-ranking military officers and landlords who had been involved in the Second Naval Revolt and the Federalist Revolution were all pardoned, the poor and illiterate residents of Canudos were massacred. The event recalls other examples in Brazilian history. The fierce repression of the Vila Rica Revolt in 1720, the Cabanagem in 1835, and the Balaiada in 1838, contrast with the leniency bestowed upon the elitist Inconfidencia Mineira in 1789, the Riograndense Farroupilha in 1845, the Liberal Revolts of São Paulo and Minas Gerais in 1842, and again the Riograndense Federalist Revolution of 1893.

Canudos and its plight would become an important theme in Brazilian literature and culture. Naturalist writer Euclides da Cunha (1866–1909) told the story of Canudos in novelistic form, questioning the validity of the Republic's discourse on modernity and progress in his *Os Sertões* (1902). While the Republic, with its narrative of modernization, set itself against what it portrayed as the backwardness and ignorance of the simple man of the countryside, da Cunha perceived the greater irrationality as lying on the side the Republic. Such irrationality was subsumed under the raging violence and lack of understanding toward the poor and oppressed inhabitants of the famine-stricken semi-arid region of the Northeast. The author thus inverted a recurring theme found in Latin American literature during the period, namely that of the dichotomy between civilization and barbarism. Ideas put forward by authors such as Argentine Domingo Faustino Sarmiento (1811–1888) and Venezuelan Romulo Gallegos (1884–1969) were reversed by Euclides da Cunha, who recognized a fallacy behind his country's discourse on progress.[12]

Prudente de Morais ended his government trying to solve the economic crisis inherited from the *Encilhamento*. The President and his economic advisors negotiated the rescheduling of Brazil's foreign debt with British bankers. With the fall in coffee's international price, high inflation, and the heavy military expenditure needed to put down two civil revolts, the country moved rapidly into a draining sovereign debt default. The result would be the taking-out of a new loan that would allow the next president to set the national economy back on track, even if only by means of highly recessive measures, such as burning currency. To that story, we will turn next.

Campos Sales (1898—1902)

Manuel Ferraz de Campos Sales (1841–1913) assumed the presidency on November 15, 1898, after an electoral process that made clear the fierce opposition between the military class and the coffee producers. The former could still be identified as Jacobins or Positivists, that is, those arguing for a centralized state. The latter were the wealthy landowners of São Paulo, whose interests lied in a decentralized federative system that allowed them to keep their revenue from coffee exports out of the hands of the central government.

The Jacobin candidate was the freemason and military commander Lauro Sodré (1858–1944), the former governor of the state of Pará who had become famous for defying Deodoro da Fonseca during his coup in 1891. His rival was Campos Sales, who had served as Deodoro's Minister of Justice from 1889 to 1891. The battle was thus clearly delineated between *Florianistas* and *Deodoristas*. Electoral victory, however, belonged to the latter and their supporting coffee producers.

Campos Sales's electoral success was a sign of the growing political clout of São Paulo and its landed aristocracy. That notwithstanding, throughout his government the President was obliged to take measures that displeased his fellow coffee barons. One of them had to do with the problem of currency devaluation and its effects on the national economy. As we have seen, the *Encilhamento*'s lavish monetary easing had produced a severe currency crisis. The symptoms of a hyperinflationary process were felt throughout Prudente de Morais's government, with the currency devaluation throwing the nation into default with its international creditors.

Campos Sales's only option was to adopt economic policies that would bring about an appreciation of the national currency. Such an appreciation, however, went against the interests of the export sector, that is, the coffee producers. As long as the national currency was devalued, Brazilian coffee remained more affordable for international buyers, thus raising the profits of the coffee barons. High inflation thus favored São Paulo's landowners who, in moments of monetary expansion, managed to retain a larger portion of the country's revenue while the general population suffered by being obliged to purchase ever more expensive imported goods.[13]

In adopting restrictive monetary policies, Campos Sales thus went against the interests of his main supporters. The President's difficulty in bringing a dependent and peripheral economy such as Brazil's into exchange-rate stability was, in any case, enormous. Since 1844, when the nation had finally freed itself from the unequal treaties of 1810 and started to take a more active role in the international economy, attempts had been made at adapting the national currency to the international standard. That should, at least in theory, have brought the country's balance of payments into equilibrium, allowing for better management of national investment and for the payment of foreign debt.

In the Brazilian case, however, the adoption of a fixed exchange rate was almost impossible. Peripheral economies based on the export of primary goods had great difficulty in adjusting to the international gold standard that prevailed among developed nations. This was due to the import coefficient of such economies, together with the constant price fluctuation of their export commodities, all of which prevented them from maintaining sufficient gold reserves to face the eventual instabilities in their balance of payments. In the specific case of Brazil, any financial downturn in the larger economies, such as that of 1893 in the United States, meant a significant fall in the country's revenue, resulting in a much harsher crisis than was ever experienced in more robust and diversified economies.

To this problem was added what economists call "deterioration in the terms of trade," that is, the situation in which, as technology develops, industrialized products tend to grow in price, while primary goods, such as the ones exported by peripheral economies, tend to maintain low exchange value.[14] The rule is not set in stone, indeed it is a subject of much debate, but it does reflect the reality of most economies marked by late industrialization and a reliance on the export of basic goods. In the case of late-nineteenth-century Brazil, a nation highly dependent on imports, the deterioration in the terms of trade did prevent the sort of equilibrium that would have allowed the adoption of the international gold standard.

Campos Sales, however, was an obstinate man. He saw all national problems as springing primarily from high inflation and exchange-rate instability, and for him adopting the gold standard seemed to be the only option. In order to solve the country's many economic problems, the government stuck to severe monetarist orthodoxy and promoted a radical deflationary policy, which included the burning of currency. Campos Sales's Finance Minister, Joaquim Murtinho (1848–1911), was put in charge of counteracting the economic imbalances inherited from Rui Barbosa's disastrous policies of the early 1890s. It was necessary to halt the unrestrained speculation in the currency market, as well as the work of arbitrageurs who had profited from the price fluctuations of export goods. Foreign debt compounded the problem. The country should not be allowed to go into default, lest the financing of coffee production, together with the maintenance of the lavish lifestyle of the coffee oligarchs, be compromised.

The procurement of a loan to finance the nation's debt with foreign banks, that is, a loan to pay a former loan, had already been negotiated between Prudente de Morais and the Rothschild bankers. Campos Sales went along with it, and in 1898 the so-called "Funding Loan" was contracted. This new credit came with a set of conditions relating to economic policies to be implemented. These amounted to an overtly recessionary package: credit restrictions, cuts in public expenditure, heavy taxation, and, as a guarantee, the revenue from the country's railroad system.

Such severe austerity promised to be particularly harsh on those who needed to look for work in the labor market. Again, the emerging middle class was to suffer most. The severely restrictive fiscal policies listed in the loan's conditions entailed the imposition of highly regressive forms of taxation. A fierce stamp duty was implemented in place of what could have been a more progressive income tax.

The initial disagreement between President Sales and São Paulo's coffee oligarchs regarding currency exchange rates was thus counterbalanced by the new loan and its poorly distributed benefits. On the one hand, Finance Minister Joaquim Murtinho's monetary contraction promoted the currency's appreciation that displeased coffee producers, but on the other hand, the Funding Loan allowed enough money to come in and be channeled directly to the agricultural sector, that is, to those who had little interest in expansionary fiscal policies and industrial incentives. In the minds of the coffee producers, industrialization tended to poach their labor force that was readily available at low cost. São Paulo's powerful landed aristocracy argued that governmental financial resources should be directed to what the country was already producing, and not to what it might produce in the future. Government-induced industrialization was regarded as competing with agriculture, and should thus be opposed. In any case, the final result of Campos Sales's policy was that the loan maintained the flow of financial resources that supported coffee production, while its borrowing scheme's mandatory fiscal contraction impaired industrial development and job creation.

In 1900, however, a new element emerged in the Brazilian economic landscape. The Amazon forest became the focus of Brazil's rubber boom, which would last for thirteen years. The fast rise in rubber exports turned the brief period from 1900 to 1913 into what is generally regarded as the golden age of Brazilian economic history. The growth in rubber exports led to a positive trade balance in 1899. It also induced remarkable urban growth in Manaus, the capital city of Amazon State, resulting in important social and political transformations in the northern part of the country. Together with the recovery of coffee's international price, the rubber boom contributed to the relative success of the difficult economic adjustments made by Campos Sales's government. These adjustments made the President very unpopular, but they would lead to the resumption of investment and the subsequent improvement in urban infrastructure at the national level. A boom in public works would start in the following administration thanks to the economic stability achieved during Campos Sales's government.

In terms of foreign policy, besides the new financial scheme contracted with British bankers, the President faced an important territorial dispute with France, the so-called *Questão do Amapá* (Amapá Dispute). Extending over an area of approximately 80,000 square miles, the region of Amapá bordered the state of Pará to the South and French Guiana to the North, lying between the limits of Portuguese and French domains as established by the Treaty of Utrecht in 1713. The Treaty had been signed in the aftermath of the War of the Spanish Succession, and, according to one of its provisions, Portugal owned the large territory that extended between the Amazon and the Oyapock river, that is, the territory of Amapá. In the early 1890s, however, the French government began to question this provision by arguing that the river referred to as "Oyapock" in the Treaty was not the one assumed by Brazil, but another watercourse located more to the South. If the claim were true, a substantial part of Amapá's territory would have to be transferred to French authority. Trying to settle matters by means of force, the French occupied the region in 1895. Campos Sales proposed a diplomatic solution and took the case to an arbitration court headed by Swiss president Walter Hauser (1837–1902) in 1900. As Brazilian representative to the court, the President appointed the aforementioned diplomat José Maria da Silva Paranhos Júnior (1845–1912), who had won the dispute with Argentina over the region of Palmas in 1895 (under the arbitration of U.S. President Grover Cleveland).

A man of aristocratic background whose father had been one of Pedro II's Prime Ministers, Paranhos Júnior was a public official known for his unshakable respect for the monarchy. Even during the present republican era, he had insisted on maintaining his nobiliary title of Baron of Rio Branco. Unlike inexperienced republicans, who showed limited ability in handling foreign affairs, Paranhos Júnior's family tradition had nurtured in him enough skill to succeed in the harsh field of diplomatic negotiations. His cultivated manners, in tandem with his deeply serene attitude, worked to disguise the shrewdness of his character, allowing him to face even the cleverest opponents across the negotiating table. The implacable Baron was thus happy to earn the hatred of his rivals. If his important diplomatic victory against Argentina had provoked the unrestrained resentment of his skillful opponent, the Argentine official Estanislao Severo Zeballos (1854–1923), now against France another powerful rival would have to be demolished, the renowned French geographer Paul Vidal de la Blache (1845–1918).

Paranhos's painstaking work in the Amapá Dispute, which exercised all his comprehensive knowledge of history and cartography, resulted in a remarkable victory over the prodigious French intellectual. President Walter Hauser's verdict favored the Brazilian claim and the outcome of the dispute set the tone for Paranhos's future political career. Maintaining to the end the title of Baron of Rio Branco, he would become a leading figure in Brazilian diplomatic history.[15]

Still in the domain of foreign relations, Campos Sales's policies followed the general republican aspiration for closer continental relations. He attempted an important rapprochement with Argentina, which was in order after years of continuous rivalry and resentment fueled by the territorial dispute of 1895. In August 1899, Argentine president Julio Argentino Roca (1843–1914) made an official visit to Brazil. Campos Sales reciprocated with a visit to Argentina the following year. This first exchange of presidential visits between the two countries started a new period in bilateral relations, laying the foundations for greater mutual trust. From then on, there would be frequent attempts to build confidence, although mutual suspicion and disagreement were never far from the surface.

The aftermath of Campos Sales's government showed little social improvement in the large and feeble South American republic. Brazil's severe problems, such as the high rate of illiteracy, the series of heavy foreign constraints, and the general lack of creativity resulting from an oligarchic structure, continued to prevent the development of a national autonomous capacity for investment and industrialization. Throughout his government, the President's only option had been to "cut off a limb to save the body," that is, to cut spending to adjust the economy. His successor, São Paulo's former senator and governor, Francisco de Paula Rodrigues Alves (1848–1919), however, would start his administration from a much better financial position than the one Sales himself had inherited from his predecessor, Prudente de Morais. Both Sales and Morais suffered the effects of the *Encilhamento*, which began to wane only after the former's severely recessive policy was followed. Put together, the Campos Sales–Rodrigues Alves period would enter Brazilian economic history as having produced a successful model for financial restructuring: a period in which initially recessive policies paved the way for investment and construction.

Rodrigues Alves (1902–1906)

Francisco de Paula Rodrigues Alves assumed the Brazilian presidency on November 15, 1902, after an easy electoral victory over his opponent, the former Foreign Minister, Quintino Bocaiuva. The new president had occupied the position of Finance Minister during Prudente de Morais's administration, being then responsible for the initial negotiations with N. M. Rothschild for the Funding Loan of 1898. Now the British banker would figure once again in the history of Brazilian finance, funding another financial scheme contracted by Rodrigues Alves, this time to solve a territorial dispute with Bolivia arising in the border territory of Acre.

The dispute over Acre is another event that features prominently in the history of Brazilian diplomacy. It presents an important early example of autonomy and political skill in the defense of an economically significant region inhabited by Brazilian citizens. Earlier instances of such well-groomed protection of the national interest appear in the Brazilian Empire's political maneuvers to maintain sovereignty over the Amazon during the 1850s, when the United States attempted to occupy it under a plan devised by the naval officer Matthew Fontaine Maury (1806–1873),[16] and the aforementioned diplomatic disputes, namely with Argentina over the territory of Palmas in the 1890s, and with France over Amapá in 1900.

The dispute over Acre revealed the pressure peripheral nations faced during a time of escalating imperialism in Europe and North America. The turn of the twentieth century was witness to the results of Bismarck's 1885 Conference of Berlin with regard to the African continent, and in the Americas the growing military clout of the United States began to be felt after the Spanish-American War of 1898. The Acre dispute, however, would signal a considerable improvement in the republican leaders' capacity for political action on the international stage.

Acre (roughly 60,000 square miles, about twice the size of Portugal) was made Bolivian territory by the Treaty of Ayacucho in 1867. The Brazilian Empire had signed the Treaty primarily as a means of buying Bolivian neutrality in the Paraguayan War (1864–1870). Given the difficult access to the region from Bolivian urban centers, however, Bolivians never occupied the area effectively. By contrast, Brazilians began to settle there after a severe drought had brought famine and devastation to the northeastern part of the country in 1877. With the drought, a substantial population shift towards the west began to occur. This migratory wave would increase significantly over the next few decades, when the aforementioned rubber boom would attract hundreds of thousands of workers to Acre.

By 1900, some 60,000 Brazilians were living in the area. As the European and North American consumption of rubber rocketed, Bolivia attempted to regain Acre's territory under the auspices of the United States. The Bolivian government signed an agreement with an American conglomerate, offering it a concession for economic exploitation of the rubber-rich territory. The corporation was called the Bolivian Syndicate. It included firms such as Cary & Withridge, United States Rubber Company, and Export Lumber, which counted among its owners a cousin of Theodore Roosevelt, then vice president of the United States.

The Bolivian Syndicate strongly resembled the colonial enterprises operating in Africa at the time. As mentioned above, the effects of Bismarck's Congress of Berlin were beginning to be felt, and in the American continent the United States' victory over Spain in 1898 paved the way for a new type of intra-American imperialism. This possibility would soon be reinforced after the assassination of President William McKinley and the rise of Theodore Roosevelt to the American presidency in 1901. President Roosevelt's corollary to the Monroe Doctrine of 1823 would result in his well-known *Big Stick* foreign policy.

In August 1902, led by a military officer from Rio Grande do Sul called Placido de Castro (1873–1908), the Brazilian residents of Acre rose up against Bolivian incursions in the region, which were commanded by

Bolivia's president himself, José Manuel Pando (1849–1917). The conflict intensified when, in December 1902, President Rodrigues Alves appointed as Foreign Minister José Maria da Silva Paranhos Júnior, the diplomat who had secured Brazilian ownership over the areas of Palmas and Amapá. Unlike his predecessors in the Foreign Office, who accepted Bolivian sovereignty over Acre as agreed in the Treaty of Ayacucho of 1867, Paranhos claimed Brazilian rights over the territory on the basis of *uti possidetis*, the old Roman law principle employed by Alexandre de Gusmão in 1750 to claim the territory of present-day Rio Grande do Sul for Portugal.

In order to counter the ongoing Bolivian military campaign in the region, Paranhos Júnior closed the Amazon River to foreign navigation, isolating Bolivian and American interests from the disputed area. Nonetheless, and in order to avoid a potentially disastrous war, Paranhos offered to buy the territory from Bolivia. Financial resources to pay the Bolivians and, most of all, the Americans, would, once again, be contracted with N. M. Rothschild, Brazil's official British banker.

As the negotiations for a new loan were set in motion, President Rodrigues Alves ordered the military occupation of Acre, provoking an immediate reaction from the Bolivian Syndicate. The local population, comprised mostly of Brazilian nationals, vowed to resist the Syndicate's attempt at armed intervention in the area. The United States government had made it clear that military force might be employed to defend the Syndicate's interests in the region. Tensions would thus not subside without a considerable amount of money being paid by the Brazilian side. Rothschild sought a peaceful and lucrative outcome to the crisis by negotiating directly with the Bolivian Syndicate. The final result was that a small part of the Brazilian loan was transferred to the government of Bolivia, and the larger part of it was given to the Bolivian Syndicate. In this way, the Brazilians and Bolivians managed to compensate the Syndicate for its "losses." Brazil thus bought the territory from Bolivia, paying for it not only with the loan contracted with the British, but also with a promise to construct a railroad that would favor Bolivian trade in the area. The dispute would come to an end with the signature of the Treaty of Petropolis in 1903.[17]

The story of Acre's acquisition is indicative of rubber's growing economic importance during the first decade of the twentieth century. Thanks to the commodity's boom, Brazil's GDP grew steadily at an annual rate of 4% during the thirteen years between 1900 and 1913. As mentioned above, the period came to be known as the country's "economic golden age." The wealth created by the rubber boom allowed for unprecedented government investments in infrastructure, which resulted in considerable modernization in various sectors. The nation's capital, Rio de Janeiro, received a thorough urban overhaul, with various new construction projects being implemented by the city mayor, Francisco Pereira Passos (1836–1913). Passos was a knowledgeable man who, during the late 1850s, had lived in Paris and witnessed Georges-Eugène Haussmann's (1809–1891) urban reforms. Haussmann was the Prefect of the Seine Department and Napoleon III's official architect. Influenced by Haussmann's style, Passos attempted to produce a tropical version of the Parisian imperial landscape in Rio de Janeiro.

However, in a city noted for social depravation, the attempt at building something similar to Haussmann's elegant Parisian boulevards soon turned into a sanitary revolution based on the demolition of slums and the removal of a mass of unemployed and homeless people from the city center. Modern urbanism and architectural refinement involved the building of elegant façades and large empty avenues from which the populace had to be excluded.

Brazil's population at the time included a large number of ex-slaves who had recently been freed and who were left abandoned in the country's major cities without any government support. It included also a large number of poor European immigrants, who continued crossing the Atlantic to escape famine in Europe and who struggled to communicate with the Portuguese-speaking locals. Pereira Passos's projects contained a comprehensive program of public health and personal hygiene, which was meant to eradicate the many illnesses proliferating throughout Rio de Janeiro's densely populated tenements. Tuberculosis, measles, typhus, leprosy, as well as frequent epidemics of yellow fever, smallpox, and bubonic plague, were some of the health problems that afflicted the city's population and detracted from the country's international image.[18]

The vast majority of Rio de Janeiro's residents did not welcome the government's reforms or their sanitation programs. Besides losing their homes, people would now have to clean up. Popular discontent rose to a climax when a mandatory vaccination law was approved in 1904. The directive allowed sanitary brigade workers to enter homes and administer smallpox vaccines by force. This applied to men and women alike and, given the prevailing Catholic mores of the time, the idea of having one's wife or daughter touched by a public servant wielding a needle provoked fear and outrage. A popular revolt, "The Vaccine Revolt," broke out in November 1904, turning the city into a battlefield. Shops were looted, tramcars were burned, and the police were attacked with rocks and sticks. The government declared a state of siege. The uprising was subdued with the suspension of mandatory vaccination. This was, however, a forerunner to various urban crises Brazilian cities would experience throughout the twentieth century.[19] With the Vaccine Revolt, social issues suddenly became visible in a society characterized by inordinate economic disparities between the various social strata and by rapid population growth among the lowers classes. Urban disorder was compounded by the continuous arrival of large numbers of European immigrants with little or no knowledge of the local language or customs. Together with their large families, they had to be accommodated in overcrowded tenements, usually known by the derogatory name, *cortiço*. The everyday hardships of those living in such tenements became a case study for naturalist literature in the hands of novelist Aluísio Azevedo (1857–1913), whose *O Cortiço* (1891) depicted the loose morals and interracial sexual relations among Rio de Janeiro's slum dwellers. Adopting the scientific-positivist perspective, Azevedo portrayed their fate as pre-determined and socially bound.[20]

Besides his difficulties in accomplishing the project of modernization and urban reform, President Rodrigues Alves had yet one further problem on his hands: coffee overproduction. The rise in rubber exports notwithstanding, the Brazilian economy depended primarily on its coffee revenues, and the commodity's high profitability had encouraged the expansion of plantations. However, overproduction resulted in the fall of international prices, with the consequent reduction in the powerful coffee barons' profits. The problem was compounded by the low price-elasticity of the product: when coffee prices plummeted, consumption did not rise, as would be expected in the case of more price-sensitive commodities. Towards the end of Rodrigues Alves's government, a scheme to sustain coffee's international price began to be concocted. Since Brazil held a virtual monopoly on the product's international market, producers asked the government to intervene in the sector with the employment of price control policies.

In February 1906, the governors of the three leading coffee-producing states, São Paulo, Minas Gerais, and Rio de Janeiro, met in the city of Taubaté, a municipality located near the historical hub of coffee farming in the Paraiba River Valley, and signed an agreement to establish a system of regulatory schemes for the commodity's price. The pact was termed "The Accord of Taubaté." Its actual implementation, however, would be contingent on President Rodrigues Alves's approval.[21]

The need for the President's approval reflected the oligopolistic scheme's inclusion of the federal government as financial guarantor for all the tampering with the production that was being planned. The pact established that the federal government would finance the acquisition of production surpluses by means of borrowed money, that is, through foreign loans. The government would retain part of the production, boosting international prices and thus sustaining the revenue of coffee producers. In order to maintain a stable exchange rate, and thus stabilize the producers' income, the State would adopt the gold standard system, creating what was called the *Caixa de Conversão*, a financial bureau that would emit paper money convertible into gold.[22] Furthermore, the federal administration would enact national policies to limit coffee production, promoting incentives for investment in other sectors.

Rodrigues Alves, however, refused to accept the scheme. He was a man of strong liberal ideas, and taking part in an oligopolistic scheme was contrary to his personal beliefs in the value of free trade and individual entrepreneurship. As we will see below, Alves's successor in the presidency would take a different approach and accept the coffee producers' proposals. In the long run, however, the scheme assembled with the Taubaté Accord would crumble. It would suffer fierce resistance from the United States, Brazil's foremost coffee client, and would finish by contributing to the end of Brazil's economic golden age in 1913.

Francisco de Paula Rodrigues Alves finished his presidency with a much higher level of popularity than did his predecessor, Campos Sales. In spite of Rio de Janeiro's riots in the Vaccine Revolt, his attempts at urban development and eradication of tropical diseases were successful. The urban reform of Rio de Janeiro helped enhance the country's international image. On July 25, 1906, Brazil hosted the third Pan-American Conference, being for the first time honored with the visit of a U.S. Secretary of State, Elihu Root (1845–1937), in what became a great national celebration.[23] The President would be re-elected for a second term in 1918. He would, however, not take office.

Afonso Pena (1906–1909)

Afonso Augusto Moreira Pena (1847–1909) became Brazil's sixth President with an electoral victory over two fierce political opponents, the military commander and freemason Laudro Sodré (1858–1944), who had raised the army against compulsory vaccination in 1904, which he thought violated individual freedom, and the former Minister of Finance, Rui Barbosa (1849–1923), the man who had been responsible for the *Encilhamento* financial crisis during Deodoro da Fonseca's presidency. The election's result displayed once again the general lack of probity prevailing in Brazilian voting culture. Afonso Pena received 288,285 votes, against 4,865 for Lauro Sodré, and 207 for Rui Barbosa. A victory that was largely implausible.

The truth was that since the Constitution of 1891 did not require a secret ballot, voters came under great pressure to support the local chieftain's favored candidate. The powerful landowners who controlled the electoral processes were called *coronel*. The term refers to a military rank and defines a powerful local landlord who controls his own militia. The concept gave rise to the notion of *coronelism*, a social and political phenomenon that characterized the power structure of the First Republic in its various regional manifestations. The *coronel* was usually part of the local oligarchy. Under his command, heavy-handed electoral fraud was widely perpetrated.[24]

Afonso Pena's candidacy had been contingent upon his acceptance of the Taubaté Accord. Only after expressing his support for the oligopolistic project concocted by the coffee barons of São Paulo, Minas Gerais, and Rio de Janeiro, was his name endorsed for the presidential poll. Pena thus became the first Brazilian president to advocate direct governmental intervention in the coffee economy. Having served as governor of Minas Gerais from 1892 to 1894, and also as vice-president to Rodrigues Alves from 1902 to 1906, Pena was an insider to the collusions that led to the Taubaté Accord. He took part in the scheme involving price fixing and agricultural subvention, practices that run counter to the liberal principles of free trade.

Under Afonso Pena's control, the federal government began to buy coffee surpluses from the powerful national producers, causing the product's international price to rise abruptly. The price rise brought immediate financial benefit for the government's associates. In the long run, however, the scheme would backfire, for the commodity's higher price started attracting foreign competitors into the market. With new producers constantly entering the sector, a snowball effect was soon generated and surpluses continued to rise. As we have mentioned, measures to promote the transfer of investments from coffee to other sectors of the economy were part of the scheme. These measures, however, could not prevent foreign producers building up new surpluses. They could work internally, but not externally. The scheme thus proved to be something of a Sisyphean task: while the federal government spent lavish sums of money buying surpluses and keeping international prices up, these very prices attracted new foreign competitors, and their production, conversely, brought international prices down.

The problem involved in the coffee valorization scheme is not uncommon in monochrome economies with narrow production-possibility curves. And a lack of economic diversification tends to be linked to a general lack of creativity in society at large. In the case of Brazil, diminished productive diversity combined with a flawed educational system to curtail any potential for diversification. The snowball effect is easily set in motion, with a lack of diversity increasing with every turn. The result, invariably, is economic frailty and dependence.

Economies such as Brazil's during Afonso Pena's presidency are extremely vulnerable to international oscillations. Their lack of allocative efficiency makes them easy prey for the constant variations in foreign demand. They also tend to produce an ever-growing concentration of wealth in the hands of those who control the production processes. This, in turn, leads to the seizure of governments by self-interested elites who tend to sabotage any attempt at diversifying the nation's use of resources. The contrast with countries such as Japan and Italy, for instance, where from the late nineteenth century the state assumed the responsibility for promoting rapid and efficient industrialization in partnership with private interests, is telling. Afonso Pena's government made it clear that in Brazil the old sesmaria mentality, which historically allowed the appropriation of outsized tracts of land by a few privileged aristocrats, would continue to reproduce itself, blurring the dividing line between the national interest and that of the hegemonic class. With the First Republic's oligarchic scheme in full flow, it was as if the holders of the hereditary captaincies had finally taken over the Crown.

Anyone looking at the Brazilian economy in 1906 might have been misled by its appearance of prosperity. Even though it appeared to be a time of bonanza, with an economic golden age driven by rubber and coffee exports, the positive financial results were clearly unsustainable; the feast could not last. For the time being, however, the President would comply with all the directives issued from the landlords of Taubaté. Pena adopted the international gold standard that had been rejected by Rodrigues Alves. The aforementioned *Caixa de Conversão* was finally established in 1906. Exchange-rate stability was thus achieved, but it made the domestic monetary offer dependent on the influx of capital from the export sector. Any imbalances in the current account would immediately be felt in the national product. In an export-dependent economy such as Brazil's, the adoption of the gold standard created a situation where trade-balance deficits provoked almost automatic economic deceleration.

The scheme enjoyed plain sailing while rubber and coffee were in high international demand. Moreover, even when things started to go awry, the federal government came to the rescue, as when the effects of a bumper coffee bumper crop in 1906 were mitigated by the government's purchases of surpluses. The production of rubber in the Amazon contributed to trade-balance stability and at the same time engendered positive effects in the capital account through the attraction of foreign long-term investments into the Amazon region. In 1907, Afonso Pena began the construction of the Madeira–Mamoré railroad, as provided for in the Treaty of Petropolis of 1903, which had put an end to the dispute over Acre. The city of Manaus experienced significant growth and a considerable level of economic prosperity. Federal programs for regional development included expeditions led by army officer Cândido Mariano da Silva Rondon (1865–1958), a man of Native American ethnic origin who would become a great supporter of Brazil's indigenous populations. In 1907, Rondon constructed the first telegraph line that linked part of the Amazon region to Rio de Janeiro. The present-day state of Rondônia is named after him.[25]

Besides the expansion of railroads and the efforts to integrate the Amazon rainforest with the rest of the country, President Afonso Pena adopted measures to facilitate immigration to Brazil. Under the motto *Governar é povoar* (To govern is to populate), the President signed contracts with private companies that would attract and transport immigrants into the country. The effort was aimed at expanding labor supply. The process of organizing a labor market after the end of slavery in 1888 was still in train, and somewhere along the way it had become entangled with pseudo-scientific theories of eugenics. Europe thus appeared as the first place to look for those who would at the same time work in the coffee plantations and "whiten" the nation. The times happened to be convenient for this purpose. During the first decade of the twentieth century, rapidly industrializing countries such as Germany and Italy were becoming exporters of people. Significant transformations in their labor markets, with the extinction of jobs resulting from the spreading of mechanized production, contributed to large-scale emigration. Adding to this was the case of Japan, where a process of rampant industrialization was also under way, and where specific cultural circumstances also contributed to significant emigration.

The case of the Japanese diaspora is especially worth noting in connection with the history of immigration in Brazil during the period of Afonso Pena's government. Starting 1868, the Meiji Revolution attempted to extinguish the traditional *shi-no-ko-sho* caste system that had prevailed in Japan since the 1580s, trying to incorporate into mainstream society a large number of former outcasts who had been confined to virtual servility throughout the Edo Period (1603–1868). The difficulty in realizing such integration, which was based on an age-old, ingrained social prejudice, led the Japanese government to offer the former outcasts incentives to emigrate. To the unwanted population, called *burakumin*, were added the historically persecuted Christians, whom the Japanese called *kakurekurishitan*. These became the undeclared focus of the Japanese government's program of incentivized emigration. Latin America became the destiny of choice after the issuing of the Gentlemen's Agreement of 1907 between the United States and Japan, whereby the latter was forced to restrict emigration to the former. The result was that in 1908 the first ship with 790 Japanese immigrants, the *Kasato Maru*, arrived in the port of Santos, officially starting a long history of Japanese immigration in Brazil.[26]

Immigrants of several other nationalities arrived in the country during Afonso Pena's presidency: Polish, Ukrainian, Czech, Syrian, and Lebanese. The case of Italians is also especially noteworthy. During the period from 1884 to 1893, 510,533 Italian immigrants arrived in Brazil. That was followed by even more, 537,784, from 1894 to 1903. The rate then fell sharply to 196,521 between 1904 and 1913. The reason for this reduction was an Italian law, issued in 1902 and known as Prinetti Decree, which prohibited subsidized emigration to Brazil. The law resulted from reported cases of mistreatment of Italian immigrants in Brazilian private farms. For centuries, Brazilian farmers had been accustomed to employing slave labor on their plantations. Their treatment of immigrant workers thus tended to be very much that which had been meted out to slaves. Brazilian landowners appeared to have inherited an aristocratic contempt for manual labor, and cases of Italian immigrants being whipped in public were reported around the world. The ensuing bad reputation soon saw the influx of immigrants slow significantly.

With the increasingly negative image of Brazil spreading abroad, the government decided to intervene in order to maintain the inflow of labor to the coffee plantations. Rodrigues Alves's Pereira Passos reforms in Rio de Janeiro had already been part of a governmental effort to improve the country's image, and thus attract visitors, investment, and immigrants. During this time, competition with Argentina to attract international workers became a question of national pride. The opening to Japanese immigration during Afonso Pena's administration should thus be understood as part of the government's attempt to overcome the decline in Italian workers entering the country after the Prinetti Decree of 1902. A treaty of commerce and friendship had been signed between Brazil and Japan in 1895, during Prudente de Morais's government, with the explicit aim of facilitating Japanese immigration. Racist resistance to accepting Asian immigrants, however, had kept the project dormant for more than a decade. After 1902, and in the context of U.S., Canadian, and Australian restrictions on Japanese immigration, Afonso Pena settled with Japan as part of the solution to the national problem of labor shortages.

In terms of more general foreign policy, the President had to face the growing rivalry with Argentina in the dispute for political hegemony in South America. Although relations between the two countries had improved with Julio Roca and Campos Sales's exchange of visits at the end of the 1890s, new developments began to alter the regional balance of power. Brazil had begun a program of naval reform in 1904, which caused great suspicion and fear in Argentina. These were times of widespread imperialism around the world, and the case of China, with its occupation by European powers, was ever present in the minds of Brazilian rulers. The appearance of Alfred Thayer Mahan's (1840–1914) theories of a U.S. manifest destiny enlarged by naval capacity and directed to overseas conquest shook the confidence of many South American leaders. Chile had become a militarily strong nation after winning the war against Bolivia and Peru in 1883, and had undergone a thorough reform of its navy in 1900. It had important frontier disputes with Argentina, the conflict over which had a negative impact on the region's stability.

The three larger Southern Cone nations, Brazil, Argentina, and Chile, sought to enhance their international prestige, and all three strived for regional hegemony. In terms of the attempts at achieving international recognition for such sought-after supremacy, Brazil secured a head start in 1905 as a result of a diplomatic crisis with Germany, which became known as "Panther Cruiser Case." While moving through the South Atlantic, the German cruiser *Panther* had been authorized by the Brazilian government to enter Brazilian waters, but not to land troops on national territory. However, in response to the desertion of a German marine near the coast of the state of Santa Catarina, part of the *Panther*'s crew disembarked in pursuit of the deserter, giving the impression of a military invasion. Santa Catarina was a region of strong German colonization, and it is possible that the marine deserted to join members of his own family. Whatever the reason, the regional authorities of Santa Catarina State protested to the federal government, and Foreign Minister Paranhos demanded an explanation from the German government. Wilhelm II's representative, the Baron Freiherrn von Treutler presented Germany's apologies to the Brazilian Foreign Minister in January 1906. This was a rare case of a European nation's recognition of a peripheral country's sovereignty. The German treatment of Brazil implied equal standing between the two nations, and the event worked to enhance Brazilian prestige in the eyes of its neighbors.[27]

The triangular dispute for South American pre-eminence between Brazil, Argentina, and Chile had a further complicating element, namely U.S. regional hegemony. The commercial treaty of 1891 signed between James Blaine and Salvador de Mendonça had turned Brazil into a virtual economic satellite of the United States, influencing the establishment of what American historian Bradford Burns called an "unwritten alliance."[28] Such an alliance placed considerable strain on the already suspicion-fraught relations between the countries of the Southern Cone. Brazil had a long history of being regarded by its neighbors as a harbinger of imperialism. As we have seen, during the process of Latin American independence the Brazilian monarchy had been seen as an agent of European re-colonization by many South American nations. Its present closeness to the United States thus revived the general impression of a Brazilian sub-imperialist disposition.

Chilean and Argentine suspicions with regard to Brazil's naval reform of 1904 were exacerbated by Afonso Pena's reorganization of the army which started in 1906. The program of military modernization was entrusted to the Minister of War, Hermes da Fonseca (1855–1923), a military commander from the bellicose state of Rio Grande do Sul who would become Brazil's next president. In the Ministry of War, Marshal Hermes da Fonseca instituted military conscription and promoted the acquisition of modern armaments. Relations with Argentina were further strained when, in 1906, Estanislao Zeballos (1854–1923), Paranho's declared enemy since the territorial dispute over Palmas in 1895, was appointed Argentina's Foreign Minister. Zeballos would become especially concerned with Brazil's naval development and would attack the Brazilian military program head-on. The issue became a subject of public debate in Argentina, where the press demanded government action to deter Brazilian military supremacy.

In 1907, Paranhos started negotiations with Chile and Argentina for the signature of a non-aggression pact, known as ABC (the initials of the three countries). The idea, however, did not mollify Zeballos's angry suspicions. The Argentine official conjectured the possibility of a secret agreement between Brazil and Chile to attack Argentina. Responding to popular demand, the Argentine Congress began to discuss a law for the modernization of Argentina's armed forces. An arms race appeared to be on its way. Zeballos's aggressive posture toward Brazil secured him the disapproval of Argentine president José Figueroa Alcorta (1860–1931). Part of the Argentine political establishment preferred a less belligerent attitude towards their neighbor.

The testy Minister resigned from office in June 1908 so that he could make public the fact that he was in possession of written proof that Paranhos intended to attack Argentina. Zeballos announced the existence of a diplomatic telegram between the Brazilian Foreign Office and its Embassy in Santiago, Chile's capital, in which Paranhos allegedly asserted Brazil's intention to go to war. Zeballos claimed that the Argentine intelligence service had intercepted the telegram and decoded it. In order to disprove Zeballos's allegations, however, Paranhos adopted an unexpected attitude rarely seen in diplomatic history. He published the codes used in the Brazilian international communications together with the telegram sent to the Brazilian Embassy in Chile on the date mentioned by Zeballos. The Argentine's claims were shown publicly to be false.[29]

Brazil and Argentina did not go to war. Paranhos had no intention of attacking Argentina. The incident did, however, shake bilateral relations. As Brazil continued its naval upgrade and began to further align with the United States, Argentine suspicion continued to rise.

In terms of domestic policy, Afonso Pena's government enjoyed the benefits of the economic boom that had continued since 1900. The President, however, was severely criticized for favoring the interests of coffee producers and for mismanaging his ministerial cabinet. Pena's ministers were humorously called "The Kindergarten." In forming his administrative staff, the President chose to surround himself with young officials who would always look up to the Head of the State and never question his ideas. More experienced men might have had better solutions to the nation's problems, but were unlikely to accept the President's commands unquestioningly. Favoring young and inexperienced politicians, Pena not only put the vigor and strength of his government in check, entrusting it to intellectually immature individuals, but also did injustice to men of more advanced age with proven capacity to serve the nation.

Afonso Pena died before the end of his term in office. On June 14, 1909, Vice President Nilo Peçanha assumed the presidency for a brief period. The contest for the 1910 presidential elction had already begun. This would be the first truly competitive presidential election in Brazilian history. The traditional opposition between the armed forces with their authoritarian, positivistic and centralizing agenda on one side, and the landed coffee oligarchs, with their federalist, liberal and decentralizing program on the other, would resurface with all its strength in 1910. The outcome, as we will see next, would be the resurgence of the political clout of the military-minded Riograndenses, who would bring their own oligarchy of southern meat curers to supersede that of São Paulo and Minas Gerais, namely the coffee and milk producers.

Hermes da Fonseca (1910–1914)

The heavy-handed army commander Hermes Rodrigues da Fonseca (1855–1923) assumed the Brazilian presidency on November 15, 1910. The new President was Marshal Deodoro da Fonseca's nephew. Born in the Riograndense town of São Gabriel, Fonseca came under the influence of the powerful senator, José Gomes Pinheiro Machado, who had skillfully orchestrated the new President's electoral campaign. Fonseca's presidency thus came to represent the military power of Rio Grande do Sul set against the civilian economic strength of São Paulo and Minas Gerais.

The rise of the military leader resulted from important developments in party politics not previously seen in Brazilian history. Pinheiro Machado had established the Republican Conservative Party early in 1910 with the aim of bringing together traditional republican politicians from different regions, such as Quintino Bocauiva from Rio de Janeiro and Venceslau Brás from Minas Gerais. In spite of being short-lived, the party became the first political organization in the country to have a national scope. It was disbanded in 1916, after the assassination of Pinheiro Machado in Rio de Janeiro.

In 1910, the Republican Conservative Party gave the Riograndenses the means to counter the political alliance between São Paulo and Minas Gerais that had been in effect since Campos Sales's government. The alliance was based on what is known as *Política do café com leite* (Coffee with Milk Politics), and it functioned under a tacit agreement between the two powerful states, São Paulo and Minas Gerais, to alternate in the presidency and work together in controlling the federal government.

The downside of such alliance politics was that it created a distorted form of federalism in the young Brazilian Republic. It made clear that some states were more powerful than others, establishing an oligopoly in the central government. Since militarily strong Rio Grande do Sul was left out of the São Paulo–Minas Gerais duopoly, men such as Pinheiro Machado and Hermes da Fonseca had to struggle to position their own regional oligarchy in the national distribution of power.

Within the Senate, Pinheiro Machado controlled the *Comissão de Verificação de Poderes* (Commission for the Confirmation of Powers), a government bureau in charge of maintaining the pact between the central government and the regional administrations in the federalist arrangement. The Commission's role was to ensure that recently elected deputies had been chosen by means of lawfully conducted polls, that is, without recourse to electoral fraud. The system, however, worked to maintain the grip of the ruling party over the national electoral process: whenever a deputy from the opposition was elected, the commission could simply accuse him of fraud and proceed to invalidate his election. The opposition was thus shackled and cut down to the size of an "allowed opposition." Under Pinheiro Machado's heavy-handed authoritarianism, this system of invalidating an elected deputy's election was suggestively called the *degola* (cut throat), recalling the form of warfare adopted in Rio Grande do Sul during the 1893 Federalist Revolution. The Senator's general resoluteness, together with his unyielding promptness in applying the *degola*, earned him the epithet in Rio de Janeiro of *Caudilho Gaúcho* (Riograndense Warlord).

Control over the Commission for the Confirmation of Powers gave Pinheiro Machado an inordinate amount of power. During the 1910 presidential campaign, he managed to gain support from a significant number of Minas Gerais's deputies. This was enough to destabilize the alliance between São Paulo and Minas Gerais. Marshal Hermes da Fonseca ran for president with Venceslau Brás, former governor of Minas Gerais, as his vice-presidential candidate. Together, they faced Rui Barbosa, who ran with Albuquerque Lins, former governor of São Paulo, for the vice-presidency. São Paulo and part of Minas Gerais thus supported Barbosa and Lins, while the new alliance between Rio Grande do Sul and the other part of Minas Gerais supported Hermes and Brás. This regional division reflected the opposition between military and civilian contenders in the contest. The so-called *militaristas*, supporters of Hermes da Fonseca, opposed the *civilistas*, supporters of Rui Barbosa.

To a great extent, the presidential election of 1910 became a personal dispute between age-old rivals: Pinheiro Machado, representing military Rio Grande do Sul, and Rui Barbosa, acting for civilian São Paulo. During the electoral campaign, Pinheiro Machado displayed his military background with pride. As a form of political self-propaganda, he would compare himself to Barbosa, saying that in their youth, while the civilian was walking around with his books under his arm, he was carrying a rifle on his back, killing Paraguayans in the Paraguayan War.[30]

Hermes da Fonseca's victory gave rise to the so-called *Política das Salvações* (Politics of Salvations), a series of federal interventions in the provincial governments through which local administrators were deposed and substituted by allies of Hermes da Fonseca and Pinheiro Machado. The operation was undertaken under the guise of an attempt to moralize politics. Its real intent, however, was unashamedly authoritarian. It reflected the positivist ideology of Rio Grande do Sul's military elite and aimed to destabilize the regional oligarchies' power through the creation of a strong centralized state. As mentioned above, Comtian political

Positivism defended the establishment of a republican dictatorship as the correct form of government. Since the times of Júlio de Castilhos, who had died in 1903, Riograndense warlords had continued to follow Comte's directive almost religiously. Their belief in the eternal truth of authoritarianism and in the uncontested necessity of dictatorship was so entrenched that renowned Brazilian historian Raymundo Faoro (1925–2003) used to refer to Rio Grande do Sul as *Comtelândia* (Comte's Land).[31]

The Federal Government's attack on the provinces should thus be understood as a logical result of positivistic militarism. Such logic, however, was bound to produce great instability in a federative system such as the one established with the First Brazilian Republic, where federal interventions were intended to be employed parsimoniously if the State itself was not to implode. The *Salvações* ended up weakening the Riograndenses' legitimacy as rulers of the nation. With the unrestrained Riograndense usurpation of elected mandates, the reconciliation between São Paulo and Minas Gerais would not be long in coming.

Before any such reconciliation could be formalized, however, two new uprisings distracted the government's attention in the first few years of Hermes da Fonseca's administration. A few weeks after taking office, the President had to face a rebellion in the navy, where a group of sailors, mostly young black men who had been forced to enter the navy and serve for a period of fifteen years, rebelled against the use of the lash in disciplining crewmen. The mutiny started on November 22, 1910, led by João Cândido Felisberto (1880–1969), a black man from Rio Grande do Sul whose parents were former slaves. Prevailing racism in the navy, together with the use of violence against the lower ranks gave the rebellion the title of "*Revolta da Chibata*" (Revolt of the Lash). The uprising soon spread from Rio de Janeiro to São Paulo. The sailors murdered several high-ranking officers and the city of Rio de Janeiro was bombed. On November 26, 1910, Hermes da Fonseca accepted the demands of the insurrectionists. Physical punishment was abolished and a pardon was promised to those willing to hand over their weapons. Soon after the agreement was settled, however, the President hesitated and two days later a new directive establishing the expulsion of undisciplined sailors was issued. The insurrectionists were pardoned, but it was clear that they were not trusted.

Hundreds of sailors were expelled from the navy. Many were killed or sent to die in the Amazon. The insurrection's leader, João Cândido, was arrested on December 13, 1910. He was sent to a high security prison and locked in a small cell with eighteen other men, seventeen of whom died by asphyxiation. After being freed a few years later, Cândido declared that 29 sailors had been executed by being buried in lime. This method of murder harked back to one allegedly applied to black soldiers in the Farroupilha Revolution in Rio Grande do Sul. In any case, the so-called Revolt of the Lash is regarded as an early social movement against racism and against the harsh working conditions imposed on the poor during the elitist First Brazilian Republic.[32]

Another large-scale rebellion brought further complications for the President. The Contestado War was a civil conflict lasting from 1912 to 1916 in a rural area close to the frontier between the states of Santa Catarina and Paraná. The region was rich in wood and yerba mate, and it was disputed by the two states, hence the war's name, *Contestado* (disputed). Besides the provincial governments' administrative disagreement over the area, the local situation was further complicated by questions of private land ownership and religious fanaticism.

In 1908, President Afonso Pena had commissioned the construction of a railroad to connect the cities of São Paulo and Santa Maria in Rio Grande do Sul. The project was contracted with the Brazil Railway Company, a North American corporation owned by a man named Percival Farquhar (1864–1953) who, in the first decade of the twentieth century, became the foremost private investor in Brazil. Together with the concession to build the railroad, the federal government offered Farquhar the right to explore the wood-rich lands bordering each side of the track. The area, however, was filled with communities of farmers who, over the last few centuries, had established a local economy based on subsistence agriculture. Together with his Brazil Railway Company, Farquhar created another corporation to explore the region's wood, the Southern Brazil Lumber & Colonization Company. In order to enhance the profitability of its investments, Farquhar's company instigated a series of expropriations. Serious financial interests were at stake and the conflict began after the dissatisfied workers of the Railway Company joined with the now landless farmers in an armed rebellion. The situation was complicated by the appearance of a series of spiritual leaders who gave the conflict a messianic dimension.

President Hermes da Fonseca's troops arrived in the region in early 1912 to control the revolt. The area in question happened to be primarily the same one disputed by the states of Paraná and Santa Catarina, and the old frontier conflict resurfaced. With federal troops on site, severe bloodshed ensued. The insurrectionists, however, were not to be put down easily. The emergence of two monks as leaders turned the conflict into a religious war with outdated demands for the re-establishment of the monarchy. The situation became very similar to that of the War of Canudos, fought some twenty years earlier in the Northeast. After a long stalemate in the fight between the local rebels and the federal troops, on February 8, 1914, a second military expedition was dispatched from Rio de Janeiro. The result, again, was hideous carnage. Contestado's holy war came to an end only in 1915 during the succeeding presidency of President Venceslau Brás (1868–1966). After years of violence and misery, the federal forces finally exterminated a population of starving men, women and children who still attempted to resist in the state of Santa Catarina. In 1916, an agreement was signed between Santa Catarina and Paraná, which also put an end to the frontier dispute.[33]

The civil conflicts taking place during Hermes da Fonseca's presidency exposed the shortcomings and vulnerabilities of the First Brazilian Republic. In the case of the Contestado, the complaints of the local population were that little had changed for them: in former times land was the property of the Portuguese Crown and only the privileged were ever granted the right to explore the vast expanse of fertile ground; now under the federal arrangement land could be transferred to foreigners, and the people continued to be exploited just the same. Throughout the conflict, the vice-governor of Paraná State, Affonso Camargo (1873–1958), served as Farquhar's attorney in defending the Southern Brazil Lumber & Colonization Company's rights to explore the region at the expense of Brazilian residents. The *uti possidetis* principle of land ownership, which had always guided Brazilian negotiations over borders with neighboring countries, seemed now not applicable to the national citizens who had fought for the Contestado region. These citizens were expelled from the land they had traditionally occupied so that a foreign company could extract the natural resources they contained. The rebellion's degeneration into a monarchist uprising was a symptom of popular dissatisfaction with what was perceived as the Republic's lack of national sentiment, as it parceled out Brazilian territory to the economic advantage of foreigners.

The Constestado uprising also reflected the economic recession experienced in Brazil during 1914. The economic golden age of 1900–1913 came to an end with the end of the rubber boom in the Amazon. Production from Dutch and British plantations in Asia contributed to the plummeting of rubber's international price. Together with the fall of rubber economy, an anti-trust legal action from the United States against those hoarding Brazilian coffee with the aim of elevating international prices forced the relaxation of the Taubaté Accord, and coffee prices also plummeted.[34] Compounding this sudden dramatic downturn, the beginning of the First World War brought an abrupt end to European investment. The

Brazilian economy was thrown into a severe recession. The government would contract a new funding loan in 1914.[35]

In terms of domestic politics, in 1913, Senator Pinheiro Machado was ready to present his candidacy for presidency in the elections the following year. Given the usual fraudulent nature of Brazilian elections, where those in power controlled the voting process, his victory was all but certain. The Senator's ambitions, however, were stymied by a formal agreement signed in 1913 between the states of São Paulo and Minas Gerais with the aim of seizing the presidency. The agreement was called Ouro Fino Pact; it established that the two states would, from then on, alternate in the presidency, that is, in a formal alliance against Rio Grande do Sul. The agreement showed, again, the fragility of Brazilian federalism. Economic discrepancies between different states made them favor distinct political arrangements. While São Paulo and Minas Gerais functioned as part of the export economy, Rio Grande do Sul produced mostly for the internal market. It thus favored a more centralized form of administration that would facilitate the marketing of its leather and beef internally. Such irreconcilable difference in economic interests made peace and understanding between the federative units practically impossible.

Besides the pact between São Paulo and Minas Gerais, the sudden economic downturn after the halt of the rubber boom also militated against Pinheiro Machado's presidential candidacy. The end of the economic golden age meant a rapid decline in Brazil's growing industrial output, which sparked a series of strikes in Rio de Janeiro beginning in the final months of 1913. The heavy-handed and authoritarian Riograndense rule of Hermes da Fonseca and Pinheiro Machado meant an aggressive attitude toward the workers' protests. The President declared a state of siege in the nation's capital. Further angry protests ensued when the government passed a law sentencing all foreigners involved in strikes to immediate expulsion.

In 1914, the oligarchs of the state of Ceará took up arms against the repeated federal interventions from the Riograndenses in their affairs. A popular local figure called Cícero Romão Batista (1844–1934) gave political support to the interests of the ruling Acioly family against the interventionism of Hermes da Fonseca and Pinheiro Machado. Known as Padre Cícero, the leader of this new regional rebellion was believed to perform miracles, and his actions recalled the religious overtones of the other popular uprisings during the First Republic. The absence of the Catholic Church from the distant Brazilian countryside, partly a result of republican secularism, left the field open for the sort of mystics who led the revolts of Canudos, Contestado, and now Ceará. In 1914, the rationality of positivist Riograndense militarism was once again countered with the faith of those who needed a messiah.

Meanwhile, São Paulo and Minas Gerais consolidated their alliance. The result was an easy electoral victory by the vice-president, Venceslau Brás who, being from Minas Gerais, had been coopted by his countrymen against the Riograndenses. During his term as vice-president, Brás had been clearly ostracized from Hermes da Fonseca and Pinheiro Machado's Riograndense government. During his term from 1910 to 1914, Brás was frequently to be found fishing in the rivers that crossed his farm in Minas Gerais, unable to break into the closed group of the Gaúchos that controlled the central government in Rio de Janeiro.

In its anti-Riograndense electoral victory, the São Paulo–Minas Gerais alliance gained further ground thanks to an incident that stymied the Gaúcho's plan for a political come back. After his group's defeat in the presidential run, Hermes da Fonseca was almost immediately elected to the National Senate representing Rio Grande do Sul, but he refused to take office when, a few days before his accession ceremony, his political godfather, Pinheiro Machado, was murdered in Rio de Janeiro. The 64-year-old Riograndense oligarch was stabbed in the back in the entrance hall of a hotel where he was to meet his adversaries from the Republican Party of São Paulo. The death of Pinheiro Machado in 1915 meant the immediate demise of his Republican Conservative Party. The Riograndenses were suddenly defeated by an act of treachery.[36] Thus began fifteen years of São Paulo–Minas Gerais combined rule until another Riograndense landlord would emerge to take the reins of the nation in 1930. From that date on, the balance of power would move again to the South, and another fifteen-year-long rule would ensue, this time under stern Riograndense dictatorship.

Venceslau Brás (1914–1918)

Venceslau Brás Pereira Gomes (1868–1966) was elected Brazil's eighth president on March 1, 1914, after winning a poll in which he competed virtually as the only candidate. Since all major political parties supported the former vice president's campaign, Rui Barbosa withdrew his candidacy with the Republican Liberal Party, but still won 8% of the vote against Brás's 91%. Although Pinheiro Machado, like Barbosa, was not registered as a candidate, he received 0.03% of the vote.

From the start, Brás's administration had to face the international constraints produced by the First World War, which had a significant impact on Brazil's export economy. Germany had declared war against

Russia exactly a month and a half before Brás assumed the presidency. On August 4, 1914 (still during Hermes da Fonseca's administration), Brazil had officially declared its neutrality vis-à-vis the conflict. Such neutrality, however, would be broken three years later, when Brazil declared war on Germany, making it the only Latin American country to take part in the First World War against the Central Powers.

Regarding the economy, in 1914 Brazil's balance of payments had been temporarily stabilized with the help of the new Funding Loan recently contracted with Rothschild Bank. The first two years of the war did not affect Brazilian exports to any great extent, as the country's commodities kept reaching Europe and the United States as usual. The biggest problem was the halt in imports. Stagnation in European industrial output produced significant shortages in the import-dependent Brazilian economy. National industrial output shrank by around 9% in 1914 as a result of the halt in the import of manufacturing inputs. A process of import substitution, that is, of national production of goods that used to be imported, began in 1915, generating a positive effect on Brazil's incipient industrialization.

But Brazil's economic situation began to deteriorate in 1915. The increase in the price of imports generated a substantial trade deficit. Problems in the trade balance further deepened as a result of foreign debt servicing starting in 1917. In the same year, Britain's prohibition on the import of coffee, which in times of war was listed as a superfluous product, threw the Brazilian economy into disarray. To make matters worse, a diplomatic dispute arose between the state of São Paulo and Germany in regard to Brazilian financial deposits retained by the German government in Belgium. The deposits were related to the scheme of coffee valorization implemented in 1906.

Relations with Germany further deteriorated when a large Brazilian steamship loaded with coffee was attacked by a German submarine, resulting in the death of three Brazilians. The vessel was traveling in accordance with the rules of neutrality and the event caused an immediate national outcry. Popular protests occurred in Rio de Janeiro, and the Brazilian Foreign Minister, Lauro Müller (1863–1926), a man of German origin, was forced to resign. In the largely German populated region of Rio Grande do Sul, attacks against citizens of German origin began to occur, resulting in the raiding, looting, and torching of several establishments owned by German descendants. The Brazilian government cut diplomatic relations with Germany on April 11, 1917 and, after three more Brazilian ships had been torpedoed by German submarines, declared war on the Central Powers on October 26, 1917.

In retaliation for the retained stocks of coffee, the Brazilian government seized 46 German and Austrian ships that were moored in Rio de Janeiro. Sectors of the Brazilian government considered military involvement in the war as potentially profitable in terms of international prestige, and a small military mission was dispatched to join the French army in Europe. A more significant force was organized by the Brazilian navy. In 1918, the Naval Division for War Operations (DNOG) was created. It consisted of a naval fleet initially tasked to patrol the Atlantic under the orders of the British Admiralty. Other uses for the fleet were discussed among the Allied forces, but indecision between Italian, U.S., and French plans, together with an epidemic of Spanish flu that claimed the lives of some 100 Brazilian sailors, delayed the DNOG and prevented its effective participation in the war. A group of military aviators was also dispatched to serve with the British Royal Air Force, created in April, 1918.[37]

As we have observed, the period from 1898 to 1910 saw a remarkable improvement in Brazil's international image, which occurred in tandem with a leaning towards the United States in terms of foreign policy. Foreign Minister Paranhos died in 1912, with that convergence as his legacy. His insistence on the idea that Latin American countries should attempt to achieve a level of development similar to that of the United States, even if by means of what he called "noble emulation," clearly indicated his recognition of U.S. superiority in the Americas.[38]

Paranhos's successors in the Foreign Office, starting with German descendant Lauro Müller, would tend to turn the Baron's aristocratic idolization of superior paradigms into a much more subservient and automatic alignment. Starting in 1912, the aforementioned "unwritten alliance" between the United States and Brazil began to move towards an embarrassing process of faltering national sovereignty, as would become clear with the incident of Brazil's recognition of the Chinese republic in 1913. Having recognized the Asian republic before the United States had done so, the Brazilian Foreign Office changed the official date of the recognition so as to avoid displeasing the northern neighbor.

This also coincided with tensions in relations with the United States as a result of the latter's prosecution of Brazilian coffee producers for their unfair trade practices. In 1913, Lauro Müller paid a visit to Washington in order to attempt reconciliation. The Brazilian representative was received with distinction, but relations between the two countries had deteriorated considerably, making the days of State Secretary Elihu Root's visit to Brazil a few years earlier seem like another age. If in 1906 the Baron of Rio Branco's nation seemed to be the dominant nation in South America, by 1910 it had lost a great part of its hard-earned international prestige.

And while Brazil declined, Argentina ascended. The latter's better economic position, achieved mostly through British investments, gave it a position of pre-eminence over the clumsy and oversized neighbor. The Argentine emergence as the leader of the South American subcontinent was crowned with the honor of holding the Pan-American Conference of 1910.

Despite the general attitude of awe towards the United States, Brazil's foremost coffee market, some Brazilians, such as the ambassador to Washington, Domício da Gama (1862–1925), defended the idea of a convergence among Latin American nations as a way to counter excessive U.S. power. Divergence between the Ambassador and Foreign Minister Lauro Müller, the champion of alignment with the United States, soon came to the fore. The Ambassador's wishes, however, would find a route to fulfillment when in 1914 the United States went to the verge of a war with Mexico. The Tampico Affair, an incident involving the U.S. Navy and Mexican forces involved in the Mexican Revolution, led to the breakdown of diplomatic relations between the two countries and to the U.S. occupation of the city of Veracruz. The city was located in a region of geopolitical interest for the United Sates, containing a settlement of U.S. citizens due to the presence of American firms in the local oil industry.

On May 20, 1914, President Woodrow Wilson called the Niagara Falls Peace Conference where Argentina, Brazil, and Chile, the so-called ABC Powers, met for diplomatic negotiations with the aim of avoiding a war between the United States and Mexico. Wilson's intention was to prevent the United States shouldering the burden of war alone. Avoiding such a situation had been an important element in U.S. foreign policy since Taft's administration. In an exchange with the Brazilian Foreign Office on January 11, 1913, Ambassador Domício da Gama commented on a recent speech by Charles H. Sherrill (1867–1936), former American ambassador to Buenos Aires, suggesting that a U.S. intervention in Mexico should be carried out together with Brazil and Argentina. Taft's government had been prepared to start a war with Mexico, and the Tampico Affair offered a good pretext. Since 1911, the nationalist policies of Mexican revolutionaries such as Venustiano Carranza (1859–1920), who defended the re-nationalization of the Mexican oil industry, were seen as a threat to American economic interests in the region.

Sherrill's suggestion that Brazil and Argentina should aid the United States in attacking Mexico seems whimsical when seen from the perspective of the two South American countries' absolute lack of interest in the region at the time. Besides an obedient following of the *Big Stick*, or of its more recent version, *Dollar Diplomacy*, Brazil and Argentina would have had scant reason to enter Mexican territory. Nonetheless, Domicio da Gama, together with Argentine and Chilean officials Romulo Naon (1875–1941) and Eduardo Suárez Mujica (1859–1922), saw in the Conference an opportunity to strengthen the ties among the Southern Cone states. Argentina, Brazil, and Chile were just emerging from a long-drawn-out naval arms race, which came to be referred to as the South American Dreadnought Race. The long awaited and eagerly hoped-for normalization of trilateral relations was reinforced with the news of a possible alliance between Colombia, Equator, Peru, Venezuela, and Bolivia, which was of immediate concern to Chile. With territorial disputes still unsettled and widespread resentment left over from the War of the Pacific (1879–1883), in which Chile had defeated Peru and Bolivia, an alliance with Brazil and Argentina was highly desirable. The three countries thus signed an agreement on May 15, 1915, affirming the principle of non-aggression and the recourse to arbitration in case of disputes. The agreement was baptized as the "ABC Pact," and it also had the implied objective of offsetting U.S. hegemony.

The U.S. occupation of Mexican territory lasted until November 1914, and it became the source of a strong resentment that would resurface in 1917, when the German Empire attempted to manipulate Mexico against the United States during the First World War. For the Southern Cone nations, however, the Tampico Affair brought some relief to their strained relations. In terms of the historical rivalry between Brazil and Argentina, the Pact is usually regarded as an early attempt at convergence, setting the tone for the future process of economic integration that started in the 1980s.

In terms of internal politics, towards the end of his government Venceslau Brás had to face a general strike that paralyzed almost the entire nation for several weeks. Started in July 1917, the strike reflected the transformations taking place in Brazilian society.[39] The great influx of immigrants during the nineteenth century, especially from Italy and Spain, had introduced socialist and anarchist ideas to the nation's working class. By the beginning of the twentieth century, many of those immigrants had abandoned the coffee farms in the distant rural areas and moved to the cities of São Paulo and Rio de Janeiro. In São Paulo, they settled primarily in an industrial neighborhood called Mooca, where soon a proletarian movement began to emerge. As anarcho-syndicalism became strong, syndicates were established as an instrument of class struggle and with them autonomous schools, daycare facilities, printing presses, and newspapers proliferated.[40]

Before the national strike of 1917, a previous general strike had occurred in 1906. This one had started in the city of Jundiaí among workers from the São Paulo Railway Company, soon spreading to other parts of the country. This earlier strike had had supporters from many walks of life, including students, merchants, and sectors of the armed forces. Public demonstrations were especially significant in the city of São Paulo, where they were severely repressed by the state secretary of justice, Washington Luís Pereira de Sousa (1869–1957), who would become Brazil's thirteenth President in 1926. The famous phrase in Brazilian political history, *Questão social é questão de polícia* (social matters are to be solved by the police), has been attributed to Luís, whose job was to control the angry crowds in both the 1906 and 1917 strikes.

In 1917, Luís had become São Paulo's mayor, and now had to face a stoppage with larger and deeper implications than that of 1906. The 1917 strike reflected the growing politicization of the Brazilian proletariat together with the influence of the Russian Revolution. In economic terms, the beginning of the First World War had entailed a remarkable rise in commodity exports to Europe, resulting in the contraction of the domestic offer of basic goods. Even if the expansion of the export sector boosted employment, the resulting inflation meant a drastic reduction in the purchasing power of the average worker. Popular dissatisfaction soon reached the level where strikes were called in all areas of the economy. Complications were compounded by the government's restrictive economic policies, which were regarded as necessary in order to tackle inflation. The effects of the First World War on the Brazilian economy were thus twofold: on the one hand, some industrial growth was achieved, while on the other, inflation and social unrest grew.

Venceslau Brás's government is also remembered for the promulgation of the first Brazilian Civil Code in 1916. Written by lawyer Clóvis Beviláqua (1859–1944), the Code reflected the values upheld by Brazilian society, or at least by those who had controlled it during the First Republic. Its provisions were primarily conservative, especially in regard to Family Law. One of its progressive aspects, however, can be seen in its recognition of the rights of foreigners. In its third article, the Code established that the Law would not distinguish between nationals and foreigners in respect to the acquisition and enjoyment of civil rights. In times of proactive governmental attempts to attract immigrants, this was a way to demonstrate the nation's openness and liberalism. Note that the article would be excluded from new Civil Code promulgated several decades later, in 2002.

As the time for new presidential elections approached, it became clear that the rules of the Ouro Fino Agreement of 1913 between Paulistas and Mineiros, that is, between the Republican Party of São Paulo (PRP) and the Republican Party of Minas Gerais (PRM), would be closely followed. According to the agreement, since the current president, Venceslau Brás, was from Minas Gerais, the next president would have to be someone from São Paulo. The chosen successor was the former president, Rodrigues Alves, who was duly elected for a second term on March 1, 1918, achieving an easy victory over Nilo Peçanha (1867–1924). Peçanha had also previously served as the nation's president, albeit only for a short period after the death of Afonso Pena in 1909. The election's result offered continued evidence of the general lack of probity in Brazilian politics: Rodrigues Alves received 99% of the vote, Nilo Peçanha 0.45%, and Rui Barbosa 0.27%.

An unexpected turn in the presidential succession came when Rodrigues Alves succumbed to the Spanish flu brought into the country by Brazilian troops returning from the First World War in Europe. The President-elect did not take office as planned on November 15, 1918. Instead, the elected vice-President, Delfim Moreira da Costa Ribeiro (1868–1920), assumed the office of the presidency on a temporary basis. Rodrigues Alves died in January 1919, and new elections were immediately called. This time the republican parties of Minas Gerais and São Paulo decided to support the candidacy of a common ally, a member of the Republican Party of Paraíba. On July 28, 1919, a president from the Northeast, supported by the powerful coffee barons of São Paulo, would take office.

Epitácio Pessoa (1918–1922)

Epitácio Lindolfo da Silva Pessoa (1865–1942) was elected the 10th Brazilian President on April 13, 1919. Rui Barbosa once again came second. Pessoa had just finished his tenure as Brazil's representative to the Conference of Paris of 1919, where he had solved the issue regarding the Brazilian coffee retained in Europe during the war. The new President had been chosen by the Minas Gerais–São Paulo alliance as an easily controllable middle ground between the two most powerful states. Being from Paraíba, a small state with only minor economic significance, the new leader had little chance of usurping the coffee (and milk) barons' supremacy. After the death of Pinheiro Machado, Pessoa had seized control over the Congress's Commission for the Confirmation of Powers. The position gave him enough visibility to boost his political career.

Without the backing of a powerful state such as Rio Grande do Sul, however, he would never obtain the same degree of power as that held by Pinheiro Machado in the same office.

Epitácio Pessoa's presidency maintained the traditional "oligarchical pact" between the central government and the provincial administrations. The pact, created during Campos Sales's government, was also known as *Política do Estados*, or *Política dos Governadores*. It was a tacit agreement between the union and the states, establishing that the federal government should intervene in the states in favor of the ruling oligarchies in exchange for the latter's support in Congress. The interventions were based on Article 6 of the 1891 Constitution, which allowed for federal interference in regional politics under specific circumstances. Virtually all the federal governments of the First Republic had applied the proviso rather lavishly. The most notable case is perhaps that of Hermes da Fonseca's government and its aforementioned *Salvações*.

In February 1920, President Pessoa dispatched a force of 10,000 soldiers to intervene in the state of Bahia, where a *coup d'état* against the ruling oligarch, J. J. Seabra (1855–1942) was under way. The federal intervention infuriated prestigious politician Rui Barbosa, now a renowned 70-year-old lawyer. Barbosa had been campaigning enthusiastically for the opposition's candidate, Paulo Fontes, who was promoting the coup. The event offers a good example of Brazilian politics during the period, with the liberal Rui Barbosa advocating a *coup d'état* as the solution to the electoral fraud carried out by Seabra under the auspices of the federal government.

With the approaching presidential elections of 1922, the electoral discredit into which the First Republic had fallen inspired a large-scale protest movement that started in the armed forces. The movement, called *Tenentismo*, emerged in the first half of 1922 as a crusade against the Republic itself, that is, against the system's oligarchic nature and its reliance on the old and unfair land distribution scheme inherited from colonial times. In the face of widespread impropriety, a group of low-ranking army officers, mostly lieutenants, started a conspiracy against the federal government. Regarding themselves as a new social force with a duty to democratize the nation, the lieutenants's agenda harmonized with that of Rio Grande do Sul's military oligarchy. They demanded the reform of the old fraudulent electoral system maintained by the elites, which presently allowed for the São Paulo–Minas Gerais political hegemony. The lieutenant's overall discourse, however, was broad, calling for the restructuring the country's very power structure.[41]

After the victory of the São Paulo–Minas Gerais alliance against Rio Grande do Sul in the 1922 presidential election (of which more below), the lieutenants' unrest reached its climax. A revolt broke out in the military headquarters of Rio de Janeiro on July 5, 1922. The event became known as the "18 of the Copacabana Fort Revolt." Early on the morning of July 5, the rebels opened fired against government bases, drawing fierce retaliation. The Fort was bombed throughout the rest of the day. The next morning, the army's command allowed the rebels to escape the siege manned by the federal forces. Although the greater part of the mutinying soldiers left the Fort under government orders to surrender, eighteen troops remained steadfast to their cause. They marched against the federal troops in a heroic gesture of self-sacrifice. Only two men survived the open fire, the lieutenants Siqueira Campos (1898–1930) and Eduardo Gomes (1896–1981). Both men would play important roles in the country's future politics.

The 18 of the Copacabana Fort Revolt stands out as an example of popular autonomy in the face of the abuses of oligarchic politics. From a more conjectural perspective, it emerged in the context of the presidential race that had started a few months earlier, when the poll to elect President Epitácio Pessoa's successor again saw the São Paulo–Minas Gerais alliance pitted against Rio Grande do Sul. In the minds of the young rebelling officers, São Paulo and Minas Gerais represented the national ruling oligarchy, while Rio Grande do Sul did not. The distinction was, however, misleading.

Rio Grande do Sul represented the power of the military establishment in which the lieutenants were professionally enlisted. Nevertheless, in Rio Grande do Sul, that military establishment was intermingled with the local landed oligarchy. The lieutenants overlooked the fact that the military leaders of Rio Grande do Sul originated among the very the landowners who, for hundreds of years, had occupied the region on large estates with the aim of wresting the territory from the Spanish. They thus saw the São Paulo–Minas Gerais against Rio Grande do Sul dispute in terms of military versus civilian, missing the fact that the contenders were, after all, nothing more than two distinct, and powerful, oligarchies.

In order to better understand the causes of the 18 of the Copacabana Fort Revolt and the Tenentista Movement to which it gave rise, we must look more closely at the electoral process leading to President Epitácio Pessoa's succession in 1922. The elections were held a few months before the uprising in Rio de Janeiro, resulting in the victory of the São Paulo–Minas Gerais's candidate Artur da Silva Bernardes (1875–1955), over Nilo Peçanha, the candidate supported by the states of Rio Grande do Sul,

Rio de Janeiro, Bahia, and Pernambuco. Bernardes was the former governor of the state of Minas Gerais, and his victory on March 1, 1922 enraged various sectors of the armed forces, above all those stationed in Rio Grande do Sul.

Immediately after the election results were made public, a group of Riograndense representatives gathered at the Military Club in Rio de Janeiro, the traditional institution founded in 1887 to foster republican ideals, and demanded an investigation into fraud in the poll. After a brief period of uncertainty, the Congress confirmed the victory of Bernardes. The furious generals continued their protest. Discontentment was further deepened when in June 1922 President Pessoa decided to conduct another federal intervention, this time into one of his rival states, Pernambuco. The intervention was heavily criticized by former president Hermes da Fonseca, one of the most prestigious figures among the top military officers at the time, and also a Riograndense. Under Pessoa's orders, Hermes da Fonseca was arrested at the Military Club, which was then closed by the federal government. This incident infuriated the military class even more.

The uprising of the younger officers in the Copacabana Fort a few weeks later thus sprang directly from the events taking place in the Military Club in the month of June. The military class had been dishonored, and it was necessary to exact revenge. Yet from a broader perspective, the crisis involving the lieutenants reflected above all, and once again, the fierce inter-oligarchical disputes taking place during the First Republic. Ultimately, the election of Bernardes or Peçanha represented nothing more than the rise or fall of one of the three major oligarchic powers in the nation: São Paulo, Minas Gerais, and Rio Grande do Sul. The difference between these oligarchies was, as mentioned above, ingrained in the military/civilian rivalry. The military vein of republican power continued to be that of Rio Grande do Sul, while civilians still comprised the political force of São Paulo and Minas Gerais.

The military/civilian dispute becomes more evident when examined under the light of another important factor that contributed to the uprising of 1922, namely the appointment of the civilian João Pandiá Calógeras (1870–1934) as Minister of War. Calógeras would the first civilian to assume that position since the founding of the Republic, and the appointment represented an open attack on the military class by the civilians of São Paulo and Minas Gerais. That, also, angered the lieutenants.

The 18 of the Copacabana Fort Revolt and its ensuing Tenentista Movement was thus linked to unswerving notions of pride and honor related to the armed forces. After the elections of 1922, the idealistic stance of the young lieutenants would be maintained with vigor as they adopted the explicit aim of overthrowing the new President, Artur Bernardes. Such idealism, however, would eventually be shattered by the harsh reality of the non-democratic Riograndense standpoint, which would come to the fore in the early 1930s. In 1922, at any rate, the Movement's emergence reflected important social changes taking place during Epitácio Pessoa's government. The young officers' acts of heroism during the Revolt earned the sympathy of an emerging middle class that was beginning to find its own voice. This class had suffered more directly the economic fluctuations experienced since the end of the First World War and harbored considerable discontent toward Pessoa's government.

In the short time span between 1918 and 1922 the economy had shifted drastically from a situation of growing prosperity to one of recession and financial instability. The year 1919 opened with an economic boom in Europe as a result of high spending on reconstruction after the end of the War. The international prices of commodities rose substantially, boosting Brazilian revenue from coffee exports. Brazil's trade balance ended with a generous surplus in 1919. The international price of coffee rose further when a frost destroyed part of the national harvest in 1918. The economic boom, however, did not last long. Escalating inflation in Europe and the United States called for drastic recessive economic policies in the central economies. The international prices of commodities started plummeting in the second half of 1920. Epitácio Pessoa had no other choice than to follow up with policies of economic austerity. These became a source of discontent among the middle classes, which would soon start supporting the Tenentista Movement.

Besides the financial predicaments derived from international constraints, Epitácio Pessoa's administration was marked also by the President's efforts to promote social and economic development in the impoverished Northeast. Being originally from the state of Paraíba, a northeastern province wracked by poverty, droughts, and frequent famine, Pessoa attempted to improve regional infrastructure, establishing an extensive program of public works to tackle water shortages. The program included the building of dams and wells, and under this aim the *Departamento Nacional de Obras Contra as Secas* (National Department of Works to Counter Droughts), known as DNOCS, was established in 1919. In spite of its goal of alleviating the suffering of destitute Brazilians in the Northeast, the program ended up simply serving the interests of the powerful local landlords, the public works being employed mostly to channel water to highly profitable agriculture. The same old oligarchies received the benefits of a central administration sustained on the *Política dos*

Estados, that is, on the exchange of favors between the federal government and the provincial elites. The general population, as was customary, continued to be deprived of their rightful governmental assistance.[42]

Another relevant aspect of Pessoa's administration related to the President's personal beliefs and to how they influenced government policies during the period. Historians tend to portray Epitácio Pessoa as a closet racist. In 1921, during the South American soccer championship in Argentina, the President prevented the selection of black soccer players for the Brazilian national team.[43] In spite of this embarrassing presidential attitude, however, racism appears to have been much less a personal failing of Epitácio Pessoa than a general tendency in Brazilian society at the time. An attitude similar to that of Pessoa has been ascribed to his successor, Artur Bernardes.

In spite of the unashamedly prejudiced views of the Brazilian presidents, a discourse on national identity that recognized the multi-ethnic nature of Brazilian society began to emerge in the clearly elitist sphere of the high arts. The avant-garde movement, which would sweep through Brazil's cultural scene during the 1920s, would attempt to portray the nation in its full ethnic diversity, standing against what it perceived as the Europeanized cultural and artistic products of the past. The *Semana de Arte Moderna* (Modern Art Week), an arts festival held in São Paulo in February 1922, established Brazilian Modernism as the national avant-garde and attempted to define the nation's very character in terms of its multi-ethnic heritage. The Brazilian avant-garde was unusual in being one of the few in the international movement of modernism where nationalism was heightened at the expense of a more internationalized, universal aesthetic. In any case, the Brazilian avant-garde appeared as a forerunner of multi-ethnic consciousness among Brazilians. It would not be until the 1930s that the preconceptions of racism would be discussed more openly in the fields of history and sociology, through works such as Gilberto Freyre's (1900–1987) *Casa Grande & Senzala* (1933), which helped establish the national discourse on racial democracy (of which more later).

Epitácio Pessoa's government was also marked by a celebratory convention of colossal dimensions assembled in the final year of his mandate, an international event that would end up putting a severe strain on the already meager resources of the National Treasury. The convention celebrated the 100th anniversary of Brazilian independence in the form of a world exposition in Rio de Janeiro. The sumptuous international exhibit took place from September 7, 1922 to March 23, 1923. It aimed at attracting foreign investment by displaying Brazil's rampant modernization. A total of fourteen countries took part, each building an extravagant pavilion to display its modern achievements. The climate of cultural and economic exchange favored the cultivation of a new image for Brazil and its capital, Rio de Janeiro, which was now portrayed as an international city that had outgrown its colonial heritage. If the Pereira Passos Reforms of 1906 had turned the Brazilian capital into an aspiring "Paris of the Americas," now the 1922 International Centennial Exhibition displayed that Parisian taste alongside the nation's new-found modernity.

While the Centennial Exhibition became an important event in the history of the country's attempts at building a positive international image, in financial terms it represented a heavy burden on the nation. The high cost of the event would contribute to the financial difficulties experienced by the next government, with the bills falling due at a very unfavorable moment. As we shall see next, after 1922 the Brazilian government would experience a period marked by continued attacks from the United States on the Brazilian coffee "valorization" schemes, as well as by a world recession that continuously stymied any influx of capital into the export-dependent South American country. The Brazilian currency, the *mil-réis*, would plummet in the second half of 1922, generating a financial crisis of huge proportions. Together with the investments in the aforementioned DNOCS, Epitácio Pessoa's lavish expenditure on the Centennial Exhibition had led to a severe fiscal crisis, and the economic downturn would have inevitably dire social and economic repercussions during the entire period from 1922 to 1926. The story of how the next President, Artur Bernardes, ruled Brazil under a state of siege during most of his four-year tenure will be told next.

Artur Bernardes (1922–1926)

Artur da Silva Bernardes (1875–1955) assumed the Brazilian presidency on November 15, 1922. His government faced fierce opposition from the Tenentista Movement and was marked by heavy social and political unrest. Upon taking office, one of the President's first tasks was to control a new revolt issuing from the ever-restless Rio Grande do Sul. The southernmost state had experienced a financial crisis under the leadership of provincial chieftain Borges de Medeiros (1863–1961), a politician who had inherited the government of Rio Grande do Sul from Júlio de Castilhos, the local dictator against whom the Federalist Revolution of 1893 had been directed.

On Castilhos's death in 1903, Medeiros became Rio Grande do Sul's official promoter of Comtean Positivism and its ideals of republican dictatorship. Castilhos and Medeiros represented the local version of

Pinheiro Machado's national Gaúcho leadership, which defended the Republic's survival by means of perpetuating its own faction's hold on power. With economic difficulties looming on the horizon for the powerful beef-curing oligarchs, however, Medeiros's rule was suddenly endangered. He had been in office since 1903, and his fifth re-election, in 1922, had angered his opponents. Led by another cattle raiser named Joaquim de Assis Brasil (1857–1938), the *Maragatos*, an old faction that fought Pinheiro Machado's *Pica-paus* in the Federalist Revolution, launched a series of attacks against the provincial government in the first weeks of 1923.

The Maragatos accused Medeiros's Riograndense Republican Party of electoral fraud. What ensued was something similar to the episode that had taken place in Bahia during Epitácio Pessoa's government, that is, after claiming electoral fraud the opposition attempted a *coup d'état*. The difference here, however, was the degree of disagreement and violence in which Rio Grande do Sul's society was traditionally mired, and how it affected the dispute. The incident awakened old resentments from the 1893 Federalist Revolution and the contending parties soon engaged in unchecked brutality and massacre. Assis Brasil and his followers inherited the agenda of the former Federalists, who had been led by Gaspar da Silveira Martins thirty years earlier: just as, in 1893, Martins's men had tried to overthrow Júlio de Castilhos, now Assis Brasil's army attempted to defeat Castilhos's successor, Borges de Medeiros.

The factions both adopted fashionable dress which bordered on the ridiculous: Medeiros's followers wore white scarves around their necks while Assis Brasil's troupe opted for a red styled cravat. With their colored mufflers, these angry mobs resumed the slaughter that had been interrupted by Floriano Peixoto and Pinheiro Machado in 1893 and that, as we have seen, had been a feature of the region's history since the establishment of the Sacramento Colony in 1680. The situation was further complicated by the fact that Medeiros had assumed an opposing stance to the recently installed government of Artur Bernardes. Contrary to the previous example in Bahia during Epitácio Pessoa's government, where the President had initiated a federal intervention to maintain the local rule of his allied oligarch, now the oligarch in power in Rio Grande do Sul was the President's political rival. During the 1921 presidential contest Medeiros had supported the candidacy of Nilo Peçanha, Bernardes's opponent and an historical ally to the Riograndenses. Added to that, the Gaúcho governor, unlike his predecessor, Júlio de Castilhos, could no longer count on the protection of Pinheiro Machado, who, using both his personal prestige as a republican senator, and his military clout as army commander, succeeded in maintaining the Castilhian local dictatorship from 1893 to 1903.

Medeiros's opposition to Bernardes thus gave the Maragatos the opportunity to attempt the coup. Assis Brasil believed that the recently elected President would not come to Medeiros's rescue, leaving the way clear for the Maragatos to seize power. The rebels, however, were unaware of Medeiros's political abilities, which altered the expected course of events. With rising pressure from the Tenentista Movement and the disturbing currency crisis that began in 1921, Bernardes had little interest in sustaining a civil war in the South to defend the interests of some local beef-curing oligarchs. He thus opted for a deal with Medeiros. Without federal support, Maragato morale soon waned and the bloody conflict came to an end in December 1923, with the signing of the so-called Pedras Altas Agreement. Borges de Medeiros would remain in power until 1928, but without the right to further re-election.[44]

The 1923 Rebellion would be called *Revolução Libertadora*, or the "Liberating Revolution," where "liberation" refered to freedom from Medeiros's local dictatorship. The uprising's outcome would have important repercussions in the future, for in 1928 Medeiros's appointed successor would seek reconciliation with the opposing faction, providing for enhanced Riograndense power and autonomy at the national level. Most importantly, the heir to the political heritage of Castilhos, Pinheiro Machado, and Medeiros would be none other than Getúlio Dornelles Vargas, the new *caudillo* who would rise to the government of Rio Grande do Sul in 1928 and then become the fiercest dictator in Brazilian history during the 1930s and 1940s.

In 1923, however, President Artur Bernardes had other more pressing problems to tend to besides those arising from the constant clashes among the southern landed gentry. The fierce attacks from the Tenentista Movement in São Paulo represented a bigger threat to the government than the discord in the South. In 1924 a second Tenentista revolt broke out. Known as São Paulo's 1924 Revolution, the uprising started on July 5, 1924, the day of the second anniversary of the 18 of the Copacabana Fort Revolt. The rebels occupied the city of São Paulo for 23 days, making the state's governor, Carlos de Campos, flee the city. President Bernardes intervened with the National Air Force. São Paulo was bombed and the rebels, led by the Riograndense General Isidoro Dias Lopes (1865–1949), retreated to the South at the end of July.[45]

By the end of October, the Tenentista Movement had also taken root in Rio Grande do Sul. There, the revolt against Bernardes came under the leadership of Luís Carlos Prestes (1898–1990), a Gaúcho brigadier who had been a sympathizer of the Maragato cause against Medeiros in 1923. Prestes commanded a first uprising in the city of Santo Ângelo, in late October 1924. Attacked by federal troops, he moved north with a group of Maragato leaders who joined his militia. In the city of Foz do Iguaçu, Paraná State, Prestes met with the rebels who had retreated from São Paulo a few months earlier and who were now under the leadership of Army General Miguel Costa (1885–1959). There, the two groups formed the so-called Luís Carlos Prestes–Miguel Costa Column, a military grouping that toured the country trying to gain recruits for the fight against Artur Bernardes and the nation's ruling oligarchies. The Column assumed a leftist ideology influenced by the ideals of the recently established Soviet Union, although Prestes himself, the movement's leader, would not become an avowed communist until later, in the 1930s.

For a long time, Brazilian historians regarded the Luis Carlos Prestes–Miguel Costa Column as part of a romantic adventure in the name of freedom. Fighting for a utopia, that is, the end of the old landed aristocracies' authoritarian rule, Prestes and his men would have set a precedent in Marxist revolutionary history, one that would have inspired Mao's Long March in China some ten years later. Recent studies, however, contradict the romantic view of the Luis Carlos Prestes–Miguel Costa Column. Evidence of rape, plunder, and murder of poor civilians along the 25,000 kilometers covered by the troops, most of them former Maragatos of Rio Grande do Sul, demand a serious re-think of the Column's history.[46]

The city of São Paulo was pacified in 1924, but Bernardes would continue to be pressed by the Column until the end of his term. Adding to the defiance against the government, which was implied in the revolutionary march that crossed the country, was a growing sense of dissatisfaction among the middle classes with the current economic situation.[47] In the final months of 1924, Bernardes began an orthodox policy of fiscal and monetary austerity. The contraction of the monetary base during 1925 achieved the government's desired deflationary results in 1926, but the political cost of the procedure was very high.

Bernardes's recessive policies of 1924 must be seen as resulting from impositions made by foreign creditors, mostly British bankers, who conditioned the adoption of fiscal austerity measures for the granting of a new loan to the federal government. Bernardes accepted all the provisions demanded by the British financial mission, the Montagu Mission, which arrived in Rio de Janeiro in December 1923. Among the demands was the transfer of the financial burden of the scheme for coffee "valorization" from the federal government to the state of São Paulo. This was completed in 1924, together with the dismissal of important São Paulo politicians from the government, such as the Minister of Finance, Rafael Sampaio Vidal (1870–1941), and the President of the Bank of Brazil, Cincinato Braga (1864–1953).

Bernardes was a man of strong liberal and industrializing convictions. As governor of his native Minas Gerais, he had promoted the incorporation of foreign capital into the establishment of the first major steel plant in Brazil, the Belgo-Mineira Metallurgy and Steel Industry, founded in 1921 with the financial support of the Belgian King, Albert I. Although a symbiotic relation between the capital derived from coffee production and that invested in the emerging national industry did exist, disagreements between the two facets of the national economy were frequent, especially with regard to the specific issues of foreign trade and tariffs.

As we have seen, since the Imperial Era, the question of tariffs saw the landlords on one side pitted against the industrialists on the other. In an export economy of primary products, tariffs and monetary policies tended to favor one sector at the expense of the other. It was thus that Bernardes's 1924 stand against São Paulo's agricultural interests was not contrary to his ideological inclinations, but the influence of the British mission was undoubtedly a determining factor in the President's decision. The *Instituto de Defesa Permanente do Café* (Institute for the Permanent Defense of Coffee), a federal organ established in 1922 to organize the scheme of coffee valorization, was transferred in 1924 to the newly created *Instituto do Café de São Paulo*, thus confirming the federal government's transfer of the valorization scheme to the province. The latter began constructing large depositories where the production surplus was kept as part of the valorization scheme. This practice contributed to non-stop overproduction, which would prove disastrous in 1929 when the influx of foreign loans that benefited coffee producers as part of the valorization scheme would suddenly halt.

In order to compensate for popular dissatisfaction at the government's deflationary and recessive economic measures, Bernardes focused on a foreign policy of international prestige centered on enhancing Brazil's position in the League of Nations. Brazil had been one of the founding members of the League in 1919 and, from the start, had pushed for permanent membership of its Council. The League Council had been established with four permanent members, Great Britain, France, Italy, and Japan, and four non-permanent members, Brazil, Belgium, Greece, and Spain. The League's Kantian/Wilsonian stance of favoring international law over balance of power as the way to build world peace hit one of

Brazil's historical foreign policy objectives, namely securing the principle of equality among sovereign states. Brazil had ardently defended the principle ever since the Hague Conference of 1907, when the many-time presidential candidate and disastrous Finance Minister, Rui Barbosa, acting as Brazil's representative, repudiated the idea of classifying nations in different ranks in the procedures of the arbitration court that was being created by the Conference.[48]

The permanent membership of the League's Council was thus a matter of prestige, one that was construed not only for Brazil itself, but also for all the "second rate" nations that had historically gravitated around the Central Powers. With the demand for permanent membership of the Council, Brazil tried to take for itself the role of leader of the weak and destitute. Even if sitting with the powerful at the Council's table would not immediately turn the former Portuguese colony into a major league player, it would at least grant it supremacy over all the other minor league ones.

Brazil's aims were thwarted when Germany re-entered the international arena after the signing of the Locarno Treaties of 1926. The Weimar Republic was immediately admitted to the League of Nations with permanent membership of the Council. This angered Bernardes, who ordered the Brazilian representatives to veto Germany's admission to the organization. In a humiliating turn of events, the Brazilian veto was repudiated and Bernardes withdrew from the League on June 14, 1926. Brazil was the first founding member to withdraw from an organization that would soon founder, incapable of realizing its declared goals. The contradiction between the ideal of equality among sovereign nations and the reality of power asymmetry in international relations became clear with the prevalence of the old Central Powers in the organization dedicated to maintaining world peace.

Bernardes completed his term in office without securing Brazil's long-sought-after international prestige. Furthermore, Prestes and his Column continued to be a source of strong opposition to the President throughout the country. Economic recession continued to incite popular dissatisfaction. The man who had assumed the presidency four years earlier under a national state of siege now passed his office to a politician from São Paulo, obeying the "coffee-and-milk" scheme agreed in the Ouro Fino Pact of 1913. Washington Luís Pereira de Sousa, the former São Paulo State Secretary of Justice and Public Safety, assumed the presidency on November 15, 1926. He would be the last ruler of Brazil's First Republic.

Washington Luís (1926–1930)

Washington Luís (1869–1957) was the sole official candidate for the presidency in the 1926 election. He was elected with 99.7% of the vote. The man who had pacified the general strikes of 1906 and 1917 now had to find a solution to the problem of Luís Carlos Prestes and his Column. Unlike his previous actions in São Paulo, however, Washington Luís now opted for a more conciliatory strategy. He freed the greater part of the political prisoners who had been taken into custody under the Artur Bernardes government. The Brazilian Communist Party, which had been outlawed immediately after its establishment in 1922, would be made legal in January 1927. The state of siege, which had been in place since the beginning of Bernardes's government, and under which the State's guarantees of individual rights had been suspended, was discontinued in most of the country, remaining in effect only in the regions directly affected by the Column. Without ever gaining the desired popular support for his revolutionary enterprise, Prestes's long march ended in 1927, when the revolutionaries disbanded near the frontier with Bolivia. The march's foremost aim of ousting Bernardes had not been achieved, and with a new president in office its reason for existing was no longer.

A period of internal peace ensued. As governor of São Paulo, Luís had become known as a great builder of roads. His motto, *Governar é abrir estradas* (To govern is to open roads), chimed well with the country's need to occupy the western part of its territory. The President's efforts at colonization would be followed up by his successor, Getúlio Vargas, who would establish the famous *Marcha para o Oeste* (March to the West), a series of governmental incentives for internal migration and the occupation of the central Brazilian plateau, which extends from the country's geographic center in the direction of Paraguay.

After Preste's Column was disbanded, the President took measures to ensure the suppression of any new revolutionary attempts springing from the Tenentista Movement. In June 1927, the National Congress approved the *Lei Celerada*, a law that imposed restrictions on the activities of the proletarian movement and allowed the government to intervene in trades unions. The bill also established heavy press censorship and restrictions on the right of assembly, creating a new class of crimes based on "ideological offenses," that is, crimes comprising any idea that incited conflict between employers and employees. With this new mood of restrictiveness, the Communist Party was again made illegal in August 1927. The issuing of the Celerada Law was indicative of the long way the nation would still have to travel before its people achieved individual liberty and freedom of expression.[49]

While social control was maintained under the grip of oppressive legal arrangements, the favorable economic position achieved in the final months of 1926 also contributed to the climate of political stability. The country had recovered from the currency crisis of 1922 and, since the end of Artur Bernardes's government, the balance of payments had shown remarkable improvement. Washington Luís maintained Bernardes's fiscal austerity, but promoted important changes in monetary and exchange-rate policies. Together with his Minister of Finance, the Riograndense Getúlio Dornelles Vargas, the new president secured Brazil's return to the international gold standard system, establishing in December 1926 the *Caixa de Estabilização*, a new organ of the Treasury similar to the *Caixa de Conversão* that had operated before the First World War. This automatic system of money supply was intended to preserve the low inflation rate that had been achieved in the past few years and to help sustain the austere fiscal policy of low government spending. A monetary reform ensued with the birth of the *cruzeiro*, a new currency that would replace the *mil-réis*.

The influx of foreign investment resumed with considerable intensity in 1926. After the recession of 1921–1922, GDP growth reached 5.6% in 1926, 10.8% in 1927, and 11.5% in 1928. Brazil's international image was improving together with its positive economic performance. In December 1928, U.S. President-elect Herbert Hoover paid an official visit to Rio de Janeiro. Hoover's administration would initiate the Good Neighbor policy in Latin America. The idea was to suggest that the times of Theodore Roosevelt's Big Stick were over. The *Realpolitik* of U.S. hemispheric hegemony and its fearful specter of military intervention in Latin America were being relaxed in favor of cultural diplomacy. Washington Luís received Hoover in Rio de Janeiro in a climate of national celebration. The "unwritten alliance" of Rio Branco's time was now consolidated by Brazil's new economic prosperity and internal calm. By all appearances, the southern giant was ready and able to become a useful and trusted ally to the United States in its quest for world power.[50]

Brazil's apparent stability, however, would soon come to an end with the world economic crisis in 1929. The country's balance of payments was sustained primarily through surpluses in the capital account, which floundered under the sudden interruption of foreign capital inflows. Without the ability to contract new loans, and with Washington Luís's insistence on maintaining the Caixa de Estabilização in full operation, the country was doomed to a new currency crisis. The Caixa de Estabilização would continue to exist until November 22, 1930, almost a month after, as we will see, the President was deposed. Its effects on the economy were harmful in that it did not allow for free monetary policy when foreign reserves began to crumble. GDP growth plummeted from 11.5% in 1928 to 1.10% in 1929, and then to a negative -2.10% in 1930. Coffee overproduction, enhanced by the valorization policies of the Coffee Institute of São Paulo, contributed to the deterioration of the commodity's international price. The contraction in foreign demand hit coffee prices still further, bringing down with it the entire undiversified Brazilian economy.

In 1929, the size and capacity of Brazilian industry still fell short of any developed nation. The period of the First World War had witnessed important growth in manufacturing plants, but as long as coffee revenues provided enough income for the ruling oligarchies, industrialization would continue to be sluggish. The need to create new industries was a hot topic of debate among economists. A significant part of the country's intelligentsia favored the traditional agricultural model at the expense of industrial growth.[51] Nonetheless, some effort at industrialization was in fact made, the most notable example being the establishment of the *Centro das Indústrias do Estado de São Paulo*, known by the acronym CIESP, in 1928. The Organization promoted the convergence of some of São Paulo's most powerful industrial capitalists and supported research on methods and procedures for enhancing industrial output and reaching markets. CIESP's first president was Francisco Matarazzo (1854–1937), a business tycoon who had arrived in Brazil in 1881 as a poor Italian immigrant hoping to make his fortune with Italian pasta. He was to become the country's richest man and foremost industrialist. CIESP appointed as vice-president Roberto Simonsen (1889–1948), a polymath who would become one of Brazil's leading politicians and intellectuals. Simonsen's father was a Jewish British banker who, after arriving in Brazil, had become involved with the coffee barons of São Paulo. The Simonsen family actually represents the growing intermingling between agricultural and industrial capital which began in the late 1920s. Simonsen's brother, Wallace Cochrane Simonsen, was one of the country's foremost coffee brokers during the First Republic. As we will see, it would not be long before coffee revenue began to be invested in industrial output.

In 1929, however, CIESP suffered a severe blow. Since the capital invested in industrial production came from two interlinked sources, coffee revenues and foreign loans, Brazilian industrialization was affected when these both faltered at the same time. It was the investments made before 1929 that enabled the nascent Brazilian industry to survive. The idle capacity previously created would contribute to the country's relatively fast economic recovery from the global crisis, which would become evident starting 1933. In any case, with the new restrictions on imports from 1929, the national industry was again called upon to undertake a process of import substitution similar to that witnessed during the First World War.

Together with the country's general financial situation, CIESP showed signs of recovery in the early years of the 1930s, although it would suffer further blows throughout the decade, when the centralizing policies of Getúlio Vargas would begin intervening in its activities. As we will see in more detail below, Vargas would turn the Brazilian State into something akin to a central syndicate to which employers and employees were compulsorily affiliated. With the rise of Riograndense totalitarianism and its Decree 19770 of 1931, known as the Syndicate Law, the CIESP would be replaced by the FIESP, a distinct organization with the function of representing the central government in its implementation of conciliatory policies between the bourgeoisie and the working class. The original CIESP would be rebuilt in 1942.[52]

1929 was thus a year of crisis for the Brazilian Republic, just as it was for most countries around the world. The peculiarity of the Brazilian case was that the crash in the New York stock market prevented the influx of capital to a nation that survived primarily on loans. The reality of São Paulo's rise to national leadership during the First Republic had been to a great extent the reality of its foreign debt. In its enthusiasm for federalism and decentralization, the 1891 Constitution had allowed for individual states to contract foreign loans independently from the central government, a proviso that São Paulo took as a blessing. The scheme of coffee valorization was thus a godsend for the coffee barons, and one they took full advantage of. It functioned as if the producer contracted a loan to buy his own production and then let someone else, meaning the central government, pay for that loan. From 1889 to 1930, the state of São Paulo contracted 25 international loans, and its debt rose to more than half that of all other Brazilian states combined. Needless to say, as long as the coffee-and-milk arrangement was preserved, that is, as long as São Paulo and Minas Gerais continued to alternate in power, São Paulo could continue its financial indulgence, for the federal government would guarantee the coffee barons' loans. The whole scheme included the Taubaté Accord and the Ouro Fino Pact as two sides of the same coin. The crisis of 1929 thus brought to the fore the unfair power structure existing among the Brazilian states. São Paulo's default meant the Brazilian Republic's default, and the cost had to be paid by all Brazilians.

After the catastrophic interlude of 1910–1914, when the southern warlords of Rio Grande do Sul managed to temporarily spoil the Paulistas' and Mineiros' joint control of Rio de Janeiro, the rule of the coffee-and-milk states had been restored, and it was clear that the bond between the two states was what kept everything else in place. In 1929, it was still evident that, even with all its might and economic prosperity, São Paulo was not yet ready to face Rio Grande do Sul by itself. Washington Luís, however, decided to let the old flame ignited in 1913 with the Ouro Fino Pact wane. He decided to break the agreement and distance himself from Minas Gerais in the upcoming presidential election.

The 1929 Crisis brought to the fore a series of profound contradictions existing among the various agricultural oligarchies of the different Brazilian states. Coffee producers from São Paulo and Minas Gerais began to diverge on whether the scheme of coffee valorization should continue to be controlled by the Coffee Institute of São Paulo. The Mineiros had finally come to the conclusion that it was necessary to limit the privileges of the Paulistas. Discontent also arose in the North and Northeast regions. Producers of cotton, tobacco and cocoa began to raise their voices against São Paulo's excessive prerogatives in what should otherwise have been a just and equal federal pact among equal partners. The cost of the coffee barons' loans had, for too long, been paid with the impoverishment of the outlying states of Brazil's pseudo federation. In Rio Grande do Sul, dissatisfaction among the beef curer/military/landowners was as high as ever. The bill they had to pay to maintain São Paulo's growing prosperity was one that they did not think they should be paying at all. Given their mostly Spanish heritage and their previous attempts at independence, even the idea of supporting São Paulo's development, which by 1929 made the southernmost state look like a large medieval fiefdom, was to them simply exasperating. Rio Grande do Sul lacked the advantages available to an export economy, to which the federal system allowed considerable autonomy. Historically, Rio Grande do Sul's meat and rice had only served the internal market. As such, the state was dependent on the demand generated by the more developed regions of the North. As we have seen, one of the major causes of the whimsical Farroupilha Revolution of 1835 had been the interruption in that very demand caused by interprovincial tariffs established with the Additional Act of 1834. In 1929, almost one hundred years later, not much had changed in the still monochrome economy run by the southern warlords. Capitalist development in Rio Grande do Sul was sluggish and subsidiary to that of São Paulo's. But this was not clearly understood by the beef curers. Drowning in their militarist-positivist-dictatorial ideology, they began plotting the occupation of São Paulo, which would be carried out by means of controlling the federal government.

The resentment of the Rio Grandenses was given an outlet when Washington Luís broke the Ouro Fino Pact during his presidential run of 1930. As we have seen, the agreement between São Paulo and Minas Gerais established that presidents from each state would alternate in power. Washington Luís now decided to support a candidate from his own state, instead of backing someone from Minas Gerais. Júlio Prestes (1882–1946), the current governor of São Paulo, was chosen by Luís as his successor with the support of all other Brazilian states except Minas Gerais, Rio Grande do Sul, and Paraíba. These formed the *Aliança Liberal*, a political coalition that advanced the agenda of the three dissident regional oligarchies together with some of the demands of the Tenentista Movement and its sympathizing urban middle classes. The entente cordiale was formed on June 17, 1929 when Minas Gerais's governor, Antônio Carlos de Andrada (1870–1946), withdrew his candidacy for the upcoming elections and gave his support to Rio Grande do Sul's governor Getúlio Dornelles Vargas (1882–1954). Supporting Vargas, Paraíba's current governor and former President Epitácio Pessoa's nephew, João Pessoa Cavalcanti de Albuquerque (1878–1930), stood for the vice-presidency. This was the second time since 1889 that Minas Gerais and Rio Grande do Sul would stand together to face São Paulo, and it would be the second time that São Paulo would be defeated.

Nevertheless, São Paulo's candidate, Júlio Prestes, won the election of March 1930, with 59.39% of the vote, ahead of Vargas's 40.41%. Contributing to the whimsicality of electoral results that was customary in Brazil's First Republic, Vargas would have received 100% of the vote in Rio Grande do Sul. Nonetheless, the Liberal Alliance's leaders contested the election as fraudulent. They began talking of an armed revolt, voicing outright rage. After a few weeks, however, tensions began to subdue. The dissident oligarchies started hesitating. It was then that an unexpected incident changed the course of events.

On July 26, 1930, the Alliance's candidate for the vice-presidency, João Pessoa, was murdered in Recife, the capital city of Pernambuco State. The murder was a crime of passion perpetrated by a political rival, the lawyer and journalist João Duarte Dantas (1888–1930). The crime resulted from Pessoa's denunciation of Dantas in the press accusing him of a love affair with a woman named Anaíde Beiriz (1905–1930), a schoolteacher and feminist who, in the eyes of conservative Paraiban society, was perceived as a libertine and as someone unsuitable for a young politician of distinguished background such as Dantas. The story ended in tragedy when, after murdering Pessoa, Dantas was found dead in prison and Beiriz died shortly after by taking poison. The Paraibans' misfortune became a political trump card in the hands of the shrewd Alliance politicians. The murder of one of their leading members served as pretext for the events which began on October 3, 1930, when a group of revolutionaries in Rio Grande do Sul assumed control of the army's headquarters in Porto Alegre, the state's capital. The following day, the entire state took up arms. Osvaldo Aranha (1894–1960), a cunning politician who during the 1923 Revolution had defended Borges de Medeiros's republican dictatorship, led the Gaúchos in a national uprising. Aranha was supported by his fellow Riograndense, Lindolfo Leopoldo Boeckel Collor (1890–1942), a German descendant who had been the Riograndense Republican Party's leader since 1919 and whose grandson, Fernando Collor de Mello (b. 1949), would become Brazil's president in 1990. Entangled from the start in the inter-oligarchic dispute, by the end of October, Minas Gerais was completely taken over by the revolutionaries. Paraíba soon joined Rio Grande do Sul and Minas Gerais under the leadership of José Américo de Almeida (1887–1980), a local political leader and novelist who would become Paraíba State's governor from 1951 to 1956.

The Tenentista Movement was also an important supporting revolutionary force throughout the country. Among its lieutenants figured some of the future military dictators who would control the nation with violence and oppression between 1964 and 1985. Emílio Garrastazu Médici (1905–1985), Artur da Costa e Silva (1899–1969), and Ernesto Beckmann Geisel (1907–1996), all three of them born in Rio Grande do Sul, were the lieutenants of 1930 who would serve as presidents in the series of military dictatorships that started in 1964. Another future president who took part in the Tenentista side of the Revolution was the Ceará-born Humberto de Alencar Castelo Branco (1897–1967). Several other future military members of Brazil's extreme right were also active in the Tenentista Movement: Juracy Magalhães (1905–2001), who would become Humberto de Alencar Castelo Branco's Foreign Minister in 1966; Juarez Távora (1898–1975), who had fought in the 1924 uprising against Artur Bernardes and later joined Prestes's Column, would run as presidential candidate in 1955 for the national right-wing party; Eduardo Gomes (1896–1981), one of the survivors of the first Tenentista revolt of 1922 in the Copacabana Fort, would be a presidential candidate in 1945 and then take part in the military *coup d'état* that would overthrow the Riograndense president, João Goulart, in 1964.

The disparity between the political standpoints of these right-wing lieutenants and that of the foremost leader of Tenentismo, Luís Carlos Prestes, reveals the Movement's complexity and lack of cohesion. While the aforementioned officers would gradually turn to the right of the political spectrum, Prestes would join the Communist Party in the early 1930s. Such a discrepancy deserves deeper analysis. Looking at how the Movement developed from an initial opposition against the established oligarchies in 1922 into a military uprising and a movement that crossed the country spreading leftist ideals in 1924, it is hard to imagine it becoming a breeding ground for future extreme-right dictators. The reality of Tenentismo's lack of cohesion suggests divisions, disagreements and ideological u-turns among its members. All lieutenants shared the same goal of overthrowing the powerful oligarchs, but their means for achieving this, and the results they expected from it, varied enormously.

In any case, the solution to the riddle of the lieutenants' shift to the right can be seen in the way Rio Grande do Sul took over the Tenentista Movement in 1930. The prevailing authoritarian doctrine of the Riograndense military schools must have played an important role in the Tenentista Movement's ideological conversion. For that same doctrinal standpoint provided the intellectual backdrop to what would be the two bloody Gaúcho dictatorships of 1930–1945 and 1964–1985.

On October 19, 1930, the Riograndense revolutionary troops entered the city of Curitiba, where Getúlio Vargas, the Revolution's leader, was received enthusiastically by the population. The state of Paraná had joined the Revolution on October 5, and its revolutionary government was under the command of General Mário Tourinho (1871–1964) who, in his younger days, had fought against the Riograndense federalists in the Lapa resistance of 1893, then under the orders of General Gomes Carneiro. Without the support of the navy, the revolutionaries under Getúlio Vargas had moved north by rail. They had met some resistance from the legalist troops of Washington Luís in the city of Florianópolis, but had finally taken that city in mid-October. A larger battle was expected to occur in the city of Itararé, at the border between the states of Paraná and São Paulo, but on October 24, Admiral Isaías de Noronha (1874–1963), together with Generals Tasso Fragoso (1869–1945) and Mena Barreto (1874–1933), the latter a Riograndense commander who had also fought against the federalists in 1893, deposed Washington Luís in Rio de Janeiro.

On the first day of November 1930, the military junta that had been established a few days earlier passed command of the nation to Getúlio Vargas. The Riograndense soldiers who had brought their *caudilho* from the far, distant, and rural Rio Grande do Sul, had vowed to tie their horses to the obelisk that stood in the capital's central avenue and raise their Gaúcho leader to the leadership of the nation. Their vow was fullfiled. The monument built during President Rodrigues Alves's Pereira Passos reforms, a symbol of São Paulo's hegemony, had now been taken over by the Riograndenses. The arrogant gesture symbolized the victory of a lineage and of an ideology whose survival depended on the total control of the central government and on the suppression of all opposition. The logic of the southern warlords Júlio de Castilhos, Pinheiro Machado, and Borges de Medeiros had finally achieved its desired conclusion in the hands of their direct descendant, the landlord from the provincial city of São Borja, Getúlio Dornelles Vargas. The first Brazilian Republic thus ended, and its demise was synonymous with the defeat of São Paulo.

Culture and Society in the First Brazilian Republic

The first Brazilian Republic witnessed the rise of São Paulo as the nation's cultural center. The city's industrial leadership and its expansion of commercial and service areas went hand in hand with its attraction of a large number of artists and immigrants. The city's ethnic make-up soon became more diversified than that of the country's capital, Rio de Janeiro. Its population growth also occurred at a much higher rate. In 1890 the city had 64,934 residents; by 1930 that number had increased more than tenfold to 822,400. Rio de Janeiro continued to be the most populated city in Brazil during the entire period, but its growth rate fell short of that of São Paulo. The nation's capital would be surpassed by São Paulo in population in the 1950s. It had started 1890 with 522,651 residents, almost ten times more than São Paulo, and by 1960 it had 3,307,163 against São Paulo's 3,825,351.

As we have seen, São Paulo's economic and population growth occurred at the expense of other Brazilian states, generating regional imbalances with greater poverty in the regions at a distance from the economic center. The legacy of the First Republic would be one in which peripheral states would be more and more deprived of their share of the national revenue and would be hindered from achieving autonomous development. São Paulo's subsidized agriculture based on coffee exports, which, as we have seen, was sustained by means of foreign loans paid by the federal government, managed to generate most of the country's income, but at the same time used up all its financial resources. The political collusion between São Paulo and Minas Gerais, in the "coffee-and-milk" arrangement, meant that the bill for their prosperity was shared by all the federal states. When this situation became unacceptable to the totalitarian and militaristic Riograndenses, the way was open to civil war.

In spite of its untenable political circumstances, the period from 1889 to 1930 saw remarkable new forms of culture and an increasingly multi-ethnic countenance appearing across the bustling tropical nation. Brazilian society showed important signs of modernization in several areas, and technology began to emerge locally in tandem with the economic prosperity of the coffee barons. One such barons, a man named Alberto Santos-Dumont (1873–1932), would dedicate most of his life to aeronautical study and experimentation, establishing in the country the beginnings of what soon became a solid aviation industry. With his airplane, named *14-bis*, Santos-Dumont would accomplish the world's first powered heavier-than-air flight made without the use of a launching rail on October 23, 1906. The flight was made in Paris, where the Brazilian aviator lived most of his life. Brazilians claim Santos-Dumont's place in the history of aviation, challenging the idea of the Wright brothers' precedence in creating a proper airplane. The First Republic's coffee wealth allowed also the emergence of pioneering women aviators in the city of São Paulo. Teresa De Marzo (1903–1986) and Anésia Pinheiro Machado (1904–1999), the latter a cousin of the powerful senator assassinated in 1915, made their first flights in 1922.

Art and technology went hand in hand as Brazil maintained strong cultural ties with Europe. In literature, the period's initial years saw the peak of Naturalism with its vigorous descriptive acumen and keen social criticism. Two masterpieces mark the crowning of Émile Zola's style in the tropics: Aluísio Azevedo's aforementioned *O Cortiço* (*The Slum*, 1890) and Euclides da Cunha's *Os Sertões* (*Rebellion in the Backlands*, 1902). The first puts Rio de Janeiro center-stage in a narrative where the city's various ethnic groups, that is, Portuguese and other European immigrants, blacks and mulattos, mingle in a lower-class tenement of the type that would be destroyed during Rodrigues Alves's Pereira Passos reforms. The second novel takes the reader to the carnage of the Canudos Rebellion and to the struggle by the poor and illiterate countrymen of Bahia against poverty, drought and political corruption during the first years of the Republic.

Os Sertões is frequently classified by Brazilian literary historians as belonging to the period called "pre-modernism," a term devised by the influential critic Alceu Amoroso Lima (1893–1983). Amoroso Lima was a conservative intellectual who would fight for freedom of expression during the dictatorial period beginning in 1964 and who would introduce the movement of Christian democracy to Brazil. Other literary scholars emerging during the First Republic would also be influential in future political and cultural developments. A brief note on literary historiography with a focus on the concept of pre-modernism will help us better understand the cultural developments in the period. Besides Amoroso Lima, the concept appears also in the works of literary historian Alfredo Bosi (b. 1936), but is undermined in the work of another important critic, Afrânio Coutinho (1911–2000). The general idea of a pre-modernism reflects the tendency of Brazilian literary critics to emphasize Modernism (of which more bellow) as a privileged standpoint from where to observe the cultural and artistic production of the first decades of the twentieth century. Instead of a more linear analysis that perceives late-nineteenth-century aesthetic tendencies such as Naturalism and Impressionism as moving into Modernism, or the avant-garde, most Brazilian critics prefer to focus on the avant-garde and then look back to what came before it as a sort of preparatory stage. Be that as it may, for our present purposes the core of what these critics call "pre-modernism" is understood as high-Naturalism, an aesthetic that flourished with remarkable intensity in the initial period of Brazil's First Republic.

Naturalism's sense of historical and sociological engagement allowed for the production of a literature that mirrored the political and economic transformations of Brazilian society at the turn of the twentieth century. Bustling city life became the very dye used on the canvas of naturalist writers such as Lima Barreto (1881–1922) and João do Rio (1881–1921). With Naturalism, social criticism became a strong feature in the literature of the period, as becomes clear from Barreto's *Recordações do Escrivão Isaias Caminha* (1909), where the author tells the story of a young man who moves to Rio de Janeiro in the hope of finding a life of excitement and success only to discover a society where the old privileges of the aristocracy and the military are preserved in a Republic that fails to fulfill its mission of democratization and egalitarianism. In Barreto's republican Rio de Janeiro, racism thrives just as it had done in the old monarchic slave system. In *Triste Fim de Policarpo Quaresma* (1911), the same author portrays the artificial nature of late-nineteenth-century urban Brazilian society, where the protagonist's nationalist fervor and distinguished literary *connaissance* contrasts with the mediocrity of his hypocritical friends and acquaintances. The novel includes several historical events, bringing the figure of Floriano Peixoto and the monarchist naval revolts of 1893 and 1894 to bear upon the protagonist's final demise. In a vein similar to that of Barreto's, João do Rio's *A alma encantadora das ruas* (1908) and *Dentro da noite* (1910) explored in a high-naturalist style themes such as human perversion, madness, and desire. Evil and anger spread through the bohemian life of the capital, where the strong French influence of *Belle Époque* style contrasts with the poverty and decay of the local night dwellers. Following the Pereira Passos reforms, the introduction of streetlighting to Rio de Janeiro in 1907 allowed for the emergence of a new urban nightlife, full of sensuality and voluptuousness, which is rendered in great detail in João do Rio's texts.

The sociological perspective of Naturalism was also present in the portrayals of life in distant provincial areas where individuals were estranged from the rapidly developing urban society of Rio de Janeiro and São Paulo. Authors Graça Aranha (1868–1931) and Monteiro Lobato (1882–1948) presented deterministic views of de-centered and economically afflicted social types. In *Canaã* (1902), for instance, Aranha portrays the life of German immigrants in the northeastern state of Espirito Santo. Depictions of the hard life of newly arrived immigrants, combined with theoretical reflections about German racial superiority, pervade this work, which had a strong impact on Brazilian literature in 1902. In *Urupês* (1918), Monteiro Lobato also adopted naturalist techniques to establish what critics defined as the school of Realist Regionalism in Brazilian narrative.[53] A collection of short stories, *Urupês* offers a non-idealized version of the indigenous Brazilian, a version that differs substantially from the nationalist portrayals of late-nineteenth-century writers. Contrary to the general trend in Brazilian Romanticism, where, especially in its *indigenista* phase, native Brazilians were celebrated according to Rousseaunian ideals of the noble savage, Lobato perceives in the *caboclo*, that is, the Brazilian Indian in its modern version, the source of all the nation's maladies. Illiteracy, lack of motivation, and the absence of governmental care produced the archetypal Brazilian rural individual, the *Jeca Tatu*. Lobato's protagonist in *Urupês* is portrayed as uncivilized, introspective, and dirty.

During the First Republic, poetry also flourished under Naturalism's scientific and empiricist approaches to reality. Here the foremost figure is Augusto dos Anjos (1884–1914). *Eu* (1912), the author's only poetry collection published during his lifetime, presents a rich textual web of themes and influences that run from nineteenth-century French Naturalism, atheism, and existentialism to Buddhism and phenomenology. The poet combines scientificism with an anti-bourgeois temperament, drawing freely on Eastern and Western traditions to express suffering and anxiety while pointing to the possibility of liberation. Both pessimism and optimism figure side by side in dos Anjos' complex and concise poetic works, which attest to the relative maturity of early-twentieth-century Brazilian literature. Other noteworthy poets of the period are Raul de Leoni (1895–1926), whose *Ode a um poeta morto* (1919) combines perfected form with expressions of weariness and the meaningless of life, and Gilka Machado (1893–1980), a celebrated female voice whose *Cristais Partidos* (1915) discloses a new perspective on female eroticism previously unseen in Brazilian writing.

The advent of *Modernismo*, the Brazilian avant-garde movement, is generally considered to be the most important cultural and artistic phenomenon of the First Republic. The movement's official start came with a large-scale arts festival held at the Municipal Theater in São Paulo from February 11 to 18, 1922. The festival was called *Semana de Arte Moderna* (Modern Art Week), and it featured the visual arts, music and literature in an all-out event that brought together some of the most representative Brazilian artists of the time. The Semana's aim was to present Brazilian modernist aesthetics to the general public. The fundamental disposition was strictly avant-garde: artists attempted to counter what they perceived as the stiffness of academicism, represented primarily by the Brazilian Academy of Letters, which was founded in Rio de Janeiro in 1897 and had as its first two presidents Machado de Assis (1897–1908) and Rui Barbosa (1908–1919).

In its classic avant-garde disposition, the Semana and its *Modernismo* attempted to break with tradition and sought to *épater le bourgeois* (shake the bourgeoisie). The paradoxical aspect of the event, however, was its being sponsored by the very bourgeoisie whose values it intended to defy. São Paulo's Municipal Theater, the Semana's venue, was a traditional meeting place for São Paulo's aristocracy. Its construction had started in 1903 with materials imported from Europe, and by 1922 it had become one of the world's best settings for the staging of operas. The Semana's audience was composed mostly of São Paulo's elite, a crowd of belle époque dandies who felt free to boo the anti-bourgeois artistic productions seen on the stage. The artists themselves were also mostly from the upper class. The complete absence of black artists in the event suggests the exclusivist nature of São Paulo's avant-garde movement in 1922.

The Semana created commotion and dissention at a time where art was defined in strict and singular terms, with little room left for deviation. Some of the so-called "pre-modernists" were quick to publish harsh public criticisms of the "modernists." The most remarkable of such criticisms came from Monteiro Lobato, whose fracas with the avant-garde had started in 1917 after the publication of his testy critique of painter Anita Malfatti (1889–1964) on the occasion of her exhibition in São Paulo. Malfatti was coming back to Brazil from a period of study in Europe and the United States and was attempting to introduce modern art to the Brazilian public. Lobato severely criticized her influences from German expressionism, which were described as the product of an epistemological distortion. An irreconcilable mutual dislike was the inevitable result.

The Semana had, as some of its most representative artists, the painters Anita Malfatti and Emiliano di Cavalcanti (1897–1976); sculptors Victor Brecheret (1894–1955) and the German born Wilhelm Haarberg (1891–1986); architects Antonio Garcia Moya (1891–1949) and Georg Przyrembel (1885–1956), the first born in Spain, the second in Poland; the composer Heitor Villa-Lobos (1887–1959) and the pianist Guiomar Novaes (1895–1979); and writers Mário de Andrade (1893–1945), Oswald de Andrade (1890–1954), Menotti Del Picchia (1892–1988), Plínio Salgado (1895–1975), Ronald de Carvalho (1893–1935), and the "pre-modernist" recently converted to the avant-garde Graça Aranha (1868–1931).[54]

Brazilian Modernism repeated the bourgeoisie-against-itself style of other national avant-garde movements, with the difference that it had a defined project of establishing a national culture capable of transcending its former European models. The high degree of nationalism involved in the aesthetic principles of the Brazilian avant-garde make it a misfit among its contemporaries around the world. While avant-garde movements across the globe strove mostly for internationalism, universality, and openness, the Brazilian movement looked for a national identity. The roots of the Brazilian avant-garde's strong nationalism must be sought in the country's own history of art, above all in the tone set during the Imperial Era by institutions such as the Brazilian Historic and Geographic Institute (IHGB) and the Imperial Academy of Art, which, as we have seen, aimed at building a sense of national belonging through the arts. One could say that the traditional nationalist vein survived into the twentieth century, producing a tendency towards self-centered expressions and the production of artworks with a diminished universalizing disposition and limited interest outside the national boundaries.

The central figure of the Brazilian nationalistic avant-garde movement was the polymath Mário de Andrade, who revolutionized Brazilian letters with his 1922 poetry collection *Paulicéia Desvairada* (Hallucinated City). The book brought the novelty of free verse to Brazilian poetry, doing away with the formal constraints of the academicism that had prevailed before. The artist's production includes novels, musicology, art history, criticism, and photography. His novel *Macunaíma* (1928) became one of the founding texts of Brazilian Modernism. In it, the protagonist is a sort of anti-hero who is portrayed as possessing the most common qualities associated with Brazilians in general, namely hedonism and laziness. These combine with the misnomer *Tupiniquim*: Macunaíma was born in a fictional indigenous tribe and had to move to São Paulo, from where culture shock and an array of misadventures followed. The work attempted to convey spoken Brazilian language in writing, and was based on the author's research in ethnography and folklore. Mário de Andrade was also a pioneer in the field of ethnomusicology in Brazil. His *Ensaio sobre Música Brasileira* (Essay on Brazilian Music, 1928) opened up the discussion of a national musical aesthetic.[55]

The second most important figure of Brazilian Modernism was probably the poet and cultural agitator Oswald de Andrade. Born into a wealthy family, Andrade used his money to support Brazilian artists and their modernist adventures in the 1920s and 1930s. With his *Pau-Brasil Manifesto* (1924), the author articulated some of the aesthetic principles of the Brazilian avant-garde, among them tropicalism and primitivism. His subsequent *Manifesto Antropofágico* (1928) sets the idea of enhancing Brazilian art's transformative power in the face of European influence: if Brazilian art could not completely shun foreign elements and aesthetic tendencies, it should intentionally devour and transform them, producing something new and expressive of the national character. The underlying idea became that of "cannibalism," thus associating the new Brazilian art with the habit of eating human flesh characteristic of some of the country's indigenous tribes.

An even more nationalistic vein of Brazilian Modernism appears with authors Plínio Salgado and Menotti del Pichia, who after 1922 created the *Movimento Verde-Amarelo* (Yellow and Green Movement), a dissident movement within the initial *Modernismo* that extolled the indigenous element of Brazilian culture with unchecked enthusiasm and exaggerated patriotism. The movement emphasized the indigenous Tupi language and culture as the true bearer of Brazilian identity. It established a close association with fascism in the 1930s, when Plínio Salgado, adding a stronger political dimension to his cultural agenda, established the so-called Integralist Movement. The parallel with Marinetti's Futurism in Italy is noticeable. In 1932, the new Yellow and Green Movement would be transformed in the *Ação Integralista Brasileira* (AIB), an outright fascist national party that would attempt a *coup d'état* in 1938.

Among modernist poets, the name of Manuel Bandeira (1886–1968) should be remembered. As a result of his poor health, Bandeira could not take part in the Semana of 1922, but he sent his poem *Os sapos* (The Frogs) to be read during the festival's opening. Poet Ronald de Carvalho (1893–1935) read the poem during the event's second evening to cat-calls and boos from the elite audience at São Paulo's Municipal Theater. Bandeira's frogs are the Parnassian poets whose verses are seen as just a rhythmic repetition of sounds without any valuable content. The poem presents one of the most emphatic attempts at a break from tradition produced by the Brazilian avant-garde.

The Semana also had an important musical dimension. Two musicians deserve particular mention in relation to the Art Week of 1922: the composer Heitor Villa-Lobos (1887–1959) and the pianist Guiomar Novaes (1895–1979). Music critics usually credit Villa-Lobos with having discovered the true Brazilian musical soul. The composer transposed to his native cultural milieu Igor Stravinsky's use of Russian folklore as a means of establishing musical modernity. His oeuvre is the foundation of the basic repertoire of Brazilian modern music with the influences of African and American Indian elements. On the first day of the Semana festival, Villa-Lobos closed his performance with the piano piece *Danças Características Africanas* (1914), a highly syncopated classical composition that, in fact, does not sound very African but which, nonetheless, led the way to a belated recognition of the African dimension in Brazilian music and culture. Villa-Lobos would become an important figure in Brazilian cultural nationalism during the 1930s, serving as the musical director to dictator Getúlio Vargas's project of a nationalist music education program.

Pianist Guiomar Novaes was a prodigious talent who achieved world fame with her interpretations of Chopin and Schumann. She performed on the evening of February 15 during the Semana, playing pieces from Émile-Robert Blanchet (1877–1943), Claude Debussy (1862–1918), and Villa-Lobos. During her participation in the Semana's events, Novaes became irritated with the inclusion in the program of the performance of *D'Edriophthalma*, a piece by Erik Satie (1866–1925) that contained a parody of the *Marche funèbre* movement of Chopin's Piano Sonata No. 2. Novaes considered Satie's music distasteful and detrimental to her own career, for she was achieving international recognition precisely for her work on the Polish Romantic master. During the event, the pianist's modernist credentials were in fact questioned; peers and public alike doubted she should have been invited. Her public expression of strong dissatisfaction with Satie's music came across as wide of the mark in the context of an avant-garde festival. Ironically, Novaes appears to have been the only performer who was well received by the Semana's audience, which, as we have seen, was mostly bourgeois. At any rate, the piano performance portion of the evening became a real point of dissent among the artists of the Semana.

In the visual arts, the event gave pride of place in the national aesthetic to a series of remarkable painters who would become the future masters of the new national visual sensibility. Together with the aforementioned Anita Malfatti, we find Tarsila do Amaral (1886–1973), the daughter of a wealthy coffee baron who financed his daughter's studies in Paris from 1920 to 1924. The painter was absent from the Semana of 1922, but in 1923 she met with Oswald de Andrade in Europe to promote the Brazilian avant-garde. The couple married in 1926. In the same year, Amaral opened her first exhibition in Paris, where her work *A Negra* (1923) was especially well received. The work, whose title translates as "The Black Woman," tells of the artist's experience with the *mucamas* on her family's farms during the period of the Brazilian Empire. Her oil painting *Abaporu* (1928), whose title in the Tupi language means an individual who eats human flesh, became the original symbol of the *Movimento Antropofágico*, the "cannibalistic" version of Brazilian Modernism theorized by Tarsila's husband, Oswald de Andrade, through his manifesto of 1928.

Another remarkable painter, and the main organizer of the Semana of 1922, was Emiliano di Cavalcanti (1897–1976). The artist would move to Paris after the Semana event, remaining in France from 1923 to 1925. On his return to Brazil, he joined the national Communist Party and started expressing in more political form his intense nationalistic feelings. In spite of his strong European influences, especially that of Pablo Picasso, Emiliano di Cavalcanti's subject matter was intensely Brazilian. Mulatto Brazilian women became one of his most favored themes, which was in line with Brazilian Modernism's pioneering tendency of recognizing the nation's African heritage.

Di Cavalcanti would take part in another modernist group formed in 1932 by painters Lasar Segall (1891–1957) and Anita Malfatti, which included architect Gregori Warchavchik (1896–1972) and several other artists. The group gathered in São Paulo and was called *Sociedade Pro-Arte Moderna* (SPAM). Its main goal was to attempt a revival of the initial avant-garde ideas of the Semana of 1922. Segall was a Jewish artist of Lithuanian origin who arrived in Brazil in 1912, bringing a strong influence of European Expressionism. Warchavchik was born in Ukraine and had adopted Brazilian nationality in 1927. Segall and Warchavchik's presence in this later re-enactment of Brazilian Modernism points to the enriching presence of immigrants in São Paulo during the First Republic.

In this regard, the most remarkable case is perhaps that of the Japanese, who, as we have seen, first arrived in 1908 under the government's scheme to replace slave labor on the coffee plantations of São Paulo. By 1935, the talented Japanese immigrants were forming their own avant-garde group called the Seibi Group. The Seibi brought together a wealth of remarkable Japanese artists whose originality and intuitive power tended to surpass that of the generally recognized avant-garde comprised of the European-educated bourgeois of the Semana. Painters such as Handa

Tomoo (1906–1996), Yoshiya Takaoka (1909—1978), Tanaka Shigeto (1910–1970), Tomioka Kiyoji (1893–1985), most of them individuals of humble origins who had to work in informal jobs to support their art, would become some of the best Brazilian painters of the twentieth century. As the group continued in the following decades, these original founders would be joined by other remarkable artists such as Okinaka Massao (1913–2000), Fukushima Tikashi (1920–2001), Manabu Mabe (1924–1997), Tomie Ohtake (1913–2015), and Flávio Shiró (b. 1928).

Together with the Seibi, another noteworthy group, the *Santa Helena*, appeared among the proletariat of São Paulo. Starting around 1930 in a more spontaneous way, the Santa Helena brought together Italian, Spanish, and Portuguese immigrants who expressed their talent in the visual arts. Alfredo Volpi (1896–1988), Fulvio Pennacchi (1905–1992), Aldo Bonadei (1906–1974), and Francisco Rebolo (1902–1980) are some of the many excellent painters that took part in the Santa Helena Group.

In spite of the elitism and prejudice that separated the SPAM Group from the more proletarian Seibi and Santa Helena, the cultural effervescence visible in these movements shows that by the end of the First Republic, São Paulo was already on its way to becoming a multicultural city. The final days of the First Republic marked the beginning of a new literary aesthetic that would thrive in Brazilian Modernism in the 1930s. This aesthetic is generally known by the term *Regionalism*. The regionalist novel had its birth in 1928 with the publication of José Américo de Almeida's *A Bagaceira*. The work tells the story of a group of destitute individuals who attempt to escape a severe drought in Brazil's northeast region in 1898. With *A Bagaceira*, the cosmopolitanism of the Modern Art Week began to be countered with views from Brazil's other regions, especially the poverty-stricken areas of the Northeast, which were part and parcel of the nation's real identity. Besides being a novelist, José Américo de Almeida was also a politician, holding governmental positions in his native state of Paraíba during the 1910s and 1920s. Two years after *A Bagaceira*'s publication in 1928, Almeida would lead his home state in the movement that took Rio Grande do Sul's oligarch, Getúlio Dornelles Vargas, to a fifteen-year period of republican dictatorship. To that story, we turn next.

CHAPTER FOUR

GETÚLIO VARGAS AND THE ESTADO NOVO (1930–1945)

The period from 1930 to 1945 saw the Riograndenses seize the central government for the second time in Brazilian history. Unlike the previous experience of 1910–1914, however, this time the Gaúcho power would enjoy a long period of control and the military-positivist ideal of a republican dictatorship would finally be achieved.

Among the many similarities existing between the two periods of Riograndense rule, 1910–1914 and 1930–1945, the most striking is perhaps the outright belief in federal intervention in the states as a valid mode of national rule. This became even stronger during the 1930–1945 period. If in 1910 Hermes da Fonseca and Pinheiro Machado enacted their interventionist politics of "Salvations" by substituting the traditional provincial leaders with their own partisans, now Getúlio Vargas, their direct descendant, would achieve a much more thorough and lasting imposition of Riograndense rule throughout the nation.

Given Rio Grande do Sul's economic backwardness and thorough dependence on the internal market, the Gaúchos saw the seizing of the central government as their sole chance of avoiding national ostracism and outright decay. They could not compete with São Paulo's export economy, which gave the Paulistas a surplus of power within the federation. Even after seizing the nation with its authoritarian leader, however, Rio Grande do Sul would never achieve the same level of economic prosperity seen in the provinces to the north.

While they would always be in second place economically and culturally, the southern warlords had the whip hand politically. The periods of 1930–1945, 1951–1954, 1961–1964, together with the major part of the twenty-year military dictatorship lasting from 1964 to 1985, all had a Riograndense ruler in power. Such political hegemony notwithstanding, Rio Grande do Sul's economic sluggishness would continue to become more and more noticeable, reaching a peak during the 1960s, when a diaspora of millions of Riograndenses migrating northwards in search of better living conditions, a phenomenon called the "Gaúcho Exodus," would emerge. Over the decades, the Riograndense dictatorship started in 1930 did not alter the southern province's overall economic situation. Rio Grande do Sul, and especially its capital city, Porto Alegre, would continue to present very low growth rates. The opposite would be the case with Rio Grande do Sul immediate northern neighbors, Santa Catarina and Paraná. Looking at GDP, by 2010 the city of Curitiba, Paraná State's capital, would have the fourth largest GDP among Brazilian capital cities, while Porto Alegre, Rio Grande do Sul's capital, would be tenth.

Back in 1930, the discrepancy between Rio Grande do Sul's military power and its economic lack thereof led the Gaúchos once again to Rio de Janeiro. That discrepancy, note should be made, was deeply rooted in the Portuguese colonial ambition for territorial expansion. As we have seen, the history of protracted disputes with Spain over the area relative to present-day Rio Grande do Sul resulted in strong regional militarization, as well as the political instability described in the previous chapters. The growing disparity between the region's military power and its economic weakness provided fertile ground for the powerful southern warlords to rise and seek national political hegemony.

A look at the territorial disposition of the Brazilian army provides a good perspective on Rio Grande do Sul's place in the national distribution of power. Brazil's Third Army, which is considered the most powerful among the nation's twelve regional divisions, is stationed in Porto Alegre, Rio Grande do Sul's capital city. The Third Army has jurisdiction over the Third Military Region, which corresponds to the state of Rio Grande do Sul. The Third Military Region is traditionally denominated "Dom Diogo de Souza's Region" in tribute to the first governor of the São Pedro do Rio Grande Captaincy, a capitaincy established in 1760 by the Portuguese Crown in the area of present-day Rio Grande do Sul.

Unlike other colonial administrative units, the Rio Grande Captaincy was officially regarded as a colonial military region, not an economic one. Its governor was always appointed as the General Military Commander of the area. This history of deep interconnection between military and political power is at the root of the very figure of the *caudilho*, the archetypal local landed warlord who would control local governments and aim to spread his power nationwide.

These southern men differed from their northern counterparts. While they were the instruments of Portuguese expansion into the southern portion of its American empire during the colonial period, they also betrayed a strong Spanish heritage. Throughout the centuries of close contact and territorial dispute between Spain and Portugal, Portuguese and

Spanish landlords intermingled. And those who were now taking over Rio de Janeiro were bringing to the nation the same Hispanic blood that the Portuguese had both feared and fought. The surnames of the new wielders of power suggest that the region corresponding to present-day Rio Grande do Sul might have remained under Spanish rule: Castilhos, Garrastazu, Luzardo, Vargas, all Spanish surnames.

The appropriation of the Spanish Missions by the Portuguese Crown in 1752 had resulted in a violent war. Subsequently, Buenos Aires Governor Pedro de Ceballos took the entire area of Rio Grande do Sul State in 1776. The territory was finally returned to the Portuguese *sesmeiros*, the future *caudilhos*, after the Treaty of Badajoz, in 1801. By then, however, the distinction between the Portuguese and the Spanish had become unclear. The region would remain in Portuguese hands, but Spanish blood would continue to course through the veins underneath the rough skin of those southern warlords. Among them, one politically skillful and intellectually shrewd landlord would rise to prominence.

The Rise of Getúlio Vargas and the 1930 Revolution

Getúlio Dornelles Vargas was born on April 19, 1882 in the municipality of São Borja, the oldest of the Spanish Missions built by the Jesuits in the seventeenth century. Founded in 1682 in an area corresponding to today's border between Rio Grande do Sul and Argentina, São Borja would also become the home of Vargas's political successor, João Goulart (1919–1976), another Gaúcho landowner who would assume the nation's presidency in 1961, to be deposed in military coup three years later.

Around 1882, São Borja was not much more than an agglomeration of a few large cattle farms along the banks of the Uruguay River. The village was known mostly for being the home of the Vargas family estate. The new president's father was one of the region's wealthiest cattle raisers and held an honorary title of Army General. Vargas's father was a follower of the two *caudilhos* from the nearby town of Cruz Alta, Júlio de Castilhos and Pinheiro Machado. The latter is said to have "discovered" the young Vargas's political talents.[1]

Brazil's new leader, after the ousting of São Paulo's coffee barons from Rio de Janeiro, had began his political career in what was called the *Juventude Castilhista*, a group of young followers of the provincial dictator, Júlio de Castilhos. In the Juventude Castilhista, the young Vargas met some key political figures who in the future would promote the Riograndense revolution we now see beginning in 1930. João Neves da Fontoura (1887–1963), Joaquim Maurício Cardoso (1888–1938), Batista

Luzardo (1892–1982), and Flores da Cunha (1880–1959) were all former *Castilhistas* who would support their fellow countryman, Getúlio Dornelles Vargas, in his rise to the presidency.

But the Riograndense invasion of Rio de Janeiro in 1930 would not be limited to the Castilhista side of southern politics. It would combine the old factions that had historically fought each other in local acts of hatred and carnage. A truce between these warlords was necessary for the joint assault on the nation's capital. This would allow them to produce a thorough revolution in the country's overall political and economic orientation. With no interest in supporting agricultural exports, as previous leaders from São Paulo had done, these southern warlords would emerge with a strong belief in industrialization. They would soon turn their 1930 Revolution into the starting point of a belated industrial revolution in Brazil.

The close relationship between the 1930 coup and industrialization was first noted by Brazilian economist Celso Furtado (1920–2004) in the seminal work *Formação econômica do Brasil* (1959). Furtado's classic analysis showed the emergence of a new process of import substitution after the crisis of 1929, with an initial autonomous transfer of capital from the coffee plantations to the industrial sector and a subsequent state-driven process of industrialization. Paradoxically, such state-driven industrialization was only made possible by the government's decision to sustain coffee production as a means of supporting national employment and investment. During the first half of the 1930s, the new Gaúcho government would adopt a fiscally expansionist policy based on the purchase of coffee surpluses and their immediate destruction. Initially, such purchases would be made with the aid of another funding loan, this one contracted in 1931. By purchasing and burning coffee crops, Vargas would operate a Keynesian expansionary policy even before British economist John Maynard Keynes (1883–1946) had presented his theories of counter-cyclical economic measures in his *General Theory of Employment, Interest and Money* (1936). This became known in Brazilian economic history as Vargas's "Keynesianism before Keynes."

Through fiscal expansion, the government managed to boost aggregate demand and promote a significant enlargement of the internal market. The sudden fall in international demand for Brazilian commodities had to be countered with an inward turn away from the traditional export economy. With the sudden slowdown in the influx of foreign capital, products previously imported now had to be produced internally, and the economy's dynamic center had to be shifted from the export sector to the internal market. An enhanced process of import substitution immediately ensued. From 1933 to 1939, Brazilian industry achieved an annual growth rate of 11.2%. Industrial output was on its way to becoming a major source of national revenue. It is true that the total value of industrial output would not surpass that of agricultural production until 1947, but the path to that goal had already been opened. The manufacturing of capital goods began in 1931. It would be significantly enhanced some ten years later with the development of the national iron and steel industry and the establishment of the Companhia Siderúrgica Nacional (CSN) in 1941.

Brazil's industrialization must be understood as a complex and difficult process during which many barriers had to be overcome. As we have seen, the importance of industrialization as a *sine qua non* of national growth and prosperity was not clear to many Brazilians during the first half of the twentieth century. Most economists and politicians supported an economic model based on agriculture. Many of them represented the traditional interests of coffee production, as well as of cotton, cocoa, and sugarcane farming. The 1930s became the stage for a new debate between agriculturalists and industrialists. The former argued that Brazil possessed a natural "agricultural vocation." They held fast to the old dictates of British economist David Ricardo and his famous theories of international trade. Industrialists, on the opposite side, called for modernization and for the expansion of the internal market. The dispute involved the difficult question of trade tariffs. As was noted above, in the case of an export economy such as Brazil's, tariffs played a dividing role in either promoting agricultural exports or protecting the national industry. How the newly empowered Riograndenses managed to solve this discrepancy, and why they opted for the industrial model is an important question that brings to light the role played by the different regional leaderships that controlled that vast and diverse territory inherited from Portugal.

The Gaúchos who rose to power in 1930 are to be credited with the country's process of industrialization, which they started. Since the greater part of the nation's wealth was concentrated in a very profitable but primarily monolithic system of coffee farming, the country lacked a strong and independent bourgeoisie capable of taking the necessary risks to promote the national industry through private investment. Industrialization was thus taken into the hands of the State. And the State now belonged to Rio Grande do Sul.

The Riograndenses lacked an export product that could benefit from low trade tariffs. What is more, they were particularly interested in the development of the internal market since their products, meat and rice, were sold internally. Rio Grande do Sul's cattle industry had never been strong enough to compete at the export level with that of Argentina, where association with British capital had promoted the development of one of the world's largest refrigeration industries as early as the 1880s. The only way left for the Gaúchos to advance their economic interests was thus by suppressing those of the Paulistas, adopting protectionist tariffs as well as regulated exchange rates.

Paradoxically, the two opposing economic interests, the agricultural and the industrial, coalesced at the point where coffee revenue was the only possible source of the capital needed not only for industrialization, but also for the nation's very survival. The Riograndenses thus had to assume control over that coffee revenue, which was in the hands of the Paulistas. Only in this way would they be able to enact the state-driven industrialization that was initially at odds with São Paulo's agricultural interests.

In order to keep São Paulo's interests in check while their own had free rein, the Riograndenses fell back on their trusted tactic of federal intervention. São Paulo, however, was nothing like the weak northeastern states that had been easily manipulated by Pinheiro Machado and Hermes da Fonseca in their Salvation Politics of 1910–1914. This time, resistance against federal intervention would not stop short of civil war. And that, as we will see in more detail below, would come through a large-scale mobilization of the Paulistas against the Gaúcho central government.

From the perspective of the historical regional imbalances inherited from the times of Portuguese colonial rule, the Riograndenses would effect on a national scale the modernization that they could not effect in their homeland. In strict economic terms, they were Keynesian through and through, even if unaware of it. In political terms, they were mostly fascist.

Several forces came into play during Rio Grande do Sul's supremacy. In the next few pages we will observe how the Gaúchos used the central state apparatus to favor their own economic interests; how they managed to control São Paulo and its powerful coffee barons; and how subsequently they forced a compromise between the emerging capitalist and proletarian classes through the establishment of an authoritarian rule based on an all-encompassing bureaucracy that would turn the nation into something akin to a syndicalist republic.

The Provisory Government (1930–1934)

On November 3, 1930, having deposed President Washington Luís, the military junta made Getúlio Dornelles Vargas head of the Provisory Government established by the Riograndense revolutionary forces. On taking office, the southern warlord, now dressed in military uniform, was eager to implement throughout the nation the rules that had prevailed historically among the meat-curing Riograndenses. The strongest blow, as the new owners of power would soon make clear, had to be against the nation's wealthiest oligarchy, the coffee barons of São Paulo. With the national army controlled by the Gaúchos, Vargas suspended the Constitution of 1891 and appointed new governors to all federal states except Minas Gerais, which emerged from the coup as an ally. The *caudillo* closed the National Congress together with provincial assemblies and municipal legislative bodies. Economic measures to enhance political centralization were immediately imposed, such as the prohibition on individual states procuring foreign loans; the establishment of a central government monopoly on currency trading; and the regulation of the agricultural sector. Together with these measures, Vargas assumed control over the workers' unions. Washington Luís and Júlio Prestes, the former president and the newly elected one, were sent into exile in Europe. The freedom of the press was suspended.

Turning the coffee oligarchs' defeat into an all-out humiliation, Vargas ousted the governor of São Paulo, Heitor Teixeira Penteado (1878–1947), replacing him with João Alberto Lins de Barros (1897–1955), one of the lieutenants who had participated in the conspiracy leading to the Tenentista Revolt of 1922 in Rio de Janeiro. João Alberto was originally from Pernambuco, and his presence was unacceptable to the São Paulo oligarchs, who saw him as an outsider and a plebeian. The "Pernabucan," as he was called in São Paulo, had moved to Rio Grande do Sul after being arrested following the 1922 rebellion in Rio de Janeiro. He then took part in the revolts that had started in Rio Grande do Sul in 1924, being thus an insider to the new Gaúcho revolutionary government. The government itself, as well as the whole Revolution, was partly run by the lieutenants who had been the fiercest enemies of the oligarchs from São Paulo and from the Northeast. Politically inexperienced, however, these low-ranking military men would soon begin to show their incompetence in conducting the State's administrative affairs, putting in jeopardy the achievement of the Revolution's stated goals.

In an attempt to calm the growing unrest produced in São Paulo by Joao Alberto's appointment, Vargas nominated Laudo Ferreira de Camargo (1881–1963) as São Paulo's new *interventor* on July 25, 1931. Ferreira de Camargo was a São Paulo-born lawyer and politician. His appointment, however, did not appease the anger of São Paulo's oligarchs. The coffee barons soon began demanding the drafting of a constitution in order to put in check Vargas's displays of force. Dissatisfied with the dictator and his lieutenants' frequent interference in the government,

Ferreira de Camargo resigned from his post in November 1931. Over the next year, two other men would assume the same position without being able to maintain a stable administration, Manuel Rabelo Mendes (1873–1945), in office from November 1931 until March 1932, and Pedro Manuel de Toledo (1860–1935), from March 1932 until October of that year. The latter was responsible for starting what came to be called the Constitutionalist Revolution of 1932, that is, São Paulo's violent reaction to, and civil war with Rio Grande do Sul.

In spite of having been appointed by Vargas to be in charge of São Paulo, Pedro Manuel de Toledo turned against the southern dictator and became the revolution's civilian leader. The course of events went as follows. A dramatic episode took place on May 23, 1932, when four young students who were protesting against Vargas's autocratic rule were murdered in a clash with federal troops. The incident lead to Pedro de Toledo assuming the leadership of the anti-Vargas movement. The local population, hungry to avenge the students' deaths, acknowledged Toledo as São Paulo's governor, officially breaking with Vargas's system of appointing his interventores to rule the state.

The São Paulo Revolution was thus ignited against the Riograndense 1930 Revolution. It started from a general feeling of outrage with the deaths of four young Paulistas protesting their province's loss of autonomy. São Paulo's population formed a clandestine civil organization called MMDC, an acronym using the names of the four deceased students. The MMDC began offering instruction in guerrilla techniques to the masses. War against Vargas and his troops was on its way.

Two dissident Riograndese military commanders, Bertoldo Klinger (1884–1969) and Isidoro Dias Lopes (1865–1949), assumed the leadership of the revolutionary forces. Klinger was a Gaúcho who had collaborated with the Tenentista Revolt of 1924. Lopes, too, was a Gaúcho who had taken part in the Federalist Revolution of 1893 against Floriano Peixoto and had joined the revolutionaries of the aforementioned Prestes's Column in 1924. Lopes had supported Vargas's Revolution two years earlier, in 1930. By 1931, however, a serious disagreement with the *caudilho* had seen the military commander change sides and join the Paulistas. The leadership of the Paulistas by two Gaúchos is symptomatic of the schism beginning to appear within Vargas's government. Accustomed to centuries of mutual confrontation, the southern oligarchs in his clique could not stay put without fighting one another. The local disputes that had divided the Riograndense landlords over the last two hundred years would not come to a halt even now, when they were finally taking over the central government. Clashes among the Gaúcho leaders in Rio de Janeiro began as early as the last weeks of 1930. By late 1931, no more than a year after the start of their national rule, some of the southern leaders began to defect and oppose Vargas. The powerful Borges de Medeiros (1863–1961) offered his support to the Paulistas and established the *Frente Única Riograndense*, a group of heavy-handed warlord/politicians ready to defend São Paulo's demand that a new constitution be drafted. Rio Grande do Sul's interventor, however, the equally powerful Flores da Cunha (1880–1959), remained loyal to Vargas. Medeiros's support had encouraged optimism in São Paulo, but Flores da Cunha's clout was lavishly displayed in the immediate suppression of Medeiros's *Frente Única Rio-Grandense*. Many a Gaúcho warlord was arrested and exiled. The same fate would befall the Mineiros who supported São Paulo, among them ex-president Artur Bernardes, who was exiled to Portugal.

São Paulo's Constitutionalist Revolution of 1932 soon became a large-scale bloody civil war. More than 200,000 combatants took to the battlefield, engaging heavy artillery, air raids, and the bombing of urban areas. Naval battles were also fought. Once again, Brazilians fought other Brazilians as they had done since the times of the War of the Emboabas in 1708 and the several uprisings that had continued throughout the former Portuguese colony's history. São Paulo was divided between the so-called *legalists*, that is, the supporters of Vargas, and the *constitutionalists*, namely the Paulistas, who demanded a new constitution. Among São Paulo's masses, voices calling for secession began to be heard and these were echoed among the State's elite, notably in calls issued by eminent literati such as Monteiro Lobato (1882–1948) and Alfredo Ellis Júnior (1896–1974). São Paulo's new nationalism was now set against its old Riograndense counterpart. São Paulo's population took the confrontation into its own hands and plunged headlong into war. The mobilization involved all sectors of society, including the upper-class ladies of distinguished families, who played their part in the conflict by donating jewelry to raise funds for military expenditure.

The situation in Rio Grande do Sul became convoluted with the anti-Vargas Riograndenses attempting to sabotage the federal troops of the Third Army that had been mobilized to move towards São Paulo. The local oligarchs, Borges de Medeiros, Batista Luzardo, and Lindolfo Collor adhered to the Paulista cause. They searched for any possible means to prevent the 18,000 men of the newly created Gaúcho Brigade of Rio Grande do Sul from moving north, but finished by being arrested by Vargas's local interventor, Flores da Cunha. Borges de Medeiros was defeated in the Battle of Cerro Alegre on September 20, 1932, coincidentally the same date that had marked the beginning of the

Farroupilha Revolution of 1835 and is celebrated as Rio Grande do Sul's local nationalistic holiday. Without support from the anti-Vargas Gaúchos, the Paulistas surrendered on October 2.[2]

While Paulistas and Gaúchos fought each other in São Paulo, Vargas also faced important challenges in matters of foreign policy. In neighboring Paraguay, another war broke out, caused by the alleged discovery of oil in the Andean foothills. The new economic dispute set several players in conflict with one another: Paraguay, Bolivia, Argentina, the Royal Dutch Shell Company, and the Standard Oil Company. The region of the Chaco Boreal, where oil seemed to have been found, was especially coveted by Bolivia. Besides its immediate economic interest, the region could provide Bolivians with access to the Atlantic by means of the Paraguay River. The country had lost its Pacific coast to Chile in the 1879 War, and its present isolation was producing severe economic restrictions in the context of the international financial crisis of the early 1930s. After a *coup d'état* that ousted President Hernando Siles Reyes (1882–1942) and the subsequent election of Daniel Salamanca Urey (1869–1935) in 1931, Bolivia threw its weight into the annexation of the Chaco Boreal.

The disputed region amounted roughly to the northern part of the Gran Chaco, a sparsely populated lowland region of the River Plate basin, occupying parts of eastern Bolivia, Paraguay, northern Argentina, and the Brazilian states of Mato Grosso and Mato Grosso do Sul. The area was claimed by Argentina during the Paraguayan War (1864–1870) as part of the old Argentine argument of Paraguay being part of the former Spanish Viceroyalty of the River Plate, and thus a legitimate part of Argentina. As we have seen, in the face of such claims, Brazil had kept its army stationed in Paraguay after the war until 1872, when the final Argentine recognition of Paraguay as an independent state was confirmed. Argentine interests in the area, however, were never fully abandoned. Immediately after 1872, unable to seize the neighboring country and effect a complete annexation, the Argentines succeeded in penetrating the Paraguayan borders economically with the skillful entrepreneurship of their bourgeoisie, which, like the Brazilian Gaúchos, comprised mostly landowning meat curers. So now the Argentines adopted a position in favor of Paraguay in the war against Bolivia, their main aim being to ensure that the northern Chaco region, with all its oil potential, should not be lost to the Bolivians.

Brazil, on the other hand, defended Bolivian ownership over the area. With the Treaty of Petropolis of 1903, Brazil had ceded a large tract of land called the *Triângulo de Terras* to Bolivia in exchange for the region of Acre. The land, as we have seen, provided Bolivians with an access to the Paraguay River. With the Chaco War, Paraguay now claimed the area as part of its own territory. Brazil was thus threatened with a possible demand to revise the Treaty of Petropolis in case of a Bolivian loss of the Triângulo de Terras. The Spanish-American nations had always regarded the Treaty as a product of Brazilian imperialism, and the former Portuguese colony's position with regard to the present war demanded tact and diplomatic ability.

Brazil thus assumed a position of official neutrality in the war. Nevertheless, this official stand hid the truth of undeclared support for Bolivia. This meant that the conflict between Paraguayans and Bolivians was once again setting in motion the opposing interests of those former enemies and eternal rivals, Brazil and Argentina. Sensing that the Chaco War might lead to what would be a catastrophic situation of continental proportions, Brazilians and Argentines opted for establishing diplomatic dialogue and promoting mutual understanding with their neighbors in dispute.

Vargas invited Argentine president, General Agustín Pedro Justo (1876–1943) to pay an official visit to Rio de Janeiro in 1933. Justo was received with a state banquet offered at the Itamaraty Palace, the seat of Brazil's Foreign Ministry, on the evening of October 7. In his welcoming speech, Vargas mentioned his being born near the frontier between Brazil and Argentina, and having since his childhood witnessed the great neighboring Republic's industrious and indefatigable people's strong friendship with Brazil. Vargas's efforts to build understanding and trust gave the event great significance in the two nations' future relations. The previous Argentine government, led by Hipólito Yrigoyen (1852–1933) and his party, the *Unión Cívica Radical*, had opted to keep its distance from Brazil, breaking with the tendency to foster closer ties initiated by President Roque Sáenz Peña (1851–1914) in the previous administration. Yrigoyen had been ousted by a military *coup d'état* that, unlike that mounted by Vargas in Brazil, reinstated the power of the country's traditional oligarchies. General José Félix Uriburu's (1868–1932) rule started what came to be known in Argentine history as "The Infamous Decade," of which Justo's government was an important part.

The landed oligarchy supporting Justo's government had significant interests in Paraguay. As we have seen, many Argentine meat curers had extended their possessions toward the neighboring country after the Paraguayan War. Justo's Minister of Foreign Relations, Carlos Saavedra Lamas (1878–1959), emerged as a central figure in furthering Argentine interests in the region. Formerly a lawyer to some of the country's most powerful families who were regaining control over the nation after the coup of 1930, Lamas was married to the daughter of former president, Roque Sáenz Peña, and followed the family tradition of recognizing the importance for Argentina of maintaining friendly ties with Brazil.

On the occasion of President Justo's visit to Rio de Janeiro, Lamas planted the seed for what would be his most important diplomatic achievement, the Saavedra Lamas Anti-War and Non-Aggression Pact. The Pact was conceived primarily as a Latin American version of the Kellogg–Briand Pact, which had been signed between France, the United States, and Germany's Weimar Republic in 1928. After securing Brazil's support in October in Rio de Janeiro, Lamas was successful in obtaining the signatures of Argentina, Uruguay, Chile, and Mexico during the meeting of the Seventh Pan-American Conference in Montevideo in December. Lamas's growing international prestige, together with that of Argentina itself, could not but fuel the Brazilians' sense of rivalry, emphasizing the urgent need to improve their country's own international image.

The Conference of 1933 brought important developments to the Americas at a time when the international scene was becoming polarized between the liberal-democratic ideals of the United States and the nationalist authoritarian rule of Nazi-fascism. United States president Franklin Delano Roosevelt (1882–1945) used the occasion to present his Good Neighbor policy, which aimed at extending American influence over Latin America in a more sympathetic way than the one enacted a few decades earlier by his cousin Theodore. This came in handy to Vargas, who was attempting to continue the course of Brazilian foreign policy established during the Baron of Rio Branco's term as Foreign Minister, that is, turning to the United States as a central economic and political partner instead of maintaining an economic dependence on Europe, as the Argentines were doing through their almost symbiotic financial relationship with the United Kingdom.

The by now traditional foreign policy of favoring the United States as the major partner notwithstanding, Vargas opted to maintain important commercial ties with Germany and Italy throughout the larger part of the 1930s. This was part of Vargas's strategy of bargaining for economic advantages for Brazil by means of keeping parallel lines of international trade running with the liberal United States on one side, and the European dictatorships on the other. Two agreements of countertrade would be signed with Germany in 1934 and 1936, while an important commercial contract would still be signed with the United States in 1935. Sensing the urge to stymy what seemed a general turn towards Europe in the American continent, the United States showed remarkable diplomatic tact in coopting Latin America to its liberal ideology. During the Montevideo Pan-American Conference of 1933, cultural diplomacy, fostering mutual understanding and cooperation, emerged as one of the main vehicles for this. After the 1933 Conference, Luso-Brazilian actress, singer, and dancer Carmen Miranda (1909–1955) would become one of the Good Neighbor Policy's main icons, making her Hollywood debut in the film *Down Argentine Way* (1940).

Besides President Roosevelt and his Secretary of State Cordell Hull's declaration of the Good Neighbor Policy, the Conference of 1933 saw the signing of The Montevideo Convention on the Rights and Duties of States, which codified the main provisos found in the region's customary international law for the diplomatic recognition of states. While the Conference established the grounds for the legitimacy of individual nations, it also opened up the possibility for them to seek enhanced international standing. In that sense, Saavedra Lamas played an important role in improving his country's profile. He took Argentina back into the League of Nations after a thirteen-year absence, established the anti-war pact of 1933, and mediated the resolution of the Chaco War.

This last feat represented a significant loss for the Brazilians, who were competing with Argentina for political hegemony in the sub-continent. Vargas and his Foreign Minister, Afrânio de Melo Franco (1870–1943), attempted to secure for Brazil the job of mediating the conflict between Paraguay and Bolivia. Argentina's interests, however, prevailed, and the war drew towards a Paraguayan victory. By the time a ceasefire was negotiated in 1935, Paraguay controlled most of the Chaco Boreal region. The Bolivian Army's German commander, Hans Kundt (1869–1939), realized his failure when the Bolivian soldiers, who had trained in the cold high lands of the Bolivian Andes, demonstrated an inability to fight in the suffocating lowlands of the Paraguayan Chaco.

The war ended with no commercial amounts of oil being found in the Chaco region. It would not be until 2012 that the Paraguayan president, Federico Franco, would announce the discovery of reserves in the area of the Pirity River. In spite of the general fiasco over oil, the war served to boost Paraguay's national pride, which had barely recovered since the war of 1864. Lamas became the first Latin American Nobel Peace Prize recipient in 1936, further emphasizing how Brazil had earned nothing from the mediation of the conflict.

The war also contributed to reducing the mutual distrust that had marked the history of Brazil–Argentina relations. In 1935, Vargas would visit Buenos Aires, returning Justo's previous visit to Rio de Janeiro. The appointment of a new Brazilian Foreign Minister, José Carlos de Macedo

Soares (1883–1968), in 1934, was part of Vargas's attempt to develop a foreign policy geared towards Latin America. In spite of the good terms achieved with Argentina, however, Brazil's apparent neutrality in the war did not succeed in hiding its undeniable leaning towards Bolivia, and this affected the building of closer relations with Paraguay. Continuous attempts at establishing closer ties between the two countries had been made since the government of President Manuel Gondra (1871–1927) started in 1920. Gondra's Liberal Party had seen in Brazil an opportunity to maintain his country's independence from Argentina, a notion that was taken up by President Eusebio Ayala (1875–1942). Ayala was favorable to Paraguay's acceptance of the Brazilian offer to cancel war debts from the confrontations of 1864–1870. The opposition, called Colorados, however, promised to prevent such a move in the Paraguayan Congress. With the end of the Chaco War, and with a new gulf emerging between the two nations, it would not be until 1943 that Vargas would finally be able to cancel Paraguay's debt with Brazil, fostering mutual understanding and cooperation in bilateral relations.[3]

The connection between the Chaco War and the Constitutionalist Revolution in São Paulo reveals some of the troublesome entanglements that Vargas was facing during the first few years of what would become his long 15-year rule in Rio de Janeiro. If the war between Paraguay and Bolivia called for a careful positioning in the international arena, the domestic revolution proved to be the source of a damaging fissure among the new Riograndense rulers of the nation. While the Constitutionalist Revolution of 1932 did not achieve its principal aim of ousting Getúlio Vargas and his Provisory Government from Rio de Janeiro, it did succeed in securing the drafting of a new constitution. The Constitution of 1934 would be promulgated on July 16 that year, and it would be very much disliked by Vargas.

The Constitutional Period (1934–1937)

The *coup d'état* that had brought Getúlio Vargas to the head of the federal government on November 3, 1930 meant the end of the legal and political system established under the Constitution of 1891. Obliged to heed the Paulista's claims, Vargas now called for the election of a constitutive assembly on May 3, 1933.

The election meant a new hope for democracy and for a cleaning-up of the nation's political process. It included significant developments in terms of the extension of civil rights to hitherto marginalized populations. For the first time in history, women were allowed to present themselves as candidates at the national level. They had been allowed to vote in the regional elections of the northeastern state of Rio Grande do Norte in 1927, but now their right to full citizenship was recognized across the country.

It would not take long, however, for the initial hope for democracy to be thwarted. The Constitutional Assembly opened on December 15, 1933, and together with its 214 elected deputies, 40 trades unions' representatives were appointed by the government to take part in the drafting of the new constitution. This appointment followed practices established by the fascist and Nazi regimes of Germany and Italy. With it Vargas was demonstrating that his concessions to democracy would not be unlimited.

While the 1891 Constitution had been modeled on the Constitution of the United States, the new Charter was based on Germany's Weimar Constitution of 1919. The new text attempted to answer some of the most pressing demands of the Tenentista Movement, whose support for Vargas on his way to Rio de Janeiro had been in great part based on the critique of the old oligarchical system and its tendency to engage in electoral corruption and fraud. The Brazilian Election Code had been decreed in 1932 and, from its foundation, the 1934 Constitution created the Brazilian Electoral Justice Department, an independent judicial body intended to oversee and defend the integrity of the future electoral processes. The Constitution also established secret voting and, following the developments seen with regard to the Constitutional Assembly, allowed votes for women. Voting was made compulsory, an obligation that remains in effect to this day in Brazil, signaling the limited democratic nature of the nation's political mentality. The legal obligation to vote interested Vargas and his upcoming totalitarian State, as it increased the number of voters in a way that facilitated the manipulation of the masses through propaganda and media control.

Besides entailing these alterations in the electoral system, the process of drafting the Constitution rekindled the old dispute between administrative centralization and decentralization. The drafting's final result tended to support the latter, and the Charter was promulgated on July 16, 1934 with provisions that diluted a great part of the central authority embodied in the figure of Getúlio Dornelles Vargas. As the new constitution enhanced the autonomy of the states with regard to the central government, it went counter to Vargas and the aims of his 1930 Revolution. The *caudilho* himself thus emerged as the Constitution's most severe critic. He claimed that the document had been prepared hastily and in a moment of political instability, when the objectives and achievements of the Revolution were still in the process of crystallization.

The 1934 Constitution established that the first presidential election following its promulgation would be held by means of indirect voting, to be carried out by the Assembly's deputies. On July 17, Getúlio Vargas was elected president, amassing an easy victory against candidates such as his fellow Riograndense Borges de Medeiros and the anti-Tenentista General Góes Monteiro (1889–1956). Monteiro was an army commander who had started his career in the Military Academy of Porto Alegre, and who had opposed the 18 of the Copacabana Fort Revolt in 1922. He would come to play a complex role in Vargas's future political life, becoming one of the military leaders who would project the Riograndense to dictatorship in 1937, and then oversee his ousting in December 1945.

The 1934 Constitution, still following the model of its Weimer equivalent, created the Justice of Labor, another independent judicial body, this one intended to defend the rights of workers. As of 2018, the body remains active in Brazil, exercising substantial control over the relation between employers and employees, with the damaging consequence of hindering the liberalization of the labor market. The Justice of Labor emerged as part of Vargas's active policy of coopting the working class for his project of a totalitarian state.

The term usually employed to define Vargas's politics in the period is *paternalism*. The leader opted to grant a series of rights to workers in order to keep them on side. Such rights reminded critics of the type of gift fathers usually gave to their children. Brazilian workers thus received without much effort the recognition of rights that had taken several decades of active political engagement for European workers to achieve. Vargas's populist tendencies would soon earn him the title of *Pai dos pobres* (Father of the Poor).

With the establishment of the nation's new legal structures, a new stage of national development was expected, but the Brazilian economy, still dependent on coffee exports, continued to suffer the effects of the world crisis that began in 1929. The situation of economic dependency was severely criticized by the left, who saw in international imperialism the main reason for the country's underdevelopment. The 1934 Constitution did adopt a few nationalistic measures, such as the nationalization of subsoil assets and waterfalls, but that was not enough to appease the demands of the most discontented leftists. Political radicalism was emerging in response to the world economic crisis. The partial liberalization of Brazilian politics saw radicals appear across the entire political spectrum. In 1932, the *Ação Integralista Brasileira* (Brazilian Integralist Action), a far-right political party of strong fascist inclination was founded by Plínio Salgado (1895–1975), a literary figure who, as we have seen, had taken part in the 1922 Modern Art Week. Salgado adapted fascist symbolism into his nationalistic version of totalitarian political conservatism. His party included a paramilitary organization partly financed by the Italian embassy. The green-shirted *Integralistas* adopted the Roman salute in tandem with the shouting of the Tupi word *Anauê*, which means "you are my brother," as their form of self-distinction. The Integralist model was based on the idea of a "Duce" with his followers, the role of the former, in this tropical version, being played by Salgado himself. Salgado's movement was one that, note should be made, remained sensible enough to avoid the overtly racist and anti-Semitic euphoria of the European Nazi-fascist original.

If right-wing extremism came from Salgado and his well-groomed followers, left-wing radicalism emerged with the establishment of the so-called *Aliança Nacional Libertadora* (ANL), a coalition of several leftist political trends led by the Communist Party. The ANL made much of its aim to fight imperialism, and counter the expansion of the *Ação Integralista*. The Brazilian Communist Party was founded in March 1922, but was outlawed in June the same year during Epitácio Pessoa's government. The Party was made legal again in 1927 and was recognized by the Comintern in 1930. The ANL soon gained a large number of followers. Its program included very idealistic claims such as the suspension of the payment of all "imperialist" debts, the immediate nationalization of all "imperialist" companies, and the immediate handing of the country's agricultural lands to the workers that cultivated them.

In 1935, Luís Carlos Prestes, the former leader of Tenentismo and of the militaristic Column in 1924, returned secretly to Brazil from exile. While in Buenos Aires, Prestes had converted to Marxism. He was now following the instructions of the Comintern, whose goal was to promote an armed uprising and establish a new revolutionary government in the country. As the ANL grew in popularity, with public demonstrations taking over the streets of several major cities, Vargas overruled the 1934 Constitution and the civil liberties guaranteed therein, promulgating the Law of National Security on April 4, 1935, which included the closure of the ANL. The Organization's closure was ordered after a large public demonstration in which a manifesto written by Prestes and calling for the overthrow of the government was presented to the nation. The manifesto echoed the Leninist motto with the cry, "All power to the ANL." The closure of the ANL was carried out with a violent display of force that included the imprisonment of activists and the prohibition of public demonstrations.

Prestes counted with the support of a small but experienced group of international revolutionaries, including the German-Jewish agent Olga Benário (1908–1942). Benário had been appointed as Prestes's bodyguard in 1934. She entered the country with false documents describing her as the Brazilian's Portuguese wife. This fake marriage turned into a real one when the two rebels fell in love with each other under the turmoil of the revolutionary struggle. The ANL attempted a *coup d'état* in November 1935. The attempt began as a military uprising in the northeastern city of Natal. The rebels gained control of the City's government, and remained there for four days while similar attempts were taking place in Recife and Rio de Janeiro. The superiority of Vargas's forces, however, soon became evident and the uprising was suppressed a few days later.

The most immediate result of the attempt, which became known as the *Intentona Comunista*, was the intensification of the state's repression of the opposition. Prestes and Olga Benário were arrested in Rio de Janeiro in January 1936. In the face of Benário's possible extradition to Germany, where she would probably have been executed under Hitler's anti-Semitic policies, an international campaign demanding that she be granted habeas corpus from Brazilian detention was initiated. In spite of her being pregnant with a Brazilian child, and of the Brazilian law's interdiction of the extradition of nationals, Vargas argued that the martial law in force at the time overruled the habeas corpus demand. Benário was thus sent to Germany in September 1936, giving birth to a girl in prison two months later. The child, after an intense international campaign, was handed to her paternal grandmother. Olga Benário was gassed at Germany's Bernburg Euthanasia Centre in 1942.[4]

Vargas did not hesitate to extract the full political benefit from Prestes's communist uprising, in the form of a widespread sense of terror purposefully spread among the population with regard to communism. Prestes's attempt gave Vargas what he needed for an expanded anti-communist government campaign. It allowed the Riograndense to maintain the state of martial law that was in force throughout the country, and to subsequently turn his war against communism into an excuse for a *coup d'état*. To that end, he found another pressure point in what became known as the Cohen Plan.

The Cohen Plan was a fictitious scheme devised by one of the extreme-right Ação Integralista's leaders, the army officer Captain Olympio Mourão Filho (1900–1972). In Mourão's fictious "plan," the communists were featured plotting in detail the ousting of Vargas and the seizing of the government. The alleged conspiracy was recorded in a written document that circulated among the high ranks of the armed forces. Vargas learned of the document by means of commander Góes Monteiro on September 30, 1937, and decided to consider the conspiracy described therein as real. From then on, it took him less than two months to arrange the coup that would overthrow the 1934 Constitution and grant him dictatorial powers. The Constitution established presidential elections to be held in January 1938. Since late 1936, candidates had begun aligning themselves for the poll. São Paulo's governor, Armando de Sales Oliveira (1887–1945), emerged as the opposition's frontrunner. Vargas presented his own candidate, the Paraiban José Américo de Almeida (1887–1980), and the Integralists presented Plínio Salgado. As we have seen, the state of Paraíba had been allied to Rio Grande do Sul and Minas Gerais during the coup that took Vargas to Rio de Janeiro in 1930. In that year, Almeida had been chosen as Vargas's interventor in Paraíba. He was subsequently appointed Minister of Transport, occupying this post until 1934. In Américo de Almeida, Vargas had a faithful follower upon whom he would be able to exert almost total control after 1938.

Being now presented with Mourão's gift of a false communist conspiracy, however, on November 10, 1937, the cunning Riograndense announced on national radio the closing of the Congress and the imposition of a new Constitution. The heavily authoritarian and repressive period known as *Estado Novo*, which would last until 1945, had begun. São Paulo's Armando de Sales Oliveira, the opposition's strongest candidate for the now canceled 1938 elections, was exiled, being allowed to return to the country only in 1945, after the end of Vargas's tropical version of a Nazi-fascist regime. With regard to the Cohen Plan, nobody ever learned who Cohen was, but the name certainly sounded Jewish.

The Estado Novo (1937–1945)

On that same day of November 10, 1937, when Vargas announced on national radio the suspension of the upcoming elections and the establishment of a new state of national security in response to the communist threat, Brazilians were presented with their new Constitution, one that this time was modeled on Poland's April Constitution of 1935.[5] Tailored to provide Poland's leader Józef Piłsudski (1867–1935) with a strong presidency, the Polish Charter provided Brazilian lawyer Francisco Campos (1891–1968) with the elements necessary to draft a new Constitution all by himself, that is, without the hindrances likely to come about from a constitutive assembly. Vargas had nominated Campos to the high executive office of Federal Consultant General in 1933, and in the years to come the lawyer would consolidate his career as one of Brazil's foremost right-wing ideologues. He would also provide faithful service to the military dictators who would take the country in 1964.

Under Campos's juristic expertise, the 1937 Constitution incorporated virtually all the provisos that the Riograndense positivists had demanded since 1889. A strongly militaristic, conservative, and authoritarian Brazilian Republic had finally come into being in which the Gaúcho, Getúlio Dornelles Vargas, enjoyed dictatorial powers. Disencumbered from the potential nuisances likely to emerge from a National Congress, or even from regional legislative assemblies, Vargas saw his way clear to fulfilling Rio Grande do Sul's manifest destiny of dictatorial control over Brazil.

Under Vargas's supreme command, a new state bureaucracy was built with a series of organs that attempted to extend the government's power throughout all areas of national life. Since Brazilians had inherited the Portuguese penchant for regulatory office-work, as well as its undeniable tendency to mistake stale, authoritarian, and uncreative bureaucratic arrangements for efficiency and rationality, the way was now open for a fully fledged enactment of a new official statism, one that mixed the nation's traditional elitist social structures with outright totalitarianism. The mixture could not but reinforce the backwardness that is typical of any country led by bureaucrats. In social terms, while those who did not work for the government would be hindered in their daily activities by the all-encompassing claws of the State, free rein was given to the power mongering of all those who craved a secure position in the governmental apparatus.

The new bureaucratic structure included agencies such as the National Department of Propaganda, known by the acronym DIP. Established in 1938, the DIP served Vargas's goal of tightening his grip on the masses. The DIP emerged with enhanced powers in relation to its predecessor government offices, the Official Department of Publicity, established in 1931, and the Department of Propaganda and Cultural Diffusion, established in 1934. Censorship was the organ's main activity, forming the axis around which all other functions were to revolve. The DIP helped the dictator to control the cultural life of the country, creating a highly centralized system where affiliated organs were established in each of the federal states. It also functioned in promoting strong feelings of nationalism through the organization of civic demonstrations, patriotic celebrations, and music concerts. Control over the media, especially radio, was thorough. The DIP's power would be further enhanced in 1939, when Vargas created the Department of Press and Propaganda, which served to organize and direct national events in tribute to the dictator, his family, and the government's senior officials. The regime was rapidly developing a cult of personality, which was being levered by the government's control of mass communications.

While the DIP encouraged nationalistic celebrations of Vargas and his clique, other government organs were created to inject the bureaucratic State's optimistic notions of efficiency and rationality into the all-encompassing governmental machine. The Administrative Department of Public Service (DASP) was established in 1938 with the aim of modernizing public administration. With it, the government's recruitment and training of civil servants was systematized. The National Institute of Statistics, created in 1934, was reformed, receiving a new name in 1938, the Brazilian Institute of Geography and Statistics (IBGE). The IBGE's role was that of an information agency that would provide statistical, geographic, cartographic, and environmental data for national state planning.

Governmental economic interventionism also increased after 1937. The logic of institutionalization, centralization and bureaucratization was also applied to the nation's economic affairs. Economic reforms and planning were carried out under the orders of Vargas's Finance Minister, the Riograndense Artur de Sousa Costa (1893–1957). Costa remained in office throughout the major part of the dictator's rule, occupying the post from 1934 to 1945.[6]

Just as with propaganda and administrative organization, several organs were created to handle specific economic areas, such as the Fund for Agricultural and Industrial Credit (1937), the National Petroleum Council (1938) and the National Council for Water and Electrical Energy (1939). The Federal Council for Foreign Trade (CFCE), created in 1934, was reformed and strengthened in 1937.

The government began to play the part of an interested and powerful mediator between the emerging industrial bourgeoisie and the working class. In its intense interventionist policies, it worked to coopt both parties. State-sponsored educational programs directed at the working class appeared with the creation of two new organs, the National Agency for Industrial Learning (Senai) and National Agency for Commercial Learning (Senac). These agencies functioned as connecting links between workers and their employers. During the second decade of the twenty-first century, these agencies continue to operate in Brazil together with several other organs created during Vargas's Estado Novo.

As we have seen, Vargas's most immediate economic goal was to promote industrialization, and for that a State-centered approach was adopted. As new government-run companies began to be established, the dividing line between the State and the economy itself became increasingly unclear. Policies for industrial incentives, however, had to be balanced with the interests of coffee producers. Brazil's economy had been dependent on coffee for precisely one hundred years. As we have seen, 1838 was the year in which the commodity rose to first place in the country's exports. And coffee's position in the Brazilian economy was not about to decline anytime soon. Coffee valorization schemes continued to be concocted, and that prompted the adoption of controlled regimes of exchange rates as a related measure.

The year 1937 had started with a troublesome trade deficit, which resulted mostly from the boost of more than 40% in imports relative to 1936. The government was forced to adopt measures for currency devaluation, largely in order to sustain the level of coffee exports. The results of these exchange controls, however, were not satisfactory. The United States, Brazil's foremost coffee buyer, was experiencing a sharp economic downturn in mid-1937, which lasted through most of 1938. At that time, more than 50% of the coffee consumed in the United States was imported from Brazil. Again, the impact of a recession in the United States was felt painfully in Brazil.

Vargas announced a sovereign debt default in mid-1937. Following his populist approach and envisaging some possible gain in the context of the rising international tension that was to lead to the outbreak of war in Europe, the Brazilian leader pointed to his country's urgent need to equip its armed forces as the main reason for stopping payment of the debt servicing. Vargas's bargaining approach to politics was once again coming into play: a sovereign debt crisis was being used to press for international credit from whoever might be willing to provide financial support and thus coopt the Latin American nation onto its side in the upcoming war. Between 1933 and 1939, Germany's share of Brazilian exports would rise from 8% to 19% while that of the United States would drop from 46% to 34%. The sovereign default could thus be seen as a clear message sent to the United States, saying that if they were not willing to maintain their financial assistance a more willing partner was waiting in the wings.

Vargas's politics of extortion gained official status with what came to be known as the *Missão Aranha*. Although the name might suggest some secret ninja or spider-like operation, the mission was conducted very much in the open. It started with an invitation from President Roosevelt to a group of Brazilian officials to visit Washington with the aim of discussing financial matters between the two countries. The mission's name derived from that of Osvaldo Aranha (1894–1960), Vargas's fellow Riograndese and Brazil's Minister of Foreign Affairs from 1938 to 1944. Aranha arrived in Washington in February 1939 accompanied by DASP's director,

Luís Simões Lopes (1903–1994), who was another member of Vargas's set of Riograndense *caudilhos*. Together with Aranha and Lopes were the banker Marcos de Sousa Dantas and a few diplomats, who participated in the discussion of Brazil's default. The idea was to try to find an amicable solution to the ending of credit resulted from the default.

The whole affair was conducted under Roosevelt's Good Neighbor Policy, and Aranha's mission was successful in guaranteeing his country a good US$50 million loan in exchange for Brazil's liberalization of its currency exchange regime and the resumption of sovereign debt services. Aranha also managed to secure the United States' support for Brazil's industrialization, support that would soon be linked with the war, and with Brazil's trading of its support. Furthermore, the Missão Aranha was important most of all in defining Brazil's position vis-à-vis the United States in a moment where commercial relations with Germany were particularly strong. Vargas used his trump card well, and his foreign policy was that of selling out to the highest bidder. On the domestic front, the dictator also seemed disinclined to slant his political position in Germany's favor.[7]

With the coup of 1937, Vargas decreed the closure of all political parties operating on Brazilian territory. The ruling affected the parties who were ideologically related to the German Third Reich, namely the Integralist Party and the Brazilian Nazi Party. The latter had been founded in 1928 in the southern state of Santa Catarina. Brazil's southern region, as we have seen, had a strong German heritage, which was fueled by its hundred-year history of German immigration. In 1940, citizens of German origin represented 22% of Santa Catarina's total population and around 19% of that in Rio Grande do Sul. Given that in that year Rio Grande do Sul's population was 3,320,689 inhabitants, the number German descendants in the state had reached almost 600,000.

Vargas's decree was met with fierce protests from the German Ambassador to Rio de Janeiro, Karl Ritter (1883–1968), who had assumed the post in July 1937. By then the Brazilian Nazi Party was the largest in the world outside Germany. Its closure was received as a frontal attack against the German government and its policies of ethnic exclusionism, which included campaigning against miscegenation in the German colonies established in Brazil. The diplomatic conflict was intensified by Vargas's nationalist policies. Severe restrictions were being imposed on the functioning of German schools in the states of Paraná and Santa Catarina, and the new nationalization campaign included the requirement of Brazilian citizenship for schoolteachers as well as the prohibition of foreign language teaching in primary and secondary education. Nationalistic policies were further implemented in 1939, when Vargas prohibited the use of foreign languages in public. Everyday speech was closely monitored, with police able to enforce a ban on the use of German and other languages in the country. State control included the seizure and destruction of documents, books, and magazines issued in languages other than Portuguese.[8]

The closure of political parties in 1937 also drew protests from the Integralist Party. In spite of having presented his own candidacy for the upcoming presidential elections of 1938, Integralist leader Plínio Salgado had supported Vargas's coup in exchange for his fascist party's enlarged political role in the new dictatorial regime. The sudden closing-down of his party was thus received with outrage and as an unacceptable form of betrayal. On March 11, 1938, the Integralists started a rebellion in the headquarters of the army located in Botafogo, Rio de Janeiro. The uprising was rapidly suppressed, but two months later, on May 11, the same rebels attempted to invade the President's official residence, the Guanabara Palace, with the aim of killing Vargas. Ironically, the Guanabara Palace was located in a street called Rua Pinheiro Machado. It stood a few blocks away from another stronghold, this one called Morro da Graça, which had belonged to Vargas's political godfather, the same José Gomes Pinheiro Machado. The older *caudilho* had bought the sumptuous building in 1897 to accommodate his family when he moved from Rio Grande do Sul to Rio de Janeiro to assume his seat in the Senate.

It is not clear whether some sort of Riograndense spirit protecting the neighborhood came to Vargas's rescue, but the fact is that the dictator managed to avoid the fate of his godfather, who, as we have seen, was stabbed in the back by a hit man. The Integralists did invade Vargas's palace, but after a ferocious exchange of fire within the building the President's guards managed to subdue the rebels and a group of seven Integralists were summarily executed at the back of the presidential residence. The massacre was conducted under the orders of Benjamin Vargas, the dictator's younger brother and political acolyte. The failed coup became known as the *Putsch Integralista*, the German word referring to the Nazi-fascist ideology at play. Plínio Salgado was not directly involved in the *Putsch*, so he was not summarily executed. He was, however, exiled to Portugal.[9]

Clashes with Germany did not stop with the closing of the Brazilian Nazi Party and the suppression of the Nazi-sympathizing Integralist Movement. After Hitler's invasion of Poland in 1939, Vargas decided it was time to go all the way with his politics of extortion directed against the United States. The Brazilian dictator wanted immediate action from the United States regarding the promises of financial support for Brazil's industrialization that had been made to Osvaldo Aranha in Washington. Vargas thus decided to send a few veiled messages to the United States in order to press for money. The first was a speech given on June 11, 1940, when, on board the Brazilian battleship Minas Gerais, the Brazilian President praised the Axis powers for their social and political achievements. Undoubtedly, Vargas was praising the totalitarian style of the political regime to which he himself subscribed. In any case, at a time when the German Blitzkrieg was gaining ground in Europe, Vargas's speech could be interpreted as a warning to the United States of a possible Brazilian alignment with the German side in the war in case U.S. financial aid was not offered promptly. Evidently, the Latin American nation did not hold any real military power that could be used either way against the Axis or the Allies, but its strategic importance in the war was still considerable, as it represented South America's gateway to Europe.

As American money remained stuck within the coffers of the Eximbank, a new veiled message was sent to President Roosevelt on April 20, 1941, in the form of a telegram from Vargas to Hitler congratulating him on his 52nd birthday. Vargas was insisting on Eximbank funding a large steel plant in Brazil, a demand that was being strongly resisted by the United States who, at the time, held a virtual monopoly on steel production. With the United States and the United Kingdom's enactment of the Atlantic Charter on August 14, however, practically bringing America into the war, Vargas's attempts to bargain economic advantages from its neutral position had to end. The Brazilian dictator was now forced to choose sides, and since there was really only one side to choose, Vargas forfeited his German trump card.

Brazil's adherence to the principles of the Atlantic Charter resulted in Germany and Italy attacking Brazilian vessels from February 1942. Vargas then found a new outlet for his brand of extortion politics, namely that of negotiating how Brazil would become involved in the war on the Allied side. The Latin American nation had a privileged geographic position in relation to Europe. What Brazilian military strategists called the *Saliente Nordestino*, that is, the salient portion of the northeastern part of the national territory facing the Atlantic, provided Vargas with a new trump card. The region's relative proximity to North Africa and Europe was highly valued when the logistics of war depended greatly on geographical factors. Vargas thus opted to offer a concession for an American military base in the area in exchange for the Eximbank's funds for a national iron factory. The result was the establishment of the *Companhia Siderúrgica Nacional* (CSN), a large steel plant built near Rio de Janeiro. The dictator also insisted on Brazilian troops being directly involved in the conflict, a move that, he hoped, would bring some future advantage to his country in case of Allied victory.

Vargas signed the Declaration by the United Nations, a follow-up of the Atlantic Charter of 1941, on August 22, 1942, officially bringing Brazil into the war against the Axis. Keeping his word on the deal with Vargas, President Roosevelt sent to Brazil a group of technical consultants for industrial development led by Morris Llewellyn Cooke (1872–1960), who arrived in Rio de Janeiro on September 27, 1942. Cooke's report was central to the establishment of Brazil's steel industry in the years ahead.

Brazil's military engagement in the war presented the United States with one more difficulty during those convoluted years. Vargas had been complaining about the need to modernize the Brazilian armed forces since the early 1930s. This need had in fact been used as an excuse for the Brazilian sovereign default announced in 1937. If Brazil were to send troops to Europe now, these would have to be trained and equipped by the United States. President Roosevelt agreed to offer training and military materials to the Brazilian troops based on the U.S. Lend-Lease policy of 1941. The Brazilian Expeditionary Force (FEB) was sent to the Mediterranean theater of war in July 1944, when the conflict was for the most part already over with the Allies victorious. Brazil's military expedition comprised a force of about 25,000 men arranged between the army and the Air Force. The troops did manage to take a significant number of Axis prisoners, mostly in Italy, suffering only 948 casualties. Brazil and Mexico were the only Latin American nations to send troops to fight overseas during the Second World War. This gave a boost to Brazilian national pride.[10]

There was an obvious contradiction in Brazil's military engagement in the conflict on the side of liberal democracies fighting Nazi fascism in Europe given the dictatorial model assumed domestically. Opposition to Vargas had long been timid, bit it was soon to awaken and turn this paradox into political profit. On October 24, 1943, a group of leading politicians in the state of Minas Gerais issued a public document called *Manifesto dos Mineiros*, pointing out the unsustainability of a domestic totalitarian regime that was engaged in a fight for democracy abroad. The manifesto was the first of a series of calls for an end to Vargas's dictatorship.

The government punished several of the manifesto's signatories. But with criticism mounting, Vargas had to bend and promise to take steps toward democratization. He vowed to call general elections as soon as the war was over. His strategy was to gain time and buy the support of the working classes so as to extend his rule after the end of the war. With that plan in mind, Vargas continued to enhance the legal apparatus that secured social rights and helped keep the masses on side. The government's situation was increasingly contradictory. Just as he was trying to maintain his own fascist dictatorship, the President was having to adopt leftist policies in order to obtain support from the working class. This angered the right-wing extremists. In 1943, he decreed a rise in the minimum wage and issued a new law called *Consolidação das Leis do Trabalho* (Consolidation of Labor Laws), whereby the nation's preexisting labor legislation, including the rules for social security established in 1935, was unified into a single document of 944 articles. The document was inspired by Mussolini's *Carta del lavoro* of 1927.

By mid-1944, the right-wing opposition was establishing a close alliance with the military class. The armed forces were gaining prestige from their operations in Europe, and the possibility that the officers who were fighting against totalitarianism abroad would promote a coup against the domestic dictatorship on their return home haunted Vargas's every thought. One of the provisional solutions adduced by the dictator's clique was to collect all armaments from the soldiers before they entered the country on their way back from Europe. That solution, however, proved to be unnecessary.

In its growing political intermingling with the armed forces, the right-wing civilian opposition started to promote the presidential candidacy of Air Force Commander Eduardo Gomes (1896–1981). The candidacy was made public in October 1944. Already, in the first days of that year, voices calling for democracy began to be heard throughout the country. They came both from the right and the left, including, in the first case, those old regional oligarchs who were now leaning on the military. Men such as Otávio Mangabeira (1886–1960), from Bahia, Júlio Prestes (1882–1946), from São Paulo, and ex-president Artur Bernardes (1875–1955), from Minas Gerais, began to gravitate toward the common idea of recovering their former power, which had been usurped by Vargas and his Riograndense warlords some fourteen years earlier. On the left, intellectuals linked to the Communist Party such as Sérgio Milliet (1898–1966), Murilo Rubião (1916–1991), and Jorge Amado (1912–2001), also started to speak out against the regime. They met on January 22, 1944, in the first Brazilian Congress of Writers and demanded democracy. In the end, only the enormous mass of working class citizens, who still regarded the old leader as their benefactor, remained loyal to Vargas.

Facing growing political isolation, the Riograndense dictator was obliged to make concessions and, on February 28, 1945, he decreed the

Constitutional Law n. 9, which called for elections to be scheduled in 90 days. On April 18, Vargas decreed a general amnesty for all those who had been charged with political crimes since July 16, 1934, the date of the promulgation of the 1934 Constitution. This freed communist leader Luís Carlos Prestes, who had been incarcerated and who could now take part in politics again, carrying the banner of his newly legalized *Partido Comunista Brasileiro* (PCB).[11]

The idea of democratization mobilized the entire nation. As the new presidential decree allowed for the re-establishment of political parties, which had been proscribed since 1937, a craze for alliances, and the hope of securing a piece of the new power to come, emerged. The old right-wing oligarchs created the *União Democrática Nacional* (UDN). Vargas himself, in his always wavering politics, gave his blessing to the establishment of two different parties, the *Partido Social Democrático* (PSD), comprised mostly of the former federal interventores who had worked to extend the dictator's power throughout the provinces over the last fifteen years, and the *Partido Trabalhista Brasileiro* (PTB), which represented the interests of the working class, so eagerly defended by the President himself throughout the period.[12] The UDN launched the candidacy of Air Marshal Eduardo Gomes (1896–1981), a heavy-handed military man from Rio de Janeiro who fiercely opposed Vargas's dictatorship from the start, while the PSD promoted that of General Eurico Gaspar Dutra (1883–1974), Vargas's Minister of War from December 5, 1936 to August 3, 1945. The Communist Party presented the candidacy of Riograndense politician Yedo Fiúza (1894–1975).

Despite having been incarcerated and having his wife handed to the Nazis in Germany by the Estado Novo's dictator, communist leader Luís Carlos Prestes decided to support the popular movement calling for the establishment of a constitutive assembly under Vargas's leadership. The constitutionalist movement began in the city of São Paulo in March 1945, soon spreading to Rio de Janeiro. By May, large public demonstrations were taking to the streets under the banner of *Queremismo*, the name assumed by the popular movement as an abbreviation of *Queremos Getúlio* (We Want Getúlio). The Queremistas demanded the continuation of Vargas's presidency, the postponement of the upcoming presidential elections, and the immediate calling of a constitutive assembly within Vargas's government. The *Queremismo* partisans also proposed that if the upcoming elections were confirmed, Vargas should run as a candidate.

In the face of the dictator's growing popular support, the military, led by Generals Góes Monteiro and Gaspar Dutra, hatched a conspiracy to overthrow Vargas. The U.S. Ambassador to Brazil, Adolf Berle, Jr. (1895–

1971), had defended the South American nation's democratization in a speech given on September 29, 1945, in the city of Petrópolis. The rebelling commanders assumed the American Ambassador's speech implied U.S. support for the ousting of Vargas. Aware of the communist support for the dictator, and looking at the example of Argentina, where Juan Domingo Perón had risen to power with the same kind of popular support presently enjoyed by Vargas, Berle Jr.'s backing of the conspirators seemed almost natural.

Whatever the case, Vargas's government was overthrown on October 29, 1945, when Generals Monteiro and Dutra forced the dictator to resign. The same military men who had brought Vargas to power in 1930, now made him step down. The ensuing democratic interlude, however, would not last long: Riograndense dictatorship would be interrupted, not ended once and for all.

Culture and Society in the First Vargas Government

The period from 1930 to 1945 marked the emergence of a new State-driven effort at building a national identity among Brazilians. The novelty now was that for the first time the mass of individuals who fell outside the privileged bourgeois class of commodity producers would be included in the cultural profile of the nation. Earlier governmental attempts at concocting a Brazilian nationality, such as the one undertaken by Emperor Pedro II and his Brazilian Historic and Geographic Institute from 1840 to 1889, had lacked a tangible perspective on citizenship. Something similar occurred during the First Republic, whose federalism and decentralizing disposition precluded the building of a uniform sense of Brazilianness emanating from the State. Furthermore, the elitist nature of both the Empire and the First Republic hindered the establishment of a notion of nationality as a shared experience common to all of those who were related to the nation by birth or residence.

If a restrictive aristocratic social arrangement precluded the transformation of the former Portuguese colonials into distinguished independent Brazilian nationals during the period from 1822 to 1889, from 1889 to 1930 the dissolution of the nationality into several regionalisms resulted in opposition between local cultures, with the final political outcome being the emergence of the authoritarian centralizing rule from Rio Grande do Sul. It is true that the First Republic's projection of feeble national unity and identity did meet with a strong reaction from the avant-garde modernists, who attempted to establish an avant-garde aesthetic based on a nationalistic disposition and on the idea of promoting a national culture that would devour and digest the old and the foreign just to excrete something new and original. That, as we have seen, was called *antropofagia*, and it implied a cultural nationalism that unconsciously recovered the identity-building aim of the imperial State in the previous century.

With Vargas and the 1930 Revolution, the relation between the State and the artists would become inverted by comparison with that previously seen with the avant-garde. Notions of citizenship and cultural identity would be imposed upon Brazilians from above as a way of holding the nation together. The Portuguese language would be emphasized, with the prohibition of foreign languages repeating the eighteenth-century policies of the Portuguese Crown and its representative, the Marquis of Pombal. In sum, the untold story of Portuguese cultural dictatorship in Brazil would regain full force during the Estado Novo regime.

Paradoxically, however, a reaction against Vargas's centralizing idea of the nation would emerge in a strong movement of regionalist literature. This notwithstanding, the dictator would still manage to co-opt a great number of artists, especially musicians, to his authoritarian project of nation building. As the cultural camp became divided, dissatisfaction among some literati, who assumed a defying, anti-Vargas position, led to a series of arrests and exiles that would leave a strong mark on the cultural history of the period.

Before we look into the artistic production of the years between 1930 and 1945 we must first observe how the Estado Novo's notion of national identity was enforced through the use of propaganda and other forms of mass control. Together with a personality cult centered upon his own figure, the dictator enforced a strongly nationalistic educational system. This system attempted to inculcate a sense of Brazilianness in the younger generation. Primary school curricula were infused with an extended program in music education. Music in particular was manipulated to fulfill the aims of the State, for it had the advantage of promoting nationalistic themes through hymns and songs, thus inspiring in students the desired emotion of love of country.

In order to implement his music education program, on April 18, 1931, Vargas decreed the obligatory teaching of Orpheonic Singing in primary and secondary schools. The following year he appointed modernist composer Heitor Villa-Lobos (1887–1959) as director of the Office for Musical and Artistic Education, another bureau in the complex web of Vargas's state-totalitarian administration. The office was conceived as part of a larger educational reform carried out by educator Anísio Teixeira (1900–1971), who subscribed to the principles of Progressive Education, a pedagogical movement that had started during the late nineteenth century in Germany and Switzerland. Progressive Education attempted to build a non-elitist educational system where experiential learning and entrepreneurship would be fostered in tandem with classical studies.[13]

Teixeira understood how far Brazilian education, especially higher education, lagged behind other Latin American countries. During the period of the Brazilian Empire, the limited offering of higher education in the country created the custom of upper class families sending their sons to attend European universities. The First Republic did very little to change the elitist nature of Brazilian education. In that context, in 1932, Teixeira published, together with 25 other men of letters, the *Manifesto dos Pioneiros da Educação Nova*. The document proposed the notion of *Escola Nova* (New School), which, much to Vargas's liking, suggested the political title of his forthcoming "Estado Novo." At a time of industrial growth and urbanization, the movement attempted to democratize education by expanding its offer to the working classes and by including curricula in professional training. Albeit deriving from a nineteenth-century European movement, the New School served Vargas's nationalism well, allowing for the direct application of his notion of nation-state building. The new education system translated perfectly the idea of a formal nationalist upbringing that would produce a skilled and dutiful proletariat in possession of a strong civic culture.

Villa-Lobos's Office for Musical and Artistic Education would play an important part in this new nationalistic educational system. The composer adapted Orpheonic Singing, which had been a part of young Brazilians' musical education since the beginning of the century, to the necessities of Vargas's all-encompassing nation state. Orpheonic singing originated in France, growing out of the ceremonial works of the Napoleonic Empire. It is distinguished from classical choral singing by its capacity to engage much larger ensembles, which perform in unison, and also for requiring no musical knowledge or vocal training from the performers. Orpheonic Singing in large groups tends to produce high levels of enthusiasm among participants, and is thus a good medium for the expression of patriotic sentiment.[14]

Villa-Lobos developed the idea of employing this form of singing to the benefit of Vargas's totalitarianism during his two extended stays in Paris (1923–24 and 1927–30), where he became acquainted with French culture. Only after having his project of nationalistic music education approved by the dictator did he decide to return to his native land from Europe. Villa-Lobos's years in Paris coincided with those of the emergence of the avant-garde around the globe, reflected in the Brazilian composer's musical output. Brazil's eccentric avant-garde nationalism would flourish in the composer's dialogue with tradition, where folk themes and songs were frequently intertwined with European classical instrumentation and form. With their simple and delicate melodies, his nine compositions entitled *Bachianas Brasileiras* (1930–1945) form an important part of Brazilian musical modernism and accord with the nationalistic disposition of Vargas's Estado Novo.[15]

While Orpheonic Singing employed themes of patriotism and lyrical sentimentalism in gigantic civic events that celebrated the regime and its leader, a less pliant artistic expression emerged in the literary form of the novel. A loose movement called *Romance Regionalista* (Regionalist Novel) or *Romance de 30* (1930s Novel) appeared in a response to the nationalistic euphoria promoted by Villa-Lobos and his music. Literary historians place the movement's starting point in 1928, with, as we have seen, the publication of José Américo de Almeida's *A Bagaceira*. The novels that followed this seminal work tended to portray the contradictions and conflicts inherent in the rapidly modernizing Brazilian society. Works from authors such as José Lins do Rego (1901–1957), Graciliano Ramos (1892–1953), Jorge Amado (1912–2001), Rachel de Queiroz (1910–2003), Cyro dos Anjos (1906–1994), and Lúcio Cardoso (1912–1968) contrasted with the official image of an urban, modern, and industrialized nation. These novelists presented Brazil's less laudable face found in impoverished and underdeveloped rural areas. The decadent provincial patriarchal society that attempted to hold fast to its waning power was depicted in these works with strong tints of social criticism. The regionalist authors distinguished themselves from the previous modernists by weaving a strong sociological dimension and avoiding aesthetic experimentation in their narratives.

The severe droughts suffered by the impoverished inhabitants of the northeastern provinces became the preferred theme in this new literary trend. In *O Quinze* (1930), Rachel de Queiroz tells the story of northeastern *retirantes*, a term that refers to poor families as they attempt to escape the drought-ridden areas of the northeastern countryside by migrating to less inhospitable regions. Their displacement is always undertaken in extremely harsh conditions, often by foot, and involves the threat of death in the semi-arid inlands. *O Quinze* is set in the author's native state of Ceará and derives the tale of the *retirantes*' struggle from real events connected to a major drought that occurred in the state in 1915. Queiroz narrates the story in simple and direct language, focusing on the present and on the plight of the main characters as they move to the state's capital, Fortaleza. The female author became involved with the Communist Party in the early 1930s and was arrested by Vargas's ideological police in 1937. Her fate at the hands of the dictator would be repeated by a great number of writers in the period.

The *retirantes* appear again as protagonists in Graciliano Ramos's *Vidas secas* (1938), a tale of survival that portrays an underprivileged family's desperate attempt to overcome its almost inhuman conditions. The narrative is written in circular form, where the end leads right back into the opening phrase, suggesting thus the cyclical and unending suffering to which the characters are submitted. Like Queiroz, Ramos also depicts the life of his native state, Alagoas, which is located to the south of Queiroz's Ceará. Also, like Queiroz, Ramos was arrested for his connections with communism. His incarceration occurred in 1936 in the craze that followed the communist revolt of 1935, which, as we have seen, started in the northeastern state of Rio Grande do Norte. The author's experience in prison forms the core of another of his novels, *Memórias do Cárcere* (1953), published posthumously. In this work, Ramos depicts a series of real events, such as Olga Benário's extradition to Germany. Both *Vidas secas* and *Memórias do Cárcere* figure among some of the most praised novels in Brazilian literary history; they were adapted into film by director Nelson Pereira dos Santos in 1963 and 1984, respectively.

The social and economic decadence of sugar cane plantations in the northeastern state of Paraíba becomes a central theme for the 1930s Regionalist Novel in the works of José Lins do Rego. Novels such as *Menino de engenho* (1932), *Bangüê* (1934), and *Usina* (1936) combine realist description with the new colloquial style that was also employed by Queiroz and Ramos, and which drew both from the modernists' experiments with original Brazilian language as well as from the late-nineteenth and early-twentieth-century naturalists' search for truth in exact description.

Menino de engenho forms a sort of *Bildungsroman* centered upon the coming of age of the young protagonist, *Carlinhos*, who is taken to live on his grandfather's plantation after the institutionalization of his father, who killed the protagonist's mother. The novel is narrated in the first person and it explores the gradual unfolding of Carlinhos's awareness of the social inequalities between the landowning gentry and the servant class. The protagonist's amorous relations with his female cousins appear against the background of local culture and folklore. The use of honest, simple language earned the novel and its author immediate critical acclaim.

A more urban perspective, albeit still set against the regionalist background of a northeastern state, appears in the novels of Jorge Amado.

Works such as *O País do Carnaval* (1931), *Cacau* (1933), *Suor* (1934), *Jubiabá* (1935), *Mar morto* (1936), and *Capitães da areia* (1937) enforced the new sense of social criticism in the novel as they depicted the slums and the lives of poor residents in the state of Bahia and its capital city, Salvador. Amado's strong Marxist leanings informed a literature sensitive to the difficulties that beset the impoverished inhabitants of the outskirts of an urban landscape where spatial exclusion of the socially destitute was the norm. *Capitães da areia* (1937), one of the author's most polemical early novels, recounts the adventures of a group of abandoned children who live as beggars and thieves on the streets of Salvador. The novel's protagonist, the orphan Pedro Bala, learns that his proletarian father was murdered while leading a strike that was brutally repressed by the police. Through the story of his father's death, the boy becomes acquainted with the notion of class struggle, an idea that permeates his life as well as the novel. Besides such Marxist subject matter, *Capitães da areia* portrays native elements of Bahian culture, such as *Candomblé*, an Afro-Brazilian religion. The religious practices of Candomblé involve a mixture of traditional Yoruba and Bantu mysticism syncretized with Roman Catholic and indigenous American beliefs, the latter involving shamanism and recalling the Siberian origin of native Americans. Candomblé officially originated in the early nineteenth century in the city of Salvador, where it continues to be an important cultural phenomenon. With his depictions of his native Bahia, Amado gave a new turn to the Brazilian regionalist novel, now mixing aspects of a regional culture with the urban dimension of a state capital. Amado thus brought to the fore the diverse cultural landscape and the deep-rooted social contradictions of a country whose authoritarian government was attempting to promote cultural unity under a monochrome notion of nationality. Like Queiroz and Ramos, Amado was also arrested by Vargas's police forces. In 1937, his books were publicly burned, having been dismissed as no more than pamphlets full of communist propaganda.

Another important writer of the period was the Mineiro Lúcio Cardoso, who, in works such as *Maleita* (1934) and *Salgueiro* (1935), maintained the sociological and realist perspective of the other regionalist writers, but who also added a deeper psychological dimension to his narratives. Cardoso's more introspective style concurred with that of his lifelong friend, novelist Clarice Lispector (1920–1977) who, in 1943, during the final years of Vargas's government, published her first book, *Perto do Coração Selvagem*, a work that turned away from the realism of regionalist fiction and brought a new existentialist dimension to the Brazilian novel. Lúcio Cardoso was also an important playwright. His *O escravo* (1937) is considered to be one of the first works of modern Brazilian theater. The play presents a dense web of disillusioned characters experiencing constant anxiety and existential misery in the face of the strong and manipulative woman who maintains her family members enslaved by her every whim. With its three acts set in a room during a tempestuous night, *O escravo* prefigures Sartre's *Huis Clos* (1944) and also the heavily existentialist content of the 1950s Theater of the Absurd. In 1947, Cardoso contributed with his play *O filho pródigo* to a theater group called "Black Experimental Theater," which had been founded in 1944 by Afro-Brazilian activist Abdias do Nascimento (1914–2011). Cardoso's play opened in Rio de Janeiro under the direction of Nascimento, who also played the role of the father in the drama based on the biblical parable of the prodigal son (Gospel of Luke, 15:11–32). Nascimento would become a major figure in the Brazilian civil rights movement, winning a seat in the Senate from 1997 to 1999. His Black Experimental Theater group was rooted in an earlier political movement called the Brazilian Black Front, founded in São Paulo in 1931. The movement acquired the status of a political party in 1936, but was closed the following year following Getúlio Vargas's coup. The Brazilian Black Front holds remarkable historical importance as the first Afro-Brazilian organization fighting against racism and demanding full rights for racial minorities in Brazilian society.[16]

Another important development in the Brazilian theater of the period from 1930 to 1945 appears in the plays of renowned dramatist, Nelson Rodrigues (1912–1980), whose first work, *A mulher sem pecado* (The Woman Without Sin, 1941), started a series of psychological dramas informed by themes such as jealousy, infidelity, hypocrisy, betrayal, perversion, incest, paranoia, and hatred. *A mulher sem pecado* portrays the life of Olegário, a man obsessed with his second wife, Lídia, and plagued by his suspicions of her matrimonial infidelity. Olegário's mental torment is furthered by his physical disability; forced to live in a wheelchair, the protagonist's suffering is intensified with each absence of his wife, whom he constantly accuses of deceit. The play is drawn to a surprising denouement when, after being assured of the faithfulness of Lídia, the audience discovers that Olegário had feigned his disability, and that now Lídia is at the point of absconding with another man.

A mulher sem pecado is the first of Rodrigues's seventeen plays of darkness and deception that portrayed the most sinister aspects of the Brazilian middle class of his day. Often charged with intense eroticism, Rodrigues's theater is marked by disturbing scenes and themes that tended to produce a strong feeling of despair in the Estado Novo's primarily

Catholic and conservative society. The author also wrote nine novels, the last of which, *O casamento* (1966), was banned by another dictatorial government that had risen to power in 1964, throwing the country into two decades of autocratic military rule. In the twenty-first century, however, Rodrigues's oeuvre gained significant popularity, as many of his plays and short stories were adapted for television, reaching a large audience in weekly Sunday-night broadcasts. Several of his plays were also adapted for film, usually erotically charged, during the 1970s and 1980s.[17]

Poetry also showed important developments during the period of Vargas's first government. The launching of poet Vinicius de Moraes's (1913–1980) career with the publication of his first collection of verse *O Caminho para a Distância* (1933) is especially noteworthy. A book later dismissed by the author as unrepresentative of his poetry, *O Caminho para a Distância* brings to verse a strong Catholic worldview that appeared as a reaction to the anti-clerical stance of the 1920s avant-garde. As the years proceeded, however, the poet became increasingly passionate about life and its pleasures, and started showing signs of what would become the life and aesthetic of a bohemian. In 1936, Moraes published *Ariana, a Mulher*, a long poem that narrates the search for an idealized woman. *Cinco Elegias* (1943) marks the birth of the author's new style, breaking away from Catholicism and engaging in enhanced sensuality and new social themes.

In the late 1950s, Vinicius de Moraes would establish a long-lasting artistic partnership with composer Antônio Carlos Jobim (1927–1994) and become an important figure in the emergence of bossa nova, a musical style that mixed the upbeat rhythms of samba music with complex harmonies and melodies, often in minor modes, creating a new, softer musical expression. The lyrics for songs such as *Chega de Saudade* (No More Blues, 1958) and *Garota de Ipanema* (The Girl from Ipanema, 1962) turned Moraes into the leading poet of the bossa nova movement.

Brazilian popular music was one of the most notable artistic developments of the 1930–1945 period. The nation's capital, Rio de Janeiro, with its strong African heritage and fast-paced urbanization, became the center of a new musical movement as middle-class neighborhoods began to bring together blacks, whites, and mestizos who lived in close proximity and who produced a highly syncretized popular musical expression. This new music was called *samba*. In it, African rhythms were combined with European harmonies and played on European instruments. The phenomenon holds similarities to the development of jazz in the United States, although here a lighter instrumentation based on guitars and flutes takes the place of the heavier brass and drums of Dixieland or Swing bands. The widespread use of the acoustic guitar in this new music was probably the result of the influence of earlier forms such as the Portuguese *fado*, which emphasized singing accompanied by strings. The sentimentality of fado informed the Brazilian *modinha*, an original musical style that existed in tandem with several forms of Afro-Brazilian musical expression, the most well known of which was the *lundu*, a song and dance form with origins among the African Bantu and colonial Portuguese peoples. Although an early and original form of samba emerged in Bahia, musicologists tend to place the genre's roots in the middle-class neighborhoods of Rio de Janeiro, where the style would have emerged as the result of a combination of modinha and lundu elements. Samba's emphasis on vocal music performed with rhythmic guitar accompaniment does suggest an inheritance from fado and modinha styles combined with the African beat of lundu.[18]

Samba soon came to epitomize the Brazilian national musical identity. Several other styles existed in the distinct regions of the country, but with Rio de Janeiro being the capital, its autochthonous music became the representative national style, that is, something that transcended the merely local. Among the middle-class neighborhoods serving as breeding grounds for this new music, Estácio de Sá was the most prominent. Named in honor of the city's founder, Estácio de Sá (1520–1567), the famous Portuguese soldier who, as we have seen, defended the city against the French invaders and their native allies in 1565, the neighborhood attracted some of the best samba musicians in the style's history. Highly talented musicians such as Angenor de Oliveira, known as Cartola (1908–1980), Nelson Antônio da Silva, known as Nelson Cavaquinho (1911–1986), Ary Barroso (1903–1964), and Noel Rosa (1910–1937) would gather in the neighborhood during the early 1930s to sing, play, and lead typically *carioca* bohemian lives. From their informal gatherings emerged what came to be known as *Turma do Estácio* (The Estácio Group), a historical/musicological construct that points to the musically rich heritage of the neighborhood.

Among the *Turma do Estácio* musicians, Cartola is considered to be the forerunner. One of his first compositions *Que Infeliz Sorte!* (1931), is also one of the first examples of the new samba music that emerged in the 1930s. The song was bought from the composer and released in 1931 by popular singer Francisco Alves (1898–1952), a Portuguese descendant who, between 1927 and his death in 1952, recorded as many as 524 78rpm gramophone albums. The song's lyrics talk of unrequited love and the ingratitude of a beautiful woman towards the composer. Francisco Alves's 1931 recording rendered Cartola's song with an instrumentation that included a tuba and several other brass instruments, producing an overall sound and rhythmic feel considerably different to what came to typify samba music, that is, a swinging melody with percussion and guitar accompaniment.

Cartola would issue his first record as a solo artist only in 1974, at the age of 66, but by then his mark on the history of samba music had already been made. As early as 1928 the singer/songwriter had been an important figure in the group of musicians that founded the Mangueira Samba School, one of the most traditional ensembles that take part in the Rio de Janeiro carnival parades. The Mangueira School was the second samba school to be established, the first being that of Estácio de Sá.

The richness of the samba music emerging in the 1930s owes a great deal to the high quality of songwriting discernable during the period. An array of songs with lyrics of high poetic density marked the musical production of Nelson Cavaquinho (1911–1986), another remarkable musician associated with the Estácio and Mangueira neighborhoods. Cavaquinho wrote more than 400 songs during his career, many of which were composed in partnership with Cartola. As a self-taught guitar player, he developed a very idiosyncratic playing style, using only two fingers of his right hand to sound chords and melodic lines. His first recorded song, *Não Faça Vontade a Ela* (1939), appeared on an album by popular singer Alcides Gerardi (1918–1978). The song's title, which in English could be translated as "Don't grant her all her wishes," or perhaps "Don't spoil her too much," suggests the content of the song, where the poet offers advice to a male friend telling him not to give too much freedom to his beloved, lest she take over his entire life.

Nelson Cavaquinho's less good-humored side appeared in songs full of nostalgia, where themes such as impermanence, old age, death, and lost love abound. A good example is his famous *Folhas Secas* (Withered Leaves), in which the poet thinks of his daily life in the neighborhood of Mangueira, and then considers a future time when old age will have prevented him from continuing to sing and play. He then states how he will miss the music and the poets of his neighborhood. The reminiscences that comprise the song's thematic core are triggered from the double meaning of the word *mangueira*. Signifying both a mango tree as well as the neighborhood where the poet lives, it is when he steps on the "withered leaves" of a mango tree that the images of the neighborhood and its poet friends emerge in nostalgic form.

Another remarkable songwriter whose work emerged in the early years of Vargas's first government was the middle-class white musician Noel Rosa (1910–1937). A dropout medical student who gave up university for the bohemian nightlife of Rio de Janeiro's red-light district, Rosa provided a bridge between the racially mixed lower-middle-class environment in which early samba music sprouted and the mainstream white society of his own neighborhood. His songs are characterized by a humorous quality not much different from that seen in Nelson Cavaquinho's *Não Faça Vontade a Ela* (1939). Rosa's first hit came in 1930. Entitled *Com que roupa?* and recorded in his own voice in the first year of Vargas's Revolution, the song told of a simple everyday event in the artist's life as a young man. While still a medical student, Rosa had attempted to go out for a samba party one night, and his mother, preventing him from leaving the house, hides his best evening clothes. He then writes the song *Com que roupa?* (With what clothes?), asking what could he possibly wear to that important evening out with his friends.

Rosa's recording inaugurated a new style in samba music. The strong tenor voice of Francisco Alves, the most popular singer of the time, was suddenly replaced by Rosa's much softer, almost subdued interpretation. Rosas's style would be mimicked in the years to come until it became part of the natural sound of Rio de Janeiro's middle-class music, the bossa nova. Rosa's songs combined the Afro-Brazilian roots of samba with the new urban and witty language of his city, portraying more faithfully the social everyday life of Rio de Janeiro's residents with their values and customs.

Rosa suffered from a congenital condition that produces facial abnormalities in humans known as Pierre Robin syndrome. His deformed chin, however, did not prevent him from being very successful with women. During his short but intense bohemian life, he had a considerable number of girlfriends. He was married in 1934 to a girl from a well-to-do family named Lindaura Martins. At the same time, however, he maintained a long-lasting love affair with a cabaret dancer named Juraci Correia de Araújo. Rosa was also a good friend of Cartola's, who, being only two years older than the reckless former medical student, frequently took care of his friend after the latter's nights of heavy drinking. On many an evening, Cartola offered Rosa shelter in his Mangueira house when his friend was in no condition to go home alone after spending long hours singing and dancing in the bohemian cabarets of Rio de Janeiro's Lapa neighborhood.

Lapa's cabarets differed significantly from their Parisian counterparts, such as the Moulin Rouge and Folies Bergère, which emerged primarily as performance venues. Lapa's cabarets, called *gafieira*, offered drinks, music and space for samba ballroom dancing. The dancing was called gafieira dancing. The dance style produced in the gafieiras was quite elegant, maintaining a remarkable sense of propriety that would virtually disappear in its modern versions. The gafieiras were places where the lower-middle-class citizens of Rio de Janeiro would spend part of their evenings at weekends to dance, have fun, and find love. Today, some clubs in the Lapa neighborhood attempt to revive the original atmosphere of the 1930s and 1940s, providing tourists with a sense of local heritage.

Together with the gafieira style of samba emerged the figure of the *malandro*, a sort of romanticized character that fits the idealized profile of the adult male who lived life to its fullest in the gafieira nights of Rio de Janeiro. Not by coincidence, Rosa's second recorded song was entitled *Malandro medroso* (The scared malandro). It tells the story of a *malandro* who attempts to seduce a girl and flees when he perceives that her father is coming his way. Rosa actually became the very archetype of the *malandro*, a sort of elegant "bad boy" who managed to get his way in always playful and attractive ways.

The excesses of nightlife started proving harmful to Rosa's health in the early 1930s. Soon the singer contracted tuberculosis and met a premature death in 1937 at the age of 26. The stereotype of the *malandro*, however, continued to echo in Brazilian society and culture. In the early 1940s, Walt Disney would create his charismatic and friendly character, the Brazilian parrot Joe Carioca, based on Rosa's *malandro* figure. Disney's creation was closely linked to President Roosevelt's Good Neighbor Policy and to the United States' attempt to win allies to fight the Second World War. Rosa's aesthetic of *malandragem* ended up being exported around the world as quintessential idea of Brazilianess.

One more popular musician whose work should be remembered with regard to the new national Brazilian culture emerging during Vargas's dictatorial period is the talented pianist and songwriter Ary Barroso (1903–1964). Born into an upper-middle-class family in the state of Minas Gerais, Barroso had the opportunity to study classical piano from early childhood and by his early teens he was already working as a pianist in Rio de Janeiro's cinemas and cafés. He went to university in 1921 in order to study Law, but was unable to reconcile his studies with the bohemian musical life he had chosen to live. Barroso dropped out of college in his second year.

Barroso's first hit appeared in 1929 under the title *Vamos deixar de intimidade*. The song was recorded by the popular singer Mário Reis (1907–1981), who had been one of Barroso's classmates in Law School. His most successful composition, *Aquarela do Brasil*, was recorded in 1939 by Francisco Alves, who was accompanied by one of the finest orchestras of the time, that of conductor Radamés Gnattali (1906–1988). *Aquarela do Brasil*'s lyrics sang of the country's beauty and of its people's gentle, sensual, and primarily good nature, giving a very idealized vision of Brazil. In its capacity to move people's hearts and at the same time exalt the nation, the song started a sub-genre of samba music called *samba-exaltação*, of which Barroso's own *Isto aqui o que é* (1942), with its claim of the Brazilian people's talent for singing and happiness, is one of the best examples. Barroso's nationalistic music was received with considerable criticism, especially from critics of a leftist orientation, for it was perceived as providing ideological support to Vargas's dictatorship.

The rise of nationalism in popular music in the 1930s coincided with the emergence of a new movement in the social sciences in which Brazilian intellectuals began to reflect upon their own country with renewed interest, as well as with enhanced interpretive skills. Three important works in Sociology, History, and Economics marked this new wave of Brazilians thinking about themselves: Gilberto Freyre's (1900–1987) *Casa Grande & Senzala* (1933), Sérgio Buarque de Holanda's (1902–1982) *Raízes do Brasil* (1936), and Caio Prado Júnior's (1907–1990) *História Econômica do Brasil* (1945). Together, these three books form the core of an analytical perspective on how Brazil came to be what it was during the fifteen years of Vargas's first administration.

Gilberto Freyre was a sociologist, anthropologist, historian, writer, journalist, diplomat, and congressman born in the city of Recife, the capital of the northeastern state of Pernambuco. His sociological treatise, *Casa Grande & Senzala* (1933), is a groundbreaking study of races and cultures in Brazil. It attempts to characterize the nation as racially conciliatory, and thus contributed to the founding of the ideology of Brazil as a racism-free country. The book's title brings together the large houses of the slave-owning gentry, the *casa grande*, with the slave quarters, called *senzalas*. These two antagonistic spaces coexisted in the landscape of northeastern sugar plantations. The book's main idea is that such coexistence resulted in the building of important emotional ties between the black slaves and their masters which, in turn, would have influenced the racial profile of the nation. Although such an idealized vision has been severely criticized on various intellectual fronts, Freyre's work is important in having found the notion of *lusotropicalism*, whereby miscegenation would have been a positive force in the establishment of Brazilian society.[19]

A less idealized vision of Brazilian culture and society appeared in the works of Weberian historian Sérgio Buarque de Holanda, who in *Raízes do Brasil* (1936) analyzed some of the psychological traits and social behavioral patterns that, according to his analysis, characterized Brazil and its people. Traits such as the tendency to employ social cordiality in order to win favor and climb the social ladder, the tendency towards paternalism and patrimonialism inherent in the nation's ingrained bureaucratic system, and the general inheritance of Portuguese *personalismo*, that is, the emphasis on political allegiances to specific persons rather than to parties or ideologies, are some of the elements analyzed by Holanda. The author insightfully uncovers such traits in order to show how they constituted an obstacle to the establishment of democracy in the country. The analysis, it should be noted, appears to be still valid several decades after the book's publication. Patrimonialism, with its essential blending of the public and private realms, still functions as a lever for corruption and authoritarianism in Brazil.

A succinct analysis of Brazilian economic history appeared in the works of Marxist historian Caio Prado Júnior. In *História Econômica do Brasil* (1945), the author analyzes the role of Portuguese mercantile capitalism in the process of Brazilian colonization. Prado Júnior stresses that even after independence in 1822, the South American country continued to be entangled in the colonial economic cycle whereby it emerged as a provider of basic commodities without enough impetus for industrial development. This would have shaped the center/periphery dialectic in which the nation would become embedded throughout its future history. Prado Júnior also notes the existence of three great aristocracies that succeeded one another during the nation's development: that of the sugar producers, or *senhores de engenho*; that of the wealthy *mineradores* of the gold cycle in Minas Gerais; and that of the coffee barons of São Paulo. The sustained strength of the latter would account for São Paulo's economic leadership in modern Brazil.

Besides the works of Gilberto Freyre, Sérgio Buarque de Holanda, and Caio Prado Júnior, as well as the aforementioned developments in music and literature, the period saw important developments in cinema with the establishment of the first major Brazilian movie companies, Cinédia, in 1930, and Atlântida Cinematográfica, in 1941. These companies countered the tendency seen during the first decades of the twentieth century toward silent movies that focused on literary adaptations. The period from 1911 to 1926 had seen the appearance of the works of Italian-Brazilian filmmaker Vittorio Capellaro (1877–1943), who translated to the medium of silent cinema literary works such as *Inocência* (1915), based on the homonymous novel by Alfredo d'Escragnolle Taunay (1843–1899), *O Guarani* (1916) and *Iracema* (1917), based on the novels by José de Alencar (1829–1877), and *O Cruzeiro do Sul* (1917), based on Aluísio Azevedo's (1857–1913) *O Mulato* (1881).

Cinédia and Atlântida started a new era of commercial and popular films. Cinédia's debut came with *Lábios Sem Beijos* (1930), a gentle story of two sisters who believed they were in love with the same man until they discovered that their lovers were not the same person, but two different persons with the same name. The film was directed by another forerunner of Brazilian cinema, Humberto Mauro (1897–1983), whose *Ganga Bruta* (1933), the story of a man who murders his bride in the bridal chamber upon discovering that she was not a virgin, became a landmark in the history of Brazilian film. Also in 1933, Mauro directed his first musical, *A Voz do Carnaval*, which gave a screen debut to the future Hollywood star, Carmen Miranda (1909–1955).

Soon large-scale productions of popular dramas and musical comedies, which were commonly referred to as *chanchada*, would dominate the national film market. Aware of the industry's growth, in 1939, President Getúlio Vargas enacted another of his nationalistic decrees, this time establishing an exhibition quota for Brazilian films in movie theaters. While state control and interventionism reached the movie industry during the early 1940s, Atlântida Cinematográfica peaked and attracted large audiences, who soon became enthralled by the new Brazilian movie stars. These stars included artists such as the Spanish-born comedian Oscarito (1906–1970) and the black comedian Grande Otelo (1915–1993), who together formed a successful comic duo. More serious actors such as José Lewgoy (1920–2003) and Zezé Macedo (1916–1999), who played both comedy and drama, were also part of Atlântida Cinematográfica's productions.[20]

The 1930s and the first half of the 1940s saw the emergence of a new popular culture in Brazil. The music, literature, and cinema of this period expressed the plight of Brazilians in both urban and rural settings. The emergence of a middle class with growing political significance encouraged the search for new themes and subject matter in theater. Sociology, History, and Economics flourished as disciplines capable of reflecting upon the nation's intrinsic qualities. A new Brazil with a peculiar and more reflective face was emerging.

In the next section, we will see how politics, art, and society developed under the new Liberal Republic. They will be times of optimism. The nation will be looked at as holding a promising future for all its citizens. The new governmental arrangement will bring democracy and freedom to Brazil from 1946 to 1964.

CHAPTER FIVE

THE LIBERAL REPUBLIC (1946–1964)

The final years of Vargas's dictatorial rule were marked by harsh economic circumstances coupled with the political instability that ultimately led to the regime's demise. By 1945, the blockade of Germany (1939–1945) had resulted in the curtailment of Brazilian imports, while exports, in particular commodities such as rubber and minerals sold to the United States, increased. The ensuing trade surplus allowed for the growth of foreign currency reserves, but it also worked negatively in helping sustain high inflation, resulting from the national industry's incapacity to supply substitutes for the now unavailable essential imports. The word *inflation* soon appeared as one of the opposition's main mottos against the maintenance of the Gaúcho ruler in power.

Between 1940 and 1945, the Brazilian economy experienced an increase of over 200% in general price levels, reaching an average annual inflation rate of 12%. In order to tackle the problem of currency devaluation, Vargas attempted measures such as price controls and the expansion of manufacturing, conflating the objectives of reducing inflation and enhancing industrialization. Such measures were taken in response both to the advances of the liberal opposition, which from early 1945 began to find enough leeway to openly criticize the dictatorial regime, as well as to the demands of the emerging working class that comprised Vargas's most important source of political support. Throughout Brazilian economic history, it would be low-wage workers who suffered most from the impact of inflation. Unable to protect their earnings from the losses of currency devaluation by means of deposits in interest-paying savings accounts, the mass of lower-middle-class workers would be immediately affected whenever inflation emerged.

Unable to control the rises in domestic prices, Vargas's government would leave a difficult economic predicament to its successor. As we will see in the next section, a new boost in imports beginning in 1946, coupled with the loss of exchange value of the foreign reserves in international markets, led the country to the verge of an economic crisis in 1947. Inflation would become a recurring problem throughout the democratic years of the new Liberal Republic (1946–1964) and beyond. Excessive borrowing and sluggish national production, as we will see, would keep pushing the economy down.

Eurico Gaspar Dutra and Economic Liberalism (1946–1951)

In spite of being the fourteenth presidential election in the nation's history, the poll carried out on December 2, 1945 is generally regarded as the first truly democratic presidential election. For the first time, no charges of fraud were made in the days following the announcement of the election's results, and the customary violence seen at previous presidential elections was absent. Army General Eurico Gaspar Dutra (1883–1974), Vargas's former Minister of War, took office on January 31, 1946, remaining in charge of the nation's presidency until January 31, 1951.

Vargas's ousting was carried out in a subdued fashion. His opponents were well aware of his popularity among the masses. As we have mentioned, this was exhibited in the public demonstrations held under the banner of *Queremismo*. The opposition thus feared the advent of large-scale popular upheavals if the former dictator were arrested or exiled after being removed from office. Furthermore, in the aftermath of Varga's fall, the natural Brazilian tendency for conciliatory politics and exchange of favors meant that Vargas offered his support to Dutra's candidacy in spite of the latter's support for Vargas's ousting. The rationale for this unlikely outcome resided in a deal negotiated by Vargas's clique in exchange for Dutra's promise not to send the former president into exile after taking office. And so it was done. Immediately after being deposed, Vargas went into a self-imposed internal exile, moving back to his fiefdom on the country's southern border with Argentina.

Together with the election of the new president in December 1945, voters also chose a new constitutive assembly, which would be comprised of 338 deputies in charge of drafting the new constitution. This new charter was promulgated on September 18, 1946. It restored the political liberties that had been safeguarded by the 1934 Constitution, but canceled by that of 1937. The new charter, that is, the 1946 Constitution, declared the equality of all citizens before the law, abolished the death penalty, and guaranteed freedom of speech.

Dutra ran as the candidate of a coalition formed by the Partido Social Democrático (PSD) and the Partido Trabalhista Brasileiro (PTB), both parties, as we have seen, had been formed under Vargas's influence, or from distinct factions formed by his political cohorts. The new president was elected with 55.39% of votes against the 34.74% of his strongest opponent, Brigadier Eduardo Gomes, who represented the right-wing party União Democrática Nacional (UDN). The communists won 9.71% of votes with their candidate, the Riograndense Yedo Fiúza.

Dutra took office at a time of mounting political polarization in the international arena. The cold war officially started in March 1947, when President Truman appeared before the United States Congress to present his containment policy, which later became known as the Truman Doctrine. Brazil's new president opted for an automatic alignment with U.S. foreign policy and on May 7, 1947, the Brazilian Supreme Electoral Court declared the Brazilian Communist Party (PCB) to be illegal. The communist presence in politics had been tolerated during 1946 and the first months of 1947 as part of the new democratic climate that swept the nation after the long dictatorial period of Vargas's rule. Communist leader Luís Carlos Prestes had been elected Senator in 1946, only to lose his seat in the Senate in 1948 as the result of what had by then become an all-out war against communism. On October 21, 1947, the Brazilian government severed diplomatic relations with the Soviet Union, relations which had been established only recently, on April 2, 1945. Brazil–USSR diplomatic relations would not be resumed until November 23, 1961, during the turbulent government of President João Goulart (1919–1976).

On the economic front, Dutra's government began under the cloud of what economic historians have called *ilusão de divisas* (currency illusion). The illusion referred to the President and his Finance Minister, Pedro Luís Correia e Castro (1881–1953), believing that the foreign reserves accumulated during the war gave their country enough leeway to promote the liberalization of the national economy prescribed by the rules established in the Bretton Woods agreements of 1944, of which Brazil was a signatory. The Bretton Woods system provided for an international scheme of fixed exchange rates and required the signatory states to commit to free trade as well as to the convertibility of their respective currencies.

Dutra's officials miscalculated the true state of Brazil's foreign reserves, which were composed mostly of nonconvertible currency. About half of the country's reserves were in pounds sterling, which by 1947 had been blocked by the British Commonwealth and thus had no exchange value for foreign trade. Added to this was the illusion that by having participated in the war on the side of democracy, Brazil would continue to be considered a key ally by the United States and that, as such, the country would receive economic assistance for development. The idea was obviously naïve and unrealistic, for the United States had more pressing issues to tend to, notably the economic reconstruction of Europe and Japan. Another misconception was the impression that with the liberalization prescribed by the Bretton Woods agreement Brazil would attract foreign investments. This expectation was also frustrated. The Brazilian government officially requested a more determined attitude from the U.S. government in promoting U.S. investments in Brazil, even suggesting that the United States should devise a Marshal Plan for Latin America. The U.S. government's response was to send to Rio de Janeiro an economic mission led by John Abbink, whose 1949 report concluded, very efficiently, that the nation needed to liberalize its economy in order to attract private foreign investment. In other words, the message was clear in saying that, unlike the case with Japan, no U.S. public money would be spent on Brazil, and that if the South American nation ever wished to see U.S. private investment, it should try hard to make itself more attractive.

The reality of shattered illusions led Brazilian Foreign Minister Raul Fernandes (1877–1967) to express his frustration with the U.S. government in a document with the pathetic title, "The Memorandum of Frustration." The document was sent to the American Ambassador in Rio de Janeiro, Herschel Johnson (1894–1966), in November 1950. There was little that Johnson could have said in response. Unable to get their hands on U.S. public money, Brazilian officials had to slow down the public works included in their new economic plan, which was aimed at improving the country's infrastructure. In May 1947, the President had presented to Congress the first effort at economic planning in the country's history. The plan was called SALTE, an acronym formed by the words "health," "food," "transport," and "education" in Portuguese. These four areas would be tackled with public investment which, in turn, would be financed through foreign borrowing. Dutra managed to include a few important projects in the plan: a hospital in Rio de Janeiro, which became the largest health facility in Latin America, was completed in 1947; a highway connecting Rio de Janeiro to São Paulo, the *Rodovia Presidente Dutra*, started to be built; and a hydroelectric power plant, the *Usina Hidrelétrica de Paulo Afonso*, was also started in Bahia.

In the aftermath of Dutra's government, however, the SALTE plan would be seen as an outright failure. The majority of its stated aims were not achieved. In the area of Education, for instance, little was done to improve the terrible conditions of national instruction. Excessive government intervention in the economy, coupled with equally excessive liberalization of foreign trade in a sort of Bretton-Woods-to-the-letter attitude, continued to push inflation upwards. Trade liberalization meant increases in imports, especially as a result of the rate at which the government fixed the Brazilian currency in relation to the dollar. The Brazilian cruzeiro was artificially overvalued at eighteen to the dollar, which inhibited exports and favored imports. Under such conditions, Dutra soon had to face the fact that his country's foreign reserves—which from the start had, in fact, been rather meager—had been used up in the purchasing of foreign consumer goods. The explosion of imports in the months immediately following the end of the Second World War, together with the ensuing exhaustion of foreign reserves, led the government to take restrictive economic measures in 1947. But, by then, things were already getting out of hand, as the effects of inflation on the living conditions of the urban working classes began to translate into public demonstrations and strikes. A large-scale upheaval took place in São Paulo in 1947, when public buildings were attacked by large crowds in confrontation with the police in a protest against a rise in public transport tariffs.

In February 1948, the government adopted a system of import licensing based on national priorities in order to contain the losses of foreign reserves and calm inflation. The policy had positive results, and trade deficits with the area of convertible currency, notably the United States, diminished. The rise in the international price of coffee in early 1949 also helped the economy to recover. At the end of his term, the general economic results of Dutra's administration seemed positive. GDP had expanded by a total of 35% during the five-year period of his government (1945–1950), against the 20% registered in the previous five years (1940–1945).

In the first weeks of 1950, the upcoming presidential election became the main theme of discussion in national politics. Dutra's initial support went to the former mayor of Belo Horizonte, the capital city of Minas Gerais, Cristiano Machado (1893–1953), who presented his candidacy with the PSD. Brigadier Eduardo Gomes was again the right-wing UDN's candidate, and Vargas emerged as a candidate with his own PTB.

The former dictator had maintained his high prestige all throughout the period of Dutra's government. Right after his ousting, Vargas had been elected Senator for both São Paulo and Rio Grande do Sul in 1945. His unabashed populism and superior talent for propaganda and self-promotion had secured him continued popular support in the years of PSD rule in Rio de Janeiro, and now the old Riograndense dictator had just found a new and useful nationalist theme that could be used in his new presidential campaign. Vargas was keen on mobilizing the nationalist sentiments that were flaring up around the theme of the nation's oil reserves. Informed by permissible state intervention, the idea of government ownership of national oil was especially attractive to Vargas whose traditionally centralizing disposition was in line with the present nationalist fervor.

The national campaign entitled *O Petróleo é Nosso* (The Oil is Ours) was immediately seized upon by Vargas's campaign. The movement against the opening of Brazil's oil market to foreign capital had started in 1947, when a group of military officers promoted a series of conferences on the subject at the Military Club, the traditional meeting place of the warrior class since 1887. The discussion regarding the need for oil nationalization spread throughout Brazilian society, setting *nacionalistas* (nationalists), i.e. those who defended the state monopoly of the national oil market, against *entreguistas* (sell-outs), those who were in favor of its liberalization. Vargas aligned with the former, which included powerful military commanders such as Júlio Caetano Horta Barbosa (1881–1965) and José Pessoa Cavalcanti de Albuquerque (1885–1959). Horta Barbosa was appointed honorary president of the *Centro de Estudos e Defesa do Petróleo* (Center for the Study and Defense of Oil), a civil institution established in 1948 with the aim of mobilizing support throughout the nation for the campaign for the state monopoly of oil.

Nationalist sentiments involving the issue of oil spread throughout all walks of Brazilian life, reaching student organizations, syndicates, and military factions. Needless to say, this was all to Vargas's advantage. So much so that on October 3, 1950 the former dictator was carried back to his second government in "the arms of the people." Vargas was elected with 48.73% of the votes under a party coalition formed between his PTB and the PSP (Partido Social Progressista), a party founded in 1946 by São Paulo's mayor and former federal interventor Adhemar de Barros (1901–1969). Barros was a politician known by the epithet *rouba mas faz* (steals but gets things done), a revealing nickname in the context of Brazilian political culture.

In second place came Eduardo Gomes with his UDN right-wing *entreguistas*, who received 29.66% of the votes. Cristiano Machado still ran for the PSD, although his party left him in the lurch a few weeks before the poll, declaring its support for Vargas. Cristiano received 9.71% of votes and from his name a new Brazilian political concept was christened, namely *cristianização*, meaning a candidate being left without support from their own party.

Vargas would assume the Brazilian presidency for the second time on January 31, 1950. His vice-president, João Fernandes Campos Café Filho (1899–1970), was a Protestant of sturdy liberal economic beliefs.

Together, they would symbolize and replicate the conflict between *nacionalistas* and *entreguistas*, a conflict that would leave a profound mark on Vargas's second government.

The Second Vargas Government and Nationalism (1951–1954)

Historians and economic analysts have frequently perceived the second Vargas administration as informed by two distinct interpretations of how the nation should proceed in order to secure acceptance into the international system of capitalism. The first interpretation defended the notion of *nacional desenvolvimentismo*, a protectionist stance based on the idea that the government should establish an "autonomous" or "national" form of capitalism from which economic development would be fostered through state-run enterprises and investments. The second interpretation defended the idea of *desenvolvimentismo associado*, or *capitalismo associado*, where development would result from the nation's "association" with foreign capital, notably through borrowing and through the attraction of foreign investment. The distinction reflected the opposition between *nacionalistas* and *entreguistas*: the first assumed a Keynesian attitude, the second a liberal one.[1]

Keynesians had remarkable influence on Vargas's administration. Their theories sprang primarily from the United Nations Economic Commission for Latin America (UNECLA), a think thank established in 1948. An all-Brazilian institute of a similar nature would appear in 1955 with the creation of the *Instituto Superior de Estudos Brasileiros* (ISEB).[2] The UNECLA had as its main theorists the German economist Hans Singer (1910–2006), the Argentine Raúl Prebisch (1901–1986), and the Brazilian Celso Furtado (1920–2004). Together they devised the aforementioned theory of the deterioration of the terms of trade between primary products and manufactured goods. The theory came to be known as the Prebisch–Singer hypothesis. It would serve as a major pillar for later research into development, notably for the so-called *dependency theory*.[3] It would also be at the root of the idea of import substitution industrialization (ISI), which emerged as the preferred system of industrial development in Brazil. ISI had in fact been applied in Brazil since the 1929 international crisis and would continue to figure in national policy until the 1980s. With such influential notions as "deterioration of the terms of trade" and "import substitution industrialization" at hand, Vargas and his economic crew could now side with the nationalists and share their perception that protectionism and state intervention were necessary for the growth of national industry.

Nevertheless, monetary orthodoxy was also a requirement if spiraling inflation was to be brought under control. The annual accumulated inflation rate registered for 1950 was 9.2%. In 1951, it rose to 18.4%. Contributing to that rise was the government's 251% increase in the minimum wage. The wage readjustment was part of a series of populist campaign promises Vargas had made with the hope of securing the support of the working classes for his candidacy. Needless to say, the increase angered the capitalist class, that is, Vargas's opposition. That anger intensified in December 1951 when the President presented to the National Congress his project for a monopolistic oil company called *Petrobras*. The project would be approved in October 1953 through the famous Law 2004, which established a state monopoly over oil exploration, refinement and transportation for the next 44 years, that is, until it was overthrown in 1995. With the establishment of Petrobras, Vargas was keeping his campaign promises and maintaining healthy popular support.

The president's understanding that inflation had to be dealt with in monetary orthodox terms was in line with the prescriptions of a new economic mission sent by the United States. The Joint Brazil-United States Economic Development Commission was based on President Truman's Point Four Program, announced in his inaugural address on January 20, 1949. The Commission was established in 1950, still during the pro-American administration of General Dutra. It arrived in Brazil in July 1951 to start a series of studies on infrastructure development, which led to the creation of 41 projects aimed at tackling some of the country's most pressing structural shortcomings. Implementation of the projects would be facilitated through loans from the Eximbank and the World Bank. As the granting of such loans invariably depends on a country demonstrating financial and monetary stability, the Brazilian government prepared itself to adopt orthodox economic measures in order to eradicate troublesome phenomena such as high inflation.

Economic historians diverge on the question of the origins of Vargas's monetary orthodoxy, pointing at times to the theoretical principles defended by Finance Minister Horácio Lafer (1900–1965) as the real element shaping the Brazilian economy during the period 1951–1954. Doctrinal controversies notwithstanding, the fact is that by mid-1951 Vargas's government had already devised a new plan to tackle financial difficulties and promote economic development. The plan was called the "Campos Sales–Rodrigues Alves Project," a sort of mixed cocktail of orthodoxy and heterodoxy intended to put the nation back on the path of sustained growth. Vargas's economic advisors looked back at the country's history to note the effective process of financial restructuring and subsequent economic growth seen in the eight years encompassing the administrations of Campos Sales and Rodrigues Alves from 1898 to 1906. As we have seen, Campos Sales had employed strict financial orthodoxy in order to eradicate the hyperinflation caused by the *Encilhamento* crisis, which had begun in 1891. Once the inflation problem had been solved, the following government, that of Rodrigues Alves, embarked on heavy public expenditure such as the Pereira Passos's urban reform of Rio de Janeiro, with resulting economic growth.

To Vargas and his economic advisors, it all seemed logical: an initial two-year phase of monetary restriction would create the resources that would not only satisfy the conditions for the Eximbank loans, but would also allow for a follow-up of intense public spending on structural development, with consequent GDP growth. Reality, however, does not always follows logic. Vargas's plan had the wind taken out of its sails when, in 1952, an international crisis in the textile industry provoked a drastic fall in Brazil's cotton exports. Cotton was by then the nation's second most important export product, after coffee, and the sudden fall in international demand had a disastrous impact on Brazil's highly indebted economy. The industry's crisis came at a time when Finance Minister Horácio Lafer had just expanded the number of import licenses, resulting in a rise of 82% in the total value of imports from 1950 to 1951. Deprived of sufficient foreign reserves, Vargas had to abandon the Campos Sales–Rodrigues Alves plan.

Added to this was a significant about-turn seen in American foreign policy with the Eisenhower administration in 1953. With President Eisenhower and his hardliners now in command, the former Point Four Program, with its promises of technical assistance and economic aid to underdeveloped countries, was abandoned. The projects of the Joint Brazil-United States Economic Development Commission, just as the Commission itself, were promptly dismissed. Vargas's nationalist policies, which amounted to an about-turn for the country with regard to the previous Dutra administration, seem to have contributed to Eisenhower's discontent with the Latin American country. On January 3, 1952, the Riograndense ruler issued a decree limiting the remittance of profits abroad to 10% of the foreign capital invested in the country, a decision that provoked protest from several American enterprises. This, it should be noted, was decided not without some good reason on Vargas's part. Several foreign companies operating in Brazil were employing a corrupt scheme whereby they managed to enter the country with small investments, raise loans from national banks, and then send part of the borrowed money back home as profit. During the five years of Dutra's administration, foreign investment into Brazil totaled US$15 million, while remittance of profits out of the country reached US$ 45 million.[4]

Another reason for Eisenhower's discontent was Vargas's refusal to send Brazilian troops to support the UN intervention led by the United States in Korea. The request for Brazilian involvement in the Korean War had been formally made through UN Secretary-General Trygve Lie (1896–1968), whose appointement had been vetoed by the Soviet Union in the Security Council but passed by the General Assembly in 1951. Vargas's rejection of Lie's request was made official in July 1951, much to the irritation of U.S. Republicans.

Without an economic plan to hand and with inflation rising to rates of 9.3% in 1952, 13.8% in 1953, and 27.1% in 1954, Vargas struggled to find a way out of his problems. As the opposition grew stronger and began to voice allegations of corruption against the government, Vargas decided to enact some changes in his ministerial cabinet, trying to surround himself with allies from Rio Grande do Sul. In June 1953, old-time Gaúcho ally Osvaldo Aranha (1894–1960) replaced Finance Minister Horácio Lafer, while Vargas's political protégé, João Goulart (1919–1976), took the place of José de Segadas Viana (1906–1991) in the Ministry of Labor and Employment.

Like Getúlio Vargas, João Goulart was born in the border town of São Borja. Like Vargas, he belonged to a wealthy family of landowners. After the death of his father in 1943, Goulart had become one of the richest and most powerful men in the region. It was then that Getúlio Vargas and his brothers, the local chieftains Manoel Viriato and Protásio, had persuaded Goulart to join their family's party, the *Partido Trabalhista Brasileiro* (PTB), which presented itself nationally as the workers' party. Goulart was elected a congressman in 1951, but soon took leave of the nation's capital to assume the office of Secretary of Justice in his native Rio Grande do Sul, under the administration of State Governor Ernesto Dorneles (1897–1964), Vargas's cousin.[5]

Against his will, Goulart would become a pivotal element in Vargas's demise. By 1953, when he assumed the Ministry of Labor and Employment, the young Gaúcho politician had built his career in the PTB as a defender of labor rights. His good relations with several union leaders led him to be regarded with great suspicion by the right-wing opposition. Added to this was the very political climate in which Goulart assumed his ministerial office. The nation was on the verge of an economic crisis and the low wages allotted to the working classes, a result of the corrosive effect of inflation, provoked frequent calls for strikes and protests. The right-wing opposition party, the *União Democrática Nacional* (UDN), had become a bastion of *anti-getulismo*, a movement that publicly condemned each and every presidential decision as wrong and ill-intentioned. Led by Rio de Janeiro Congressman Carlos Lacerda (1914–1977), the most radical members of the UDN formed an avant-garde group ironically referred to as *Banda de Música* (music ensemble) for the noise generated at their protests against the President.

Lacerda was an ex-communist who had supported the failed *coup d'état* of 1935 and who, after realizing the communists' penchant for authoritarianism and dictatorship, made a radical political shift in the early 1940s, abandoning communism and becoming a stout conservative, as well as one of the most resolute defenders of right-wing ideologies. His hooked-nosed appearance and opportunism in preying on the waste of his fallen enemies granted him the sobriquet, "The Raven." From mid-1953, João Goulart became one of Lacerda's choice targets for political accusations. According to the leader of the UDN radicals, Goulart possessed unchecked influence over the working classes, which made him capable of inciting them at will to strikes and popular demonstrations. Lacerda also suggested that the new Minister of Labor and Employment secretly planned to establish a syndicalist republic in Brazil similar to the one created by Juan Domingo Perón (1895–1974) in Argentina. He alleged that Vargas had held secret talks with Perón, and that they hoped to establish an anti-United States pact between Argentina, Brazil, and Chile.

Lacerda's attacks on Vargas turned into more concrete accusations when he denounced an alleged scheme of corruption in which the Bank of Brazil was facilitating credit to the enterprises of a powerful journalist named Samuel Wainer (1910–1980) in exchange for political support for the President. Wainer was an old friend of Vargas and owned an important newspaper called *Última hora*, the only paper that at this point still openly defended the government. A Parliamentary Investigation Committee (CPI) was established in the Congress to investigate Lacerda's accusations. During the five months of the Committee's operation, 27 witnesses were called to present their testimonies in what became highly publicized media events. At the end of its work, the Committee concluded that it could not find sufficient evidence for an indictment of the President, but the long media circus turned out to be profoundly damaging to Vargas's image and morale. During those five long months, the charges of corruption turned into talk of presidential impeachment, making the aging President feel more and more trapped by a situation from which no escape seemed possible.

By late-1953, the young Congressman, Lacerda, and his band members had become keen on securing the support of powerful military leaders with the same right-wing outlook to help in their anti-Vargas campaign. The military commanders became particularly enraged when in January 1954 Minister João Goulart sent to Congress a project proposing a 100% increase in the minimum wage. Reacting angrily against what they saw as the Minister's socially progressive policy, on February 20, a memorandum signed by 82 army colonels, called *Manifesto dos Coronéis*, was made public through the press. The military leaders attacked Vargas directly by arguing that the national defense forces were being neglected by the federal government, that military facilities and equipment were obsolete, that the average Brazilian officer's salary was blatantly inferior to that of officers in other countries, and that the 100% increase in the minimum wage could not be perceived as anything other than an aberration in that it would raise the salary of an unskilled worker to the level of that of an army officer, which was an insult to the armed forces.

Despite their absurd line of reasoning, Vargas knew that the discontent expressed by the high military officers meant one more serious threat to his government. Given the circumstances, the *Manifesto dos Coronéis* could be seen as an omen of his fall. To gain time and appease at least some of the colonels' anger, Vargas opted to dismiss Goulart from his ministerial post on February 23, 1954. However, the old Riograndense landlord, now approaching his seventy-second year, was not willing to capitulate entirely. Vargas was born and raised in the historically conflictive region of Western Rio Grande do Sul, a large and desolate territory that for centuries had been scarred by bloody disputes between Portuguese and Spanish colonizers. Although given to populism, and with the melodramatic posture honed over years of public appearances, the stout, unbending, and violent character of the Gaúcho had never stopped working underneath Vargas's conciliatory garb. Getúlio Dornelles Vargas was a southern warlord, a chieftain. He had always shown the capacity to weigh out his chances, and act accordingly in order to sustain what was becoming a twenty-year rule over one of the largest nations in the world, so he would be even less likely to bend and accept defeat now that advanced age and the inevitability of death made cowardice unacceptable and retreat pointless.

On May 1, 1954, in the midst of the Workers' Day celebrations, Vargas chose to remain faithful to his populism and to the masses that for almost half a century had supported him, the masses for whom he had been given the title *Pai dos pobres*, the father of the poor. The leader who had toiled a lifetime to build the legacy of *trabalhismo*, a politics of recognizing the value of work, of dignity in everyday labor, decided now to extend his hand in a last gesture of defiance and generosity. Against all his enemies and in acceptance of the odds of an oncoming civil war, Vargas signed Decree 35.450, doubling the minimum wage.

Despite the possibility of positive effects from the move in enhancing the aggregate demand of the economy and stimulating productivity, Vargas's wage policy was received with outright rage by the nation's business class. To the Brazilian political and financial elites, policies of wealth distribution were seen as nothing more than communist abominations. The abhorrence for anything that reeked of social or class equality suggested the subliminal play of a collective unconscious filled with perverse feelings of superiority and hatred enduring from the colonial times of slavery with unchecked cruelty. Combined with the long-standing dissatisfaction of the military class, the attacks from the business class on Vargas made his situation unsustainable.

This state of affairs was made even more dramatic by one last event that would bring the President into final, irreconcilable despair. On the night of August 5, 1954, Carlos Lacerda, the angriest and loudest among all of Vargas's opponents, received a gunshot wound in an attempt on his life that killed his bodyguard, the Air Force Major Rubens Florentino Vaz. Historians debate the veracity of the account that became the accepted version of the incident. Climério Euribes de Almeida (1910–1975) and José Antônio Soares (dates unknown), both members of Vargas's personal guard, supposedly hired Alcino João Nascimento (b. 1921) as the hit man. The planning of the attempt was attributed to an old-time foreman of the Vargas family, a man named Gregório Fortunato (1900–1962). Born in São Borja into a family of enfranchised slaves, Fortunato had become a soldier in a military campaign led by Colonel Benjamin Vargas, the President's brother, in 1932. Subsequently, he was employed as chief of Vargas's personal guard, which was created in 1938 after the Integralist attack on the President. Almeida, Soares, Nascimento, and Fortunato were arrested a few days after the murder of the air force official. They would be tried in 1956.

A different version of the incident suggests that the first shot hitting Lacerda's bodyguard could have come from Lacerda's own pistol, which was never examined in the investigations following the crime. The shot that allegedly hit Lacerda in the foot was also never confirmed. In any case, whether the attempt was planned and executed according to what became the official version, or whether it was part of a conspiracy seized upon by the opposition to further damage Vargas's reputation, the fact is that the episode led to a major political crisis. The death of an Air Force officer enraged the military class, especially Brigadier Eduardo Gomes, the Air Force Commander and UDN presidential candidate who had lost the last election to Vargas. The UDN, Lacerda, Eduardo Gomes, and the military found themselves as one in their opposition to the President.

The National Air Force established an independent investigation parallel to the official police procedures in order to determine who was responsibile for the crime, producing what appeared as a self-standing power structure separate from and challenging the official federal administration centered on the presidency. The military scheme was ironically called *República do Galeão*, suggesting a defiant separate state within the limits of Rio de Janeiro's national airport, the Galeão Airport. Both the military and the press started a defamatory campaign against the President with the aim of bringing down his government.

The last straw in this mounting humiliation was the military leaders' formal request for the President's resignation. On August 22, 1954, the army issued a memorandum signed by nineteen commanders called *Manifesto dos Generais*. The document ordered Vargas's immediate resignation from the presidency. The manifesto's idea came from hardline officer Golbery do Couto e Silva (1911–1987) who, at the time, served at the *Escola Superior de Guerra* (ESG), the Brazilian version of the American National War College. Couto e Silva would soon become one of the nation's most powerful figures through the application of his Doctrine of National Security, a theory that would guide the Brazilian armed forces in their twenty-year dictatorial rule starting in 1964.

Deprived of any means to negotiate with the military, Vargas found himself in a blind alley. Politically isolated, with public opinion turned against him by the continuous campaign in the press, he agonized over how to maintain the nation's constitutional order and avoid a coup that could bring only chaos. In the evening of the day following the publication of the *Manifesto dos Generais*, the President decided to take a fatal step that would plunge the entire nation into a state of upheaval. After a last ministerial meeting in the presidential palace that had continued into the evening, Vargas retired to his chambers and wrote a note stating that the time had come for him to leave his life and enter history. In the note, he said that the insults and abuses to which he had been subjected, and which he had endured in silence, had been the product of the greed of those who, allied to the interests of international capitalists, could not accept his social policies or the ideas of freedom and social equality they entailed. In a heartrending message written in almost intimate terms to the Brazilian working classes, the seventy-two-year-old defeated politician beseeched his impoverished people to remember him and to feel his presence whenever hunger and humiliation besieged them. In short punctuated phrases, he pleaded with them to live in hope and to find the strength to fight on in spite of the injustice and suffering to which they would continue to be subjected.

Vargas shot himself in the chest before daybreak in the early hours of August 24, 1954. The public opinion that had abused him for so long now saw things differently: accusations turned to remorse. The President's enemies were themselves stunned. Carlos Lacerda had to flee the country to avoid the angry crowds, who came after him as soon as they learned of the President's fate. But nonetheless, within a few days, the government would be handed to a conservative politician who had never concealed his sympathy for and connections with those who had brought Vargas to his brutal end.

Café Filho and the Return of Liberalism (1954–1955)

Vice-President João Augusto Fernandes Campos Café Filho (1899–1970) assumed the presidency on August 24, 1954 a few hours after Vargas's suicide was made public. In his first official address, the new President attempted to calm the general shock caused by the publication of a suicide note that revealed an ongoing conspiracy against the now deceased leader. Café Filho affirmed his commitment to follow Vargas's policies, favoring the poorer members of society and the working classes.

In spite of this initial speech, however, the new President would immediately diverge from Vargas's nationalism and social welfare policies. Café Filho established a conservative ministerial cabinet and promoted an immediate return to alignment with U.S. interests in both foreign and domestic policy, resuming the political line established during Eurico Gaspar Dutra's government. State-led developmental policies were suppressed by more liberal-minded officials, who were ready to do away with the Vargas legacy of *trabalhismo*.

The framework of the Bretton Woods agreements resurfaced in the adoption of a resolutely liberal exchange-rate policy meant to facilitate foreign investment in the country. The most notable instrument in this return to economic liberalism was the Normative Instruction 113 issued in January 1955 by the country's monetary authority, the *Superintendência da Moeda e do Crédito* (SUMOC). The Superintendency was a government department established in 1945 in compliance with demands from the IMF and the World Bank. Its purpose was to work as a preparatory step to the establishment of a national central bank (Brazil's Central Bank, the BACEN, would not be established until December 1964).

The SUMOC's Normative Instruction 113 has been a recurring theme of debate among Brazilian economic historians since its adoption in 1954. (It operated until 1961, when another Instruction, this one numbered 204, made the 113 mostly inoperative.) In any economy that is largely dependent on exports, such as that of Brazil in the 1950s, exchange-rate policies reflect not only prevailing ideological factors, but also the pre-eminence of the interests of specific economic sectors. In the case at hand, the 113 Instruction allowed for the importation of capital goods without currency exchange cover, that is, as direct foreign investment. This had several implications in the nation's process of industrialization. On the one hand, it facilitated the establishment of foreign companies in national territory, allowing them to bring in important machinery and equipment and thus operate at lower costs. But, on the other hand, it tended to hinder domestic industrial development, as native companies had little incentive to produce domestically the capital goods that were now being easily imported. The policy thereby obstructed the process of import substitution industrialization (ISI) that had been the developmental banner of Vargas and the nationalists since the early 1930s. The instruction also had the negative effect of allowing foreign enterprises to import goods without paying import duties. The absence of monetary disbursements in such operations was seen as desirable, for it promoted the expansion of capital goods in the national territory without affecting the country's balance of payments. The most evidently negative aspect of the policy, however, was that it allowed only foreign companies to import goods without currency coverage, leaving national businesses at a blatant competitive disadvantage.

Determining the actual results of the Instruction 113 in terms of its benefits and downsides to national economic development involves the sort of measurement and data analysis that cannot be undertaken here. Defending or condemning the policy would mean to enter the polarized ideological debate that rages to this day among Brazilian economists regarding state interventionism. Suffice it to note, however, that Instruction 113 meant the assumption of a new official position with regard to foreign capital. The instruction remained in effect for several years, and would be used lavishly and liberally by the next administration, that of President Juscelino Kubitschek, as the legal basis for a new form of industrialization wherein the national productive forces would be closely associated with foreign capital. Instruction 113 thus holds an important historical and symbolic dimension in Brazilian economic history: for some, it meant a mature realization of the nation's incapacity to promote its own industrialization in an autarchic fashion; for others, a cowardly bending to the power of foreign capital and to the national profiteers ready to associate with it.[6]

The new directive in industrial policy resulted in great measure from the work of new Finance Minister Eugênio Gudin (1886–1986), who held the office from August 1954 to April 1955. Gudin was an unbendingly liberal-minded economist who had fiercely opposed Vargas on all possible fronts, especially in the establishment of Petrobras and the state monopoly of oil in 1953. His Normative Instruction 113 was combined with staunch monetary orthodoxy. Upon assuming the Finance Ministry, Gudin's stated goal was to counter the rising inflation of 1954, and for that end he adopted austere fiscal and monetary policies. As excessive monetary orthodoxy is often prone to produce unwanted effects, however, Gudin's austerities ended up in a series of bankruptcies in Rio de Janeiro and São Paulo. After the insolvency of two large banks and the persistence of rising inflation, he was dismissed from the government in April 1955.[7]

The post of Finance Minister was given to José Maria Whitaker (1878–1970), who occupied it from April to October 1955. Whitaker was a lawyer from São Paulo who early in his life had made a fortune in the coffee trade. He had served as Finance Minister from 1930 to 1931, during Vargas's first government, having been the mastermind behind Vargas's coffee valorization schemes implemented to counter the effects of the world crisis in 1929. Back to the Finance Ministry twenty-five years later, the old coffee baron tried to impose a new directive on the national economy. Countering Gudin's excessive monetary orthodoxy, he promoted the expansion of credit and solved the country's impending liquidity crisis. Whitaker also proposed a liberal reform in exchange rates that would favor coffee exports and result in the total nullification of Vargas's nationalist-developmental project. In the end the reform was not approved, but it brought about an important debate that revealed the interests and economic forces still at play in Brazil at the time. Whitaker's argument was that the nation could very well prosper as a provider of primary goods for the international market, and that industrialization was not a *sine qua non* of economic prosperity. The argument hid an age-old debate that divided agriculturalists and industrialists in Brazil, two sectors that always found themselves at odds when the theme of exchange rates emerged. In any case, what is most important to note is that the Gudin-Whitaker dissent emerging in Café Filho's government reveals that agricultural, and most notably coffee, interests were still strong and ready to apply a backward pressure against industrialization as late as 1955.

Café Filho's alignment with U.S. interests in domestic economic policy was reproduced in foreign policy. The President reinstated Dutra's former Foreign Minister, Raul Fernandes, the one who had drafted the aforementioned "Memorandum of Frustration." Fernandes signed a controversial agreement on atomic energy with the United States. The agreement provoked nationalist outrage for agreeing the sale of Brazilian uranium to the United States without including any form of technological cooperation in the transaction, that is, without providing the Brazilians with any sought-after transfer of technology. Most surprisingly, uranium would be exchanged on an equivalent basis with wheat. The treaty does look like the product of an outright surrender of sovereignty when set against the terms that Germany was offering Brazil. This potential became stalled because of ideological barriers. Negotiations with Germany had been undertaken by Navy Admiral Álvaro Alberto da Mota e Silva (1889–1976), who had received Vargas's permission to proceed with the transactions in 1953. The Admiral was the founder and first president of the National Research Council (CNPq), an institution established in 1951 to promote the advancement of science in Brazil. The agreement with Germany involved the purchase of three uranium enrichment centrifuges, which were, in fact, intercepted by the United States without ever reaching Brazil. After the agreement signed by Café Filho in 1954 the enraged Admiral Álvaro Alberto resigned from his post at the CNPq.

In terms of domestic politics, Café Filho is usually credited with having made a magnanimous effort to maintain the electoral calendar established in the 1946 Constitution, under which a new presidential election was due in 1955. Early that year, the climate was of political disorder and soon voices demanding the postponement of the poll began to be heard. The nation was still haunted by the trauma of Vargas's suicide and the UDN conservatives were not willing to allow another *nacional-desenvolvimentista* to assume the presidency. As the candidates started aligning themselves along ideologically divided party lines, fear of a new *coup d'état* arose.

A party coalition was formed between the PSD, the PTB and four other smaller parties. The coalition presented as candidates for the presidency and vice-presidency Juscelino Kubitschek de Oliveira (1902–1976) and Vargas's former minister of labor, João Goulart. Kubitschek was an experienced politician from Minas Gerais who had served as the state capital's mayor from 1940 to 1945, and then as governor from 1951 to 1955. His keenness for industrialization was seen in the establishment of the first state-run electricity company in Minas Gerais, the CEMIG, in 1952, and also in his building of five hydroelectric power plants during the period. With the champion of social welfare, the Riograndense João Goulart, at his side running for the vice-presidency, Kubitschek's candidacy could not avoid severe resistance from the right-wing conservatives. Adding to the leftist tinge of Kubitschek's candidacy was the open support from the Brazilian Communist Party (PCB). Early in 1955, communist leader Luís Carlos Prestes had taken to the streets to defend the Mineiro's candidacy, much as he had done in support of Vargas in 1945.

From then on, the UDN and the high military ranks made every possible effort to hinder Kubitschek's candidacy. Carlos Lacerda was back as a member of parliament and he proposed the establishment of a state of exception with the adjournment of the upcoming presidential elections. The man who, on June 1, 1950, had published in his newspaper, the *Tribuna da Imprensa*, a note saying that "Senator Getúlio Vargas shall not be a candidate for the presidency; if a candidate, shall not be elected; if elected, shall not take office; if he takes office, a revolution must be enacted so that he will not rule," was now repeating his litany against Kubitschek. He employed whatever means he could find in order to try to impugn the Mineiro's candidacy, including the publication of a letter appearing to be from an Argentine congressman, Antonio Jesus Brandi, to João Goulart mentioning a plan devised between the latter and Juan Domingo Perón to establish a syndicalist republic in Brazil. The letter, which was later found to be false, mentioned a supposed negotiation for the purchase of armaments in case a revolution emerged in Brazil.

In spite of Lacerda's defamatory campaign, presidential elections were held on August 3, 1955. Kubitschek's victory was achieved with 35.68% of the votes against the 30.27% received by General Juarez Távora (1898–1975), the UDN, and Lacerda's, candidate. Lacerda immediately attempted to challenge the election result, arguing that Kubitschek could not be considered the poll's winner because he had not received the majority of votes. The argument was deeply fallacious, for the 1946 Constitution was silent on any required ratio for victory. Nevertheless, President Café Filho, who had supported Távora's candidacy, was sympathetic to Lacerda's argument. As rumors of a coup circulated in the military, the Minister of War, General Henrique Teixeira Lott (1894–1984), publicly stated that the Constitution should be observed, and that, if necessary, the nation's constitutional order would be promptly defended by the armed forces.

The higher ranks of right-wing officers paid little heed to the Minister of War's statement and continued to talk of an operation to prevent Kubitschek from taking office. On November 8, Café Filho went on leave from the government, alleging health reasons. The leader of the House of

Representatives, Carlos Luz (1894–1961), assumed the presidency *ad interim*. A coup was on the way. The absence of a duly elected figure in the presidency produced a power vacuum that would facilitate the seizing of the central government by the right-wing military officers.

It was thus that General Lott, after presenting letter of resignation from the post of Minister of War to the incumbent president Carlos Luz, ordered the seizure of the Catete Palace, the official presidential residence. Luz attempted to escape in a naval vessel, the Cruiser Tamandaré, accompanied by a select group of anti-Vargas turned anti-Kubitschek individuals which included Carlos Lacerda himself. The army fired on the Tamandaré which surrendered almost immediately. Luz was deposed and the Head of the Senate, Nereu Ramos (1888–1958), assumed the presidency *ad interim*.

The way was now open for Juscelino Kubitschek de Oliveira to assume the presidency. The new head of state would repeat Vargas's developmental and industrializing policies. To the surprise of his opponents, however, he would do so without turning his back on foreign capital.

Juscelino Kubitschek and Liberal Development (1956–1961)

Juscelino Kubitschek de Oliveira assumed the Brazilian presidency on January 31, 1956 in a climate of great popular celebration. Brazilians were enthusiastic about their new president; the masses were particularly enthralled by his campaign slogan, "Fifty years in Five." The promise was of rapid economic growth, rapid industrialization, and the rapid achievement of prosperity. To this end, the new president announced his national development plan, the *Plano de Metas* (Objectives Plan), the second general executive program of national scope to be devised in Brazilian economic history, following Dutra's 1950 SALTE.

Kubitschek's plan included 31 stated aims geared towards economic, industrial, and infrastructural development. The first 30 aims were arranged in five major areas: energy, transportation, food and agriculture, heavy industry, and education. The 31st aim stood beyond these as a 'last but not least' goal. It was stylishly called *meta-síntese*, and it amounted to nothing less than the building of a new capital city right in the middle of Brazil's enormous territory.

The Plano de Metas's main purpose was to tackle those issues that were holding back the country's economic development, such as the inadequacy of roads for commodity transportation, the reduced provision of electricity, deficiencies in agricultural mechanization, and the lack of regional integration in the national territory. The actual planning of concrete structural projects was based on previous studies carried out since the early 1940s, including those produced by the Joint Brazil-United States Economic Development Commission during the period 1951–1953. One of Kubitschek's main strategies was to consolidate a national automobile industry in collaboration with international companies by means of foreign direct investment. This was part of the President's stated aim of promoting a national industry of durable consumer goods, a real novelty in comparison to former government efforts at industrialization, which had focused primarily on heavy industry.

It was thus that, unlike the former *desenvolvimentismo nacionalista* that had characterized President Vargas's economic program (which, thanks to its more autarchic style, was dubbed "Prussian style"), Kubitschek favored the notion of *desenvolvimentismo associado*, that is, national development associated with foreign capital. Under this new mindset, the President's economic team devised the idea of an "economic tripod" as the model for the new official program. Each leg of the tripod would correspond to a sustaining portion of the new economic foundation: the State would execute projects in infrastructure and heavy industry; the national private business sector would invest in non-durable consumer goods, such as food and clothing; and foreign enterprises would operate in areas of higher aggregate value, that is, in the production of durable consumer goods, such as automobiles and electronic equipment.

Under this new arrangement, in September 1956, the President inaugurated the first truck factory capable of producing vehicles equipped with motors produced domestically. The motors were produced by Mercedes-Benz in a manufacturing plant built in the city of São Bernardo do Campo, in São Paulo State, which would become home to the largest industrial park in Latin America. Alongside the establishment of a national automobile industry, the plan envisaged the building of roads to complement the new auto manufacturing under way. This represented an option for road transportation that would be severely criticized by Brazilian economists and policymakers in the future. According to them, the heavy emphasis placed upon the automobile industry and on the building of highways during Kubitschek's government prevented the expansion of the national railroad system, thus hindering the emergence of a more dependable and economically efficient mode of transportation.

In any event, roads kept being built, and by the end of Kubitschek's government the country's federal highway system had expanded by more than 20,000 kilometers. Many of these new routes would be linked to the new capital being constructed right at the geographical center of the territory. The Belém–Brasília and Brasília–Acre Highways, which would become important physical connectors between the Southeast and the more underdeveloped North, are cases in point in regard to the new transportation vectors that emerged from the building of the new capital.

Kubitschek also promoted the naval industry and built important hydroelectric power plants, notably Três Marias and Furnas, both in his native state of Minas Gerais. Attempts to improve economic conditions in the Northeast, an area frequently beset by severe droughts, were made through the establishment of a specialized governmental agency called *Superintendência do Desenvolvimento do Nordeste* (SUDENE), whose command was assigned to UNECLA's economist Celso Furtado. Given the persistence of a remarkable economic disparity between the Northeast and the Southeast in the following decades, however, the SUDENE's overall accomplishments tend to be considered meager.

In any case, the massive amount of investment deployed by Kubitschek's government resulted in overall positive numbers for the economy. From 1956 to 1961, GDP increased at an average annual rate of 7.8%, easily surpassing the average of 5.2% from 1945 to 1955. Industrial output rose at an even higher rate, an annual average of 10.7%. Inflation, however, remained high, at an annual average of 24.7%. The rising inflation was directly related to the government's options and decisions in financing its colossal Plano de Metas. The heavy borrowing taken on to support such a lavishly expansive fiscal policy came initially from foreign banks, but when the spring ran dry, bouts of highly inflationary monetary easing became the norm. This is what historians refer to when they describe Kubitschek's economic model as "growth with growing foreign debt," or "inflationary growth."

During the first half of his term, the President made every possible effort to secure international credit for his governmental enterprise. Kubitschek saw a great opportunity for requesting American financial aid when on May 13, 1958, U.S. Vice-President Richard Nixon (1913–1994) was accosted by an angry Venezuelan mob during an official visit to Caracas. Nixon's troubles during the visit reflected the Venezuelans' anger over U.S. military support for political coups in Central America. Kubitschek pretended to see the incident as a function of economic underdevelopment and as the product of a machination devised by leftist groups. He then decided to launch his Operation Pan America, an economic development program for Latin America that would prevent the region from falling into the hands of the communists.

Kubitschek sent a letter to President Eisenhower presenting his "Operation" and asking for U.S. support. As the word "support" meant, above all, "financial support," the Brazilian President argued that economic development, or more precisely the eradication of poverty, was the most efficient way to prevent leftist ideologies from spreading among the United States' southern neighbors. Eisenhower was primarily unaffected by the missive, which he must have regarded as yet another Brazilian attempt at scooping up a Latin American Marshal Plan, an idea that had always been refused by the United States. However, after observing recent developments in Cuba, where Fidel Castro was on the verge of succeeding in his revolutionary aims, the American President reconsidered and ceded the point to Kubitschek.

Secretary of State John Foster Dulles (1888–1959) was sent on an official visit to Brazil in August 1958, but conversations regarding the Operation Pan America were kept low key. Kubitschek had been in the process of co-opting an important ally for his Operation, the recently elected Argentine President Arturo Frondizi (1908–1995). Frondizi had been elected in February 1958, and visited Brazil in April. Talks with Kubitschek had positive results in promoting the two countries' mutual understanding and political rapprochement. The two presidents shared common ideological assumptions. Both relied on the ideas put forward by UNECLA, which recognized the need for industrialization in Latin America. Both presidents also understood economic development as a necessary shield against communism. Under the auspices of an Operation Pan America that was only getting lukewarm support from the United States, Brazil and Argentina joined forces and promoted the establishment of the Inter-American Development Bank (IDB). The Bank was formally created on April 8, 1959, when the Organization of American States drafted the Articles of Agreement establishing the institution.

However, the Operation Pan America would not bring the results Kubitschek and Frondizi had hoped for. Support from the United States fell well short of what could be described as a Latin American Marshal Plan, and the Operation itself served more as a starting point for the establishment of the Inter-American Development Bank than as a real motor for Latin American development. Kubitschek was thus obliged to find financing for his Plano de Metas elsewhere. Brazil's economic conditions were becoming increasingly unfavorable as time went by. The country's excessive spending soon started to look suspicious in the eyes of the IMF. Attempting to gain time and continue the borrowing, the President asked his Finance Minister, Lucas Lopes (1911–1994), to devise an orthodox plan aimed at quelling the rising inflation that was already reaching an annual rate of 22.60%. Lopes responded with the so-called *Plano de Estabilização Monetária* (PEM), which was sent to the National Congress on October 27, 1958. The plan, however, was not well received by the IMF, who expected a less gradualist attempt at inflation control than the one proposed by Lopes. Unable to comply with the Organization's demand, which in fact entailed halting the Plano de Metas, in 1959 Kubitschek unilaterally broke away from the IMF. This meant that the loans laboriously contracted with the Eximbank would, in the end, simply not be conceded.

The break with the IMF was presented politically as striking a blow for Latin American autonomy vis-à-vis the United States, in particular, and imperialistic capitalism, in general. In hyperbolic fashion, the move was seen as a Brazilian voice of liberty resounding throughout the Latin American landscape in the mode of a Bolivarian cry for brotherly unity. On learning of Kubitschek's decision, Frondizi immediately expressed his support for the Brazilian President. Another symbol of Latin American independence would surface the following year, with the establishment of the Latin American Free Trade Association (LAFTA) in 1960, which was co-signed under the Treaty of Montevideo by Argentina, Brazil, Chile, Mexico, Paraguay, Peru, and Uruguay. These countries believed that, united, they could promote regional development themselves. The truth, however, was that the LAFTA, with all its ambitious aims, would be largely ineffective. Kubitschek was thus left in the lurch with no external source of funding to complete his Pharaonic project of national modernization.

Things started looking even worse when the initial popular enthusiasm for the "Fifty years in Five" slogan began to wane and the working classes began to feel the cold blast of inflation in their lives. To urban discontent were added the increasingly loud voices of the Peasant Leagues, social organizations of sharecroppers, subsistence farmers, and other small agriculturalists who demanded land reform. The Leagues were founded in the rural areas of the Northeast in the late 1940s with the support of the Communist Party. They aimed at the impossible, that is, to overthrow the powerful landowners who had always controlled the region, as well as most of the country. Despite being at a huge disadvantage with regard to the wealthy and greedy *ladifundiários* that would never yield any of their land for the sake of some social justice, the Leagues gained strength in the early 1960s as they spread through the Northeast under the influence of the Cuban Revolution and the leadership of Francisco Julião Arruda de Paula (1915–1999), a lawyer who dedicated most of his life to defending the rights of the peasants.[8]

President Kubitschek found himself in an uncomfortable position on the issue of agrarian reform. His party, the PSD, had strong links with the conservative landlords of the Northeast and the President had to maintain his own party's support. It is true that a minority group within the PSD called the *ala moça* (youth wing) assumed a more progressive stance, but in the end the conservatives had the lead within the party and the much-needed agrarian reform was simply not advanced during Kubitschek's administration. Given the fact that approximately 70% of the Brazilian population lived in rural areas at the time, the President's indifference to land reform just added to the growing popular dissatisfaction with his government. It was thus that, without any more external funding, with an increasingly dissatisfied population, and with an obsession to conclude the construction of the new capital in time for it to be inaugurated within his administration, a feat that would crown his entire mandate and boost his image for posterity, the President decided to resort to the only possible option available for financing his project: printing money.

Kubitschek's gigantic debts and inflationary policies would become a nightmare for his successor, but for the Mineiro President the dream overcame logic, and the monumental works already under way in the Brazilian central highlands had to continue. Building continued at a fast pace. By the end of 1959 time was running out. The electoral campaigns for the following year's presidential elections were already under way and the public was losing interest in the President's great inauguration, which was scheduled for early 1960. If the new capital were not ready in time for the inauguration, the result would be embarrassment rather than prestige.

The idea of transferring the capital to the center of the territory was an old one. It had been around since colonial times, with frequent arguments about its potential benefits in terms of strategic defense and territorial integration. Article 3 of the first republican Constitution in 1891 stated that a new capital should be built in the nation's central plateau. As a result, President Floriano Peixoto had established an exploratory commission to study and map out the area where the new capital would be located. In 1892, Floriano's commission set out on an expedition commanded by French astronomer Louis Ferdinand Cruls (1848–1908), who at the time served as director to the Brazilian National Observatory in Rio de Janeiro. Cruls presented his report to the President, pointing to roughly the same area that in 1877 had been suggested by Brazilian historian Francisco Adolfo de Varnhagen (1816–1878) as an adequate location for the new capital. The area comprised a large expanse of land in the Brazilian central plateau, covered by the Cerrado biome, an ecosystem characterized by tropical savannas and gallery forests forming long lush green corridors along rivers and wetlands. After the 1892 Expedition, the area became known as the "Cruls Rectangle."

During the first Vargas administration, the central government established a program called *Marcha para o Oeste* (March to the West), which attempted to promote the colonization of the interior in the direction of the future capital's agreed location. The first agricultural colony was settled in the state of Goiás in 1941, and from 1943 a large exploratory expedition called *Expedição Roncador-Xingu* advanced through the virgin territory entering the southern part of the Amazon forest. There, remarkable discoveries were made throughout the region's dense hydrographic network, and contacts with previously unknown indigenous tribes were established. In 1944, the leaders of the Roncador-Xingu Expedition founded the city of Nova-Xavantina, named after the local indigenous population, the Xavantes.[9]

Despite these earlier attempts at colonization, when President Kubitschek began the construction of Brasilia what he found was still a distant, isolated, and largely unpopulated area. His grandiose personality, however, would not allow any wavering in the face of difficulties. Following the Brazilian penchant for making public projects look impartial and credible, on March 12, 1957 the government started the selection of the projects that had been submitted to the public tender established for the building of the new capital. However, such arrangements barely function with any sense of honor or probity given the local culture of patrimonialism and back-scratching. In the end, the jury was composed of several personal friends of the eventual winner, architect Lúcio Costa (1902–1998), who received all the votes in the ballot. The *Concurso Público* or *Licitação*, as such tenders are generally called in Brazil, saw several unhappy bidders leave the competition even before it had finished.[10]

Before the actual capital was constructed, hundreds of miles of roads had to be built so that building materials could reach the area. With this completed in near record time, the land relative to the Cruls Rectangle began to see the arrival of trucks and heavy machinery with thousands of men flocking in to work in what became a non-stop, 24-hour hustle of building frenzy. Unemployed and impoverished men from the Northeast, the so-called *candangos*, soon arrived in hundreds of thousands looking for a job and hoping to find a means of subsistence. The job of designing the city was given to architect Oscar Niemeyer (1907–2012), one of the members of the jury that had unanimously chosen the project of his friend, Lúcio Costa, for the urban plan of the new capital.

After three years of uninterrupted work, astronomical expenditure, and not a few accusations of overbilling, President Kubitschek's dream came true on April 21, 1960. The inauguration of the capital occurred on schedule and on the symbolic date of the national holiday that is celebrated annually in tribute to Joaquim José da Silva Xavier, the leader of the Inconfidência Mineira Revolution who was hanged and dismembered by the Portuguese colonial government in 1792. The event thus assumed a revolutionary tone of self-proclaimed freedom and autonomy.

It cannot be ignored that since its inauguration, the city of Brasilia has been widely criticized for its shortcomings and inadequacies in terms of engineering work and urban planning. Criticisms range from expressions such as "city without citizens" and "phantom city" to "city of bureaucrats" and "fantasy-island." A lack of coherent urban planning, together with the reliance on a futuristic architectural vision of a dream world that was never converted into reality, account for the city's lack of organic functionality. Perhaps its best feature lies in its geographical location: occupying the country's central highlands at an elevation of 1,172 meters, Brasilia has a cooler climate than other Brazilian cities which, despite being located in more southern areas, have higher temperatures and humidity levels. Natural endowments thus compensated for human incompetence.[11]

By the time of the new capital's inauguration ceremony, campaigning for the upcoming presidential elections scheduled for October 3, 1960 was already in full swing. The government maintained the PSD-PTB party coalition and presented as their candidate the former Minister of War, Marshal Henrique Teixeira Lott, who had supported Kubitschek's rise to the presidency in 1956. Vice-President João Goulart was to stand again for the same post. Teixeira Lott lacked the charisma required to sustain a fiercely contested presidential run, especially after the rise of a new political sensation, the young governor of São Paulo, Jânio da Silva Quadros (1917–1992).

Born in Campo Grande, capital city of Mato Grosso State, but raised in the conservative city of Curitiba, the capital of Paraná State, Quadros moved in his late teens to São Paulo where he worked as a secondary school teacher and later became a municipal deputy, taking office in 1948 to replace the communist officials who had been ousted by President Dutra's move to ban the Communist Party. Quadros became mayor of the city of São Paulo in 1953 and the State's governor two years later, in 1955. His rapid political rise was due to an irresistibly populist charisma and to his reputation as an unrelenting fighter against corruption. As a symbol of his presidential campaign, Quadros used a broom with which he promised to sweep away the country's corruption.

"Vassourinha" (little broom), as Quadros was called, ran for President for a small party called *Partido Trabalhista Nacional* (PTN), which had made a coalition with another small party, the *Partido Democrata Cristão*

(PDC). Given its strong conservative character and the rising popularity of Quadros, the UDN opted to support Little Broom rather than put up a candidate of its own. The strongest right-wing party in the country had been showing signs of a change in attitude since at least 1958, when the younger generation of the organization had launched what was called the "Bossa Nova Manifesto," a statement of purpose whose contents were ironically in direct contrast with the basic principles of the "Banda de Música," the loud anti-Vargas faction of the party's older generation, represented above all by Carlos Lacerda. The humorous musical metaphor referred to the option of taking a softer line: the term "bossa nova" suggested the more mellow tone of the national popular music that was rapidly gaining a larger audience in the country during the late 1950s. The new Bossa Nova faction of the UDN wanted to present itself as being like the new music i.e. softer and smoother in comparison to the old Banda de Música faction which was faster paced and highly syncopated like the traditional samba and chorinho styles.

Among the UDN's Bossa Nova partisans were important young politicians such as future president José Sarney (b. 1930) and future governor of the state of Sergipe, João de Seixas Dória (1917–2012). These conservatives had been very lenient towards Kubitschek's administration but they now decided to support the President's rival, Jânio Quadros. Quadros won by a landslide with 48.27% of the votes against Lott's 32.93%. This time the UDN would not question the election's result, even though, again, the winner did not receive the majority of votes. Carlos Lacerda was elected governor of the state of Guanabara, of which the capital city was Rio de Janeiro. The Raven would now be in a better position to plot against the communists.

Quadros would take office on January 31, 1961, receiving the presidential sash from Kubitschek. It would be the first time in Brazilian republican history that an incumbent president peacefully transferred power to an elected member of the opposition. However, from the start, Quadros would not hold back from blaming Kubitschek for the terrible inflation he now had to deal with.

Brazilians tend to regard Juscelino Kubitschek de Oliveira's government with sympathy. The five years from 1956 to 1960 are frequently dubbed "Brazil's golden years." The country achieved remarkable economic growth and modernization, although the social costs caused by inflation were extremely high. For that reason, Kubitshek's program is what analysts call "conservative modernization," the characteristic Brazilian mode of economic development based on a strong and centralized state from where fierce social control and economic decisions emanate.

Undoubtedly, the term "conservative" also carries class connotations, suggesting the maintenance of power structures that had continued since colonial times.[12]

The "golden years" of Kubitschek's government are thus primarily the heyday of an emerging middle class that began experiencing the delights of the consumer society. The social gap between the rich and the poor, whether in the urban environment of cities like São Paulo and Rio de Janeiro, or in the rural areas still ruled by landed aristocracies, tended to be intensified as Brazil's modernization established an even sharper dividing line between those who controlled resources, and those who did not. Looking back at the years of Kubitschek's government and seeing that the outstanding rates of economic growth were not matched by any improvement in living conditions for a large portion of the population, allows us to conclude that, in Brazil, material progress and modernization often bear little relation to social equality. The disparity seen during this period in how much different layers of society benefited differently from economic growth suggests that Brazilians still lacked the sense of a common destiny pursued with a shared sense of citizenship within the boundaries of the national territory. The self-interested use of public institutions, unchecked corruption, exchanges of favors, abuse of power, disregard for individual merit, and the enormous difficulty in recognizing the equal rights of all fellow Brazilians was and would continue to be the underlying social and cultural conditions that determined the development of Brazilian history.

Jânio Quadros and High Populism (January–August 1961)

On the evening of the day he assumed the presidency, Jânio da Silva Quadros went on national radio to criticize Juscelino Kubitschek's government as incompetent, riddled with corruption, shameful, and fully responsible for the high inflation and onerous foreign debt which he, the new President, was now faced with. In the days that followed, Quadros would repeat his dramatic speeches, filled with exaggerated populism, and impose a series of minor political and legal measures aimed at expanding his media coverage and retaining popular attention. The President ordered a ban on cockfights, on the wearing of bikinis in beauty contests, and on the use in carnival parties of *lança-perfume*, a euphoria-inducing perfume aerosol.

The new president was attempting to contrive a moralizing public image that would appeal to the conservatives who had supported his campaign. His anti-corruption posturing and austere outlook provided for the creation of a persona that was at the same time reassuring and daring. His somewhat convoluted usage of the Portuguese language, with its mix of archaisms and complex semantic structures, called attention to the correctness and self-disciplined dignity of the former schoolteacher. The strict educator would now bring order and morality to the unrestrained chaos and debauchery reigning in the country.

Quadros acted against certain privileges held by public officials and curtailed some of the benefits extended to the military class. His aim was to further centralize power in the presidency, enlarging the areas under the direct responsibility of the Executive and underplaying the role of the Congress. He had good reason for doing this, for having been elected as the candidate of a small party, the new president had scant political support within the national legislative body. His survival in office thus depended on the strength of the Executive.

In March 1961, Quadros announced his new economic program and a currency exchange-rate reform. The reform was carried out through a new normative instruction issued by the SUMOC, Instruction 204. This new policy extinguished the system of foreign currency auctions and multiple exchange rates that had been established after the currency crisis of 1952, when President Vargas had had to relinquish his "Campos Sales–Rodrigues Alves Plan." In 1953, the Minister of Finance Osvaldo Aranha and the President of the Brazilian Bank, Marcos de Sousa Dantas, had devised and issued SUMOC's Normative Instruction 70. The instruction established four different quoting prices for the dollar, three of which were subsidized by the government with a view to favoring exports. The Normative 70 worked as a protectionist tariff that promoted industrialization. Quadros's Normative 204 now eliminated the trade barriers imposed in 1953 and moved toward the unification of currency exchange rates. The sudden reform favored foreign creditors and provoked a crisis in the already highly indebted economy. The opposition immediately criticized the exchange-rate reform, while foreign creditors, pleased with the new set-up, proceeded to offer new loans. In other words, the borrowing had resumed.[13]

Quadros's attitudes, which strongly appealed to the economic and psychological interests of right-wing conservatives, began to appear at odds with his more progressive stance on foreign policy issues. The President assumed an audacious posture in international affairs, contrasting with his essentially conservative domestic position. The formal title of his new foreign policy summarized Quadros's daring approach: *Política Externa Independente* (PEI).

The idea of independence in foreign policy involved grand and symbolism-laden gestures such as a visit to Fidel Castro's Cuba in March 1960 (still during the presidential campaign), an instruction to his Foreign Minister, Afonso Arinos de Melo Franco (1905–1990), to start negotiations to resume diplomatic relations with the Soviet Union in April 1961, and a ceremony in honor of Argentine revolutionary Ernesto Che Guevara (1928–1967) in Brasilia in August of the same year, an act that provoked the fury of the conservatives.

Quadros's PEI reflected the profound changes taking place in international politics at the time. In the process of decolonization occurring in Africa and Asia, Brazilians saw an excellent opportunity for international trade and capitalist expansion. The country would refrain from taking part in specific third-world associations, such as the Non-Aligned Movement that was gradually developing through a series of international conferences, notably Bandung (1955), Cairo (1957), and Belgrade (1961). Nevertheless, Brazilians still attempted to assume an equivalent autonomous position in relation to the two opposing poles of the cold war, the United States and the USSR. Quadros's grandiose foreign policy thus had a double intent: on the one hand, to stay attuned to the general principle of non-alignment and, on the other, to present Brazil as a suitable economic and political partner to the newly free nations emerging from the international decolonization process.

The President went on to promote the opening of new embassies in various African countries, most notably in Senegal, Nigeria, Ethiopia, and the Ivory Coast. The resumption of diplomatic relations with socialist nations, such as Hungary, Romania, and Bulgaria, was also achieved. In May 1961, the President received in Brasilia the first commercial mission from the People's Republic of China, and in July, a mission from the Soviet Union arrived. On this occasion, honors were presented to USSR astronaut Yuri Gagarin (1934–1968) in a ceremony that furthered Brazil's image of independence vis-à-vis the United States.

Quadros's displays of autonomy and political prowess made the right-wing conservatives' hair stand on end. The unions and the Peasant Leagues were gaining strength and their support for the nation's new foreign policy further enhanced conservative discontent. Anger peaked when Quadros sent Vice President João Goulart on an official visit to China. The rightists perceived Goulart primarily as a disguised syndicalist-communist leader, and his present mission was seen as a definitive shift to the left for the government. The real boiling point, however, was reached with the honoring of Che Guevara. This was, in fact, the result of a humanitarian act, rather than a political statement. Trying to curry favor with the nation's most conservative sectors, notably the Catholic Church, but also with one eye on his own international image, Quadros asked Guevara to grant clemency to a group of Catholic priests who were on death row in Cuba. The Vatican's diplomatic representative in Brazil had asked the President to intercede with Guevara over the case. The ceremony in Brasilia was thus meant as an opportunity for Quadros to show gratitude to Guevara for the mercy shown toward the priests.

The opposition, however, did not interpret the event as a story of mercy. The liberals were dissatisfied with the President's recent nationalist measures in domestic policy, especially the withdrawal of a concession granted to the American company Hanna Mining to explore iron ore in Minas Gerais. Quadros's new anti-trust law, which had recently been sent to Congress, was also a point of discord. The military, expecially the lower ranks, were particulary agitated by the ceremony in honor of Che Guevara. Some of the most powerful men in the country spoke out against the President. Carlos Lacerda accused Quadros of preparing a leftist coup.

On August 25, 1961, the government's powerful military ministers pressed Quadros to resign from the presidency. A face-to-face meeting with Marshal Odílio Denys (1892–1985), Brigadier Gabriel Grün Moss (1904–1989), and Admiral Sílvio Heck (1905–1988), quickly persuaded Quadros to step down. Those were men whose powers reached much beyond those of the President. Quadros, however, agreed to resign thinking that the Congress would not accept his leter of resignation. Quadros's logic was that, since the next in line for presidency was the leftist Vice-President who was presently visiting communist China, the entire Congress would ask him to stay on. He would then make a comeback in grand style, with popular support.

But the President had miscalculated his congressional support. He had forgotten that he had been elected at the head of a small party with little representation in the Congress. The very election process that took him to the presidency had been based on undermining traditional party politics. The euphoria he expected from his people was betrayed by a mild acceptance of the facts in the days following the publication of his letter of resignation.

By August 28, 1961, Quadros's charismatic rule had come to an end. That morning, the ousted President boarded a vessel called "Uruguay Star" and sailed to the United Kingdom. A new President was on his way back from China, with no one knowing for sure whether he would actually take office.

João Goulart: Parliamentarism and the Left (1961–1964)

The short seven-month presidency of Jânio da Silva Quadros produced a major transformation in the traditional aims and procedures of Brazilian foreign policy. The country's new non-alignment to the United States went a step further than similar previous attempts at autonomy, such as the policy of pursuing the national interest by trying to play the United States and Germany off against each other during the Second World War. President Kubitschek had also attempted to create an alternative to being aligned to the United States after President Eisenhower's rejection of the Operation Pan America. The effort at establishing commercial ties with Eastern Europe was partially an example of his timid attempt at autonomy. With Quadros, however, a new national position was clearly delineated in global terms, and from then on the country would continue to assert its autonomy, suggesting along the way its capacity for regional leadership.

In terms of domestic affairs, however, the Quadros administration was much less successful. After his resignation, the country was left in a situation of great instability, with sheer chaos looming on the horizon. The presidency was occupied *ad interim* by the Head of the House of Representatives, Ranieri Mazzilli (1910–1975), but real power remained in the hands of the military ministers who had forced the President's resignation. Affairs were complicated further when these powerful officers announced their opposition to Vice-President João Goulart's return to the country, sparking a ferocious dispute between left and right. In Goulart's Rio Grande do Sul, Governor Leonel Brizola (1922–2004) started what was called the "legality campaign," a military mobilization aimed at securing Goulart's return from China and his assumption of the presidency. Governor Brizola was João Goulart's brother-in-law, having married the Vice-President's sister in a ceremony at which Getúlio Vargas had been the best man. Adding to his political clout was his control of the Brazilian Third Army, now known as the "Southern Military Command," which, as we have seen, was the most powerful branch of the national army. Just as it had been to men such as António Gomes Freire de Andrade (1685–1763), José Marcelino de Figueiredo (1735–1814), Rafael Pinto Bandeira (1740–1795), José Gomes Pinheiro Machado (1851–1915), Júlio Prates de Castilhos (1860–1903), and Getúlio Dornelles Vargas (1882–1954), Rio Grande do Sul was to Leonel Brizola a significant powerbase.

On August 29, 1961, the military ministers who now controlled the central government threatened an air raid against Brizola's Piratini Palace in Porto Alegre. The palace was named after the short-lived, if not completely fictitious republic that had been declared in the region during the Farroupilha Revolution of 1835–1845. The commanders' order from Brasilia was to attack and kill the Gaúcho governor. The Third Army, however, led by General José Machado Lopes (1900–1990), learned of the plan in advance and invaded the air base located in the neighboring city of Canoas, from where the attack would start. Faced with the superiority of the infantry, the air corps was forced to capitulate. The Third Army then started to march northwards, in the direction of the capital, Brasilia.

In tandem with the military mobilizations in the south, a political quick fix to calm everyone's temper was being negotiated in the Congress. The approval of a constitutional amendment altering the government's regime from presidentialism to parliamentarism appeared as the compromise solution to enable Goulart to assume the presidency albeit with restricted powers. Under the parliamentary system the President would act as head of state, not as head of government, which would represent more limited authority. The Constitutional Amendment 16/1961 was approved on September 2, 1961. Forced to accept this new arrangement, João Goulart arrived in Brazil on September 5 and took office on September 7, the national day of independence.

That year of 1961 would see the beginning of a struggle to maintain order in a nation that was becoming chaotic. Upon returning from China, Goulart was faced with a country still growing at an 8.6% annual rate, but where inflation was at 33.2% annually. After 1961 the slide into complete economic stagnation would continue at a fast pace, with GDP growth falling to 6.6% and inflation rising to 49.4% in 1962; 0.6% and 72.8% in 1963; and 3.4% and 91.8% in 1964. The classical analysis of the crisis in the period is that of the aforementioned UNECLA economist Celso Furtado (1920–2004). In 1962 Furtado was appointed Minister of Planning and was instructed to devise an emergency program to tackle inflation and restore GDP growth. The plan was called *Plano Trienal* (of which more below), and it resulted in outright failure. An article by Furtado in 1965, "Obstáculos políticos ao crescimento econômico no Brasil" (Political Obstacles to Economic Growth in Brazil), showed that the process of industrialization found in Brazil during the three previous decades had been an indirect result of policies aimed at the defense of traditional export agriculture. The absence of a strong class of industrial entrepreneurs equipped with a liberal and constructive ideology turned industrialization into a function of the interests of the landed aristocracy that controlled politics. Industrialization was thus centered upon non-essential sectors of the economy, notably in the import substitution of some consumer goods that suffered eventual import restrictions and which were destined primarily for consumption by the upper echelons of society, that is, those who derived their wealth from land ownership.

Furtado emphasized that industrialization was not accompanied by matching investments in urban infrastructure and basic services, which could improve the working classes' standard of living and promote citizenship and human development. Concurrent with the lack of effective urbanization was the belated, imported, and highly mechanized process of industrialization that produced social exclusion and prevented the natural development of an internal market capable of pushing forward the industrial cycle. The political prevalence of conservative forces in society was thus a hurdle to development policies. The very 1946 Constitution worked to preserve traditional oligarchical power through a federal system in which small and backward states were given inappropriate strength in the Senate. These small federal units were precisely the places where agricultural interests were keener to obstruct industrialization, and through the federal system they were able to hold back industrialization across the whole nation.

Furtado also noted the prevalence of the landowning class's interests in the House of Representatives, this being a result of the 1946 Constitution's awarding of greater weight to the votes of electors in small states with higher rates of illiteracy. These, again, were precisely the states that relied more on traditional export agriculture. To Furtado's analysis, we could add the terrible consequences of the compulsory voting established with the 1946 Constitution, which facilitated the use of economic power and propaganda to win voter support, especially among the less well educated.[14] In his essay, Furtado concluded by noting that under such an arrangement, the National Congress itself posed a major obstacle to economic growth. The dreadful consequence was that the conflict between a progressive Executive and a conservative Legislature produced the conditions for military arbitration. The political and economic crisis was thus seen as the result of ill-conceived institutional arrangements that were deep-rooted in the country's federative profile.

In the middle of such a complex web of mutually exclusive interests, a new president had to take office. On doing so, under the newly concocted parliamentary scheme, João Goulart attempted a politics of reconciliation, hoping to quell the angry dispute between the aforementioned power triangle: the progressives, the conservatives, and the military. A fourth, but no less important, wrestler in the ongoing political match appeared no less in need of reassurance: the United States. In order to keep the powerful northern neighbor calm, Goulart maintained Quadros's appointment of Roberto Campos (1917–2001) to the Brazilian Embassy in Washington.

Campos had built his bureaucratic career as a defender of alignment with the United States and of liberal policies with regard to foreign capital, a position that had earned him the sobriquet of "Bobby Fields" (a literal translation of his name into English). Since President Goulart was eager to continue the new globalist and non-aligned stance of the PEI, the management of good diplomatic relations with the United States was of utmost importance. As Minister of Foreign Relations, Goulart appointed Francisco Clementino de San Tiago Dantas (1911–1964), a man who would become a key figure in the ensuing Brazilian attempt at sustained autonomy in foreign policy. Dantas was a former lawyer and university professor who had good relations with both sides in the liberal–nationalist debate. Unlike the largely uncreative bureaucrats who spend their lives climbing the greasy pole in the public administration, the new Foreign Minister had had a long career in the private sector, notably as attorney to the Moreira Salles Group, a family-run corporation that controlled part of the nation's banking industry. Later, Dantas became the owner of his own newspaper, the *Jornal do Comércio*, from the pages of which he defended the policies of *trabalhismo* and *desenvolvimentismo* implemented by Getúlio Vargas.

From such middle ground between the mutually opposing forces that had been vying to seize the country since the early 1930s, Dantas could proceed with the PEI without causing the same alarm as Quadros. In November 1961, albeit not without receiving some criticism from the conservatives, the new Foreign Minister completed the process of resuming diplomatic relations with the USSR. In January 1962, during a meeting of the Organization of American States in Punta Del Este, Uruguay, Dantas expressed Brazil's disagreement with a proposal from United States to expel Cuba from the Organization. Together with Argentina, Bolivia, Chile, Ecuador, and Mexico, Brazil abstained in the vote that resulted in the U.S. proposal being approved. Although abstentions are often seen as a weapon of cowards who fail to take a stance in the face of danger, Dantas's position during the Conference is still regarded as a display of autonomy by most historians of Brazilian diplomacy.[15]

Another point of disagreement with the United States emerged in February 1962, when Rio Grande do Sul's governor Leonel Brizola decided to nationalize two American companies, Bond and Share, and IT&T. He argued that their concession contracts had expired and they were refusing to make new investments in the region. Since companies tend not to invest without the prospects of making a profit, Brizola's argument seemed to beg the question. In any event, the incident caused an important rift in Brazil–U.S. relations, and Dantas had to work hard to keep a visit to the United States scheduled for Goulart the following month on track. Goulart had a successful meeting with President John F. Kennedy in April 1962, despite the apparent attempts of his anti-American brother-in-law to complicate the visit. Goulart and Kennedy agreed that the nationalization of American enterprises should be done peacefully, with prior negotiation, and with a recognition of the right to recompense. Goulart also praised Kennedy's Alliance for Progress, a U.S. economic assistance program to Latin America that had started in 1961.

In June 1962, Prime Minister Tancredo Neves (1910–1985) resigned his post and Goulart appointed San Tiago Dantas to the office. The conservatives, however, vetoed Dantas's appointment in Congress and a member of Brizola's clique, the Riograndense politician Francisco Brochado da Rocha (1910–1962), assumed the post of Prime Minister on July 12, 1962. San Tiago Dantas left the Foreign Ministry that same day, being replaced by Afonso Arinos de Melo Franco (1905–1990). After a constitutional referendum was held on January 6, 1963, whereby the presidential system was reinstated with João Goulart as President, Dantas was appointed Minister of Finance, where he worked side by side with Celso Furtado in implementing the latter's hastily conceived economic plan, the aforementioned Plano Trienal.

After Dantas stepped down from the Foreign Ministry, Brazilian foreign politics looked erratic, reflecting the growing instability of domestic politics at the time. During what remained of Goulart's government as many as four people held the post of Foreign Minister. The rise of conservative forces in the Ministry became evident in the new position Brazil adopted with regard to the decolonization process in Africa. Although the country maintained its former position in favor of the right of nations to self-determination, in reality a different tone emerged when it came to the question of the Portuguese colonies in Africa. In January 1962, the question of the independence of Angola was debated at the UN and the Brazilian stance was favorable to Portuguese interests. António de Oliveira Salazar's (1889–1970) government had demanded Brazil's support, invoking a pact of friendship signed in 1953. Salazar ruled his country during a bewildering period of 36 years, from 1932 to 1968, and as long as he lived he would not be willing to let go of his colonies. The Brazilian position in 1962, however, was determined not by Salazar's demands, but by the remarkable political influence held by the Portuguese community residing in Brazil. Adding to the complexity of the question was the fact that the Angolan process of decolonization was assuming a strong leftist character with the rapid ascension of the communist People's Movement for the Liberation of Angola (MPLA). In any case, the contradiction between the Brazilian position in favor of African decolonization and its pro-Portugal position at the UN showed how much the old Portuguese colonial influence still held sway among Brazilians at the time.

One last important event in Brazilian foreign politics during Goulart's administration was the definition of the country's nuclear policy. The emergence of a nationalist movement against the export of uranium during Kubitschek's government had led to the establishment of the National Commission for Nuclear Energy (CNEN), and the country began to assert its right to nuclearize. On September 19, 1963, the new Foreign Minister, João Augusto de Araújo Castro (1919–1975), gave a speech at the UN asserting three key points of Brazilian foreign policy: disarmament, development, and decolonization. The speech became know in the country's diplomatic history as the "3D's Speech," and it gave an important indication as to the direction of Brazilian nuclear policy in the following years. The word "disarmament" employed in the speech was heavily charged with Brazilian claims with regard to the Treaty on the Non-Proliferation of Nuclear Weapons (NPT), which had been proposed by Ireland in 1958. The need for such a treaty became more urgent after the Cuban Missile Crisis of 1962. Brazil noted that among the three pillars discussed as the basis for the treaty, namely non-proliferation, disarmament, and peaceful use, the first was gaining ground over the others. This foreshadowed a future when the five recognized nuclear States (China, France, the Soviet Union, the United Kingdom, and the United States) would use the treaty to prevent other states from nuclearizing while avoiding compliance with the disarmament provisions it contained. Araújo Castro's speech set the tone for Brazilian autonomy with regard to the international regime of nuclear non-proliferation. Brazil would not sign the NPT until 1998.

Back on the domestic front, a constitutional referendum was called for January 6, 1963 to select the form of government for the country, following the changes made immediately after Quadros's resignation. President João Goulart still enjoyed considerable popular support. The government set out on a monumental advertising campaign, arguing for the return of the presidential system and Goulart secured almost 80% of votes. Empowered as the head of the newly reinstated presidential system, the President could now implement the social policies that had made up the core of his political program since his time as Minister of Labor in Vargas's administration. These policies were brought together in a single program called *Reformas de Base*, which comprised restructuring programs in several areas, such as finance and the banking system, urban planning, government administration, taxation, education, and, most importantly, land reform. This last aspect of the package represented a high risk for the government, for it meant altering the country's oligarchical structure that had survived since colonial times. So far, such changes had proved impossible. The 1930 Revolution had been carried out under the banner of dislodging from the government the oligarchical power rooted in the nation's agrarian structure, but it never dared to suggest land reform. In the end, the Revolution only substituted Rio Grande do Sul's oligarchy for São Paulo's in the central government.

The reform package was linked to the economic plan devised by Celso Furtado and presented in late 1962. The Plano Trienal established a series of aims to be achieved in the remaining three-year period of Goulart's administration (1963–1965). Given the rising inflation seen in 1961 and 1962, the plan established measures of fiscal and monetary austerity, with public deficit control and restrictive monetary policies. The plan's orthodox nature conflicted with the aim of the nationalists, which was to continue the scheduled state-run projects of structural development. The solution was to attempt the maintenance of the funding of these projects by means of foreign loans. These were being negotiated by the now Minister of Finance, San Tiago Dantas. The plan's monetary orthodoxy appeared thus as a precondition to the approval of such loans. The whole scheme with the Plano Trienal, however, proved to be unfeasible, and the plan's failure became noticeable by the end of 1963, when the annual GDP growth rate fell from 6.6% the previous year to a contraction of 0.6%. Analysts have blamed several different causes for the plan's failure, such as the exhaustion of the process of industrialization based on import substitution, lack of political support, the breakdown of political populism and its capacity to mobilize the masses, as well as sheer incompetence. Whatever the causes of its failure may be, the fact is that the Plano Trienal's demise would throw Goulart's government into a maze of confusion from which it would never extricate itself.

At the beginning of 1963, however, the government still had hopes regarding the plan's success. Goulart's dangerous attempt at land reform was still on course and his first victory came in March 1963 with the congressional approval of a bill called The Rural Workers' Statute. The Statute established the extension of labor rights to rural workers. Until then, the legislation of *trabalhismo* had been applicable only to urban employees who, since 1943, had enjoyed certain benefits such as vacation time and regulated work hours. For the first time in the country's history rural labor would be entitled to the same rights. Needless to say, the new law provoked anger among the most conservative sectors of society. In truth, however, the law turned out to be almost completely ineffective due to the resistance it received from the powerful landowners who would not allow its enforcement in the distant rural areas. Although the Statute would be revoked in 1973 during the military regime, it did represent an important political victory for the struggling President in 1963.[16]

By mid-1963 Goulart's reform program had reached a point where its maintenance depended on a change to the constitution. The President had presented a preliminary draft of his land reform project to the Congress in April, and since it contained a scheme for land expropriation with the use of government bonds, only a consensual legislative determination could allow it to move forward. The Congress, however, did not approve the project. This time the leftists were the ones moved to outrage.

As popular movements demanding the reforms gained momentum, the government found itself pressured from all sides. The urban workers unions, for instance, albeit supporting the President's Base Reforms program, called for repeated strikes in order to force the government to act faster and in a more resolute manner. In August 1962, syndicate leaders met in São Paulo and established the *Comando Geral dos Trabalhadores* (CGT), a unified national movement encompassing all the country's syndicates. The CGT supported the government, but at the same time opposed it whenever the syndicates' claims were not immediately heeded. The conservatives, on the opposite pole, continued accusing Goulart of being involved with the CGT in an attempt to follow Perón's example in Argentina and establish a syndicalist republic in Brazil.

The climate of ideological radicalization became even more noticeable in September 1963, when a revolt of low-ranking military officers broke out in Brasilia. The soldiers rebelled against the Supreme Federal Court's decision to maintain the 1946 Constitution's provision that established the ineligibility of military officers for election to the legislative body. The officers were in favor of the President's program and frustrated with the congressional rejection of the land reform project, hence their desire to enter politics.

Enthusiasm for social and political reform was also found in the realm of culture and the arts. In the movie industry, a new movement called *Cinema Novo* embraced social criticism and produced a series of works highly influenced by leftist ideology. The turbulent years of 1963 and 1964 saw the height of the Cinema Novo movement in works such as *Vidas Secas* (1963), by Nelson Pereira dos Santos, *Deus e o Diabo na Terra do Sol* (1964), by Glauber Rocha, and *Os Fuzis* (1964), by Ruy Guerra. All three films narrated stories set in the poverty-stricken Northeast, presenting negative portrayals of the mighty landlords who appeared responsible for the subhuman living conditions of the rural population. The nation's abominable agrarian structure was also a recurrent theme in the productions of the *Centro Popular de Cultura* (CPC), a movement established in 1962 in Rio de Janeiro by a group of left-wing artists and intellectuals, among whom figured playwright Oduvaldo Vianna Filho (1936–1974), filmmaker Leon Hirszman (1937–1987), and poet Ferreira Gullar (b. 1930).

While the President gained some support from the nation's less organized sectors, such as the Peasant Leagues, the CGT, and the urban artists and intellectuals, the much more powerful conservative upper middle class joined the Catholic Church in a movement against the government. As the economic situation deteriorated, the year 1964 opened with the President politically isolated in a country where general dissatisfaction had become evident. The PSD was moving in the direction of Carlos Lacerda's UDN, as both parties feared the PTB's growth and the candidacy of Rio Grande do Sul's Leonel Brizola for the upcoming presidential election of 1965. The Riograndense leaders, Goulart and Brizola, were now regarded as embodiments of the communist threat in what could only be a surreal historical shift from traditional Gaúcho right-wing *caudilhismo* to left-wing dictatorship of the proletariat. Recalling Stalin's *caudilho* profile, however, the shift might after all not have been that surreal.

In any case, Goulart was now in no position to step back. On March 13, 1964, he spoke to a large popular assembly gathered in Rio de Janeiro's Central Railroad Station. The event brought together a crowd of some 150,000 people who occupied the entire central area of the country's former capital. A few hours before the event, the President had signed two decrees, the first ordering the expropriation of land in a tract of ten kilometers through the margins of highways and railroads, and the second establishing the nationalization of five oil companies operating in the country. Goulart started his speech at 8pm facing the hopeful crowd who had waited for him the whole day. Facing also three tanks carefully pointed in his direction by the State Governor, Carlos Lacerda, the President spoke of land reform, comparing it to the abolition of slavery. He spoke also of human dignity as a Christian principle, of the right of all Brazilians to freedom and democracy, and of the suffering of those who endured impoverished lives in the distant fields of the countryside.

For the discontented right wing, his assertion of an unyielding commitment to land reform was a step too far. His speech amounted to the sealing of a pact with the left. The conservatives took his words as an act of direct aggression and the PSD immediately withdrew its support from the government. That meant the end of the President's coveted constitutional reform, for together the PSD and the UDN controlled more than 50% of the Congress, this in spite of the PTB's strong showing in the elections of 1962.

The situation became more complex still when the conservatives began to suspect that, now bereft of congressional support, the President's only option to continue his desired reforms would be to mount a coup and close the Congress. A climate of paranoia emerged among all walks of conservatism. As the elections of 1965 approached, the United States began financing candidates from the opposition, using anti-communist think thanks such as the *Instituto Brasileiro de Ação Democrática* (IBAD) and the *Instituto de Pesquisas e Estudos Sociais* (IPES) as a means to transfer funds to pro-U.S. politicians. Relations between the United States and the Brazilian government had worsened after September 1962 with the Brazilian congressional approval of a law restricting the remittance of profits abroad. In October that year, one month after the approval of the law, President Kennedy and American Ambassador to Brazil, Lincoln Gordon (1913–2009), appointed United States Army officer Vernon A. Walters (1917–2002) as Army Attaché to the American Embassy in Brasilia. Walters had friendly relations with high-ranking Brazilian military officers such as General Humberto de Alencar Castelo Branco (1897–1967), whom he had met in Italy in 1944 in the context of U.S.–Brazil joint military operations of the Second World War. Castelo Branco would become the first military president in the dictatorial regime initiated a few months later. After November 1963, Lyndon Johnson's administration would turn away from Kennedy's more conciliatory position with regard to Latin American nationalist policies that, they believed, harmed American interests. Ideological radicalization and the emerging political crisis were clearly moving Brazil towards a potentially hazardous and unpredictable outcome.[17]

President Goulart, however, seemed oblivious to the real danger of his situation. In the next few days following his fatal public speech, he continued to push the opposition hard, insisting on the subject of land reform and social policy. Looking back at Brazilian history, we can see that Goulart lacked the strategic ability of his Riograndense predecessors. While Pinheiro Machado and Vargas had known how to measure the extent and limits of their power and act accordingly, Goulart relied on the sincerity of his intentions and on the certainty of acting in the interests of his people. He seemed unaware of the need to achieve a minimum level of agreement among the different forces in society if he was to avoid his whole enterprise coming to a dead end.

On March 19, 1963, the conservatives organized a large public demonstration in São Paulo to protest against the President's communistic aims stated a few days earlier in Rio de Janeiro. São Paulo saw 200,000 protesters take to the streets in what was called the *Marcha da Família com Deus pela Liberdade* (March of the Family with God in the Name of Freedom), the first of a series of rallies promoted by São Paulo State Governor, Ademar de Barros, together with important members of the clergy and some women's associations. These associations, it should be noted, were feminine but not feminist. They were comprised of women of good society, and financed also by the IBAD and the IPES. Groups such as the *Campanha da Mulher pela Democracia* (Women's Campaign for Democracy), *União Cívica Feminina* (Feminine Civic Union), and *Fraterna Amizade Urbana e Rural* (Fraternal Urban and Rural Friendship) took to the streets to protest against the President's leftist policies. Walking side by side through the large avenues of São Paulo with these newly "empowered" Brazilian women was none other than Carlos Lacerda, The Raven, who had flown from Rio de Janeiro to support the demonstration.

A fierce response to the high-society ladies of São Paulo came immediately from the Steelworkers' Syndicate. On March 25, a group of 2,000 marines gathered at the Syndicate's headquarters to defy the orders of the Minister of the Navy, Admiral Sílvio Mota (1902–1969), who had banned their association claiming it was a political group. The marines gathered to celebrate the anniversary of their now illegal syndicate, the *Associação dos Marinheiros e Fuzileiros Navais*. Important attendees at the event were former Rio Grande do Sul Governor, Leonel Brizola, now serving as a Congressman, and João Cândido, the leader of the Revolt of the Whip of 1910. In a remarkably odd historical turn, the Afro-Brazilian Riograndense João Candido, who had served as a foot soldier under Riograndense General Pinheiro Machado's command in the Federalist Revolution of 1893, and had been betrayed by Riograndense President Hermes da Fonseca in 1910, was now supporting the Riograndense President João Goulart side by side with Riograndense Congressman Leonel Brizola.

The event opened with a speech from marine leader José Anselmo dos Santos (b. 1942), known as Cabo Anselmo, who bravely stated the Association's intention to fight for the President's reforms and against the people's misery and exploitation. Admiral Silvio Mota moved a naval infantry command to the location with an order to arrest the rebels. Upon arriving at the Steelworkers' Syndicate, however, the soldiers decided to join their comrades in revolt. President Goulart took the side of the marines, causing the immediate resignation of the Minister of the Navy, who was angry at seeing his authority violated by the President. The marines' mutiny lasted throughout the following day. On March 27, the President officially pardoned the rebels.

Goulart had now openly defied the military. But he still managed to make his situation even worse. On March 30, the President attended a meeting of army sergeants in the Automobile Club of Rio de Janeiro. In an impassioned speech, Goulart intensified his populist position, polarizing the rich and the poor, and drawing a clear dividing line between those who defended his reforms and those who did not. The speech began by recognizing the present national crisis as being caused by a minority of privileged individuals who feared the integration of all Brazilians into the economic, social, and political life of the nation. Such individuals, the President continued, were the same Pharisees who in 1961 had attempted to tear up the 1946 Constitution and prevent his rightful assumption of the presidency. Now, Goulart continued, they paraded a false zeal for that same Constitution, opposing its lawful amendment. Advancing his argument for the legality of the constitutional reform, the President cited the Charter's Article 217 which contained the modification provision. He then continued his polarizing speech, condemning the opposition's misappropriation of Catholic sentiments in their attempt to counter his project of social reform. The President recalled Pope John XXIII's encyclical *Mater et magistra*, promulgated in 1961, and invoked the progressive sectors of the Catholic Church against the ideological maneuvers of the opposition's wealthy proprietors, who wanted to bury the nation under a fascist dictatorship, acting under the guise of defenders of Catholic values. Goulart then cited the priest Dom Hélder Câmara (1909–1999), an advocate of Liberation Theology who had recently been designated by the Pope to serve as Archbishop of Olinda and Recife. From there the President's speech moved from religious to financial matters, calling on the sergeants to note that all the money invested in the grand advertising campaigns against his government came from those who gained with the remittance of profits abroad and who were now bound by his Law of 1962. That money, he continued, also came from international oil interests in collusion with national companies that opposed his law that had given the oil import monopoly to Petrobras. The President finished by blaming real estate speculation for the current inflationary crisis and by accusing foreign pharmaceutical laboratories of attempting to destabilize his government.

Goulart's speech to the sergeants in Rio de Janeiro was the final straw that broke the camel's back of military patience. In the early morning of the following day, Army General Olympio Mourão Filho (1900–1972) ordered the Fourth Infantry Division to march from Minas Gerais and occupy the city of Rio de Janeiro. Mourão was the powerful commander who had devised the anti-communist Cohen Plan used by Vargas to establish his Estado Novo dictatorship in 1937. His prestige among the high ranks of the armed forces was such that while his troops were leaving the Infantry Division's headquarters and beginning the march to Rio de Janeiro a few telephone calls to other military commanders throughout the country were enough to start the coup. With military mobilizations already under way, Mourão received full support from the governor of Minas Gerais, Magalhães Pinto (1909–1996), whose participation in the events that followed, together with that of other civilian politicians, turned the coup into a civilian-military affair. In the states of São Paulo and Guanabara, Governors Ademar de Barros and Carlos Lacerda immediately offered their unreserved support to what was dubbed the "Popeye Operation," a reference to Mourão's habit of pipe smoking. By the evening of that same day, May 31, 1964, the military commanders had taken control of the streets of Rio de Janeiro and President Goulart was forced to flee the Laranjeiras Palace, where he had been accommodated after attending the sergeants' meeting the day before.

Goulart arrived in Porto Alegre in the early hours of April 1, being received by Rio Grande do Sul's Third Army Commander, General Ladário Pereira Teles. Leonel Brizola arrived a few hours later to take control of Rio Grande do Sul State's government, replacing the oppositionist governor, Ildo Meneghetti (1895–1980), who had fled the capital in fear of a military takeover from Goulart and Brizola. Meneghetti's fear was not without foundation. With the support of the Third Army, Brizola tried to convince Goulart to resist and fight the right-wing military rebellion that was gaining control of the country. The President, however, decided to avoid what would become a bloody civil war and fled to his native São Borja, from where he entered Uruguay requesting political asylum.

The Brazilian Liberal Republic had come to an end. On April 2, 1964, the National Congress declared the absence of João Belchior Marques Goulart from the presidency and handed the post to the Head of the House of Representatives, Congressman Ranieri Mazzilli. A period of severe political repression would ensue. During the next two decades, harsh military rule would be combined with astounding GDP growth and inadequate income distribution. Severe wealth concentration would result from development policies focused on a model of industrialization that would prove socially exclusionary and economically unsound. At the end of the period, the nation would be experiencing high inflation and acute economic recession, with immeasurable social costs and humanitarian losses.

Brazil would continue to be a country disfigured by social injustice. Most Brazilians would continue to live and work under semi-servile conditions. The two-faced nation would appear in its urban guise with poorly built cities, densely populated by struggling middle classes and their domestic servants, while in its rural countenance immense estates the size of small countries would continue to house a minority of wealthy landowners and their miserable semi-slaves. After 1964, anyone who challenged this structure would be tortured and murdered, with some members of the upper classes happy to pay to watch the torture and the executions.

By the end of the Liberal Republic, it was very clear that President Dutra's illusions, which had marked the beginning of the period, were in fact mere wishful thinking, dreams that could never come true. The Marshal Plan for Latin America, just as a Marshal Plan for Brazil, would never arrive. Brazilians might ask themselves why there was never a Marshal Plan for Brazil, why the Second World War enemies, Germany and Japan, were reconstructed with the aid of the powerful and wealthy United States, while Brazil, the ally, was not granted the same help. Put another way, why would the Germans and the Japanese be allowed to enjoy high standards of living and social justice in the future, while Brazilians would be denied them. And the answer involves the sad reality that in a country where the upper classes abhorred social policies, where wealthy landowners still functioned with a slave-trade mentality, where influence peddling and back-scratching prevailed over individual talent, where the public sector was used as private property, where corruption flourished in all areas of economic life, where social injustice reached astronomic levels, where greed and envy became the norm in the absence of a meritocratic system favoring individual growth, where education was undermined in order to facilitate mass mind control, where infrastructure was poorly developed as financial resources became entangled in webs of corruption, where the electoral system was designed to enable the use of economic power to win polls, where a sense of citizenship and nationality was weak, where a bureaucratic system favored laziness and unreliability, and where human capital was wasted in hypocrisy and state patronage, a Marshal Plan simply could not be implemented.

The military coup that ousted the lawful occupant of the Brazilian presidency in 1964 was the result of an agrarian-minded and highly stratified society based on semi-feudal power structures being suddenly confronted with a modernization that it needed but could not accept. The ghost of land reform threatened those very power structures, semi-feudal and conservative, while the incipient industrial sector reproduced the landowners' mores. Both urban and rural capitalists needed foreign capital, and in its primarily parasitic nature, foreign capital was always ready to collude. With the President's threat by the two-edged sword of land reform and nationalist capital regulation, capitalists, both urban and rural, were suddenly asphyxiated.

Historians debate the role of the United States in the military overthrow of the constitutionally elected President. In their zeal for conspiracy theories and spy-thriller narratives, many Brazilian writers, most of them eager to sell books, attempted to establish a direct link between the U.S. government and the events leading to Goulart's fall. The most common of such links is the one referred to as *Operação Brother Sam*, an operation supposedly ordered by President Lyndon Johnson to offer logistical support to the rebelling Brazilian military in case they found resistance from Goulart's supporters. Goulart's decision to present no resistance, and thus to avoid a civil war, it has been argued, was influenced by his knowledge of a possible American intervention.

That Goulart's government was not in tune with U.S. interests is an obvious truism. That the U.S. government supported the military insurgents is also evident. The coup, however, was solely a Brazilian affair. Its only cause was the country's inability to maintain extended self-government under a sustained legal arrangement. The coup represented the nation's failure at democracy and reconciliation, and also its immaturity and lack of self-determination.

And now darkness would set in *manu militari*. If the Liberal Republic, in all its liberality, had not been capable of advancing the values of freedom and social justice, now the weapons of authority would show that those values had been, from the beginning, only an illusion. The innermost fears of President Vargas, who, in an attempt to avoid what was presently coming into being, shot himself in the chest, were turning into reality. The nation was to fall into a silent chaos of anguish and disillusion. And there was no one to blame but the Brazilians themselves.

Culture and Society in the Liberal Republic

The period from 1945 to 1964 saw the gradual emergence of an urban culture in Brazil that was directly influenced by the State's deliberate attempt at industrialization. The rising middle class, with its still conservative and Catholic attitudes, would make up the internal market for the durable goods that were finally being produced by domestic industry.

Cars and electric appliances would become status symbols in the incipient consumer society that began to experience the delights of capitalism and industrialization. Enthralled by the benefits of progress and city life, bourgeois Brazilians supported the Liberal Republic's attempt at introducing their country into the international community of free and technologically advanced nations.

In reality, however, looking away from the feigned modernity of a few urban centers, the country was still primarily agrarian. At least until the first years the 1970s, the size of the rural population would continue to surpass that of city residents. If in 1940 only 30% of Brazilians lived in cities, by 1960 that number had still reached only 45%. The processes of industrialization started by Getúlio Vargas and Juscelino Kubitschek allowed for the emergence of an internal market based on the southeastern part of the country, to where a large migration wave was immediately set in motion. The central portion of the territory also received a remarkable number of new residents, most of them coming from the Northeast in search of work and of a better life in the new capital under construction.

In spite of their deficient infrastructure, however, Brazilian cities kept growing. The city of Brasilia, founded in 1960, was already the tenth largest municipality in the country ten years after its inauguration, reaching 537,492 inhabitants in 1970. By 2010, Brasilia would have become the fourth largest city in Brazil, with 2,455,903 residents.

São Paulo finished the period of the Liberal Republic as the largest city in the nation. Its population surpassed that of Rio de Janeiro at some point in the 1950s. Census numbers indicate 2,198,096 residents in São Paulo against 2,377,41 in Rio de Janeiro in 1950. As we have seen, numbers for 1960 put São Paulo ahead with 3,825,351 compared with Rio's 3,307,163.

São Paulo's population growth reflected its higher rate of industrialization. Since the 1910s the city had shown signs of higher industrial diversification in comparison with Rio de Janeiro or any other Brazilian city, and by 1950 it had reached national leadership in industrial output. A larger number of European immigrants settling in São Paulo since the late nineteenth century had also provided more skilled labor than in Rio de Janeiro, allowing for the emergence of a more consistent consumer market. European immigration to the city also produced a higher level of entrepreneurship, as exemplified in the large industries established by the Italians Matarazzo and Crespi, the Lebanese Jafet, and the Lithuanians Klabin.

The question of education proved to be a thorny issue during the Liberal Republic period. Education became the source of an intricate and highly polarized debate after Vargas's fall in 1945. The 1946 Constitution established free schooling, but only at primary level. A fierce debate emerged between the defenders of public schools and the supporters of a stronger presence of the private sector in education. Economic interests were set in motion and here again left- and right-wing ideologues disagreed. The debate became even more polarized when, to the left-against-right ideological battles, were added the questions of lay-versus-religious education. The clash between the two propositions reflected an old dispute between the Brazilian government and the Catholic Church initiated with the establishment of the First Republic in 1889. Until then, the nation's education system had been entrusted to the Catholic Church, but under the First Republic the public sector began to take that responsibility upon itself. Five decades later, the Liberal Republic was faced with a private sector that defended religious education, and a public one that called for laicism.[18]

In order to comply with the 1946 constitutional provision ordering the formulation of a law to regulate the country's educational system, President Dutra's Minister of Education, the Bahian Clemente Mariani Bittencourt (1900–1981), formed a commission of educators from various ideological dispositions. Academics such as Pedro Calmon (1902–1985), Alceu Amoroso Lima (1893–1983), and Lourenço Filho (1897–1970) were brought together to devise the country's new schooling regulations. Some of these men represented the old *Escola Nova* group, which defended public education and which had prevailed during Vargas's government; others supported the Catholic religious tendency with an emphasis on private education. The commission's first draft of the new law was issued in 1948 under the rubric of *Projeto Mariani*, but a lack of consensus and fierce ideological polarization in the Congress resulted in it not being promulgated until 1961, and then only with substantial amendments. The most important of these alterations came in 1959 from none other than the UDN right-wing leader Carlos Lacerda who, in his "Lacerda Substitutive," fiercely defended private education with strong religious indoctrination. What was really at stake in Lacerda's proposal was the financing of private schools with public funds. The politician argued that since parents had the right to choose between public and private schooling for their children, so the State had the obligation to transfer the same amount of money to both types of institution. Lacerda thus managed to completely alter the course of the debate regarding the new educational law. His proposal would evidently result in the transference of public funds to the private sector. Alarmed with Lacerda's "Substitutive," a group of progressive thinkers established a national campaign in defense of the public school system. Among them were sociologist Florestan Fernandes (1920–1995), anthropologist Darcy Ribeiro (1922–1997), internationally acclaimed educator Paulo Freire (1921–1997), and the founder of the Escola Nova in Brazil, Anísio Teixeira (1900–1971).[19] But despite their efforts, Lacerda's proposal was successful in a Congress dominated by the conservative right-wing parties, the PSD and the UDN. The Law 4.024/61, promulgated in the first year of João Goulart's government, established the directives of national education with significant support for private interests.

During the 1960s, the Brazilian education system's shortcomings appeared more and more pressing. When João Goulart assumed the presidency in September 1961, Brazil had a population of 70,779,000 of which 39.5% were illiterate, and only 2% of those who started primary school reached higher education. After the victory of Lacerda's proposal in the Congress, some civil organizations began to promote free educational programs on their own. The *União Nacional dos Estudantes* (UNE) created the *Centros Populares de Cultura* (CPCs), where cultural and artistic productions such as theater performances, music concerts, and literary events were offered free of charge to the general public. The UNE was a general union of students enrolled in higher education, established in 1938 with President Vargas as official sponsor. During Goulart's administration, the UNE vehemently supported the President's social policies.[20]

Goulart's government established the *Movimento de Educação de Base* (MEB) in 1961, a foundation program in basic education linked to the President's *Reformas de Base* program and executed with the help of progressive sectors of the Catholic Church, most notably the *Conferência Nacional dos Bispos do Brasil* (CNBB), a religious organization founded by Bishop Dom Hélder Câmara (1909–1999) in Rio de Janeiro in 1952. The CNBB became very influential within the Liberation Theology Movement, which started with The Second Vatican Council under Pope John XXIII in 1962. The Movement was based upon a Christian scriptural hermeneutic founded on the idea of poverty as suffering and of liberation from suffering as salvation. Salvation was thus regarded as possible through social action and improvement. The doctrine's proponents never denied its compatibility with aspects of Marxism, and its adoption by President Goulart earned the Brazilian politician renewed charges of communism.

In any case, starting during Goulart's government, the CNBB created the so-called *Comunidades Eclesiais de Base* (CEB), a grassroots movement that attempted to promote social policies in poor neighborhoods and villages, with special attention to evangelization in connection with cultural and educational programs for literacy and basic learning. These programs were favored by the methods of the aforementioned educator Paulo Freire (1921–1997), who had developed a basic literacy teaching technique in the late 1950s. Freire's experiments had led him to teach a large group of sugarcane cutters to read in only 45 days in his native Pernambuco. Freire then developed his notion of Pedagogy of Liberation, where education is seen from a critical perspective and put to work in the service of social transformation. Since education had an important political role in João Goulart's governmental program, upon learning of the gifted pedagogue who had worked in the impoverished northeastern backlands, the President called Freire to Brasilia an invited him to supervise the drafting of the government's National Program for Literacy (NPA), which was established on January 21, 1964 only to be extinguished a few months later by the military leaders who mounted the *coup d'état* ousting João Goulart.[21]

The years of the Liberal Republic also witnessed the emergence of the works of important intellectuals who re-examined the cultural foundations of Brazilian society. Especially important in this respect are the works related to the aforementioned *Instituto Superior de Estudos Brasileiros* (ISEB), which was established in Rio de Janeiro in 1955 and closed down immediately after the 1964 coup, with most of its members being sent into exile by the new regime. The ISEB was linked to the Ministry of Education and it began its activities after Juscelino Kubitschek assumed the presidency. Kubitschek's ideas of rapid industrialization with strong reliance on foreign capital, subsumed in his "tripod" model, were attuned to the developmental notions of the Institute's members. Among them figured individuals such as Nelson Werneck Sodré (1912–1999), Helio Jaguaribe (b. 1923), Anísio Teixeira (1900–1971), Gilberto Freyre (1900–1987), Alberto Guerreiro Ramos (1915–1982), and Roland Corbisier (1914–2005). These intellectuals provided a theoretical formulation for the socioeconomic ideology known as *nacional desenvolvimentismo*.

The ISEB functioned as an autonomous think thank and its members embraced vigorously the political polarization of the Liberal Republic, interpreting the national situation in terms of a clear distinction between *nacionalistas* and *entreguistas*. The former were the ones who defended a thorough involvement by the State in the economy against the domination of North Atlantic hegemonic capitalism; the latter were those who favored the private sector with an openness to foreign capital. ISEB members had invariably belonged to the first group, until dissent arose in 1958 with the publication of Helio Jaguaribe's *O nacionalismo na atualidade brasileira* (Nationalism in present-day Brazil). The book questioned the radicalism of those who saw in foreign capital the root of all evil, and thus set in motion a severe institutional crisis that provoked an ideological split among the Institute's members. Jaguaribe's critique was in fact attuned to Kubitschek's nationalistic program, which, as we have seen, was not averse to foreign capital. The book was, above all, an attempt to reconcile the President's policies with an increasingly discontented left.

Among the works of ISEB members, those of Nelson Werneck Sodré are especially important for our present purpose of understanding the cultural developments experienced during the Liberal Republic. Sodré's first book, *História da literatura brasileira: seus fundamentos econômicos* (1938), produced a turning point in Brazilian literary studies with the introduction of a Marxist approach to literary history. Sodré's departure from traditional historical analyses such as Araripe Júnior's (1848–1911) *Cartas sobre a literatura brasileira* (1869), Sílvio Romero's (1851–1914) *Introdução à história da litteratura brasileira* (1882), and José Veríssimo's (1857–1916) *História da Literatura Brasileira* (1916) reveals an important intellectual attunement to the political developments taking place in the 1930s and 1940s. The author observed the structural contingencies of the colonial system as a determining factor in the country's literary production, identifying colonial literature as an embryonic stage in Brazil's literary development. According to Sodré, imported ideas and transculturation become the norm in a second stage, marked by the adoption of Parnassianism and Symbolism. A truly national literature arrived only with the advent of a third stage, when economic and social conditions allowed for a new period of autonomy that saw a doubling in the country's literary production with genuinely national forms of expression. Sodré's Marxist analysis would be reinforced during his term in the ISEB, when his subsequent works, notably *As Classes Sociais no Brasil* (1957) and *O Naturalismo no Brasil* (1965) would produce a new form of literary analysis based on the realities of social conflict and the interconnection of power structures.

The literary works of the period also tended to adopt a Marxist epistemology. Direct depictions of the nation's sorrowful realities of extreme poverty and class conflict were present in poetry, theater, and drama. Social inequality and economic domination appear as recurrent themes in late-modernist verse and narrative, with remarkable examples in the works of poet João Cabral de Melo Neto (1920–1999) and novelist Guimarães Rosa (1908–1967). Melo Neto was born in the northeastern state of Pernambuco but spent most of his life abroad serving in different Brazilian diplomatic missions. His first mission was in Barcelona, where he arrived in 1947. Spain, and most notably the city of Seville, would come to figure prominently in the poet's works. Melo Neto's first collection of verse, *Pedra do Sono* (1942), showed the initial influence of Surrealism on the artist, presumably the result of contact with the work of the Spanish surrealists, the *Generación del 27*. The surrealist aesthetic, with its depictions of dream-like states and symbolist imagery, was subsequently abandoned in favor of a more realist epistemic stance. This became evident in his *Morte e Vida Severina* (1955), a long poem considered to be one of the landmarks of Brazilian literary history. The poem restated the theme of the plight of the *retirantes* found in previous literary works such as Rachel de Queiroz's *O quinze* (1930) and Graciliano Ramos's *Vidas Secas* (1938). Constructed as a narrative poem told in the first person with a tight structure of short verses and charged rhyming, *Morte e Vida Severina* tells the story of a common man from the drought-ridden backlands of the state of Pernambuco and of his struggle to reach the coastal capital, Recife, thus escaping hunger and death. The poem's title plays with the persona's name, Severino, who starts addressing the reader by presenting himself and explaining the origin of his name. "Severino" is a common name, and as such lacks individuality. So the narrator provides more detail, saying that he could be called "Severino of Zacarias," adding the name of his father to explain who he is. But most men in his birthplace, the narrator continues, are "Severinos of Zacarias," as many descend from a landlord called Zacarias, who was the oldest landowner in the region. "Severinos," he then concludes, are all those poverty-stricken men who suffer the constraints of social injustice, moral abuse, and climatic harshness. All those "Severinos" share a common fate, the fate of a cruel life and of a terrible death in hunger and pain. The poem's title, *Morte e Vida Severina* (Severina Life and Death), thus changes the proper noun "Severino" into an adjective that qualifies "life" and "death," suggesting the terrible birth and demise shared by all the "Severinos."

    The Brazilian novel also saw remarkable developments during the period of the Liberal Republic. A Marxist aesthetic emerged most notably in the works of a novelist from Minas Gerais, Guimarães Rosa (1908–1967). Like Melo Neto, Rosa belonged to the Brazilian diplomatic corps, assuming his first position abroad in Germany in 1938. As a diplomat, the author became known for having supported Jewish immigration to Brazil during the years of Nazi rule in Germany. His novels and short stories are usually set in the dry backlands of the Brazilian Northeast, and present an important example of modernist aesthetics in the Portuguese language with extensive use of linguistic experimentation, vernacular localisms, and neologisms. Rosa's usage of language has been compared to that of James

Joyce, and his oeuvre is usually cited as the Brazilian example of the Latin American literary boom of the 1960s. During a time when political leaders constantly promoted the ideology of *desenvolvimentismo*, Rosa showed the complex reality of the Brazilian rural landscape with all its mysticisms, violence, ignorance, cruelty, and domination, but also as a unique space filled with remarkable culture and outstanding human value. Rosa's backlands are a place where the peasant's wisdom thrives freely and produces a magical sense of reality akin to those found in other corners of Latin America. The enlarged sense of the real, experienced by his characters, saw his novels figure among the magical realist aesthetic that led Latin American literature to world prominence in the twentieth century.

Among Rosa's novels, *Grande sertão: veredas* (1956) is usually cited as his most representative work. The novel tells the story of the friends Riobaldo and Diadorim as they move through the private wars set in motion by their landowning bosses, engaging in tales of cruelty, rivalry, and revenge. Through Riobaldo and Diadorim, Rosa depicts the life and mores of the *jagunço*, a type of bodyguard and hitman hired by wealthy farmers for protection against invaders and feudal enemies. Filled with local folklore, the narrative reveals Riobaldo's philosophical questioning of good and evil, God and the Devil, the meaning of life and death. The novel is constructed around such contrary poles, providing the reader with a psychological and, at the same time, ethnographical record of the *jagunço*'s mental landscape as he encounters and questions the realities of his environment through the hermeneutic tools made available to him by his cultural setting. The sacred and the profane intermingle in the narrator's mind, and religiosity becomes a defining element in the contrast between the urban modern and the rural traditional. In his close friendship with his partner, Riobaldo begins to have subtle homoerotic feelings for Diadorim, who is depicted as an androgynous individual, embodying thus the ambiguities and paradoxes that besiege Riobaldo's mind. Only after Diadorim's death, does Riobaldo discover that his friend was in reality a woman.

The magical realism of Rosa's novels, just as with their Spanish-American counterparts, derives in great part from national folklore and religiosity, with their tendency to impinge a sense of wonder upon perceived reality. Some literary critics have tried to trace magical realism's roots to German expressionism and the aesthetics of *Neue Sachlichkeit*, but the original worldviews of Latin American indigenous religions appear a more reliable starting point for the style's history, as is argued in the works of the Cuban novelist and critic Alejo Carpentier (1904–1980).

A distinct literary tendency, this one channeled toward urban reality and middle-class existential conflict, also emerged in the Brazilian novel during the period. Perhaps the most noteworthy example is that of Ukrainian-born author Clarice Lispector (1920–1977), who, as we have seen, introduced to the Brazilian novel a new introspective style linked to the stream of consciousness technique. After her *Perto do coração selvagem* (1943), novels such as *A maçã no escuro* (1961) and *A paixão segundo G. H.* (1964) brought a new dimension to the country's literary production, with narratives that are closely connected to philosophical developments in phenomenology and existentialism. In *A maçã no escuro*, the Sartrean thesis that existence precedes essence underlies the protagonist's adoption of a new identity after taking refuge in a farm without knowing for sure if he has killed his wife. The protagonist's new life and exchanges with the three women who inhabit the estate establish the notion that existence is created out of nothing, and that the choices that appear at every single instant are a form of incessant existential renewal. In *A paixão segundo G. H.*, Lispector presents her reader with a circular monologue narrated in the first person. The female narrator, identified only as G.H., tells obsessively of her unstable psychological state after crushing a cockroach the previous day. The fragmentary nature of the narrative discloses a psychological crisis that soon moves into chaos and the absurd. The mental action takes place in the maid's room of the narrator's elegant Rio de Janeiro apartment. The maid has just quit her job, and when the owner starts to clean out the servant's room, expecting to find it filthy and disordered, she is startled to find it clean and deserted, with nothing in it but a cockroach. She then experiences a breakdown after crushing the insect in the door of a wardrobe and seeing the entrails of its still-living, squirming body begin to ooze out. The narrator then undergoes an existential transformation as she traverses each circular re-enactment of the story. After her identity is completely shattered, she somehow mingles with the writhing insect as she takes the cockroach's excreted fluid in her hands and eats it. The book's shocking denouement suggests a heavy charge of social criticism with posthumanist overtones, with the disturbed owner debasing herself in mingling with the cockroach in the absence of the black maid who hated her. The owner and the cockroach are now one, and the maid may never have existed. Lispector's *A paixão segundo G. H.* also recalls instances of the Theater of the Absurd, notably Jean Genet's *The Maids* (1947), where class conflict, cruelty, and madness assumed heavy existential connotations.[22]

While Lispector's existentialism opened the way for a new aesthetic in the Brazilian novel, the poetry of Ferreira Gullar (1930–2016) transformed Brazilian verse through the adoption of a renewed avant-garde disposition. Born in São Luís, the capital city of the northeastern state of Maranhão, Gullar moved to Rio de Janeiro in 1951 after winning a poetry competition. The publication of his first collection, *A luta corporal* (1954), immediately set him at the forefront of Brazilian poetry. The volume starts with a series of powerful prose poems that recall *Les Chants de Maldoror* (1868), the famous work of one of Surrealism's forerunners, Isidore-Lucien Ducasse (known as Comte de Lautréamont, 1846–1870). *Les Chants de Maldoror*'s direct conversational tone aimed at various interlocutors to whom the poem's persona discloses his misanthropist, skeptic, and, at the same time, truthful and straightforward personality resonates in some of Gullar's pieces such as "*Carta de amor ao meu inimigo mais próximo*" (Love letter to my closest enemy) and "*Os ossos do soluço*" (The sob's bones), where a mythical, timeless existence makes the first person narrator seem to hover in a morally empty limbo constructed beyond life and death.

After his successful attempts at prose poetry, Gullar adopted a progressively experimental disposition, turning away from meaning and deconstructing language's capacity to signify. Poems such as "*Roçzeiral*" attracted the attention of São Paulo-based avant-garde artists Décio Pignatari and the brothers Augusto and Haroldo de Campos, who invited Gullar to join their Concrete Poetry Movement. The movement would become an important element of Brazilian cultural history in the twentieth century. Diverging personal opinions and incompatible aesthetic views, however, would soon provoke a split between Gullar and his colleagues from São Paulo. Gullar had joined the *concrete* Paulistanos after being advised by some friends not to let the São Paulo poets take all the credit for the innovations he was producing. Joining the group was thus a way to guarantee the recognition of his achievements. The break-up came when the São Paulo *concretistas* began defending the application of mathematics to poetry composition.

Free from the brainy brothers of São Paulo, in 1959, Gullar published his *Manifesto Neoconcreto*, as well as his *Teoria do Não-objeto*, by means of which he launched his own movement, which was called *Neoconcretismo*. Gullar's Movement valued subjectivity and expressiveness in opposition to the stale intellectualism of the São Paulo brothers. Two opposing avant-garde movements were thus established in the early 1960s: one based in Rio de Janeiro and centered around Gullar, and another based in São Paulo and led by the de Campos brothers. Artists such as Lygia

Clark (1920–1988) and Hélio Oiticica (1937–1980) joined Gullar's Neo-Concrete Movement in Rio de Janeiro. Clark was a painter who believed that painting was no longer sustainable in its traditional material form. She turned to installation work with strong influence from Russian Constructivism and from the works of her former teacher, the avant-garde landscape architect Roberto Burle Marx (1909–1994). Going a step further from Clark's revolutionary ideas in the visual arts, Oiticica attempted to completely disconnect art from its object, establishing an intimate dialogue with Gullar's non-object theory, which announced the death of painting and called for the creation of "special objects" produced "outside of all artistic convention and which would reaffirm art as the primordial formulation of the world."[23]

Gullar's aesthetic theory, filled with Heideggerian overtones, was very influential in this new *carioca* avant-garde, and Oiticica relied on it in his own turn towards performance art. Oiticica questioned traditional ideas of aesthetics by considering the spectator in his work, which he described as an "experimental exercise in freedom." This new avant-garde soon assumed a strong leftist political orientation. Gullar and his followers were strongly supported by prestigious art critic Mário Pedrosa (1900–1981), who is said to have initiated the discipline of modern art criticism in Brazil. Aligned to a strong Trotskyst orientation, Pedrosa opposed the traditionally Stalinist Socialist Realism and favored abstract art, becoming a mentor to the Rio de Janeiro Neo-Concrete avant-garde.[24]

An even more radical shift to the left occurred when Gullar decided to move away from abstractionism into a more politically engaged form of poetic expression in which meaning could be restored to the poem in favor of its new role in the social struggle. In 1962, Gullar joined the National Student's Union (UNE) to establish the aforementioned *Centro Popular de Cultura* (CPC) under the banner of civil society's rightful attempt to play its part in support of President Goulart's reform program, which was being stalled in the Congress. With the CPC, Gullar turned to a more popular sort of poetics, adopting traditional forms from his native Maranhão such as the *Literatura de cordel*, a genre whose origins date back to the Portuguese sixteenth-century renaissance, when the oral poetry of the medieval troubadours began to appear in print in the form of booklets or pamphlets that were hung from strings and displayed by vendors to attract potential buyers. Gullar's ideological shift was accompanied not only by his election to the presidency of UNE's CPC in 1963, but also by an engagement with Francisco Julião's Peasant Leagues, as well as with an affiliation to the Brazilian Communist Party. Ideology, however, weighed heavily on Gullar's poetic expression. Unlike the Marxist aesthetic of João

Cabral de Melo Neto and Guimarães Rosa, which was more a part of these men's natural intellectual and sentimental disposition than the product of a conscious attempt at producing a specific form of literature, Gullar's ideological engagement and shift to Cordel Literature produced poetry of lesser strength in comparison to his former work. An example is his *História de um Valente* (1966), which was written in answer to a request from the Communist Party. In any case, Gullar's literature would soon regain its former power and luster to the extent of turning him into one of the greatest poets in the Portuguese language.

A strong leftist orientation is also found in Brazilian cinema during the period. As we have seen, the ideological polarization at the end of the Liberal Republic was reflected in the country's film production through a movement called *Cinema Novo*. Highly influenced by Italian Neorealism and the French *Nouvelle Vague*, Brazil's *Cinema Novo* opposed the national cinema's traditional emphasis on the production of musical comedies in a Hollywood style. The movement's foundation was set during the First Congress of National Cinema, held in September 1952, when artists and film-industry technicians discussed the possibilities of producing a new form of cinema with clearly national characteristics. The first such film was Nelson Pereira dos Santos's (b. 1928) *Rio, 40 Graus* (1955), a semi-documentary that tells the real-life story of a group of young men from a shantytown in Rio de Janeiro who survive by selling peanuts in the city. Nelson Pereira dos Santos was born in São Paulo and held a Law degree from the local university. With *Rio, 40 Graus* he started a long career, becoming the forerunner of the new Brazilian cinema movement. His *Boca de ouro* (1962) brought to the screen an adaptation of the homonymous play by the aforementioned dramatist Nelson Rodrigues (1912–1980). *Boca de ouro* told the story of a powerful Rio de Janeiro gambling gangster who had all his teeth made of gold. The story provides a literary rendition of Rio de Janeiro's underground power struggles, showing a new urban perspective of contemporary national culture. The filmmaker's next work, *Vidas Secas* (1963), was also based on a homonymous literary work, this time the novel by Graciliano Ramos (1892–1953) published in 1938. As we have seen, the miserable lives of northeastern *retirantes* forms the central theme of *Vidas Secas*. The film version was nominated for the 1964 Cannes Film Festival. In later years, Nelson Pereira dos Santos would become one of the most respected Brazilian documentary film directors, with remarkable works that told of important aspects of the national culture. Some of his most notable titles are *Casa Grande & Senzala* (2000), *Raízes do Brasil* (2004), and *A Música segundo Tom Jobim* (2012).[25]

Brazil's *Cinema Novo*'s most representative artist, however, was the filmmaker Glauber Rocha (1939–1981). While still in his teens, Rocha became involved with leftist art and politics in his native Bahia. The artist held a strong anti-American disposition and also a fierce apocalyptic vision of the world, which is evidenced in his famous trilogy, *Deus e o Diabo na Terra do Sol* (1964), *Terra em Transe* (1967), and *O Dragão da Maldade Contra o Santo Guerreiro* (1969). This last production earned him the award for Best Director at Cannes in 1969. All three films were laden with intense social criticism. *Deus e o Diabo na Terra do Sol* was especially critical of the Brazilian agrarian social structure. The film tells the story of the impoverished ranch hand Manoel and his wife, Rosa. Manoel makes a deal with his powerful estate-owning boss: he would take his boss's cattle to be sold in the city, and the profit would be divided between the two. While traversing the dry region of the backlands, however, a great number of the animals perish, and when the time for the division of the profit comes, the boss asserts that the dead cattle was all Manoel's, thus cheating him out of his compensation. Enraged, Manoel kills his boss and joins a religious group led by a black saint who fights a white devil. Hence the English translation of the film's title, *Black Saint, White Devil*. The film blends mysticism, religion, and popular culture in a symbolic drama loaded with Marxist overtones. First screened in 1967, *Terra em Transe* is another landmark film in Glauber Rocha's career, and in the Cinema Novo movement. It was the first of the director's productions finished after the coup that ousted Goulart in 1964. The film parodied the country's political history in the years leading up to the coup. Its screening was initially prohibited by the new dictatorial regime, whose severe censorship would silence many works of art after 1964.

Another important director associated with the Cinema Novo movement is Ruy Guerra (b. 1931). Guerra was born in Maputo, Mozambique, but moved to Brazil in 1958. His first film, *Os Cafajestes* (1962), brought to the screen an urban drama centered upon a wealthy family living in Rio de Janeiro. On finding out that his father is going bankrupt, a young man attempts to blackmail his rich uncle. The film raised an important polemic in the Liberal Republic's conservative society for presenting the first nude scene in the history of Brazilian cinema. The scene was a long shot of actress Norma Bengell (1935–2013), who in the narrative is betrayed by her boyfriend and left naked on a beach, being then photographed by the film's protagonist for blackmail purposes. The long scene starts with composer Luiz Bonfá's (1922–2001) sensual music, which soon turns into a fast saxophone solo when the woman realizes she is being cheated. The music then degenerates into a schizophrenic proliferation of laughter and car noises when the helpless naked woman cries while being photographed on the sand. In another film, *Os Fuzis* (1964), Ruy Guerra approached the Cinema Novo's recurrent theme of life in the Northeast. Here a group of soldiers is called into a poverty-stricken neighborhood to prevent a starving crowd from plundering a food storage warehouse. The film was awarded the Silver Bear Extraordinary Jury Prize at the 14th Berlin International Film Festival in 1964.

Another important film director of the period was Anselmo Duarte (1920–2009). A handsome leading man during the previous era of Hollywood-influenced films, Duarte had an ideological argument with the leftist filmmakers of the Cinema Novo movement. That, combined with unreserved jealousy for his international acclaim, condemned him to ostracism from the leading filmmakers of the period. As of 2018, Duarte's *O Pagador de Promessas* (1962), based on a play written by dramatist Dias Gomes (1922–1999), is the only Brazilian film to have won the *Palme d'Or* at the Cannes Film Festival. The film tells the story of a poor man in the backlands of Bahia who owns a small farm and a donkey, and who makes a promise to a Candomblé saint that if his donkey recovers from illness he will give away his land to the poor and carry a cross all the way to the capital, Salvador, in penitence. The film opens with the naïve peasant arriving in the state capital city carrying a cross on his back and being followed by his wife, Rosa. Throughout the development of the story, the keeper of the promise is cheated and humiliated in many ways: his wife is seduced by a sleazy man with whom she spends the night; the local priest condemns him for having breeched Catholic rules by making a promise to a Candomblé saint; the newspapers make sensationalist use of his story, saying that he gave away his land because he was a communist. The poor peasant meets a tragic end in a maze of religious and political disputes.[26]

The Liberal Republic also saw important developments in popular cinema, the most remarkable example being perhaps the debut of actor and director Amácio Mazzaropi (1912–1981), whose first film, *Sai da frente*, appeared in 1952. Mazzaropi represented an immanent drive within the emerging Brazilian middle-class society to represent itself in a simple and humorous way. The actor-director worked as if on a parallel line that contrasted with the intellectualized Cinema Novo, with the two never intersecting. His films were received with certain prejudice by critics, who preferred renderings of Brazilian life in film in a mode more attuned to their ideological principles and beliefs. Mazzaropi's works only started gaining recognition as an important part of Brazilian cultural history in the

1990s, when the Museum Mazzaropi was inaugurated in the city of Taubaté in São Paulo State.[27]

Besides a rich cinematic production, the period of the Liberal Republic also showed remarkable developments in popular music, the most noteworthy of which being probably the advent of bossa nova, a new musical style that combined the earlier samba and chorinho forms with a richer, jazz-influenced harmonic base and softer rhythms. Bossa nova emerged in the mid-1950s from the informal gatherings and artistic collaboration of Rio de Janeiro's young middle-class musicians, who had at their disposal an immense array of samba and jazz music to draw from. It was from playing samba with a more sophisticated knowledge of music theory and of jazz harmony that these musicians started writing their own songs, which reflected more refined tastes and an enhanced capacity for the employment of complex musical structures. Their music owed much to an earlier sub-style of samba called *samba-canção*, which emerged in the 1930s out of the new urban, modern life that began to thrive in the nation's capital.[28]

Musicologists suggest that *samba-canção* succeeded the earlier *modinha* as the basic model for romantic music during the 1930s. The style, in any case, was never a completely separate genre, but one of the many denominations of samba music, which included other sub-styles as well, such as the *samba de roda*, a traditional form originated in Bahia in the nineteenth century and usually associated with the Afro-Brazilian capoeira, the *samba de raiado*, a form brought to Rio de Janeiro also from Bahia and characterized by the use of clapping and dancing, and the *samba de partido-alto*, which originated early in the twentieth century and is rhythmically akin to musical expressions found in the Congo and Angola. As it developed from the 1930s and 1940s onwards, *samba-canção* assumed a stronger lyrical dimension and became associated with the emerging recording industry, as well as with urban life, becoming commercially successful in a way that other sub-styles of samba did not.

Several of the traditional samba songwriters from Rio de Janeiro produced remarkable pieces in the samba-canção style, as is the case of Noel Rosa's *Pra que mentir* (1937), Cartola's *As rosas não falam* (1974), and Nelson Cavaquinho's *A flor e o espinho* (1957). The style, however, also developed signature artists of its own. Given its commercial appeal as a form of romantic ballad, the development of *samba-canção* became closely related to the emergence of the phonographic industry, and several professional singers appeared who specialized in the style. Urban culture and the radio era began to demand elegant and highly orchestrated arrangements, and crooners like Orlando Silva (1915–1978) and Vicente

Celestino (1894–1968) became very popular in the 1930s. In the 1940s, as *samba-canção* reached larger theaters and ballrooms, a singer named Farnésio Dutra e Silva, known as Dick Farney (1921–1987), emerged as one of the biggest stars of the moment. From 1941 to 1944, Farney worked as a crooner in the orchestra that performed nightly at Rio de Janeiro's Urca Casino, where he adopted an American style in his performances. Farney had started his career at a very young age as a jazz pianist, and became one of the greatest jazz singers in the country. In 1946, he issued the recording of the song *Copacabana*, which set the tone for the new mix of *samba-canção* and jazz.

The *samba-canção* style also adopted influences from Spanish-American rhythms, such as bolero and tango. From that line of development, the style gradually moved towards the genre of romantic songs filled with a melancholy tone. In 1948, singer Francisco Alves (1898–1952) issued the recording of a landmark song in the genre: *Esses moços*, a lyrical piece marked by nostalgic pessimism and sadness, written by a new composer called Lupicínio Rodrigues (1914–1974). Rodrigues became one of the forerunners of the new bolero-styled *samba-canção* of the 1950s. The lyrics to his hit song talked of the uselessness of being in love, and created the notion of *dor-de-cotovelo*, a famous expression coined by Rodrigues himself to refer to the pain one feels in one's elbows after leaning for hours over a table in a bar alone while lamenting one's lost love. Rodrigues's revolutionary song is structured around a call-and-response melodic pattern presented in moderate tempo and forming an overall A and B form. Each A and B section is subdivided into four subsections, where the lamenting melodic motive develops diatonically and with little repetition, thus turning the overall melody of each section into long through-composed units. A modulation from the major key in the A section to its relative minor in the B section further enhances the tune's melodic and harmonic variety without, however, stepping out of the original key center.

Lupicínio Rodrigues's *Esses moços* opened the way to the golden years of *samba-canção*. The mid-1950s were the times of Juscelino Kubitschek's *desenvolvimentismo associado*, with, as we have seen, openness to foreign capital and to things foreign in general. Full of optimism about the President's promised fifty years of development in five, the Brazilian middles classes were eager to embrace modernity and started copying the lifestyles of developed nations, above all the United States. With the emerging national automobile industry, the mid-social strata could now own cars and mimic the fashionable life provided by the consumer society. The golden years of the Liberal Republic were thus the same ones of *samba-canção*'s stylistic primacy in music and general sensibility. Great female singers appeared as the style's representatives. Artists such as Maysa (1936–1977), Ângela Maria (b. 1929), Dalva de Oliveira (1917–1972), and Elizeth Cardoso (1920–1990) brought the genre to its zenith.

Singer and songwriter Maysa is perhaps the most remarkable female artist of the period. Possessed of a very strong character, the singer married into a powerful family of industrial tycoons, the aforementioned Matarazzos. She became a national icon after her difficult separation from her handsome millionaire husband in 1957. Maysa represented the new strong woman who suffered from the break-up of her family but remained on her feet with uncompromising dignity. Lupicínio Rodrigues's *dor-de-cotovelo* became Maysa's *fossa*, a word that translates literally as *cesspool* or *sewer*, but that meant primarily "the blues." Brazilians were thrown into their *fossa* whenever romantic relationships fell apart. Such collapses were taken with great seriousness and usually meant excruciating emotional and psychological anguish, an understandable outcome for individuals raised in a very conservative Catholic society where divorce was not legalized until 1977. Maysa was the first Brazilian singer to perform in Japan (in 1959). In the video recording of her performance, one can see her singing *Meu mundo caiu* (My world fell apart), a terribly sad *samba-canção* filled with a deep sense of despair. In the video recording, the singer is seen offering a caveat to the Japanese audience before the performance. Maysa explains that carnival in Brazil was what it was, but that the samba that she sang had nothing to do with carnival. That seemed like an apposite qualification, for how would the Japanese have otherwise coped with Maysa's sorrowful samba that sounded just like the saddest enka song?

It was in the late 1950s that all these rich musical developments came to crystalize into a new style. The melodic sambas of Noel Rosa, Cartola, and Nelson Cavaquinho; the jazz piano chords and Americanized interpretations of Dick Farney; and the sorrowful melodies of Lupicínio Rodrigues and Maysa's *samba-canção*, all came to coalesce in the elegant songwriting and new rhythmic style of the young middle-class Rio de Janeiro musicians who created bossa nova. As we have mentioned, as a cultural and artistic movement, bossa nova started from informal gatherings of musicians in the city's *zona sul*, the southern and richer municipal district of Rio de Janeiro. The gatherings recalled those of previous decades in the Estácio de Sá neighborhood, when Noel Rosa, Cartola, and Nelson Cavaquinho had created the earlier style. Such informal musical gatherings can be seen as part of the country's age-old musical tradition, wherein musical gatherings recall the medieval and renaissance practices of the minstrel. The Portuguese *sarau*, a traditional cultural gathering that takes place in private homes, might be seen as a cultural forerunner.

Music historians usually cite August 1958 as bossa nova's official starting point. The date refers to the release of Bahian musician João Gilberto's (b. 1931) recording of Antônio Carlos Jobim's song *Chega de Saudade*. With its distinguished vocal texture and novel rhythmic feel, Gilberto's performance, recorded in a compact 78 rpm record, became a landmark in the history of the music. Gilberto's solo performance technique, doubling on voice and guitar, would become very important to the new style's development. Early in his career, the musician realized that by singing softly he could delay or anticipate the melody in relation to the rhythmic and melodic accompaniment he himself was providing with the guitar. Transferred to a regular combo, Gilberto's approach provided new possibilities for more creative forms of syncopation, allowing for greater freedom in the rhythm section. Coupled with the more intimate overall quality of the music, new rhythmic patterns were devised to fill in under the new subdued tone of the voice. With the emergence of harmonies more complex than those found in the previous *samba-canção* compositions, bossa nova was ready to conquer the world.

Bossa nova's ensuing success owed much to the incomparable talent of one man above all: Antônio Carlos Jobim (1927–1994). The gifted musician was raised in Rio de Janeiro's southern district of Ipanema, a neighborhood famous for its homonymous beach and astonishing coastal scenery where the sea extends along the adjacent beaches of Copacabana and Leblon, forming a long shoreline that mingles tropical blue skies and bustling urban life. Jobim started his musical studies under the guidance of the German music teacher Hans-Joachim Koellreutter (1915–2005), who had moved to Brazil in 1937 after becoming dissatisfied with Nazi rule in his native country. The German flutist and conductor helped found Brazil's National Symphonic Orquestra (OSB), being also credited with the introduction of dodecaphonism to the country.

After studying classical harmony with Koellreutter, and thus equipped with the sort of theoretical knowledge that was unavailable to older musicians, Jobim could devise a thorough musical revolution for his time. Impressionism and atonality would echo throughout his performances and compositions. The soft symbolism of Debussy's *Prélude à l'après-midi d'un faune* would resurface in Jobim's collaborations with the aforementioned poet Vinicius de Moraes (1913–1980), who would make up for Mallarmé in the duo. Also, whole tone scales, non-functional harmony, altered chords, and dreamy sequences of repeated notes would gain currency in the composer's pieces, performances and orchestrations.

Jobim's new harmonic sophistication could be sensed already in his first landmark bossa nova song, the abovementioned *Chega de Saudade* (1958). The song brings a very innovative harmonic style to Brazilian popular music, presenting new chromatic movements and interesting modulations. The first of such chromaticism can be heard in the melody's descending a half step from the second to the third bar, and then ascending an equivalent half step from the fourth to the fifth bar, establishing thus a graceful motivic development with the chromatic interval. As other chromatic passages abound throughout the composition, the song's overall tonal structure is also innovative. It starts in the relative minor of the key of F and then goes to a very bright bridge in the key of D major, creating an overarching movement from D minor to D major that is also quite unique.

Adding to Jobim's new harmonic sophistication was his personal elegance as a performer. The musician's refined style would represent well the new face of modern Brazil in its Kubitschek golden years. After a memorable performance in Rio de Janeiro in 1962, Jobim and his bossa nova friends would attract the attention of American saxophonist Stan Getz (1927–1991) and his guitarist partner Charlie Byrd (1925–1999), who would issue the commercially successful album *Jazz Samba* the same year, bringing bossa nova into the mainstream of American music. The album presented two songs by Ary Barroso, *É Luxo Só* and *Baia*, suggesting the continuity between bossa nova and the earlier, more traditional samba style.

In that same year of 1962, the Brazilians made their first appearance at Carnegie Hall. After that performance, Jobim remained in the United States recording new compositions for the American market. From then on bossa nova would become more and more a lyrical fusion of samba and jazz. American greats, such as Quincy Jones, Coleman Hawkins, Dizzy Gillespie, Miles Davis, Lee Morgan, Hank Mobley, Dexter Gordon and many others would soon venture into the new, soft, melodious, side-to-side/two-feeling, and exotically Latin groove that provided a pleasing contrast to the straight-ahead, forward-moving swing. These great musicians' approach would be very different from that seen in the previous decade, when jazz fans could hear Latin songs inserted in bebop recordings, such as Charlie Parker's *Tico Tico no Fubá* (1951). From now on, the regular jazz repertoire would have one more consistent rhythmic style merged into its already rich sound palette.

Back in Brazil, bossa nova would not be free from the ideological polarization holding sway over the nation in its immediately post-Kubitschek years. Some of the musicians involved in the movement also became involved in the UNE's CPC, and began to criticize the new jazz influence on the Brazilian musical form. These musicians proposed a return to the samba roots of bossa nova, engaging older artists such as Nelson Cavaquinho and Cartola in recordings and concerts. Carlos Lyra (b. 1936), an important bossa nova singer and songwriter, was one of the founders of the CPC. Together with poet Ferreira Gullar and playwright Oduvaldo Vianna Filho (1936–1974), Lyra's political engagement was effectively transferred to the bossa nova movement through his 1961 composition, *Samba da legalidade* (Samba of lawfulness), whose lyrics openly defended João Goulart's rise to the presidency after Jânio Quadros's resignation.

Music historians tend to agree on the year 1966 as that of the bossa nova movement's demise. From that year on, a new Brazilian musical expression would emerge under the umbrella concept of *Música Popular Brasileira* (MPB). This would be a time when popular music, together with virtually all other artistic forms, would be caught in a complex, and at times irreconcilable, relationship with the vicious and fearsome new military dictatorship initiated in 1964.

CHAPTER SIX

THE MILITARY DICTATORSHIP (1964–1985)

The final years of the Liberal Republic were marked by an even worse economic situation than that which had contributed to Vargas's fall in 1945. In 1964, Brazil's annual GDP growth rate was 3.4%, having made a slight recovery from the 0.6% of 1963, but it would fall again to 2.4% in 1965. The inflation rate for 1964 was 91.8% and the general rise in price levels enhanced the sense of instability that foreshadowed President João Goulart's fall on April 1.

After Vargas's tragic death in 1954, another Riograndense had now been ousted as the result of a conspiracy that began in the high ranks of the armed forces. This time the military leaders acted in consort with the governors of Minas Gerais, São Paulo, and Rio de Janeiro. The old regional division of forces that had produced repeated revolutionary uprisings throughout the country's history seemed to be in full force, with the southern warlords set against the chieftains of the Southeast. But time had worked its transformations. Power relationships were now embedded in the constraints of a new urban society. A new type of split between the civilian political leaders and the commanders who controlled the military machine ensued from the new social reality of cities and their urban masses striving for a political voice.

In 1964, Governors Magalhães Pinto, Adhemar de Barros, and Carlos Lacerda, who together had attempted to depose Vargas ten years earlier, thought they could manipulate the high commanders of the armed forces into seizing power from the President and handing it to them. They were wrong. They would soon discover that those commanders simply did not accept orders from civilians.

The military leaders who ousted President João Goulart would establish themselves in power and hold fast to their brutal dictatorship from April 1, 1964 until March 15, 1985. The civilian leaders would be outraged when they learned of the secondary role they would have to play in the nation's new political arrangement. Ironically, after realizing that his military partners would not step down, Carlos Lacerda, one of the fiercest right-wing opponents of the Riograndenses, joined his former enemy, João

Goulart, to launch a national movement against the military coup in November 1966. By then, however, it was too late. The new military rulers responded by immediately suspending Lacerda's political rights. They had already done the same to Kubitschek's in June 1964. Civilians would now occupy a lower position in the country's political power structure. And they would be fiercely oppressed, if need be. The new triad for democracy, Lacerda, Kubitschek, and Goulart, would meet strange deaths at almost the same time in 1976 and 1977. In those years, as we shall see, the military president, Ernesto Geisel (1907–1996), was losing control over the extreme right wing of the armed forces. The three men would meet their ends at a time of chaos. The cause of their deaths would never be fully clarified.

It is to this new reality of right-wing terror, of state-induced murder, of authoritarian and conservative development policies, of severe wage reductions and the resulting unprecedented economic growth, of astronomical foreign debt, of economic crisis and stagflation, of slackening education and general impoverishment, and of state propaganda and mass mind control, that we turn now.

Marshal Castelo Branco and the PAEG (1964–1967)

Marshal Humberto de Alencar Castelo Branco (1897–1967) assumed the Brazilian presidency on April 15, 1964. He had been appointed the Army's Chief of Staff by President Goulart himself in 1963, and the following year had become one of the conspirators who brought the President down. Castelo Branco's rise to the head of the government represented the final triumph of the armed forces since their initial rise in prestige after the Paraguayan War. With a military president now enjoying virtually unlimited powers, the soldier class was ready to surpass the former iron rule it had imposed upon the nation immediately after the overthrow of the Empire and the Proclamation of the Republic in 1889.

Starting in 1964, the new military government began exerting its new rule through a series of decrees. These were called *Ato Institucional* and were used as mechanisms to legitimize the new government's political acts. Through these rulings, the military commanders availed themselves of extra-constitutional powers, establishing a façade of lawfulness wherein dictatorial acts were legally based on presidential decrees.

The first of these acts was issued during the *ad interim* term in office of Ranieri Mazzilli, the Head of the House Representatives who had assumed the presidency after Goulart's ousting on April 2, 1964. On April 9, the first Institutional Act appeared with eleven articles, establishing, among other things, the suspension of the political mandates of those who opposed the new government and the ending of employment stability for public servants. Only a small opposition controlled by the government would be allowed in Congress. This first Act also ordered the holding of indirect presidential elections on April 11. The new president would rule until January 31, 1966, thus finishing the five-year mandate initiated by Jânio Quadros in 1961. It was under this order that the splintered National Congress elected Marshal Humberto de Alencar Castelo Branco, who assumed the presidency on April 15, 1964.

The new military ruler's stated aim was to enact a transition from Jânio Quadros's interrupted mandate to the next presidential election, following the schedule established in the 1946 Constitution. Unexpected gains by the opposition in the provincial elections of October 3, 1965, however, would change the course of events. The state of Guanabara, present-day Rio de Janeiro, elected Francisco Negrão de Lima (1901–1981) as its new governor. Negrão de Lima was a member of the PSD who had been Minister of Justice during Vargas's second administration and also Minister of Foreign Affairs during Juscelino Kubitschek's presidency. The state of Minas Gerais elected Israel Pinheiro (1896–1973) as state governor, a man who belonged to Kubitschek's Mineiro faction. Among other connections, Pinheiro had presided over Novacap, a public company established in 1956 by Kubitschek to coordinate the construction of the new capital, Brasilia. Pinheiro had also been the first president of the Vale do Rio Doce mining company, a large enterprise founded by the Brazilian Federal Government in Minas Gerais in 1942, that is, by President Vargas. Just like Negrão de Lima, Pinheiro was thus enmeshed in the Vargas-Kubitschek clique, of which João Goulart was the present leader. Needless to say, this new turn of events set alarm bells ringing for the new military dictators.

Castelo Branco reacted against the disturbing results of the October 3 provincial elections by issuing a new decree, the Institutional Act 2 (AI-2), which was announced on October 27, less than 25 days after the publication of the regional electoral results. With the AI-2 the regime was keen to show its aggressiveness. It comprised 33 articles, which, among other rulings, dissolved all political parties, established indirect elections for president, allowed the government to close the Congress at will, and granted the President the right to intervene in the states and to dismiss public servants who proved incompatible with the regime.

Calling itself "revolutionary," the new regime established a two-party system. Together with all other political associations, the three main parties that had existed since 1945, namely the left-wing populist Brazilian

Labor Party (PTB), the liberal Social Democratic Party (PSD), and the conservative National Democratic Union (UDN) were closed down and replaced by the official right-wing and pro-government National Renewal Alliance (ARENA) and the mildly oppositional Brazilian Democratic Movement (MDB). The two-party system would last until 1979.

Two other Institutional Acts would be issued during Castelo Branco's administration, the AI-3 and the AI-4. All four acts issued up to then would remain in effect until March 15, 1967, when a new Constitution would be imposed upon the nation. The AI-3 was announced on February 5, 1966, extending the two-party system to the provincial and municipal levels. The Decree also ordered presidential and parliamentary elections to be held on October 3 and November 15, 1966, respectively. On October 3, the National Congress elected as the new president the government's candidate, Marshal Artur da Costa e Silva (1899–1969), a tough hardline commander from Rio Grande do Sul.

Following Costa e Silva's election, Castelo Branco decreed the closure of the National Congress on October 20, 1966. The dictatorial act caused great indignation among the civilian members of the Parliament. The Head of the House of Representatives, Congressman Adauto Lúcio Cardoso (1904–1974) attempted to maintain the doors of the plenary assembly open in an act of defiance against the Executive's diktat. President Castelo Branco then ordered the army to invade and close the building. The Congress remained closed until November 22, a few days after the parliamentary elections of Novemeber 15, which had resulted in an impressive victory for the regime's party, the ARENA.

On December 7, 1966, the President issued the Institutional Act 4 (AI-4), which ordered the Congress to vote and promulgate the new Constitution that would replace the 1946 Constitution. The new Charter was presented to the Congress in its final version, which had been prepared by lawyer Francisco Campos (1891–1968), the same man who had written the authoritarian 1937 Constitution, as well as the totalitarian Institutional Act 1 (AI-1). The fifth Constitution in the history of the Brazilian Republic, the 1967 Constitution, was published on January 24, 1967. It attempted to institutionalize the dictatorial regime, enhancing the influence of the Executive over the Legislature and Judiciary. A centralizing hierarchy was thus established by granting virtually unlimited powers to the military rulers: presidential elections would be indirect, held in the Congress every five years; crimes against national security could now be punished with the death penalty; the workers' right to strike was curtailed.

On February 9, 1967, a few weeks before the new president took office on March 15, Castelo Branco approved the *Lei de Imprensa* (Press Law), which restricted the freedom of the press. Together with fierce censorship, new mechanisms of repression were being devised and put to the service of the regime's despotism. A national intelligence agency had been created in June 1964 under the name *Serviço Nacional de Informações* (SNI). Its creator, General Golbery do Couto e Silva (1911–1987), another Riograndense military hardliner, would continue his recurrent outbursts of creativity in many and varied forms, such as the literary, as expressed in his 1966 book entitled *Geopolítica do Brasil* (Brazilian Geopolitics), where he argued for a doctrine of national security that would connect the State and the economy against leftist ideology. The SNI's heavy hand would play an important role in the ensuing torture and murder that would blemish the country's history during the following twenty years of military dictatorship. The full extent of political repression that took place in that first year of military rule would not come to light until almost fifty years later, when a national high-level government commission established by the Federal Law 12.528 of 2011 would disclose the estimated number of 50,000 politically motivated arrests in 1964 alone.

As could be expected, fierce far-right anti-communism, violent repression, and arbitrariness soon resulted in the rise of leftist armed reaction. Drawing on the so-called *Foco Theory* of guerrilla warfare formulated by French officer Régis Debray (b. 1940), revolutionary groups began to appear and line up against the increasingly tyrannical regime. The first of these groups was the one launched by Leonel Brizola in Uruguay. Immediately after Goulart's fall, Brizola began receiving funds from the Cuban government to organize a guerrilla force. Another revolutionary movement started inside the very armed forces, where a group of low-ranking officers created the *Movimento Nacionalista Revolucionário* (MNR). The *Organização Revolucionária Marxista Política Operária* (POLOP) emerged among young socialists in major cities such as Rio de Janeiro, São Paulo, and Belo Horizonte. The POLOP joined the MNR in the first successful attempt at forming a guerrilla army to fight the dictatorial regime. The movement came to be called *Guerrilha do Caparaó*, named after its encroachment in the Caparaó Mountains, which are located in the northern part of Minas Gerais State. The *Vanguarda Popular Revolucionária* (VPR), another left-wing guerrilla movement, was formed in 1966 from dissidents who left the POLOP and the MNR. It later became integrated into the *Comando de Libertação Nacional* (Colina), another important guerrilla group. The *Movimento Revolucionário 8 de Outubro* (MR8) was formed in 1964 among members of the Brazilian Communist Party, many of them university students from Rio de Janeiro. The group would be responsible for the kidnapping of U.S. Ambassador Charles Burke Elbrick (1908–1983) in 1969. Some of its members became famous as intrepid revolutionaries. Carlos Lamarca (1937–1971), a former army captain, commanded the kidnap of Swiss Ambassador Giovanni Enrico Bucher (1913–1992) and was killed by government agents in 1971. His lover, Iara Iavelberg (1944–1971), a young and beautiful university lecturer from a rich Paulistano family, became one of the MR8's leaders and was also killed a few weeks before her boyfriend's execution. As a valiant freedom fighter (and as different forms of freedom can sometimes overlap), Iavelberg became a sort of left-wing guerrilla sex symbol after adopting the principle of free love and engaging romantically with more than a few idealistic revolutionaries. Another renowned freedom fighter associated with MR8 was Dilma Rousseff (b. 1947), the future Brazilian president.[1]

The series of terrorist acts perpetrated by these groups began during Marshal Castelo Branco's government. The first major attempt occurred in July 1966, with a bomb attack inside Recife International Airport. The attack aimed to kill the then presidential candidate Artur da Costa e Silva. The bomb failed to hit its target, but ended up killing a journalist and a navy officer. Another fourteen people were severely wounded. The government responded with more political repression.

In the first months following the coup in April 1964 persecution and torture were employed by the new government to suppress leftist movements. The government's initial repression hit the most vulnerable members of the opposition. Since many participants in the emerging leftist groups were young university students, the military concentrated their initial acts of terror on college campuses, as was the case with the Federal Rural University of Rio de Janeiro (UFRRJ), where two students who had promoted Marxist ideas through their Academic Center were abducted and tortured in May 1964.

The higher administrative and professorial levels of the universities also became an important target for the regime. The Federal University of Rio Grande do Sul, alma mater to Getúlio Vargas and João Goulart, is a case in point. There, the regime promoted a large purge of university professors, with seventeen summary expulsions in 1965. In the same year, the building of a new campus on the outskirts of the capital city, Porto Alegre, was ordered. The new facilities would house the Humanities Department, thus transferring the most potentially subversive academic courses, Philosophy and History, away from the city center. The campus was built with classrooms equipped with openings in the higher part of the walls, which allowed for the content of classes to be heard by federal inspectors who circulated through the corridors constantly. Obviously, that allowed also for sound leakage between classrooms, making teaching in these buildings almost impossible.

Under the dictatorial regime, the official notion of education would come to be equated with that of indoctrination. The regime's anger towards ideas became clear within hours of its establishment. Even before President Goulart had been ousted, on the evening of March 30, 1964, government forces invaded the UNE's headquarters in Rio de Janeiro and set them on fire. As we have seen, the UNE was created in 1938 under Vargas's patronage and was part of the dictator's attempt to coopt the nation's young urban students to his totalitarian plans. As anything that resembled the Vargas-Goulart duo was immediately demonized by the new regime, the attack on the UNE symbolized the new government's vengeance on *varguismo*. This first state-terrorist attack against students foreshadowed what was to come over the next two decades. On April 5, 1964, the government passed a law called *Lei Suplicy de Lacerda*. The Law was named after the new incoming Minister of Education, Flávio Suplicy de Lacerda (1903–1983), and it prohibited political activities in student associations, making the UNE illegal. The fierce opposition between right and left in high politics was being immediately transferred into society at large and reaching the younger population, a situation that would ignite a future sense of general dislike for militarism and authoritarianism among Brazilian university students.

Political and social chaos mirrored the ongoing economic instability. As we have seen, the annual inflation rate for 1964 had reached 91.8%, with an accompanying low 3.4% of GDP growth. The military commanders who seized the government in April had to hurry to devise an emergency plan to control the rise in prices. Castelo Branco's economic advisors, Roberto Campos and Otávio Gouvêa de Bulhões, produced a new economic plan called *Programa de Ação Econômica do Governo* (PAEG). The PAEG consisted of a series of economic measures aimed at taming inflation, which the government saw as preventing growth and hindering the country's international credibility. Moreover, inflation was preventing endorsement from the IMF, which was needed for contracting new foreign loans. Since Campos and Bulhões' diagnosis identified the current rise in prices as the result of a demand-pull inflation which, according to Keynesian theory, arises when aggregate demand in an economy outpaces aggregate supply, they assumed that measures of fiscal austerity were in order. The concrete causes of the inflation were identified as: 1) the large and recurrent public deficits; 2) the recent expansion of credit; and 3) the rise in wages above productivity gains, this latter cause suggesting also a cost-push inflation inherent in the demand-pull price increases. (Put simply, the diagnosis suggested the inadequacy of Goulart's wage policies.) Such elements were seen as provoking the expansion of the money supply, a view that itself salvaged the orthodox monetarist perspective and its ensuing call for monetary restraint. The PAEG Plan thus became famous for combining a Keynesian diagnosis of the inflationary process with the old monetary austerity prescribed by liberal orthodoxy. In any case, the country once again set off on the road of monetary restraint.

The country's economy had seen four previous attempts at monetary austerity in the last two decades: the first during Café Filho's administration when, under the guidance of Finance Minister Eugênio Gudin, the currency exchange crisis of 1952 was tackled restrictively; the second during Kubitschek's government, with the plan devised by Minister Lucas Lopes but which in the end was abandoned in favor of fiscal and monetary expansion adopted to maintain the funding of the President's grandiose public works; the third in Jânio Quadros's administration, with Minister Clemente Mariani's austere fiscal measures, which helped secure important foreign loans; and the fourth during Goulart's administration, included in Celso Furtado's failed *Plano Trienal*. After so much austerity with so few results, a new attitude towards inflation was now needed, even if with the same orthodox and monetarily restrictive mindset.

The new "Bobby Fields" way of dealing with inflation included the adoption of some very creative new dogmas, such as that asserting the necessity of "learning to live with inflation."[2] This beautiful, generous, almost selfless way of facing the excruciating and poverty-producing effects of the general rise in prices led to the establishment of something called *correção monetária* (monetary adjustment), an economic malignant tumor that, in the long run, would drag the nation into hyperinflation and chaos. "Correção monetária" meant the thorough indexation of the economy, a technique to adjust prices and income payments according to a price index. The mad-cap idea simply could not work in a large economy such as Brazil, in which it is virtually impossible for the government to exercise full price control. Under the employment of monetary adjustment techniques, inflation did fall at first, but that was due mostly to the heavy authoritarian nature of the regime and its severe policies of wage contraction. In the long run, this new approach to inflation reduction, generally termed "gradualist," would destroy the economy's capacity to order value in terms of price. Thanks in great part to Roberto Campos and

Castelo Branco's system of indexation, Brazil's annual inflation rate would reach the astronomical number of 2,708% in 1993.

Other aspects of Castelo Branco's PAEG were less inept than the "monetary adjustment" mechanism. The Program promoted a reform in the nation's financial system, creating a central bank in December 1964, the BACEN. The new financial institution allowed for better monetary control, assuming the functions that were formerly performed in conjunction by the SUMOC, the Bank of Brazil, and the National Treasury. The Bank of Brazil was especially problematic at the time. Prior to the establishment of the BACEN, it operated in various and at times conflicting areas, being at the same time a central bank, a funding institution for structural projects, an agent of the treasury, and a commercial bank. This multi-functionality allowed for considerable influence peddling, bad management, and corruption. The establishment of the BACEN represented an important step towards autonomy and safety in monetary policy. Monetary decisions were now less vulnerable to the influences of the various interests encircling the Bank of Brazil's administration.

The PAEG also carried out a financial reform related to the economy's external sector. The import substitution model adopted until 1964 had tended to promote great pressure on the balance of payments because technology had to be imported every time a new product began to be produced internally. The contradiction of import substitution industrialization (ISI) rested, among other things, on the fact that such technologies were always capital-intensive, that is, they required ever more skilled labor and ever fewer natural resources in order to be produced, precisely the opposite of what was available in the country. In this sense, the import-substitution process increased income concentration. Its exhaustion as a feasible economic model has been regarded as one of the reasons for the political upheavals that led to Goulart's fall in 1964.[3]

Castelo Branco now proposed an about-turn in the nation's industrialization program. The government adopted measures to enhance foreign trade and attract foreign investments. Fiscal incentives were offered to the export sector as an attempt to stimulate and diversify international exchanges. Official agencies for foreign trade, such as the *Carteira de Comércio Exterior* (CACEX), created in 1953, were given new roles and expanded functions. Exchange rates were gradually simplified and unified, and import controls were drastically reduced.

Economic liberalization measures were also applied to foreign investment. A new agreement establishing guarantees for foreign capital was negotiated together with the rescheduling of foreign debt services. A new law allowed private companies to borrow directly from foreign banks and funding institutions, while domestic commercial banks could also seek financing from the international market. Such measures meant an important step in the financial internationalization of the country. They were certainly attuned to Castelo Branco's shift towards the United States in foreign policy, a move that became clear through his unconditional signing-up to the aims of the Alliance for Progress, President Kennedy's ten-year plan for Latin America started in 1961.

The Alliance Charter included a clause that committed Latin American governments to facilitate the flow of foreign investments into the region. Castelo Branco followed the dictate. The nationalists soon raised objections, arguing that American corporations were withdrawing more money from the country than they were investing in it. In any case, the liberalization continued.

President Castelo Branco's foreign policy has famously been called *um passo fora da cadência* (a step outside the line), an expression coined by Brazilian historian Amado Luiz Cervo (b. 1941) to express the disparity of the new government's policies in relation to those of the preceding and the following administrations.[4] Castelo Branco's first measure in foreign policy was to immediately dismantle the diplomatic principles of independence and autonomy established during the administrations of Jânio Quadros and João Goulart. Under the leadership of new Foreign Minister, Vasco Leitão da Cunha (1903–1984), Brazilian diplomacy returned to unconditional alignment with the United States, establishing what the same Leitão da Cunha called a "purposeful redressing." The Foreign Minister based his new directives on a theory developed by the aforementioned dictatorial ideologue General Golbery do Couto e Silva called *Teoria dos Círculos Concêntricos*. As could be expected, the theory was not very complex; it simply acknowledged the existence of a hierarchy of themes and geographical spaces that should be tackled in terms of national defense against communism. Its most immediate implication was that the country could not stay impervious to ideological polarization and the cold war, and that consequently not bending to the United States was not an option.

Following the hardliner's line of thought, Brazilian Ambassador to Washington, Juracy Magalhães (1905–2001), would pronounce the infamous phrase: "What is good for the United States, is good for Brazil." Despite this shameful surrender of sovereignty, which still produces considerable amusement among American diplomats and researchers of Brazilian diplomatic history, Magalhães would take Leitão da Cunha's place in January 1966, becoming Castelo Branco's second Foreign Minister. The government following that of Castelo Branco's, namely that led by General Artur da Costa e Silva, would return to a more independent foreign policy, whence Amado Cervo's depiction of the awkwardness of Castelo Branco's directives in the overall history of Brazilian diplomacy.

During Marshal Castelo Branco's government, the surrender of sovereignty was justified as realism. Independence and autonomy were labeled as cowardly neutrality. Distortions and misrepresentations became the norm. Castelo Branco's policymakers claimed that a country as important as Brazil should not stay oblivious to the current undeclared war between the countries that faced each other from the world's ideological poles. Brazilian defense strategists paid special attention to the South Atlantic and to the western coast of Africa. They regarded the rise of communism in West Africa as a major threat to national security. The maintenance of the Portuguese colonial system in that region began to be regarded as a guarantee against communism, and a new pro-Salazar, meaning pro-colonial, attitude emerged. In exchange for support for its colonial system, Salazar offered the Brazilians a trade agreement that facilitated Brazilian commerce with Portuguese African colonies.[5] In the minds of the new regime's rulers, economic and political interests thus prevailed over the values of freedom and the people's right to self-determination.

On assuming the presidency, one of Castelo Branco's first measures in foreign policy had been to sever diplomatic ties with Cuba. The decision was made under Leitão da Cunha's influence. The Foreign Minister opposed the President's intention to wait for a meeting of the OAS before announcing the break. Castelo Branco seemed unwilling to take any diplomatic action without first receiving permission from the United States. In line with his submissive position, the President sent 1,130 Brazilian troops to the Dominican Republic to take part in the military occupation of that country initiated on April 28, 1965. That was more than enough for the old Spanish-American fear of Brazilian sub-imperialism to resurface.

Faced with growing suspicion from its neighbors, the Brazilian government attempted to improve sub-continental relations. To that end, Castelo Branco saw a rapprochement with Paraguay as especially profitable. The two countries had been in the process of strengthening diplomatic ties since at least 1954, when the rise of Alfredo Stroessner (1912–2006) to the Paraguayan presidency entailed a diplomatic shift in Paraguayan diplomacy away from Argentina and towards Brazil. Relations were strained, however, when, in 1962, the Brazilian government showed interest in exploiting the hydroelectric potential of the frontier region between the two countries, the so-called Sete Quedas. Paraguay immediately claimed sovereignty over the area, leading to considerable discord. The Paraguayans argued that the Treaty of 1872, signed in the aftermath of the Paraguayan War, did not specify Brazilian sovereignty over the region. The Brazilians knew the truth to be otherwise, and so did the Paraguayans. Unable to defend the Paraguayan claim on a legal basis, however, Stroessner used the notion of sub-imperialism to pressure for a concerted solution. Given the Brazilian involvement in the Dominican Republic and the bad feelings it had produced among its neighbors, instead of engaging in a problematic frontier dispute with Paraguay, President Castelo Branco decided to co-opt the neighbor back to the Brazilian side of the Latin American entanglement. In July 1966, Foreign Minister Juracy Magalhães signed the Iguaçu Treaty with Paraguayan Foreign Minister Raúl Sapena Pastor (1908–1989). The Treaty was based on the idea that building a bi-national hydroelectric power plant in the disputed area would be the best solution for the emerging conflict. The energy eventually produced would be divided equally between the two countries, and each nation would be allowed to buy part of the other's surplus.[6]

One of the most important corollaries of the agreement was the suspicion and jealousy it provoked in Argentina. The rapprochement with Paraguay meant an important stimulus to the growth of Brazilian geopolitical influence in the region. The river where the power plant was to be built also passed through Argentine territory. The Argentines would soon begin questioning the legality of the construction of a hydroelectric dam that would retain part of the river flow that should reach their country after passing through Brazil and Paraguay. The situation would escalate into a diplomatic crisis in the years that followed, and relations between Brazil and Argentina would not recover until at least 1979.

Castelo Branco's foreign policy showed a few instances of independence and autonomy from U.S. views and policies, such as in its attempt to enhance commercial ties with the USSR and in the refusal to send troops to Vietnam. Otherwise, Brazil maintained a position of unconditional alignment to the United States throughout the period. This, however, would change considerably in the next administration, that of General Artur da Costa e Silva.

Marshal Artur da Costa e Silva and the Hardline (1967–1969)

Marshal Artur da Costa e Silva (1899–1969) was the first of a series of Riograndense military leaders to occupy the Brazilian presidency during the dictatorial period of 1964–85. His two successors would also be Gaúchos.

They would enforce the anti-Vargas/Goulart directive both at the national and the regional levels, showing that, in as late as 1967, the old disputes among southern warlords, as well as the far-reaching clout of Rio Grande do Sul's military class was as solid as ever. Three Riograndense commanders would thus rule the nation with an iron fist over the next twelve years, from 1967 to 1979.

Costa e Silva represented the hardline faction of the armed forces. Relying on the prestige of powerful army generals such as Emílio Garrastazu Médici (1905–1985), Olympio Mourão Filho (1900–1972), and Sylvio Frota (1910–1996), the hardline embodied a fiercely anti-communist stance ready to pursue a witch-hunt and to destroy anyone who did not follow the regime's ideological orientation. Assuming a fiercely populist discourse against political destabilization, Costa e Silva's government would promote police investigations ostensibly to uncover subversive activities, but actually to harass and undermine the opposition. The suppression of civil liberties and sheer state brutality soon became the norm.

The new Marshal assumed the Brazilian presidency on March 15, 1967. On the same day, the new Constitution entered into effect, canceling the four Institutional Acts decreed during the former administration. By 1967, Castelo Branco's PAEG had had positive results in reducing inflation. Price instability was still a problem, but, as we will see in more detail below, inflation rates had gone from 91.8% in 1964 to 28.3% in 1967, due mostly to the authoritarian government's capacity to depress salaries. International rates for 1967 showed 5.6% in Japan, 3.0% in the United States, and 0.7% in Germany. Although the economic objectives of the plan were not fully met, GDP had recovered substantially in comparison with the years prior to 1964. Percentages for 1966 and 1967 were 6.7% and 4.2% respectively.

On the political side, however, the overall situation became increasingly convoluted. On March 28, 1968, a terrible massacre of students occurred in a university cafeteria owned by the Ministry of Education in Rio de Janeiro. The students were protesting in the street against the high price of the cafeteria's meals, and a confrontation with the military police ensued. After an initial clash outside the cafeteria, where the police forces were attacked with sticks and stones, the students moved inside. The policemen then forced entry into the building and as the large crowd of students dispersed, several of them were shot from various directions. Edson Luís de Lima Souto (1950–1968), a poor student from the northern state of Pará who had come to Rio de Janeiro to enter high school, fell dead from a shot in the chest. Another student, twenty-year-old Benedito Frazão Dutra, was also shot and died in hospital a few hours later. Two other people died and six more were severely wounded. The massacre produced a state of uproar across the country. Several demonstrations were organized to protest against the violence. A Roman Catholic mass held on April 4, 1968, in memory of Edson Luís de Lima Souto gathered a large number of followers who were also confronted by the military police. In the days that followed, skirmishes between students and the government resulted in several arrests throughout the country. A harsh struggle between the State and the population had begun, with frequent displays of mutual distrust and rising hostility. Public dissatisfaction reached its climax on June 26, 1968, when a large popular protest against the military dictatorship took to the streets of Rio de Janeiro. The demonstration was called *Passeata dos Cem Mil* (The March of the Hundred Thousand) and was organized by the student movement with the support and participation of artists, celebrities, and intellectuals. The *Passeata* became one of the largest popular protests in the country's history. Brazilian society mobilized around a series of demands, such as the release of the students who had been arrested, the end of censorship, and the restoration of democratic freedoms. As President Costa e Silva refused to bend, the country began to fall into chaos. Another massacre of students took place in the state of Goiás, and in the next few months more than 800 students would be arrested across the country.[7]

On the same day as the *Passeata dos Cem Mil*, the leftist guerrilla group *Vanguarda Popular Revolucionária* (VPR) carried out a terrorist attack, exploding a car bomb in the headquarters of the Second Army, in São Paulo. Casualties included one officer, who died immediately from the explosion, and six other soldiers, who were severely wounded. Leftist guerrillas were beginning to assume an attitude of open defiance of the dictators. On October 12, 1968, Charles Rodney Chandler (1938–1968), a U.S. Army officer who lived in Brazil as an international student and was enrolled in the prestigious Fundação Armando Álvares Penteado (FAAP)'s School of Sociology, was murdered by the VPR. Coupled with popular dissatisfaction, these terrorist acts resulted in the emergence of an apparatus of ferocious political repression. Faced with leftist guerrilla terror, the government responded with state terror. Faced with popular dissatisfaction, the government responded with intimidation and censorship. Faced with strikes in the factories of São Paulo and Minas Gerais, the government responded with the arrests of workers.

The exploitation of fear thus became a weapon of the state, with kidnappings, torture, and murder. Tensions further increased on September 2, 1968, when the National Congress expressed its disagreement with the government's terror-like methods. Congressman Márcio Moreira Alves (1936–2009) spoke in the Parliament, criticizing the military leaders and their policies. His speech sparked a severe political crisis. The Minister of Justice, Luís Antônio da Gama e Silva (1913–1979), demanded the Supreme Court indict the congressman, but according to the law no prosecution could be started, for Moreira Alves's speech had been made in the exercise of his public legislative function. The Supreme Court's pronouncement was that only the House of Representatives itself could prosecute the congressman. The Minister of Justice then proceeded to pressure the Parliament to revoke Moreira Alves's mandate and banish him from Congress. On December 12, 1968, in an unexpected act of autonomy, the House of Representatives decided to defy the military regime and maintain the congressman's parliamentary immunity. The commanders who ruled the nation with their firearms and tanks were infuriated. An all-out war had begun.

On December 13, 1968, the day following the House of Representative's decision to maintain Congressman Márcio Moreira Alves's mandate, President Costa e Silva summoned the National Security Council and decreed the Institutional Act 5 (AI-5), the fifth and most ferocious Act in the history of the military dictatorship. The Act amended the 1967 Constitution and extended the President's power to close the Congress, indict its members, and undertake unchecked political repression. In only twelve articles, the AI-5 represented a severe tightening of authoritarianism, with the suppression of civil liberties and individual rights. The suspension of the writ of habeas corpus in regard to "political crimes" resulted in the immediate curtailment of human rights, civil rights, and general freedoms. Many newspapers and publications were censured and closed, while a large number of artists and intellectuals were exiled, a measure that would severely damage the nation's intellectual and critical capacities.

Institutionalized repression ignited the guerrilla groups into more violence and terror. On September 4, 1969, U.S. Ambassador Charles Burke Elbrick (1908–1983) was kidnapped by a group of activists connected to two organizations, the *Movimento Revolucionário 8 de Outubro* (MR8) and the *Ação Libertadora Nacional* (ALN). The MR8 was a Marxist-Leninist organization named after the day on which Ernesto "Che" Guevara (1928–1967) had been captured in Bolivia, that is, October 8, 1967. The ALN was a socialist group founded in February 1968 by Carlos Marighella (1911–1969), a factory worker born in the state of Bahia who had become an anti-dictatorship activist in the 1930s during the first Vargas administration, when he was repeatedly arrested and tortured. During Costa e Silva's government, Marighella became the regime's number one enemy. He was executed in a police operation commanded by officer Sérgio Paranhos Fleury (of whom more below) on November 4, 1969. Marighella was not directly involved in Elbrick's abduction, but the ALN assumed responsibility for the crime. The Ambassador was released on September 6, 1969 after a negotiation with the kidnappers and the release of fifteen political prisoners.[8]

The government had been tightening its grip on national security since mid-1969. On July 2 of that year, the Armed Forces and the Governor of São Paulo, Roberto Costa de Abreu Sodré (1917–1999), had launched the *Operação Bandeirante* (OBAN), an information system aimed at integrating the different mechanisms of political repression and vigilance. The OBAN received funding from several private companies, including U.S. multinationals as well as national corporations that operated in high profit sectors such as banking, civil construction, energy, and transportation. The war against communism was mirroring the dispute between liberalism and nationalism. Among the OBAN's corporate CEO sponsors was the Danish-born Henning Albert Boilesen (1916–1971), president of the Ultra Group, a high-profile corporation that operated in the fuel distribution sector. Boilesen was identified by leftist activists as someone who would have spent large sums of money to watch sessions of torture against alleged communists detained in the OBAN's center in São Paulo. After becoming a preferred target for the leftist guerrilla groups, the businessman was executed on April 15, 1971 in the same place where Carlos Marighella had been murdered two years earlier. The ALN assumed responsibility for the execution, openly recognizing it as an act of revenge.

Among the most brutal acts of torture executed in the OBAN center in São Paulo was the one committed against a 24-year-old Dominican preacher and student leader, Tito de Alencar Lima (1945–1974). At the age of 18, Frei Tito, as he was known, became a leader of the Catholic Student Union in his native Fortaleza, the capital of Ceará State. A few years later he moved to Pernambuco and then to São Paulo, where he joined the National Student Union (UNE) in 1968. He was arrested for the first time that same year for taking part in a clandestine reunion of student activists. On November 4, 1969, Frei Tito was arrested again, this time by police officer Sérgio Paranhos Fleury (1933–1979) on a charge of being connected with Carlos Marighella, who, as we have seen, would be executed by Fleury later on that same day. Sérgio Fleury was in charge of the *Departamento de Ordem Política e Social* (DOPS), a police department established in 1924 to promote "social order" and which had been connected with political repression and torture since Vargas's Estado

Novo dictatorial period (1937–1945). Now, enlarged with the support of the OBAN, the DOPS became the civilian police arm of the paramilitary apparatus built to promote ideological cleansing and communist persecution. Fleury was known for the use of extreme brutality in his communist hunts. During the 1970s he would allegedly be involved in some the most inhumane crimes committed by the dictatorial regime, among which figure the 1976 *Chacina da Lapa* (Lapa Massacre), where three leaders of the Communist Party were murdered and six others arrested and tortured. Fleury appeared also to be involved in the various operations of the *Esquadrão da Morte* (Death Squad), which exterminated more than 200 individuals between 1969 and 1971.

Under Fleury's orders, Frei Tito was detained for thirty days starting on November 4, 1969 at the DOPS police station, where he was repeatedly beaten and tortured. He was then transferred to the Tiradentes Penitentiary, located in the central region of the city of São Paulo, where he was kept for a few weeks before being transferred again on February 17, 1970, this time to the OBAN center. The OBAN was located at the back of São Paulo's 36th Police District, in a quiet part of the distinguished Paraíso neighborhood. There, Frei Tito was received by Captain Maurício Lopes Lima (b. 1936), who allegedly told him that he was about to enter "a subsidiary of hell." The young Catholic priest was tied to what is called a *cadeira do dragão* (dragon's chair), an electric chair in which the victim receives electric shocks in various parts the body. Electric wires were attached to Frei Tito's ears, tongue, and genitals, being also pushed inside his body through his urethra. Water was thrown over his body in order to enhance the power of the electric shocks, which were intermingled with punches and kicks. Over the next few months, Frei Tito was held captive in the OBAN facilities, being subjected to several forms of physical and psychological torture. One of them was the so-called *pau-de-arara*, an old Portuguese torture technique widely used during the times of slave trade. The victim is tied with his or her ankles and wrists fastened together, being then hanged naked upside down on a bar that is kept stable horizontally. In such vulnerable position, the victim is subjected to a combination of torture procedures, such as the extraction of nails from the toes and fingers, skin burning, electric shocks, and sexual abuse. The profound psychological trauma produced by the *pau-de-arara* tends to be permanent.

Frei Tito was repeatedly tortured in this most inhumane and traditionally Brazilian way in order to provide the police with information about communist groups. Unable to bear any more suffering, he attempted suicide, cutting his wrists with a razor blade. Wary of the possible repercussions of the young man's death, the police transferred Tito to a hospital. The young man was deported to Chile on January 13, 1971, after having suffered daily physical and psychological abuse for more than a year. After the coup against Salvador Allende (1908–1973) in Chile in 1973, Frei Tito had to seek asylum in Europe. He was eventually received by the Dominicans of the Saint-Jacques Monastery, in Paris, and began studying at the Sorbonne. Suffering severe psychological damage and presenting signs of increasing emotional and psychological instability, however, he had to be transferred to the Sainte-Marie de la Tourette Monastery, located near the city of Lyon. There he committed suicide by hanging himself on August 10, 1974 at the age of 28.[9]

The fate of Tito de Alencar Lima matches that of countless Brazilians during the period from 1964 to 1985. Before being deported, Frei Tito identified as his main torturer Captain Maurício Lopes Lima (b. 1936), who would be identified also by future president, Dilma Rousseff, as one of her main torturers during her two years in detention from 1970 to 1972 in the OBAN and the DOPS facilities. In 2011, a national government commission was established to investigate the thousands of cases of torture and murder committed during the period of the military dictatorship. On November 11, 2011, the Brazilian Supreme Court ruled against Maurício Lopes Lima's legal prosecution, founding its decision on the Law 6.683 of August 28, 1979. The Law, known as the "Amnesty Law," was published during General João Baptista de Oliveira Figueiredo's (1918–1999) government, when a process of détente between the ideological poles dividing Brazilian society began to emerge. The Law was intended to grant total amnesty for political crimes. Its initial purpose was to allow for formerly persecuted individuals who had been banished to return to the country. However, the rule soon became distorted and by 2011 it was being used to provide a legal basis for the regime's crimes to remain unpunished. The "amnesty" suggested in the Law came to be considered as applicable also to the government agents who had committed murder and torture during the period.

In any event, in that year of 1969, the state-driven slaughter was just beginning. The military leaders were tightening their grip on the central government and beginning a purge of civilians from the centers of decision-making. In August 1969, President Costa e Silva suffered a cerebral thrombosis and retired from the presidency. According to the 1967 Constitution, the Vice-President should have assumed the presidency. The individual in question however, was a civilian, the former deputy from Minas Gerais Pedro Aleixo (1901–1975). Suspicious that Aleixo might seek to re-establish democratic liberties and call new elections, the three armed forces ministers, General Aurélio de Lira Tavares (1905–1998), Admiral Augusto Rademaker Grünewald (1905–1985), and Brigadier Márcio de Sousa e Melo (1906–1991), assumed the presidency in Aleixo's place in the form of a military junta. In order to do so within the boundaries of a legal arrangement, they issued a new Institutional Act, the AI-12. Through national radio and television, the military leaders informed the population that the seriousness of the present situation prevented Vice-President Pedro Aleixo's investiture, for the communist menace demanded a strong military hand in command of the nation. Enacting this coup within a coup, on September 5, 1969, the military junta issued the Institutional Act 13 (AI-13), which banished from the national territory anyone considered harmful to national security. The Act was decreed one day after Charles Burke Elbrick's kidnapping. In the same vein, on September 10, the government issued the Institutional Act 14 (AI-14), establishing the use of the death penalty in cases of revolutionary or subversive war.

With a strengthened legal apparatus devised to persecute the left, the government could also extend its repressive capabilities to control workers and force the economy to move ahead. As we have seen, President Castelo Branco's economic plan, the PAEG, had been successful in reducing inflation in 1967. During Costa e Silva's administration, the relatively low 28.3% reached in that year would continue to fall, reaching 22% in 1968 and 19.31% in 1969. Working to the regime's advantage, GDP would grow as inflation fell, rising steadily from 1968 to 1973 and allowing the period to be dubbed the "Brazilian Economic Miracle." GDP growth rates were 9.8% for 1968, 9.5% for 1969, 10.4% for 1970, 11.3% for 1971, 11.9% for 1972, and 13.9% for 1973. Per capita, however, the Brazilian GDP grew at a much lower rate, reaching 6.7% in 1968, 6.5% in 1969, 7.4% in 1970, 8.4% in 1971, 9.0% in 1972, and 11.0% in 1973. Brazil's nominal per capita GDP was US$ 371 in 1968, while that of Argentina was US$ 1,136. Japan's was US$ 1,451 and that of the United States US$ 4,491 in that year. Five years later, in 1973, those numbers would be: Brazil US$ 768, Argentina US$ 2,083, Japan US$ 3,873, United States US$ 6,462.

These numbers show that, in spite of its remarkable production boost during the period from 1968 to 1973, in the end the results of Brazil's economic expansion remained far below that of more developed nations. What is worse, the condition of general poverty was actually exacerbated by a growth in production that promoted fierce wealth concentration. Adding to the country's problems, population growth appeared as an important factor in the growing economic disparity. If in 1960 the country had 70 million inhabitants, by 1970 that number had reached 94 million, and the benefits of GDP growth were obviously not shared by the entire population.

The credit for the so-called "Brazilian Economic Miracle" is generally attributed to a man named Antônio Delfim Netto (b. 1928), the Minister of Finance appointed by President Costa e Silva in 1967. Netto saw in the authoritarian regime's repressive capabilities a useful instrument to exert control over the economy so that a production boost could be carried out in spite of the interests of the majority of the population. The economist, who would later become an emeritus professor at the University of São Paulo, served as Finance Minister from 1967 to 1974, as Minister of Agriculture in early 1979, and then as Minister of Planning from mid-1979 to 1985. Netto is one of the most influential and controversial figures in Brazilian economic history. During his term as Finance Minister, strict measures of wage reduction were imposed upon workers in favor of the accumulation of corporate capital. The Minister's famous motto, "to make the cake grow before sharing it," came across as a bad joke in the face of the growing social gap that polarized the starving on one side and the extremely wealthy and corrupt on the other.

One of Netto's first acts as Finance Minister was to introduce tax reform through a regulation called Complementary Act 40, which was published on December 30, 1968. The Act reduced the provincial share of the national tax distribution system and concentrated the greater part of the national revenue in the hands of the central government. This allowed the regime to maintain its high spending on public works as well as its subsidies for wealthy landowners and friendly corporations. Public works were carried out through private companies owned by the government's friends so development policy soon became a vehicle for the accumulation of corporate capital. Most of these public works were extremely onerous to the state, racking up more and more governmental debt. The President Costa e Silva Bridge, for instance, which is commonly known as the Rio-Niteroi Bridge, is a case in point. The bridge crosses the Guanabara Bay, connecting the city of Rio de Janeiro and the municipality of Niterói. On its completion in March 1974, the overpass was the second largest in the world, surpassed only by the Lake Pontchartrain Causeway, in Louisiana, United States. The bridge was a monument to the new era of Brazilian development that was being publicized by the military regime. The project's financing came from Brazil's oldest banker, N. M. Rothschild & Sons, who signed the loan with Defim Netto in London in 1968. The works began that same year with a ceremony attended by the Queen Elizabeth II of the United Kingdom. Some of the Brazilian corporations involved in the enterprise were the very ones whose CEOs were suspected of financing the OBAN in São Paulo. In any case, accusations of irregularities and embezzlement of public funds abounded with regard to the bridge's construction.[10]

The Trans-Amazonian Highway, a 4,000 km route that would be built during the subsequent administration, was another problematic idea from the Brazilian government. The highway was conceived as a means of transferring population from the drought-ridden Northeast to the Amazon thus alleviating one of the country's most pressing social problems. Severe droughts had afflicted the northeastern states in 1969 and 1970, prompting the government to launch a program called *Plano de Integração Nacional* (PIN), under which the enormous demographic vacuums of the Amazon forest would be filled with the impoverished inhabitants of the northeastern backlands. The plan was part of the regime's attempt to give the appearance of social policy and agrarian reform. Trying to make up for the sudden cuts to Goulart's social programs, on November 30, 1964, the military rulers issued the Law 4.504, known as *Estatuto da Terra* (Land Statute). The Law ordered the promotion of agrarian reform, but from the start it was a dead letter, just as many other laws in the nation's history (the most famous being the 1831 anti-slave traffic law mentioned above, dubbed, as we have seen, "Law to fool the British").

The Land Statute gave birth to various development programs such as the aforementioned *Programa de Integração Nacional* (PIN), established in 1970, the *Programa Especial para o Vale do São Francisco* (PROVALE), established in 1972, and the *Programa de Pólos Agropecuários e Agrominerais da Amazônia* (POLAMAZÔNIA), established in 1974. The Trans-Amazonian Highway was included in the first of these programs. All programs involved high expenditure, extensive corruption, lavish propaganda, and few results. The PIN, however, transcended all standards of administrative ineptitude and governmental venality. It was initially publicized as a program for territorial integration based on nationalistic propaganda with mottos such as *integrar para não entregar*, a play on words that translates literally as "to integrate so as to not hand over," that is, to integrate the Amazon to the national territory so as to not be obliged to surrender its resources to the United States. The Trans-Amazonian Highway was probably the most ineffective of all the actions promoted by the PIN. Large amounts of money were invested in the construction of a road that had terrible environmental impact, did not function as a useful means for transferring the population, and, in the end, was actually abandoned. As of 2018, the construction of the Trans-Amazonian Highway has not been completed.[11]

Minister Delfim Netto controlled several offices at the top of the regime's administrative structure. At one time he held the position of President of the National Monetary Council, President of the Commission for Financial Planning, Finance Minister, and member of the National Security Council. During a gap in his government activity he was appointed Brazilian Ambassador to Paris. With so much power in his hands, accusations of corruption and influence peddling abounded, the most publicized of which being one related to the supply of government funds to the owner of two corporations called Coroa and Brastel. The Brazilian Supreme Court did not accept the charges that were made against the Finance Minister, but the incident generated substantial media coverage and provoked considerable anxiety in the government.[12]

Economic historians have dubbed the developmental programs initiated in Costa e Silva's government "conservative modernization." The concept was coined by American political sociologist Barrington Moore Jr. (1913–2005) to account for the model of capitalist development adopted in Germany and Japan, where a political pact between the emerging industrial bourgeoisie and the old financial oligarchy led to highly militarized totalitarian states hell-bent on industrialization. The result of these countries' conservative modernization programs was the emergence of a strong bourgeois class of independent entrepreneurs. In the case of Brazil, however, the same process faced structural and cultural deficiencies that led to the emergence of a weak bourgeoisie that was strongly dependent on foreign capital and that did not have the required creativity to promote innovation. The Brazilian state-led modernization was held back by an agrarian structure that had maintained its original features largely intact since the sixteenth century. While Germany and Japan adapted industrialization to urbanization, agrarian Brazil's growing mechanization of large estates dedicated to export agriculture led to the expulsion of rural populations into urban centers that were not prepared to receive them.

Finance Minister Delfim Netto's "conservative modernization," however, served the government's purpose of creating an international image of Brazil's rapid development and economic growth. The international projection of this new national image was entrusted to Foreign Minister José de Magalhães Pinto (1909–1996), the former governor of Minas Gerais who had supported the initial military maneuvers leading to the ousting of President João Goulart's in 1964. Magalhães Pinto's foreign policy was dubbed "diplomacy for prosperity." It revived some of the diplomatic principles from the years of Jânio Quadros-João Goulart, namely independence and autonomy in foreign relations. That meant a volte-face from Castelo Branco's excessive fawning over the United States. The most evident sign of this autonomy came in 1968 when, as we have seen, Brazil refused to sign the Non-Proliferation Treaty (NPT), causing considerable annoyance and irritation in the U.S. government. Magalhães Pinto argued that the Treaty prevented developing nations from having access to important, i.e. nuclear, technology. As we have mentioned, Brazil would not sign the pact until 1998. Brazil did, however, sign a series of bilateral agreements on the subject, among which a nuclear cooperation pact with India in particular annoyed the United States. In 1967, Indira Gandhi had become India's prime minister and under her administration India's nuclear program had resumed with renewed vigor. China had just exploded a thermonuclear device and the cold war was at its height. Under these circumstances, Costa e Silva's main strategy was to establish new ties with these developing nations in order to advance Brazil's own nuclear program. The second United Nations Conference on Trade and Development (UNCTAD), held in New Delhi in March 1968, facilitated a rapprochement with Gandhi. A nuclear cooperation treaty between Brazil and India was signed in December of that year in Rio de Janeiro.

Ensuing from his efforts at rapprochement with developing nations, Costa e Silva also attempted to establish stronger ties with his Latin American neighbors. In 1969, Brazil sponsored the River Plate Basin Treaty, an international agreement signed in Brasilia between Brazil, Argentina, Bolívia, Paraguay, and Uruguay. The Treaty aimed at fostering mutual understanding and promoting joint projects between these countries for the use of natural resources. The Brazilian government attempted to bind the neighboring nations under a common set of regulations for the area, hoping above all to reduce Argentina's dissatisfaction with the Brazilian-Paraguayan engagement on Iguaçu. In spite of meeting with several obstacles in terms of the actual implementation of its joint projects, the Treaty was important in the history of Latin American integration. It meant an initial impetus in the efforts toward convergence before a sudden halt would result from the rise of various military dictatorships in the region. Latin American military governments would tend to be suspicious of, and mostly unfriendly to, each other. The stall in regional convergence was thus inevitable.

Costa e Silva's foreign policy has been dubbed "third world multilateralism." His successor, General Emílio Garrastazú Médici, would continue an independent foreign policy, establishing commercial ties with communist China and with Eastern European countries. To the specifics of Médici's government, we turn next.

General Emílio Garrastazu Médici and the *Brasil Potência* (1969–1974)

General Emílio Garrastazu Médici (1905–1985) assumed the Brazilian presidency on October 30, 1969. Five days before his investiture ceremony, the hardline officers ordered the National Congress to be reopened and for the congressmen to vote for, and thus legitimize, the new president. Presenting himself as the only candidate in this electoral farce, on the afternoon of October 25, 1969, Emílio Médici would be elected with 293 votes in his favor. There were 75 abstentions, but no one dared to vote against the General. Fearing for their lives, all 369 Brazilian congressmen failed in their duty to act in the service of the nation on that shameful day.

Emílio Médici was the second in a series of Riograndense military heavyweights who led the nation into terror and chaos after 1964. Born in the small city of Bagé near the border with Uruguay, Médici descended from a rich landowning family of Italian and Basque origins. A close ally of Costa e Silva and his hardline associates, from 1967 to 1969 he had succeeded General Golbery do Couto e Silva as the head of the regime's intelligence agency, the National Information Service (SNI). Médici's rise to the SNI's command followed Couto e Silva's stepping down from the agency to take the post of president of the American Dow Chemical Corporation in Brazil. Drawing on his experience in the SNI, General Emílio Médici set about an all-out communist witch-hunt, with all the characteristics of a war of extermination. By the end of his term in 1974, he had succeeded in suppressing all urban and rural guerilla groups operating in the country.

The General's term in office became know as the *anos de chumbo* (years of lead). Shielded by fierce censorship imposed upon all forms of communication, the regime was supported by a paramilitary terrorist group called *Comando de Caça aos Comunistas* (Command for Communist Hunting). The group staged violent attacks against leftist artists and personalities, breaking into theaters and performances and producing a cultural censorship program of its own. In 1970, President Médici's anti-communist police arm was strengthened with the establishment of two agencies directly connected to the army: the Department of Information Operations (DOI) and the Center for Internal Defense Operations (CODI). Together, these agencies formed the fearful DOI-CODI, a political police force that took over some of the functions of the OBAN with enlarged powers and carte blanche to persecute, arrest, torture, and murder anyone who dared defy the regime. The DOI-CODI meant the actual federalization of the OBAN, that is, it adopted the basic idea of the original institution that was being funded by the private sector and transformed it into a governmental office.

The DOI-CODI functioned as a centralized anti-dissent bureau where information gathering, data analysis, strategic planning, military coordination, police operation, persecution, intimidation, detention, punishment, torture, and murder were, for the sake of convenience, brought together under a single institution. The DOI-CODI's agencies were spread throughout various parts of the country, with offices established in virtually all major cities, São Paulo's being the best known. Located on Tutóia Street, in the respectable Paraíso district, it was commanded by officers Carlos Alberto Brilhante Ustra (1932–2015) and Audir Santos Maciel (b. 1932). Official records point to fifty deaths and more than 6,700 politically motivated arrests by the agency from 1970 to 1973. In 2008, Carlos Alberto Ustra would become the first army officer prosecuted in Brazil for torture during the dictatorial period.

The DOI-CODI's operations were based on General Golbery do Couto e Silva's strategies for national security, which were formulated in his think thank, the National Information Service (SNI). The General drew on his experience acquired at the Fort Leavenworth War School, in Kansas, where he studied in 1944. The DOI-CODI's techniques of torture were also learned and developed from technologies developed by the CIA, notably in the Project MKUltra and the KUBARK Manual. The Manual lists the results of experiments on humans using drugs and other forms of physical and psychological intervention in procedures of interrogation and torture.[13]

Another important liaison with the United States in the field of political repression came through the so-called *Operação Condor* (Operation Condor). The term refers to a series of operations implemented by the various South American dictatorships during 1970s involving intelligence procedures, assassination of opponents, and general state terror. It is widely accepted that the actions of Operation Condor received technical support and military aid from the United States government, but due to their clandestine nature, the precise actions involved, as well as the number of deaths they caused are all heavily disputed. In the Brazilian case, the Operation's activities have been linked to the deaths of João Goulart, Juscelino Kubitschek, and Carlos Lacerda, which, as we have seen, occurred between 1976 and 1977, during the government of Emílio Médici's successor, General Ernesto Geisel (1907–1996).[14]

The fierce political repression exerted by the OBAN and later by the DOI-CODI provoked an immediate reaction from the leftist guerrilla groups toward the end of 1969. Their most common form of resistance was the kidnapping of diplomats. Following the taking of the U.S. Ambassador Charles Burke Elbrick in 1969, Japanese Consul Oguchi Nobuo (b. 1917) was abducted in March 1970, German Ambassador Ehrenfried von Holleben (1909–1988) was kidnapped in June of the same year and in December the *Vanguarda Popular Revolucionária* (VPR) took Swiss Ambassador Giovanni Enrico Bucher (1913–1992) hostage. The latter operation was carried out on the orders of Carlos Lamarca, the regime's number one enemy. The kidnappings, note should be made, were usually solved promptly. The government tended to bend to the terrorists' demands, which generally involved the freeing of political prisoners.[15]

To counter this leftist terror, Emílio Médici's government targeted its own terror at important intellectuals and politicians. One of the most remarkable cases was that of the former congressman for the state of São Paulo, Rubens Paiva (1929–1971). Paiva was elected for the leftist PTB in 1962. His political rights were revoked by the military junta established in 1964. The politician maintained contacts with former president, João Goulart into the late 1960s, and worked as director for the newspaper *Última Hora*, which had been subjected to a parliamentary investigation for providing support to Getúlio Vargas during his second administration. Paiva struggled to provide financial help to some of the Brazilian intellectuals who had been sent into exile by the dictatorial regime, and soon the DOI-CODI officers began to suspect him of having connections with Carlos Lamarca. The suspicions were unfounded, but Paiva was still hounded and captured. He was arrested at his house in the presence his wife and children in 1971 and taken into custody. He was subsequently tortured and murdered in Rio de Janeiro's DOI-CODI headquarters. His body was transferred to several different places before it was finally thrown into the ocean. Paiva's case received great media coverage after the end of the dictatoship, becoming the focal point for a cut-throat political and judicial dispute between the former military murderers and the outraged civil society. In May 2014, the Brazilian Federal Justice would accept the charges issued by the Federal Prosecutor's Office against five commanders accused of Paiva's murder. The Prosecutor's argument was that the Amnesty Law of 1979 (of which more below) was not applicable to regular crimes such as that committed against the former congressman. Paiva's murder, according to the Prosecutor, was not based on any of the regime's legal acts, making it thus a general offense against humankind that, according to international treaties on human rights signed by the Federative Republic of Brazil and incorporated in the nation's legal corpus, could not be included in the amnesty. Supreme Court Minister

Teori Albino Zavascki (b. 1948), however, suspended the criminal prosecution against the five military officers in September 2014, citing, again, the Amnesty Law of 1979. Once again, the Law ended up exculpating government agents of the torture and murder committed during the period.

State persecution and murder was obviously transcending the interests of the regime to be committed on the sole basis of personal cruelty and psychopathic rage. According to the National Truth Commission established by the Chamber of Deputies in 2011 to investigate human rights violations during the military dictatorship, Paiva's murder can be ascribed to army lieutenant Antônio Fernando Hughes de Carvalho (1942–2005). Paiva's capture and torture were allegedly carried out by the Air Force under the orders of Third Aerial Zone Commander Brigadier João Paulo Moreira Burnier (1919–2000). According to the testimony of Federal University of Bahia Professor João Augusto de Lima Rocha, Burnier had a secret plan to exterminate all Brazilian intellectuals during the dictatorship.[16] In 1959, Burnier had allegedly commanded the so-called Aragarças Revolt, an attempted coup against President Juscelino Kubitschek initiated together with other National Air Force commanders.[17] In 1968, he was accused of leading the so-called Para-Sar case, a plan involving bomb attacks from a special Air Force command against Rio de Janeiro's water and gas supply systems with the aim of creating enough chaos to facilitate the murder of 40 important political personalities, among whom figured Carlos Lacerda, Jânio Quadros, Juscelino Kubitschek, and Bishop Dom Hélder Câmara. Burnier was also accused of being involved in the torture and murder of Stuart Edgart Angel Jones (1946–1971), a student who participated in the MR8, and in the death of educator Anísio Teixeira (1900–1971), who had introduced the *Escola Nova* into the Brazilian educational system during Getúlio Vargas's first government.[18]

One of the most ignominious cases of human rights violation registered during Emilio Médici's government was that of left-wing activist Inês Etienne Romeu (1942–2015). Romeu was arrested in São Paulo on May 5, 1971 by members of Detective Sérgio Fleury's police station under charges of taking part in the kidnapping of Swiss Ambassador Giovanni Bucher. Romeu was taken to the DOPS, where she was tortured in the *pau-de-arara* in the hope that she would inform on her comrades. Unable to bear the pain, she attempted to fool the police officers by suggesting she make an appointment with a guerrilla member who the police could arrest. While she was being taken to the proposed meeting place, however, she attempted suicide, throwing herself underneath an urban bus. Her suidide attempt failed, leaving her severely wounded; she was taken to hospital where she received a blood transfusion and was kept alive. Once she had recovered enough she was again tortured for information on her group members. Romeu was then taken to a place in the mountains on the outskirts of Rio de Janeiro, an old house that came to be known as "The House of Death." There she was repeatedly raped and beaten during the course of the next three months until her face became unrecognizable. Romeu attempted suicide four times before she was finally convinced by her torturers to become an informant against her fellow guerrilla members. She denounced her torturers after the end of the dictatorship in 1985. In 2003, at the age of 61, she was found in her house drowning in blood, victim of a severe beating from which she suffered brain damaged and lost her ability to speak. Suffering from severe aphasia, Romeu passed away in 2015 without being able to tell the story of her assault. In 2011, the Brazilian Federal Government issued the results of an investigation showing that at least nineteen people had suffered the same sort of torture by Romeu at the House of Death.[19]

The arrest and torture of Inês Etienne Romeu, together with the deaths of Rubens Paiva, Stuart Edgart Angel Jones, Anísio Teixeira, Flávio Carvalho Molina, Francisco José de Oliveira, Luiz Almeida Araújo, Frederico Eduardo Mayr, Grenaldo de Jesus da Silva, the brothers Denis and Dimas Antônio Casemiro, as well as many other men and women, most of them in their mid-twenties, made that horror-filled year of 1971 an infamous time in Brazilian history. The worst, however, is that the carnage was just beginning. In that same year the mayor of São Paulo, Paulo Salim Maluf (b. 1931), a conservative politician closely connected to the military dictators, began the construction of a large cemetery on the outskirts of the city. The Dom Bosco Cemetery was built in a suburban neighborhood called Perus. Its original project contained a special zone marked for "terrorists" and also a plan for a crematorium to be used according to new legislation allowing for the cremation of bodies without the approval of the deceased's family. The project also aroused suspicion for not having a designated area for a chapel. In 1990, journalist Cláudio Barcellos (b. 1950) began investigating police violence in the city of São Paulo and in the process discovered a clandestine common grave in the Dom Bosco Cemetery that seemed to be used for the concealment of human corpses, notably those of people whose forensic reports were marked with a letter "T" for *terrorista*. In 1995, São Paulo's Mayor Luiza Erundina de Sousa (b. 1934) ordered the opening of what came to be called *Vala de Perus* (Perus Common Ditch), the clandestine burial ground in which the mortal remains of more than 1,400 unidentified people were found. In 2009 the

Federal Prosecutors Office started a lawsuit against São Paulo's former mayor, Paulo Maluf, DOPS Director Romeu Tuma (1931–2010), and coroner Harry Shibata (b. 1927), who were accused of several crimes, including that of concealing human corpses. None of them was ever convicted. In any case, what the *Vala de Perus* story illustrates is that the all-out war promoted by the Brazilian State might be moving in the direction of genocide.[20]

In 1972, Emilio Mécidi's government started military deployments to put down an armed rural Maoist movement called *Guerrilha do Araguaia*. The movement was established in 1967 in the Araguaia river basin, a region in the northern part of the country corresponding to today's Tocantins State. The area was chosen for its potential to attract a large number of followers, above all the impoverished and dissatisfied inhabitants of the Northeast. The Araguaia Guerrilla Movement attempted to re-ignite opposition to dictatorial rule after the suppression of the urban movements by the armed forces. The Araguaia area was particularly unstable because of the constant clashes between the deprived peasants on one side and the new miners and public works contractors on the other. The latter began entering the region after the discovery of large reserves of iron ore in the nearby Carajás Mountains. The discovery had been made by the United States Steel Corporation in 1962, but by 1969 the Brazilian government had gained control over investment in the area, and from 1973 the economic exploitation of the iron ore reserves would be carried out in partnership with Japanese capital. The guerrilla movement was thus enmeshed in a dispute for the country's natural resources in one of the richest mineral areas in the world.

Combat operations between the guerrillas and the Brazilian army lasted from 1972 to 1974. At the beginning of 1975, already under the government of President Ernesto Geisel (1907–1996), the armed forces would begin an operation to hide all traces of what had been a large-scale massacre. Torture, decapitation, and mutilation of body parts were some of the procedures used by the armed forces to scare the local civilian population into informing on the rebels and thus suppress the movement. Once again, the shadow of Canudos and Contestado seemed to hover over a poverty-stricken population inhabiting the lawless countryside. Brazilians went on killing Brazilians, this time with the army deploying napalm against its own population.[21]

In March 2001, family members of the men and women who had vanished as the result of movement's suppression appealed to the Inter-American Commission on Human Rights for the establishment of an investigation into extrajudicial killings in Araguaia. The Commission declared the case admissible in terms of violations of the American Human Rights Conventions and, in December 2012, the Inter-American Court of Human Rights ruled that Brazil had violated the American Convention on Human Rights in the case of the Araguaia Guerrillas. The Brazilian Supreme Federal Court, however, upheld once again the 1979 Amnesty Law, preventing the prosecution of the offenders and turning the Brazilian nation into a pariah in the international community of states that recognize international law as the basis for justice and respect among sovereign entities.

With the greater part of its population living in fear, Emilio Médici's Brazil was submerged into a circus of official propaganda and everyday bad faith. Devastated by the state's repressive psychopathy and suffering from what seemed to be a collective psychological trauma, Brazilians suffered bouts of self-deception, accepting tacitly a reality that no one wanted to acknowledge as real. State propaganda succeeded in inciting nationalistic pride in a population eager for self-assurance. The victory in the 1970 soccer World Cup was celebrated as a colossal national achievement, all the while official violence and terror continued to infiltrate everyday life at every street-corner in every district in every city.[22]

In 1972, the military government promoted a huge national celebration for the 150th anniversary of Brazilian independence. Showing that their morbid mindset was not limited to delighting in crimes of torture and murder against their fellow citizens, the military leaders ordered the first Brazilian emperor's dead body to be brought from Portugal for the ceremony. It was hard to tell if there was anything left of D. Pedro I's mortal remains, but his coffin was received with full state honors. Bringing the morbid spectacle in person was none other than Américo Thomaz (1894–1987), Portugal's military president and the last of Salazar's proxies who were doing to the African colonies much the same kind of work that the military dictators were doing to Brazil. As the celebratory mood spread throughout the country, an elegant hymn was composed especially for the occasion, its beautiful lyrics describing Brazil as a "potency of love and peace." The National Museum of Fine Arts in Rio de Janeiro promoted a special exhibition of nationalistic art arranged chronologically so as to demonstrate the nation's brilliant past and suggesting a promising future. Even a mini-World Cup was assembled, in the belief that, despite all its unchecked triteness, basic unsophistication, and openness to nationalistic manipulation, sport brings people closer together. The Brazil Independence Cup opened with twenty national teams competing against each other in honor of a great nation's independence. As if arranged in advance, the final match brought together Brazil and

Portugal themselves. Brazil won 1-0, with a goal scored in the last minute. The tournament obviously appears to have been a farce, and the final game a pre-arranged theatrical performance. The event suggests how much professional soccer, as well as professional sports in general, are nothing but a mass consumption product capable of arousing petty individualistic and nationalistic feelings that are easily manipulated by political groups.

Overestimating the value of GDP growth was one more self-deceiving method favored by the dictatorship in the 1970s. The country was urbanizing, that is, people were being constantly thrown out of the countryside to swell the cities where they lived in poverty. But GDP growth was presented as the government's uncontestable proof of success. The myth of *Brazil Potência* appeared alongside the encouragement of unchecked nationalism and chauvinistic euphoria. The "Brazilian Economic Miracle" began to be publicized as the result of the dictatorship's new economic plan, the "National Development Plan" (PND). The plan was in effect from 1972 to 1974, being substituted in the following administration by the creatively named "Second National Development Plan" (PND II). The Minister of Planning, João Paulo dos Reis Velloso (b. 1931), devised the program as an instrument of aggressive state interventionism, promoting lavish public investment in transportation, telecommunications, naval and petrochemical industries, and steel. The plan's target for GDP growth was easily achieved until October 1973, when the international oil crisis, set in motion by OPEC's embargo, hit Brazil hard. The crisis caught the Brazilian government off guard. Thereafter, all its colossal public works, such as the Rio-Niterói Bridge, the Trans-Amazonian Highway, and the Itaipu Hydroelectric Power Plant, would suddenly have to move on unfinanced.

The government saw in the Carajás iron ore reserves a possible way out of the crisis. In November 1973, the powerful Finance Minister Antônio Delfim Netto would be found in Tokyo signing a contract with the Japanese government for the construction of the Tucuruí Hydroelectric Power Plant, which would facilitate the economic exploitation of the Carajás mines. These also contained large amounts of bauxite, which is the common raw material for the production of metallic aluminum. In the early 1970s, Japan had become the world's largest importer of the metal, and their idea was to keep getting it from Brazil. Aluminum's extremely energy-intensive production process demanded a hefty power generator in order to function appropriately. A hydroelectric power plant would fit the bill, so the Tucuruí dam was built.

The idea of trade and cooperation with Japan in connection to the Brazilian mineral resources was not new. In the early 1960s, the Minister of Mines and Energy to President João Goulart's government, Eliezer Batista da Silva (b. 1924), had the idea of using the Brazilian iron ore reserves to get involved in the reconstruction of Japan's industrial infrastructure, which had been greatly damaged during the Second World War. Batista had been appointed directly by President Jânio Quadros as Director of Vale do Rio Doce Corporation (CVRD) in 1961. The CVRD was a public company that had been created by Getúlio Vargas in 1942 after the dictator's nationalization of the Brazilian subsoil mineral assets and the expropriation of American tycoon Percival Farquhar's (1864–1953) Itabira Iron Ore Company, which had been established in 1911. In 1962, Batista signed a series of iron ore export contracts with twelve Japanese steel corporations. Brazilian iron ore would be transported from the mines of Minas Gerais to the Port of Tubarão, which began construction that same year of 1962 in the city of Vitória (Espírito Santo State). Now with the discovery of the Carajás reserves in the North, a new system of logistics was put into effect with investments in infrastructure, namely the construction of the Port of Itaqui in the city of São Luís (Maranhã State), started in 1966, and the building of the aforementioned Tucuruí Hydroelectric Power Plant in the Tocantins River, started in 1975.

Finance Minister Delfim Netto's trip to Japan in 1973 resulted in the creation of the Albras Alumínio Brasileiro S.A. in 1978. The company emerged from a series of negotiations between the CRVD and the Japanese Aluminum Resources Development Corporation (ARDECO), an aggressive bauxite mining initiative that had been in operation in Africa and South America since the late 1960s. Sponsored by the Metal Mining Agency of Japan (MMJ), the ARDECO sent several technical missions to Brazil to prospect the country's bauxite reserves and analyze the various mines already being explored, including the ones that belonged to the British-Australian multinational Rio Tinto Zinc, which controlled the reserves found in the city of Paragominas (Pará State) through its Brazilian subsidiary, the Mineração Vera Cruz. The ARDECO entrusted its Brazilian venture to Mitsui Aluminum, whose president, Kawaguchi Isao, established the Nippon Amazon Aluminium Company (NAAC) in 1976 as a subsidiary of Mitsui. To that end, Kawaguchi counted on the political support of Japanese Prime Minister Miki Takeo (1907–1988).

The deals with Japanese capital had been regarded as a high priority by the military dictators. After Delfim Netto's initial trip to Tokyo in 1973, a presidential visit to Japan was arranged during the next administration in order to close the deals started by the Minister of Finance. President Ernesto Geisel, who would be commander in charge from 1974 to 1979, met with Prime Minister Miki in Tokyo on September 17, 1976. The

Brazilian President was received with enthusiasm and extensive media coverage. The Asahi Shimbun spoke of Brazil as Brazil spoke of itself: a nation on its way to becoming one of the greatest economic powers of the twenty-first century. Among the large number of high officials included in the Brazilian delegation was Minister of Mines and Energy Shigeaki Ueki (b. 1935), a Brazilian Nisei cleverly appointed by President Geisel in 1974 to conduct the negotiations with the Japanese government. Geisel and his entourage returned home from Japan in a state of quasi-euphoria, after signing a US$ 9 billion contract with Miki. For the Japanese side, the arrangement was vital, for after the oil shock of 1973 the country had been obliged to forsake its attempt to end its reliance on aluminum imports. The energy-intensive nature of the production process of aluminum meant this was impossible after the oil crisis.

Albras was thus born from that deal. The company, however, produced only meager benefits to Brazil, especially to the state of Pará, where it was built. The Albras project was sold to the Brazilian population as part of the military government's aforementioned *Programa de Integração Nacional* (PIN), which was one of the initiatives for development in the Amazon contained in the official economic plan, the PND. In truth, however, the company became part of an enclave economy, that is, an export-based industry controlled by international capital that produces little advantages for the local population. The problems with the Albras included its complex relationship with another company that was fundamental to the actual production of aluminum, the Alunorte, which since the project's beginning should have produced alumina, or aluminum oxide, the intermediary product that would be transformed into aluminum by the Albras. The difficulty with the establishment of the Alunorte was that the Japanese were not interested in alumina, only in aluminum. So the Alunorte, which should have started operations several months before the Albras, so that entirely home-grown aluminum could be produced, was simply not financed. The Alunorte had its construction completely stalled for no less than ten years after the Albras began operating. During all this time, the Albras had to import alumina to Brazil and then transform it into aluminum to send it to Japan. Besides the lack of investment from Japan, the establishment of Alunorte was also delayed by the intensive lobbying of the American company Alcoa Inc., which was one of the world's leading alumina producers and did not want to see new competitors entering the market. Alunorte did not begin operations until 1995, only to be sold to the Norwegian Norsk Hydro in 2010, after the CVRD, which had been in charge of the Alunorte, was privatized in 1997.

With all this coming and going, it is no wonder Brazil remains a poor country. Besides not producing any effective economic results, either nationally or locally, the military government's deal with the Japanese involving the Amazon was counterproductive in that it opened up the territory to foreign interests and imperialist covetousness. Japanese interests in the area continued to be advanced in the decades that followed through actions that found support in the Japanese community in Manaus, Amazon State's capital city. Japanese immigration to the area had started in the 1930s in connection with the production of jute and intensified with the creation of the *Pólo Industrial de Manaus* (PIM), a free economic zone established in 1967 during Humberto de Alencar Castelo Branco's government and in which Japanese capital was heavily invested. Japanese biopiracy would emerge as a local problem in the years that followed, the most notable case being the Japanese Asahi Foods Co.'s registering of the cupuaçú, a local plant, as a trademark in 1998. Since the military regime had openned the area to Japan, the Asian country began to penetrate the Amazon region both culturally and economically with heavy investments and cultural projects. As of 2018, the *Câmara de Comércio e Indústria Nipo-Brasileira do Amazonas*, established in 1987, counts with more than fifty associated Japanese corporations acting in the area. Special Japanese interest in the Amazon region is also demonstrated by the presence of the Japan Foundation, the Japanese government's institution for the dissemination of Japanese culture abroad. The Japan Foundation has targeted the area through several cultural programs aimed at promoting Japanese culture locally. These receive support from the *Associação Pan-Amazonia Nipo-Brasileira* (APANB), established in 1960. As a cultural arm of the Japanese Ministry of Foreign Affairs (MOFA), the Foundation has been charged with cultural imperialism in its attempts to promote Japanese national ideas in developing countries.[23] The notion of "cultural imperialism," however, is misleading in that it suggests that Japan's focus is solely on enhancing its "soft power," that is, it overlooks the complexity of Japan's defense problems and its interest in extending influence over resource-rich areas located in underdeveloped, vulnerable nations. Facing the Chinese and North Korean threats, the Japanese government, and hence the Japan Foundation's actions cannot be dismissed lightly as the product of mere "cultural" imperialism. The concept itself is flawed in that that there is no such thing as "cultural" imperialism, but only *imperialism*, which may assume various forms under distinct conditions.

The Japan Foundation, note should be made, relies heavily on very meticulously devised methods for promoting is nationalistic image of Japan abroad. Its policies are geographically selective, made according to

Japan's geopolitical interests. Different programs are devised for different peoples and areas of the world, and the programs pursued vary according to the participants' origins and to the aims and racial views of the bureaucrats and politicians that control the institution. While programs aimed at recruiting scholars from developed nations include generous research grants, programs devised for developing countries include training in large facilities located in Japanese territory, with elements of brainwashing and indoctrination aimed at the trainee's assimilation of values and behavioral patterns based on notions of Japanese cultural, social, and racial superiority. Any citizen from a developing nation taking part in one of the Japan Foundation's "training" programs tends to feel as if entering a group of foreign mercenaries being prepared to fight for a re-enactment of the *Daitōakyōeiken* (Greater East Asia Co-Prosperity Sphere). The euphemism implied in the notion of "cultural imperialism" thus hides a much more complex reality connected to the right-wing disposition of the Japanese leading political party, the LDP. In the case of Brazil, its place as one of the world's leading producers of commodities such as iron ore, niobium, and soybean, as well as its possessing one of the world's largest reserves of potable water (the Guarani Acquifer) makes it an attractive target for a country like Japan that faces constant threat from its neighbors and that, with the LDP's rightist pro-American inclination, as of 2018 is pursuing constitutional reform to allow rearmament.

Another project emerging in connection with Japan during the period of the military dictatorship is the "Japanese and Brazilian Cooperation Program for Cerrado's Agricultural Development," known in Portuguese as the *Programa de Desenvolvimento do Cerrado* (PRODECER). The program started with a technical visit to Brazil by members of the Japanese federal agricultural union, the Zenkoren, in 1970, during Emilio Médici's government. The Japanese technicians identified remarkable agricultural potential in the Brazilian Cerrado region, a vast tropical savanna spreading through the Brazilian central plateau, occupying the greater part of the states of Goiás and Minas Gerais at an average altitude of 1,100 meters. After the 1973 U.S. soybean exports embargo on Japan, known as the "Nixon Shock," the Japanese government intensified its negotiations with Brazil for the establishment of a joint project aimed at the production of soybean in the Cerrado. In the same year, the *Empresa Brasileira de Pesquisa Agropecuária* (EMBRAPA) was established and in 1974 the PRODECER was celebrated as a joint project between the Japan International Cooperation Agency (JICA) and the EMBRAPA. A subsidiary of the Brazilian company, called EMBRAPA SOJA, was established in 1975 in Londrina (Paraná State). After President Geisel's visit to Japan in 1976, the introduction of soybean farming into the Cerrado was initiated with the use of liming, an agricultural technique that had been employed by the Japanese in Hokkaido since 1926. In the next few years the Brazilian soybean output would grow exponentially. The 1.5 million tons produced in 1970 rose to 15 million in 1979. The EMBRAPA would become a world-class research institution in the fields of sustainable development and agribusiness, and the PRODECER would turn Brazil into the second largest soy producer in the world in 2010. The incongruence, however, is that, mainly for cultural reasons, the consumption of soy as food in Brazil is very low. As of 2018, about 50% of the Brazilian grains are exported (of which more than 70% go to China), and the other half is used mostly as fodder. This suggests that the benefits of soy production are not directly shared with the majority of the Brazilian population. Given the nation's agricultural model based on large estates and highly mechanized production, an inheritance of the country's old land ownership disparity, the large soybean producers, together with Japanese and Chinese consumers, are the ones who have profited most from projects and investments such as the ones involved in the PRODECER.

Another problem we find in all these joint ventures has to do with the low aggregate value of Brazilian exports, of which iron ore and soybeans are the clearest examples. The Brazilian inability to aggregate industrial value to its exports, which has deep roots in the nation's poor higher education and the resulting lack of the capacity to foster originality and creativity, makes projects such as the Carajás, Albras, PRODECER, and many others look like a series of public parties to which only a few selected guests are ever invited. Money pours in, and stays in the pockets of a few.

Back to the first half of the 1970s, President Emílio Médici's foreign policy presented itself as continuing the line of independence and autonomy adopted during President Costa e Silva's administration. Médici's Foreign Minister, Mário Gibson Barbosa (1918–2007), called his own policies *Diplomacia do Interesse Nacional* (Diplomacy for the National Interest), which meant that Brazil would look for opportunities to expand its commercial and economic interests, taking advantage of such opportunities whenever and wherever they appeared, independently of ideological constraints. Undoubtedly, a new leeway for autonomy was now being allowed by the growing détente between the Soviet Union and the United States (started with the Nixon administration in 1969). The Nixon Doctrine, which aimed for an outsourcing of conflict resolution among nations, as well as for the American withdrawal from Vietnam, allowed for countries such as Brazil to assume a more determined attitude in foreign relations.

In 1971, President Médici paid an official visit to the United States, where he had a private meeting with President Nixon. The meeting took place in the White House on December 9. The United States National Security Advisor, Henry Kissinger, and the former Military Attaché to the United States Embassy in Brazil, General Vernon Walters, were also present. President Médici dispensed with the involvement of Brazilian diplomats in the meeting, which, to this day, remains inexplicable to most Brazilian foreign affairs analysts. Some such analysts believe that Médici discussed with Nixon the Brazilian role in the upcoming ousting of President Salvador Allende in Chile. The Brazilian President had already supported General Hugo Banzer's (1926–2002) coup in Bolivia in August 1971 and was getting ready to do the same for Juan Bordaberry (1928–2011) in Uruguay in mid-1973.[24]

During the period from 1969 to 1974 Brazilians attempted to expand and diversify the country's trade partnerships. Here again the détente was helpful, notwithstanding continued strong resistance from the military to the establishment of lines of communication beyond the cold war's ideological frontiers. When in mid-1972 the Brazilian Minister of Commerce Marcus Vinícius Pratini de Moraes (b. 1939) approached President Médici with a proposal to sell Brazilian sugar to communist China, the President was startled, asking how could possibly Brazil sell sugar to communists. The Minister felt obliged to inform the President that the sale was a matter of commerce, not politics. After some thought, probably trying to figure out the difference, the President consented to the negotiations. Thus began a long trade partnership. Neither Médici nor Pratini de Moraes, however, could foresee that forty years later China would become the foremost client for Brazil's iron ore and soybeans, producing a situation in which the South American nation would become economically dependent on the Asian one. Even worse, Brazil would be selling primary products to China and buying back high aggregate-value goods, just as it had always done with the North Atlantic nations.[25]

In any case, in 1972 General Emílio Médici's government continued to search for new sources of trade. Eastern Europe became the target for a commercial mission that was sent to nine countries of the Soviet block in order to negotiate trade agreements. The group was part of the Commission for Trade with Eastern Europe (COLESTE), established in 1968. Africa was also included in the government's trade expansion plans, with visits from Foreign Minister Mário Gibson Barbosa to the Ivory Coast, Ghana, Gabon, Cameroon, Nigeria, and Senegal. During his trip to

Africa, however, the Minister avoided visiting areas under Portuguese rule so as to avoid confrontations on colonial issues. The Brazilian Foreign Ministry would be relieved of its Portuguese commitments only in 1974, when the Portuguese *Revolução dos Cravos* (Carnation Revolution) would overthrow Portugal's dictatorship and Portuguese troops would start withdrawing from Guinea-Bissau, Cape Verde, Mozambique, São Tomé and Príncipe, and Angola. After the oil shock of 1973, Brazil had been put on Nigeria's black list of pariah countries subjected to oil embargos for offering support to Portuguese colonial rule in Africa. Now, with the end of Portuguese control across the African continent, Brazil could try to improve its relations with Nigeria in order to resume buying the oil that was needed for the maintenance of its "Economic Miracle."

As we will see in the next section, during General Ernesto Geisel's rule, Brazilian foreign policy would be shaped by the country's dependence on oil imports. Brazil would attempt to establish new ties with Arab nations and move away from Israel. The Foreign Ministry would call this new stance "diplomacy of responsible pragmatism."

General Ernesto Geisel and the Castelista Group (1974–1979)

General Ernesto Beckmann Geisel (1907–1996) was the third Riograndense military leader to occupy the Brazilian presidency during the 1964–1985 period of dictatorship. Geisel was born into a Lutheran family of German immigrants in Bento Gonçalves, a city located in the northern part of Rio Grande do Sul State. Having received a very rigorous education from his German parents, Geisel graduated from the Military High School of Porto Alegre, Rio Grande do Sul's capital, in 1925, and then moved to Rio de Janeiro, where he attended the prestigious Realengo Military School. In 1964, he became Military Chief of Staff to President Humberto de Alencar Castelo Branco's administration. As we have seen, Castelo Branco's initial aim on assuming the presidency in 1964 was to establish a transitional period of restricted democracy, after which the nation would return to civilian administrative control. Geisel subscribed to this line of thinking, which came to be known as *castelismo*.

The *castelista* faction of the armed forces was opposed to the hardline group which, as we have seen, included commanders such as Artur da Costa e Silva, Emílio Médici, Olímpio Mourão Filho, Sylvio Frota, and Newton Cruz. The more moderate *castelistas* included Castelo Branco, Ernesto Geisel, and Golbery do Couto e Silva, among others. Through Couto e Silva, the castelistas had strong links with the think thank *Escola*

Superior de Guerra (ESG), which gave them the ironic title of "The Sorbonne Group." The title came from the hardliners, who saw the castelistas as too intellectual and soft.

The relative political moderation of the castelistas, however, did not represent any lessening of their hatred of communism. The castelistas' position was based primarily on the recognition that the dictatorship could not last forever, and that some level of political consensus among the various social fronts acting nationally was in order if chaos and the possible failure of the state were to be avoided. The castelistas were, in sum, much less willing to face a civil war than the hardliners.

The rise of Costa e Silva to the presidency and the issuing of the AI-5 in 1968 had represented a hard blow for the castelista group. Dissatisfied with the turn of events, the powerful Head of the National Information Service (SNI) and theoretician of the National Security Doctrine, General Golbery do Couto e Silva, left the government and, as we have mentioned, assumed the presidency of the Brazilian branch of the American Dow Chemical Corporation. Couto e Silva presided over the Corporation from 1968 to 1973. In that year, the Minister of the Army, Orlando Beckmann Geisel (1905–1979), appointed his younger brother, Ernesto, for the next presidency. The military leaders accepted the prestigious Brazilian-German commander as the next president with the supposition that Couto e Silva would remain distanced from the government. With the rise of castelista Ernesto Geisel, however, General Couto e Silva would no longer stay behind the scenes. He would assume the office of Chief of Staff of the Presidency of the Republic to ratify the new government's *Abertura*, that is, the internal détente aimed at a gradual return to democracy. The hardliners, nevertheless, would not be willing to accept Geisel's and Couto e Silva's new democratic overtures so easily, and a serious, potentially catastrophic, split emerged between the military rulers of the nation.

Just like Ernesto Geisel, Couto e Silva was a powerful Riograndense disciplinarian whose practices focused above all on national security and anti-communist geopolitics. Together, the two Gaúchos would attempt the difficult task of protecting the nation from the mounting international charges of human rights abuses while still keeping the communist menace under control. Geisel assumed the presidency in a climate of popular dissatisfaction. The world recession that had begun with the 1973 oil shock had brought an end to the country's "Economic Miracle." GDP annual growth rates had fallen from 13.97% in 1973 to 8.15% in 1974, and would reach 5.17% in 1975. Inflation was back, rising from 16.2% in 1973 to 33.8% in 1974. In the last year of Geisel's administration, 1979, it would reach 76.8%.

The energy crisis demanded immediate action so that the massive investments initiated during the 1968–1973 period could be kept on course. Geisel had been chosen to assume the presidency in great part due to his experience in the oil industry, having served as president of Petrobras from 1969 to 1973. During that time, the General had maintained a strong nationalistic stance and prevented foreign capital from taking part in the company. Without those foreign investments, however, the company's production could not satisfy the domestic demand, and Brazil remained highly dependent on oil imports. In the face of the crisis that had started in 1973, the new government had only two options: either slow down the process of state-sponsored growth, which meant accepting an economic recession with all the social and political costs involved, or move ahead with all the massive public investments of the previous period and try to find ways to finance them at any cost. Geisel chose the second option, and that meant falling into what Brazilian analysts call *crescimento com endividamento externo* (growth with foreign debt).[26]

Financing public works, and its accompanying debt, came from what is generally called "petrodollar recycling," that is, the OPEC nations' lending to developing countries the surplus dollars amassed with the 1973 oil price rise. With new money coming in, Geisel's administration issued another development plan, the PND II. The aim was a sustained annual industrial development rate of 12% from 1974 to 1979 with an import-substitution strategy based on lavish incentives for the production of capital goods. Since more than 80% of the oil consumed domestically was imported, a reduction in oil dependency became an immediate goal. The PND II thus included a series of special programs designed for the development of a more diversified national energy matrix. The expansion of nuclear power was seen as a priority and in 1974 the government established the Brazilian Nuclear Enterprises (Nuclebrás), a public company charged with implementing the national nuclear program. Under the supervision of Nuclebrás, the construction of the Angra Nuclear Power Plant (Angra II) reactor began in Rio de Janeiro in 1976. The new reactor resulted from a cooperation agreement signed with West Germany involving technology transfer.

Ethanol fuel was another important element in the government's energy strategy. The National Alcohol Program, called Pró-Álcool, was launched in 1975. Brazil had a long history of cultivating sugarcane, which was the first commercial product introduced in the Portuguese colony in 1532. Now the same product could be used to produce ethanol fuel, and the government started investing heavily in the development of new technologies that would allow for its widespread use. Brazilian carmakers, namely the local subsidiaries of Fiat, Volkswagen, and Ford, began modifying gasoline engines to be able to take hydrous ethanol. By 1979, gasoline stations in the country were already supplying the new fuel, and thirty years later Brazil would have become the world's second largest producer and the world's largest exporter of ethanol.

Urban development also figured prominently in the PND II. São Paulo's metro was inaugurated in 1975, and Rio de Janeiro's in 1979. Other costly public works included the Sanegran Project, which aimed at the improvement of São Paulo's sewage treatment system; the Jaíba Project, a gigantic irrigation system that would bring development to deprived areas in the north of Minas Gerais State; the Açominas Siderurgy, a large steel plant constructed with foreign loans from German, French, and British banks; the Ferrovia do Aço, a large railway that passed through more than one hundred tunnels in the mountainous inlands of Minas Gerais State to transport iron ore to São Paulo; the nuclear power plants Angra II and Angra III; the expansion of Embraer, the Brazilian aircraft and aerospace corporation; the Camaçari Petrochemical Conglomerate, a large industrial plant built in the state of Bahia to house dozens of companies operating in the chemical sector; the IMBEL, a national arms industry linked to the Ministry of the Army; the hydroelectric power plants of Tucuruí and Itaipu, and many others.

Such a colossal and expansive fiscal policy prevented the country from falling into economic recession. The public sector, however, soon became the largest borrower. The government's soaring debts were inflated by the fact that the government itself assumed the role of guarantor to the foreign loans contracted by the private sector. This came to be called the "statization of the external debt," an iniquitous move that transferred to society at large the burden of public debt.

The regime's rulers understood that the growing external deficit could not be sustained indefinitely. The Brazilian government was borrowing lavishly and at floating interest rates. The bill would have to be paid sooner or later. The present situation revealed the sad reality that, historically, Brazilian industrialization had had to be financed either through recourse to the government's inflationary monetary policies or through its external debt, practices that could not provide sustained support for economic development. In the long run, the lack of a strong private sector endowed with autonomous creativity and organizational capacity would force the national industry to continuously lag behind international standards, constantly requiring renewed state intervention and financing. Furthermore, the lack of adequate infrastructure would continue to weigh on the national production, forming what came to be called the "Brazil cost."

General Geisel's statization of the external debt would appear more clearly and in all its undesirability after the second oil crisis in 1979. This crisis provoked an unexpected rise in international interest rates, caused primarily by the Federal Reserve's attempt to counter inflationary pressures in the United States. The Brazilian debt was contracted with floating interest rates, meaning that the amount owed could vary according to the whims of the international finance market. From 1978 to 1980, Brazil's total debit balance almost tripled. In 1982, the Mexican moratorium would produce an overarching debt crisis that spread throughout Latin America. The Brazilian government would have to resort to the IMF to negotiate interest payments. In the end, the excessive borrowing and expenditure of the 1970s would turn the 1980s into what has been called Brazil's lost decade.

On the domestic side, the President's program for democratization, which, as we have seen, was called *Abertura*, was a process that the government said should be "slow, gradual, and safe." Even at its gradual pace, however, the *Abertura* was not without its setbacks. Relaxing the regime's excessive authoritarianism had in fact been General Golbery do Couto e Silva's idea; the Chief of Staff of the Presidency was widely known as the real political force behind the President's decisions. In spite of the government's democratizing disposition, however, congressional mandates and political rights were constantly being abrogated whenever they went too far against right-wing rule. The government's project of internal détente received an initial shock with the congressional elections of November 15, 1974. The permitted opposition party, the MDB, made a remarkable recovery from its debacle in the previous elections of 1970, and the military leaders immediately realized that their democratizing process would have to be balanced with some authoritarian measures. In June 1976, the government issued a law called *Lei Falcão*, which proscribed political debate in the media during electoral campaigns. The situation became ever more bizarre: radio and television channels were obliged to offer air time to candidates but these were not allowed to speak; instead, only their biographies were presented by a narrator and accompanied, in the case of television, by their photographs.

The more Generals Geisel and Couto e Silva talked of political détente and gradual re-democratization the more it angered the hardliners. Another serious blow to the castelista enterprise came on October 25, 1975, when journalist Vladimir Herzog (1937–1975) was found dead in the offices of the DOI-CODI in São Paulo. Herzog was born in Yugoslavia to a Croatian

Jewish family that had immigrated to Brazil in the early 1940s to escape Nazi persecution. Later he became a well-known newspaperman active in the civil resistance against the military dictatorship. On October 25, 1975, Herzog was summoned by the military police to be interrogated with regard to the actions of the then illegal Brazilian Communist Party (PCB), of which he had been a member. The journalist promptly presented himself at the DOI-CODI in São Paulo for an interrogation that would soon turn into a torture session. On the same day, Herzog's body was found hanging in his prison cell. The police officers published a poorly arranged picture of the dead man in what was officially termed a "suicide by hanging." The image shows a man who could not have hanged himself, as his legs were bent and touching the floor while his body was half-raised by a rope.

The forged suicide generated a wave of protest that soon gathered international attention, becoming the starting point for a movement in defense of human rights in Brazil. Geisel and Couto e Silva became infuriated with the hardliners. The President and his Chief of Staff knew that the type of action carried out against the journalist could only weaken military rule.

On January 17, 1976, out-of-control torturers dealt another blow to the government. Early that morning, factory worker Manuel Fiel Filho (1927–1976) was arrested in front of his wife and two daughters and taken to the same DOI-CODI offices in São Paulo where Vladimir Herzog had been killed a few months before. There he was also tortured until he died. Just as in Herzog's case, the cause of Manuel Filho's death was announced by the DOI-CODI's officers to be "suicide by hanging." In response to the incident, the President dismissed General Ednardo D'Ávila Mello (1911–1984) from his post of Commander of the Second Army, the military branch of which the DOI-CODI was a part. The President's action caused an irreconcilable split between the two rival tendencies in the armed forces, the castelistas and the hardliners.

After Herzog's death, the President had made it clear that he would no longer tolerate crimes being committed inside the army. The examples of Herzog and Manuel Filho were not isolated cases. There had been many assassinations reported inside the DOI-CODI offices since its creation in 1970. The Student Movement's leader Alexandre Vannucchi Leme's (1950–1973) death in March 1973 is a case in point. The murder of the 22-year-old student created a state of national commotion. The seventh-day mass held by Archbishop Dom Paulo Evaristo Arns (b. 1921) after his death drew around 5,000 people in São Paulo's central cathedral demanding justice and the end of state terror.

Even military officers themselves were not above suspicion in the DOI-CODI's anti-communist activities. On August 8, 1975, Lieutenant José Ferreira de Almeida (1911–1975) died after more than a month of beatings and electric shocks in the military agency's offices. Something similar occurred to Colonel José Maximino de Andrade Netto (1913–1975) ten days later. The torture and assassination of these officers were part of a cleaning-up operation against leftist members of São Paulo's military police forces. During 1974 and 1975, more than 60 officers who were targeted as having connections with the PCB were arrested and tortured by the DOI-CODI. The repression was part of the so-called *Operação Radar*, a military police operation aimed at annihilating all PCB members before the re-democratization could be put into effect. According to the final report from the National Truth Commission established by the Presidency of the Republic and the House of Representatives in 2011, Operation Radar was the responsibility of the Chief of Staff of the First Army, the Riograndense General Leônidas Pires Gonçalves (1921–2015).[27] The report, published in 2014, also points to Colonel Audir Santos Maciel (b. 1932) as the Operation's commander.[28] Also allegedly involved in Operation Radar were Major Carlos Alberto Brilhante Ustra and Detective Sérgio Paranhos Fleury.[29]

In any case, Operation Radar resulted in hundreds of unlawful arrests and cases of human rights abuse throughout the country. On December 16, 1976, Fleury allegedly commanded the aforementioned Lapa Massacre, an operation against communist leaders in São Paulo's Lapa neighborhood, resulting in the killing of three people with the subsequent arrest and torture of a further five. The individuals murdered on this occasion were João Baptista Franco Drummond (1942–1976), Ângelo Arroyo (1928–1976), and Pedro de Araújo Pomar (1913–1976).

1976 also saw the deaths of former Presidents Juscelino Kubitschek and João Goulart. Kubitschek died on August 22, Goulart on December 6. In both cases the cause of death is disputed and the hypothesis of murder seems plausible. Kubitschek died in a car accident, the circumstances of which have been the source of an ongoing debate.[30] In Goulart's case, the official version suggests death by heart attack while in exile in Uruguay, but members of Goulart's family defend the thesis of poisoning. In 2008, the Legislative Assembly of Rio Grande do Sul's Commission for Citizenship and Human Rights conducted an investigation into charges that President João Goulart had been murdered by poisoning with President Geisel's acquiescence.[31] The charges were based on the declarations of a Uruguayan citizen, Ronald Mario Neira Barreiro. Barreiro claimed to have taken part in Operation Condor to kill João

Goulart. The investigations and later exhumation of the former President's body were inconclusive regarding poisoning. Historian Luiz Alberto Moniz Bandeira suggests the inexistence of concrete evidence to justify the theory of murder by poisoning.[32] In any case, if the thesis of murder is valid, and President Geisel did acquiesce in the crime, then we would be facing what looks like an atavistic and bitter re-enactment of the old history of Riograndenses killing Riograndenses, that is, the history we have seen as a maze of mutual distrust, betrayal, and ferocious factionism, plagued with unrestrained hatred and summary executions, as exemplified in the revolutions of 1835, 1893, and 1923.

In any event, the beginning of a series of repressive actions carried out throughout South America as part of Operation Condor in that year of 1976 reinforces the thesis of conspiracy in the deaths of the former presidents. In Argentina, the rise to power of a military junta headed by General Jorge Rafael Videla (1925–2013) in March 1976 marked the intensification of the so-called *Gerra Sucia* (Dirty War) and its large-scale employment of state terror. From 1976 onwards, the Chilean *Dirección de Inteligencia Nacional* (DINA) and the Argentine *Secretaría de Inteligencia* (SIDE) cooperated in the persecution and assassination of political opponents. The forces of repression in Uruguay and Brazil also cooperated in the surveillance of political refugees in each other's territories. The alleged poisoning of João Goulart in 1976 would have been carried out with the support of the Uruguayan civic-military dictatorship established under Juan María Bordaberry (1928–2011) in 1973. In the same way, the attempted kidnap of Uruguayan opposition activists Universindo Rodriguez Díaz (1952–2012) and Lilian Celiberti de Casariego (b. 1950) with their two children in Porto Alegre in 1978 by the Uruguayan intelligence service would have been supported by the Brazilian military government.[33]

During their exile in Uruguay, João Goulart's family members repeatedly reported to the Uruguayan government that they were being monitored, without any action being taken on the part of the Uruguayans. Under the circumstances of cooperative political repression among Southern Cone dictatorships, the coincidence in the deaths of Juscelino Kubitschek and João Goulart in 1976, together with that of Carlos Lacerda the following year suggests the possibility of a conspiracy. Lacerda died on May 21, 1977 in a clinic in Rio de Janeiro where he checked in because of a head cold. The officially publicized cause of death was generalized infection.[34]

During the 1970s, the harshest of all Latin American dictatorships seems to have been the one established in Argentina. The number of deaths and abductions there is appalling when compared to those verified in its neighbors. An estimate for the number of people killed and missing in the Southern Cone republics reaches 2,000 in Paraguay; 3,196 in Chile; 297 in Uruguay; 366 in Brazil; and more than 30,000 in Argentina.[35] In the case of Brazil, President Ernesto Geisel's and Chief of Staff Golbery do Couto e Silva's attempts at internal détente helped prevent anti-communist repression reaching the fierceness seen in other Latin American countries. Even if the two Riograndenses did not favor democracy over what they perceived as the need to undermine the communist threat, it is plausible to surmise that in their efforts to control the summary executions carried out by the DOI-CODI, as well as in their *Abertura* re-democratization program, they helped contain right-wing repression in Brazil, preventing it from reaching the level of violence experienced in the Argentine Dirty War.

President Ernesto Geisel's castelista policies, however, did not prevent Brazil from being charged internationally with human rights violations on several occasions. The President himself was seen as condoning violence, and for that he was severely criticized. The United States began an active foreign policy of defending human rights in Latin America after Jimmy Carter became President in 1977. First Lady Rosalyn Carter's visit to Brazil that same year produced a confrontation with Geisel on the subject. In response to criticism from Carter, Geisel responded by calling attention to the absence of racism and religious prejudice in Brazil, implying that the same could not be said of the United States.[36] Dissatisfied with the U.S. government's criticism of his regime's human rights record, President Geisel canceled the Military Assistance Agreement that had been in effect between the two countries since 1952. A Nuclear Cooperation Agreement signed with Germany in 1975, which led to the building of the Angra II nuclear power plant, had already affected the Brazil-United States relations, and the cancelation of the 1952 military agreement meant further distancing at the behest of the Brazilian side.

In terms of domestic policy, Geisel had to balance his attempts at détente with the reality of a political opposition growing stronger. On April 13, 1977, the President closed the Congress and issued six decrees that came to be known as *Pacote de Abril* (April Package), wherein the rules for the upcoming congressional elections were altered in order to favor the government's party, the ARENA. According to the new regulations, a portion of the seats in the House of Representatives would be elected by indirect voting and a proportion of the new senators would be appointed by the government. This step backward in Geisel's democratization process was a response to the fears experienced by the hardliners. The internal dispute between the two opposing factions within the high military ranks was gathering momentum with the approach of Geisel's succession in 1979, and the government's immediate goal was to diminish dissent. Still, in 1977, the hardliners appointed the Minister of the Army, General Sylvio Frota (1910–1996), as their candidate for the indirect presidential election scheduled for October 1978. Geisel and the castelistas presented the Chief of SNI, General João Baptista de Oliveira Figueiredo (1918–1999), as their candidate. The internal dispute was ferocious, and Geisel was not willing to concede any ground to his adversaries. On October 12, 1977, the President took an unexpected decision and dismissed General Frota from the post of Minister of the Army. Enraged, the dismissed General attempted to organize a coup against Geisel, but lacking support ended up accepting his dismissal.

On October 15, 1978, the National Congress elected General João Baptista de Oliveira Figueiredo as the new President. On January 1, 1979, in a symbolic act meant to suggest the dawn of a new era, President Geisel revoked the AI-5, the fearsome Institutional Act that had served as the legal basis for the political persecution, torture, and summary execution of many Brazilians. As we will see in the following pages, even with the electoral defeat and the rise of another castelista to the presidency, the hardliners were not yet ready to give up.

General João Figueiredo and the End of Military Rule (1979–1985)

General João Baptista de Oliveira Figueiredo (1918–1999) took the oath of office as Brazil's 30th President on March 15, 1979. Born in Rio de Janeiro, Figueiredo was the first non-Riograndense President to take office since 1967, when General Castelo Branco finished the first military mandate of the dictatorial period. That notwithstanding, the new President had started his military career as a student in the Military Academy of Porto Alegre, having moved to Rio Grande do Sul as a child to accompany his father, an army general who had been transferred to the rural town of Alegrete.

General Figueiredo's term would be marked by the effects of the international economic crisis that resulted from the oil shock of 1979. The ensuing rise in international interest rates would bring the Brazilian economy to a virtual standstill, putting an end to a long era of state-centered developmental programs. Escalating inflation rates and sluggish productivity soon turned into the feared phenomenon of stagflation. Mounting foreign debt and unemployment rates brought the nation to the verge of economic chaos. While the GDP growth rate plummeted from a 9.2% rise in 1980 to a terrible -4.3% recession in 1981, inflation rose from 77.2% in 1979 to 110.2% in 1980, lowering slightly to 95.2% in 1981 only to rise again and reach 211% in 1983 with a -2.9% GDP retraction. 1984 closed with a 238.8% inflation rate, 7.1% unemployment, and a GDP recovery marking 5.4%.

From 1981 to 1983 the industrial sector experienced a general contraction of 52%. In the first semester of 1979, the new Minister of Planning, the aforementioned Mario Henrique Simonsen (1935–1997), pointed to the impossibility of maintaining the current policies of extensive growth cycles combined with the postponement of macroeconomic adjustments. In other words, the adoption of recessive monetary, fiscal, and exchange-rate policies was needed. The Minister's diagnosis of the external deficit as the result of disproportionate domestic absorption justified his adoption of measures that would reduce GDP growth. Simonsen had understood that the model of *desenvolvimentismo*, that is, of state-driven industrialization under import-substitution programs, had come to an end. Brazilian capitalists and policymakers, however, needed some time to accept the economic exhaustion of their long-lasting model. The Minister's fiscal adjustment and credit contraction policies displeased the larger part of private investors, as well as a portion of the government. In August 1979, Antônio Delfim Netto, who had occupied the post of Minister of Agriculture since March of that year, took Simonsen's place in the Ministry of Planning.

What nobody expected was that Delfim Netto would arrive with a stimulus package that would end up exploding the entire economy. In the first months of 1980, the new Minister promoted a 30% maxi-devaluation of the cruzeiro in order to stimulate exports. This meant a heterodox shock that was difficult for the economy to absorb, as well as the end of the more sensible mini-devaluation of the currency that had been established by Netto himself during Costa e Silva's administration. Subsidized agriculture entered the package with a nationalistic advertising campaign under the slogan *Plante que o João Garante* (Plant, for President John will guarantee). Since this was an era before agriculture had become part of the discussions at the WTO, government incentives could be offered lavishly. A new indexation system promoted salary rises every six months, which conflicted with the freezing of contracts and financial assets. The economy entered an inflationary spiral and investors experienced a sudden panic that simply paralyzed the economy.

The return of effective economic activity only came in 1984 thanks mostly to the United States' financial recovery and to its renewed demand for Brazilian exports. The national industrial output, which had contracted sharply by 52% between 1981 and 1983, showed a substantial revival, managing 4% growth in 1984. The economic recovery was also due to the government's understanding that the initial diagnosis of Mario Henrique Simonsen was, after all, correct and that heterodox shocks would have to be replaced by recessive adjustments. This understanding came together with the aforementioned Latin American debt crisis that began with the Mexican moratorium of 1982, which led Brazilian policymakers to seek help from the IMF and its emergency funds in order to maintain debt payments. By 1983, the government was modeling its economic decisions according to the demands of the IMF.

The exhaustion of *desenvolvimentismo* as a state-induced economic developmental model exposed the fatigue of the military rule as a sustainable political arrangement. On August 29, 1979, President Figueiredo had promulgated the Amnesty Law, which had been long demanded by Brazilian civil society. At a deep psychological level, the Law represented a recognition on the part of the regime that its rule could not be perpetuated indefinitely, and that the end of the dictatorial period was imminent. With this recognition as background, the Law officially pardonned not only those who had perpetrated acts of "subversion," but, as we have seen, those who had repressed those acts. The amnesty in question was defined as "ample, general, and unrestricted." Evidently, with the regime's end fast approaching amid the rubble of the economy, the castelistas were opting for a pre-arranged conciliatory pact between the military and civil society. The rulers' attitude was, just like the long dictatorship itself, cowardly and venal.

But before political power could be transferred to a civilian government, the military rulers had to weaken the left as much as possible. On December 20, 1979, President Figueiredo decreed a new electoral law, which disbanded the two national parties, the ARENA and the MDB, and established a multiparty system. The aim of the Law was to divide and weaken the left, which up to then had been concentrated in one large party, the MDB. From early 1980 onwards, the left would be diluted into several small and weak parties.

The national party structure bifurcated as follows. While right-wing ARENA gave birth to the Social Democratic Party (PDS), the center-left MDB spawned the Brazilian Democratic Movement Party (PMDB), the Popular Party (PP), the Brazilian Workers' Party (PTB), the Democratic Workers' Party (PDT), and the Workers' Party (PT). The PMDB emerged under the leadership of Congressman Ulysses Guimarães (1916–1992), a former PSD deputy of conservative orientation; the PP was built around former MDB Senator Tancredo Neves (1910–1985); the PTB around Getúlio Vargas's niece, Ivete Vargas (1927–1984); the PDT around Leonel Brizola (1922–2004); and the PT around trade union leader Luiz Inácio Lula da Silva (b. 1945). In 1980 the government announced direct elections for state governors to be held in 1982.

The hardliners' reaction against the President's democratizing policies emerged promptly and with a vengeance. A wave of terrorism spread through the country's major cities. A total of 28 bomb attacks were commited in 1980 and other 19 in 1981. The first terrorist attempt was on January 18, 1980, when a bomb was discovered and deactivated at the Hotel Everest, in Rio de Janeiro, where PDT leader Leonel Brizola was staying. In April 1980, a series of bomb attacks against newsstands that sold leftist newspapers and magazines started in the cities of Brasília, Porto Alegre, Curitiba, Belo Horizonte, Belém, Rio de Janeiro, and São Paulo. In August 1980, bomb attacks against a PMDB Deputy in Rio de Janeiro and against the President of the Order of Attorneys of Brazil (OAB) provoked national panic. On April 30, 1981, an attack against Rio Centro, a large pavilion hall where a crowd of 20,000 people were watching a music concert, became a turning point in the regime's history. The concert was being held in celebration of International Workers Day, bringing together famous artists such as Chico Buarque, Caetano Veloso, Gilberto Gil, Milton Nascimento, Elba Ramalho, Gonzaguinha, and Gal Costa. The sheer incompetence of the army officers who planned the attack made the bomb explode inside their car, killing Sergeant Guilherme Pereira do Rosário (1946–1981) and leaving Captain Wilson Luís Alves Machado, who was never punished for the attempt, wounded.

The Rio Centro attempt, together with the other bomb attacks, was not properly investigated by the armed forces, and no responsibility was ever assumed by the hardline terrorists. The situation of widespread violence springing from the army against the population saw General Golbery do Couto e Silva resign from his office in protest. The powerful commander had been re-appointed to the post of Chief of Staff in President Figueiredo's administration and now he decided it was time to step down from politics altogether. The man who had formulated the strategy of political détente during President Geisel's administration left office discretely, with no announcement, saying simply that he was not coming back. The fate of the transition to civilian rule was now in the hands of the new President, a man who knew his army and its hardliners very well.

General Figueiredo understood that army officers feared the wrath of the civilian population and the likelihood of revenge when a civilian government came to power. With that in mind, the President realized that announcing a series of punishments against his fellow officers could only further hamper the political transition to civilian rule. And that transition, he knew, had to be achieved at all costs. For the military had gradually lost prestige during the twenty years of dictatorial rule, and the growing popular dissatisfaction, fueled by the severe economic situation, had brought the top brass to the understanding that their grip on power could not be sustained much longer. For the hardliners, however, the fear of what could come next made the defensive position still appear to be the best strategy.

Starting in March 1983, a popular movement demanding the calling of direct presidential elections spread throughout the country in a wave of public protests and mass mobilizations. The movement was initiated in the state of Pernambuco among the ranks of the PMDB and soon spread towards the central and southern parts of the country with the support of other leftist parties. Public protests took place in the cities of Goiânia in June and São Paulo in November. Early in 1984, the movement reached the city of Curitiba, spreading subsequently to Salvador, Campinas, João Pessoa, Olinda, Maceió, and emerging again in São Paulo, with a large demonstration of 300,000 people on the day of the city's anniversary, January 25. In February, demonstrations started in Rio de Janeiro, Cuiabá, Rio Branco, and Belo Horizonte, and by March the entire country was aflame under a unified national movement for democracy. On March 2, Congressman Dante de Oliveira (1952–2006) presented to Parliament a proposal for Constitutional Amendment 5, which demanded that direct presidential elections be called immediately. The *Diretas Já* Movement (Direct Elections Now) was born. The word "democracy" was now on everyone's lips, in all social classes and all walks of life.

The *Emenda Dante de Oliveira*, as the proposed Amendment was called, was scheduled be voted on April 25, 1984. It seemed as if the entire nation took part in demonstrations that day in a desperate attempt to make the military leaders understand the strength of people's longing for citizenship and freedom. On April 10, approximately one million demonstrators gathered in downtown Rio de Janeiro in what became the largest public demonstration in the nation's history. On April 16, São Paulo's demonstration superseded that of Rio de Janeiro, congregating one-and-a-half million people around the city's cathedral. All Brazilians gathered hand in hand with intellectuals, celebrities, musicians, religious leaders, and progressive politicians in an event that perhaps for the first time in almost 500 years suggested a sense of nationality and of a common destiny underlying the lives of those Iberian, African, Indian, Central and Northern European, Asian, Turkish, Arab, and Jewish descendants that for some reason or another had been born or had decided to come and live in that large South American nation inherited from the Portuguese colonizers.

The Amendment was voted on April 25, 1984. A few hours before the congressional session began a gigantic power shortage left the entire south and southeast regions of the country without electricity. This prevented the population in those areas hearing directly about the day's events on the media. Since the beginning of the week, Brasilia had been occupied by the armed forces. On the day of the vote, the army surrounded the National Congress in order to repel any acts of civil disobedience. The residents of Brasilia had planned a car-horn-honking parade during the plenary session. They kept hoping for a positive decision in favor of democracy, and wanted to try until the last minute to press the Congress into heeding the people's wishes. The horn-honking idea, however, was thwarted when hardline General Newton Cruz took to the streets of Brasilia atop his white stallion and began whipping the hoods of cars that dared honk their horns. If this seemed laughable, the mood quickly turned to heart-rending disappointment when Brazilians heard the result of the vote on the Amendment.

With the opposition intimidated by the military deployment encircling the Congress, the dictatorial hardliners had a head start in the voting. As is always the case, little can be done against an unprincipled display of military force against those who are unarmed and untrained. The Dante de Oliveira Amendment received 298 votes in favor against only 65 against. However, a political maneuver by the dictators managed to ensure the absence of a large number of congressmen from the plenary session, so that the vote fell short of the one required for the Amendment to be approved. The hardline's unabashed employment of threats and extortion led to a dirty and deceitful victory. The frustration of the entire country's hope for democracy provoked a deep sense of national disillusionment and a dramatic and widespread sadness. On that day, Brazilians experienced a profound sense of impotence in the face of dictatorial power. Coupled with economic recession and astronomical inflation rates reaching 238.8%, the disenchantment with the Amendment's rejection made 1984 a memorable landmark in the nation's recognition of its own limitations. After twenty years of silence in the face of abuse, of fear and intimidation, the people's movement, its great demonstrations, protests, and pleas full of hope and sincerity, were simply not heard. Brazilians understood that, in the end, the people themselves did not matter. Power was the same as it had always been, the same power that had held all there was captive within its closed hands since the first day of colonial rule: the power that existed only to serve itself.

Brazilians, once again, would have to watch silently the Congress choose the next president. In mid-1984, President João Batista Figueiredo called presidential elections to be held by means of indirect vote on January 15, 1985. On that day, the Electoral College met for the last election held under the military regime and under the 1967 Constitution. During the *Diretas Já* campaign, political parties had begun announcing their candidates. The right-wing PDS had presented São Paulo's governor, Paulo Salim Maluf; the center-left PMDB appointed Ulysses Guimarães, one of the leaders of the re-democratization campaign; and the PP presented Tancredo Neves, former Minister of Justice to Getúlio Vargas's final administration. With the *Diretas Já*'s debacle, however, a new arrangement was established. The PP merged with the PMDB, and Tancredo Neves was chosen as the candidate in place of Ulysses Guimarães. The PDS, which represented a reconfiguration of the right-wing ARENA, was divided between two candidates, Paulo Maluf and Mario Andreazza (1918–1988), the latter a Riograndense military officer who had served as Minister of Transportation during the hardline Costa e Silva and Médici administrations. In that office, Andreazza had been in charge of the Rio-Niterói Bridge and the Trans-Amazonian Highway works. Paulo Maluf won the contest with the support of General Golbery do Couto e Silva, but met great opposition from the northeastern landlords, who had supported the military government through a series of exchanges of favors that could not be maintained by the civilian Maluf. After the latter's victory over Andreazza in the PDS, the northeastern chieftains broke with the party and formed the so-called Frente Liberal, from which emerged the *Partido da Frente Liberal* (PFL).[37] The PFL then joined the PMDB in what was called the Democratic Alliance, which presented as candidates PMDB's Tancredo Neves, for President, and PFL's José Sarney (b. 1930), for Vice President. The PDS presented as candidates Paulo Salim Maluf and Congressman Flávio Marcílio (1917–1992) for President and Vice President, respectively. On January 15, 1985, the Electoral College elected PMDB's Tancredo Neves for a six-year presidential mandate.[38]

The last dictatorial administration left the country in a severe economic crisis and with a general feeling of resentment among the great majority of the population. Faced with terrible economic conditions in the politically convoluted South American nation, by 1985, foreign capital had completed its retreat. Hyperinflation, combined with the near-standstill of the colossal public works left unfinished around the country, contributed to a general climate of desolateness and waste.

In that last military administration of President Figueiredo, foreign policy had also been erratic. On assuming the Foreign Ministry in 1979, Ramiro Saraiva Guerreiro (1918–2011) had proclaimed his new "diplomacy of universalism." Being "universalist" meant the continuation of President Geisel's policies of independence vis-à-vis the United States. Under the severe restrictions imposed by its foreign debt crisis, however, Brazil had its hands tied with regard to foreign action. In 1983, Guerreiro attempted to strengthen the Cartagena Group, an arrangement among Latin American nations for a collective negotiation of the region's foreign debt. The idea was that if united in a single bloc the Latin American nations would be in a stronger position when negotiating payments. Saraiva Guerreiro and the members of the Foreign Ministry challenged the Minister of Planning, Delfim Netto's policies with regard to the nation's gigantic foreign debt, forming a rift within the government. In the end, Guerreiro's idea of collective negotiations was not successful, and the foreign debt of Latin American nations was treated on a country-by-country basis.

President Figueiredo's foreign policy achieved better results in its attempts to improve relations with the neighboring countries. During President Geisel's administration, relations with Argentina had worsened substantially. The former Spanish colony had started an international campaign against the Brazilian-Paraguayan construction of the Itaipu Hydroelectric Power Plant on the Paraná River near the border between the two countries. The plant was projected to be the world's second largest hydroelectric facility, and the enormous amount of water retained in its dam was regarded by the Argentines as a threat to their security. All three countries in the area, namely Paraguay, Brazil and Argentina, were under military dictatorships, and mutual distrust was high. Argentina feared that, in the event of a conflict, Brazil could open the dam's floodgates, flooding the city of Buenos Aires. The Argentine government began a fierce international campaign denouncing the Brazilian imperialistic attitude in the region. An important diplomatic settlement was reached with the signing of the *Acordo Tripartite Itaipu-Corpus* in October 1979. The three countries agreed that the hydroelectric potential of the region would be exploited in a way that did not cause harm to any of the interested parties. The agreement was especially important for Argentina, which was involved in territorial disputes with Chile over the Beagle Channel and with the United Kingdom over the Malvinas/Falkland Islands. A third dispute with Brazil would have made the country's situation untenable.

The Acordo Tripartite saw a new page turned in the history of Brazil-Argentina relations. In May 1980, President Figueiredo visited Buenos

Aires and signed an important agreement with Argentina on the use of nuclear energy for peaceful purposes. The agreement became the foundation for future nuclear cooperation programs established between the two countries. In 1991, the two nations would establish the *Agência Brasileiro-Argentina de Contabilidade e Controle de Materiais Nucleares* (ABACC), which allowed for confidence building measures in terms of nuclear energy development and employment. The 1979 pact also allowed for the emergence of a new sense of shared destiny between the two nations, which in the 1990s would begin an important process of economic integration under the MERCOSUL. In 1982, Brazil would reiterate its long-standing support for Argentina's claim to sovereignty over the Malvinas/Falkland Islands during the conflict with the United Kingdom.[39]

During President Figueiredo's term, Brazil continued its policy of rapprochement with Arab nations. The new friendship had started during President Geisel's administration, inspired by the country's need for oil in the aftermath of the 1973 shock. In an attempt to curry favor with the Arabs, in 1975 Brazil cast its vote in favor of the United Nations General Assembly Resolution 3379, which declared Zionism to be a form of racial discrimination. In 1979, Geisel allowed the Palestine Liberation Organization (PLO) to establish an office in Brasilia. Joint ventures for oil extraction were established between Petrobras and the governments of Algeria, Libya, Iraq, and Saudi Arabia. Cooperation also reached the Brazilian military-industrial complex, with the beginning of arms and missile sales to Iraq. The sales were carried out through the Brazilian ENGESA, a private company founded in 1963 to operate in the national armaments sector. During the 1970s, Iraq became one of the company's foremost clients, and one of Brazil's foremost commercial partners. Illegal sales of Brazilian yellowcake (oxide of uranium ore) to Saddam Hussein (1937–2006) began during General Figueiredo's term. In 1982, the assassination of journalist Alexandre von Baumgarten (1930–1982), who allegedly produced a dossier disclosing the involvement of São Paulo's government, together with that of a group of high-ranking military officers, in the illegal uranium sales, brought the case into the open. São Paulo's governor and future presidential candidate supported by the military regime, Paulo Salim Maluf, came close to being associated with the case, given the apparent support of São Paulo's government for the ENGESA, the company that produced and sold arms to Iraq.[40] The Chief of SNI, General Newton Cruz, the same man who from his white stallion would two years later ride the streets of Brasilia whipping car hoods during the vote on the Dante de Oliveira Amendment, was accused of ordering Baumgarten's assassination. In 1992, the General was prosecuted but acquitted for lack of sufficient evidence to prove his involvement in the murder.[41]

During General Figueiredo's term, Brazil initiated important new relations with several countries and increased the use of presidential diplomacy. The first presidential visit to Africa in Brazilian history occurred in 1983. These belated high-level visits took the Brazilian President to Nigeria, Senegal, Guinea-Bissau, Cape Verde, and Algeria. In 1984, President Figueiredo visited China. His meeting with Deng Xiaoping (1904–1997) foreshadowed a new era of cooperation between the two large countries. Cultural and technological exchanges between Brazil and China would become a symbol of the new South-South relations initiated in the 1990s. By the end of that decade, Japan would be immersed in a long economic recession and China would have become Brazil's most important trading partner after the United States.

Culture and Society in the Dictatorial Period

The years between 1964 and 1985 saw the spread of an unbalanced urbanization that left the entire country with an appalling record of social problems, including urban violence, spatial exclusion, income disparity, social alienation, and environmental degradation. By the early 1980s, more than 70% of Brazilians lived in cities. These lacked effective infrastructure, with systems of public health, transportation, water treatment, law enforcement, and education that were either deficient or non-existant, except in selected areas occupied by high-income residents. Urbanization was not accompanied by improvement in the general population's living conditions or levels of formal education. While the city of São Paulo, for example, grew from 5,924,615 residents in 1970 to 8,493,226 in 1980, the national rate of illiteracy only fell from 33.6% to 25.5% in the same period, a mere 8.1% that still left one in four Brazilians unable to read or write. Regional imbalances also became more accentuated with most of the national wealth concentrated in the southern and southeastern areas, while other regions became increasingly impoverished.

The phenomenon of fast-paced and unplanned urbanization was fueled by a dramatic exodus from rural areas that saw the cities swell to the point of virtual collapse. The military government's stalling of the land reform programs planned during President João Goulart's administration generated a large and sudden population flight from rural areas. All throughout the twenty years of military rule, every day hundreds of starving families that were no longer able find work in the gigantic and newly mechanized farms of the countryside would arrive in the urban centers with nothing to offer and only fit for the most menial jobs. The figure of the domestic servant became the clearest sign of a terrible social gap that spread like a plague among Brazilians living in cities. Usually young women in their late teens coming from the countryside, these individuals would arrive at their potential patron's house carrying a suitcase or a bag that usually contained everything they owned. If they were lucky and were willing to work hard, they might find employment that could last for a couple of months. No contracts would be offered, and being chased away from the houses where they would both work and live would occur at the patron's will. These women would normally be lodged in a small room at the back of the patron's house or apartment, usually located close to the kitchen, and start the day early serving breakfast, then cleaning the house, cooking, washing dishes, babysitting, doing laundry, preparing dinner, cleaning again, and then going to bed late after the last soap opera that, again, if they were lucky, their patron would allow them to watch on the kitchen television. That same routine, with hardly any change, would start again early in the morning of the next day. When their patron decided to change servants, these women would just have to pack up and leave. In the best case, they might be given a letter of recommendation, which in most cases they were not able to read.

Without any form of labor rights, female servants would generally have only Sunday afternoons free, sometimes not even that. Their lack of legal support meant they were vulnerable to all sorts of abuse from their patrons. Psychological harassment was more the norm than the exception. Sexual harassment was frequent. The degree of alienation suffered by these individuals was generally translated into severe loneliness, self-loathing, depression, intellectual deprivation, and a lack of trust in human beings.

This heartrending reality, which replicated itself through the lives of hundreds of thousands of young Brazilian women living in urban centers, clearly reproduced some of the patterns found in the country's former slave system. The brutal semi-servile conditions under which these individuals were forced to exist throughout their entire lives furthered the social gap that became the hideous mark of Brazil in the twentieth century and beyond. With the country's public education system in a parlous state, illiteracy was common among these young maidservants, further increasing the divide between them and their patrons. The contrast between two disjointed classes became so obvious that the use of the Portuguese language in each group started to differ remarkably. The intermingling between the contrasting social strata was thus further hindered by a communication gap rooted in an economic and educational situation that fostered exclusion. The inhumane result was that two distinct and primarily incompatible types of individuals began to coexist within the same country. Middle-class Brazilians hardly saw their domestic servants as fellow citizens entitled to the same rights as themselves. They did not perceive of these individuals, who lived in the back rooms of their homes, as equals belonging to a single nation with a shared common future. The very houses or apartment complexes built in major cities almost invariably contained what was called a *dependência de empregada*, that is, a maidservant's room that functioned like a slave quarter. Brazilian homes were thus constructed in a way that reproduced the national culture of exclusion and exploitation, a culture that had remained in place through centuries of social oppression and that was intensified with every economic downturn. In this sense, even Brazilian architecture and civil engineering could be said to have complied with the abhorrent social divide that had continued throughout the centuries and that further intensified during those twenty years of military rule.

Brazil's social division was thus exacerbated by the two most damaging results of the military government's policies: rural exodus and failed public education. The dictatorial regime's war on education started in the first few days after the ousting of President João Goulart. One of General Castelo Branco's first acts in the field of schooling was to abandon the National Education Plan (PNE), a program for mass instruction that had been started during Goulart's administration. The PNE had been conceived by educator Anísio Teixeira (1900–1971) and contained within it the National Program for Literacy, an emergency plan for reading and writing instruction authored by the aforementioned educator Paulo Freire (1921–1997). Together with ending the PNE, Castelo Branco conducted a witch-hunt against university professors throughout the country. Eight days after the coup, Teixeira was ousted from his post of Dean at the recently founded National University of Brasilia (UNB). The following day, 2,000 troops invaded the University and 223 professors were dismissed from their posts. Teixeira would continue to be persecuted throughout the next few years; he would be found dead under mysterious circumstances in 1971. Freire was immediately arrested in his hometown, Recife, and after being incarcerated for 70 days was sent into exile in Bolivia. The dictators' higher education reform came in 1968 with the *Lei de Reforma Universitária* (Law 5.540/68), which established that university deans would from then on be appointed directly by the government. Departmentalization was emphasized as a means of fragmenting and isolating knowledge. An authoritarian educational model based on technical learning immediately replaced the liberal educational system that had been conceived by Teixeira and Freire. Critical thinking was strongly discouraged and schools were obliged to adopt something closer to a military model of teaching.[42]

Together with the suppression of the academic and intellectual class, the dictatorial government emphasized private education to the detriment of public schools. If in 1965, 53% of higher education institutions were part of the public system, by 1974 that number had decreased to 38%. The consequences of curtailed government funding were even more noticeable in elementary and secondary education. By the end of the dictatorial period, public schools would have lost their former prestige. From the 1980s onwards, middle-class parents started making every possible effort to send their children to private schools. Access to higher education depended more and more on the quality of education that became unavailable in the impoverished public school system. The Law 5.540/68 also promoted social exclusion in higher education by extending its reforms to the university entrance examination system. The so-called *vestibular*, a general term for college admission exams, was established in 1911 by the Law 8.659/11, known as the Reforma Rivadávia Corrêa. The 1911 Law's primary aim was to break the state monopoly and allow for the establishment of private institutions of higher education in the country. The *vestibular* emerged as a way of granting autonomy to these new private institutions in their selection of candidates for admission. The 1968 reform unified the entrance examination system, creating the *Comissão Nacional de Vestibular Unificado* (CONVESU), which prepared exams that tested a unified body of knowledge based on a multi-disciplinary curriculum instead of allowing for the examination of specific areas or disciplines related to a candidate's intended field of study. This put students from the lower social classes at a disadvantage as they now had to compete with economically privileged students who could spend more time and money in preparing for the increasingly demanding exams.

The ossification of higher education and the devaluing of creativity and individuality in the entrance examination system promoted the disturbing situation of weakening Brazilian universities at all levels. The dimension of the problem of access to higher education in Brazil becomes clear when national numbers are compared with those of other Latin American countries. According to data collected by UNESCO, while only 10.8% of the total population reached higher education in Brazil in 1975, in Bolivia that rate was of 12% and in Argentina 26%. By 1985, the rate in Brazil had fallen to 10%, while in Bolivia it had risen to 18.7% and in Argentina to 36.4%. In 2003, the rate in Brazil was 20%, in Colombia 24.3%, in Peru

31.9%, in Uruguay 37.4%, in Bolivia 39.4%, in Venezuela 40.2%, in Chile 42.2%, and in Argentina 59.8%. Note that, in 2003, among Latin American nations only Guyana, at 6.1%, had a lower rate than Brazil. The above figures suggest that something was not right with the Brazilian educational system. Widespread illiteracy was another problem that brought even more out into the open the country's critical social and educational situation. Following the 1964 coup, the military leaders instituted their own literacy program, the MOBRAL, which replaced Paulo Freire's National Program for Literacy that was part of Anísio Teixeira's PNE. The MOBRAL (*Movimento Brasileiro de Alfabetização*) was officially established in 1967, but only started functioning three years later. It attempted to introduce reading, writing, and basic mathematics skills to individuals who were beyond the normal schooling age. Perhaps the foremost difference between the MOBRAL and Paulo Freire's literacy program was that the former did not emphasize individuality, freedom, or creativity. It also established a standardized and nationalistic curriculum based on uniform materials that did not take into consideration the regional and cultural differences between learners. By 1985, when the program was abandoned after the end of dictatorial rule, the MOBRAL had reduced the national rate of illiteracy by only 8.1%. Since its closure, the program has been the subject of a highly contentious, ideologically driven debate. While most left-wing intellectuals portray it as complete failure, rightist analysts tend to point to its good results. The persistently high illiteracy rates registered as late as 1985 do, however, confirm the leftist appraisal. One of the saddest aspects of the MOBRAL story, and this one not necessarily the fault of its military ideologues, is that the program also provided Brazilians with a new concept to employ in their everyday acts of social prejudice, which increased in tandem with the widening of the nation's social gap and income inequality during the 1970s and 1980s. Throughout the time of its operation, the program's acronym became a popular derogatory term used to refer to individuals with little or no formal education. The way in which the very word entered the lexicon of the middle classes suggests that the country's problems of illiteracy and social injustice had deeper, perhaps more psychological roots than is generally recognized.[43]

The arts in the dictatorial period reflected the ideological polarization that took hold of Brazilian society as a whole during those twenty years. In the visual arts, the experimental works of Hélio Oiticica (1937–1980), the engravings of Alex Flemming (b. 1954), and the oil paintings and woodcuts of Antônio Henrique do Amaral (b. 1935) represented a cry for freedom and a reaction against authoritarian rule.[44] In cinema, during the first few years of the period the Cinema Novo managed to continue presenting its allegories of left and right power struggles. Glauber Rocha's *O Dragão da Maldade Contra o Santo Guerreiro* (1968) restated the theme of class conflict in the northeastern outback, creating a sequel to the aforementioned *Deus e o Diabo na Terra do Sol* (1964). Another cinematic allegory of the chaos generated by military dictatorship appeared in Joaquim Pedro de Andrade's (1932–1988) *Macunaíma* (1969), an adaptation of the 1928 homonymous novel by Mário de Andrade (1893–1945), one of the high points of Brazilian Modernism. Nelson Pereira dos Santos's (b. 1928) *Como Era Gostoso o Meu Francês* (1971) is also a noteworthy production from the period. The film is unique in the history of Brazilian cinema for its careful historical reconstruction of the French invasions of the late 1500s and for presenting dialogue in the Tupi language, the lingua franca used throughout Brazil during the colonial era.

As censorship went hand in hand with the dictatorship, much less politically engaged cinema gradually emerged. The government's censorship program was institutionalized through the Law 4.483 of November 16, 1964, which placed special emphasis on films. The Law established the *Serviço de Censura de Diversões Públicas* (SCDP), which was subordinated to the Federal Police Department. Until the publication of the AI-5 on December 13, 1968, the SCDP focused its censorship criteria on issues of morality, especially on scenes containing sex and vulgar language. This allowed for politically charged films such as Arnaldo Jabor's documentary *Opinião Pública* (1967) and Glauber Rocha's *O Dragão da Maldade Contra o Santo Guerreiro* (1968) to reach the public. After the AI-5, however, the SCDP started a crackdown on films with political content and filmmakers were obliged to move in other directions. The establishment of the *Empresa Brasileira de Filmes* (Embrafilme) in 1969 helped the regime to co-opt filmmakers and avoid the presentation of social or political themes on the big screen.

With Embrafilme, directors and producers were catered for with generous funds provided by the company, funds which, ironically, ended up primarily in the pockets of Rio de Janeiro's moviemakers who had been connected with the defiant Cinema Novo movement. This helps explain the Cinema Novo's silence after 1970. Now, with plenty of money in their hands to invest in more mild films, former Cinema Novo avant-gardists turned into politically moderate artists.

While Embrafilme became responsible for organizing and funding the national film production, a system of taxation was imposed on the profits of foreign film distributors, the resources from which were used for financing national cinema. Since political themes were ruled out from the company's production menu, eroticism became the favored subject. With heavily erotic dramas played on screen by popular soap opera celebrities, the Embrafilme managed to attract large audiences to movie theaters while avoiding political polemics.

One of the favored approaches to the new erotic drama genre was the production of screen adaptations of the erotic plays by the aforementioned dramatist Nelson Rodrigues (1912–1980). The approach made sense in terms of a turn towards non-politicized cinema. Rodrigues was known for his conservatism and political support of the military dictatorship, a stance that reflected clearly in his tales, which were marked by a distinctively male point of view. As many as seventeen of Rodrigues's works were turned into film between 1964 and 1985, among them *O Beijo* (1965), by Flávio Tambellini (1925–1976); *A Falecida* (1965), by Leon Hirszman (1937–1987); *Toda Nudez Será Castigada* (1973) and *O Casamento* (1975), by Arnaldo Jabor (b. 1940); *A Dama do Lotação* (1978) and *Os Sete Gatinhos* (1980), by Neville de Almeida (b. 1941); *O Beijo no Asfalto* (1980), by Bruno Barreto (b. 1955); and *Bonitinha mas Ordinária* (1981), *Álbum de Família* (1981), and *Perdoa-me por me Traíres* (1983), by Braz Chediak (b. 1942).

Another important moviemaker that embarked on the erotic drama genre was the São Paulo-born Walter Hugo Khouri (1929–2003). Born to a Lebanese father and an Italian mother, Khouri presented his viewers with a strange form of eroticism full of mixed feelings of love, hate, jealousy, and anger. Among the 26 films that make up his catalog appear *O Anjo da Noite* (1974), *Eros, o deus do amor* (1981), and *Amor Estranho Amor* (1982). Arnaldo Jabor's (b. 1940) *Eu te amo* (1981) and *Eu Sei que Vou Te Amar* (1986) belong to the same category of psychological eroticism. Perhaps one of the most obvious characteristics of the erotic dramas of the 1970s and 1980s was their use of polemics in the treatment of themes such as prostitution, betrayal, machismo, and homosexuality. After watching some of these films, one gets a sense of how strongly conservative Brazilian society's sexual mores were at the time.

Together with erotic dramas, a more open style of soft pornography also flourished. Known by the general term of *pornochanchada*, the genre assumed a clearly commercial, and much less aesthetic, style. The 1970s *pornochanchada* is usually regarded as a development of the earlier erotic industry developed in São Paulo's *Boca do Lixo*, a red-light district in the city's Luz neighborhood. Some of the most successful filmmakers of Embrafilme's erotic drama style started their careers in the *pornochanchada* milieu, as is the case of Carlos Reichenbach (1945–2012) and the aforementioned Walter Hugo Khouri. The first pornographic Brazilian film to reach the country's big screen was *Coisas Eróticas* (1982), directed by Rafaelle Rossi (1938–2007).[45]

Besides the wave of light pornography, elegant literary adaptations also emerged as a new trend in the politically feeble national film production of the 1970s. Works such as *O Meu Pé de Laranja Lima* (1970), based on the 1968 *Bildungsroman* by José Mauro de Vasconcelos (1920–1984) and directed by Aurélio Teixeira (1926–1973), and *Inocência* (1983), based on the 1872 novel by Alfredo d'Escragnolle Taunay (1843–1899) and directed by Walter Lima Junior (b. 1938), are cases in point. One important film from the period is Tizuka Yamazaki's (b. 1940) *Gaijin* (1980), a story centered on the theme of Japanese immigration to Brazil during the early twentieth century. The film tells the story of Japanese and Italian immigrants who upon arriving at a coffee plantation in the countryside of São Paulo learn that the traditional forms of exploitation inherited from centuries of slave labor in the region still continue, and that their own work will be treated according to those patterns of domination. The film is an important example of the growing cultural and artistic contribution of the Japanese diaspora to Brazilian culture in the twentieth century.

The avoidance of political themes by Brazilian filmmakers would come to a halt only in 1982 with the production of Roberto Farias's (b. 1932) *Pra Frente Brasil* (Go Ahead, Brazil). The film became a landmark in the history of Brazilian cinema for being the first work to openly portray political repression during the dictatorial regime. *Pra Frente Brasil* tells the story of an average and politically indifferent middle-class man mistakenly kidnapped by an extremist right-wing group. The protagonist is subjected to repeated sessions of torture from which he attempts to escape. In the end, however, he expires from the severe physical injuries suffered in a setting that looks like the DOI-CODI's headquarters. The SCDP attempted to censor the film; Embrafilme's president, Celso Amorim (b. 1942), was dismissed for having supported the film's production (Amorim would later occupy the post of Foreign Minister from 2011 to 2015). *Pra Frente Brasil* was finally screened in an uncut version in 1983, bringing to the public a fictional story that was extremely close to the real events that all Brazilians knew from their experience of everyday life but that the regime insisted on denying. The protagonist's torturers, for instance, were presented in the film as being financed by a group of wealthy businessmen, forming a clear parallel with the real OBAN; the murder of one of the businessmen in the movie also recalled the real case of the assassination of Henning Albert Boilesen in 1971.

Unlike cinema, theater productions managed to maintain a more defiant attitude towards the dictatorship for a longer period of time. São Paulo's *Teatro de Arena* is a case in point. The company was established in 1953 when theater director José Renato (1926–2011) gathered a group of professional actors interested in producing an original repertory of national works as an alternative to the lavishly produced spectacles of the *Teatro Brasileiro de Comédia* (TBC), founded in 1948.[46] The Arena emerged with a strongly defiant political disposition when Italian-born actor and playwright Gianfrancesco Guarnieri (1934–2006) joined the company in 1958 and debuted his famous play *Eles não usam black-tie* (They Don't Wear Black-Tie). The production was directed by José Renato with Guarnieri in the leading role of a young factory worker who suffers a series of moral compunctions after learning that his girlfriend is pregnant. The protagonist faces a dilemma between joining a strike and remaining faithful to his political beliefs or breaking the same strike and being able to feed his family. The text was adapted for the screen in 1981 by film director Leon Hirszman (1937–1987), again with Guarnieri playing the lead role. Hirszman's film won the Grand Special Jury Prize in the 38th Venice International Film Festival in that same year of 1984. Back in 1958, the play's box office success allowed the Arena Theater to continue producing plays with high political content. From 1964 onwards, the group became a breeding ground for resistance against the dictatorial regime. In 1969, the Arena produced Bertolt Brecht's *The Resistible Rise of Arturo Ui* (1941) under the direction of Augusto Boal (1931–2009), who would later develop the *Theatre of the Oppressed*, a theatrical form that drew on the ideas of educator Paulo Freire. The production of another of Brecht's plays, *Drums in the Night* (1919), lead to a police crackdown on the Theater and to its closure in 1972.[47]

The Arena was by no means the only theater group during the period that attempted to resist dictatorial rule and suffered as a result. São Paulo's Ruth Escobar Theatre also suffered a vicious attack in July 1968 from the extremist right-wing organization *Comando de Caça aos Comunistas* (CCC). The organization emerged around 1963 as a paramilitary group formed mostly by upper-middle-class college students. The CCC attracted members from the universities that tended to favor right-wing ideology, most notably São Paulo's Mackenzie Presbyterian University (established in 1870). The group also included members of the *Opus Dei*, an ultra-conservative Catholic movement of right-wing political orientation founded in Spain in the late 1920s, and with some students from the Pontifical Catholic University of São Paulo (established in 1946). On July 18, 1968, the CCC invaded the Ruth Escobar Theatre and attacked the actors who were staging a play entitled *Roda Viva*. The play was written by Francisco Buarque de Hollanda (b. 1944) and directed by José Celso Martinez Corrêa (b. 1937). It narrated the story of a popular singer who is manipulated by the phonographic industry and suffers the negative effects of the consumer society. After the attack, the military government prohibited the staging of the play. In October 1968, the CCC was involved in what came to be called *Batalha da Maria Antônia*, a series of violent confrontations between leftist students from the University of São Paulo and rightist ones from Mackenzie Presbyterian. During the confrontations, one student was killed with a gunshot to the chest. The CCC launched further attacks in the cities of Porto Alegre and Recife, where they are believed to have murdered Antonio Henrique Pereira Neto (1940–1968), a 28-year-old Catholic priest.

Like theater, popular music also maintained a defiant stance in the face of the dictatorial regime. The *Tropicália*, a movement that emerged in the late 1960s, is a case in point. The movement included art forms such as theater, dance, and poetry, and combined popular and avant-garde elements, thus assuming a marked anti-bourgeois, socially defiant outlook. Popular musicians engaged in Tropicália included Caetano Veloso (b. 1942), Gilberto Gil (b. 1942), and Torquato Neto (1944–1972). The movement revitalized the historical Brazilian avant-garde's notion of antropofagia to suggest the assimilation of foreign influences, such as rock music, in the process of expressing originally national ideas. The 1968 album *Tropicália: ou Panis et Circencis* served as a musical manifesto as well as a direct attack on the regime. The expression *Panis et Circencis* in the title, Latin for "bread and circus," referred to the dictatorship's cultural policies of offering great amounts of light entertainment to the people as a way of keeping them under control. The fifth song on the album, *Parque Industrial* (Industrial Park), a composition by Bahian composer Tom Zé (b. 1936), gave a sharply satirical take on the regime's notion of Brazil as a country on its way to achieving high industrialization and economic development. The song's title came from the 1933 homonymous novel by Patrícia Galvão (1910–1962), a modernist author and Communist Party member who became Oswald de Andrade's (1890–1954) second wife in 1930. Galvão's novel was the first work of proletarian literature in the country's history; its use by the "tropicalists" emerged as another point of defiance with regard to the right-wing dictatorship. In 1969, Veloso and Gil were arrested and forced to seek exile in the United Kingdom, being allowed to return to Brazil only three years later, in 1972.[48]

Another important musician who openly defied the dictatorial regime was samba singer and composer Francisco Buarque de Hollanda (b. 1944).

Born into a family of renowned artists and intellectuals, Hollanda produced a new form of samba music that mixed clever and highly articulated lyrics with a gentle, almost nonchalant type of singing. A few months after the performance of his 1968 play *Roda Viva* was attacked by the right-wing CCC and subsequently banned by the government, Hollanda sought exile in Italy. After his return to the country in 1972, the musician began composing songs that lamented the ongoing political repression while at the same time jeering at the military leaders. His subtle use of language and ingenious employment of mockery managed to deceive the regime's censors most of the time. Hollanda's *Apesar de Você* (In spite of You) became one of the landmarks of artistic resistance to the government's tyranny. The song's lyrics have the form of a missive directed to the military dictators, saying that in spite of them the future still holds the prospect of a better life. In broader terms, Hollanda's elegant and unique style brought another tint of high culture to samba music. The songwriter would assume a very prominent position in Brazilian culture over the following decades, with his works conveying a new depth and elegance to Brazilian music in general.

The emergence of Brazilian jazz is also a noteworthy cultural development of the period. Unlike countries such as France and Japan, for instance, where jazz was already being heard in its original American form as early as the first decades of the twentieth century, in Brazil jazz emerged primarily through a blending with national forms and styles. France had an important early relationship with jazz, which relates to its cultural ties with New Orleans and the Louisiana colony, ties that persisted even after the sale of the 828,000 square-mile territory by Talleyrand to Robert Livingston in 1803. Less than a decade later, American soldiers and musicians introduced the new twentieth-century sound to French audiences during the First World War. Japan, in its turn, took to jazz in the first decades of the twentieth century. The music arrived from the Philippines following the Spanish-American War of 1898, when Filipino musicians who were exposed to the music performed by American soldiers began travelling to Japan. Jazz in Japan further developed in its original American swing form throughout the Taishō Period (1912–1926), though it started being suppressed during the fascist era initiated in the 1930s. Jazz in Japan then experienced a new boost during the American occupation years of 1947–1952.[49]

In Brazil, differently from the French and Japanese cases, a combination of factors led to a more syncretic emergence of jazz. The existence of compatible native forms, such as choro and samba, promoted transculturation. The rise of bossa nova, which became popular among the middle classes and the intellectual milieu, worked to fill the space traditional swing jazz was occupying in other countries in the 1950s and 1960s. These elements made it difficult for jazz to be acculturated among Brazilian musicians. It was thus that while in Europe and Japan big band jazz, and later modern jazz, emerged in the traditional swing style, Brazilian musicians adopted jazz more as an "influence" than as a finished form, blending it with national rhythms and sub-styles.

Another factor to consider with regard to the emergence of jazz in Brazil is the strong musical nationalism prevailing among musicians. Presumably another instance of the strong nationalist feeling characterizing the country's artists and intellectuals since the times of the IHGB, in music indigenous forms and rhythms constantly resurfaced when foreign styles were introduced. Jazz played by Brazilians thus tended to be highly "Brazilianized." American influence became more evident in the works of a few specific artists associated with *samba-canção* and bossa nova. Musicians such as Dick Farney (1921–1987), Johnny Alf (1929–2010), Romeu Silva (1893–1958), Paulo Moura (1932–2010), and Leny Andrade (b. 1943), for instance, borrowed more directly from jazz, but still with a strong emphasis placed on national aesthetic elements. Well into the twenty-first century, being more "Brazilian," that is, playing with a strong Brazilian rhythmic feel and primarily using a national repertoire, would continue to be a highly praised quality among Brazilian jazz musicians. The *transculturation* of jazz, to use Cuban anthropologist Fernando Ortiz's (1881–1969) term, was a phenomenon that clearly distinguished the Brazilian version of jazz from that of other non-American ones.[50]

Under the pressure of such musical nationalism, the emergence of modern jazz, namely bebop and beyond, in Brazil would come only in the 1970s, and this as a result of the work of two outstandingly talented musicians, namely the alto saxophonist Victor Assis Brasil (1945–1981) and the trombonist Raul de Souza (b. 1934). These two performers were probably the first Brazilians to thoroughly master the bebop language on their instruments. Assis Brasil recorded his first album in Brazil in 1966 and in 1969 moved to the United States to study at Berklee College of Music. Raul de Souza's first album appeared in 1965. He moved to the United States around the same time as Assis Brasil. When these musicians came back to their country a few years later, they brought with them something new, that is, a highly developed bebop vocabulary that, when mixed with local rhythms, became the root of Brazilian jazz. One could say that Victor Assis Brasil and Raul de Souza played for jazz in Brazil a similar role to that played by trumpet player Fumio Nanri (1910–1975) and saxophonist Sadao Watanabe (b. 1933) in Japan, that is, they brought the music from abroad and incorporated it into the national musical landscape, although Brazilians did so engaging their country's own native sounds and styles.[51]

Together with Brazilian jazz, the period from 1964 to 1985 also saw the development of a new form of instrumental music that mixed popular and avant-garde elements and would develop in close contact with the national jazz over the coming decades. This new music emerged from the works of two uncommonly talented artists, Egberto Gismonti (b. 1947) and Hermeto Pascoal (b. 1936). Gismonti recorded his first album in 1969 in Paris, where he studied composition and worked with French singer Marie Laforêt (b. 1939). The artist's strongly experimental aesthetic soon began to receive attention from the European music market and from 1977 Gismonti recorded fifteen albums for the Norwegian label ECM.

Pascoal recorded his first album in 1966 with a quartet called Quarteto Novo, formed by bassist Théo de Barros (b. 1943), guitarist Heraldo do Monte (b. 1935), and drummer Airto Moreira (b. 1941). His performance on Miles Davis's *Live-Evil* (1971) brought him immediate attention from the international jazz-fusion market. Together with the aforementioned bebop instrumentalists, Victor Assis Brasil and Raul de Souza, the more experimental avant-gardists, Egberto Gismonti and Hermeto Pascoal, would become the forerunners of a rich contemporary jazz-fusion Brazilian music that, as we will see in more detail in the next chapter, achieved a considerable degree of popularity in the years immediately following the fall of the military dictatorship.

Brazilian classical music also showed important developments during the period, perhaps the most remarkable being the works of composer and conductor Claudio Santoro (1919–1989). Born in the city of Manaus, Santoro was a musical prodigy who played his first concert at the age of twelve. At the age of eighteen, Santoro was already a professor at the National Conservatory of Rio de Janeiro. The musician began studying the compositional methods of Paul Hindemith and Arnold Shoenberg with Hans-Joachim Koellreuter in 1940 and in 1947 received a scholarship from the French government, embarking on a successful career with several international prizes and honors. In 1962, he became the head of the Department of Music at the recently founded University of Brasilia, resigning from his post in 1965 in protest against the purges of the University's faculty enacted by the military government. With the rise of military dictatorship Santoro moved to Europe, where he became a professor of conducting at the National School of Music at Mannheim, in Germany. The composer returned to Brazil only in 1978 to resume his post at the University of Brasilia. Santoro wrote a total of fourteen symphonies and several chamber works. In 1989, he was honored by the Brazilian Senate, which promulgated a law changing the name of the National Theatre of Brasilia to National Theatre Claudio Santoro.[52]

Just as with theater and cinema, literary narrative was also heavily persecuted by the dictatorial regime's fierce censorship. The initial sexually moralizing intent registered during the pre-AI-5 period, that is, from April 1964 to December 1968, also reached the domain of the novel. The cases of the works of two women writers, Cassandra Rios (1932–2002) and Adelaide Carraro (1926–1992), are especially noteworthy. Rios was a best-selling author of erotica who openly approached female homosexuality in popular fictional form. Carraro's eroticism was more conventional than Rios's, but her works also featured prominently on the best-seller lists. Both authors were considered pornographic and their works were ferociously hounded by the military. The dictatorship's political conservatism had a social dimension that translated into vigorous machismo and severe sexual repression. The Manichean moralism of the new military rulers incorporated the same right-wing tendencies and whims whose satisfaction had been the aim of President Jânio Quadros's prohibitions in 1961. Those tendencies had resurfaced in the aforementioned June 1964 "March of the Family with God in the Name of Freedom." Now under military rule, those tendencies re-emerged with a vengeance to crack down on anything that was considered immoral.[53]

As we have mentioned, after the AI-5, sexual content became less of a problem in the eyes of the censors, who started focusing on themes such as urban violence and police brutality. A case in point appears in the short stories of Rubem Fonseca (b. 1925), a former police officer who would become an internationally acclaimed fiction writer. Fonseca depicted the general psychopathy of Brazilian urban life, portraying the new urban centers with all their disorderly growth, wretched class conflicts, and widespread insensitivity. His *Feliz Ano Novo* (1975) was censored by the regime due to its subject matter that included armed robbery, gang rape, marginalization, and crimes of passion. A similar case is that of Dalton Trevisan (b. 1925), who depicted the same sort of dehumanization, now with the city of Curitiba as a background. The city's cold climate and frequently dark, cloudy skies, a result of its high altitude and peculiar topography, allowed Trevisan to establish a new sense of mysteriousness in Brazilian literature.[54] Like Fonseca, his short stories depict the most sordid aspects of their characters' personalities, thus forming an aesthetic that could be seen as recovering some of the naturalist principles of late-nineteenth century writers, such as Aluísio Azevedo, Inglês de Souza, and

Adolfo Caminha. Trevisan's short story collection, *O Vampiro de Curitiba* (1965), brings an obsessive and clearly pathological male sexuality to the fore under the author's characteristically minimalist aesthetic.

Besides Fonseca and Trevisan, the dictatorial period saw the emergence of a rich network of writers of various styles and tendencies. Authors such as Fernando Sabino (1923–2004), Rubem Braga (1913–1990), and Sérgio Sant'Anna (b. 1941) are just a few examples of novelists and short story writers who entered the Brazilian canon under the general term of "contemporary." By 1985, Brazil was turning a new page in its almost 500-year history. That was the year of the publication of *A Polaquinha*, Dalton Trevisan's only novel. The work brought back the strong literary eroticism that had been subjected to censorship since the first years of the dictatorial period. With it, a cycle appears to have been concluded. The novel's title refers to the unnamed protagonist, a young blonde woman, most likely of Polish origin, who becomes a prostitute in the city of Curitiba. The strong wave of Polish immigration to the city makes the protagonist appear an exemplar of the majority of the female population, thus dissolving the character into an archetypal figure. As this blonde, rustic girl is pushed around and humiliated by her numerous male partners, she suffers a series of psychological breakdowns but remains steadfast seeking the possibility of freedom. At that point in the country's history, her freedom seemed to recall the same freedom that all Brazilians hoped they would see, starting in this year of 1985.

CHAPTER SEVEN

THE NEW REPUBLIC (1985–2010)

The period in Brazilian history starting in 1985 is commonly referred to as the New Republic or the Sixth Republic. Historians tend to regard the period of the First Republic as the one beginning with the fall of the monarchy in 1889 and ending with the 1930 Revolution. That period was succeeded by what we have seen as the Vargas Era, which comprised two distinct periods, namely the initial and allegedly democratic one, extending from 1930 to 1937 and considered to be the Second Republic, and the one established with Vargas's coup in 1937 and ending in 1945, that is, the Third Republic. More generally referred to as the *Estado Novo*, the Third Republic thus amounts to the timespan of Vargas's period of official dictatorship. The Fourth Republic would be that of the liberal democracy, which was sustained, albeit with great difficulty, from 1946 to 1964. The Fifth Republic followed this liberal interlude, it amounts to the military dictatorship stretching from 1964 to 1985. The Sixth Republic is thus the one started when the military dictators left the central government and moved back to their headquarters.

Six republics in less than one hundred years can mean nothing other than great political instability. And political instability, as we know, is not good for business. Conversely, the result of protracted bad business was precisely what came to characterize that hope-laden year of 1985. National GDP registered growth of 7.8%, but only at the expense of a 235% inflation rate coupled with an, as usual, astronomical foreign debt.

And more political instability was on its way: presidents who died before taking office; others who were ousted on charges of corruption; playboy vice-presidents and their scandalous girlfriends; terrible privatization deals; venality at all levels. Brazil was stepping out of a dictatorial period to enter a new stage where the State had to be built anew, but the builders were the same old characters. Previous rules no longer applied, but when a new constitution was drafted, the drafters were the same as before.

The new constitution would retain the infamous authoritarianism implied in compulsory voting. The first paragraph of its Article 14 would uphold the onerous obligation that had been in effect since the 1932

Electoral Code. Once again, the State would prevail over the individual. While this meant the tutorship of the State over the political conscience of individuals, compulsory voting satisfied the aims of a professional class of politicians who could gather enough financial resources to influence voters through propaganda and inducements in the mass media. In a country marked by terrible deficits in formal education, compulsory voting would continue to facilitate mass mind control. It would continue to reek of a gift given by politicians to themselves.

Nevertheless, in those first months of 1985, the nation still believed it was entering a new era. It would take some time before it could realize that nothing had actually changed. No effective land reform would ever be enacted; no real wealth distribution would ever take place; the social gap between the rich and the poor would keep widening; populism would continue to prevail; thwarted expectations would repeat themselves to the point where people began expecting to be deceived.

José Sarney and the Cruzado Economic Plan (1985–1990)

On January 15, 1985, the congressional Electoral College selected PMDB leader Tancredo Neves as President. His term in office was supposed to last for six years starting on March 15, 1985. Neves would be the first civilian Head of State since the ousting of João Goulart in 1964. He represented the nation's hopes for change. He also represented an end to suffering for those who had been abused by the cowardly military tyrants. The worn-out nation saw in the old civilian politician a symbol of novelty and reconciliation.

The dignified man who had remained steadfast in his loyalty to Getúlio Vargas and João Goulart, but who, at the same time, had enough prestige as an unwaveringly honest civil servant to avoid being persecuted by the military regime, appeared as a harbinger of peace and understanding in that critical moment of political transition. On March 14, 1985, however, the day before his investiture ceremony, Neves suffered a physical breakdown and was rushed to hospital in Brasilia. There began a national drama of fear and resistance. The entire nation was engulfed in a state of panic, thinking that, if Neves were to die, the dictators might not transfer the presidency to the civilian Vice-President-elect, José Sarney (b. 1930). Neves himself doubted the intentions of President João Figueiredo, and tried to gather forces to attend his own investiture ceremony the following day. He was, however, in a critical condition and unable to attend the ceremony. The media avoided broadcasting the real cause of Neves's hospitalization, a terminal cancer at an advanced stage from which no recovery would be possible. The oath of office thus had to be taken by the Vice President, a situation that enraged the military leaders. President Figueiredo had seen José Sarney move from the PDS who supported the government, to the opposition in a way that seemed surreptitious and self-serving. The old military disciplinarian saw in Sarney the worst of civilian venality and refused to pass the presidential sash to someone he considered unworthy. In the end, Sarney assumed the presidency, but General Figueiredo refused to take part in the ceremony, leaving the presidential palace angrily through a side entrance.

On that day, Brazilians still hoped for the recovery of Tancredo Neves. They prayed to all their Catholic saints and Candomblé *orixás*, lit millions of candles at every possible crossroad, went though sessions of penitence, and made countless religious promises, but their prayers and offers went unheard. On April 21, 1985, Tancredo Neves passed away leaving Brazilians with one more deception to endure. The already battered people had no other choice than to accept and trust someone who they were not sure deserved their trust.

As the weeks went by, Brazilians displayed openheartedness and generosity, showing great willingness to support whatever measures the new civilian President decided to employ in order to set the country straight. And setting the country straight meant, above all, solving the terrible problem of inflation, a plague that corroded the lives of the most vulnerable and widened the appalling social gap that had expanded during those twenty years of military rule.

It was thus that, with full popular support, on March 1, 1986, President José Sarney launched his first economic plan aimed at bringing down inflation and starting a process of economic recovery. The Cruzado Plan was the responsibility of Finance Minister Dilson Funaro (1933–1989) and his economic advisors, who correctly diagnosed inflation as inertial, that is, the result of all prices in the economy being continuously adjusted in relation to a price index. This situation had been created during President Castelo Branco's administration, where, as we have seen, the problem of inflation had been confronted with what was called a "gradualistic" stance, namely one in which price adjustments were officially dictated. Brazilians indeed had had to learn to "live with inflation."[1]

Minister Funaro's measures to reduce inflation, however, were somewhat outlandish. The Finance Minister and his assistants decided to assume a fundamentalist Keynesian attitude and proceeded to a series of heterodox shocks in the economy in order to bring price instability to a halt. Such measures included a radical freeze in prices, exchange rates, and salaries. Since the economy was no longer bound to the former indexation methods, a price table was issued in order to allow for the price adjustment of specific products. The economic situation generated by this was almost surreal. On an everyday basis, Brazilian housewives would go out on the streets carrying the government's "price table" to make sure business owners were not unlawfully raising their prices beyond the government's dictated levels. They became know was the *Fiscais do Sarney* (Sarney's Feminine Inspectors). With such great popular support, inflation rates did plummet quickly and steadily. That notwithstanding, the Plan had a fundamental shortcoming that Minister Funaro and his team tried to hide at all costs: the unavoidable necessity of salary adjustments. They knew that whenever salaries were raised an explosion of consumption would ensue and inflation would be back with a vengeance. Attempting to gain time before that happened, the Plan's creators established the so-called *gatilho salarial* (salary trigger), a legal device establishing that whenever inflation crossed the 20% threshold salaries would be raised automatically and accordingly. But to ensure that salaries were not raised accordingly, however, the government set about manipulating inflation rates.

Through this manipulation, Sarney and Funaro managed to maintain the impression of low inflation for a few months, fooling the entire country into believing that economic stability had finally been achieved. The reason for this maneuver was that general elections were scheduled to take place in the near future, when state governors, senators, and federal deputies would be elected together with the members of the National Constitutive Assembly. The government thus made every effort to maintain the appearance of the Plan's success, which translated directly into unrestricted popular support. As a result of such unabashed act of deceit, the government party, the PMDB, scored a major victory in the November 15, 1986 elections, proving that the whole arrangement had paid off. Six days after the elections, however, no longer able to manipulate the inflation rates, the government decreed the end of the price freeze through the issuing of a new economic plan, the Cruzado II. Inflation was back.[2]

This unseemly event will forever be cited in Brazilian history books as a warning for future generations. Social scientists and economic historians tend to describe the arrangement as a mixture of electoral larceny and bad fiscal and monetary policy. The Plan's lack of any fiscal reform that could restrain government expenditures and curtail aggregate demand resulted in a consumption boom when salaries were adjusted to their correct level while prices were unnaturally being forced down. In the face of the economy's feeble supply capabilities, the whole country experienced severe shortages, including of food and basic necessities. Sarney and

Funaro's Cruzado Plan turned the country's economy upside down, with the only favorable result being the one earned by the government itself, that is, the PMDB's electoral victory in virtually all states.[3]

The Plan's demise meant a first blow to the people's trust, patience, and hopes. More and more, political corruption came to the fore as Brazilians in general developed a deep distrust of the country's civilian political class. Sarney's government's second economic plan, the Cruzado II, was announced by Minister Funaro on November 21, 1985, six days after the polls. Besides the general liberalization of prices, indexation was reinstated. The price adjustment of domestic rents was particularly problematic, and popular protests occurred a few days after the Plan was publicized. The Cruzado I had produced significant trade deficits, and the balance of payments was another problem the government had to deal with. The exchange-rate freeze had kept the currency overvalued, creating a rise in imports and curtailing exports. Foreign reserves reached a critical point in February 1987, and the government announced a moratorium on foreign debt payments. Minister Funaro's position became unsustainable and on April 29, 1987, Luis Carlos Bresser Pereira (b. 1932) was appointed as the new Finance Minister. The "Bresser Plan" was immediately issued. It contained emergency measures aimed at reducing the public deficit and controlling inflation, which was on the rise again. Minister Bresser Pereira was an experienced economist who could have solved some of the most pressing economic issues at the time, but his ideas found no political support, especially for what he suggested in terms of fiscal reform. Inflation just kept rising and 1987 finished with an annual rate of 363%.

In January 1988, a new finance minister, Maílson da Nóbrega (b. 1942), took office. Again, a heterodox package was issued in what was another desperate attempt to control inflation. The fourth and last of President Sarney's economic plans was called *Plano Verão* (Summer Plan); just like the previous ones, it ended in total failure. In 1989, the annual inflation rate reached an astonishing 1,782%. Hyperinflation had set in, and that meant nothing other than economic chaos.

Brazilians were once again faced with nothing to live on but hope. Presidential elections had been scheduled for November 15, 1989. With no expectation that President Sarney's administration could improve the current economic situation, massive optimism was invested in what would be the first direct presidential election since 1960. With the choice of the new president now in the hands of the people, the general idea was that the new democracy could rescue the nation and finally bring the peace and security that had been lost during the last 25 years of authoritarian rule.

But the magic of democracy, as Brazilians would soon understand, depended on a level of citizenship that the country had yet to attain, if it ever could.[4]

The principles of citizenship, however, seemed to be well established in the new Constitution. The Constitutive Assembly elected in 1986 while the government was pretending that inflation was low and that economic prosperity was on its way, certainly had the wherewithall to transform the country into a democratic state based on the rule of law. But in the former Portuguese colony where people were used to laws being made only "to fool the British," the new Constitution's well-wrought principles would end up having little effect.

In that moment of intense political debate, however, the 1988 Constitution appeared to be a source of hope. Although the political force prevailing in the aftermath of the Constitutive Assembly's elections of November 1986 had been primarily the ruling PMDB–PFL, that is, a disguised ensemble of the military dictators' civilian friends, the new Constitution did manage to move away from the excessive conservatism of the dictatorial period and into a more liberal form of state based on the rule of law. Fundamental rights were given considerable importance and mechanisms for the protection of individuals from abuse by the State were clearly established in the fifth Article. Article 37 established an important set of principles that should guide public administration: morality, neutrality, transparency, and efficiency. If correctly observed by public officials, these principles should do away with the old patrimonialism, abuse of power, and influence peddling that had characterized Brazilian governments since colonial times. A general tendency to regard principles as mere ideals, however, would prove that, in spite of the Legislators' understanding of the principles of good government, nothing short of a revolution in mentality could turn Article 37's provisions into anything remotely effective.

Such progressive elements notwithstanding, more conservative positions also succeeded in being included in the legal document. Besides the aforementioned cancer of compulsory voting, land reform appeared particularly problematic in the treatment it was given by Articles 184 through 191. These Articles were written in such abstract terms that they could not be a basis for any real land reform to ever take place. Article 185 determined that productive land would not be expropriated, leaving the definition of "productive land" open. The Article is often seen as a political victory of the *União Democrática Ruralista* (UDR) in the ideological disputes underwriting the Constitutive Assembly of 1987.

The UDR is a group of politicians and legislators established in 1985 to bring together large landowners who expressly reject land reform. The group would become known as *Bancada Ruralista* (Ruralist Contingent), and would acquire enormous political clout starting the years immediately following the promulgation of the Constitution. Members of the UDR have been blamed for numerous episodes of violence in rural areas. The Ruralists' fierce defense of private property tends to provoke constant clashes with the aforementioned Landless Workers' Movement (MST). Unlawful actions by UDR militias resulted in the death of 640 people between 1985 and 1989. Class conflict in rural areas related not only to land reform, but also to environmental issues. The UDR was accused of involvement in the murder of rubber tapper and environmentalist Francisco Alves Mendes Filho (1944–1988), known as Chico Mendes. Mendes had embarked on a public campaign to preserve the rainforest and the rights of peasants and indigenous peoples in the Amazon region. His assassination in December 1988, that is, in the first years of the supposedly new freedom-based historical moment, provoked a national outcry.[5]

Besides the emergence of the rural right-wing UDR, the politics of the Constitutive Assembly of 1987 revealed the alignment of other political forces that would characterize the greater part of the New Republic. Before the Constitution was promulgated on October 5, 1988, an important split occurred in the PMDB, the largest party at the time and the one to which the deceased President Tancredo Neves had belonged. In the 1986 polls, the PMDB had won 53% of the seats in the House of Representatives, as well as 38 of the 49 seats in the Senate and 22 of the 23 state governorships. The split occurred when a group dissatisfied with President Sarney's administration, that is, with, among other things, the "Plano Cruzado" farce, decided to form a new party. Senator Mário Covas (1930–2001), a well-respected politician famous for his unwavering probity as a civil servant, gathered a group of social democrats and established the Brazilian Social Democratic Party (PSDB) in June 1988. Covas had had his political rights suspended in 1969 after the promulgation of the AI-5, the same having happened to his new associates, José Serra (b. 1942) and Artur da Távola (1936–2008). Another member of the PSDB group, Fernando Henrique Cardoso (b. 1931), had gone into exile immediately after the coup of 1964. The mark of anti-dictatorship and political persecution gave the PSDB an initial leftist disposition, which contrasted with the PMDB's increasingly right-wing orientation, expressed in the congregation of conservative politicians in the party's so-called *Centrão* (The Big Center). The PSDB had a social-democratic agenda marked by the defense of the parliamentary system of government and economic policies associated with the Third Way movement. Its center-left positioning in the political spectrum contrasted with the more left-wing posture of the *Partido dos Trabalhadores* (PT), which was launched in 1980 and officially recognized in 1982. Led by Luíz Inácio Lula da Silva (b. 1945), a trade unionist who started his life as a factory worker in the automobile industry, the PT brought together socialists, left-wing intellectuals, artists, and Catholics affiliated with Liberation Theology. Together, the PSDB and the PT would dominate Brazilian politics during the first decade of the twenty-first century, when they would become bitter rivals.

In the upcoming elections to be held on November 15, 1989, however, the strongest parties were the PT and PRN. Under the name *Partido da Reconstrução Nacional*, the PRN represented a right-wing tendency of neoliberal economic orientation. Its leaders were emerging politicians keen to establish themselves in the new political landscape. They were men such as Federal Deputy for the state of Alagoas, Renan Calheiros (b. 1955), telecommunications tycoon from Paraná State, José Carlos Martínez (1948–2003), Minas Gerais Governor, Itamar Franco (1930–2011), and Alagoas State Governor, Fernando Collor de Mello (b. 1949). Initially, the PRN did not seem to be a threat to the larger parties. This, however, was to change.

A total of 22 candidates were officially registered for the upcoming poll in what became a fierce dispute marked by the proliferation of new and diverse political positions and ideologies, most of which had been almost completely suppressed during the previous 20 years of military rule. Since the 1988 Constitution had established the two-round system, the first round scheduled for November 15 was marked by political fragmentation. While the PRN presented Fernando Collor de Mello for President and Itamar Franco for Vice President, the PT presented Luíz Inácio Lula da Silva and socialist Senator José Paulo Bisol (b. 1928) for the same posts. The deceased former President João Goulart's brother-in-law, Leonel Brizola, ran for the PDT; Mário Covas entered the fray for his PSDB; former Governor of São Paulo, Paulo Salim Maluf, ran for the official rightist PDS; Ulisses Guimarães represented the PMDB; private sector CEO Guilherme Afif Domingos represented the PL; and even the Communist Party, the PCB, had its candidate, Federal Deputy Roberto Freire (b. 1942).

The first electoral round featured the first live broadcast of a presidential debate on television. The televised debates would achieve astonishing audience rates, as Brazilians for the first time in 30 years were getting ready to elect a President. Seeing their candidates vying against each other on live TV was a new thrill, and no one wanted to miss it. During the broadcasts, most of the candidates tried to improve their profile by attacking their opponents with insults and jokes. Duels emerged between ideologically opposed candidates, such as Paulo Maluf against Luíz Inácio Lula da Silva, and right-wing Liberal Party Guilherme Afif Domingos against Leonel Brizola. The latter was particularly fond of ridiculing his opponents. Brizola attacked even ideologically compatible rivals. His Riograndense accent and mannerisms also gave him great publicity, especially when he called Luiz Inácio Lula da Silva a "Bearded Toad," Paulo Salim Maluf a "Dictator's Puppy," and Guilherme Afif Domingos a "Political Yuppie." The presidential debates soon turned into media events that appealed to the Brazilian sense of humor.

The newly democratized Brazilians voted with enthusiasm in this overpublicized "first presidential election in 30 years." On November 15, 1989, Fernando Collor de Mello and Luiz Inácio Lula da Silva qualified for the second round, setting in motion an all-out war between the right and the left. The Riograndense Leonel Brizola, who had disparaged Lula da Silva a few days earlier, now expressed his support for the PT candidate. He did so, quoting an old phrase from his fellow Riograndense, Senator Pinheiro Machado, who had once remarked that politics is, to a great extent, the art of "eating toads," that is, being sycophantic. And now Brizola had to eat a bearded one. Since the Gaúcho had no choice but to make every effort to bring the left to power, the First Republic's *caudilho*'s saying seemed apposite.[6]

Although the right's candidate, Fernando Collor de Mello, did not display the same fascist right-wing ideology that had ruled the country during the dictatorial period, his new, neoliberal disposition was still anathema to the left. This was a time when the Soviet Union was about to implode and leftist thinkers and politicians were beginning to experience a crisis of confidence. Fernando Collor represented above all the Washington Consensus's market fundamentalism that was feared and abhorred by men like Leonel Brizola, whose mindset was still positivistic, centralizing, and Riograndense.

Even before the election was finished, however, it was already clear that Brazilians were not yet ready for a leftist government. During the presidential campaigns, the middle classes began to freeze in panic thinking that once in power the communist former factory worker, Lula da Silva, would make the well-to-do bourgeoisie share their houses with the poor. Housewives experienced fear and delusion, abhorring the idea of waking up every morning and sharing their breakfast table with their housemaids. For if Lula da Silva won the poll, they thought, everyone would be equal and the same. Something similar to the 1964 "March of the Family with God in the Name of Freedom" was set in motion, and many middle-class Brazilians lit candles and prayed for Fernando Collor's victory.

That victory came on December 17, 1989, when the handsome forty-year-old politician from Alagoas won the poll with considerable ease against his rival. Collor de Mello secured victories in nineteen States, losing only in seven: Rio Grande do Sul, Santa Catarina, Rio de Janeiro, Bahia, Pernambuco, Rio Grande do Norte, and the Federal District (Brasilia). Although during his campaign the now President-elect had constructed the image of a new type of political figure who was not involved in the old dealings of professional politicians, in truth his election indicated the victory of the traditional political establishment against the more novel forces that were emerging from the left. Collor de Mello was the heir to a tradition of political hardliners who had played an important role in the country's history of authoritarianism. But Brazilians did not care to look back two or three generations in order to decide who to vote for. They did not consider personal heritage or family traditions as possible factors in someone's behavior or political decisions. What is more, their lack of a democratic political culture, which had been demolished during that long period of dictatorship, made them choose whoever fooled them best with effective advertising campaigns, voting being compulsory.

Collor de Melo's electoral victory can also be regarded from the perspective of the left's international discredit after the fall of the Berlin Wall one month before the rightist candidate's triumph in December 1989. The Brazilian Left was shaken by the sudden loss of any esteem for international communism. With the approaching dissolution of the Soviet Union, which would occur in 1991, and the debacle of 1989, national leftists would immediately draw closer to their Latin American counterparts. The main pillar for the construction of an all-Latin American supranational communism would be an anxious Cuba that was in search of a way out of is growing isolation. After an agreement between Lula da Silva and Fidel Castro in July 1990, the defeated Brazilian Worker's Party would promote the so-called São Paulo Forum, the starting point of a leftist international movement aimed at reconstructing in the tropics what was about to crumble in Eastern Europe. The Forum gathered a number of political leaders from several Latin American nations, most of them men and women who in the next decade would rise to power in their countries, promoting the virtual hegemony of the Left in the subcontinent.

The Forum counted with the problematic presence of members of the Revolutionary Armed Forces of Colombia (FARC), which gave it a violent and guerrilla-oriented dimension. It would be the starting point for a confused Latin American leftism emerging in the first decade of the twenty-first century when the interests of the FARC, the Bolivian government under Evo Morales (b. 1959), and international drug trafficking would converge. The forum would also become a stage for anti-U.S. hysteria and general populism, with the idea of Bolivarianism taking hold from the start.[7]

It was thus that in 1990, while the defeated Lula da Silva and the Worker's Party would start looking for allies among the country's neighbors, the new President, Fernando Collor de Melo, would begin a government that looked promising at first, but that in truth was ill-fated, ending up marred by scandal and corruption. This time, however, country was no longer the same as it had been in 1985, when its most immediate aim was to break free from military rule. Brazilians had come a long way in just five years, and now much less tolerance was readily available.

In the eyes of other nations, the democratic elections made Brazil appear as a more reliable political entity, one that no longer held to the obstinately defensive position assumed by the military governments. The country's new image had been carefully constructed throughout President Sarney's five-year term. Brazil had enacted a foreign policy focused on bringing the nation under the regimes of international law. Compliance with the international human rights regime had been announced during President Sarney's opening speech to the 40th session of the United Nations in 1985. Procedures for the signing of treaties such as the International Covenant on Civil and Political Rights of 1966 (ratified in 1992), the United Nations Convention against Torture of 1984 (ratified in 1989), and the International Covenant on Economic, Social and Cultural Rights of 1966 (ratified in 1992) were also announced.

In its attempt to present Brazil as a new supporter of human rights, President Sarney's administration distanced itself from South Africa and its apartheid regime. The defense of Namibian independence brought Brazil closer to West Africa, a region regarded as having fundamental geopolitical importance. In 1986, Brazil pressed for the UN's approval of Resolution 41/11, which created the South Atlantic Peace and Cooperation Zone (ZOPACAS), a regional agreement that made the South Atlantic an area free of the military presence of countries from other regions. The idea of the ZOPACAS found resistance from the United States, but the Brazilian proposal succeeded in the General Assembly. The Resolution

41/11 foreshadowed the Declaration on the Denuclearization of the South Atlantic adopted by the South American states in Brasilia in 1994.

Starting in 1985, Brazil began to emphasize South-South economic relations as a primary aim of its foreign policy. In this regard, cooperation with China was regarded as especially important. In July 1988, President Sarney met with Chinese leader Deng Xiaoping (1904–1997) and signed the first protocol for the development of the China-Brazil Earth Resources Satellites (CBERS), which at the time was the most advanced technological cooperation program ever to have been undertaken between two developing nations.

Still under its South-South banner, President Sarney's government reestablished diplomatic ties with Cuba in 1986 (relations had been stalled since 1964) and signed the Iguaçu Declaration, a protocol on economic integration, together with Argentina's President Raúl Alfonsín (1927–2009). The Declaration became the legal basis for the launching of the Southern Common Market (MERCOSUL) in 1991. The MERCOSUL began as a free trade agreement that aspired to become the foundation for higher levels of economic integration. Its ultimate aim was to establish a political union among Southern Cone nations in a format similar to the European Union.

President Sarney's administration is usually regarded as a transitional period, a bridge between the years of military dictatorship and those of a new era of democracy and the primacy of the rule of law. Historians tend to consider the success of this transition as the President's most important achievement. During José Sarney's government, especially in its early months, people were not certain that military dictatorship had really ended. They feared greatly the return of dictatorial rule. Five years later, the direct election of Sarney's successor proved that the President had brought the democratization process to a satisfactory end.

Fernando Collor de Mello and the Impeachment (1990–1992)

Fernando Collor de Mello (b. 1949) assumed the Brazilian Presidency on March 15, 1990 after an ideologically polarized contest with the Workers' Party leader, Luiz Inácio Lula da Silva (b. 1945). The youngest man to assume the presidency in Brazilian history, Collor de Mello's aristocratic origins and personal elegance sharply contrasted with Lula da Silva's humble background and more popular charisma. The election contest had mirrored two versions of Brazilian society, two facets of the same people who faced each other constantly in everyday life but who could not mingle. Collor de Mello's loftiness, his supercilious and falsely moralizing calls against corruption, made him look like a new type of disciplinarian. This time, however, the discipline would not come from an army general, but from someone whose eloquence was informed by an upbringing and personal taste that the great majority of the population lacked but still admired. The 1989 presidential election made it clear that Brazilians were not ready to see themselves represented by someone with such humble countenance as Luiz Inácio Lula da Silva's: their trust had to be bestowed on someone who seemed to have the higher qualities that they themselves could only aspire to.

If the impoverished majority of the population could not see in the Workers' Party candidate someone whom they could trust and elect as president, this was all the more so among the middle classes. The former factory worker born in the remote drought-ridden lands of Pernambuco State was seen as the type of person middle-class Brazilians were used to having as their gardener or janitor, but not as their president. During the presidential campaign, the press disparaged Lula da Silva as someone whose lack of formal education should prevent him from even aspiring to the post he was seeking. Collor de Mello, on the contrary, was someone Brazilians could look up to. His impassioned speeches against what he called the *marajás*, that is, the civil servants he identified as having the same sort of privileges given to Indian monarchs, gave him an image of probity and dignity. He built the image of a new type of non-professional politician who would put an end to corruption. Brazilians feigned not to know of Collor de Mello's origins in a family of statesmen who were very well established in the country's political history. The new President's father, Arnon Afonso de Farias Mello (1911–1983), was a conservative politician who served under the right-wing UDN as Governor of Alagoas from 1951 to 1956 and then as Senator from 1963 to 1983, this time under the military dictatorship's party, the ARENA. Arnon de Mello, as he was known, was the son of a powerful northeastern landlord who owned two large sugar plantations but who lost his fortune when sugar exports halted during the First World War. The new President's father reshaped the family's wealth by marrying the daughter of powerful Rio Grande do Sul politician Lindolfo Boeckel Collor (1890–1942), a resolute German descendant who served as Minister of Labor in Getúlio Vargas's first administration. After entering a family of politicians and embarking on his own successful political career, Arnon de Mello became famous for committing a terrible crime in the National Congress in 1963, when he shot and killed Senator José Kairala (1924–1963). Kairala received the fatal wound after Arnon de Mello missed his target, the Senator for

Alagoas, Silvestre Péricles de Góis Monteiro (1896–1972). The infamous incident showed the extent to which Brazil was still an oligarchic republic as late as 1963. Given his parliamentary immunity, Arnon de Mello was never prosecuted for his crime.

Fernando Collor de Mello was thus simply not the non-professional politician he claimed to be. Both from his mother's, as well as from his father's side he descended from top-tier political figures. In ideological terms, his politics were, nonetheless, very erratic. The new President had launched his political career in 1979, when he joined the dictatorial regime's ARENA and was appointed mayor in the capital city of Alagoas State, Maceió. Shortly after, he continued a right-wing career, joining the PDS and being elected federal deputy in 1982. With the PDS, he supported Paulo Salim Maluf's candidacy in the indirect presidential elections of 1985. His about-turn came in 1986, when he joined the center-left PMDB, which, given the aforementioned political and economic circumstances, was the only party that could elect him governor in his home Alagoas. After being elected governor, Collor de Mello built his own party, the PRN, under which he ran for president in 1989.

The new President took office with the country experiencing the harshest economic crisis in its history. Inflation had reached an annual rate of 1,782% in 1989. During his investiture ceremony on March 15, 1990, the new President promised a renewed series of price control measures. What no one expected was that the following day such measures would include a severe heterodox shock that would virtually paralyze the entire economy. Through his newly appointed Finance Minister, the São Paulo-born economist Zélia Cardoso de Mello (b. 1953), the President announced the Collor Plan, a recessive economic package that included the immediate freezing of all accounts over 50,000 cruzeiros. This was the second time in Brazilian history when a government seized its people's money in such a direct an unabashed way (that is, counting from the 1821 incident perpetrated by the Braganza King). With inflation still high, Brazilians could not but be shocked at the sudden decree, knowing that their financial assets, even with the government's promise of indexation and eventual repayment, were devaluing every day.

Together with the government's appropriation of the population's financial assets, the Collor Plan introduced a series of neoliberal measures that further punished the country's already shaky economy. The President and his financial advisors were defenders of the market fundamentalism launched in the so-called Washington Consensus. They took very seriously the Consensus's commandment to remove the state from the economy. Fiscal incentives for national industry were at once eliminated, privatizations of public companies were undertaken in haste, and extravagant trade liberalization measures were immediately decreed, provoking a virtual collapse in the country's industry. Annual GDP growth rates fell from a positive 3.1% in 1989 to a negative -4.3% in 1990. With the drastic reduction in money supply, inflation rates initially dropped, but in the face of the radical decline in economic activity re-monetization became an immediate necessity. And when re-monetization came about, inflation returned with a vengeance. The year 1990 finished with a 480.2% inflation rate, which was on its way up to the 1,158% registered in 1991.

With hyperinflation refusing to be tamed, Georgetown University graduate and former Brazilian ambassador to the United States Marcílio Marques Moreira (b. 1931) was called to replace Finance Minister Zélia Cardoso de Mello. Moreira launched another plan, this one called the Marcílio Plan. A less heterodox approach was chosen: high interest rates were combined with a restrictive fiscal policy in the usual monetary austerity program prescribed by the IMF. A US$2 billion loan was secured, allowing for the shoring up of international currency reserves. The Plan's implementation, however, was interrupted with the sudden end of Fernando Collor de Mello's government.

In May 1992, the President's brother, Pedro Collor de Melo (1952–1994), revealed a corruption scheme allegedly taking place in the federal government involving the President and his campaign treasurer, Paulo Cesar Farias (1945–1996). The scheme consisted of widespread bribery and trafficking of influence, where businessmen interested in dealing with the government paid high sums to Farias, who would keep 30% of the negotiated amount and allegedly transfer the remaining 70% directly to the President. The accusations from the President's brother also involved more personal elements, such as drug use and domestic violence. On May 27, 1992, a Parliamentary Committee was formed to investigate if the President had a case to answer on the corruption charges. The country had again been set aflame and street protests against the President took place in the major cities. The National Students Union (UNE) started a movement called *Fora Collor* (Collor Out!) and extensive media coverage turned the House of Representatives into a stage for the country's history-in-the-making. On September 29, 1992, the President's impeachment was voted and approved. Collor de Mello resigned the presidency on the same day. He hoped that by avoiding being formally ousted he would be able to maintain his political rights. The Senate, however, proceeded with the President's prosecution, imposing upon Collor de Mello the penalty of disqualification from holding public office for eight years. In 1994, the Brazilian Supreme Court tried Collor de Mello for the criminal corruption charges connected with Paulo Cesar Farias. A procedural flaw in the police investigations, however, allowed the ex-President's lawyers to have important pieces of evidence that might have led to a prison sentence declared non-admissable. The Brazilian Supreme Court found Collor de Mello not guilty. On June 23, 1996, Paulo Cesar Farias was found dead in his home in Maceió together with his girlfriend, Suzana Marcolino. Both had been shot in what police investigations somewhat hastily concluded to be an act of murder-suicide. Charges of irregularities in the police work abounded in this highly politicized case that received extensive media coverage. Whether or not witness elimination was the purpose behind the couple's "murcer-suicide," after the eight years in which he was prevented from holding public office, in 2006 the former President was back with a public mandate, being elected to the Brazilian Senate representing the state of Alagoas.[8] Here again we can intuit that the Brazilian electoral system, with its reliance on compulsory voting, plays a major role in results from states such as Alagoas, where extremely high rates of poverty and illiteracy facilitates the influencing of voters.

Fernando Collor de Mello's short government, which lasted from March 15, 1990 to October 2, 1992, produced profound changes in the country's economy. Perhaps the most remarkable of such changes had to do with the neoliberal policies championed by the President and his economic advisors. As we have seen, under Collor de Mello, Brazil went through a vast program of economic liberalization. Barriers to foreign trade were virtually eliminated, producing a wave of imports. After the two decades of austere nationalistic development policies imposed by the military governments, the new and sudden market liberalization provoked a wave of consumerist euphoria among Brazilians. The middle classes could now buy those products they had dreamed of in the past but could not afford because of prohibitive import taxes. Now, owning an imported automobile became possible for the emerging bourgeoisie, who sought to enhance social status by increasing consumption. Starting with Collor de Mello's administration, it became a little easier for Brazilians to imitate the patterns of consumption of rich countries.

The President's own personal style encouraged his people's desire for luxury goods. Collor de Mello constructed a public image centered on his youth and personal elegance. He was constantly seen engaging in sporting activities. He jogged, raced cars, and went parachuting. Together with his young and beautiful First Lady, he sometimes allowed himself to be photographed by the paparazzi at the beach, showing off his well-honed body to the amazement and pride of his people. The President's concocted public image also aimed to promote the new Brazilian image abroad. To that purpose, Collor de Mello complied with the international requirements on nuclear policy, putting an end to Brazil's secret attempts to develop an atomic bomb; promoted a rapprochement with equally neoliberal-minded and equally *charmant* Argentinian President Carlos Menem, signing in 1990 the integration pact *Ata de Buenos Aires*; and established new cultural ties with Portuguese-speaking countries with the signature of the Portuguese Language Orthographic Agreement of 1990.[9]

In terms of domestic politics, the story of Collor de Mello's fall holds important similarities to that of the resignation of Jânio Quadros in 1961. Both Presidents assumed office claiming to be non-professional politicians who would do away with corruption. Both emerged from small parties, and were elected mostly on the basis of their personal charisma, rather than on their personal history as public servants. Under these small parties, both Presidents had little political support in the National Congress. The result was that both fell. Considered side-by-side, the stories of the two leaders show that, given the tradition of populism in domestic politics, Brazilian leaders tend to overestimate their personal appeal, forgetting that without a strong party to back them in Congress they become extremely vulnerable.

Itamar Franco and the Plano Real (1992–1994)

Itamar Augusto Franco (1930–2011) was sworn in as Brazil's President on December 29, 1992. Unlike Collor de Mello, Franco started his career in the leftist PTB during Juscelino Kubitschek's administration, moving through the MDB and the PMDB toward the right-wing Liberal Party (PL), which he joined in 1986. Two years later, he formed the PRN together with Collor de Mello, but due to differences over economic policy, he broke with the President and moved back to the PMDB in 1992.

Franco had made his career in the state of Minas Gerais, which he had represented as Federal Senator almost uninterruptedly from 1975 to 1990. Upon assuming the Presidency, he too was faced with a nation in a terrible economic condition. GDP had shrunk by 0.5% in 1992, with an almost surreal inflation rate of 1,158%. And matters were not going to get better any time soon. The economic stagnation of 1992 gave way to a mild GDP recovery, reflected in the 4.9% growth in 1993, but only with an accompanying, and ruthless, 2,780% inflation rate.

The economic downturn stoked a social crisis. Cases of violence spread throughout the country, plaguing the nation with hideous murders and massacres. These started on the very day of the new President's investiture. It seemed that, as Presidents rose and fell, chaos ensued from the sense of political failure.

On October 2, 1992, at the very time Vice President Itamar Franco was assuming the presidency after Collor de Mello had had his presidential mandate suspended by the Congress, a terrible massacre was taking place in the Carandiru Penitentiary, a prison located in the northern part of the city of São Paulo. The massacre started when a division of São Paulo's military police reached the penitentiary building in order to put down a prisoner revolt. The revolt had escalated from a fight between prisoners of rival gangs, both trying to control drug traffic inside the penitentiary. According to the judicial reconstruction of the incident, the fight began at 13h30, when two prisoners were severely wounded. Unable to control the violence, the prison administration requested police intervention at 14h30. The military police arrived at 15h00, receiving authorization to enter the penitentiary complex at 16h15. In the next 30 minutes, 102 prisoners were shot dead, while nine others were stabbed. A further 86 were severely wounded. No police officer was killed. The Governor of São Paulo, Luiz Antônio Fleury Filho (b. 1949), and the Public Safety Secretary, Pedro Franco de Campos, were responsible for ordering the police to storm the facility, but never faced criminal charges. The operation involved 362 policemen commanded by Colonel Ubiratan Guimarães (1943–2006), a hardline police officer who had fought left-wing guerillas during the dictatorial period and defended stricter rules for detainees in penitentiaries. In the aftermath of the massacre, 85 policemen were charged with murdering the prisoners, but only 52 received jail sentences, and that only in 2014. The operation's commanding officer, Colonel Ubiratan Guimarães, was initially sentenced to 632 years in prison, but here again procedural mis-handlings invalidated the sentence. The commander had been wounded and taken to hospital during the initial moments of the police operation, a fact that was accepted by the Court in his defense. In the years following the massacre, Colonel Guimarães appeared as a public hero, receiving substantial media coverage and starting a political career with public safety as his main banner. He was elected State Deputy to São Paulo's House of Representatives in 2002.[10]

The story of the Carandiru Massacre is indicative of the level of brutality to which Brazilian society had sunk in the years following the end of the military regime. The discriminatory treatment of the poor by law enforcement officers recalled the fierce governmental suppression of popular revolts during the colonial period, which, as we have seen, contrasted with the lenience bestowed upon elite groups. The historically discriminatory treatment of the poor led to the coinage of the concept of *social apartheid* to characterize Brazilian society in the 1990s.[11]

The Carandiru prison slaughter of 1992 was not an isolated case. On the night of July 23, 1993, another hideous incident took place in the surroundings of Rio de Janeiro's Candelária Cathedral, where eight homeless children were shot dead by a group of policemen engaged in an unexplained execution operation. Several other street children were severely wounded in the attack. Only two policemen ever received prison sentences and both of them were granted parole after a few months of confinement.[12]

In that same month of July 1993, another massacre occurred in the northern state of Roraima. Here the violence assumed the dimension of genocide as it was directed by a large group of *garimpeiros* (gold miners) against a Yanomami indigenous tribe. The Yanomami are a large group of indigenous people who live in more than 200 villages in the Amazon rainforest near the border with Venezuela. They form a warrior society in which outbursts of violence and inter-village warfare are not uncommon. Anthropologists such as Napoleon Chagnon (b. 1938) and Marvin Harris (1927–2001) have reported that rape and child murder sometimes feature in Yanomami warfare.[13] In a response to pressures from human rights activists, in 1978 the Brazilian military government initiated plans for the demarcation of large tracts of land to be reserved for the Yanomami. The actual demarcation was concluded during Fernando Collor de Mello's administration, but with a new gold rush, which began in the region in 1987, as well as a lack of adequate enforcement to prevent the entry of outsiders into reserved areas, conflict between the indigenous populations and the *garimpeiros* mounted. From 1987 onwards, the murders of individual Yanomami became frequent. Other indigenous tribes were also harassed in different areas of the country in conflicts related to reserve demarcations. In March 1988, the Tikuna tribe was subjected to an attempted genocide when the National Foundation for the Indians (FUNAI, est. 1967) initiated land demarcations in the Amazonas State. Local squatters who disputed the area killed four people, with another nineteen being wounded and ten disappearing in the Solimões River. The Guarani-Kaiowás, an indigenous people that traditionally inhabited parts of Paraguay and the Brazilian Mato Grosso do Sul State were also expelled from their lands. The rise of demarcated reserves in the early 1990s was further complicated by the mounting influence of foreign religious groups working among native Brazilian communities. These groups began fostering nationalistic sentiments among the natives, encouraging them to establish independent political entities in the reserved areas, notably in parts of the Amazon rainforest. Resulting from these conflicting interests with regard to the demarcation of reserves, in July 1993 another massacre took place. The carnage became known as the Haximu Massacre. It involved an attack by gold miners who entered the Yanomami land illegally and executed a group of sixteen native Brazilians, including women and children. The invaders did not leave the area before burning down the entire village.[14]

Clashes between native inhabitants and gold prospectors had proliferated in Brazilian territory since colonial times. This made the Haximu Massacre seem like the product of historical atavism, or perhaps of the country's backwardness and its failure to move on. Together with all of the other cases of harassment of indigenous populations, the Haximu massacre assumed clear historical overtones. It showed that, in many respects, the Brazil of 1993 had changed little from that of the 1500s.

Besides the massacres of Carandiru, Candelária, and Haximu, another slaughter took place in Rio de Janeiro in 1993, again involving police brutality. In an act of retaliation for the killing of four policemen by drug dealers in a Rio de Janeiro shantytown known as Vigario Geral, a death squad of 36 hooded men entered the neighborhood on the night of August 29, 1993, and murdered 21 residents, none of whom had criminal records or any reported involvement with drug trafficking. After the case was investigated, only seven policemen were convicted for the crime and among them only one was still in prison ten years later.[15]

The rise in urban and rural violence in the first half of the 1990s mirrored the virtual failure of the Brazilian State to counter economic and social decline. Together with the political catastrophe of Collor de Mello's impeachment, the economic crisis destroyed Brazilian hopes for peace and prosperity. In a desperate attempt to control hyperinflation, in May 1993 President Itamar Franco transferred the Minister of Foreign Relations, Fernando Henrique Cardoso (b. 1931), to the post of Minister of Finance. Cardoso was a social scientist and co-founder of the Brazilian Social Democracy Party (PSDB), having occupied a seat in the Federal Senate as São Paulo State's representative from 1983 to 1992. He was the fourth politician to assume the Finance Ministry in less than seven months, and he did so with a promise of ending hyperinflation. The new Minister gathered a group of high-profile economists and set about creating a new economic plan. The so-called *Plano Real* was presented to the nation on February 20, 1994. The program was based on a diagnosis of the price instability as a case of inertial inflation, that is, the phenomenon of distortion in price adjustments that follows the employment of an indexation system. As we have seen, the Brazilian currency's indexation structure was implemented in President Castelo Branco's economic program, the PAEG. Over time, the system became disoriented and economic agents began raising their prices before the indexes were stipulated. This was caused by these agents' need to protect themselves from inflation-related monetary losses. The vicious circle of competitive price raises combined with the country's dire structural conditions and accounted for diminished supply capacity and high production costs.

The Plano Real's most immediate goal was to promote the de-indexation of the economy, which was undertaken in three distinct phases. The first phase consisted of structural reforms subsumed under the so-called *Plano de Ação Imediata* (PAI). The PAI program included public expenditure cuts, rises in tax revenue, new banking regulations, and the privatization of public companies. This was intended to leave the government with enough funds to promote a thorough currency reform. The second phase of the plan consisted of the creation of a non-monetary currency that existed in parallel with the actual exchange monetary unit, the cruzeiro. This currency was called *Unidade Real de Valor* (URV) and its value was set at approximately one U.S. dollar. This allowed for prices quoted in URVs to remain stable over time. Once people became accustomed with dealing in URVs, a new currency called the *real* was introduced on July 1, 1994. That was the third part of the *Plano Real*. The new currency was pegged to the U.S. dollar, forming a fixed exchange-rate anchor that pulled prices downwards. In a context where trade barriers had been virtually eliminated (a condition previously imposed upon Brazil when it had contracted Brady Bonds), the currency peg lowered the price of imported goods, obliging national producers to contain their own prices in order to remain competitive in the internal market. This was neoliberalism at its fiercest. Unable to compete with cheaper imports, many national companies went bankrupt. Since the currency peg could only be sustained with high international reserves, interest rates were kept very high, which worked both in attracting foreign capital as well as in discouraging private investment. Overall the entire policy was primarily recessive. The year 1994 ended with a GDP growth of 5.8%, 1995 with 4.2%, and 1996 with 2.6%. Inflation, however, did subside. The 1,093% of 1994 plummeted to 14.7% in 1995, 9.3% in 1996, 7.4% in 1997, and 1.7% in 1998.

Minister of Finance Fernando Henrique Cardoso was the great political winner with the Plano Real. A few weeks after the Plan's launch, Cardoso left the Finance Ministry to run for the presidency in the elections scheduled for October 3, 1994. The Real Plan's execution was entrusted to the new Minister of Finance, Rubens Ricupero (b. 1937), who had been one of the key political figures in implementing the economic plan. The way was now open for Cardoso's rise. The rapid fall in inflation had made him very popular and almost guaranteed his victory in the upcoming poll. In reality, however, the *Paulistano* politician deserved much less of the credit for the Plan's success. Its conception had been the work of experienced economists who did all the work that the public now believed emanated directly from the Finance Minister. Men such as Pérsio Arida (b. 1952), an MIT PhD in Economics, Pedro Malan (b. 1943), a Berkeley PhD in Economics, Edmar Bacha (b. 1942), a Yale PhD in Economics, and Winston Fritsch, a Cambridge University PhD in Economics had been the real minds behind the Real Plan. Fernando Henrique Cardoso, on the other hand, was a University of São Paulo sociologist whose knowledge of Economics was reputed to be limited.

The political profit Cardoso earned from the Plan, that is, by taking for himself the credit for having controlled inflation, was widely criticized by opponents and supporters alike. It was generally believed in the government at the time, however, that the foremost left-wing candidate, the Workers' Party leader Luiz Inácio Lula da Silva, had to be defeated at any cost. The credit for the Plan's economic results was thus given to Cardoso, albeit not without considerable jealousy in various quarters.

With the approaching election, Cardoso's PSDB moved rapidly to the right. A coalition was established with the right-wing PFL, as well as with the PTB, which since the end of the military regime had lacked a strong ideological basis, tending to support anyone who was in power (the PTB would accept the affiliation of ex-president Fernando Collor de Mello in 2007). The left went to the polls divided between the candidacies of Lula da Silva (PT), Leonel Brizola (PDT), and Orestes Quércia (PMDB). Facing a weakened and divided left, Cardoso's was an easy victory. The contest was decided in the first round, and the former Finance Minister won in all states except Rio Grande do Sul. The way was open for a new sort of personality to assume the presidency and begin a process in which the leader's populist attitudes would attempt to present Brazil as an important nation in the international concert of States.

Fernando Henrique Cardoso and the New Price Stability (1995–2002)

Fernando Henrique Cardoso (b. 1931) was sworn in as Brazil's 34th President on January 1, 1995. His administration would be marked by an international financial crisis, a series of controversial privatizations, a sequence of polemical political maneuvers to alter the Constitution and allow for his re-election, energy shortages that left the country in the dark, and, worst of all, a series of humiliations at the hands of leaders of more developed countries.

Cardoso's administration focused on maintaining price stability, a *sine qua non* of his presidency. Price stability, however, and as we all know, cannot be equated with economic prosperity. Large amounts of foreign reserves were spent in maintaining the national currency's overvalued exchange rate, something that prevented the government from using monetary policy to achieve macroeconomic stability. As interest rates were kept very high, private investment was strongly discouraged. In the absence of trade barriers, the overvalued currency ended by destroying large portions of the nation's industry. During Cardoso's government, the country witnessed a string of bankruptcies like nothing it had seen before. Furthermore, unemployment grew 35% between 1995 and 2001.

Cardoso justified his neoliberalism on the basis of an alleged collapse of the ideological frontiers between communism and capitalism, and on the exhaustion of state-led development as an economic model. In his address to the National Congress on December 14, 1994, the President-elect sustained that the years of authoritarianism in the country had come to an end and a new democratic state was emerging from the 1994 elections. The new President associated the end of authoritarianism with an agenda of "modernization," which implied the liberalization of foreign trade and the elimination of restrictions on foreign capital. The main idea behind Cardoso's policy was that *nacional desenvolvimentismo*, that is, the development policies initiated in the Vargas Era, had finally run out of steam and needed to be replaced. The new President's words seemed to suggest that Riograndense Positivism and its republican dictatorial disposition was now finally being substituted by the Paulistano First Republican liberal project, which could now be revived to pick up where it had left off in 1930. Seen under the light of his electoral defeat in Rio Grande do Sul, Cardoso's congressional address suggests that in as late as 1994 the old Rio Grande do Sul-São Paulo opposition still pulsated underneath Brazil's political skin.

In order to do away with what he perceived as the "inheritances" of the Vargas Era, Cardoso began a fierce program of privatization, which was identified as one of the most important parts of a general reform of the State. Cardoso's denationalization of several major public companies was among the most controversial acts of his government. A large privatization program had been initiated during Fernando Collor de Mello's administration under the so-called National Privatization Program (PND), when 68 companies were slated for denationalization, but, of these, only sixteen were actually sold. There were, however, important differences between Collor de Mello's PND and Cardoso's new program. One of them is that Collor de Mello's administration accepted government bonds as currency to pay for privatized companies. This meant that the sale of public property would not finance the government's deficit, but would only purchase back the public debt. And since most of the bonds used in the transactions referred to debts that would not be honored by the government, that is, since the public companies were being exchanged for toxic assets, much of what was privatized during Collor de Mello's administration amounted to a direct transfer of public property into private hands without any direct benefit to the state or the nation.

Cardoso's administration, on the other hand, focused on privatization as a means to finance the public deficit. Preference was given to foreign capital in the purchase of national companies, a strategy intended above all to keep the domestic currency overvalued. The actual sales would be entrusted to the self-regulatory capabilities of the market and special supervision agencies would be created to oversee the functioning of these new, now private, enterprises. The results of the actual sale of the national companies, however, were risible. Several large public enterprises, especially in the energy sector, attracted no interest from private capital. Facing the government from the opposing camp of the old ideological battleground, social movements and political parties protested against the privatization schemes, claiming various irregularities such as bribery and influence peddling. This led to countless judicial processes against the government and its officials. The continuous disputes, accusations, and criminal charges in relation to the privatization procedures of Fernando Henrique Cardoso's government point to the gradual transformation of the former ideological dispute between different governmental and economic models and projects into the simple workings of insidious gang warfare.

As the gangs began taking over the country's government, a new reconfiguration of power emerged around the PSDB and its privatization project. Cardoso bestowed on the creators of the Plano Real leading positions in the government bureaucracy. Pedro Malan was appointed Minister of Finance; José Serra was given the Ministry of Planning; and Persio Arida was presented with the presidency of the Bank of Brazil. The new PSDB hegemony irritated the left, which was growing stronger by the day thanks to the growing popularity of the Workers' Party (PT). The PT elected 50 federal deputies in 1994, 59 in 1998, and 91 in 2002. The absence of agrarian reform continued to be an important argument for the left against the rightist PSDB government.

In 1995, land disputes led to new conflicts and massacres in rural areas. On August 9, sixteen people lost their lives in what became known as the Corumbiara Massacre. The incident occurred when a group of around 600 peasants occupied a rural area in the countryside of the state of Rondônia, close to the border with Bolivia. The Rondônia State police, joined by bodyguards of the region's landowners, attacked the peasants, inflicting beatings and killing twelve people, including an infant. The actual number of casualties, however, appeared to have been much higher than that officially reported; the remains of incinerated human bones found in the area suggested a much larger carnage.

Another massacre occurred in 1996, this time in the municipality of Eldorado dos Carajás, in the state of Pará. Here the state's police troops left nineteen people dead. The landless farmers were demonstrating to demand the federal appropriation of a private estate where the Landless Workers' Movement (MST) had set up a large camp with almost 2,000 families. The government considered the camp to be an invasion of private property. The peasants protested by closing a highway. The confrontation reached its climax when the military police open fire on the protesters.[16]

A similar situation to the Corumbiara and Eldorado dos Carajás massacres occurred in Rio Grande do Sul in 1989. There, another police incursion left nineteen people dead in the municipality of São Gabriel, a small township located near the border with Uruguay and First Republic's President Hermes da Fonseca's birthplace. The slaughter came to be called the Santa Elmira Massacre. It resulted from the occupation of the farms belonging to the powerful local landowner Alfredo William Losco Southall. Southall's estate would again be involved in controversy in 2003 when, after being selected for expropriation in the national land reform program established by the then newly elected President Luiz Inácio Lula da Silva, it was returned to Southall's possession by the ruling of Supreme Federal Court Judge Ellen Gracie Nortfleeth (b. 1948). The judge had made her career in Rio Grande do Sul and had family ties with Southall's wife, Maria da Graça Palmeiro da Fontoura Southall. State Deputy Sérgio Antônio Görgen accused Judge Nortfleeth of impropriety and bias in the case.[17]

Landowners holding a surplus of power thanks to family ties with Supreme Court judges is just part of the problem facing the Brazilian rural structure. Another part of the problem lies in the country's federative organization, where agrarian reform is entrusted to the federal government but the maintenance of public order is assigned to provincial administrations, which tend to reproduce the power structures centered upon the local oligarchies. State governors are elected with the financial support of landowners, that is, with their patronage and blessing. Local members of the judiciary are also appointed according to the interests of the local chieftains. Ultimately, it is the responsibility of local state governors to control local police and military corps, as well as to deal with police brutality. That responsibility, however, soon becomes diluted in a maze of finger pointing and laying blame, with local judicial courts stalling investigations and prosecutions.

The responsibility for the massacres in Corumbiara, Eldorado dos Carajás, and São Gabriel thus became just another dead letter of Brazilian lawlessness. At the time of the incidents, the incumbent state governors were Valdir Raupp (b. 1955) in Rondônia State, Almir Gabriel (1932–2013) in Pará State, and Antônio Britto Filho (b. 1952) in Rio Grande do Sul State. Needless to say, none of these politicians were ever questioned about what became just one more instance of the Brazilian State killing its own people.

By the middle of 1998, President Cardoso's government's popularity was still holding up, thanks largely to continued low inflation. Brazilians were happy with 1997's 7.4% mark and almost burst into fits of joy with 1998's 1.7%, even if GDP remained stagnant, with a miserly 0.1% growth that year. In any case, the control of inflation helped President Cardoso achieve his greatest ambition, re-election. To begin with, of course, re-election was proscribed by the Constitution. But for politicians who never respect any Constitution, or for the country famous for its, again, "law to fool the British," the Constitution did not present a problem: all that the President had to do was change it. And that came about on June 4, 1997, when the Constitutional Amendment 16 was promulgated and it was plain sailing for Cardoso's second term of office. As one might expect, however, the Amendment negotiations were not free of corruption. Even before the amendment was promulgated, two congressmen, Ronivon Santiago (b. 1950) and João Maia (b. 1940), both affiliated with the PFL, were recorded saying that they had been procured to sell their votes for the amendment. President Cardoso defended himself saying that the amendment also favored provincial governors, who could now also be re-elected, and that they were the ones who bought the congressmen's votes. As usual, nothing happened to anyone, that is, no one was charged with anything. And it was thus that on June 4, 1997, Cardoso again posed for the media as the winner in the amendment process.

The re-election amendment provides a useful lesson for understanding how politics functions in Brazil. Since its promulgation in 1997, all presidents have been re-elected at the end of their first mandates: Cardoso in 1998, Luis Inácio Lula da Silva in 2006, and Dilma Rousseff in 2014.

The coincidence with the politics of liberals and conservatives during the Brazilian Empire is, to say the least, amusing. As we have seen, one of the greatest problems with the election system initiated in 1840 was that invariably the party in power managed to win the next election. And that happened because the party in power could control the electoral system. More than 150 years later, things seemed not to have changed much. The incumbents still have an enormous advantage in elections because of their capacity to divert public funds to their campaigns, grant favors to their supporters, influence the media, and exert control over voters, all of this, of course, aided by the hideous effects of the undemocratic compulsory voting.

On that day, June 4, 1997, President Cardoso thus celebrated his victory, earning the right to compete for a second mandate. But not all was favorable for the President. The Asian financial crisis that started in July 1997 set off alarm bells among Brazilian economic administrators. They knew that the artificially overvalued real would be easy prey for speculative attacks, and fear of contagion rose rapidly. The 1994 Mexican crisis and its tequila effect was very much at the forefront of everyone's mind and the dark cloud of sweeping capital flight seemed to be looming on the horizon. Fears of a worldwide economic meltdown were enhanced with the Russian financial crisis that started in August 1998. Presidential elections were scheduled for October 4 of that same year and Cardoso immediately put his intelligence to work to find a way to profit personally from the situation. He soon realized that victory would come easily by threatening Brazilians with the collapse of the Plano Real and the consequent end of the current low inflation paradise if he was not re-elected. Cardoso's campaign for the 1998 presidential run was as undemocratic as it could possibly be. Claiming that he was too busy taking care of the looming financial crisis, the President refused to take part in televised debates with the other candidates. Together with the re-election amendment, the law provided further support for re-election in not requiring incumbent presidents to leave their office in order to start presidential campaigns. Cardoso could thus refuse to engage in a democratic debate with his opponents while at the same time profiting from the exposure received as the incumbent president.

The President's candidacy was supported by a coalition of center-right parties: the PFL, the PPB, and the PTB, together with the major part of the PMDB, supported Cardoso's PSDB. The opposition was divided between Luíz Inácio Lula da Silva's PT and Ciro Gomes's (b. 1957) Partido Popular Socialista (PPS). Gomes had been one of the founding members of the then center-left PSDB, but with the party's shift to the right he had moved to the PPS in 1996. Lula da Silva and Gomes stood no chance in the face of the PSDB's control of the electoral process. Cardoso's was an easy victory in the first round. The President won in all states besides Rio Grande do Sul, Rio de Janeiro, and Ceará.

President Cardoso's second term began in January 1999. His campaign had been based on a narrative that linked economic stability to the maintenance of a steady currency with sturdy purchasing power. In other words, the President's campaign promise was to keep the national currency overvalued and thus sustain low inflation. Brazilians would soon discover, however, that once again the promise would not be honored. The country had fallen again for the same electoral gambit that had been enacted during the Cruzado Plan. A few days after his re-election, Cardoso's economic team altered the country's exchange regime, allowing the currency to float. By March 1999, the real had lost more than half of its value. The artificial overvaluation sustained since 1994 had reached its limit. Continuous trade balance deficits coupled with a capital flight initiated after the Ruble Crisis of 1998 left the government without enough reserves to sustain the currency at its high level. President Cardoso's government had to procure a loan from the IMF, which was signed in December 1998, a few months after the re-election had been secured on October 4. The devaluation of the Brazilian currency irritated the United States, which would have to face losses in trade with Brazil. On the occasion of a meeting of international leaders in Italy in November 1999, President Bill Clinton severely scolded the Brazilian president for the lack of honesty in Brazil's financial system. The Brazilian press did not broadcast Cardoso's shameful lecture from Clinton in that meeting in Florence, called "Seminar on Progressive Governance." Cardoso managed to present himself to his people as a great leader, or as the man who for the first time could win for Brazil a seat at the top table of world leaders. But, in the end, Brazil's attendance at the banquet was an occasion for national humiliation.

Starting in July 1999, Brazil had replaced the fixed exchange rates adopted since the beginning of the Plano Real with an inflation target regime operated by the Brazilian Central Bank. The former exchange-rate anchor was transformed into what was called a monetary anchor, that is, monetary policy was now the sole instrument for keeping inflation down. The target for 1999 was set at 8.0% and the Central Bank's new president, Armínio Fraga (b. 1957), celebrated the 8.9% achieved at the end of that year. In reality, however, inflation had gone from the 1.7% of the previous year to its present level of 8.9%, which was not a small rise. Added to this was the fact that GDP growth had moved from a sorry 0.1% to an equally disappointing 0.8% in the same period. But the economic downturn was not the only example of the Cardoso administration's bad management. In March 1999, the first of a series of major power outages occurred and over the next few years the country would be left in the dark on several occasions. On March 11, 1999, about 70% of Brazil became "powerless" and from July 2001 to February 2002 what Brazilians called *Crise do Apagão* (Blackout Crisis) swept the country, provoking severe economic losses.

In spite of the growing economic difficulties on the domestic front, President Cardoso's administration attempted to present Brazil as a modern emerging economy. The left-wing opposition constantly criticized Cardoso for what they perceived as his excessive use of presidential diplomacy, which comprised a large number of international visits carried out throughout his two terms.[18] Calling his diplomacy "Autonomy by means of Participation," the President attempted to advance Brazil's candidacy for a permanent seat at the UN Security Council. Aware of the country's lack of real influence in international affairs, however, the President insisted on the concept of "soft power" developed by Joseph Nye during the late 1980s. In Cardoso's mind, Brazil could use its "peaceful" history to gain influence in the world. Betting on the strength of non-military power, Cardoso signed the NPT in 1998 and attempted a global projection together with what was termed a "consensual hegemony" in Latin America.

That hegemony, however, was far from consensual. Especially in his first term, Cardoso focused on strengthening alliances with developed countries, an attitude that, again, provoked discomfort among Brazil's neighbors, who, as we have seen, since 1822 feared a sub-imperialist attitude in the former Portuguese colony. In his second term, however, regional conditions forced Cardoso to attempt an improvement in relations with the Southern Cone nations. The Brazilian currency devaluation of 1999 had provoked dangerous imbalances in the region, threatening to put an end to the MERCOSUL. A lack of macroeconomic coordination between Brazil and Argentina led to the latter losing ground in the Brazilian market after Cardoso's currency devaluation. The situation contributed to an economic downturn in Argentina and to the peso crisis of 2000. Argentina became irritated by Brazil's lack of concern with the regional agreements that had been painstakingly weaved together over the past 10 years. In an attempt to appease his neighbors' anger and desire for redress, Cardoso launched the Initiative for the Integration of the Regional Infrastructure of South America (IIRSA), an important structural program destined to promote trade among South American nations. The

MERCOSUL, which had lost much of its relevance after the currency devaluation, would have to be relaunched in 2003, during Luíz Inácio Lula da Silva's government.[19]
By 2002 inflation was again on the rise, with a 12.5% increase against a target of 3.5%. Presidential elections were held on October 6 and the polls showed the Brazilian people's desire for change. The first round led to a run-off between the Workers' Party candidate, Luiz Inácio Lula da Silva, and the Social Democracy Party's leader, José Serra (b. 1942). Marked by fierce ideological polarization, the contest ended on October 27, 2002 with a massive victory for the left. The PT and its leader had finally taken hold of the Planalto Palace in Brasilia. Corruption, violence, and bad administration, however, would not subside.

Luiz Inácio Lula da Silva: Finally the Left (2003–2010)

In 1985, when the nation was coming out of that long period of brutal dictatorship, Brazilians could not possibly imagine that less than twenty years later the union leader who had little formal education and was famous for suffering police persecution during strikes in São Paulo's industrial district would win a huge victory in a presidential campaign against a Cornell University PhD from the center-right. Luiz Inácio Lula da Silva (b. 1945) was an electoral phenomenon. His personal charisma appealed to a new side of Brazilian sensibilities. For the first time, the majority of the people saw that it was possible to have a leader who had a background similar to their own. For the first time Brazilians seemed to be perceiving value and dignity in what they actually were, and to be voting accordingly with a sense of self-esteem.

Lula da Silva was a man with a humble background. The new President had left school as a young boy to work and help his family. He started working as a street vendor at the age of 12; factory work came a few years later. Da Silva joined the labor movement in the early 1970s. During the military regime, he was jailed for organizing strikes. He founded the *Partido dos Trabalhadores* (PT) in February 1980 and in 1986 won a seat as Federal Deputy in the House of Representatives. He came second in the 1989 presidential race against Fernando Collor de Mello, and then again against Fernando Henrique Cardoso in 1994. In 2002, the left-wing candidate's rise was regarded as a threat in right-wing circles worldwide. Fear that, once elected, he would not honor Brazil's sovereign debt commitments grew in Europe and in the United States.

Such fears were not without foundation. Lula da Silva's rise followed that of Hugo Chávez (1954–2013) in Venezuela in 1999, a populist leader with a heavy, if not completely hysterical, anti-American, anti-capitalist, and anti-imperialist discourse. In the next decade, several members of the aforementioned São Paulo Forum would rise to the presidency in Latin American countries: Néstor Kirchner (1950–2010) in Argentina (2003); Nicanor Duarte (b. 1956) in Paraguay (2003); Michelle Bachelet (b. 1951) in Chile (2006); Evo Morales (b. 1959) in Bolivia (2006); Cristina Kirchner (b. 1953) in Argentina (2007); Daniel Ortega (b. 1945) in Nicaragua (2007); Rafael Correa (b. 1963) in Ecuador (2007); and José Alberto Mujica (b. 1935) in Uruguay (2010). All these leaders would, to a greater or lesser extent, repeat Chaves's anti-American and anti-imperialist discourse. Standing center-stage at the São Paulo Forum, they would preach a Latin American integration that would bring autonomy to the region vis-à-vis the United States and world capitalism. They would also create new institutions, such as the UNASUL and the Bank of the South, the latter a regional monetary fund aimed at achieving local independence from the IMF and the World Bank. The Workers Party's new foreign policy would wrest MERCOSUL and the IIRSA from their original liberal economic purpose and put them to work in the service of a new state-led Latin American integration.

Members of the Workers Party such as Celso Amorim (b. 1942) and Marco Aurelio Garcia (b. 1941) would come to the fore to defend the President's new turn away from the United States in foreign policy by citing the 1988 Constitution's Article 4, which urged Latin American integration. With such well-founded justification, Lula da Silva's government would have free rein to implement the São Paulo Forum's accords. The latter's anti-Americanism and anti-liberalism certainly created a sense of unease among foreign investors. To the U.S. government, however, the Forum looked much less threatening. The possibility of Latin America, and even more of South America, coming under the rule of international communism was not seen as much of a threat by the United States even at the height of the cold war, let alone now, when international communism was at a low historical point. Latin American nations had always been economically and militarily weak, and even under the fiercest anti-American communism no threat was likely to emerge from them.

In order to appreciate the U.S. historical perception of Latin American leftism, and thus better understand the empty populism inherent to the Forum's leader's discourse, consider the U.S. policies directed to Asia since the end of the Second World War in comparison to those dispensed to Latin America. U.S. efforts to reconstruct Japan were seen as vital in avoiding the latter's falling under the influence of the USSR, a situation that, had it taken place, might prove disastrous to American security.

Coopting the Japanese to the American side in the context of the cold war represented and enormous burden on the U.S. treasury. Concessions had to be made on various fronts, including the transferring of lavish amounts of public money to the Japanese (under the idea of "reconstruction"), accepting the maintenance of the imperial household (a deal cut with the defeated fascists in order to maintain the symbolic status quo), as well as dispensing a relatively light treatment to war criminals.[20]

Latin America, on the other hand, as we have seen in the past chapters, was easily manipulated and even, when need arose, militarily invaded in order to clean up anti-American tendencies. The region was never of enough interest so as to entail the necessity of economic aid for capitalist consolidation. If over the centuries it had never offered any threat to American hegemony, now its leaders' anachronistic ideologial discourse emanating from the São Paulo Forum was almost laughable.

The Forum's anti-American stance would become an issue to the United States only when its participating leftist governments began to show that some of their interests converged with those of international criminal organizations and with drug trafficking. In order to finance their electoral ascension and state-led corrupt enterprises, not a few of these governments would begin to collude with such organizations, creating a strange mix between terrorism, arms and drug trafficking, and the so-called South-South cooperation. Soon some of these leftist Latin American leaders would begin establishing close ties with men such as Libya's Muammar Gaddafi (1942–2011) and Iran's Mahmoud Ahmadinejad (b. 1956).

In his first year of government, however, and lest foreign investors simply disappear from the country, Lula da Silva needed to present himself in a more politically conciliatory, and less anti-American light. He immediately reaffirmed his intention to continue the policies of the Plano Real and to continue servicing Brazil's sovereign debt. On assuming the Presidency on January 1, 2003, he appointed Henrique Meirelles (b.1945), a PSDB economist, as head of the Brazilian Central Bank. Meirelles was a former CEO of the BankBoston with an MBA from Harvard. His rise to the nation's central financial institution indicated the conciliatory position of the new President.

Reconciliation was also in order with the country's largest communication's network, the Rede Globo. The media conglomerate had held unparalleled power over Brazilian society since its inception in 1965 as a television network owned by media mogul Roberto Marinho (1904–2003). Under the auspices of the military dictatorship, Marinho built his empire, becoming one of the richest and most powerful men in Latin

America during the 1970s. The 1993 British documentary film *Beyond Citizen Kane*, directed by independent filmmaker Simon Hartog (1940–1992), shed light on the extent to which the Brazilian media tycoon held sway over the country's culture, society, and politics during the second half of the twentieth century. The Globo Group prospered through the construction of its image as a corporate heavyweight and the use of continued self-promotional schemes broadcast on their own airwaves. Always right-wing in its leanings, the conglomerate had historically opposed left-wing politicians, although a façade of impartiality was generally maintained. With the end of the military dictatorship, left-wing presidential candidates such as Leonel Brizola and Lula da Silva began opposing the company's hegemony over Brazilian telecommunications. Employing subtle techniques of mass mind control on a large population comprised mostly of illiterate individuals, Rede Globo's power transcended a simple capacity to influence public opinion and reached the level of shaping Brazilians' very notion of reality. Attacked by left-wing politicians, the company fought back. One of the most publicized attempts by the conglomerate to undermine the left emerged in the final moments of the 1989 presidential race, when Rede Globo's vice president, José Bonifácio de Oliveira (b. 1935), deliberately favored Fernando Collor de Mello against Luiz Inácio Lula da Silva in the last televised debate of the campaign.[21]

Since his first presidential candidacy, in 1989, Lula da Silva had spoken of the need to demolish Rede Globo's media hegemony as being a *sine qua non* of democracy in the country. After reaching the presidency, however, the politician and his Workers Party realized that the conglomerate's power was unshakable, and soon conciliatory measures began to be undertaken. In July 2005, Lula da Silva appointed former Rede Globo journalist Hélio Costa (b. 1939) as Minister of Communications. Given Costa's prominent position within the Globo Group, the appointment suggested the intention to develop good relations with the conglomerate. In October 2007, however, President Lula da Silva signed the creation of the *Empresa Brasil de Comunicação* (Brazil Communication Company, EBC), which aimed to provide an alternative to Rede Globo's virtual monopoly of the Brazilian media market. The EBC, however, proved unable to threaten the conglomerate's hegemony.

In his feeble attempt to fight Rede Globo's dominance, the President tried to favor the company's foremost rival, the Rede Record, a media conglomerate controlled by Edir Macedo Bezerra (b. 1945), an evangelical leader and media mogul who founded the Pentecostal Universal Church of the Kingdom of God in Brazil in 1977. Macedo was one of the country's most powerful spokesmen against Rede Globo's hegemony in telecommunications, but the recurrent money laundering, conspiracy, and tax evasion charges against him made it difficult for politicians like Lula da Silva to have him openly as an ally.

President Lula da Silva's weakness in producing any significant reform of the country's media's power structure began to be seen as evidence of personal interests taking precedence over the fulfillment of his populist electoral promises. This view was enhanced by the growing social and political instability during the second year of his term of office. In spite of his unquestioned popularity, allegations of widespread corruption in his government shackled his ability to face down such a powerful adversary as Rede Globo.

Corruption charges against high public officials connected directly to the President came under what was called the *Mensalão* scandal. The term referred to Federal Deputy Roberto Jefferson's (b. 1953) accusation that the President's party, the PT, paid high monthly sums to congressmen in exchange for their voting for legislation favored by the party. The scandal emerged in June 2005 and was heavily publicized by Rede Globo, which began dedicating an increasingly large portion of its evening news program to cover the developments in the case. Rede Globo's sensationalist reports on the *Mensalão* scandal were intensified with the discovery of new cases of bribery in the National Congress involving PT politicians. Talk of presidential impeachment emerged, but with no hard evidence of any involvement by Lula da Silva himself. The government, however, could not prevent an all-out witch-hunt against the PT's high officials. The Finance Minister, Antonio Palocci (b. 1960), was accused of administrative impropriety, but investigations were stalled. Only in 2012 would the Federal Supreme Court rule that PT leaders José Dirceu (b. 1946), José Genoíno (b. 1946), and Delúbio Soares (b. 1955) were guilty of the crime of bribery. Accusations of the President's personal involvement in the *Mensalão* corruption scheme persisted.[22] In 2016, suspicion would emerge suggesting Lula da Silva's involvement in corruption also at the national oil company, Petrobras, from an investigation conducted by the Federal Police and commanded by Brazilian federal judge Sérgio Moro (b. 1972). In July 2017, Lula da Silva would be found guilty and sentenced to nine and a half years in prison by the same judge.[23]

Back in 2005, in spite of the Mensalão corruption scandal, the President's popularity continued to grow among the lower classes as a result of his social policies and programs. In 2003, his first year in office, President Lula da Silva launched the *Fome Zero* (Zero Hunger) program, a cash transfer scheme that attempted to guarantee poor Brazilians the right of access to food. The program's implementation was entrusted to the *Ministério do Desenvolvimento Social e Combate à Fome* (Ministry of Social Development and Fight against Hunger), which was established in January 2004 to oversee the several schemes contained in the program, most notably the *Bolsa Família* (Family Allowance), which helped families out of conditions of extreme poverty. The *Fome Zero* was successful in diminishing Brazil's terrible rates of hunger and misery. The extreme poverty rate fell around 15% during the program's first 5 years and the relative social improvement became noticeable. The program also provided incentives for education. Participation in the cash transfer scheme was contingent on having one's children registered for school attendance. After ten years of the scheme, young Brazilians who would probably never have attended school were entering the job market with a formal education due to the stimulus provided by the *Bolsa Família*. The former reality of domestic servants who moved to the urban centers from rural areas to work in conditions of semi-servitude diminished considerably. With the government's help, the better social standards achieved by the sons and daughters of those former maidservants after formal schooling became a new reality.

Not all, however, was paradise. Income inequality persisted and perhaps the most evident downside of the money transfers is that they did not come from the highest layers of society towards the lowest. They came from the middle. During Lula da Silva's government, while the very poor became a little less miserable, the very rich became much richer. The middle class was the one who lost part of its share in the national income; and a middle class that has to fight for every bit of its share of the national income tends to become very greedy, envious, and dishonest. The Brazilian middle class, with all its bourgeois pretensions of achieving a lifestyle similar to that of economically developed nations, became extremely competitive and frequently resentful of the lower class's economic improvement. Criticism of the *Bolsa Família* program normally came from middle-class individuals, who dismissed it as a populist strategy meant to support the left-wing administration's electoral position.

Be that as it may, the fact is that the poverty rate fell considerably during President Lula da Silva's first term, and that alone might have brought him an easy victory in the upcoming presidential elections on October 1, 2006. Politics, however, does not follow simple logic. The proliferation of corruption scandals coupled with a new rise in violence throughout the country made voters unsure of the PT's real accomplishments.

The increase in violence started in 2005, with cases of political disputes involving murder springing up in both rural and urban areas. The case of Roman Catholic nun Dorothy Mae Stang's (1931–2005) cold-blooded murder in the state of Pará shocked the entire country. The nun worked as an advocate for the rural poor, seeking to protect peasants against abuse from wealthy ranchers. Dorothy Stang was executed, receiving six gunshots, after receiving numerous death threats from loggers and local landowners.[24] Urban violence rates also rose in the period, with an outbreak of terror taking place in São Paulo in 2006. Attacks directed against security forces from a criminal organization called *Primeiro Comando da Capital* (First Command of the Capital, PCC) occurred in May and soon spread to other major cities. The PCC is a large criminal group with more than 10,000 members that emerged from a series of prison riots related to the abovementioned 1992 Carandiru Massacre in São Paulo. The organization was established after a prison fight in São Paulo State's Taubaté Penitentiary in 1993, when the inmates decided to make a pact and create a group to demand improvement in the country's penitentiary system and avenge the death of the 111 prisoners of Carandiru that had occurred the previous year. Through the use of cell phones, which were permitted in prisons until 2009, inmates began establishing connections with criminals on the outside to build a large organization that could act in society at large, rather than just inside the penitentiaries. In 2001, PCC leaders coordinated simultaneous riots in 29 prisons in São Paulo State. An alliance with another criminal organization acting in Rio de Janeiro, the *Commando Vermelho* (Red Command), was established the same year. The Red Command dated back to the 1970s, when left-wing political prisoners and regular criminals began conspiring inside prisons to rebel against the military dictatorship. The cooperation between men convicted for drug dealing and political prisoners made drug trafficking emerge as a source of finance for leftist gerrilas. From the 1980s onwards, the Red Command became responsible for a large part of the arms and drug trafficking in Rio de Janeiro. By the early years of the decade of 2000, it would be suspected of having direct connections with the PT and with the São Paulo Forum, which further suggested an interconnection between the FARC, drug trafficking in Colombia and Brazil, and emerging Latin American leftist politicians.

Coupled with the PCC, the Red Command now began to spread violence throughout a great part of the country. Terrorism emerged in São Paulo on the night of May 12, 2006, spreading to other state capitals in the days that followed. Initially, the acts of violence were directed primarily against law enforcement officers, but civilian casualties rose as the terror progressed. Official reports counted 128 dead and 59 wounded in the clashes occurring between Friday, May 12 and Wednesday, May 17 in the states of São Paulo, Minas Gerais, Bahia, Mato Grosso do Sul, and Paraná. More recent studies conducted by Rio de Janeiro State University (UERJ) sociologist Jose Ignacio Cano, however, point to 569 dead, of which 59 were police officers and 505 civilians. The number of 110 wounded adds to the count.[25]

The widespread violence posed a serious difficulty for President Lula da Silva's 2006 presidential campaign. As time progressed, his poll rating, that had been 51% at the start of the year, continued to fall. As the bouts of violence increased in the city of São Paulo, however, the situation began to have a more ambiguous effect on the President's popularity. Since São Paulo's governor at the time was precisely the opposition's strongest candidate, the PSDB's Geraldo Alckmin (b. 1952), voters could not decide who was to blame for the chaos, the President or the Governor. In any case, the proliferation of scandals related to the PT's administration since 2003 continued to weaken Lula da Silva's re-election campaign. Together with the Mensalão Scandal, other corruption schemes involving PT officials came to the fore. The Bingos Scandal, the Post-Office Scandal, the Dossiê Scandal, and the Ambulances Scandal pointed, if nothing else, to the President's lack of control over his party members' "avidity." Added to this was the fact that the powerful Rede Globo television network was adopting an increasingly biased attitude against the President's re-election, using its news programs to expose the most negative aspects of the PT administration. Attacks from the network against what was portrayed as the President's lack of personal refinement proliferated. The First Lady's decision to acquire Italian citizenship for herself and her children during this time was also not helpful to her husband's popularity. The case was ridiculed by the yellow press, which publicized that when asked why she had decided to request Italian citizenship for herself and her family, the First Lady, Marisa Letícia Lula da Silva (b. 1950), would have replied "because I want to give a better future to my children." Many commentators pointed out that, with the prospect of future corruption charges against her husband, Italian citizenship might indeed prove to be very useful.

Besides the jokes at the expense of the First Lady's and her untimely decision to settle her citizenship matters, another problem in the President's campaign was Lula da Silva's refusal to take part in televised debates during the first round of the campaign. This anti-democratic attitude was the same as that of his predecessor, Fernando Henrique Cardoso. The irony, however, was that the absence of Lula da Silva from the televised debates badly affected his public image. Analysts suggest that the absence of the President from the debates contributed to his failure to be elected in the first round. His victory in the second round, however, was an easy one, with 60% of the votes in his favor.

President Lula da Silva's second term would be marked by a series of bad political choices, persisting corruption scandals, an international economic crisis that put the brakes on national economic growth, all compounded by terrible mistakes in foreign policy. In 2007, the government launched the *Programa de Aceleração do Crescimento* (Growth Acceleration Program, PAC), a large infrastructure program consisting of financial policies and investment projects aimed at boosting economic growth. Several sectors were selected to receive massive government investments, such as energy, sanitation, transportation, and logistics. The program included important subprojects, such as the *PAC das Crianças* (PAC for the Children), which brought investments to fight child abuse and promote social integration, and the *PAC das Cidades Históricas* (PAC for Historical Cities), which dedicated funds for the preservation of the nation's artistic and cultural heritage in historical sites. Together with the PAC, the government launched the *Plano de Desenvolvimento da Educação* (Plan for the Development of Education, PDE), which established projects for the expansion of the public education system such as the *Plano de Reestruturação e Expansão das Universidades Federais* (Plan for the Restructuring and Expansion of Federal Universities, REUNI).

During the last four years of President Lula da Silva's term, the PAC generated great controversy, especially with regard to financial irregularities in the execution of the infrastructure projects and in relation to the low completion rate of such projects. In 2012, the *Tribunal de Contas da União* (Court of Audit of the Union, TCU), an independent court established in 1890 by the then Minister of Finance Rui Barbosa (1849–1923) to oversee executive action, revealed that, out of the more than 13,000 governmental projects included in the PAC, less than 3,000 had actually been completed by the end of President Luiz Inácio Lula da Silva's government in 2010. The President was also accused of using the PAC's public works to promote the presidential campaign of his successor, Dilma Rousseff (b. 1947), who, as Chief of Staff during the President's administration, was frequently featured together with Lula da Silva at events that celebrated the launching of PAC public works.[26]

In spite of all the controversy, President Lula da Silva's government ended with positive results in terms of economic growth. In 2002, the last year of President Cardoso's administration, Brazil had figured as the world's 13th largest economy; by 2010, the last year of President Lula da Silva's administration, it had risen to 7th place. One of the most consistent indicators of the country's new financial solidity was its capacity to recover rapidly from the world financial crisis experienced in 2008. During the crisis, the Brazilian Central Bank assumed a Keynesian stance and expanded the monetary base with a concurrent expansionary fiscal policy. The economy did go into recession in 2009, but by 2010 it was growing again, recording 7.5% GDP growth for the year.

Another noteworthy aspect of Lula da Silva's economic policies relates to the Brazilian position with the IMF. Historically, the PT had demonized the financial institution as one of the clearest embodiments of North Atlantic capitalist domination. Initially, Lula da Silva honored the commitments to the Fund that had been assumed during Cardoso's administration. Starting in 2005, however, the President began to indicate his intention not to renew the contracts still in effect with the institution. At the end of that year, the government's objective of disentangling the Brazilian economy from the Fund became clear with the advance repayment of roughly US$ 15 billion in special drawing rights (SDR) relative to previous loans. The government insisted on the necessity of expanding the country's autonomy with regard to the Fund, an autonomy that it said would increase international trust and lower the nation's risk classification. The repayment was made possible by the rise in international reserves accumulated over the previous years, and in January 2006 the President addressed the nation to say that Brazil had paid its debt to the IMF. This new narrative was cleverly constructed to obscure in the people's minds the difference between the two notions of "debt with the IMF" and "foreign debt." It was thus that from 2006 onwards many Brazilians started thinking that their country had miraculously become a creditor in the world.

From 2008, President Lula da Silva's economic team started a new strategy in relation to the IMF and Brazil began requesting a reform of the Fund's governance that would allow emerging nations more decision-making power. The demand was linked to other requests, such as those related to the UN Security Council and to the WTO. The campaign for these reforms comprised an important part of the new Brazilian profile in foreign relations. With the emergence of the BRICS concept and the exaggerated international attention given to the emerging economies, which in the case of Brazil spawned a series of economic prophecies of future greatness, Lula da Silva appeared to have started believing that his country was actually rising to a prominent position in the international system. Together with the President, Brazilian officials started overestimating their country's power. Ridiculous as it may seem, they started suggesting that Brazil could contribute to solving the Middle East crisis, bringing an end to the suspicions regarding the Iranian nuclear program. Lula da Silva started a rapprochement with Iranian president, Mahmoud Ahmadinejad, and the two leaders exchanged visits in 2009 and 2010. The rapprochement, however, hid more complex aims and interests emanating from the São Paulo Forum and its declared goal of advancing an anti-capitalist, and anti-United States, stance internationally. Iran was seen as an ally in that crusade.

Another, more psychological factor, seemed also to be at play in the rapprochement between Lula da Silva and Ahmadinejad. After being treated with derision by the Brazilian press throughout most of his political life, Lula da Silva seemed to believe that he was finally proving his capacity to bring his country to a more autonomous and sovereign position in the international arena than had been the case with his more formally educated predecessor. The truth, however, was that neither Luiz Inácio Lula da Silva nor Fernando Henrique Cardoso reached anything like the heights they believed they had on the world stage. They were not, and would never be, the world-class statesmen of their dreams. Looking at Cardoso's pathetic debacle with Bill Clinton in Italy in 1999, and then at Lula da Silva's now shameful attempt at international self-promotion with Ahmadinejad in 2010, one had to agree with the international analysts who felt that Brazil should take care of its own domestic problems and leave international security affairs to the big players.[27]

President Lula da Silva's government ended with the best outcome he could possibly have expected, namely the electoral victory of his political protégée, Dilma Rousseff. The daughter of a prosperous Bulgarian businessman who arrived in Brazil in the late 1930s, Rousseff was raised in an upper-middle-class household in Minas Gerais. Following the 1964 coup, she joined a leftist urban guerrilla group to fight against the military dictatorship. She was eventually captured and taken to São Paulo's OBAN in 1970, where she was reportedly tortured at the hands of detective Fleury and his men. After being jailed for two years, Rousseff moved to Porto Alegre, Rio Grande do Sul's capital, where she received a degree in Economics from the local university and began a political career in Leonel Brizola's PDT. In 1993, Rousseff became Secretary of Energy to Rio Grande do Sul State in the PDT administration of Governor Alceu Collares (b. 1927). Rousseff's politics thus had their roots in the breeding ground of Brazilian dictatorship, that is, in the home of hardline politicians such as Deodoro da Fonseca, Júlio de Castilhos, Hermes da Fonseca, José Gomes Pinheiro Machado, Getúlio Vargas, João Goulart, Emílio

Garrastazu Médici, Artur da Costa e Silva, Ernesto Geisel, Golbery do Couto e Silva, Leonel Brizola, Lindolfo Collor, and many others. Starting in 2010, it would not be difficult to perceive the old Riograndense political clout working behind the female President's hardline position.

The 2010 presidential elections presented the novelty of not having Luiz Inácio Lula da Silva as candidate. Since 1989, the leader of the PT had competed in all the polls. The election's first round took place on October 8, 2010, with the two great rivals, the PT and the PSDB, the left and the right, qualifying for the second round. Ideological polarization was, as usual, strong. Brazilians had not understood that the difference between the left and the right in their country was practically irrelevant. They had not grasped the fact that what moves Brazilian politicians above all is their desire to perpetuate themselves in power, and that ideological allegiances are unstable and feeble. The old saying remained valid: in Brazil, there is nothing that resembles a conservative more than a liberal in power.

In the second round of the 2010 presidential elections, Dilma Rousseff faced José Serra, who had served as São Paulo's governor from January 2007 to April 2010. Rousseff won with 56% of the vote. The PT should have at least eight more years ahead of itself to try to govern the unruly former Portuguese colony.

Culture and Society in the New Republic

The end of the military regime in 1985 marked the beginning of a new political, commercial, and cultural openness to the outside world in Brazil. The previous twenty years of dictatorial rule had been carried out under heavy economic protectionism and with nationalist policies hindering the country's direct contact and exchange with other societies and cultures. Those years of autarchic development had left the nation backward, with technology and industrial output lagging behind that of modern societies. In 1985, Brazilians new that their country was part of the so-called "Third World," and they were eager to leave that stigma behind.

The process of re-democratization meant the beginning of a gradual movement towards cultural exchange and internationalism. Brazilian culture had for a long time been introspective and endogenic. Since the rise of the avant-garde, or what was called *Modernismo*, in the early 1920s, the idea of "Brazilianness" and the search for a national identity had taken hold of the country's artistic output. As we have seen, the *Antropofagia* movement proposed the absorption of foreign influences only as a means of creating something new and national: the foreign had to be "deglutinated," that is, destroyed, and only then could something new emerge. The contrast with other Latin American nations such as Chile and Argentina, for instance, where European movements such as Surrealism and Existentialism were integrated into the national literary and artistic landscape, is remarkable.

After the heyday of the avant-garde in the 1920s, cultural and artistic nationalism would continue to be hegemonic. The Vargas Era saw the emergence of nationalist classical music in the works of composer Heitor Villa-Lobos and of regionalist literature in the novels of José Américo de Almeida and José Lins do Rego. Brazil itself was always the preferred theme in the arts. The Liberal Republic of 1946–1964 showed a mild attempt at cultural cosmopolitanism, especially in music, with the rise of bossa nova and the acceptance of a limited influence of jazz. In cinema, however, the emergence of the Cinema Novo movement in the late 1950s showed that the search for a national expression was still the primary driving force operating underneath the Brazilian artistic mind. The question of "what is Brazil?" prevailed inside anything that could be construed as artistic innovation and experimentation. Subsequently, the military regime's isolation and entrenched recourse to state terror prevented Brazilian art from reaching for the universal, except in the case of psychological eroticism and soft pornography in cinema, although even then the mores portrayed and discussed were clearly national. In the 1970s, the Tropicalia Movement and the Marxist-oriented theater of Augusto Boal emerged with their focus on present social reality and criticism, confirming the national experience as the preferred underlying theme in the arts.

The year 1985 marked an important break with nationalism, one that, while not everlasting, ushered in a moment of freshness and openness to foreign culture. The sudden end of cultural isolation allowed Brazilian artists to move away from aesthetic autarchy and be influenced by international trends and styles. The exchange with foreign artists allowed for new techniques to be incorporated into the various artistic fields and helped Brazilians to move towards more universal forms of expression. Three large arts festivals launched between 1985 and 1987 advanced this new stance of openness and exchange, namely the Rock in Rio, the Free Jazz Festival, and the Carlton Dance Festival.

Rock in Rio was a remarkable event that showcased several superstars of commercial music during ten days in January 1985. The event was devised and produced by marketing and advertising executive Roberto Medina (b. 1949), who built what was called the "City of Rock" in Rio de Janeiro, a large facility that hosted 1,380,000 people over the course of those ten days. It was the first time a music concert of that magnitude had taken place in South America. The Rock in Rio line-up included bands and solo artists such as Queen, James Taylor, George Benson, Rod Stewart, Yes, Ozzy Osbourne, and Iron Maiden. The all-night concerts were balanced with up-and-coming Brazilian rock-pop groups such as Paralamas do Sucesso, Blitz, Kid Abelha, and Barão Vermelho. The Festival opened a new venue for Brazilian commercial music. It became a recurring event, spreading to Lisbon and Madrid in 2004, and reaching the United States in 2015.

Better quality music, and more refined overall tastes, were also favored in that year of 1985 with the launching of the Free Jazz Festival. This event was the brainchild of producer Monique Gardenberg (b. 1958), who became a pioneer in Brazil in combining cultural products with merchandising techniques. Gardenberg brought together the image of jazz and that of a new cigarette brand called "Free." The "Free Jazz Festival" was born. The cigarette brand belonged to the tobacco company Souza Cruz, a subsidiary of British American Tobacco. Souza Cruz's marketing executives liked Gardenberg's idea of advertising through a cultural product, and besides the jazz festival the brand also promoted the Carlton Dance Festival starting in 1987. The jazz festival was held sixteen times from 1985 to 2001, with each guest artist performing both in Rio de Janeiro and São Paulo. After the Brazilian government's prohibition of tobacco advertising in the country, Gardenberg found a new sponsor in a mobile phone company, and the Free Jazz Festival became the Tim Jazz Festival. A few years later, it would become the BMW Jazz Festival, and then the Brazil Jazz Fest.

The Free Jazz Festival's first staging in 1985 brought to the stages of Rio de Janeiro's Hotel Nacional Theater and São Paulo's Maksoud Plaza Hotel Theater outstanding jazz musicians such as Bobby McFerrin (b. 1950), Chet Baker (1929–1988), Joe Pass (1929–1994), McCoy Tyner (b. 1938), Pat Metheny (b. 1954), Sonny Rollins (b. 1930), and many others. On the Brazilian side, musicians such as Egberto Gismonti (b. 1947), Hélio Delmiro (b. 1947), Luiz Eça (1936–1992), Ricardo Silveira (b. 1956), Paulo Moura (1932–2010), and Márcio Montarroyos (1948–2007) were featured. Musical collaboration between Brazilian and American artists was an important part of the Festival. In its first edition, the most memorable case of this artistic exchange came in Chet Baker's concert, where the legendary trumpet player had two Brazilian musicians in his band, pianist Rique Pantoja (b. 1955) and bassist Sizão Machado (b. 1956). Baker and Pantoja had started collaboration back in 1980, when they recorded the album *Chet Baker and the Boto Brasilian Quartet*

(Dreyfus Jazz/Sony Music). The Boto Quartet was led by drummer José Bôto (b. 1945), who started playing with Pantoja at Berklee College of Music, where both musicians studied in the late 1970s. The 1980 album with Chet Baker featured six songs composed by Pantoja. Baker tended to favor the Flugelhorn in recordings with the Brazilian musicians, achieving a quiet lyricism throughout. Some critics defined the album as too "easy listening," but after the Free Jazz Festival concert in Brazil a second album, titled *Rique Pantoja & Chet Baker* (WEA/Musiquim), recorded in 1987, became a Brazilian jazz classic.

The Free Jazz Festival was not free from Brazilian cultural nationalism and its attempts at promoting a national aesthetic identity. Most Brazilian musicians, especially horn players, could not demonstrate the same level of virtuosity as the Americans. This tended to establish a barrier between what was termed *Música Instrumental Brasileira* (Brazilian Instrumental Music) and jazz. As the word "jazz" implied the idea of virtuosity, Brazilian musicians who could not display a sufficient level of technical proficiency preferred to stay within the more secure realm of what was conceived as Brazilian Instrumental Music. As mentioned above, the notion of "Brazilianness" was construed as a positive quality among Brazilian instrumentalists. Some of the established players even criticized younger musicians who studied, or wanted to study, at Berklee College of Music in Boston. Their claim was that after studying at Berklee, musicians started playing the same musical patterns, all sounding alike, and also that they tended to lose the "roots" of Brazilian music. The attitude of those who could not boast a Berklee pedigree ranged from mild jealousy to outright hatred. In any case, over the years, the Free Jazz Festival assumed the dimension of an important transnational encounter, fostering understanding and friendship between Brazilian and American artists. The results were very positive. The Festival figures as a great cultural achievement and deserves to be further studied from the point of view of transculturation, cultural diplomacy, and general musicology.

Another cultural enterprise that was successfully developed by the talented Monique Gardenberg was the Carlton Dance Festival. With its first staging in 1987, the Festival brought to Brazil some of the world's leading artists and companies, such as the Americans Martha Graham (1894–1991) and Merce Cunningham (1919–2009), the Israeli Batsheva Dance Company (est. 1964), the Dutch Nederlands Dans Theater (est. 1959), the Japanese Sankai Juku (est. 1975), and the Canadian La La La Human Steps (est. 1980). Among the Brazilian companies featured in the Festival over the years were Ballet do Terceiro Mundo (est. 1980), Victor Navarro Dance Company (est. 1982), Deborah Colker Company (est.

1994), and Grupo Marzipan (est. 1982). The Carlton Dance Festival obviously had a more international scope than the Free Jazz, which was more limited to artists from Brazil and the United States. The Dance Festival lasted from 1987 to 1997 and fostered the internationalization of Brazilian dance. In 2013, Gardenberg signed a sponsorship contract with a large Brazilian cosmetics company to start a new dance festival to replace the Carlton, which had been absent from the country's stages for more than ten years. In the second decade of the twenty-first century, Gardenberg remains one of Brazil's most successful arts producers. She is also a successful theater and film director. Among many notable works, her staging of the play *The Seven Streams of the River Ota*, by Canadian writer Robert Lepage (b. 1957), in 2002, was especially well received by critics.

While Gardenberg provided Brazil with a clearly liberal and cosmopolitan perspective on the arts after the end of the military dictatorship in 1985, the same was not the case with all artists and producers. The case of cinema presented an exception to the sudden rise in artistic cosmopolitanism. On the big screen a national orientation continued to prevail in place of the more outward-looking tendencies seen in music and dance. Productions that centered on social reality and views of the nation still dominated throughout the late 1980s and 1990s.

The years immediately following the end of the dictatorial period were marked by the foreign debt crisis that started in 1982, and economic restraints curtailed the national movie industry's output. The few films produced in those years maintained the national or regionalist themes of the previous decades. *A marvada Carne* (1985), by André Klotzel (b. 1954), *O Beijo da Mulher-Aranha* (1985), by Héctor Babenco (b. 1946), *Avaeté, Semente da Vingança* (1985), by Zelito Viana (b. 1938), *Com licença, eu vou à luta* (1986), by Lui Farias (b. 1958), *Vera* (1987), by Sérgio Toledo Segall (b. 1956), *Feliz Ano Velho* (Happy Old Year, 1987), by Roberto Gervitz (b. 1957), *Ele, o boto* (1987), by Walter Lima Jr. (b. 1938), *Luzia Homem* (1987), by Fábio Barreto (b. 1957), and *Kuarup* (1989), by Ruy Guerra (b. 1931) are cases in point. *A Marvada Carne* (The Evil Flesh) told the story of a naïve country girl and her desire to get married; *O Beijo da Mulher-Aranha* (Kiss of the Spider Woman) was based on the homonymous novel by Argentine author Manuel Puig (1932–1990), it narrated the relationship between a political prisoner and a homosexual, both of whom shared a prison cell during the dictatorial period; *Avaeté, Semente da Vingança* (Avaete, Seed of Revenge), told the story of the terrible massacre of the Cinta-Larga indigenous tribe by gold diggers in Mato Grosso State in 1963; *Com licença, eu vou à luta* (Excuse me, I Need to Move Ahead) brought to the screen a tale of teenage angst in a proletarian setting in Rio de Janeiro; *Vera* questioned the efficacy of the national juvenile prison system through adaptation for the screen of the true story of a transsexual youth who was sponsored in a public job by the then State Deputy Eduardo Suplicy (b. 1941) and who ended up committing suicide; *Feliz Ano Velho* was a screen adaptation of the homonymous biographical novel by Marcelo Rubens Paiva (b. 1959), the son of the of Federal Deputy Rubens Beyrodt Paiva (1929–1971), who was executed by the military regime in 1971; *Ele, o boto* (The Dolphin), narrated a legend from the Amazon in which a mythical Amazon River Dolphin comes out of the water at night to seduce young peasant women; *Luzia Homem* was a screen adaptation of the homonymous 1903 naturalist novel by Domingos Olímpio (1851–1906), which tells the story of a woman in the backlands of impoverished Ceará State who attempts to avenge the murder of her parents; *Kuarup* was the screen adaptation of the novel by Antônio Carlos Callado (1917–1997), which told the story of a missionary who lived in the Xingu region (Mato Grosso State) and opposed the military dictatorship. Virtually all these films followed the realist tendency based on national themes and social motifs characteristic of the previous decade. The tendency culminated with *Sargento Getúlio* (1983), by Hermanno Penna (b. 1945), a screen adaptation of the homonymous and also regionalist novel by João Ubaldo Ribeiro (1941–2014).

A work from the New Republic's initial period that is especially worth mentioning is *Um trem para as estrelas* (Subway to the Stars, 1987), by Carlos Diegues (b. 1940). The film tells the story of a young saxophone player from a suburban area of Rio de Janeiro who moves through the city at night trying to find his missing girlfriend. The story is beautifully told by Diegues, who was one of the founders of Brazil's Cinema Novo. The film starts with the protagonist practicing Charlie Parker's solo from *Ornithology* and mentioning his dream of becoming a great musician. He does so looking at the picture of his deceased father on the wall, who was also a saxophone player. The story is very much of a piece with jazz's emerging popularity in the country at that time, boosted, as we have seen, by Gardenberg's festivals which started in 1985. Gilberto Gil (b. 1942) composed the film's music score, which included lush saxophone solos by Zé Luis Oliveira (b. 1957).

With the emergence of Fernando Collor de Mello's government in 1990, the national film industry virtually collapsed, along with several other sectors of the country's productive chain. Deprived of funding from 1990 to 1994, Brazilian cinema plummeted into what is considered the deepest crisis in its history. Very few films were delivered in the period. Worth noting is *A Grande Arte* (High Art), by Walter Salles Jr. (b. 1956), possibly the only significant film produced in 1991, and maybe during the entire four-year period of the Collor/Franco administration. The work consisted of a screen adaptation of the homonymous novel by Rubem Fonseca (b. 1925), telling the story of an American photographer in Rio de Janeiro who gets involved with members of an underworld criminal group. Salles belonged to a wealthy family of bankers and his financial influence is frequently mentioned to explain the production of this film, which is spoken in English. *Vagas para Moças de Fino Trato* (Room for Elegant and Refined Ladies, 1993), by Paulo Thiago (b. 1945), a much lower-budget production, is another of the few films produced duting that period. It brought to the screen a drama about a middle-aged woman who rents rooms in her apartment to two younger women and attempts to establish a motherly relationship with them. The film reflects the reality of urbanizing Brazil, with its mores and human needs.

In 1992, President Itamar Franco appointed Antônio Houaiss (1915–1999), a prestigious philologist and diplomat, as Minister of Culture. Houaiss understood the need to promote national cinema through the creation of new legislation, and in 1993 the Law 8.685/93, known as *Lei do Audiovisual*, was promulgated, conferring tax exemptions on individuals and companies investing in national film production. The Audiovisual Law followed the principles of the previous Law 8.313/91, known as *Lei Rouanet*, which had established the same form of fiscal incentive to multiple areas of the so-called national "cultural expression." Since the Rouanet Law did not discriminate among art forms, it ended up including gospel music, fashion shows, and circus. The obvious criticism was that the Law should promote art, and not just "everything." Another criticism was that it transferred to private companies the decisions over what type of "cultural products" to incentivize, resulting in famous popular singers receiving the larger portion of available public funds. While the Rouanet Law had proved to be little more than a missed opportunity to advance the Brazilian arts, the Audiovisual Law has done better for the country's film industry since its publication in 1993.

The film *Carlota Joaquina, Princesa do Brasil* (1995), by Carla Camurati (b. 1960), is generally regarded as one of the works that "relaunched" Brazilian cinema after the drought that started in 1990. Camurati was a versatile actress who appeared successfully in a range of productions, from erotic films to TV dramas. She had become especially famous after posing nude for Playboy Magazine in 1982 and then starting a career as film director. Her *Carlota Joaquina* was a mocking historical piece that looked with irony at the transfer of the Portuguese Court to Rio de Janeiro in 1808.[28] Together with Camurati's piece, Fábio Barreto's (b. 1957) *O Quatrilho* was another important film released in 1995. Barreto came from a family of filmmakers that included his father, Luiz Carlos Barreto (b. 1928), and his brother, Bruno Barreto (b. 1955). *O Quatrilho* was also regionalist in outlook, it told the story of a colony of Italian immigrants in Rio Grande do Sul in the early 1910s. The same sort of regionalism was seen in Barreto's earlier work, *Índia, a Filha do Sol* (1982), a film that narrated a love story between a young native Brazilian woman and a white man amid the violence triggered by the gold rush in the Amazon River basin. In 1996, Walter Salles Jr.'s *Terra Estrangeira*, a black and white film funded by the city of Rio de Janeiro, gave new strength to this resurrection of national cinema. The film narrated the story of a trumpet player who decided to move to Europe after being deprived of his funds when President Collor de Mello froze all bank deposits in the country in 1990. One of the film's merits lies in its approach to then very up-to-date theme of Brazilian emigration. The film's music by José Wisnik (b. 1948) is particularly remarkable. In 1997, *O Que É Isso, Companheiro?* (Four Days in September), by Bruno Barreto (b. 1955), brought another true story to the screen, this time that of the 1969 kidnapping of the American Ambassador to Brazil, Charles Burke Elbrick (1908–1983). In 1998, another film by Walter Salles Jr., this one a Franco-Brazilian production, once again brought a social realist story to the screen: *Central do Brasil* (Central Station). The film's beautifully conceived narrative, with its sincere approach to pressing themes such as poverty, illiteracy, and regional disparities made it especially meaningful in terms of consciousness raising and social criticism.

The greater part of the Brazilian film production from 1985 to 1998 was made of realist works that looked to the country's social and economic situation as a source of audiovisual narratives. Regional legends, folk tales, and historical settings were part of the "Brazilianness" favored by filmmakers. This emphasis on the national precluded the emergence of works with more universalizing aesthetics and themes. The country had difficulty in producing generic variety in its cinematic output and although several high-quality films were released, overall diversity was lacking. Such prevailing social realism in the 1985–1998 years had a few noteworthy exceptions. Perhaps the most remarkable ones were José Antônio Garcia (1955–2005) and Ícaro Martins's (b. 1954) *Estrela Nua* (1985) and Guilherme de Almeida Prado's (b. 1954) *A Dama do Cine Shangai* (1987). *Estrela Nua* (Naked Star) starts with a dream sequence in which a nude woman is lying on a beach where she starts bleeding and appears to be in agony. The sequence ends when the main character wakes up having fallen asleep reading a novel by Clarice Lispector (1920–1977). The sequence sets the tone for the psychological narrative that follows. *Estrela Nua* was the last of a series of erotic films by Garcia and Martins that included *O Olho Mágico do Amor* (1981) and *Onda Nova* (1983), films that presented a large number of lesbian scenes featuring Carla Camurati in the leading role. After *Estrela Nua*, Garcia moved on to an individual career as a film director and into more overt engagements with Clarice Lispector's literary works. His film *O Corpo* (1991), as well as his staging of Lispector's only extant play, *A Pecadora Queimada e os Anjos Harmoniosos* (1948), are examples of such engagement. If *Estrela Nua* represented a fresh break with the nationalist-regionalist thematic hegemony of the period by presenting a psychological narrative with more universalizing overtones, *A Dama do Cine Shangai* (1987) brought a new film noir aesthetic to the screen, producing another break with the prevailing tendencies. The film is a mystery drama in which a man is enticed into investigating a murder case by a beautiful woman he meets in a movie theater.[29]

The years 1997 and 2001 marked two important developments in the Brazilian film industry and in its legal underpinnings. The creation of Globo Filmes in 1997 and of the *Agência Nacional do Cinema* (Ancine) in 2001 transformed the Brazilian movie industry, providing it with new funding opportunities and fostering aesthetic dynamism. Globo Filmes, as the name suggests, is closely connected to the communications conglomerate, Rede Globo. As should be expected, the influence on Brazilian cinema exerted by Globo Filmes is not without controversy. The company faces much criticism for having established a monopoly over the production and distribution of national films. Globo Filmes allegedly takes advantage of the economic and political clout of its mother company, the Rede Globo, as well as of the laws that provide fiscal incentives to cinema, in order to monopolize the market.

According to the Audiovisual Law of 1993, in order to be eligible to receive funds from the tax exemption scheme, the producer must be "independent," that is, a legal entity that has no direct legal relation with mass communication enterprises. In Brazil, mass communication enterprises have the legal status of concessionaries of public services. This makes Rede Globo and Globo Filmes ineligible to receive funding directly from the scheme in order to finance their productions. The conglomerate can, however, invest in the projects of independent companies by using the Law's tax exemption system. Given its massive financial resources, which translate into large sums applicable through the Law's scheme and channeled to its chosen productions, Rede Globo, and consequently Globo Filmes, end up gaining control over the production of its "independent" associates. The market has grown accustomed to the enterprise's clout. Ironically, among insiders to the sector the term "independent" began to be reserved only for those films and filmmakers who are not financed by Globo Filmes. Besides all the comings and goings with the gaps in the Audiovisual Law, Globo Filmes has been criticized for exercising a monopolistic stance in the market by effectively controlling several of the links in the chain of a film's production. Using the extended reach of its mass telecommunications parent company, it can influence a film's advertising campaign by bringing actors and directors into its high-audience TV talk shows, thus providing them with important media exposure that in turn can be charged back on to "independent" partners as advertising air time.[30]

Monopolistic behavior could be investigated and perhaps prevented by the Agência Nacional do Cinema (Ancine), a federal regulatory agency established in 2001 under President Fernando Henrique Cardoso's privatization program.[31] The agency's main purpose was to foster, regulate, and supervise the national film industry. Filmmakers criticize the body for its severe bureaucratization of film production, which slows and at times even prevents the conclusion of projects from small and independent producers. In terms of its regulating capabilities, the Ancine seems to be ineffective with regard to complaints about Globo Filmes's alleged monopoly of the national film industry. The fact remains that between 1997 and 2007 Globo Filmes's portfolio contained 90% of the most successful films in the country. Its expensive productions, or rather, the productions of its "independent" partners, tend to feature the same actors and directors that become popular celebrities through the Rede Globo's television soap operas. Criticism of Globo Filmes/Rede Globo's supremacy in the industry also refers to the commercial aesthetic favored by its productions. The case of Globo Filmes's support through public funding schemes of works such as *Cazuza, O Tempo Não Pára* (Cazuza, Time Doesn't Stop, 2004), *2 Filhos de Francisco* (Two Sons of Francisco, 2005), and *Antônia* (2006), films centered upon mass cultural products, shows that the strategic promotion of art films is being thwarted in favor of commercial success and financial gain. The fiscal incentive scheme provided by the Audiovisual Law should follow the obvious logic that less commercial artworks, which generally have a higher need for financial support, should be the ones favored. The abovementioned three films provide sorry examples of how art is downplayed in the entire process. The film *2 Filhos de Francisco* is especially noteworthy. The movie became Brazil's biggest box office hit in twenty years by telling the story of two country singers who are not only alive and millionaires, but who also produce a type of country music with an American influence that is not at all rooted in any Brazilian tradition. The case is perhaps even worse with *Antônia*, which more than a musical film seems to be a promotional piece for an Afro-Brazilian hip-hop girl group. The promotion of low quality music through the film industry, as is also the case with *Cazuza, O Tempo Não Pára*, thwarts the educationally and culturally enhancing aims of the public funding apparatus. The claim is that all this lack of greater control over content is excused by the demands of "democracy," or perhaps of "cultural democracy."

A few examples of meaningful works that have emerged from the duo Globo Filmes/Audiovisual Law are Fernando Meirelles's (b. 1955) *Cidade de Deus* (City of God, 2002), Héctor Babenco's (b. 1946) *Carandiru* (2003), and Vicente Amorim's (b. 1966) *Corações Sujos* (Dirty Hearts, 2011). Nevertheless, projects that do not receive Globo Filmes's favor tend to face extreme difficulty in reaching a larger public. This is the case of fine works such as Cláudio Assis's (b. 1959) *Amarelo Manga* (Yellow Mango, 2002), Gustavo Pizzi's (b. 1977) *Riscado* (Craft, 2010), Kleber Mendonça Filho's (b. 1968) *O Som ao Redor* (Neighboring Sounds, 2012), and many others.

For better or worse, after the inception of the Audiovisual Law in 1993, and of Globo Filmes in 1997, Brazilian cinema experienced a boom. Among films that were not produced or distributed by Globo Filmes but that were commercially and artistically successful are *Villa-Lobos, Uma vida de paixão* (Villa-Lobos, A Life of Passion, 2000), by Zelito Viana (b. 1938), *Bufo & Spallanzani* (2001), by Flávio Tambellini (b. 1952), *Tropa de Elite* (Elite Squad, 2007), by José Padilha (b. 1967), and *Bruna Surfistinha* (2011), by Marcus Baldini (b. 1974). *Villa-Lobos* (2000) narrates the life of the classical composer through a well-researched and musically rich perspective. *Bufo & Spallanzani* (2001) is a film noir based on the 1986 novel by Rubem Fonseca (b. 1925). The film is outstanding in its capacity to bring an example of the country's finest literature to the screen with considerable originality. *Tropa de Elite* (2007) is a realistic account of the life of a member of the *Batalhão de Operações Policiais Especiais* (BOPE), the special police operations squad of Rio de Janeiro's Military Police. Mixing social realism and psychological investigation, the film offered a clear picture of Brazilian reality in areas dominated by drug trafficking. *Bruna Surfistinha* is a well-directed movie based on the autobiography of Raquel Pacheco (b. 1984), a former prostitute who left the profession to get married to a client. Pacheco's book is part of what could be called "call-girl confessionary," a popular literary genre emerging in several countries from former prostitutes who profit in the book market by sharing their experiences with readers.[32] Marcus Baldini's film is handsomely conceived and executed. It approaches the theme of prostitution from the perspective of loneliness and tenderness, questioning important aspects of human interaction and psychological alienation. More importantly, it provided a view of how Brazilians can sometimes unearth gentleness and kindness in the harshest conditions.

One noticeable aspect of the new Brazilian cinema emerging after the crisis of the early 1990s is the continuity of the same narrative realism and national subject matter that prevailed during the 1985–1990 years. Following the same tendency verified in the previous period, after 1990 one still notices the scarcity of experimental works that transcend the narration of mere factual reality and move into a more universalizing aesthetic. The prevailing social realism appears to reflect a commercial attitude assumed by filmmakers. The works of director Arnaldo Jabor (b. 1940) provide a case in point. The filmmaker's transition from adaptations of playwright Nelson Rodrigues's profoundly intricate dramas in *Toda nudez será castigada* (1973) and *O casamento* (1976), or from psychologically complex original screenplays such as *Eu te amo* (1981) and *Eu sei que vou te amar* (1986), into a commercial production full of hackneyed sentimentality such as *A Suprema Felicidade* (The Supreme Happiness, 2010) reflects the decline in subject matter and creative capacity marking the commercial boom that started in 1997. Another example of this decline appears in the work of filmmaker Walter Lima Júnior (b. 1938), who went from beautifully composed and culturally insightful works such as *Inocência* (1983) and *Ele, o boto* (1987) to a high-cost commercial blunder such as *Os Desafinados* (2008). In the same vein, film director Ana Carolina (b. 1943) went from the deep existential inquiries of *Das Tripas Coração* (1982) and *Sonho de Valsa* (1987) to *A Primeira Missa* (2014), a metanarrativistic historical comedy that demands that the viewer "reflect upon Brazil" in a way that is superficial and aesthetically uninteresting.

Several factors are at play in the aesthetic decline seen in the work of such notable filmmakers. Undoubtedly, the banalization of sexuality characteristic of contemporary society precludes the former aestheticized eroticism found in the films of artists such as Walter Hugo Khouri, Arnaldo Jabor, Ana Carolina, Ruy Guerra, and Neville d'Almeida, works where jealousy and betrayal played an important function within the general psychology of erotic dramatization. But even if the former psychological investigations of love and sexual desire no longer seem possible, new forms of introspectiveness, thematic depth, and narrative originality should still be. The excessive commercialism of post-1997 Brazilian cinema seems to be the element that is hindering more creative output. Such commercialism translates above all in the employment of soap opera TV celebrities in expensive movie productions, which tend to result in shoddy sentimentalism and histrionics.

Brazilian cinema provides a good vantage point to observe important aspects of the process of political and economic liberalization that started in 1985. The strange mixture of nationalism and the desire to emulate the lifestyles of more economically developed societies taking hold of the Brazilian middle classes after the end of the dictatorial period appears nowhere more clearly than in the very business of national cinema. Filmmakers and public alike crave big productions in a Hollywood style, but they want it translated into what is familiar and confortable. The goal seems to be that of creating luxury dreams that are maintained close enough to the national reality lest they begin appearing too unattainable. When the filmmaker's disposition is leftist, however, the illusion of luxury turns into nationalist expressions of debased and backward mass culture. Looking at the big picture, the ghost of being part of the developing world has obviously not disappeared. The story of Brazilian film shows that emerging economies, which in previous decades were part of the so-called "Third World," will keep striving to look like the rich ones. The vocabulary changes, but the dreams remain the same.

Conclusion

Brazil after 2010

Just like any other country, Brazil is a product of its history. In the preceding pages, we have looked into some of the most basic aspects of Brazilian history, drawing attention to important developments that took place in culture, society, and politics throughout the centuries. Our narrative was presented in chronological order and our end point is 2010. Looking at what, in that year, amounts to a 510-year history, we find the nation full of imbalances, social problems, and terrible injustices that we probably already expected to find at the beginning of our story. But perhaps now we can understand the sources of those imbalances, social problems, and terrible injustices somewhat more clearly.

Brazil is a nation that has lived through a constant and indefatigable search for development. The word has several meanings and all of them point to distinct forms of scarcity. Economic development is the general term that includes human, social, educational, moral, technological, individual, political, cultural, artistic, and many other forms of development. However, in Brazil, economic development is frequently understood in terms of only a few of its many aspects. This allows government officials and state bureaucrats to promote selected forms of development to the detriment of others, thus producing further imbalances. Furthermore, the excessive power held by Brazilian government officials and state bureaucrats, illustrating how the State is too large and overbearing, also hinders overall development. The paradox is that the bureaucrats who are responsible for advancement are the ones who hinder it the most.

Throughout this book I have suggested that Brazilian growth has been hobbled by the excessive authoritarianism inherited atavistically from the Portuguese colonial bureaucratic apparatus. I have also suggested that such authoritarianism was boosted by an inordinate military power concentrated in Rio Grande do Sul, where the adoption of a republican dictatorial ideology imposed authoritarianism at the national level. My analysis concluded that an imbalance between economic backwardness and military clout led the southernmost province to rise and virtually take control of the entire nation throughout most of the twentieth century. This analysis will probably not be found in the average Brazilian history book; my hope is that future researchers will consider it and study the subject further.

The role of Rio Grande do Sul's military and political power in the construction of the Brazilian State translates into the authoritarianism that, as was suggested, hinders development. And one of the most preposterous faces of such authoritarianism, I argued, is compulsory voting. Under an electoral system plagued by authoritarianism and compulsion, the word "democracy" becomes a weak and empty concept.

Another aspect of the Brazilian administrative arrangement that prevents the possibility of effective democracy is the virtual monopoly on the media entrusted to a single corporation, namely Rede Globo. Throughout the decades, nothing has been done, and probably never will be, to change this situation.

Again, Brazil is the product of its history. And in 2010 the terrible results of Brazilian history could be easily seen in a comparison with other countries. Looking at numbers from the United Nations Development Program's (UNDP) Human Development Index (HDI), in 2010 Brazil occupied a mere 11th position among Latin American nations. In the world ranking for that year, Brazil was number 73rd (0.699) while Chile was 45th (0.783) and Argentina 46th (0.775). In 2012, Brazil had fallen to 85th in the world (0.735), while Chile and Argentina had risen to 40th (0.819) and 45th (0.811), respectively.

Regional disparities were especially problematic to Brazilian development. The South and Southwest continued to figure way ahead of the other regions. In 2010, no state from the North or Northeast figured among the ten highest Brazilian states in IDH (measured as City Development Index, CDI). Even within regions and states, development was unequal. In the South, the capital cities of Paraná and Rio Grande do Sul, Curitiba and Porto Alegre, respectively, showed remarkable differences. While both cities had similar populations, Curitiba with 1,746,896 residents and Porto Alegre with 1,409,939, in 2010 Curitiba figured as the 10th highest IDH in the country (0.823), while Porto Alegre was 28th (0.805). In 2013, Curitiba had maintained its 10th position while Porto Alegre had fallen to 33rd.

Among Brazilian cities, São Paulo continued its leadership as the country's financial and intellectual center. From a population of 8,587,665 in 1980, the city grew to 11,253,503 in 2010, in a country that in that year reached 190,755,799 residents. In 2015, São Paulo figured as the 10th highest GDP city in the world (using purchasing power parity). The city's initial industrial character, developed during the First Republic (1889–

1930), has been replaced by an economy based on the tertiary sector. The focus on services and businesses makes São Paulo the economic motor of Brazil. The city is also the political center of the nation.

In 2013, São Paulo became the initial stage for a series of protests against the rise in public transportation fares. The demonstrations spread throughout the country, threatening the stability of President Dilma Rousseff's government and giving rise to what some analysts called a "Brazilian Spring." In 2015, São Paulo saw the birth of another political movement, this one part of a more organized intent called *Movimento Vem pra Rua* (Come to the Streets Movement). The *Vem pra Rua* was started by a man named Rogério Chequer (b. 1968) who, through the use of social media such as twitter and facebook, created a mass movement of protest against the government. On March 15, 2015, the movement attracted around 2 million people onto the streets in 252 cities across the country in what qualified as the largest protest in the nation's history. The Movement's demands ranged from the end of corruption to the impeachment of President Rousseff. The ruling party, the PT, denounced the movement as part of a rightist strategy to disrupt the government. It was revealed that Chequer was involved in businesses in the United States, which, leftists claimed, suggested his rightist disposition. Some contended that he was taking part in an international conspiracy to promote a coup in Brazil.

In spite of its vociferous protests against corruption, the movement was peaceful and its demonstrations occurred without recourse to violence. The protests against corruption referred primarily to the results of what was called the *Operação Lava Jato* (Operation Car Wash), a Brazilian Federal Police investigation started in March 2014 that uncovered widespread corruption taking place at Petrobras, the Brazilian state-owned oil company. The corruption scheme became one of the greatest scandals in the country's history. It involved the public company's high executives, private corporations, and top politicians serving in the Planalto Palace and in the National Congress. The police operation started with the arrest of a *doleiro*, that is, a dealer managing the illegal remittance of currency abroad. As is usually the case in countries that impose capital controls on their territory, the operation of sending currency abroad without approval from the Central Bank, known as "currency evasion," is proscribed in Brazil. From the investigations of *doleiro* Alberto Youssef's (b. 1967) activities, the Federal Police discovered a scheme wherein funds were being diverted from the construction of the Abreu e Lima Refinery, a large industrial plant owned by Petrobras in Pernambuco State. The construction of the refinery was part of the aforementioned public investments program *Programa de Aceleração do Crescimento* (PAC) launched by President

Luíz Inácio Lula da Silva in 2007. The initial estimate for the construction was US$ 2.5 billion, but a few years later that number had reached US$ 18.5 billion. Petrobras executives justified the increase by citing the new technologies being added to the project, as well as estimated factors such as currency exchange variations. The truth, however, is that the increase was part of an overpricing scheme. Since the refinery's construction was made with public funds, the budget estimate increase depended on congressional approval, which led to the bribing of politicians. At the other end of the bribery chain from the politicians were the contractors who provided services for Petrobras in the refinery's construction process. In the middle of the chain were the Petrobras executives. Soon the bribery scheme became a web of interconnected deals. The engineering companies bribed Petrobras executives to be favored in public tenders; they bribed again to overprice their contracts; executives, in turn, bribed politicians to approve higher budgets; politicians were also bribed directly by the engineering companies for their influence in tendering and budgeting. When everyone had fully lined their pockets, they called Alberto Youssef and other *doleiros* to send their dollars outside the country illegally.

In March 2014, Petrobras Director Paulo Roberto Costa (b. 1954) was arrested after the Federal Police investigation revealed his connections with Youssef. In September 2014, Costa signed a plea bargain that contained an agreement to receive judicial leniency in exchange for information on the individuals involved in the corruption scheme. Among the accused were the President of the Congressional House of Representatives, Federal Deputy Henrique Eduardo Alves (b. 1948, PMDB), the President of the Senate, Senator Renan Calheiros (b. 1955, PMDB), Minister of Mines and Energy Edison Lobão (b. 1936, PMDB), former Minister of Finance Antonio Palocci (b. 1960, PT), Chief of Staff of the Presidency of the Republic Gleisi Helena Hoffmann (b. 1965, PT), Federal Deputy Cândido Vaccarezza (b. 1955, PT), Federal Deputy João Pizzolatti (b. 1961, PP), former Rio de Janeiro State Governor Sérgio Cabral (b. 1963, PMDB), former Pernambuco State Governor Eduardo Campos (1965–2014, PSB), former President Fernando Collor de Mello (b. 1949, PTB), and Maranhão State Governor Roseana Sarney (b. 1953, PMDB). On December 10, 2014, Maranhão State Governor Roseana Sarney, the daughter of former President José Sarney (b. 1930), resigned her post and fled to the United States. She was accused of receiving approximately US$ 500,000 from Alberto Youssef in exchange for the approval of a payment of nearly US$ 65 million to the construction company Constran, owned by "soy king" Olacyr de Moraes (b. 1931). On December 18, eight days after Roseana Sarney's move to the United

States, the incumbent Governor of Maranhão State and lifelong affiliate of the Sarney family, Arnaldo Melo (b. 1954, PMDB), granted by decree a life pension to Sarney. As much as this may sound like a mistake, it is not. According to the Brazilian Public Prosecutor's Office, more than one billion dollars were diverted from Petrobras in the overall corruption scheme. Among the construction companies allegedly involved in the Abreu e Lima Refinery scandal are Camargo Corrêa (est. 1939), presided over by Dalton dos Santos Avancini (b. 1966), Odebrecht (est. 1944), owned by Marcelo Odebrecht (b. 1968), OAS (est. 1976), owned by César Mata Pires (b. 1949), Mendes Júnior (est. 1953), owned by Sérgio Cunha Mendes (b. 1956), Andrade Gutierrez (est. 1948), owned by Sergio Lins Andrade (b. 1948) and presided over by Otávio Marques de Azevedo (b. 1951), and Queiroz Galvão (est. 1953), owned by Antônio de Queiroz Galvão (b. 1923). Some of these executives figure in the Forbes Magazine 2014 list of the world's billionaires. In 2015, some of them were arrested, accused of forming a cartel. Allegedly, Ricardo Ribeiro Pessoa (b. 1951), director of UTC-Engineering (est. 1974), was the cartel's coordinator. Together with charges against the construction companies' executives, Petrobras public servants Renato Duque (b. 1955) and Pedro Barusco (b. 1956) were also prosecuted. Petrobras President Maria das Graças Silva Foster (b. 1953) and five other members of the company's administrative board resigned their positions in February 2015. In 2016, former President Luiz Inácio Lula da Silva was accused of taking part in the bribery scheme. He was convicted in 2017.

The Petrobras corruption scandal weighed heavily on Brazilian society. In 2015, some of the major international credit rating agencies lowered the company's investment grade to the lowest value. Considering that Petrobras is a public company, this means a curtailment in foreign investment that affects all Brazilians. The private construction companies involved in the scandal also lost a considerable part of their value on the stock market. This also results in losses for the country. But worst of all is that the entire corruption scheme was enacted from the misuse and appropriation of taxpayers' money. This is what, above all, the Rogério Chequer's *Movimento Vem pra Rua* was protesting against. Whether or not the Movement's leader had the specific political aim of attempting a rightist coup is not clear. The Movement's main shortcoming, in any case, was to remain ignorant of the real causes of the widespread corruption in Brazil. The present Petrobras scandal is just one of the many schemes involving bribery, money laundering, and a lack of administrative integrity by public officials taking place throughout the country every single day. One could say that the Petrobras scandal's roots date back to the country's very birth. The scandal is part and parcel of the enormous Brazilian State that was inherited from the first centralized national bureaucratic apparatus that ever existed in Europe, the Portuguese State. Corruption exists first of all because its conditions are present. In the case of Brazil, one of these conditions lies in the enormity of the public sector, which allows for the handling of taxpayers' money in ways that are not possible in modern countries around the world. The size and scope of the public sphere in Brazil, if not the direct cause, provides fertile ground for corruption to grow.

The enormity of the Brazilian public sector, with its virtual control over the entire economy, has deep roots in the nationalism that was examined in the earlier pages. The history of the role of the state in the economy in Brazil is informed by the surviving Portuguese colonial bureaucratic mentality, of which nationalism is the clearest psychological expression. In colonial times, since the Portuguese Crown owned the entire nation, the idea of defending the Crown was equated with defending the nation. However, since the Crown was not in the territory, being across the Atlantic in Lisbon, the state bureaucracy became equated with the Crown. In other words, the de-territorialization of the center of power made its proxy, the bureaucracy, assume control over the territory and be identified as the core of the nation. Hence defending the state bureaucracy became the same as defending the nation. Nationalism and the public sector, or the state bureaucracy, have thus been inextricably linked in the minds of most Brazilians since the country's inception as a Portuguese colony in 1500. The lack of a real break with Portugal and its monarchy at the moment of the independence in 1822 provided for a continuation of the colonial bureaucratic-public-nationalist mentality that is still at work in "modern" Brazil. Without that understanding, any movement that calls for the end of corruption, for respect for taxpayers' money, for more public education, and for more public healthcare is doomed to be ineffective.

In 2015, the demands and complaints of Rogério Chequer's Movement appeared either naïve or ill-intentioned when they moved into vague and populist calls for honesty and respect in the face of socially costly corruption. The word "respect" is used as part of an empty discourse that calls for more public education and public health in general terms without ever getting to the bottom of the national shortcomings in those areas, which issue precisely from the demand for public intervention in the economy. As we have seen, the question of public education became part of a public-private dilemma that emerged after the end of the first Vargas government. That dilemma was never fully resolved. The Movement's use of the word "respect," in any case, is particularly problematic when the conditions for mutual respect among Brazilians are absent and the understanding of such absence is lacking. Mutual respect within a nation supposes a strong sense of citizenship that can only be built through an efficient education system. In the absence of the latter, the average Brazilian emerges as not educated enough to understand the need to respect others in terms of citizenship and the building of the nation, that is, in terms of acting according to the law and respecting each other's rights. This forces the Brazilian notion of "respect" to rely primarily on natural morality rather than on any dimension of civic observance of the law as the desirable logic to be followed (as per the surviving mentality of the "law to fool the British"). To put it more bluntly, Brazilians are uneducated in civic terms because an efficient educational system was never accomplished in the country; and that happened because, among other things, education became enmeshed in a public-private dispute laden with nationalistic and self-interested overtones, that is, in an *either/or* that reveals the historical Brazilian lack of intellectual flexibility and administrative imagination. As long as education remains the missing link that prevents territorialized power from developing into a nation, disrespect and its corollary, corruption, will not be overcome by the simple phenomenon of public demonstrations, nor from a simple change of government, which only substitutes one group of corrupt individuals for another.

The problem with "respect" is thus much more complex than Rogério Chequer and his two million followers can surmise. Looking at the missing link, one cannot even say that the Brazilian educational system is failed or obsolete: in Brazil education cannot be said to have collapsed because it was never truly built as an efficient and socially enhancing structure. All levels of what is called the Brazilian education system show terrible flaws that hinder the establishment of the country as a modern nation. And perhaps the most blatant evidence of the virtually non-existent Brazilian education system can be found in higher education. The arrangement pits public and private institutions against each other in a way that renders both largely ineffective. Public universities lack competition and hence competitiveness. They are financed by the State and generally any form of non-governmental funding is aggressively rejected. Public university education is offered free of charge, but the highly competitive entrance examinations normally require years of study in expensive preparatory private schools, which makes public institutions accessible primarily to wealthy students. Affirmative action programs have been implemented, only to founder as unprepared students enter higher education without the grounding of adequate basic formal schooling.

Adding to the general chaos, the rejection of external funding for public institutions creates a series of problems that range from the lack of adequate material structure to the control of the institution by the student body. Public universities are poor, their facilities are shoddy, and lack of administrative creativity is the norm. Since private enterprises are generally not allowed to operate on campus, good services are not offered, and campuses become dull places far removed from the lively environments supportive of intellectual exchange that universities should be. The public nature of the institutions also allows students to assume an attitude of ownership over them. The case of the University of São Paulo's ongoing problems with campus surveillance provides a case in point. The University's main campus, located in São Paulo's Butantã neighborhood, occupies a large forested area with several buildings standing at a distance from one another. After continued reports of violence on campus, which houses more than 50,000 students, the murder of Economics major Felipe Ramos de Paiva (1987–2011) as a result of an armed robbery in one of the parking lots on May 18, 2011 led the University administration to sign an agreement with the São Paulo State Police Force to increase security on campus. The agreement, for a strengthening of the police presence on the University's premises, was signed on September 8, 2011 between the University Dean, João Grandino Rodas (b. 1945), the Military Police General Commander, Colonel Álvaro Batista Camilo (b. 1961), and the State Secretary for Public Security, Antônio Ferreira Pinto (b. 1943). Dissatisfied with the agreement on the grounds of not wanting the "repressive" police force on campus, students immediately started confrontations with the law enforcement officers when they arrived at the University. The truth behind the students' rejection of the police monitoring the campus, however, was that several students wanted to be able to freely consume illegal drugs at the university's premises, an activity that was hindered by the presence of the police. In the afternoon of October 27, 2011, the arrest of three undergraduate students for possession of illegal drugs on campus provoked a violent confrontation between the students and the police. Clashes continued into the evening, when a group of 500 students invaded the building of the Faculty of Philosophy and Letters, breaking windows and committing acts of vandalism. On November 2, a group of 70 students occupied the University's main administrative building, controlling the area for 6 days until a police operation was ordered to evict the students by force. Confrontations between students and the police, however, did not subside. Intimidated by recurrent acts of aggression from the student body, in early 2012 the State Police Force discontinued campus surveillance. From then on reports of robbery, kidnapping, and rape inside the University's premises multiplied. On July 2, 2014, fifteen students were victims of an armed robbery in the student cafeteria. As of 2018, the police task has not yet returned to monitor the campus.

The University of São Paulo's recent history shows the potential shortcomings of public education when the public space is misinterpreted as the personal property of a specific group. It also shows the problem of limited funding when no external resources outside of government provision are allowed to contribute to the financing of the institution. In the case of the University of São Paulo, funding comes from the State Sales Tax (ICMS), which can vary according to economic fluctuations. The gravity of the situation becomes clear when one observes the University's financial crisis, which leads to recurrent strikes by professors, administrative officers, and even students. Data shows that between 1989 and 2014 the University's student body grew by 96%, while the number of faculty grew by only 6.8%. One might think that searching for new forms of financing should solve the problem. But things are not so simple. Consider for instance an incident in 2011 when Dean João Grandino Rodas, who directed the University from 2010 to 2014, accepted the equivalent of roughly US$ 500,000 in donations from two major law firms whose owners were University of São Paulo alumni. The donations were destined to the reform and maintenance of two large auditoriums in the Department of Law which, in exchange, were symbolically named after the donors. After a public protest of more than 1,000 students, who demonstrated against what they called "the appropriation of public spaces by individuals and firms," São Paulo's Court of Justice ordered the names of the donors to be removed from the refurbished auditoriums.

The disputes between students and the administration at the University of São Paulo gain renewed significance when one considers the fact that Dean João Grandino Rodas had been appointed to his post by the then Governor of São Paulo, José Serra, despite finishing second in the University's own internal elections for the position. The Dean's connections with the Governor's party, the PSDB, in a university with a leftist majority, may have influenced the course of these events. It is evident that the major issue at stake, however, is the public nature of the University itself, which in the context of a country whose society is still informed by clear ideological frontiers, ends up falling prey to disputes between political parties. In any case, students preventing the police from monitoring the campus so they can be free to use illicit drugs, and bringing down memorial plates from classroom doors so as not to forfeit the supremacy over "their" space, shows that something is obviously not right with the Brazilian educational system.

The situation becomes even worse when it comes to more academic questions. The legal system that limits the possible forms of financing public universities, that is, the imposition of exclusive reliance on public funds, results in the lack of competition between institutions and promotes academic sluggishness. The teaching and research profession is deprived of economic stimulation for academic production. Without anything similar to an academic market where professors could aim at improving their careers through outstanding contributions to knowledge and through services offered to different institutions of various levels, the profession becomes stale and lethargic. The lack of mobility between institutions is almost absolute. Under this situation, the public university promotion schemes fall prey to a bureaucratization that is almost laughable. In the absence of a tenure system, public university professors gain job stability by being regular civil servants, and their promotion schemes are based on points earned according to books or articles published and class hours taught. The points are calculated every two years with the help of a point table.

But that is not all. Since public university professors are regular public servants, they are obliged to pass a civil service examination in order to be granted a university position. This means that, after finishing their doctorate, academics have to compete with other professionals in a session with written paper examinations and mock classes that are graded from 0 to 100. It is difficult to understand the criteria that can establish a taught class as worth, say, 74 and not 75 points. If the academic decides not to sit these pointless exams, which are costly, can take weeks, and in which the selected candidate is usually predetermined, however, they still have the option of applying for a job at a private university. But here things get much worse. For just like public universities, private institutions have no tenure system. Added to the fact that one does not become a civil servant in a private university, such institutions cannot offer any job security. What is worse is that someone with a PhD will cost a private university more than someone with, say, only an MA or an undergraduate degree. The chances of someone with a PhD getting a job at a private university, then, tend to be lower. Worse still is that private universities are generally obliged to rely on their students' tuition fees for financing. That means that professors are even more prey to their students in the private than in the public sector. Courses that are not profitable are simply not offered, and professors have to please their students at all times so as to not get fired.

One can see that the Brazilian higher education system is not particularly conducive to the production of the sort of knowledge that would foster development and the emergence of mutual respect in society. For one thing, in the national education system, a clear understanding of ethics and of the need for law-abiding attitudes gets lost in partisan infighting, acts of vandalism against the public facilities, disrespect for knowledge and for the figure of the professor, illicit drug use, anger, and widespread violence. The link between a failed education system and the corruption cases seen among politicians, public companies, and private enterprises is not difficult to draw.

It took 515 years, one empire and six republics, for two million Brazilians to take to the streets to demand mutual respect and the end of corruption. If this is the result of such a long history, prospects for the future do not seem bright at all.

The aforementioned developments in Brazilian society and politics since 2010 suggest an answer to some of the questions we have posed throughout this book: the question of why there was never a Marshal Plan for Latin America; the question of why Brazil had to express its "frustration" with the United States in 1947; the question of why the country had to go through a vicious dictatorial period lasting more than twenty years; the question of why Brazilian presidents continue to suffer from delusions of grandeur and insist on assuming self-agrandizing attitudes in international fora; the general question of why the country continues to be a theater of murder, of social injustice, of land disputes, of mass media mind control, and of patronage and power abuse.

Not wanting to finish on a dark note, however, I hope that the reader will find the information and critical perspectives presented in this book useful as reference for further study and research. My aim with these pages was to provide future scholars and researchers in Brazilian and Latin American Studies with a critical and interdisciplinary introduction to Brazilian history. I hope the reader will find that this objective has been met. In any case, my opinion is that the most interesting aspect of Brazilian society lies in its art and culture. Many developments in those areas could not be discussed in these pages, such as the rich Afro-Brazilian religions, with their peculiar art and music, the more recent literature and poetry, the arts of the Asian diaspora, and the new developments in contemporary art. I hope the reader will find interest in pursuing studies in those areas with an enhanced background gained from the information provided in this book.

NOTES

Chapter One

[1] An interesting analysis of the usage of Victor Meirelles's painting in Brazilian cinema can be found in Carmen Nava and Ludwig Lauerhass, *Brazil in the Making: Facets of National Identity* (Rowan & Littlefield Publishers, 2006, pp. 164–167). Readers of Portuguese can find an in-depth analysis of the role of Victor Meirelles's works in the building of the Brazilian national identity in Giselle Martins Venâncio's article "Pintando o Brasil: artes plásticas e construção da identidade nacional (1816–1922)," in *Revista História em Reflexão*, vol. 2, n. 4, UFGD, Dourados Jul/Dec 2008, pp. 1–18. The subject of national ideology and Victor Meirelles's paintings also figures in the works of Isis Pimentel de Castro, "Pintura, memória e história: a pintura histórica e a construção de uma memória nacional," in *Revista de Ciências Humanas*, n.38, EDUFSC, Florianópolis, October 2005, pp. 335–352, and of Maria Inez Turazzi, *Victor Meirelles, novas leituras* (São Paulo: Studio Nobel, 2009). A collection of the painter's works is found in the Victor Meirelles Museum, located in the Brazilian city of Florianópolis, birthplace of the artist.

[2] Pero Vaz de Caminha's report on the newly found territory parallels also the one produced by Christopher Columbus in 1493 and addressed to the registrar of the Catholic Kings of Spain. A careful comparison between the two reports appears in Claude Hulet, "The Columbus Letter of February 15, 1493, and the Pero Vaz de Caminha Letter of May 1, 1500: A Comparison," in *Mester*, Vol. xxiv, No. 1, Spring 1995, pp. 107–124.

[3] An informed discussion in English of Caminha's account and of its role in the forging of the Brazilian nationality can be found in Eduardo Mayone Dias, "Brazil's Birth Certificate: The Letter of Pero Vaz de Caminha" (*Pacific Coast Philology*, Vol. 27, No. 1/2, Sep. 1992, pp. 10–15). An English version of Caminha's work appears in Stuart B. Schwartz (ed.), *Early Brazil: A Documentary Collection to 1700* (Cambridge University Press, 2010, pp. 1–9).

[4] For an informed account of the emergence of a patrimonial state in Portugal and of its transmission to Brazil see Raymundo Faoro's *Os Donos do Poder: formação do patronato político brasileiro* (Porto Alegre: Editora Globo, 1958). Faoro's work is masterful in its analysis of the Brazilian political system, providing an in-depth analysis of the role of the cultural and political disposition inherited from Portugal in the establishment of a fiercely bureaucratic state in Brazil.

[5] For a discussion in English about the captaincy system in Brazil see H. B. Johnson, Jr., "The Donatary Captaincy in Perspective: Portuguese Backgrounds to

the Settlement of Brazil," in *The Hispanic American Historical Review*, Vol. 52, No. 2, May 1972, pp. 203–214.

[6] For an analysis of the transposition of the legislation regarding the sesmaria system from Portugal to its South-American colony in the sixteenth century see Nelson Nozoe, "Sesmarias e Apossamento de Terras no Brasil Colônia," in *Economia*, Brasília, v.7, n.3, Sep/Dec 2006, pp. 587–605.

[7] The political importance of the War of the Mascates during the Brazilian colonial era is mentioned in Colin M. MacLachlan, *A History of Modern Brazil: The Past Against the Future* (Wilmington: Scholarly Resources Inc, 2003). Readers of Portuguese can find a more detailed account of the war in Mário Melo, *A guerra dos Mascates como afirmação nacionalista* (Recife: Imprensa Oficial, 1941). A more recent analysis of the war is found in Evaldo Cabral de Mello, *A fronda dos mazombos: Nobres contra mascates, Pernambuco, 1666–1715* (São Paulo: Editora 34, 2003). The War of the Mascates also figures in the Brazilian literary canon as background to the romantic novel of José de Alencar (1829–1877), *A Guerra dos Mascates* (1871).

[8] The French presence in the Brazilian colonial territory has been examined in detail in the works of Brazilian historian and diplomat Vasco Mariz (b. 1921). Among his works figure *Villegagnon e a França Antártica* (Rio de Janeiro: Nova Fronteira, 1999), and *La Ravardière e a França Equinocial – Os Franceses no Maranhão (1612–1615)* (Rio de Janeiro: Topbooks, 2007), which were written in collaboration with the French writer Lucien Provençal.

[9] The theme of the Dutch territorial occupation and its interpretation in Varnhagen's work is treated in Demétrio Magnoli, *O corpo da pátria: imaginação geográfica e política externa no Brasil (1808–1912)* (São Paulo: Unesp, 1997, pp. 97–102). The author observes Varnhagen's work as an important part of the Brazilian Empire's effort in establishing a "civilizational" process in the newly independent nation during the first half of the nineteenth century. Magnoli also notes the influence of Robert Southey's (1774–1843) *History of Brazil* (first published in London in 1810) on Varnhagen's work. Regarding the Dutch occupation of the Brazilian colonial territory, the foundational work is Charles Ralph Boxer's *The Dutch in Brazil, 1624–1654* (Clarendon Press, 1957). For an analysis of the Dutch influence on Brazilian culture see Michiel van Groesen (Ed.), *The Legacy of Dutch Brazil* (Cambridge University Press, 2014). Also of interest to the subject is Evaldo Cabral de Mello's *Olinda restaurada: Guerra e açúcar no Nordeste, 1630–1654* (São Paulo: Editora 34, 2007). For an appraisal of the Guararapes Battle from the point of view of Brazilian military history see Cláudio Moreira Bento, *As Batalhas dos Guararapes: Descrição e Análise Militar* (Recife: Universidade Federal de Pernambuco, 1971).

[10] For an overview of the occupation of the Amazon region from the perspective of diplomacy and foreign policy see the work of Brazilian historian and diplomat Synesio Sampaio Goes Filho, *Navegantes, bandeirantes, diplomatas: Aspectos da descoberta do continente, da penetração do território brasileiro extra-Tordesilhas e do estabelecimento das fronteiras da Amazônia* (Brasília: Fundação Alexandre de Gusmão, 1991). For a general account of the history of the Amazon see Anísio

Jobim, *O Amazonas: sua história, ensaio antropogeográfico e politico* (Companhia editora nacional: 1957).

[11] The area where the historical *quilombo* existed is today part of a memorial site called Parque Memorial do Quilombo dos Palmares. The site was established in 2007 by the Instituto do Patrimônio Histórico e Artístico Nacional (Iphan), a heritage register of the Brazilian federal government created in 1937 shortly after the *coup d'état* that gave rise to the Estado Novo regime. For analysis of the republican characteristics of the Quilombo dos Palmares see the next note.

[12] A rich research literature exists in Portuguese regarding the Quilombo dos Palmares. Two important works for further reference are Décio Freitas, *Palmares: a guerra dos escravos* (Rio de Janeiro: Graal, 1982) and João José Reis and Flávio dos Santos Gomes (Eds.), *Liberdade por um fio: história dos quilombos no Brasil* (São Paulo: Companhia das Letras, 1998), published in English as *Freedom by a Thread: The History of Quilombos in Brazil* (Diasporic Africa Press, 2016). See also Flávio dos Santos Gomes, *Histórias de Quilombolas: Mocambos e comunidades de senzalas no Rio de Janeiro, século XIX* (Companhia das Letras, 2006).

[13] An in-depth discussion of the slave labor system implemented in the region of the mines can be found in Laird Bergad, *Slavery and the Demographic and Economic History of Minas Gerais, Brazil, 1720–1888* (Cambridge University Press, 1999).

[14] For an analysis of the political conditionings that led to the Filipe dos Santos Revolt see João Dornas Filho, *O ouro das Gerais e a civilização da Capitania* (São Paulo: Companhia Editora Nacional, 1957) and Carlos Guilherme Mota and Adriana Lopez *História do Brasil: Uma interpretação* (São Paulo: Editora 34, 2015).

[15] Important historiographical research on the Treaty of Madrid appears in the work of Portuguese historian Jaime Cortesão, *Alexandre de Gusmão e o Tratado de Madrid, 1695–1735* (Instituto Rio Branco, 1950). See also Mário Clemente Ferreira, "O Mapa das Cortes e o Tratado de Madrid: a cartografia a serviço da diplomacia," in *Varia História*, Belo Horizonte, vol. 23, n. 37, Jan/Jun 2007, pp. 51–69.

[16] For a historical study of the Tupi language and the Nheengatu, its modern version, please refer to the French text of Ozias Alves Jr, *Parlons Nheengatu: Une langue tupi du Brésil* (Paris: L'Harmattan, 2010).

[17] For a closer view on Pombal's reforms in the eighteenth century see Sandra Aparecida Pires Franco, "Reformas Pombalinas e o Iluminismo em Portugal," in *Fênix – Revista de História e Estudos Culturais*, Vol. 4, 2007, pp. 1–14. The implementation of a secular education taken into the hands of the State is frequently cited as one of the most important aspects of Sebastião José de Carvalho e Melo's reforms. In this regard, see Dermeval Saviani, *História das idéias pedagógicas no Brasil* (Campinas: Autores Associados, 2007, pp. 107–111). The foundational study of Pombal's life and works in English is Kenneth Maxwell's *Pombal, Paradox of the Enlightenment* (Cambridge University Press, 1995).

[18] Two works are especially worth mentioning regarding the revolts of this period of Brazilian history, Kenneth Maxwell's *Conflicts and Conspiracies: Brazil and Portugal, 1750–1808* (Routledge, 2004) and Gabriel Paquette's *Imperial Portugal in the Age of Atlantic Revolutions: The Luso-Brazilian World, c. 1770–1850* (Cambridge University Press, 2013).

[19] For an interesting study on poetry in the colonial period see Ivan Teixeira's *Mecenato pombalino e poesia neoclássica* (São Paulo: EDUSP, 1999). A biography of poet Cláudio Manuel da Costa can be found in Laura de Mello e Souza, *Cláudio Manuel da Costa: O Letrado Dividido* (Companhia das Letras, 2011).

[20] For an analysis of the ethnic make-up of Bahia during the period, as well as the local struggle for freedom from slavery see Dale Torston Graden, *From Slavery to Freedom in Brazil: Bahia, 1835–1900* (University of New Mexico Press, 2006).

[21] Two important works for further information on the conspiracy in Bahia are Donald Ramos, "Social Revolution Frustrated: The Conspiracy of the Tailors in Bahia, 1798," in *Luso-Brazilian Review 13*, no. 1, 1976, pp. 74–90; and Stuart B. Schwartz, *Sugar Plantations in the Formation of Brazilian Society: Bahia, 1550–1835* (Cambridge University Press, 1985).

[22] A clear example of such a humorous rendering in popular culture can be seen in the film *Carlota Joaquina, Princesa do Brazil* (1995), directed by Carla Camurati.

[23] A detailed account of the event can be found in Kirsten Schultz, *Tropical Versailles: Empire, Monarchy, and the Portuguese Royal Court in Rio de Janeiro, 1808–1821* (Routledge, 2001).

[24] Rodrigo de Sousa Coutinho is mentioned in the monumental work by Otávio Tarquínio de Sousa, *História dos Fundadores do Império do Brasil* (Editora José Olympio, 1957), re-edited in 2015 by Senado Federal, Conselho Editorial.

[25] An in-depth analysis of John VI's policies for the Platine Region after his arrival in the Brazilian territory in 1808 can be found in Ronaldo Bernardino Colvero, *"Bajo su Real Protección": as relacões internacionais e a geopolítica na região do Rio da Prata, 1808–1812* (Porto Alegre: EDIPUCRS, 2015).

[26] For an analysis of the educational institutions established by John VI in Bahia see Edivaldo M. Boaventura, *A Construção da Universidade Baiana: Objetivos, Missões e Afrodescendência* (Salvador: Edufba, 2009).

[27] For an in-depth analysis of the Holy Alliance and its activities in Europe see Mark Jarrett's *The Congress of Vienna and its Legacy: War and Great Power Diplomacy after Napoleon* (London: I. B. Tauris, 2014).

[28] For a detailed account of the consolidation of Braganza absolutism in Portugal see Glenn J. Ames, *Renascent Empire?: The House of Braganza and the Quest for Stability in Portuguese Monsoon Asia, ca. 1640–1683* (Amsterdam University Press, 2000).

Chapter Two

[1] In this regard, see the works of Amado Luiz Cervo, *Depois das Caravelas: as relações entre Portugal e Brasil, 1808–2000* (EDU/UNB, 2000); *História da política exterior do Brasil* (Brasília: UNB, 2011); and *A Parceria Inconclusa: as relações entre Brasil e Portugal* (Belo Horizonte: Fino Traço, 2012).

[2] Regarding the war in Bahia see Luís Henrique Dias Tavares, *A independência do Brasil na Bahia* (Salvador: EDUFBA, 2005).

[3] An extensive bibliography exists in Portuguese on José Bonifácio de Andrada e Silva. Especially worth noting in chronological order are Vicente Barretto's *Ideologia e política no pensamento de José Bonifácio de Andrada e Silva* (Zahar Editores, 1977); Miriam Dolhnikoff's (Ed.) *Projetos para o Brasil, José Bonifácio de Andrada e Silva* (São Paulo: Cia. das Letras, 1998); Ana Rosa Cloclet da Silva's *Construção da nação e escravidão no pensamento de José Bonifácio: 1783–1823* (Campinas: Editora da Unicamp, 1999); Berenice Cavalcante's *José Bonifácio: razão e sensibilidade: uma história em três tempos* (Rio de Janeiro: FGV, 2001); and Miriam Dolhnikoff's *José Bonifácio* (São Paulo: Cia. das Letras, 2012). Also of special interest is the section on José Bonifácio found in Emília Viotti da Costa, *Da monarquia à república: momentos decisivos* (São Paulo: UNESP, 1998, pp. 61–130). For an English version of the book see Emília Viotti da Costa, *The Brazilian Empire: Myths and Histories* (The University of North Carolina Press, 2000).

[4] See Leslie Bethell, *Brazil: Empire and Republic, 1822–1930* (Cambridge University Press, 1989, p. 45).

[5] See José Murilo de Cavalho, *A construção da ordem: a elite política imperial* (Rio de Janeiro: Campus, 1980) and *Teatro das sombras: a política imperial* (São Paulo: Edições Vértice, 1988).

[6] The document produced by the Constituent Assembly in 1823 came to be known as *Constituição da Mandioca*, or "Cassava Constitution," a humorous rendering that indicates the unsuccessful attempt at ascertaining Brazilian interests over Portuguese ones in the new nation. The rejected Charter's text, drafted by the Brazilian faction, established the rules for "censitary suffrage," that is, for the electoral system in which a person's rank determines his or her right to take part in the ballot. Among such rules was one which established the right to vote only for individuals who could prove a minimum income derived from their cassava plantations. This rule was actually a stratagem concocted by the Brazilians to exclude the Portuguese from the political process, for most Portuguese citizens tended to work as merchants and did not own land, unlike the Brazilians. For José Bonifácio's own description of the so-called "Night of Agony" see Jorge Caldeira (Ed.), *José Bonifácio de Andrada e Silva* (São Paulo: Editora 34, 2002, pp. 244–247).

[7] For an analysis of the division of power established in the 1824 Constitution and its usage by the Brazilian monarchs see José Murilo de Carvalho, *A Monarquia brasileira* (Rio de Janeiro: Ao Livro Técnico, 1993). For a more general view on

the Brazilian monarchy and its political intentions see Roderick Barman, *Brazil: The Forging of a Nation: 1798–1852* (Stanford University Press, 1994).

[8] For book-length discussions of the 1817 Pernambucan Revolution see Manuel Correia de Andrade, *A Revolução Pernambucana de 1817* (São Paulo: Ática, 1995) and Gonçalo de Barros Carvalho e Mello Mourão, *A revolução de 1817 e a história do Brasil: um estudo de história diplomática* (Brasília: Fundação Alexandre de Gusmão, 2009). The original historiographical work on the Revolution is that of Francisco Muniz Tavarez (1793–1876), *História da Revolução de 1817* (Recife: Typ. Imparcial de L. I. R. Roma, 1840).

[9] The 1824 attempt at sedition is treated at length in Alexandre José Barbosa Lima Sobrinho, *Pernambuco: da Independência à Confederação do Equador* (Recife: Conselho Estadual de Cultura, 1979); Ulisses Brandão, *A confederação do Equador* (Recife: Instituto Arqueológico, Histórico e Geográfico Pernambucano, 1924); Evaldo Cabral de Mello, *A outra independência: o federalismo pernambucano de 1817 a 1824* (São Paulo: Editora 34, 2004); and Amy Caldwell de Farias, *Mergulho No Letes: Uma Reinterpretação Político-Histórica da Confederação do Equador* (Porto Alegre: EDIPUCRS, 2006).

[10] On the life and works of Joaquim da Silva Rabelo see Evaldo Cabral de Mello, *Frei do Amor Divino Caneca* (São Paulo: Editora 34, 2001).

[11] Historians debate whether the idea of establishing a joint Portuguese-Spanish realm was not originally Carlota Joaquina's. Regarding the personality and politics of the Queen see Francisca L. Nogueira de Azevedo, *Carlota Joaquina na corte do Brasil* (Editora Record, 2003).

[12] A considerable bibliography exists on the life and works of Felisberto Caldeira Brant. In chronological order: Antônio Costa Aguiar, *Vida do marquês de Barbacena* (Rio de Janeiro: Imprensa Nacional, 1896); João Pandiá Calógeras, *O marquês de Barbacena* (São Paulo: Companhia Editora Nacional, 1936); Lúcia Maria Guimarães, "Felisberto Caldeira Brant (Marquês de Barbacena)," in Ronaldo Vainfas (Ed.), *Dicionário do Brasil Imperial (1808–1889)* (Rio de Janeiro: Objetiva, 2002); and Fabiano Vilaça Santos, "O marquês de Barbacena e o reconhecimento da Independência," in Claudia Heynemann e Renata Vale (Eds.), *Temas Luso-Brasileiros* (Rio de Janeiro: Arquivo Nacional, 2010).

[13] See Brian Vale, "English and Irish Naval Officers in the War for Brazilian Independence," in *Irish Migration Studies in Latin America*, Vol. 4, No. 3, July 2006, pp. 102–144.

[14] An in-depth analysis of the establishment of the national frontiers in the River Plate region can be found in Luiz Alberto Moniz Bandeira, *O Expansionismo Brasileiro e a Formação dos Estados da Bacia do Prata: da colonização à guerra da tríplice aliança* (Editora UNB, 1985). For a view on the position assumed by the United States regarding the Platine Questions see Antônia F. de Almeida Wright, "Brasil-Estados Unidos, 1831/1899," in Sérgio Buarque de Holanda (Ed.), *História Geral da Civilização Brasileira, Tomo II, Volume 6* (Rio de Janeiro: Bertrand Brasil, 2004. pp. 202–239; first edition São Paulo: Difel, 1974).

[15] For a study on the Algarve-born Brazilian army officer Carlos Frederico Lecor see Fábio Ferreira, *O General Lecor, os Voluntários Reais e os Conflitos pela*

Independência do Brasil na Cisplatina (1822–1824) (Doctoral Dissertation, Universidade Federal Fluminense, Instituto de Ciências Humanas e Filosofia, Departamento de História, 2012).

[16] A careful inquiry on Rio Grande Sul's salt-beef industry and its economic determinants can be found in Stephen Bell, *Campanha Gaúcha: A Brazilian Ranching System, 1850–1920* (Stanford University Press, 1998).

[17] For an analysis of the political life of Pereira de Vasconcelos see Théo Lobarinhas Piñeiro, "Bernardo Pereira de Vasconcelos e a Construção do Império," in *Passagens. Revista Internacional de História Política e Cultura Jurídica*, Rio de Janeiro: vol. 6, no.3, setembro-dezembro, 2014, pp. 415–438. For two book-length studies on the Brazilian politician see Octávio Tarquínio de Sousa, *Bernardo Pereira de Vasconcelos* (Editora Itatiaia, 1988) and José Murilo de Carvalho (Ed.), *Bernardo Pereira de Vasconcelos* (Editora 34, 1999).

[18] For detailed information on the life of Domitila de Castro do Canto e Melo please refer to the works of Paulo Rezzuti, *Titília e o Demonão. Cartas Inéditas de d. Pedro I à Marquesa de Santos* (São Paulo: Geração Editorial, 2011); *Domitila, a verdadeira história da Marquesa de Santos* (São Paulo: Geração Editorial, 2013); and *D. Pedro, a história não contada: O homem revelado por cartas e documentos inéditos* (São Paulo: LeYa Brasil, 2015). For a study on Pedro I's character see Isabel Lustosa, *D. Pedro I: um herói sem nenhum caráter* (São Paulo: Companhia das Letras, 2006).

[19] For a detailed account of the incident see Chico Castro, *A Noite das Garrafadas* (Brasília: Senado Federal, 2012).

[20] For an account of Pedro de Alcântara's final years after his departure from Brazil see Sérgio Corrêa da Costa, *As quatro coroas de D. Pedro I* (Rio de Janeiro: Paz e Terra, 1995).

[21] For an analysis of the National Guard and of the Regency Period see Marco Morel, *O Período das Regências (1831–1840)* (Editora Zahar, 2003).

[22] Regarding the emergence of Brazilian federalism in the period of the regency see Miriam Dolhnikoff, *O pacto imperial: origens do federalismo no Brasil* (Rio de Janeiro: Editora Globo, 2005).

[23] Regarding the Cabanagem Revolt see the works of Júlio José Chiavenato, *Cabanagem, o povo no poder* (São Paulo: Brasiliense, 1984); Denise Simões Rodrigues, *Revolução cabana e construção da identidade amazônida* (Belém: EDUEPA, 2009); and Marcos Reis, *Cabanos, a História* (Belém: Maguen, 2011).

[24] For the role of Italian immigrants in Rio Grande do Sul's revolution see Laura de Leão Dornelles, *Risorgimento e Revolução: Luigi Rossetti e os Ideais de Giuseppe Mazzini no Movimento Farroupilha* (Porto Alegre: EdiPUCRS, 2012).

[25] Some historians from Rio Grande do Sul maintain that the Farroupilha Revolution's leader, David Canabarro, did not betray his black soldiers, allowing them to die at Porongos. In this vein see Cesar Pires Machado, *Porongos: Fatos e Fábulas* (Porto Alegre: Matriz, 2011) and Cláudio Moreira Bento, *O Negro e seus Descendentes na Sociedade do Rio Grande do Sul* (Porto Alegre: IEL, 1975). Less biased historians recognize the existence of what is called "The Porongos Massacre." See especially Spencer Leitman, "Negros farrapos: hipocrisia racial no

sul do Brasil," in José Hildebrando Dacanal (Ed.), *A Revolução Farroupilha: história e interpretação* (Porto Alegre: Mercado Aberto, 1985), and Moacyr Flores, *Negros na Revolução Farroupilha: traição em Porongos e farsa em Ponche Verde* (Porto Alegre: EST Edições, 2004). For an analysis of the economic aspects of black slavery in Rio Grande do Sul see Fernando Henrique Cardoso, *Capitalismo e escravidão no Brasil meridional: o negro na sociedade escravocrata do Rio Grande do Sul* (São Paulo: Difel, 1962). For a bibliography on the theme see Regina Célia Lima Xavier (Ed.), *História da Escravidão e da Liberdade no Brasil Meridional: guia bibliográfico* (Porto Alegre: UFRGS, 2007) and Luiz Aranha Corrêa do Lago, *Da Escravidão ao Trabalho Livre: Brasil, 1550–1900* (São Paulo: Companhia das Letras, 2014).

[26] The imbalance between military and economic power is, I would argue, the main cause of Rio Grande do Sul's ex-centric place within the Brazilian nation in its various historical phases. The secondary nature of Rio Grande do Sul's economy is analyzed in Roger Kittleson, *The Practice of Politics in Postcolonial Brazil: Porto Alegre, 1845–1895* (Unversity of Pittsburgh Press, 2005). Kittleson writes, "In both its formative and mature stages, Rio Grande do Sul was in essence a secondary economy within Brazil, mainly producing goods for consumption in the export agriculture centers of the Northeast and Center-South regions" (p. 16).

[27] For an analysis of the aspects of racial tension and economic distress in the Sabinada see Paulo César Souza, *A Sabinada* (São Paulo: Companhia das Letras, 2009).

[28] Regarding the Malês Revolt see João José Reis, *Slave Rebellion in Brazil: The Muslim Uprising of 1835 in Bahia* (Johns Hopkins University Press, 1995).

[29] For an in-depth analysis in English of the conservatives' plight in the period see Jeffrey Needell, *The Party of Order: The Conservatives, the State, and Slavery in the Brazilian Monarchy, 1831–1871* (Stanford University Press, 2006).

[30] Brazil and Argentina, however, were moving ahead of several countries in terms of railway construction. The most remarkable contrasting case is perhaps that of Japan, whose first railroad was only finished in 1872, connecting the area of Shimbashi, in Tokyo, to Yokohama, a distance of 23.8 km.

[31] For a thorough analysis of the Brazilian two-party system sustained during most of the Second Empire see Ilmar Rohloff de Mattos, *O Tempo Saquarema* (São Paulo: HUCITEC, 1987).

[32] A discussion of the electoral processes carried out during the period of the Brazilian Empire can be found in Fernando Limongi, "Revisitando as Eleições do Segundo Reinado: Manipulação, Fraude e Violência," in *Lua Nova*, São Paulo, 91, 2014, pp. 13–51.

[33] For a study in English on the life and political career of Pedro de Alcântara see Roderick Barman, *Citizen Emperor: Pedro II and the Making of Brazil* (Stanford University Press, 1999). In Portuguese see Pedro Calmon, *História de D. Pedro II* (5 vols.) (São Paulo: Editora José Olympio, 1975).

[34] A thorough discussion of the Aberdeen Act appears in Leslie Bethell's *The Abolition of the Brazilian Slave Trade: Britain, Brazil and the Slave Trade Question* (Cambridge University Press, 1970).

[35] Amado Luiz Cervo and Clodoaldo Bueno, *História da política exterior do Brasil* (Brasília: UNB, 2011).

[36] For detailed information on the Viscount of Uruguay see José Murilo de Carvalho (Ed.), *Visconde do Uruguai* (São Paulo: Editora 34, 2002).

[37] For a view on the position assumed by the United States in regard to Brazilian slave traffic see Antônia F. de Almeida Wright, "Brasil-Estados Unidos, 1831/1899," in Sérgio Buarque de Holanda (Ed.), *História Geral da Civilização Brasileira, Tomo II, Volume 6* (Rio de Janeiro: Bertrand Brasil, 2004. pp. 202–239; first edition São Paulo: Difel, 1974).

[38] See Leslie Bethell, *The Abolition of the Brazilian Slave Trade: Britain, Brazil and the Slave Trade Question 1807–1869* (Cambridge University Press, 1970, pp. 315–321).

[39] The original historiographical work in Portuguese on the Platine War is Gustavo Barroso's *A Guerra dos Rosas: 1851–1852* (São Paulo: Companhia Editora Nacional, 1929). Highly recommendable for an understanding of the so-called Platine Questions and of the wars fought in the period is Francisco Doratioto's *Maldita Guerra: Nova história da Guerra do Paraguai* (São Paulo: Companhia das Letras, 2002).

[40] For an important work in Brazil-Argentina comparative history see Boris Fausto and Fernando J. Devoto, *Brasil e Argentina: Um ensaio de história comparada (1850–2002)* (São Paulo: Editora 34, 2004).

[41] See Francisco Doratioto, *O Brasil no Rio da Prata: 1822–1994* (Brasília: FUNAG, 2014, pp. 30-35) and Paulo Roberto de Almeida, *Formação da diplomacia econômica no Brasil: as relações econômicas internacionais do Império* (São Paulo: Editora Senac, 2001).

[42] For an analysis of Gobineau's influence in Brazil and of his theories of scientific racism see Demétrio Magnoli, *Uma Gota de Sangue: história do pensamento racial* (São Paulo: Editora Contexto, 2009). Regarding Positivism in Brazil see Oséias Faustino Valentim, *O Brasil e o Positivismo* (Rio de Janeiro: Editora Publit, 2010) and Mozart Pereira Soares, *O positivismo no Brasil: 200 anos de Augusto Comte* (Porto Alegre: Editora AGE, 1998). For an analysis of the influence of Positivism in Brazilian education see Roque Spencer Maciel de Barros, *A Ilustração Brasileira e a Ideia de Universidade* (São Paulo: EDUSP, 1986).

[43] The allied defeat at Curupayty was preceded by an important victory in the Battle of the Riachuelo, a naval combat fought on June 11, 1865. The Battle of the Riachuelo represented a turning point in the war from the previous Paraguayan victories into allied preeminence. It is especially important as a symbol of Brazilian nationalism, having become the subject of a famous painting by the aforementioned artist Victor Meirelles. The painting was commissioned in 1872; it can be seen at the National Historical Museum in Rio de Janeiro.

[44] Here the recommended work is, again, Francisco Doratioto's *Maldita Guerra: Nova história da Guerra do Paraguai* (São Paulo: Companhia das Letras, 2002).

[45] On the life and times of the Duke of Caxias see Adriana Barreto de Souza, *Duque de Caxias: o homem por trás do monumento* (Rio de Janeiro: Civilização Brasileira, 2008).

[46] For an analysis of the intellectual climate during the decade of 1870 see Ângela Alonso, *Idéias em movimento: a geração 1870 na crise do Brasil Império* (São Paulo: Paz e Terra, 2002).

[47] The Law n. 2040 of 09/28/1871 was called *Lei do Ventre Livre*. It followed the previous abolitionist laws of 1831 and 1850, the latter proscribing the slave trade in Brazil. The 1871 Law established that the children of a slave woman should be raised by her mother's owner until reaching 8 years of age, when the owner could opt between receiving an indemnification from the State for granting the child's freedom or employing the child in compulsory labor until the age of 21 years old. As it becomes evident, in practice the law only postponed the end of slavery to a distant future. That notwithstanding, the Bill was severely opposed by the coffee producers of São Paulo, Minas Gerais, and Rio de Janeiro in the plenary voting at the Chamber of Deputies. For the abolitionist laws of the period see the works of Robert Edgar Conrad: *Destruction of Brazilian Slavery, 1850–88* (University of California Press, 1973); *Brazilian slavery: An annotated research bibliography* (G. K. Hall, 1977); *World of Sorrow: The African Slave Trade to Brazil* (Louisiana State University Press, 1986); and *Children of God's Fire: A Documentary History of Black Slavery in Brazil* (Penn State University Press, 2000).

[48] See Roque Spencer Maciel de Barros, "A Questão Religiosa," in Sérgio Buarque de Holanda (Ed.), *História Geral da Civilização Brasileira, Tomo II, Volume 6* (Rio de Janeiro: Bertrand Brasil, 2004. pp. 392–423; first edition São Paulo: Difel, 1974). For an analysis of the Religious Question from the point of view of United States and Protestant influence in the Brazilian Empire see Davis Gueiros Vieira, *O Protestantismo, a Maçonaria e a Questão Religiosa no Brasil* (Brasília: Editora Universidade de Brasília, 1980).

[49] Brazilian historian José Murilo de Carvalho points to the peculiarities of the province of Ceará and to the general role of the State in the abolition process. See "A política da abolição: o rei contra os barões," in *Teatro das sombras: a política imperial* (São Paulo: Edições Vértice, 1988). Differently from Carvalho's view, Richard Graham emphasizes the role of individuals and urban societies in the final collapse of slavery. See "As causas da abolição da escravatura no Brasil," in *Escravidão, reforma e imperialismo* (São Paulo: Perspectiva, 1979).

[50] The event happened around 1883, when the beautiful widow, Maria Adelaide Andrade Neves Meirelles, the Baroness of Triunfo, appears to have enticed the lust of both men. Maria Adelaide was born in Rio Pardo, Rio Grande do Sul, as the daughter of José Joaquim de Andrade Neves (1807–1869), Baron of Triunfo, who died during combat in Asunción, Paraguay. She married Miguel Pereira De Oliveira Meirelles, taking the last name of her husband. For a popular rendering of the affair see Laurentino Gomes, *1889: Como um imperador cansado, um marechal vaidoso e um professor injustiçado contribuíram para o fim da Monarquia e a Proclamação da República no Brasil* (Editora Globo, 2013). Miguel Pereira De Oliveira Meirelles, Maria Adelaide's husband, is mentioned in Stephen Bell's aforementioned *Campanha Gaúcha: A Brazilian Ranching System, 1850–1920* (Stanford University Press, 1998, p. 139).

[51] Readers of Portuguese can find an introduction to Brazilian literary history in Alfredo Bosi, *História Concisa da Literatura Brasileira* (São Paulo: Cultrix, 2003). Also of interest is Antônio Cândido's *Formação da Literatura Brasileira* (Editora Itatiaia, 2000). For informed discussions on Brazilian literature and culture in English see João Cezar de Castro Rocha (Ed.), *Brazil 2001: A Revisionary History of Brazilian Literature and Culture* (Tagus Press at UMass Dartmouth, 2000). For a bilingual anthology of Brazilian poetry from the colonial period to the twentieth century see Frederick G. Williams, *Poets of Brasil* (Luso-Brazilian Books, 2004).

[52] The critical bibliography on this third generation of romantic poets is too extensive to be treated here satisfactorily. Introductorily see Euclides da Cunha, *Castro Alves e seu tempo* (Rio de Janeiro: Imprensa Nacional, 1907); Luiza Lobo, *Épica e modernidade em Sousândrade* (Rio de Janeiro: 7 Letras, 2005); and Paulo Leminski, *Vida: Cruz e Sousa, Bashô, Jesus e Trótski* (São Paulo: Companhia da Letras, 2013).

[53] Perhaps the most commendable work on Brazilian Parnassianism is Luís Augusto Fischer's *Parnasianismo brasileiro: entre ressonância e dissonância* (Porto Alegre: EDIPUCRS, 2003). See also Sânzio Azevedo, *Roteiro Da Poesia Brasileira: Parnasianismo* (Global, 2006).

[54] This title is usually given to Machado de Assis, who tends to be highly overrated by Brazilian literary historians. Assis's works portrayed the Brazilian nineteenth-century bourgeoisie with clever language but lack of real depth, ignoring social issues such as slavery and poverty. His realism is limited and his mores conservative and restrictive. Assis tends to be liked by critics who wish to construct an idealized view of Brazil and its literature, presenting the country as capable of reaching the level of European high art in literary matters. For such an idealized vision of Machado de Assis see Roberto Schwarz's *Um Mestre na Periferia do Capitalismo: Machado de Assis* (São Paulo: Duas Cidades, 1990), in John Gledson's English translation, *A Master on the Periphery of Capitalism: Machado de Assis* (Durham: Duke University Press, 2002). As the title suggests, even in its peripherality, Brazil is still capable of producing a literary master. Gledson's original works on Assis may also be of interest: *Machado de Assis: ficção e história* (Paz e Terra, 1986); *Machado de Assis: impostura e realism* (Companhia das Letras, 2005); and *Por um novo Machado de Assis* (Companhia das Letras, 2006). For the foundational literary biography on Aluísio Azevedo, a much better writer than Assis, see Jacque-Yves Mérian, *Aluísio Azevedo: Vida e Obra* (Rio de Janeiro: Garamond, 1988). The French inheritance of Azevedo's Naturalism may account for its meager critical reception in English. An important work in English from the field of comparative literature featuring Azevedo's *The Slum* is João Sedycias, *The Naturalistic Novel of the New World* (University Press of America, 1993). For a reading of Machado de Assis, José de Alencar, and Aluísio Azevedo from the perspective of what the author calls the Brazilian *bildungsroman* see Zephyr Frank, *Reading Rio de Janeiro: Literature and Society in the Nineteenth Century* (Stanford University Press, 2016).

[55] For a discussion of Brazilian Naturalism in English see the works of Eva Paulino Bueno, *Resisting Boundaries: The Subject of Naturalism in Brazil* (Routledge, 1995) and "Brazilian Naturalism and the Politics of Origin," in *MLN* Vol. 107, No. 2, Hispanic Issue (Mar. 1992), pp. 363–395. In Portuguese see Nelson Werneck Sodré, *O naturalismo no Brasil* (Civilização Brasileira, 1965).

[56] On the history of Brazilian theater see Mario Cacciaglia, *Pequena História do Teatro no Brasil* (São Paulo: Edusp, 1986); Edwaldo Cafereiro and Carmem Gadelha, *História do teatro brasileiro: de Anchieta a Nelson Rodrigues* (Rio de Janeiro: UFRJ/Funarte, 1996); Sábato Magaldi, *Panorama do teatro brasileiro* (Global, 1998.); as well as the works of Décio de Almeida Prado, *Teatro de Anchieta a Alencar* (São Paulo: Perspectiva, 1993) and *História concisa do teatro brasileiro* (São Paulo: EDUSP, 1999). For a view on nineteenth-century popular theater see *Salvyano Cavalcanti de Paiva, Viva o Rebolado! Vida e Morte do Teatro de Revista Brasileiro* (Rio de Janeiro: Nova Fronteira, 1991). An analysis of Rio de Janeiro's cultural climate at the turn of the twentieth century is offered in Tatiana Oliveira Siciliano, *O Rio de Janeiro de Artur Azevedo: Cenas de um Teatro Urbano* (Rio de Janeiro: Faperj, 2015).

[57] Regarding the life and works of Castro Lobo see the works of musicologist Paulo Castagna (b. 1959). Castanha suggests the influence of Antonio Rosetti's (1750–1773) vocal works in the works of the Brazilian musician. See especially "Produção musical e atuação profissional de João de Deus de Castro Lobo (1794-1832): do desaparecimento de seus autógrafos à transmissão de sua música pelas redes sociais," in *Opus: Revista Eletrônica da ANPPOM*, v.18, n.1, jun. 2012, pp.9–40. In English see Paulo Castagna and Jaelson Trindade, "Chapelmasters and Musical Practice in Brazilian Cities in the Eighteenth Century," in Geoffrey Baker and Tess Knighton (Eds.), *Music and Urban Society in Colonial Latin America* (Cambridge University Press, 2011, pp. 132–150). For general histories of Brazilian music see Vasco Mariz, *História da música no Brasil* (Civilização Brasileira, 1981) and José Geraldo Vinci Moraes and Elias Thomé Saliba (Eds.), *História e Música no Brasil* (São Paulo: Alameda, 2010).

[58] A comprehensive biography of Carlos Gomes is found in Marcos Góes, *Carlos Gomes: a força indômita* (Belém: Secult, 1996). For a more literary rendering of the composer's life see the work of novelist Rubem Fonseca, *O Selvagem da Ópera* (Rio de Janeiro: Nova Fronteira 1994).

[59] Such dialectic must be understood in terms of the depreciation of labor as a human activity in the nation's value system. Such depreciation follows from several factors, such as the Portuguese aristocratic culture that historically underrated manual labor, as well as the assessment of labor as undesirable and even humiliating in the context of a slave-based economy. A discussion of the subject appears in Lúcio Kowarick, *Trabalho e Vadiagem: A Origem do trabalho Livre no Brasil* (Editoria Brasiliense, 1987).

[60] For a detailed discussion of the subject see Thomas Holloway, "Immigration and Abolition: The Transition from Slave to Free Labor in the São Paulo Coffee Zone," in Dauril Auden and Warren Dean (Eds.), *Essays Concerning the Socioeconomic*

History of Brazil and Portuguese India (Gainesville: University Press of Florida, 1977).

[61] Note that the notion of eugenics was developed not by Gobineau, but by the English Victorian psychologist Francis Galton (1822–1911) in his book *Hereditary Genius* (1869).

[62] For detailed inquiries on Brazilian immigration see the works of Jeffrey Lesser, *Negotiating National Identity: Immigrants, Minorities, and the Struggle for Ethnicity in Brazil* (Duke University Press, 1999); *A Discontented Diaspora: Japanese Brazilians and the Meanings of Ethnic Militancy 1960–1980* (Duke University Press, 2007); *Immigration, Ethnicity, and National Identity in Brazil: 1808 to the Present* (Cambridge University Press, 2013). Note that the Jewish presence in Brazil should be considered as a special case that resists the use of the word *immigration*. Such presence is closely connected to the history of the Iberian Peninsula and to the expulsion of the Jews from there during the reign of Philip II of Spain (1527–1598), who repeated the procedure of the Catholic Kings, Isabella I of Castile and Ferdinand II of Aragon, enacted in 1492. Following the Lisbon Pogrom of 1506, during the Iberian Union many Sephardic Jews fled to the Portuguese South American colony, trying to escape Philip II's persecution. There they had to conceal their religion or convert to Roman Catholicism, thus receiving the denomination of New Christians. The first Jewish community to emerge openly in the Brazilian territory was the one established in Recife, Pernambuco, in the early 1630s, during the period of Dutch occupation, which was marked by religious freedom. After Brazilian independence, the 1824 Constitution maintained Roman Catholicism as the official religion but conceded religious freedom in the Empire. For a detailed analysis of Jewish communities in Brazil see Jeffrey Lesser's *Welcoming the Undesirables: Brazil and the Jewish Question* (University of California Press, 1995). For a historical perspective on Judaism in Brazil see Anita Novinsky, Daniela Levy, Eneida Ribeiro, and Lina Gorenstein, *Os Judeus que Construíram o Brasil: Fontes Inéditas para uma Nova Visão da História* (Editora Planeta, 2015). For a comparative view on South American Immigration see May E. Bletz, *Immigration and Acculturation in Brazil and Argentina: 1890–1929* (Palgrave Macmillan, 2010). For an analysis of Italian immigration in Brazil see Angelo Trento, *Do outro lado do Atlântico: um século de imigração italiana no Brasil* (Studio Nobel, 1989).

[63] For a discussion in English on chattel slavery in Brazil see Richard Graham, "Another Middle Passage? The Internal Slave Trade in Brazil," and Robert W. Slenes, "The Brazilian Internal Slave Trade, 1850–1888: Regional Economies, Slave Experience, and the Politics of a Peculiar Market," in Walter Johnson (Ed.), *The Chattel Principle: Internal Slave Trades in the Americas* (Yale University Press, 2005). See also Mary C. Karasch, *The Slave Life in Rio de Janeiro, 1808–1850* (Princeton University Press, 1987); Stuart B. Schwartz, *Slaves, Peasants, and Rebels: Reconsidering Brazilian Slavery* (University of Illinois Press, 1995); David Barry Gaspar and Darlene Clark Hine (Eds.), *More Than Chattel: Black Women and Slavery in the Americas* (Indiana University Press, 1996); Mieko Nishida, *Slavery and Identity: Ethnicity, Gender, and Race in Salvador, Brazil, 1808–1888*

(Indiana University Press, 2003); Laird Bergad, *The Comparative Histories of Slavery in Brazil, Cuba, and the United States* (Cambridge University Press, 2007); and Katia de Queirós Mattoso, *To be a slave in Brazil* (Rutgers University Press, 1986), published originally in French as *Être esclave au Brésil, XVIe–XIXe siècles* (Paris: Hachette, 1979). A brief list of relevant works in Portuguese would include: Emília Viotti da Costa's *Da Senzala à Colônia* (São Paulo: UNESP, 1966) and *A Abolição* (São Paulo: UNESP, 1987); Manolo Florentino's *Em Costas Negras – Uma história do tráfico de escravos entre a África e o Rio de Janeiro* (Companhia das Letras, 1997); and Alberto da Costa e Silva's *Francisco Félix de Souza, Mercador de Escravos* (Nova Fronteira, 2004).

[64] Numbers from the IBGE (Instituto Brasileiro de Geografia e Estatística) published in *Recenseamento do Brazil em 1872* (Rio de Janeiro: Typ. G. Leuzinger, 1874).

[65] Regarding the institute of the *escravo de ganho* see David Baronov, *The Abolition of Slavery in Brazil: The Liberation of Africans Through the Emancipation of Capital* (Westport: Praeger, 2000, p. 181). See also Luiz Carlos Soares, "Os Escravos de Ganho no Rio de Janeiro do Século XIX," in *Revista Brasileira de História*, March 1988, vol. 8, n. 16, pp. 102–142 and Thomas Ewbank, "Cruelty to Slaves," in Robert M. Levine and John J. Crocitti (Eds.), *The Brazil Reader: History, Culture, Politics* (Duke University Press, 1999, pp. 138–142).

[66] For an analysis of urbanization in nineteenth-century Brazil see Emília Viotti da Costa, *Da monarquia à república: momentos decisivos* (São Paulo: UNESP, 1998, pp. 233–270).

[67] An excellent biography of the poet can be found in Alberto da Costa e Silva, *Castro Alves, um poeta sempre jovem* (São Paulo: Companhia das Letras, 2006).

[68] As Leslie Bethell and José Murilo de Carvalho have noted, *O Abolicionista* lasted for only thirteen months, between 1882 and 1884. The journal's closure was caused by lack of financial support. Regarding the journal, as well as the exchanges between Brazilian and British abolitionists during the period see Leslie Bethell and José Murilo de Carvalho, "Joaquim Nabuco e os abolicionistas britânicos. Correspondência, 1880–1905," in *Estudos Avançados*, vol.23, n.65, São Paulo, 2009. Joaquim Nabuco was one of Brazil's most remarkable intellectuals during the nineteenth century. A well-informed biography can be found in Angela Alonso, *Joaquim Nabuco: Os Salões e as Ruas* (Companhia das Letras, 2007).

Chapter Three

[1] Regarding the general influence of Positivism at the dawn of the Brazilian Republic see José Murilo de Carvalho, *A Formação das Almas: O imaginário da República no Brasil* (São Paulo: Companhia das Letras, 1990).

[2] The naturalization of foreign residents is an important part of the process of building a sense of citizenship in Brazil at the end of the nineteenth century. Instituted by the Law 200-A of February 8, 1890, it became known as the *Grande*

Naturalização. See José Murilo de Carvalho, *Os Bestializados: O Rio de Janeiro e a República que não foi* (São Paulo: Companhia das Letras, 1987). For an inquiry on the influence of the naturalization law upon Brazil-Portugal relations see Amadeu Carvalho Homem, Armando Malheiro da Silva, Artur Cesar Isaia (Eds.), *Progresso e religião: a república no Brasil e em Portugal 1889–1910* (Universidade de Coimbra, 2007, pp. 127–132).

[3] Regarding the economic experience of the *Encilhamento* see Gail D. Triner, *Banking and Economic Development: Brazil, 1889–1930* (New York: Palgrave, 2000) and Ignacy Sachs, Jorge Wilheim, and Paulo Sérgio Pinheiro (Eds.), *Brazil: a century of change* (University of North Carolina Press, 2009, p. 58).

[4] Regarding the theme of corruption in Brazil from a historical perspective see José Murilo de Carvalho, "Passado, presente e futuro da corrupção brasileira," in Leonardo Avritzer, Newton Bignotto, Juarez Guimarães, Heloisa Maria Murgel Starling (Eds.), *Corrupção: ensaios e críticas* (Editora UFMG, pp. 237–242).

[5] For a general view on Floriano Peixoto's administration see Lincoln de Abreu Penna, *O Progresso da Ordem: o florianismo e a construção da República* (Rio de Janeiro: Sette Letras, 1997).

[6] The Brazilian government had to purchase a new naval force in order to counter the rebellion of the navy. A series of small battleships were bought from the United States. The affair is described by Joaquim Nabuco (1849–1910) in *A Intervenção estrangeira durante a revolta de 1893* (Brasília: Senado Federal, 2010).

[7] For a closer look at the 1893 Federalist Revolution in English see Joseph Love, *Rio Grande Do Sul and Brazilian Regionalism 1882–1930* (Stanford University Press, 1971). In Portuguese see Wenceslau Escobar, *Apontamentos para a história da Revolução Rio-Grandense de 1893* (Brasília: UNB, 1983).

[8] See Suely Robles Reis de Queiroz, *Os radicais da República* (São Paulo: Brasiliense, 1986) and Gladys Sabina Ribeiro, "O jacobinismo nos primeiros anos da República: seus ódios, suas razões e a criação de uma idéia de nação," in *História: Questões & Debates*, Curitiba, v. 10, n. 18–19, 1989, pp. 261–282.

[9] The dispute became known as *Questão de Palmas*. See Adelar Heinsfeld, *Fronteira Brasil/Argentina: A questão de Palmas (de Alexandre Gusmão a Rio Branco)* (Passo Fundo: Méritos, 2007). The Brazilian representative, José Maria da Silva Paranhos Júnior (of whom more below), offered President Cleveland an extended defense of the Brazilian argument. See *Obras do Barão do Rio Branco I: Questões de Limites República Argentina* (Brasília: FUNAG, 2012).

[10] The determinants and exigencies of the Blaine-Mendonça treaty are discussed in Steven Topik, *Trade and Gunboats: The United States and Brazil in the Age of Empire* (Stanford University Press, 2000). For an analysis of the Brazilian Republic's leaning towards the United States in opposition to Great Britain see Antonia Fernanda Pacca de Almeida Wright, *Desafio Americano À Preponderância Britânica no Brasil 1808–1850* (Rio de Janeiro: Editora Trio, 1972).

[11] See David M. Pletcher, *The Diplomacy of Trade and Investment: American Economic Expansion in the Hemisphere, 1865–1900* (University of Missouri Press,

1998, p. 263). For a contemporary source see W.J. Lauck, *The causes of the panic of 1893* (Cambridge: The Riverside Press, 1907, p. 112).

[12] On the Canudos Revolt in English see Robert M. Levine, *Vale of Tears: Revisiting the Canudos Massacre in Northeastern Brazil, 1893–1897* (University of California Press, 1995) and Patricia R. Pessar, *From Fanatics to Folk: Brazilian Millenarianism and Popular Culture* (Duke University Press, 2004). See also Milton Tosto, *The Meaning of Liberalism in Brazil* (London: Lexington Books, 2005). A large body of critical work exists on Euclides da Cunha's novel. See especially Frederic Amory, "Historical Source and Biographical Context in the Interpretation of Euclides da Cunha's Os Sertões," in *Journal of Latin American Studies*, vol. 28, n. 3, 1996, pp. 667–685; and Maria Zilda Ferreira Cury, "Os Sertões, de Euclides da Cunha: Espaços," in *Luso-Brazilian Review*, vol. 41, n. 1, 2004, pp. 71–79. The novel's English translation, by Samuel Putnam, is titled *Rebellion in the Backlands* (University of Chicago Press, 1957).

[13] The recommended works on Brazilian economic history are Amaury Patrick Gremaud, *Economia Brasileira Contemporânea* (Editora Atlas, 2009); Fabio Giambiagi, Lavínia Barros de Castro, André Villela, and Jennifer Hermann, *Economia Brasileira Contemporânea, 1945–2010* (Elsevier, 2011); and Marcelo de Paiva Abreu (Ed.), *A Ordem do Progresso: Dois Século de Política Econômica no Brasil* (Elsevier, 2014).

[14] The notion of "deterioration of the terms of trade" is part of what is known as the "Prebisch-Singer Hypothesis." See David I. Harvey, Neil M. Kellard, Jakob B. Madsen, and Mark E. Wohar, "The Prebisch-Singer Hypothesis: Four Centuries of Evidence," in *Review of Economics and Statistics*, Vol. 92, N. 2, 2010, pp. 367–377.

[15] For a more detailed discussion of the Amapá Question see Arthur Cézar Ferreira Reis, *Limites e Demarcações na Amazônia Brasileira: A Fronteira Colonial com a Guiana Francesa* (Belém: SECULT, 1993) and Demétrio Magnoli, *O corpo da pátria: imaginação geográfica e política externa no Brasil (1808–1912)* (São Paulo: Moderna, 1997).

[16] Maury wrote a book about the Amazon titled *Amazon, and the Atlantic Slopes of South America* (1853). An account of his interests in the region appears in the aforementioned work by Amado Cervo and Clodoaldo Bueno, *História da Política Exterior do Brasil* (Brasilia: UNB, 2011, pp. 110–117). See also Gerald Horne, *The Deepest South: The United States, Brazil, and the African Slave Trade* (New York University Press, 2007, pp. 107–127).

[17] See Luiz Alberto Moniz Bandeira, "O Barão de Rothschild e a questão do Acre," *Revista Brasileira de Política Internacional*, vol.43, n.2, Brasília, 2000.

[18] Regarding Pereira Passos's reforms see Paula de Paoli, *Entre Reliquias e Casas Velhas: a Arquitetura das Reformas Urbanas de Pereira Passos no Centro do Rio de Janeiro* (Rio de Janeiro: FAPERJ, 2013).

[19] See Theresa Meade, "'Civilizing Rio de Janeiro': The Public Health Campaign and the Riot of 1904," in *Journal of Social History*, Vol. 20, No. 2 (Winter, 1986), pp. 301–322.

[20] For a perspective on the period's society see the works of Sidney Chalhoub, *Trabalho, lar, botequim: o cotidiano dos trabalhadores no Rio de Janeiro da Belle Époque* (São Paulo: Brasiliense, 1986) and *Cidade febril: cortiços e epidemias na Corte imperial* (São Paulo: Companhia das Letras, 1996). See also Magali Gouveia Engel, *Os delírios da razão: médicos, loucos e hospícios, Rio de Janeiro, 1830–1930* (Rio de Janeiro: Editora Fiocruz, 2001). For a perspective on the period's society and literature see Sophia Beal, *Brazil under Construction: Fiction and Public Works* (Palgrave Macmillan, 2013).

[21] Regarding the Accord of Taubaté see Mauricio A. Font, *Coffee and Transformation in Sao Paulo, Brazil* (Rowman & Littlefield, 2010). A detailed discussion of the financial determinants of the Accord appear in Chapter 5, especially pages 132–135. See also Thomas Holloway, *The Brazilian Coffee Valorization of 1906: Regional Politics and Economic Dependence* (Madison: The Society Press of the State Historical Society of Wisconsin, 1975) and Joseph Love, *São Paulo in the Brazilian Federation, 1889–1937* (Stanford University Press, 1980). In Portuguese see Edgar Carone, *A Primeira República (1889–1930): texto e contexto* (São Paulo: Difel, 1973). An important work on the subject is that of Brazilian economist Celso Furtado, *Formação econômica do Brasil* (Rio de Janeiro: Fundo de Cultura, 1959), published in English as *The Economic Growth of Brazil: A Survey from Colonial to Modern Times* (University of California Press, 1963). Furtado, as we will see later, presents a cogent analysis of Brazilian industrialization in its relation to the decline of the prevalence of coffee export interests in the national economy after the 1930 Revolution.

[22] On the *Caixa de Conversão* see José Marcos Nayme Novelli, *Instituições, política e idéias econômicas: o caso do Banco Central do Brasil, 1965–1998* (São Paulo: Anna Blume/FAPESP, 2001, pp. 52–53). See also Maria Teresa Ribeiro de Oliveira and Maria Luiza Falcão Silva, "O Brasil no padrão-ouro: a Caixa de Conversão de 1906–1914," in *História Econômica & História de Empresas*, vol. 4, issue 1, 2001, pp. 83–114.

[23] The importance of the conference for the historical development of Brazilian diplomacy is analyzed in Luís Cláudio Villafañe, *O Brasil entre a América e a Europa: o Império e o interamericanismo (do Congresso do Panamá à Conferência de Washington)* (São Paulo: UNESP, 2004)

[24] In regard to *coronelism*, see Maria de Lourdes Mônaco Janoti, *Coronelismo: uma política de compromissos* (São Paulo: Brasiliense, 1981) and Victor Nunes Leal, *Coronelismo, enxada e voto* (São Paulo: Alfa-Ômega, 1986).

[25] An excellent biography of Marshal Cândido Rondon is found in Todd A. Diacon, *Stringing Together a Nation: Cândido Mariano da Silva Rondon and the Construction of a Modern Brazil, 1906–1930* (Duke University Press, 2004).

[26] The subject of Japanese emigration to Latin America involving Japanese imperialism and social prejudice is treated in Toake Endoh, *Exporting Japan: Politics of Emigration to Latin America* (University of Illinois Press, 2009). For a perspective on Japanese immigration from the point of view of the Brazilian Foreign Office see Valdemar Carneiro Leão Neto, *A Crise da Imigração Japonesa no Brasil, 1930–1934: Contornos Diplomáticos* (Brasília: FUNAG,

1990). See also the aforementioned work by Jeffrey Lesser, *A Discontented Diaspora: Japanese Brazilians and the Meanings of Ethnic Militancy 1960–1980* (Duke University Press, 2007).

[27] The case is analyzed in João Paulo Soares Alsina Júnior, *Rio-Branco: grande estratégia e o poder naval* (Editora FGV, 2015). See also Adelar Heinsfeld, "Rio Branco e a modernização dos mecanismos de defesa nacional," in *História: Debates e Tendências*, v. 10, n. 2, 2010, pp. 264–276; Max Justo Guedes, "O Barão do Rio Branco e a Modernização da Defesa," in Carlos Henrique Cardim and João Almino (Eds.), *Rio Branco, a América do sul e a Modernização do Brasil* (Rio de Janeiro: EMC, 2002); and José Joffily, *O Caso Panther* (Paz e Terra, 1988).

[28] See E. Bradford Burns, *The Unwritten Alliance: Rio-Branco and Brazilian-American Relations* (Columbia University Press, 1966). A general history of Brazil is also available by the same author under the title *A History of Brazil (Myth and Poetics)* (Columbia University Press, 1971).

[29] Regarding the professional disputes and mutual dislike between Paranhos and Zeballos see Adelar Heinsfeld, *Fronteira e Ocupação do Espaço: A Questão de Palmas com a Argentina e a Colonização do Vale do Rio do Peixe-SC* (São Paulo: Perse, 2014). See also from the same author *Fronteira Brasil/Argentina: a Questão de Palmas – de Alexandre de Gusmão a Rio Branco* (Passo Fundo: Méritos, 2007) and "Falsificando telegramas: Estanislau Severo Zeballos e as relações Brasil-Argentina no início do século XX," in *Vestígios do passado: A história e suas fontes* (IX Encontro Estadual de História, Associação Nacional de História, Seção Rio Grande do Sul – ANPUH-RS).

[30] A biography of the politician appears in Cyro Silva, *Pinheiro Machado* (Rio de Janeiro: Tupã Editora, 1951).

[31] See Raymundo Faoro, *Os Donos do Poder: formação do patronato político brasileiro* (Porto Alegre: Editora Globo, 1958). See also Joseph Love, *Rio Grande do Sul and Brazilian Regionalism, 1882–1930* (Stanford University Press, 1971) and, in Portuguese, Nelson Boeira, "O Rio Grande de Augusto Comte," in José Hildebrando Dacanal and Sergius Gonzaga (Eds.), *RS: cultura e ideologia* (Porto Alegre: Mercado Aberto, 1980, pp. 34–59). Two Brazilian historians who assumed an early anti-Positivist posture and criticized Rio Grande do Sul's ideology are Sílvio Romero (1851–1914) and Capistrano de Abreu (1853–1927). For a historiographical analysis see Letícia Nedel, "A recepção da obra de Gilberto Freyre no Rio Grande do Sul," in *Mana*, vol. 13, n. 1, Rio de Janeiro, 2007.

[32] For two book-length studies of the revolt see Joseph Love, *The Revolt of the Whip* (Stanford University Press, 2012). See also Zachary R. Morgan, *Legacy of the Lash: Race and Corporal Punishment in the Brazilian Navy and the Atlantic World* (Indiana University Press, 2014).

[33] For an in-depth analysis of the conflict see Todd A. Diacon, *Millenarian Vision, Capitalist Reality: Brazil's Contestado Rebellion, 1912–1916* (Duke University Press Books, 1991).

[34] The anti-trust action was based on the Sherman Act of 1890. See Enrique Cardenas, José Antonio Ocampo, Rosemary Thorp (Eds.), *An Economic History of*

Twentieth-Century Latin America: Volume I: The Export Age (Palgrave, 2000, pp. 41–43).

[35] Regarding the funding loan of 1914 see Bill Albert and Paul Henderson, *South America and the First World War: The Impact of the War on Brazil, Argentina, Peru and Chile* (Cambridge University Press, 1988, pp. 134–138).

[36] Senator José Gomes Pinheiro Machado was murdered by Francisco Manso de Paiva Coimbra, who was arrested immediately after the incident. Coimbra was born in Rio Grande do Sul, in a city called Cacimbinhas. After the Senator's assassination, Cacimbinhas's administrator, Ney Lima Costa, changed the city's name to Pinheiro Machado, as it remains to this day. To the end of his life, Francisco Manso de Paiva Coimbra maintained that he had acted alone, and the Senator's rivals from São Paulo were never formally accused of ordering the crime.

[37] On the Spanish Influenza and its effects in Brazil during the First World War, see Robert L. Scheina, *Latin America: A Naval History, 1810–1987* (Naval Institute Press, 1987).

[38] The famous notion of "noble emulation" (*nobre emulação*) appears in the Foreign Minister's address at the III Latin American Scientific Congress (Rio de Janeiro, 1905). The text is found in *Obras do Barão do Rio Branco, Vol. IX* (Rio de Janeiro: Imprensa Nacional, 1946, pp. 76–77). See Eliana Zugaib, *A Hidrovia Paraguai-Paraná e seu Significado para a Diplomacia Sul-Americana do Brasil* (Brasília: FUNAG, 2006, p. 45). See also Paulo Fagundes Visentini, *A Projeção Internacional Do Brasil* 1930–2012 (Rio de Janeiro: Elsevier, 2013).

[39] For the 1917 strike and its ramificaions see Cláudio Henrique de Moraes Batalha, *Movimento Operário na Primeira República* (Rio de Janeiro: Jorge Zahar Editores, 2000). See also Robério Santos Souza, *Tudo pelo trabalho livre! Trabalhadores e conflitos no pós-abolição (Bahia 1892–1909)* (EDUFBA, 2011) and Paulo Sérgio Pinheiro, "O Proletariado Industrial na Primeira República," in Boris Fausto (Ed.), *O Brasil Republicano: Sociedade e Instituições (1889–1930)* (Rio de Janeiro: Bertrand, 1990, pp. 140–154). The general strike reached as far as Rio Grande do Sul, where it had a strong influence on the emergence of Trabalhista Movement. See Miguel Bodea, *A Greve de 1917: As origens do trabalhismo gaúcho* (Porto Alegre: L&PM, s/d). The influence of the Russian Revolution in Brazil has been analyzed by Luiz Alberto Moniz Bandeira in *O Ano Vermelho: A Revolução Russa e seus Reflexos no Brasil* (Rio de Janeiro: Editora Civilização Brasileira, 1967).

[40] For a study on Anarchism in Brazil see John Foster Dulles, *Anarchists and Communists in Brazil, 1900–1935* (University of Texas Press, 1973). Regarding the general development of the Labor Movement in the country see Robert J. Alexander, *A History of Organized Labor in Brazil* (Praeger, 2003).

[41] Much has been written on the Tenentista Movement. See Edgard Carone, *O Tenentismo* (São Paulo: Difel, 1975); Virgilio Santa Rosa, *O sentido do Tenentismo* (São Paulo: Alfa-Ômega, 1976); Jose Augusto Drummond, *O Movimento Tenentista: a intervenção militar e conflito Hierárquico (1922–1935)* (Rio de Janeiro: Graal, 1986); Paulo Sérgio Pinheiro, "A crise dos anos vinte e a

Revolução de 1930," in Paulo Sérgio Pinheiro (Ed.), *O Brasil Republicano. Volume 2: sociedade e instituições (1889–1930)* (Rio de Janeiro: Bertrand Brasil, 1997).

[42] Note that the *Departamento Nacional de Obras Contra as Secas* received this denomination only in 1945. It was created in 1909 as *Inspetoria de Obras Contra as Secas* (IOCS), and in 1919, during Epitácio Pessoa's government, was federalized, receiving the new name, *Inspetoria Federal de Obras Contra as Secas*. The DNOCS still functions as of 2016 with its head office in the city of Fortaleza, Ceará. See Manuel Correia de Oliveira Andrade, *O Nordeste e a questão regional* (Editora Ática, 1988). For discussions on the present policies of the DNOCS see Delma Pessanha Neves, Ramonildes A. Gomes, Pedro Fonseca Leal (Eds.), *Quadros e programas institucionais em políticas públicas* (Campina Grande: EDUEPB, 2014). Regarding the region's human and natural geography see Aziz Ab'Sáber, "Sertões e Sertanejos: uma geografia humana sofrida," in *Estudos Avançados*, v. 13, n. 36, 1999, pp. 7–59.

[43] See Heloisa Turini Bruhns, *Futebol, carnaval e capoeira: entre as gingas do corpo brasileiro* (Campinas: Papirus, 2000) and Marco Antonio Villa, *A História das Constituições Brasileiras: 200 Anos de Luta Contra o Arbítrio* (São Paulo: Leya, 2011).

[44] For the 1923 Revolution in Rio Grande do Sul see Aline Brandt, *De Borges a Getúlio: Transição Política nas Páginas de O Nacional* (Masters Thesis, University of Passo Fundo, Brazil, 2008) and Jonas Balbinot, *Relações de Poder: Getúlio Vargas e Borges de Medeiros (1922–1928)* (Master Thesis, University of Passo Fundo, Brazil, 2008).

[45] Regarding the 1924 Revolution in São Paulo see Ilka Stern Cohen, *Bombas sobre São Paulo, A Revolução de 1924* (São Paulo: Editora Unesp, 2006). See also Anna Maria Martinez Corrêa, *A Rebelião de 1924 em São Paulo* (São Paulo: Hucitec, 1976).

[46] The idea of historical revisionism regarding the Luis Carlos Prestes-Miguel Costa Column started with the publication of the work by Eliane Brum, *Coluna Prestes: o avesso da lenda* (Porto Alegre: Artes e Ofícios, 1994). See also Lira Neto, *Getúlio: dos anos de formação à conquista do poder (1882–1930)* (São Paulo: Companhia das Letras, 2012).

[47] Regarding the country's economic situation during Bernades's government see Winston Fritsch, "1922: A Crise Econômica," in *Estudos Históricos*, Rio de Janeiro, vol. 6, n. 11, 1993, pp. 3–8.

[48] Carlos Henrique Cardim, *A Raiz das Coisas: Rui Barbosa, O Brasil no Mundo* (Civilização Brasileira, 2010).

[49] Regarding the Celerada Law see Vito Giannotti, *História das lutas dos trabalhadores no Brasil* (Rio de Janeiro: Editora Mauad, 2007, pp. 101–103).

[50] Regarding the diplomatic relations between Brazil and the United States in the twentieth century see the work of Monica Hirst, *Brasil-Estados Unidos: desencontros e afinidades* (São Paulo: FGV, 2009).

[51] See Ricardo Bielschowsky, *Pensamento econômico brasileiro: o ciclo ideológico do desenvolvimentismo* (Rio de Janeiro: Editora Contraponto, 1995).

⁵² Regarding the CIESP and its role in the Brazilian process of industrialization see Ben Ross Schneider, *Business Politics and the State in Twentieth-Century Latin America* (Cambridge University Press, 2004, pp. 102–105) and Mauricio Augusto Font, *Transforming Brazil: A Reform Era in Perspective* (Rowman and Littlefield, 2003, pp. 130–133). An overview of industrialization in Brazil can be found in Anne G. Hanley, "Financing Brazil's Industrialization," in Jeff Horn, Leonard N. Rosenband, Merritt Roe Smith (Eds.), *Reconceptualizing the Industrial Revolution* (The MIT Press, 2010, pp. 251–270).

⁵³ See, for instance, Lúcia Miguel Pereira, *Prosa de Ficção (1870–1920)* (Belo Horizonte: Editora Itatiaia, 1950) and Antônio Cândido, *Literatura e Sociedade: Estudos de Teoria e História Literária* (São Paulo: T. A. Queiroz, 2002). See also Gilberto Mendonça Teles, *Contramargem: estudos de literatura, Volume 1* (Editora PUC-Rio, 2002, pp. 306–308).

⁵⁴ On the Brazilian avant-garde and the Modern Art Week see Mário da Silva Brito, *História do modernismo brasileiro: antecedentes da semana de arte moderna* (Civilização Brasileira, 1974) and Maria Augusta Fonseca, *Oswald de Andrade: Biografia* (Editora Globo, 2007). In English see John Nist, *The Modernist Movement in Brazil: A Literary Study* (University of Texas Press (November 15, 2014). See also Charles A. Perrone, *Seven Faces: Brazilian Poetry Since Modernism* (Duke University Press, 2012) and Fernando Luiz Lara, *The Rise of Popular Modernist Architecture in Brazil* (University Press of Florida, 2008).

⁵⁵ Recommended articles on Mário de Andrade's modernism in English are: Kimberle S. López, "Modernismo and the Ambivalence of the Postcolonial Experience: Cannibalism, Primitivism, and Exoticism in Mário de Andrade's Macunaíma," in *Luso-Brazilian Review*, vol. 35, n. 1, 1998, pp. 25–38; Bruce Dean Willis, "Necessary Losses: Purity and Solidarity in Mário de Andrade's Dockside Poetics," in *Hispania*, vol. 81, n. 2, 1998, pp. 261–268; Sarah Hamilton-Tyrell, "Mário de Andrade, Mentor: Modernism and Musical Aesthetics in Brazil, 1920–1945," in *Musical Quarterly*, vol. 88, n. 1, 2005, pp. 7–34.

Chapter Four

¹ Regarding Pinheiro Machado's influence on Vargas's political career, see Luciano Aronne de Abreu, *Getúlio Vargas: a construção de um mito, 1928–30* (Porto Alegre: EDIPUCRS, 1996, pp. 33-37). A biography of Getúlio Dornelles Vargas in English can be found in John W. Foster Dulles, *Vargas of Brazil: A Political Biography* (University of Texas Press, 1967).

² Regarding the 1932 Constitutionalist Revolution, see Stanley E. Hilton, *A guerra civil brasileira: história da Revolução Constitucionalista de 1932* (Editora Nova Fronteira, 1982) and Holien Gonçalves Bezerra, *O Jogo do Poder: revolução paulista de 32* (São Paulo: Moderna, 1988). Regarding the 1930 Revolution, see Boris Fausto, *A Revolução de 1930: Historiografia e História* (São Paulo: Companhia das Letras, 1997) and Thomas E. Skidmore, *Politics in Brazil 1930–1964: An Experiment in Democracy* (Oxford University Press, 1967). Regarding

the Tenentista Movement and its revolutionary intents, see Vavy Pacheco Borges, *Tenentismo e Revolução Brasileira* (São Paulo: Brasiliense, 1992) and Anita Leocádia Prestes, *O Tenentismo Pós-1930: Continuidade ou ruptura* (São Paulo: Paz e Terra, 1999).

[3] Regarding the Chaco War and its diplomatic implications see William R. Garner, *The Chaco Dispute: A Study in Prestige Diplomacy* (Washington: Public Affairs Press, 1966). From the perspective of military history see Bruce W. Farca, *The Chaco War: Bolivia and Paraguay, 1932–1935* (Praeger, 1996). An informative ilustrated book on the War can be found in Alejandro de Quesada, *The Chaco War 1932–1935: South America's Greatest Modern Conflict* (Oxford: Osprey Publishing, 2011).

[4] A biography of Olga Benário Prestes is found in Fernando Morais, *Olga: Revolutionary and Martyr* (Grove Press, 2007), translated by Ellen Watson. For an account of Jewish women moving to Brazil in order to avoid German persecution see Katherine Morris (Ed.), *Odyssey of Exile: Jewish Women Flee the Nazis for Brazil* (Wayne State University Press, 1996).

[5] For an in-depth discussion of the Estado Novo and its policies see Dulce Pandolfi (Ed.), *Repensando o Estado Novo* (Rio de Janeiro: FGV, 1999).

[6] For an analysis of the Brazilian bureaucracy see Maria Rita Loureiro, *Burocracia e Política no Brasil* (Rio de Janeiro: FGV, 2010). See also Luiz Carlos Bresser Pereira, *A sociedade estatal e a tecnoburocracia* (São Paulo: Editora Brasiliense, 1981) and Fernando Luiz Abrucio, Maria Rita Loureiro, and Regina Silvia Pacheco (Eds.), *Burocracia e política no Brasil: desafios para o Estado democrático no século XXI* (Rio de Janeiro: FGV, 2010).

[7] For an account of Osvaldo Aranha's Mission, see Ricardo Antônio Silva Seitenfus, *A entrada do Brasil na Segunda Guerra Mundial* (Porto Alegre: EDIPUCRS, 2000, pp. 175–177). Vargas's policy of using Brazil-Germany relations for bargaining his support to the allies during the Second World War has been famously analyzed by Gerson Moura, who defined the dictator's stance as "pragmatic equidistance." See Gerson Moura, *Sucessos e ilusões: relações internacionais do Brasil durante e após a Segunda Guerra Mundial* (Rio de Janeiro: FGV, 1991). See also from the same author *Autonomia na dependência: a política externa brasileira de 1935 a 1942* (Editora Nova Fronteira, 1980).

[8] See Giralda Seyferth, "Os imigrantes e a campanha de nacionalização do Estado Novo," in Dulce Pandolfi (Ed.), *Repensando o Estado Novo* (Rio de Janeiro: FGV, 1999, pp. 199–228).

[9] Regarding the Integralista Revolt see Hélio Silva, *O ciclo de Vargas: 1938, Terrorismo em Campo Verde* (Rio de Janeiro: Civilização Brasileira, 1971).

[10] For a detailed study of Brazil's role in the Second World War see Neill Lochery, *Brazil: The Fortunes of War – World War II and the Making of Modern Brazil* (Basic Books, 2014). Regarding Brazil-U.S. relations in the period and beyond see Luiz Alberto Moniz Bandeira, *Presença dos Estados Unidos no Brasil: (dois séculos de história)* (Rio de Janeiro: Civilização Brasileira, 1973) and *Brasil, Argentina e Estados Unidos (Da Tríplice Aliança ao Mercosul, 1870–2003)* (Rio

de Janeiro: Revan, 2003). See also Roberto Sander, *O Brasil na Mira de Hitler* (São Paulo: Editora Objetiva, 2007).

[11] Regarding Brazil-Soviet Union relations in the period see Stanley E. Hilton, *Brazil and the Soviet Challenge 1917–1947* (University of Texas Press, 1991).

[12] The establishment of the Partido Trabalhista Brasileiro tends to be regarded as the crystallization of Brazilian *Trabalhismo*. See Angela Maria De Castro Gomes, *A invenção do trabalhismo* (São Paulo: FGV, 2005). See also the aforementioned work by Miguel Bodea, *A Greve de 1917: As Origens do Trabalhismo Gaúcho* (Porto Alegre: L&PM, n/d).

[13] Regarding the works of Anísio Teixeira see Luis Vianna Filho, *Anísio Teixeira: A polêmica da educação* (Rio de Janeiro: Nova Fronteira, 1990). As we will see in more detail later, Anísio Teixera's ideas were influential in the debate regarding the establishment and maintenance of public education in Brazil. In this regard see Diana Couto Pinto (Ed.), *Trajetórias de liberais e radicais pela educação pública: Anísio Teixeira, Darcy Ribeiro, Fernando de Azevedo, Florestan Fernandes* (São Paulo: Edições Loyola, 2000). Readers interested in the history of Brazilian education can find useful information in Maria do Carmo Guedes's edition of José Ricardo Pires de Almeida's *História da Instrução Pública no Brasil 1500–1889* (São Paulo: EDUC, 2000). Pires de Almeida's work was originally published in French in 1889. The author analyzes the educational regulations established throughout the Imperial Period and praises Jesuit education in Brazil. For the subject of education during the republican period see Maria Auxiliadora Cavazotti, *O Projeto Republicano de Educação Nacional na Versão de José Veríssimo* (São Paulo: Anna Blume, 2003). Still regarding Anísio Teixeira see a comparative approach to his ideas and those of Paulo Freire (1921–1997) in Sérgio C. Fonseca, *Paulo Freire e Anísio Teixeira: Convergências e Divergências 1959–1969* (Jundiaí: Paco Editorial, 2011).

[14] See Alessandra Coutinho Lisboa, *Villa-Lobos e o canto orfeônico: música, nacionalismo e ideal civilizador* (Masters Thesis, Universidade Estadual Paulista, UNESP, São Paulo, 2005) and Ludwig Lauerhass Júnior, *Getúlio Vargas e o Triunfo do Nacionalismo Brasileiro* (Rio de Janeiro: Editora Itatiaia, 1986).

[15] On Heitor Villa-Lobos see Gerard Béhague, *Villa-Lobos: The Search for Brazil's Musical Soul* (University of Texas Press, 1994) and Simon Wright, *Villa-Lobos* (Oxford Oxford University Press, 1992). The reader interested in the Brazilian composer's life and works can find useful information in David P. Appleby's *Heitor Villa-Lobos: A Bio-Bibliography* (New York: Greenwood Press, 1988).

[16] See Paulina L. Alberto, *Terms of Inclusion: Black Intellectuals in Twentieth-Century Brazil* (The University of North Carolina Press, 2011).

[17] For an analysis of Rodrigues's theater see David Sanderson George, *Nelson Rodrigues and the Invention of Brazilian Drama* (Latin American Theater Review Press, University of Kansas, 2010)

[18] A lot has been written on the history of samba music. See particularly Hermano Vianna, *The Mystery of Samba: Popular Music and National Identity in Brazil* (The University of North Carolina Press, 1999); Marc A. Hertzman, *Making*

Samba: A New History of Race and Music in Brazil (Duke University Press, 2013); Idelber Avelar and Christopher Dunn (Eds.), *Brazilian Popular Music and Citizenship* (Duke University Press, 2011); Bryan McCann, *Hello, Hello Brazil: Popular Music in the Making of Modern Brazil* (Duke University Press, 2004); and Peter Fryer, *Rhythms of Resistance: African Musical Heritage in Brazil* (Wesleyan, 2000).

[19] The Brazilian deceptive ideology of racial democracy has been severely criticized on several fronts. See Abdias do Nascimento, "The Myth of Racial Democracy," in Robert M. Levine and John J. Crocitti (Eds.), *The Brazil Reader: History, Culture, Politics* (Duke University Press, 1999, pp. 379–381); France Winddance Twine, *Racism in a Racial Democracy: The Maintenance of White Supremacy in Brazil* (Rutgers University Press, 1998); and Edward E. Telles, *Race in Another America: The Significance of Skin Color in Brazil* (Princeton University Press, 2006). On the theme of affirmative action in Brazil see A. Cicalo, *Urban Encounters: Affirmative Action and Black Identities in Brazil* (Palgrave Macmillan, 2012) and Rosana Heringer, Ollie Johnson, and Ollie A. Johnson III (Eds.), *Race, Politics, and Education in Brazil: Affirmative Action in Higher Education* (Palgrave Macmillan, 2015). For a perspective from the field of media studies see Samantha Nogueira Joyce, *Brazilian Telenovelas and the Myth of Racial Democracy* (Lexington: Lexington Books, 2012).

[20] For a chronological history of Brazilian cinema see Lisa Shaw and Stephanie Dennison, *Brazilian National Cinema* (Routledge, 2004). For a view on the building of a Brazilian national identity in film see Tatiana Signorelli Heise, *Remaking Brazil: Contested National Identities in Contemporary Brazilian Cinema* (University of Wales Press, 2012). See also the works of Richard A. Gordon, *Cannibalizing the Colony: Cinematic Adaptations of Colonial Literature in Mexico and Brazil* (Purdue University Press, 2008) and *Cinema, Slavery, and Brazilian Nationalism* (University of Texas Press, 2015).

Chapter Five

[1] Regarding the notion of *desenvolvimentismo* see Luiz Carlos Bresser-Pereira, *Desenvolvimento e Crise no Brasil 1930–1967* (Rio de Janeiro: Zahar Editores, 1968). See also Paulo Nogueira Batista Jr., "Nacionalismo e desenvolvimento," in Luiz Carlos Bresser-Pereira (Ed.), *Nação, câmbio e desenvolvimento* (Rio de Janeiro: FGV, 2008). For the specificities of Brazilian economic liberalism see Maria Angélica Borges, *Eugenio Gudin, capitalismo e neoliberalismo* (São Paulo: Educ, 1996) and Ricardo Bielschowsky, "Eugênio Gudin," in *Estudos Avançados*, vol. 15, n. 41, São Paulo, Jan/Apr 2001.

[2] The ISEB played an important role in the development of public policies during the second half of the twentieth century. As we will see in more detail later, among the ISEB's members figured important intellectuals such as Hélio Jaguaribe (b. 1923), Nelson Werneck Sodré (1911–1999), Antonio Cândido (b. 1918), Celso Furtado (1920–2004), Gilberto Freyre (1900–1987), Heitor Villa-Lobos (1887–

1959), and Miguel Reale (1910–2006). See Caio Navarro de Toledo, *ISEB: fábrica de ideologias* (Porto Alegre: Ática, 1977); Luiz Carlos Bresser-Pereira, "O Conceito de Desenvolvimento do ISEB Rediscutido," in *Textos para Discussão da Escola de Economia de São Paulo da Fundação Getulio Vargas*, Texto para Discussão 137, August 2004; and Caio Navarro de Toledo (Ed.), *Intelectuais e política no Brasil: A experiência do ISEB* (Rio de Janeiro: Revan, 2005). See also Edson Rezende de Souza, "O ISEB e o nacional-desenvolvimentismo: A intelligentsia brasileira nos anos 50," in *Contemporâneos: Revista de Artes e Humanidades*, UFABC, n. 4, May/Oct 2009.

[3] Vincent Ferraro, "Dependency Theory: An Introduction," in Giorgio Secondi (Ed.), *The Development Economics Reader* (London: Routledge, 2008, pp. 58–64).

[4] See Ana Cláudia Caputo and Hildete Pereira de Melo, "A industrialização brasileira nos anos de 1950: uma análise da instrução 113 da SUMOC," in *Estudos Econômicos*, vol. 39, n. 3, São Paulo, July/Sept 2009.

[5] For an analysis of the continuities in the politics of Vargas and Goulart see Pedro Cezar Dutra Fonseca and Sérgio Marley Modesto Monteiro, "Credibilidade e populismo no Brasil: a política econômica dos governos Vargas e Goulart," *Revista Brasileira de Economia*, Rio de Janeiro, vol. 59, n. 2, Apr/Jul 2005. In this regard, the idea of *populismo* as a defining feature of the period is especially relevant. See José Dantas Filho and Francisco Fernando Monteoliva Doratioto, *A República Bossa-nova: A Democracia Populista (1954–1964)* (São Paulo: Atual, 1991) and Octavio Ianni, *O colapso do populismo no Brasil* (Rio de Janeiro: Civilização Brasileira, 1968).

[6] See Edson de Oliveira Nunes, *A gramática política do Brasil: clientelismo e insulamento burocrático* (Rio de Janeiro: Jorge Zahar, 1997, pp. 107–133) and Luciano Aronne de Abreu and Helder Gordim da Silveira (Eds.), *De Vargas aos Militares: Autoritarismo e desenvolvimento econômico no Brasil* (Porto Alegre: EDIPUCRS, 2014).

[7] See the aforementioned works by Maria Angélica Borges, *Eugenio Gudin, capitalismo e neoliberalismo* (São Paulo: Educ, 1996) and by Ricardo Bielschowsky, "Eugênio Gudin," in *Estudos Avançados*, vol. 15, n. 41, São Paulo, Jan/Apr 2001.

[8] Regarding the emergence of the Peasant Leagues in Brazil see Cliff Welch, "Keeping Communism Down on the Farm: The Brazilian Rural Labor Movement during the Cold War," in *Latin American Perspectives*, vol. 33, n. 3, 2006, pp. 28–50, and Leila de Menezes Stein, *Trabalhismo, circulos operários e politica: a construção do sindicato de trabalhadores agrícolas no Brasil (1954 a 1964)* (São Paulo: FAPESP, 2008). For a biography of Francisco Julião see Cláudio Aguiar, *Francisco Julião: Uma Biografia* (Civilização Brasileira, 2014).

[9] Regarding the occupation of the western portion of the Brazilian territory see Orlando Vilas Bôas and Claudio Vilas Bôas, *A Marcha Para o Oeste: A Epopeia da Expedição Roncador-Xingu* (São Paulo: Companhia das Letras, 2012).

[10] Regarding the theme of corruption in the building of Brasília see Jeferson Tavares, *Projetos para Brasília e a cultura urbanística nacional* (Masters Thesis, São Carlos, USP, 2004) and *Projetos para Brasília: 1927–1957* (IPHAN, 2014).

See also from the same author "50 anos do concurso para Brasília – um breve histórico," in *Arquitextos*, ano 08, Jul 2007. Tavares mentions the Companhia Urbanizadora da Nova Capital do Brasil, NOVACAP, the company in charge of the public works involved in the building of the new capital, as well as Carlos Lacerda's attempts to establish a Parliamentary Inquiry Commission in the National Congress to investigate possible cases of corruption related to the construction works. Regarding Kubitschek's government more generally see Ronaldo Costa Couto, *O Essencial de JK* (Planeta do Brasil, 2013).

[11] For an analysis of Brasília see James Holston, *The Modernist City: An Anthropological Critique of Brasilia* (University of Chicago Press, 1989).

[12] Regarding the concept "conservative modernization" see Wladimir Pomar, *Era Vargas: A Modernização Conservadora* (Editora Ática, 2002).

[13] For a detailed discussion of the SUMOC's Instruction 70, as well as of Brazilian economic history in general, see Werner Baer, *The Brazilian Economy: Growth and Development* (Praeger, 1995). See also Marcio Holland and Yoshiaki Nakano, *Taxa de Câmbio no Brasil: Estudos de uma Perspectiva do Desenvolvimento Econômico* (Rio de Janeiro: Campus/Elsevier, 2011).

[14] Regarding the theme of compulsory voting in Brazil see Timothy J. Power, "Compulsory for Whom? Mandatory Voting and Electoral Participation in Brazil, 1986–2006," in *Journal of Politics in Latin America*, vol. 1, n. 1, 2009, pp. 97–122. See also Gabriel Cepaluni and F. Daniel Hidalgo, "Compulsory Voting Can Increase Political Inequality: Evidence from Brazil," in *Political Analysis*, 2016.

[15] A large body of texts has been produced in regard to the Conference and to the Brazilian position in it. See Alceu Amoroso Lima, "A Posição do Brasil em Punta del Este," in *Revista Brasileira de Política Internacional*, ano V, n. 17, Rio de Janeiro, Instituto Brasileiro de Relações Internacionais, March 1962; Renato Archer, "San Tiago e a Política Externa Independente," in José Vieira Coelho (Ed.), *San Tiago vinte anos depois* (Rio de Janeiro: Paz e Terra, 1985); Luiz Alberto Moniz Bandeira, *De Martí a Fidel: a Revolução Cubana e a América Latina* (Rio de Janeiro: Civilização Brasileira, 1998); and Hélio Franchini Neto, "A Política Externa Independente em ação: a Conferência de Punta del Este de 1962," in *Revista Brasileira de Política Internacional*, vol. 48, n. 2, Brasília, July/Dec 2005.

[16] In regard to the extension of labor rights to rural workers during João Goulart's government see Luiz Alberto Moniz Bandeira, *O Governo João Goulart – As Lutas Sociais no Brasil (1961–1964)* (Rio de Janeiro: Editora Civilização Brasileira, 1977).

[17] Regarding the IBAD and the IPES, as well as the entire process leading to the 1964 coup see René Armand Dreifuss, *1964: A Conquista do Estado* (Porto Alegre: Editora Vozes, 1981).

[18] Regarding this debate, see Sofia Lerche Vieira e Isabel Maria Sabino de Freitas, *Política educacional no Brasil: introdução histórica* (Plano Editora, 2003) and Otaiza de Oliveira Romanelli, *História da Educação no Brasil* (Editora Vozes, 2007). See also Ester Buffa, *Ideologias em conflito: escola pública e escola privada* (São Paulo: Cortez e Moraes, 1979).

[19] In this regard see the aforementioned work by Diana Couto Pinto (Ed.), *Trajetórias de liberais e radicais pela educação pública: Anísio Teixeira, Darcy Ribeiro, Fernando de Azevedo, Florestan Fernandes* (São Paulo: Edições Loyola, 2000).
[20] The CPCs had an important role in claiming a social function for the arts during the period. See Miliandre Garcia, "A questão da cultura popular: as políticas culturais do centro popular de cultura (CPC) da União Nacional dos Estudantes (UNE)," in *Revista Brasileira de História*, vol. 24, n. 47, São Paulo, 2004.
[21] An extensive bibliography exists on the works of Paulo Freire, who became a world-renowned educator during the second half of the twentieth century. For introductory purposes in English see Ana Maria Araujo and Donaldo P. Macedo (Eds.), *The Paulo Freire Reader* (Continuum International Publishing Group, 2000) and Peter Leonard and Peter McLaren (Eds.), *Paulo Freire: A Critical Encounter* (Routledge, 1992).
[22] For a biography of Clarice Lispector in English see Benjamin Moser, *Why This World: A Biography of Clarice Lispector* (Oxford University Press, 2009).
[23] In this regard see the aforementioned work by Charles A. Perrone, *Seven Faces: Brazilian Poetry Since Modernism* (Duke University Press, 1996) and Sérgio B. Martins, *Constructing an Avant-Garde: Art in Brazil 1949–1979* (MIT Press, 2013).
[24] See Gloria Ferreira and Paulo Herkenhoff (Eds.), *Mário Pedrosa: Primary Documents* (Duke University Press, 2016).
[25] For a study of the filmmaker's career see Darlene J. Sadlier, *Nelson Pereira dos Santos* (Papirus, 2012). Regading the Cinema Novo movement see Randal Johnson, *Cinema Novo x 5: Masters of Contemporary Brazilian Film* (University of Texas Press, 1984) and Lúcia Nagib, *Brazil on Screen: Cinema Novo, New Cinema, Utopia* (I. B. Tauris, 2007). For an in-depth historical analysis of Brazilian cinema see Robert Stam, *Tropical Multiculturalism: A Comparative History of Race in Brazilian Cinema and Culture* (Duke University Press, 1997).
[26] See Waldir Salvadore, *São Paulo em preto & branco: cinema e sociedade nos anos 50 e 60* (São Paulo: Anna Blume, 2005).
[27] Regarding Brazilian popular cinema see Stephanie Dennison and Lisa Shaw, *Popular Cinema in Brazil: 1930–2001* (Manchester University Press, 2004). For a careful study of Mazzaropi's cinema see Eva Paulino Bueno, *Amácio Mazzaropi in the Film and Culture of Brazil: After Cinema Novo* (Palgrave Macmillan, 2012).
[28] For an account in English of the development of bossa nova see Ruy Castro and Julian Dibbell, *Bossa Nova: The Story of the Brazilian Music That Seduced the World* (Chicago Review Press, 2012). See also David Treece, *Brazilian Jive* (Reaktion Books, 2013); Bryan McCann, "Blues and Samba: Another Side of Bossa Nova History," in *Luso-Brazilian Review*, vol. 44, n. 2, 2007, pp. 21–49; and Martha Tupinambá de Ulhôa, Cláudia Azevedo, and Felipe Trotta (Eds.), *Made In Brazil: Studies In Popular Music* (Routledge, 2014). In Portuguese see Paulo Sergio Duarte e Santuza Cambraia Naves, *Do Samba-canção à Tropicália* (Rio de Janeiro: Relume Dumará, 2003) and José Ramos Tinhorão, *História Social da Música Popular Brasileira* (São Paulo: Editora 34, 1998). Also of interest is the

Chapter Six

[1] Regarding the guerrila movements in Brazil during the period see Elio Gaspari, *A Ditadura Escancarada: As ilusões armadas* (São Paulo: Companhia das Letras, 2002); Claudinei Cássio de Rezende, *Suicídio Revolucionário: a luta armada e a herança da quimérica revolução em etapas* (São Paulo: Unesp, 2010); and Maria Helena Moreira Alves, *State and Opposition in Military Brazil* (University of Texas Press, 1988). See also the book by Catholic Church Cardinal and human rights activist Dom Paulo Evaristo Arns, *Brasil Nunca Mais* (Editora Vozes, 1996); the English version is entitled *Torture in Brazil: A Shocking Report on the Pervasive Use of Torture by Brazilian Military Governments, 1964–1979 (Translated by Jaime Wright; Edited with a new preface by Joan Dassin)* (University of Texas Press, 1998). The book documents episodes of torture under the military dictatorship between 1964 and 1979, relating the cases of more than 15,000 victims. Regarding the role of Dom Paulo Evaristo Arns, the Catholic Church, and Liberation Theology in the resistance to the dictatorship see Ricardo Carvalho, *O Cardeal da Resistência: As Muitas Vidas de Dom Paulo Evaristo Arns* (Instituto Vladimir Herzog, 2013).

[2] The idea of "learning to live with inflation" would support the government's option of economic indexation that would result in the highly problematic process of inertial inflation. On this subject see Alkimar R. Moura, *Paeg e Real: Dois Planos que Mudaram a Economia Brasileira* (FGV, 2007).

[3] See Jennifer Hermann, "Reformas, Endividamento Externo, e o 'Milagre' Econômico (1964–1973)," in Fabio Giambiagi (Ed.), *Economia Brasileira Contemporânea* (Elsevier, 2011, pp. 49–71).

[4] See the aforementioned work by Amado Cervo and Clodoaldo Bueno, *História da política exterior do Brasil* (São Paulo: Ática, 1992). In regard to the foreign policies enacted during the dictatorial period see also Paulo Fagundes Visentini, *A política externa do regime militar brasileiro* (Porto Alegre: UFRGS, 2004); Williams da Siva Gonçalvez and Shiguenoli Miyamoto, "Os Militares na política externa brasileira: 1964–1984," in *Revista Estudos Históricos*, vol. 6, n. 12, Rio de Janeiro, 1993, pp. 211–246; Gelson Fonseca Jr, *A legitimidade e outras questões internacionais: Poder e ética entre as nações* (São Paulo: Paz e Terra, 1998); and Letícia Pinheiro, *Política Externa Brasileira* (1889–2002) (Rio de Janeiro: Jorge Zahar, 2004). See also Miriam Gomes Saravia e Tullo Vigevani, "Política Externa do Brasil: Continuidade em meio à descontinuidade, de 1961 a 2011," in Daniel Aarão Reis, Marcelo Ridenti, and Rodrigo Patto Sá Motta (Eds.), *A ditadura que mudou o Brasil: 50 anos do golpe de 1964* (Jorge Zahar, 2014) and Thomas E. Skidmore, *The Politics of Military Rule in Brazil, 1964–1985* (Oxford University Press, 1990).

⁵ See José Flávio Sombra Saraiva, *O lugar da África: A dimensão atlântica da política externa brasileira, de 1946 a nossos dias* (Brasília: UNB, 1996) and Pio Penna Filho and Antônio Carlos Moraes Lessa, "O Itamaraty e a África: As Origens da Política Africana do Brasil," in *Revista Estudos Históricos*, vol. 1, n. 39, Rio de Janeiro, Jan/Jul 2007, pp. 57–81.

⁶ For an in-depth study of Brazil-Paraguay relations see Francisco Doratioto, *Una relación compleja: Paraguay y Brasil, 1889–1954* (Assunción: Tiempo de Historia, 2011).

⁷ The Brazilian student movement and its resistance of the military dictatorship has been analyzed in the works of João Roberto Martins Filho, *Movimento estudantil e ditadura militar* (Campinas: Papirus, 1987) and *Rebelião estudantil: 1968 – México, França e Brasil* (Campinas: Mercado de Letras, 1996).

⁸ Several works were written about the life of the revolutionary. See especially Mário Magalhães, *Marighella: O guerrilheiro que incendiou o mundo* (São Paulo: Companhia das Letras, 2012) and Frei Betto, *Batismo de Sangue: Guerrilha e Morte de Carlos Marighella* (Rio de Janeiro: Rocco, 2006). Frei Betto, as is known Carlos Alberto Libânio Christo (b. 1944), is a Roman Catholic Priest and Dominican friar; his book was adapted for film by director Helvécio Ratton (b. 1949) in *Batismo de Sangue* (2007). See also the documentary film about the revolutionary by filmmaker Silvio Tendler (b. 1950), *Marighella – Retrato Falado do Guerrilheiro* (2001).

⁹ For a study on the life of Tito de Alencar Lima see Leneide Duarte-Plon and Clarisse Meireles, *Um Homem Torturado: Nos Passos de Frei Tito de Alencar* (Rio de Janeiro: Civilização Brasileira, 2014). See also Lucas Figueiredo, *Olho por Olho: Os Livros Secretos da Ditadura* (São Paulo: Record, 2009).

¹⁰ See Geraldo Cantarino, *A Ditadura que o inglês viu* (Editora Mauad, 2014) and Heloisa Maria Murgel Starling, "Ditadura Militar," in Leonardo Avritzer, Newton Bignotto, Juarez Guimarães, and Heloisa Maria Murgel Starling (Eds.), *Corrupção: ensaios e críticas* (Editora UFMG, pp. 251–251).

¹¹ Regarding the *Programa de Integração Nacional* see Gerd Kohlhepp, "Conflitos de interesse no ordenamento territorial da Amazônia brasileira," in *Estudos Avançados*, vol. 16, n. 45, São Paulo, May/Aug 2002, and Neli Aparecida de Mello, *Políticas territoriais na Amazônia* (São Paulo: Anna Blume, 2006). See also Octávio Ianni, *Ditadura e agricultura: o desenvolvimento do capitalismo na Amazônia, 1964–1978* (Rio de Janeiro: Civilização Brasileira, 1979). For an analysis of the economy in the Amazon region in the twenty-first century see Francisco de Assis Costa, *Elementos para uma economia política da Amazônia: historicidade, territorialidade, diversidade, sustentabilidade* (Belém: NAEA, 2012). Regarding the Amazon and geopolitics see the works of Bertha Koiffmann Becker (1930–2013), especially *Amazônia: Geopolítica na Virada do III Milênio* (Rio de Janeiro: Editora Garamond, 2004). On the Trans-Amazonian highway see Nigel J. H. Smith, *Rainforest Corridors: The Transamazon Colonization Scheme* (University of Califonia Press, 1982).

¹² See Herbert Lowe Stukart, *Ética e corrupção* (São Paulo: Nobel, 2003, p. 49).

[13] See United States Select Committee on Intelligence, *Project MKULTRA, the CIA's program of research in behavioral modification* (University of Michigan Library, 1977).
[14] See J. Patrice McSherry, *Predatory States: Operation Condor and Covert War in Latin America* (Rowman & Littlefield, 2005) and Stephen G. Rabe, *The Killing Zone: The United States Wages Cold War in Latin America* (Oxford University Press, 2015).
[15] Regarding the rebel Carlos Lamarca see Emiliano José and Oldack de Miranda, *Lamarca: O Capitão da Guerrilha* (São Paulo: Global Editora, 2000).
[16] See interview with UnB Agência (National University of Brasília), Débora Cronemberger, Secretaria de Comunicação da UnB, 08/10/2012. University of Bahia Professor João Augusto de Lima Rocha is the biographer of educator Anísio Teixeira, whose death seems to be connected with the repressive activities of National Air Force agents under Burnier's command. João Augusto de Lima Rocha is the author of *Anísio Teixeira e a Cultura* (Brasília: UNB, 2014).
[17] See Hernâni Donato, *Dicionário das batalhas brasileiras* (São Paulo: Ibrasa, 1996, p. 190).
[18] See João Luiz de Moraes, *O calvário de Sonia Angel: Uma história de terror nos porões da ditadura* (MEC Editora, 1994) and Cecília Maria B. Coimbra, "Gênero, Militância, Tortura," in Marlene Neves Strey, Mariana Porto Ruwer de Azambuja, Fernanda Pires Jaeger (Eds.), *Violência, gênero e políticas públicas* (Porto Alegre: EDIPUCRS, 2004, pp. 45–54).
[19] Romeu was kept alive for the successive beatings from the military police with the alleged help of medical doctor Amílcar Lobo Moreira da Silva (1939–1997), who served as military physician at Rio de Janeiro's DOI-CODI from 1970 to 1974. In 1981, Romeu recognized Lobo as one of her torturers. In 1989, the physician published a book relating his subjection to military orders during sessions of torture at the DOI-CODI. See Amílcar Lobo, *A hora do lobo, a hora do carneiro* (Petrópolis: Vozes, 1989). In regard to the "House of Death," see Diego Grossi and Roberto Schiffler, "A Casa Da Morte de Petrópolis: A importância da (re)construção de uma memória além da "Cidade Imperial" para a consolidação democrática," in *Acesso Livre*, n. 2, Jul/Dec 2005, pp. 5–18; and Rogério Medeiros e Marcelo Netto, *Memórias de uma Gerra Suja* (Rio de Janeiro: Topbooks, 2012). See also Maria Helena Moreira Alves, *State and Opposition in Military Brazil* (University of Texas Press, 1988); Lucas Figueiredo, *Ministério do Silêncio; a história do serviço secreto brasileiro, de Washington Luís a Lula 1927–2005* (Rio de Janeiro: Record, 2005, pp. 207–208); and Reinaldo Cabral e Ronaldo Lapa (Eds.), *Desaparecidos Políticos: Prisões, Sequestros, Assassinatos* (Edições Opção, 1979).
[20] See Ignacio Cano and Patricia Salvão Ferreira, "The Reparations Program in Brazil," in Pablo De Greiff (Ed.), *The Handbook of Reparations* (Oxford University Press, 2006, pp. 102–152). See also the works of Janaína de Almeida Teles, "A constituição das memórias sobre a repressão da ditadura: o projeto Brasil Nunca Mais e a abertura da vala de Perus," in *Anos 90*, Porto Alegre, v. 19, n. 35, 2012, pp. 261–298, and *Desarquivando a Ditadura: Memória e Justiça no Brasil*

(São Paulo: Hucitec, 2009). See also Edson Teles and Renan Quinalha, "Scopes and Limits to the Transitional Justice Discourse in Brazil," in Nina Schneider and Marcia Esparza (Eds.), *Legacies of State Violence and Transitional Justice in Latin America: A Janus-Faced Paradigm?* (Lexington Books, 2015, pp. 19–36).

[21] See Leigh A. Payne, *Unsettling Accounts: Neither Truth Nor Reconciliation in Confessions of State Violence* (Duke University Press, 2008, pp. 197–203) and Elio Gaspari, *A Ditadura Escancarada: As Ilusões Armadas* (São Paulo: Companhia das Letras, 2002).

[22] See João Batista de Abreu, *As Manobras da Informação: análise da cobertura jornalística da luta armada no Brasil (1965–1979)* (Rio de Janeiro: Mauad, 2000); Beatriz Kushnir, *Cães de guarda: Jornalistas e censores, do AI-5 à Constituição de 1988* (São Paulo: Fapesp, 2004); and Alexandre Ayub Stephanou, *Censura no Regime Militar e Militarização das Artes* (Porto Alegre: EDIPUCRS, 2001).

[23] For a critique of the Japan Foundation's cultural imperialism in India see P. A. George (Ed.), *Japanese Studies: Changing Global Profile* (New Delhi: Northern Book Centre, 2010, pp. 52–54). For the same theme in regard to China see Utpal Vyas, "The Japan Foundation in China, An Agent of Japan's Soft Power?" in *The Electronic Journal of Contemporary Japanese Studies*, 15 August 2008. For a general history of the Japan Foundation, especially in regard to coming under the jurisdiction of the MOFA in 2003 see Jan Melissen and Yul Sohn (Eds.), *Understanding Public Diplomacy in East Asia: Middle Powers in a Troubled Region* (Palgrave Mcmillan, 2016). See also Nissim Kadosh Otmazgin, "Geopolitics and Soft Power: Japan's Cultural Policy and Cultural Diplomacy in Asia," *Asia-Pacific Review*, Volume 19, 2012, Issue 1, pp. 37–61. Regarding Japanese patents on Plao Noi, a local herb with medicial properties found in Thailand, see Daniel F. Robinson, *Confronting Biopiracy: Challenges, Cases and International Debates* (London: Earthscan, 2010, pp. 63–67). See also Ikechi Mgbeoji, *Global Biopiracy: Patents, Plants, and Indigenous Knowledge* (Toronto: UBC Press, 2006), as well as Aaron Schwabach, *International Environmental Disputes: A Reference Handbook*, (Oxford: ABC-Clio, 2006, p. 178).

[24] See Matias Spektor, *Kissinger e o Brasil* (Rio de Janeiro: Jorge Zahar, 2009).

[25] See Henrique Altemani de Oliveira, "Brasil-China: trinta anos de uma parceria estratégica," in *Revista Brasileira de Política Internacional*, vol. 47, n. 1, Brasília, Jan/Jun 2004.

[26] See, for instance, Fernando Veloso, *Desenvolvimento Econômico: Uma Perspectiva Brasileira* (Elsevier, 2012, pp. 187–190).

[27] General Pires Gonçalves was given the post of Minister of the Army from 1985 to 1990, during the government of José Ribamar Sarney (b. 1930), which immediatelly followed the end of the dictatorial period.

[28] The National Truth Commission was established by the Law 12528/2011 to investigate human rights violations during the period 1946–1988. See www.cnv.org.br. See also Eduardo Loureiro Lemos, *Justiça de Transição: Análise da efetivação da justiça histórica e criminal no Brasil* (Belo Horizonte: D'Plácido Editora, 2013).

[29] Carlos Alberto Brilhante Ustra was a Riograndense army colonel born in Santa Maria, a municipality located in the central part of Rio Grande do Sul State. In 2008, Ustra became the first government agent to be recognized by a Brazilian court as a torturer during the dictatorial period. On the Operação Radar see Edson Teles and Vladimir Pinheiro Safatle, *O que resta da ditadura: A exceção brasileira* (São Paulo: Boitempo, 2010, pp. 271–275); Milton Pinheiro (Ed.), *Ditadura: o que resta da transição* (São Paulo: Boitempo, 2014); and José Paulo Netto, *Pequena história da ditadura brasileira (1964–1985)* (São Paulo: Editora Cortez, 2014). Regarding the Lapa Massacre see Pedro Estevam da Rocha Pomar, *Massacre na Lapa: Como o Exército liquidou o Comitê Central do PCdoB* (São Paulo: Editora Fundação Perseu Abramo, 2006) and Wladimir Pomar, *Pedro Pomar: uma vida em vermelho* (São Paulo: Editora Xamã, 2003).

[30] See Carlos Heitor Cony, *JK e a Ditadura* (Objetiva, 2012).

[31] The investigation was coodinated by deputy Adroaldo Mousquer Loureiro (1948–2016). See Assembleia Legislativa do Rio Grande do Sul, Comissão de Cidadania e Direitos Humanos, Subcomissão para investigar as circunstâncias da morte do ex-Presidente João Goulart – RDI 11/2008.

[32] See Luiz Alberto Moniz Bandeira, *O governo João Goulart: As lutas sociais no Brasil 1961–1964* (São Paulo: Unesp, 2010).

[33] See John Dinges, *The Condor Years: How Pinochet And His Allies Brought Terrorism To Three Continents* (The New Press, 2005).

[34] See John Watson Foster Dulles, *Carlos Lacerda, Brazilian Cruzader, Volume Two: The years 1960–1977* (University of Texas Press, 1996). See also Carlos Heitor Cony and Ana Lee, *O Beijo da Morte* (São Paulo: Objetiva, 2003).

[35] Numbers from data collected by Brazilian investigative journalist Nilson Mariano (b. 1958); see his *As Garras do Condor* (São Paulo: Vozes, 2003).

[36] Geisel's assertion, obviously, did not correspond to the truth. The declaration, however, did provoke a reaction from Rosalynn Carter. See the transcription for the Geisel-Rosalynn Carter meeting on June 7, 1977. APGCS/HF. See Elio Gaspari, *O Sacerdote e o Feiticeiro: A ditadura encurralada* (Rio de Janeiro: Editora Intrínseca, 2002) and Maria Celina d'Araújo and Celso Castro (Eds.), *Tempos modernos: João Paulo dos Reis Velloso: memórias do desenvolvimento* (Rio de Janeiro: FGV, 2004, p. 188).

[37] São Paulo's former Governor, Paulo Salim Maluf, was President Figueiredo's preferred candidate. Maluf's image, however, was severely tainted by several charges of corruption, which made him unpalatable for members of his own party. That was also one of the causes of the rupture in the PDS. See Wendy Hunter, *Eroding Military Influence in Brazil: Politicians Against Soldiers* (The University of North Carolina Press, 1997, p. 38).

[38] See George A. Lopez and Michael Stohl (Eds.), *Liberalization and Redemocratization in Latin America* (Greenwood Press, 1987).

[39] For the dispute over the islands see César Caviedes, "Conflict Over The Falkland Islands: A Never-Ending Story?" in *Latin American Research Review*, vol. 29, n. 2, 1994, pp. 172–187. Brazil remained neutral in the war of 1982, but reaffirmed its recognition of Argentine sovereignty over the islands expressed in

1833. The islands are located within what Argentina claims as its maritime territory. Its inhabitants claim their right to self-determination but do not seek the establishment of an independent state. Their understanding of "right to self-determination" seems to be confused with the right to maintain British citizenship, a right that, needless to say, should not be affected in case the islands were recognized as Argentine. The distortion of the notion of "self-determination" to accommodate allegiance to a specific state and discard the principle of independence there contained appears deceitful. From a Latin American perspective, the British claim to the islands can hardly be seen as anything other than a remnant of European imperialism.

[40] The ENGESA was onwed by engineer José Luiz Whitaker Ribeiro, who was also appointed president of the state-owned IMBEL. The ENGESA declared bankruptcy in 1993. Regarding the company's sales of arms to Iraq see James S. Henry, *The Blood Bankers: Tales from the Global Underground Economy* (Four Walls Eight Windows, pp. 158–163). Whitaker is mentioned in Gerald Horne's *The Deepest South: The United States, Brazil, and the African Slave Trade* (New York University Press, 2007, p. 251).

[41] Baumgarten's dossier assumed the form of a novel titled *Yellowcake*. See Jacques Alkalai Wainberg, *Império de palavras* (Porto Alegre: EDIPUCRS, 1997, pp. 233–234) and José Argolo and Luiz Alberto Machado Fortunato, *Dos quartéis à espionagem: caminhos e desvios do poder militar* (Rio de Janeiro: Editora Mauad, 2004).

[42] See Antonio Paim, *A UDF e a Ideia de Universidade* (Rio de Janeiro: Tempo Brasileiro, 1981); Roque Spencer Maciel de Barros's "O desenvolvimento da idéia de Universidade no Brasil," in his own *Estudos Brasileiros* (Londrina: Editora da UEL, 1997); and Rodrigo Patto Sá Motta, "A Modernização Autoritário-Conservadora nas Universidades e a Influência da Cultura Política," in Daniel Aarão Reis, Marcelo Ridenti, and Rodrigo Patto Sá Motta (Eds.), *A ditadura que mudou o Brasil: 50 anos do golpe de 1964* (Jorge Zahar, 2014).

[43] For a history of Brazilian education see Cynthia Greive Veiga and Thais Nivia de Lima Fonseca (Eds.), *História e Historiografia da Educação no Brasil* (Belo Horizonte: Autêntica, 2003).

[44] See Irene V. Small, *Hélio Oiticica: Folding the Frame* (University of Chicago Press, 2016); Elena Shtromberg, *Art Systems: Brazil and the 1970s* (University of Texas Press, 2016); and Claudia Calirman, *Brazilian Art under Dictatorship: Antonio Manuel, Artur Barrio, and Cildo Meireles* (Duke University Press Books, 2012).

[45] The film caused great agitation in the conservative society of Brazil's dictatorial period. See the book by Denise Godinho and Hugo Moura, *Coisas Eróticas* (São Paulo: Panda Books, 2012). See also the entry "Pornochanchada," in Peter H. Rist, *Historical Dictionary of South American Cinema* (Rowman & Littlefield, 2014, p. 460). For Brazilian marginal cinema see Fernão Ramos, *Cinema marginal (1968/1973): a representação em seu limite* (São Paulo: Brasiliense, 1987); Cláudio da Costa, *Cinema brasileiro, anos 60–70: dissimetria, oscilação e simulacro* (Rio de Janeiro: 7 Letras, 2000), and Marcel de Almeida Freitas, "Entre

Estereótipos, Transgressões e Lugares Comuns: notas sobre a pornochanchada no cinema brasileiro," in *Intertexto*, n. 10, Programa de Pós-graduação em Comunicação e Informação, Universidade Federal do Rio Grande do Sul, 2004.

[46] Regarding the Teatro Brasileiro de Comédia see Alberto Guzik, *TBC: Crônica de um Sonho* (São Paulo: Editora Perspectiva, 1986.)

[47] Regarding the Arena Theatre see David Sanderson George, *Flash & Crash Days: Brazilian Theater in the Postdictatorship Period* (Garland Publishing, 2000, pp. 134–144). See also Izaías Almada, *Teatro de Arena* (São Paulo: Boitempo, 2004) and Rosangela Patriota, "A escrita da história do teatro no Brasil: questões temáticas e aspectos metodológicos," in *História*, vol. 24, n. 2, Franca, 2005.

[48] See Christopher Dunn, *Brutality Garden: Tropicalia and the Emergence of a Brazilian Counterculture* (The University of North Carolina Press, 2001).

[49] See the works of E. Taylor Atkins, *Blue Nippon: Authenticating Jazz in Japan* (Duke University Press, 2001) and *Jazz Planet* (University Press of Mississippi, 2003). For Jazz in the Philippines see Richie C. Quirino, *Pinoy Jazz Traditions* (Anvil Publishing, 2004). See also the documentary film by Richie Quirino and Collis Davis, *Pinoy Jazz: The Story of Jazz in the Philippines* (2006). Regarding the history of Jazz in France see Jeffrey H. Jackson, *Making Jazz French: Music And Modern Life In Interwar Paris* (Duke University Press, 2003).

[50] Regardin Ortiz's differentiation between *transculturation* and *acculturation* see Fernando Ortíz, *Cuban Counterpoint: Tobacco and Sugar*, Translated by Harriet de Onís (Duke University Press, 1995) and Elizabeth Kath, "On Transculturation: Re-enacting and Remaking Latin Dance and Music in Foreign Lands," in Julian Lee (Ed.), *Narratives of Globalization: Reflections on the Global Condition* (Rowman & Littlefield, 2015). Regarding the question of nationalism in Brazilian jazz see Acácio Tadeu de Camargo Piedade, "Brazilian Jazz and Friction of Musicalities," in E. Taylor Atkins, *Jazz Planet* (University Press of Mississippi, 2003, pp. 41–58). See also Marina Beraldo Bastos and Acácio Tadeu Piedade, "Análise de improvisações na música instrumental: em busca da retórica do jazz brasileiro," in *Revista eletrônica de musicologia*, Volume XI, Sept 2007. Together with Camargo Piedade, Stuart Nicholson notes that Brazilian jazz musicians are sensitive to the potentially humiliating effects of cultural imperialism and strive to avoid contamination by the bebop paradigm, seeking a musical expression that is more rooted in Brazil and drawing, for instance, on local elements such as *chorinho*. See Stuart Nicholson, *Is Jazz Dead?: Or Has It Moved to a New Address* (Routledge, 2005, p. 172).

[51] Regarding the works of Victor Assis Brasil see Jairzinho Teixeira, *"Nada será como antes": a música de Victor Assis Brasil no álbum Pedrinho*, Masters Thesis, Campinas, Unicamp, 2014).

[52] See Vasco Mariz, *Cláudio Santoro* (Rio de Janeiro: Civilização Brasileira, 1994). See also from the same author, *A música clássica brasileira* (Rio de Janeiro: Andrea Jakobsson Estúdio, 2002).

[53] See Elizabeth Ginway, "Literature under the Dictatorship," in Robert M. Levine and John J. Crocitti (Eds.), *The Brazil Reader: History, Culture, Politics* (Duke University Press, 1999, pp. 248–253).

⁵⁴ The city of Curitiba is located 900 meters above sea level in a plain encircled by two mountain ranges, the Serra do Mar and the Serra de São Luiz do Purunã. The mountains provide for the stalling of mist and thus for the hight nebulosity in the area, making the city of Curitiba's frequently dark skies a rare case among Brazilian cities.

Chapter Seven

¹ See Luiz Carlos Bresser-Pereira and Yoshiaki Nakano, *The Theory of Inertial Inflation* (Boulder: Lynne Rienner Publishers, 1987).
² For a detailed account of the Cruzado Plan see the chapter "Economic Growth is the Priority," in Albert Fishlow, *Starting Over: Brazil Since 1985* (Brookings Press, 2013, pp. 33–86)
³ For a detailed economic history of Brazil see the aforementioned work by Werner Baer, *The Brazilian Economy: Growth and Development* (Praeger Publishers, 1995). See also Patrice Franko, *The Puzzle of Latin American Economic Development* (Rowman & Littlefield, 2007) and Francisco Vidal Luna and Herbert S. Klein, *The Economic and Social History of Brazil since 1889* (Cambridge University Press, 2014).
⁴ Regarding the complex theme of citizenship in Brazil see José Murilo de Carvalho, *Cidadania no Brasil: O longo caminho* (Civilização Brasileira, 2001).
⁵ See Andrew Revkin, *The Burning Season: The Murder of Chico Mendes and the Fight for the Amazon Rain Forest* (Island Press, 2004) and Miguel Carter, *Challenging Social Inequality: The Landless Rural Workers' Movement and Agrarian Reform in Brazil* (Duke University Press, 2015). See also Sue Branford and Jan Rocha, *Cutting The Wire: The Story of the Landless Movement in Brazil* (Latin America Bureau, 2002).
⁶ See Chico de Gois and Simone Iglesias, *O lado B dos candidatos* (Rio de Janeiro: Leya, 2014).
⁷ On the theme of Bolivarianism see Barry Cannon, *Hugo Chávez and the Bolivarian Revolution: Populism and democracy in a globalised age* (Manchester University Press, 2009).
⁸ On the death of Paulo Cesar Farias see Robert M. Levine, *The History of Brazil* (Greewood Press, 1999, p. 140). For an account of the impeachment process and the alleged crimes included therein see Lucas Figueiredo, *Morcegos Negros: PC Farias, Collor, Máfias e a História que o Brasil não Conheceu* (Record, 2000). Regarding Pedro Collor's denunciations see Pedro Collor de Mello, *Passando a limpo: a trajetória de um farsante* (Record, 1992). For an analysis of the political implications of the impeachment see Keith S. Rosenn and Richard Downes (Eds.), *Corruption and Political Reform in Brazil: The Impact of Collor's Impeachment* (University of Miami North South Center Press, 1999).
⁹ Regarding Collor the Mello's nuclear choice see Marshall C. Eakin, *Brazil: The Once and Future Country* (St. Martin's Griffin, 1997, p. 207); Britta H. Crandall, *Hemispheric Giants: The Misunderstood History of U.S.-Brazilian Relations*

(Rowman & Littlefield, 2011, p. 150); and Tânia Malheiros, *Brasil, a bomba oculta: O programa nuclear brasileiro* (Rio de Janeiro: Gryphus, 1991). Regarding the more recent Brazilian nuclear submarine program see Togzhan Kassenova, "Brazil and the Global Nuclear Order," in Oliver Stuenkel and Matthew M. Taylor (Eds.), *Brazil on the Global Stage: Power, Ideas, and the Liberal International Order* (Palgrave Macmillan, 2015, pp. 117–142) and João Roberto Martins Filho, "O projeto do submarino nuclear brasileiro," in *Contexto Internacional*, vol. 33, n. 2, Rio de Janeiro, Jul/Dec 2011.

[10] The massacre is described in a novel-memoir format published by Brazilian medical doctor Drauzio Varella (b. 1943). Varella was a volunteering physician at Carandiru Penitentiary during the time of the massacre. See Drauzio Varella, *Estação Carandiru* (Companhia das Letras, 1999), English version *Lockdown: Inside Brazil's Most Dangerous Prison* (Simon & Schuster UK, 2012). The book became one of the all-time best-sellers in Brazil, being adapted for film by director Héctor Babenco (b. 1946) in *Carandiru* (2003).

[11] The concept appears to have been coined by Maria Helena Moreira Alves. See her "São Paulo: the political and socioeconomic transformations wrought by the New Labor Movement in the city and beyond," in Josef Gugler (Ed.), *World Cities Beyond the West: Globalization, Development and Inequality* (Cambridge University Press, 2004, pp. 299–326). Moreira Alves provides an important analysis of the distinct economic conditions experienced between internal migrants of indigenous or African-slave descent and European immigrants throughout the twentieth century. While the former lacked governmental support, the latter tended to receive assitance from their home countries. The contrast is cited as contributing to the economic dispartity between the two social types. See also Brodwyn Fischer, *A Poverty of Rights: Citizenship and Inequality in Twentieth-Century Rio de Janeiro* (Stanford University Press, 2010). Regarding the social effects of the economic debacle in the period see Ben Ross Schneider, "Brazil under Collor: Anatomy of a Crisis," in Roderic Ai Camp (Ed.), *Democracy in Latin America: Patterns and Cycles* (Rowman & Littlefield, 1995, pp. 225–248).

[12] See the book by Amnesty International researcher Julia Rochester, *The Candelaria Massacre: How Wagner dos Santos Survived the Street Children's Killing that Shook Brazil* (London: Vision, 2008). One of the massacre's survivors, Sandro Rosa do Nascimento (1978–2000), was killed a few years later by the Rio police when he hijacked a city bus, taking hostages in what seemed to be an act of insanity. The incident was recorded on national television. Sandro Nascimento screamed to the cameras about social injustice in Brazil while holding a hostage. After being detained Sandro was asphyxiated by the police officers. The incident is portrayed in the critically acclaimed documentary *Bus 174* (2002) by director José Padilha (b. 1967) and in the movie *Last Stop 174* (2008) by Bruno Barreto (b. 1955). See also Gilberto Dimenstein, *Brazil: War on Children* (Latin America Bureau, 1991), in Portuguese *A Guerra Dos Meninos: Assassinatos de Menores No Brasil* (Editora Brasiliense, 1995), and *Meninas da noite: A Prostituição de meninas escravas no Brasil* (Editora Ática, 1997). See also from the same author

Democracia em Pedaços: Direitos Humanos No Brasil (Companhia das Letras, 1996).

[13] Considerable controversy arose in the field of Anthropology regarding the claims of Chagnon and Harris. See Rob Borofsky, *Yanomami: The Fierce Controversy and What We Can Learn from It* (University of California Press, 2005) and the polemical book by Patrick Tierney, *Darkness in El Dorado: How Scientists and Journalists Devastated the Amazon* (W. W. Norton & Company, 2000). The controversy appears also in the documentary film by Brazilian director José Padilha, *Secrets of the Tribe* (2010). See also Brian Ferguson, *Yanomami Warfare: A Political History* (Santa Fe: School for Advanced Research Press, 1995).

[14] See Jan Rocha, *Murder in the Rainforest: The Yanomami, the Gold Miners and the Amazon* (Latin America Bureau, 1999), published in Portuguese as *Haximu: O Massacre dos Yanomami e as suas Consequências* (São Paulo: Casa Amarella, 2007) and Davi Kopenawa, "Appendix D: The Haximu Massacre," in Davi Kopenawa, *The Falling Sky: Words of a Yanomami Shaman* (Belknap Press of Harvard University Press, 2013). See also Jonathan W. Warren, *Racial Revolutions: Antiracism and Indian Resurgence in Brazil* (Duke University Press, 2001); Jan Hoffman French, *Legalizing Identities: Becoming Black or Indian in Brazil's Northeast* (The University of North Carolina Press, 2009); and Tracy Devine Guzmán, *Native and National in Brazil: Indigeneity after Independence* (The University of North Carolina Press, 2013).

[15] See Maria Helena Moreira Alves, *Living in the Crossfire: Favela Residents, Drug Dealers, and Police Violence in Rio de Janeiro* (Temple University Press, 2011); Janice Perlman, *Favela: Four Decades of Living on the Edge in Rio de Janeiro* (Oxford University Press, 2010); Enrique Desmond Arias, *Drugs and Democracy in Rio de Janeiro: Trafficking, Social Networks, and Public Security* (The University of North Carolina Press, 2006); and R. Ben Penglase, *Living with Insecurity in a Brazilian Favela: Urban Violence and Daily Life* (Rutgers University Press, 2014). For a more personal account of Rio de Janeiro's drug trafficking see Misha Glenny, *Nemesis: One Man and the Battle for Rio* (Alfred A. Knopf, 2015), which tells the life story of drug dealer Antônio Francisco Bonfim Lopes (b. 1976).

[16] See César Barreira, *Trilhas e atalhos do poder: conflitos sociais no sertão* (Rio de Janeiro, Rio Fundo Editora, 1992).

[17] See Antonio Canuto, Cássia Regina da Silva Luz, and José Batista Gonçalves Afonso (Eds.), *Conflitos no Campo: Brasil 2003* (Goiânia: Comissão Pastoral da Terra, 2004) and Antônio Canuto and Leandro Gorsdorf, "Direito humano à terra: a construção de um marco de resistência às violações," in Daniel Rech (Ed.), *Direitos humanos no Brasil 2: diagnóstico e perspectivas* (Rio de Janeiro: Mauad, 2007, pp. 167–194). Regarding the Santa Elmira Massacre see the works of Frei Sérgio Antônio Görgen, *O massacre da fazenda Santa Elmira* (Petrópolis: Vozes, 1989) and *Marcha ao Coração do Latifúndio* (Petrópolis: Vozes, 2004). See also Mitsue Morrisawa, *A História da Luta Pela Terra e o MST* (São Paulo: Editora Expressão Popular, 2008). For a view on land conflict on the Amazon region see

Glenn Alan Cheney, *Promised Land: Nun's Struggle against Landlessness, Lawlessness, Slavery, Poverty, Corruption, Injustice, and Environmental Devastation in Amazonia* (New London Librarium, 2013).

[18] Here the popular gag was to call the President "Viajando Henrique Cardoso," a play on words with his first name, "Fernando." For a study on the use of presidential diplomacy in Brazilian history see Sergio França Danese, *Diplomacia Presidencial* (Rio de Janeiro: Topbooks, 1999).

[19] See Ministério do Planejamento, Brasil, *IIRSA: Iniciativa para implantação da infraestrutura regional da América do Sul* (Brasília, Secretaria de Planejamento e Investimentos Estratégicos, MPOG, 2002). Lula da Silva's relauching of the MERCOSUL deserves a special chapter. It followed the emergence of the Left in Latin America and the directives of regional integration established by the São Paulo Forum and its Bolivarian mindset. Under Lula da Silva's government, the MERCOSUL's original idea of liberal economic intergration would give way to an attempt at establishing Latin American self-suficiency under the economic program of the São Paulo Forum and international communism, that is, under a state-oriented position.

[20] Consider, for the instance, the facilities granted to Japan for its payment of war debts. The General Headquarters (Supremme Commander for the Allied Powers) got the payments stopped as early as June 1946, which allowed for the creation of Japan's Reconstruction Finance Bank in that same year. See Mark Metzler, *Capital as Will and Imagination: Schumpeter's Guide to the Postwar Japanese Miracle* (Cornell University Press, 2013, pp. 87).

[21] See Mauro Porto, *Media Power and Democratization in Brazil: TV Globo and the Dilemmas of Political Accountability* (Routledge, 2012) and Paulo Henrique Amorim, *O quarto poder: Uma outra história* (São Paulo: Hedra, 2015).

[22] See Jan Rocha and Sue Branford, *Brazil Under the Workers' Party: From euphoria to despair* (Practical Action Publishing, 2015) and Timothy J. Power and Matthew M. Taylor (Eds.), *Corruption and Democracy in Brazil: The Struggle for Accountability* (University of Notre Dame Press, 2011). In Portuguese see Lucas Figueiredo, *O Operador: Como (e a mando de quem) Marcos Valerio irrigou os cofres do PSDB e do PT* (Editora Record, 2006).

[23] For an account of the *Operação Lava Jato* (Operation Car Wash), the Federal Police investigation on cases of corruption, see the book by Rede Globo journalist Vladimir Netto, *Lava Jato: O Juiz Sérgio Moro e os Bastidores da Operação que Abalou o Brasil* (Sextante, 2016).

[24] See Roseanne Murphy, *Martyr of the Amazon: The Life of Sister Dorothy Stang* (New York: Orbis Books. 2007) and Binka Le Breton, *The Greatest Gift: The Courageous Life and Martyrdom of Sister Dorothy Stang* (New York: Doubleday, 2008).

[25] See Ignacio Cano, "Violence and Organized Crime in Brazil: The Case of 'Militias' in Rio de Janeiro," in Heinrich-Böll-Stiftung and Regine Schönenberg (Eds.), *Transnational Organized Crime: Analyses of a Global Challenge to Democracy* (Bielefeld: Transcript Verlag, 2013, pp. 179–188) and Ignacio Cano

and Nilton Santos, *Violência letal, renda e desigualdade no Brasil* (Rio de Janeiro: 7 Letras, 2007).

[26] For a brief overview of the PAC see Marcelo de Oliveira Passos, "O Programa de Aceleração do Crescimento (PAC): Pontos positivos e falhas de origem, in *Revista Economia & Tecnologia*, ano 03, vol. 08, Curitiba, Jan/Mar 2007, pp. 23–26.

[27] Brazil has been called the very home of unfulfilled promises. See Alfred P. Montero, *Brazil: Reversal of Fortune* (Polity, 2014) and Michael Reid, *Brazil: The Troubled Rise of a Global Power* (Yale University Press, 2014). See also James Holston, *Insurgent Citizenship: Disjunctions of Democracy and Modernity in Brazil* (Princeton University Press, 2009).

[28] See Leslie L. Marsh, *Brazilian Women's Filmmaking: From Dictatorship to Democracy* (University of Illinois Press, 2012).

[29] See Antônio Márcio da Silva, *The "Femme" Fatale in Brazilian Cinema: Challenging Hollywood Norms* (Palgrave Macmillan, 2014).

[30] Regarding the controversy surrounding Rede Globo and Globo Filmes see Valério Cruz Brittos and César Bolaño (Eds.), *Rede Globo: 40 anos de poder e hegemonia* (São Paulo: Paulus, 2005). See also Fernando Antônio Azevedo, "Mídia e democracia no Brasil: relações entre o sistema de mídia e o sistema político," in *Opinião Pública*, vol. 12, n. 1, Campinas, Apr/May 2006.

[31] Regarding the theme of regulatory agencies in Brazil see Edson de Oliveira Nunes, *Agências reguladoras e reforma do Estado no Brasil: inovação e continuidade no sistema político institucional* (Editora Garamond, 2007).

[32] Besides Pacheco's work, see Samantha Moraes, *Depois do Escorpião* (Seoman, 2006), Vanessa de Oliveira, *O Diário de Marise* (Matrix, 2006), the Spanish Alejandra Duque's *La agenda de Virginia* (Booket, 2006), as well as the American forerunner, Dolores French, *Working: My Life As a Prostitute* (Victor Gollancz, 1997).

INDEX

18 of the Copacabana Fort Revolt, 158, 159, 164, 174, 201
1824 Constitution, 60, 69, 78, 95, 433
1834 Additional Act, 69, 70, 73, 77
1891 Constitution, 157, 171, 200
1924 Revolution, 164, 448
1930 Revolution, 26, 188, 200, 215, 267, 365, 445, 449
1934 Constitution, 200, 202, 204, 213, 230
1937 Constitution, 205, 298
1946 Constitution, 230, 246, 247, 263, 268, 272, 276, 297,
1967 Constitution, 298, 309, 312, 347
1988 Constitution, 370, 372, 395
A Polaquinha (novel), 364
Abdias do Nascimento, 220, 451
Aberdeen Act (1845), 78, 81, 86, 106, 436
Abertura (détent politics, Geisel government), 333, 336, 340
Abolitionist Movement, 108
Ação Integralista Brasileira (AIB), 182, 201
Acordo Tripartite Itaipu-Corpus (1979), 348
Acre Dispute, 132
Admiral Álvaro Alberto, 246
Adolf Berle, Jr., 213
Afonso Pena, 136, 138, 142, 156
Afrânio Coutinho, 178
Agência Nacional do Cinema (Ancine), 413
Agustín Pedro Justo, Argentine President, 196
Airto Moreira (drummer), 362

Albras Alumínio Brasileiro S.A., 326, 327, 330
Alceu Amoroso Lima, 177, 277, 454
Alexandre de Gusmão, 30, 133, 431, 446
Alfred Thayer Mahan, 141
Alfredo Bosi, 178, 438
Alfredo d'Escragnolle Taunay, 100, 227, 357
Alfredo Stroessner, Paraguayan President, 305
Aliança Liberal (1929), 173
Aliança Nacional Libertadora (ANL), 202
Alliance for Progress (John F. Kennedy), 265, 304
Aluísio Azevedo, 101, 104, 109, 135, 177, 227, 363, 439
Alves Branco (tariff, 1844), 74, 78
Amácio Mazzaropi, 288, 455
Amado Luiz Cervo, 80, 304, 432
Amapá Dispute (with France), 129, 130, 133, 444
American Civil War, 83, 124
Amnesty Law (1979), 319, 320, 321, 324, 343
Ângela Maria (singer), 291
Anísio Teixeira, 215, 279, 321, 322, 352, 354, 451, 454, 458
Anita Malfatti, 180, 181, 183, 184
Anselmo Duarte (filmmaker), 288
Antônio Carlos Jobim, 221, 292
Antônio Conselheiro, 124
António de Oliveira Salazar, 265
Antônio Delfim Netto, 314, 325, 342
Antônio Francisco de Paula de Holanda Cavalcanti, 76

Antônio Francisco Lisboa, Aleijadinho, 37
Antônio Houaiss, 411
Apesar de Você (song), 360
Aquarela do Brasil (song), 225
Aragarças Revolt (1959), 321
Argentine Confederation, 63, 80, 88
Arnaldo Jabor (filmmaker), 355, 356, 416
Artur Bernardes, 160, 162, 164, 168, 174, 194, 212
Artur Azevedo, 102, 440
Artur da Costa e Silva, 174, 298, 300, 305, 306, 332, 405
Arturo Frondizi, Argentine President, 251
Ary Barroso, 222, 225, 293
Atlântida Cinematográfica, 227, 228
Auguste Comte, 84, 85, 112, 146, 162
Augusto dos Anjos, 179
Bachianas Brasileiras (Heitor Villa-Lobos), 217
Balaiada, 73-125
Bancada Ruralista (Ruralist Contingent), 371
banda de música (UDN), 239, 256
Banda Oriental, 43, 61
bandeirantes, 17, 23, 24, 27, 430
Bank of Brazil, 46, 47, 55, 66, 166, 239, 303, 388
Baron Wilhelm Ludwig von Eschwege, 45
Bartolomé Mitre, 88, 89, 92
Battle of Curupayty, 89, 90, 437
Battle of Guararapes, 21, 22, 104, 430
Battle of Porongos, 72, 435
Battle of Tacuarembó, 61
Beckman Brothers uprising, 70
Belgo-Mineira Metallurgy and Steel Industry, 166
beneplácito, 95
Benjamin Vargas, 209, 241
Bernardino Rivadavia, 62, 63

Bernardo Pereira de Vasconcelos, 66, 67, 69, 70, 86, 435
Beyond Citizen Kane (1993 documentary film by Simon Hartog), 397
Bill Clinton, United States President, 392, 404
Black Experimental Theater, 220
Blaine-Mendonça Treaty of 1891, 122, 443
Boca do Lixo (São Paulo district), 356
Bolivian Syndicate, 132, 133
bossa nova, 5, 221, 224, 289, 291, 292, 293, 294, 360, 361, 406, 455
Bossa Nova Manifesto (UDN), 256
Bradford Burns, 142, 446
Braganza dynasty, 2, 46, 49, 56
Brazil cost, 336
Brazilian academicism, 44
Brazilian Academy of Letters, 180
Brazilian baroque, 36, 37, 45, 99
Brazilian Black Front, 220
Brazilian Communist Party, 168, 202, 231, 247, 285, 300, 337
Brazilian Democratic Movement (MDB), 298, 343
Brazilian Expeditionary Force (FEB), 211
Brazilian Historic and Geographic Institute (IHGB), 21, 72, 361
Brazilian Institute of Geography and Statistics (IBGE), 206
Brazilian Island, 11
Brazilian jazz, 360, 361, 407, 408, 462
Brazilian Nazi Party, 208, 209
Brazilian Positivist Church, 84
Brazilian Social Democratic Party (PSDB), 371
Brazilian War of Independence, 62
Brazil-USSR diplomatic relations, 231, 159, 264
Brazilwood, 11
Bresser Plan (1987), 369

Bruno Barreto (filmmaker), 412
burakumin, 140
bureaucracy, 12, 33, 76, 191, 295, 388, 423
Cabanagem, 71, 435
Cabo Anselmo, 271
cadeira do dragão (dragon's chair), 311
Caio Prado Júnior, 226, 227
Caixa de Conversão (gold standard), 136, 138, 169, 445
Caixa de Estabilização (gold standard), 169
Câmara dos homens bons, 16, 104
Manuel Ferraz de Campos Sales, 126
candangos, 254
Candelária Massacre, 383
Cândido Rondon, 139, 445
Candomblé, 219, 288, 367
Canudos, 124, 125, 148, 149, 177, 323, 443
capitação, 27
captaincy, 13, 14, 20, 23, 34, 102, 187, 429
Carandiru Massacre, 382, 384, 400, 415, 464
Carlos Diegues (filmmaker), 410
Carlos Frederico Lecor, 53, 61, 65, 434
Carlos Gomes, Antônio, 103, 440
Carlos Lacerda, 239, 241, 243,247, 248, 256, 260, 269, 271, 273, 277, 295, 319, 321, 339, 453, 460
Carlos Lamarca, 300, 320, 457
Carlos Marighella, 309, 310, 457
Carlos Saavedra Lamas, 196
Carlota Joaquina of Bourbon, 51, 61, 411, 434
Carta de doação, 13
Cartola (Angenor de Oliveira), 222, 223, 224, 289, 291, 294
Casa Grande & Senzala (1933), 161, 226, 286
Castro Alves, 100, 109, 439, 442

Castro Lobo, João de Deus de, 102, 103, 440
Catholic Church, 10, 36, 84, 94, 95, 149, 260, 269, 277, 278, 456
Celso Furtado, 189, 235, 250, 262, 265, 267, 302, 445, 452
Censorship, 44, 168, 205, 287, 299, 308, 318, 355, 363, 364
Centro Popular de Cultura (CPC), 269, 278, 285, 294, 454
Cerro Corá Battle, 91
Chacina da Lapa (1976), 311, 338
Chaco War, 89, 92, 195, 196, 198, 449, 450
chanchada (cinema), 228
Charles Burke Elbrick, 300, 309, 313, 320, 412
Charles Rodney Chandler, 308
Chega de Saudade (song, 1958), 221, 292, 293
Chichorro da Gama, 79
China-Brazil Earth Resources Satellites (CBERS), 376
Chinese immigrants, 44
Cícero Romão Batista, 149
Cinédia, 227
Cinema Novo, 268, 286, 288, 355, 406, 410, 455
Cipriano Barata, 38
Cisplatine War, 25, 64, 65, 66, 71, 80
Clarice Lispector, 219, 283, 413
Cláudio Manuel da Costa, 34, 37, 101, 432
Claudio Santoro (composer), 362, 363
Clemente Mariani Bittencourt, 277
Clóvis Beviláqua, 155
Coffee Barons, 76, 79, 93, 98, 117, 126, 135, 156, 170, 177, 188, 191, 277
Cohen Plan, 203, 273
Collor Plan (1990), 378
Colônia do Santíssimo Sacramento, 24, 25, 31, 43, 53, 62, 163

Comando de Caça aos Comunistas (CCC), 318, 358
Comando de Libertação Nacional (Colina), 299
Comando Geral dos Trabalhadores (CGT), 268
Comintern, 202
Commando Vermelho (criminal organization), 400
Como Era Gostoso o Meu Francês (1971), 355
Companhia Geral de Comércio do Maranhão, 32, 70
Companhia Siderúrgica Nacional (CSN), 190, 210
compulsory voting, 263, 365, 366, 370, 380, 391, 419, 454
Comtean republican dictatorship, 113
Comunidades Eclesiais de Base (CEB), 278
Concrete Poetry Movement, 284
Confederation of the Equator, 59
Conference of Berlin (1885), 132
Conferência Nacional dos Bispos do Brasil (CNBB), 278
Congress of Vienna of 1815, 46, 47, 432
Conjuração Baiana, Conspiracy of Bahia, 38, 39
Consolidação das Leis do Trabalho (CLT), 212
Constitutionalist Revolution of 1932, 193, 194, 199, 449
Constitutive Assembly of 1987, 370, 371
Contestado War, 147, 323, 446
Copacabana (song), 390
coronelism, 137, 445
Corumbiara Massacre, 389
Crise do Apagão (2001), 393
Cristóvão Jacques, 12, 13
Cruls Rectangle (Brasília), 253, 254
Cruz e Sousa, 100, 439
Cruzado Plan (1986), 367, 369, 392, 463

Custódio José de Melo, 118
Dalton Trevisan (author), 363, 364
Dalva de Oliveira (singer), 291
Dante de Oliveira, 345
Darcy Ribeiro, 278, 451, 454
David Ricardo, 30, 190
Deng Xiaoping, 350, 376
Deodoro da Fonseca, 97, 109, 113, 114, 116, 118, 126, 136, 144, 404
Departamento de Ordem Política e Social (DOPS), 310
dependency theory, 235, 453
derrama, 34, 35
desenvolvimentismo associado, 235, 249, 290
desenvolvimentismo nacionalista, 249
Dias Gomes (playwright), 288
Dick Farney (singer), 290, 291, 361
Dilma Rousseff, 300, 312, 390, 402, 404, 405, 420
Diogo Antônio Feijó, 70, 71
Dionísia Gonçalves Pinto, *Opúsculo Humanitário*, 84
Diplomacia dos Patacões, 82
Diretas Já Movement, 345, 347
Doctrine of National Security, 242, 299
DOI-CODI (governmental agencies), 318, 319, 458
Dom Hélder Câmara, 272, 278, 321
Dom Paulo Evaristo Arns, 337, 456
Domingos Faustino Sarmiento, 91
Domingos Jorge Velho, 23, 24
Dorothy Mae Stang, 400
Dutch West India Company, 19, 20
Egberto Gismonti (musician), 362, 407
Eldorado dos Carajás Massacre, 389, 390
Eleições do Cacete, 77,
Eliezer Batista da Silva, 326
Elizeth Cardoso (singer), 291
emboabas, 27, 194
Emiliano di Cavalcanti, 181, 184

Emílio Garrastazu Médici, 174, 307, 318, 404
Empresa Brasileira de Filmes (Embrafilme), 355, 357
Empresa Brasileira de Pesquisa Agropecuária (EMBRAPA), 329
Encilhamento Crisis (Economy), 115, 120, 126, 131, 237, 442
Enlightenment, 32, 38, 431
Ernesto Beckmann Geisel, 174, 296, 319, 327, 332, 337, 340, 344, 348, 405, 460
Ernesto Che Guevara, 259, 260, 309
Escola Superior de Guerra (ESG), 242, 333
escravo de ganho, 108, 442
Esses moços (song), 390
Estácio de Sá, 19, 222
Estácio de Sá (neighborhood in Rio de Janeiro), 222, 291
Estado Novo, 204, 206, 213, 215, 220, 273, 365, 431, 450
Estanislao Zeballos, 130, 142, 143, 446
Euclides da Cunha, 125, 126, 177, 439, 444
Eurico Gaspar Dutra, 213, 243
Eusébio de Queirós, 79, 81, 106
Evaristo da Veiga, 67
Expedição Roncador-Xingu, 254, 453
Farroupilha Revolution, 25, 65, 71, 72, 77, 80, 90, 125, 147, 172, 195, 262, 435
Federalist Revolution, 117, 119, 125, 145, 162, 163, 193, 271, 443
Felisberto Caldeira Brant Pontes, 54
Fernando Collor de Mello, 174, 372, 374, 376-83, 394, 397, 410, 412, 421, 463
Fernando Henrique Cardoso, 371, 384-88, 394, 401, 404, 414, 435
Ferreira Gullar, 269, 284, 294
Fidel Castro, 251, 279, 374
Filipe dos Santos, 27, 28, 35, 431
Florestan Fernandes, 278, 451, 454
Floriano Peixoto, 114-20, 123, 163, 178, 193, 253, 443
Foco Theory (guerrilla warfare), 299
Fome Zero (Zero Hunger Program), 398
Foral, 13
Formação econômica do Brasil (1959), 189, 445
France Antarctique, 18, 19
France Équinoxiale, 19
Francis I, 12, 18
Francisco Adolfo de Varnhagen, 21, 22, 253, 430
Francisco Alves Mendes Filho (Chico Mendes), 371, 463
Francisco Buarque de Hollanda, 359
Francisco Campos, 204, 298
Francisco de Lima e Silva, 61, 69
Francisco de Vitoria, 16
Francisco Julião Arruda de Paula (Peasant Leagues), 252, 285, 453
Francisco Matarazzo, 170
Francisco Pereira Coutinho, 15
Franklin Delano Roosevelt, United States President, 197, 207, 208, 211, 225
Free Jazz Festival, 406-09
Freemasonry, 84, 94, 95
Frei Caneca, Joaquim da Silva Rabelo, 60
French Artistic Mission of 1816, 44, 99
Fructuoso Rivera, 62
Funding Loan, 55, 128, 131, 149, 151, 189, 446
gafieira, 224, 225
Gaspar da Silveira Martins, 98, 118, 163
George Canning, 53, 54
Getúlio Dornelles Vargas, 26, 92, 107, 164, 168, 173, 183, 185, 188-94, 197-205, 207-15, 220-

27, 238-49, 258, 261, 264, 270, 273, 275, 297, 300, 307, 320, 326, 344, 365, 404, 449-54
Gianfrancesco Guarnieri (actor), 358
Gilberto Freyre, 161, 226, 279, 446, 452
Gilka Machado, 180
Glauber Rocha (filmmaker), 268, 287, 355
Globo Filmes, 413-15, 467
Gobineau, Joseph Arthur de, 85, 105, 437, 440
Golbery do Couto e Silva, 242, 299, 304, 318, 332, 333, 336, 337, 340, 344, 347, 405
Golpe da Maioridade, 74
Gonçalves Dias, 99
Good Neighbor Policy, 169, 197, 198, 208, 225
Governo Geral, 15, 16, 17, 20
Graça Aranha, 179, 181
Graciliano Ramos, 217, 281, 286
Grande sertão: veredas (1956), 282
Gregório de Matos e Guerra, 36
Gregório Fortunato, 241
Grover Cleveland, United States President, 121, 130
Guarani War, 25, 31
Guerrilha do Araguaia (1967), 323
Guerrilha do Caparaó (1966), 299
Guimarães Rosa, 280, 281, 286
Haitianism, 73
Hans-Joachim Koellreutter, 292
Haximu Massacre (1993), 384, 465
Heitor Villa-Lobos, 181, 183, 215, 406, 451, 452
Helio Jaguaribe, 279, 280, 452
Hélio Oiticica, 285, 354, 461
Henning Albert Boilesen, 310, 357
Herbert Hoover, United States President, 169
Hermes da Fonseca, 119, 142, 144-50, 157, 159, 186, 191, 271, 389, 404
Hermeto Pascoal (musician), 362

Hipólito Yrigoyen, Argentine President, 196
História da literatura brasileira: seus fundamentos econômicos (1938), 280
História Econômica do Brasil (1945), 226, 227
Holy Alliance, 47, 54, 432
Honório Hermeto Carneiro Leão, 70, 82, 86
House of Aviz, 12
Humberto de Alencar Castelo Branco, 174, 270, 296-306, 313, 317, 328, 332, 341, 352, 367, 385
Humberto Mauro (filmmaker), 228
Iara Iavelberg (MR8 guerrilla member), 300
Iberian Union, 17, 22, 24, 30, 57, 441
Ibicaba Farm Revolt, 106
ilusão de divisas (currency illusion), 231
Imperial Academy of Fine Arts, 44
Import Substitution Industrialization (ISI), 235, 244, 303
Inácio Luís Madeira de Melo, 52, 53
Inconfidência Mineira, 33, 255
Inês Etienne Romeu, 321
Initiative for the Integration of the Regional Infrastructure of South America (IIRSA), 393, 395, 465
Institutional Act (*Ato Institucional*), 296
Institutional Act 12 (AI-12), 313
Institutional Act 13 (AI-13), 313
Institutional Act 14 (AI-14), 313
Institutional Act 2 (AI-2), 297
Institutional Act 4 (AI-4), 298
Institutional Act 5 (AI-5), 309, 333, 341, 355, 363, 371, 459
Instituto Brasileiro de Ação Democrática (IBAD), 270, 271, 454
Instituto de Pesquisas e Estudos Sociais (IPES), 270, 271, 454

Instituto Superior de Estudos Brasileiros (ISEB), 235, 279, 280, 452,
Integralist Movement, 182, 209
Intentona Comunista, 203
Inter-American Development Bank (IDB), 251
inverted parliamentarism, 78
Ipanema (neighborhood in Rio de Janeiro), 292
Irineu Evangelista de Sousa, Baron of Mauá, 75
Isabel Cristina Leopoldina de Bragança, 96
Itamar Franco, 372, 381-84, 411
jagunço, 282
James Monroe, United States President, 54
James Norton (British naval officer), 64
Jânio da Silva Quadros, 255, 257-61, 263, 266, 294, 297, 302, 304, 321, 326, 363, 381
Japan Foundation, 328
Japanese biopiracy, 328
Japanese Cultural Imperialism, 328, 329, 459
Japanese Immigration, 140, 328, 357, 445
Jazz Samba (album, 1962), 293
Jean-Andoche Junot, 42
Jean-Baptiste Debret, 44, 99
Jeca Tatu (social stereotype), 179
Jimmy Carter, United States President, 340
João Baptista de Oliveira Figueiredo, 312, 341, 343, 347-50, 366, 460
João Cabral de Melo Neto, 280, 286
João Cândido (Revolt of the Whip, 1910), 146, 271
João do Rio, 178, 179
João Gilberto (musician), 292
João Goulart, 174, 188, 231, 238-40, 246, 255, 259, 261-63, 265, 271, 278, 294, 295, 297, 300, 304, 316, 319, 320, 326, 338, 339, 350, 352, 366, 372, 404, 454, 460
Joaquim José da Silva Xavier, Tiradentes, 34, 255
Joaquim José Rodrigues Torres, 79, 90
Joaquim Nabuco, 109, 442, 443
Joaquim Silvério dos Reis, 35
John F. Kennedy, United States President, 265
John Foster Dulles, 251, 447
John Maurice of Nassau, 21
John Pascoe Grenfell, 53
John VI of Portugal, 40, 42, 43-48, 51-53, 55, 58, 60-62, 88, 99, 103-05, 432
Johnny Alf (musician), 361
Jorge Amado, 212, 217, 218
José Américo de Almeida, 174, 185, 204, 217, 406
José Bonifácio de Andrada e Silva, 56, 59, 68, 108, 397, 433
José de Alencar, 100, 103, 227, 430, 439
José de Anchieta, 101
José do Patrocínio, 109
José Figueroa Alcorta, Argentine President, 142
José Gervasio Artigas, 61
José Gomes Pinheiro Machado, 118-20, 144, 145, 149, 150, 156, 157, 163, 164, 176, 186, 188, 191, 209, 261, 270, 271, 373, 404, 446, 449
José Joaquim Carneiro de Campos, 69
José Lins do Rego, 217
José Manuel Pando, Bolivian President, 133
José Maria da Silva Paranhos Júnior, Baron of Rio Branco, 130, 133, 152, 169, 197, 443
José Murilo de Carvalho, 58, 433, 435, 436, 438, 442, 443, 463

José Sarney, 256, 347, 366, 376, 421
Juan Antonio Lavalleja, 62, 63
Juan Domingo Perón, Argentine President, 214, 239, 247, 268
Juan Manuel de Rosas, 71, 80, 93
Júlio de Castilhos, 116, 118, 146, 162, 176, 188, 404
Júlio Prestes, 172
Julio Roca (Argentine president), 92, 141
Juscelino Kubitschek, 57, 244, 246, 248, 256, 257, 276, 279, 290, 297, 319, 321, 338, 381
Justice of Labor, 201
Justo José de Urquiza, 82, 88
kakurekurishitan (Japan), 140
Kasato Maru (Japanese immigration), 140
Korean War, 238
Latin American Free Trade Association (LAFTA), 252
Lei Áurea (1888), 109
Lei Celerada (1927), 167
Lei de Imprensa (1967), 299
Lei do Audiovisual (1993), 411
Lei Falcão (1976), 336
Lei Interpretativa do Ato Adicional de 1834 (1840), 77
lei para inglês ver (Law to fool the British), 81, 315, 390
Lei Rouanet (1991), 411
Lei Suplicy de Lacerda (1964), 301
Leny Andrade (singer), 361
Leonel Brizola, 262, 264, 269, 271, 273, 299, 344, 372, 373, 386, 397, 404, 405
Liberation Theology, 272, 278, 372, 456
Libero Badaró, 66
Libertas Quae Sera Tamen, 35
Liga Progressista, 86, 90
Lima Barreto, 178
Lindolfo Collor, 194, 405
Lord John Ponsonby, 64
Louis Ferdinand Cruls, 253

Luís Alves de Lima e Silva, Duke of Caxias, 73, 80, 90, 92, 437
Luis Carlos Bresser Pereira, 369
Luís Carlos Prestes, 164, 165, 168, 175, 202, 213, 231, 247
Luís Carlos Prestes-Miguel Costa Column, 165, 167, 168, 174, 193, 202, 448
Luís Filipe Gastão de Orléans, Count d'Eu, 91
Luiz Alberto Moniz Bandeira, 339, 460
Luiz Inácio Lula da Silva, 344, 373, 377, 386, 389-92, 394-99, 402, 404, 421, 422, 466
Lupicínio Rodrigues (composer), 290
lusotropicalism, 226
luzias, 76
Machado de Assis, 101, 180, 439
Macunaíma (1928), 189
Magalhães Pinto, 273
malandro, 225
Malês Revolt, 73, 436
Manabu Mabe, 185
Manifesto Antropofágico (1928), 182
Manifesto dos Coronéis (1954), 240
Manifesto dos Generais (1954), 242
Manifesto dos Mineiros (1943), 211
Manifesto Neoconcreto (Ferreira Gullar, 1959), 284
Manuel Alves Branco, 74, 78
Manuel Bandeira, 182
Manuel Congo Revolt, 73
Manuel de Carvalho Paes de Andrade, 60
Manuel Luís Osório, Marquis of Herval, 89
Manuel Oribe, 81
Mao's Long March, 165
Maragatos, 165
Marc Ferrez, 44
Marcha da Família com Deus pela Liberdade (1963), 271
Márcio Moreira Alves, 309

Maria Leopoldina, 66
Mário Covas, 371, 372
Mário de Andrade, 181, 182, 355, 449
Mario Henrique Simonsen, 342
Marquis of Pombal, 29, 31, 32, 101, 215
Martim Afonso de Sousa, 14
Mary I of Portugal, 33, 40
Matthew Fontaine Maury, 131
Max Weber, 13
Maysa (singer), 291
Mem de Sá, 19
Memorandum of Frustration (Raul Fernandes), 232, 246
Memórias do Cárcere (1953), 218
Mensalão Scandal (2005), 398
MERCOSUL, 349, 376, 393, 395, 450, 466
Miki Takeo, Japanese Prime Minister, 326
Military Club (Clube Militar), 97, 159, 234
Military Question, 94, 97
Ministério da Conciliação, 82
Ministério dos Marqueses, 68
Missão Aranha, 207
MOBRAL, 354
Modernismo (Brazilian Avant-garde), 7, 180, 182, 405, 449
Monique Gardenberg (arts producer), 407
Monroe Doctrine, 132
Montagu Mission (1923), 165
Monteiro Lobato, 179, 180, 194
Moreira César, Army Officer, 119, 125
Morte e Vida Severina (1955), 281
Movimento de Educação de Base (MEB), 278
Movimento Nacionalista Revolucionário (MNR), 299
Movimento Revolucionário 8 de Outubro (MR8), 299, 309, 321
Movimento Vem pra Rua, 420

MST (Landless Workers' Movement), 371, 389, 465
Música Popular Brasileira (MPB), 294
nacional desenvolvimentismo, 235, 279, 387
Nathan Mayer Rothschild, 54
National Department of Propaganda (DIP), 205
National Guard, 69, 97, 435
National Information Service (SNI), 318, 333
National Privatization Program (PND), 387
National Renewal Alliance (ARENA), 298
National Research Council (CNPq), 246
Naturalism (literature), 101, 102, 177, 178, 179, 439
Nelson Cavaquinho, 222-24, 289, 291, 294
Nelson Pereira dos Santos (filmmaker), 218, 268, 286, 355, 455
Nelson Rodrigues (playwright), 220, 286, 356, 416, 439, 451
Nelson Werneck Sodré, 279, 280, 439, 452
neoclassicism, 33-37, 44, 45
Neoconcretismo (Ferreira Gullar), 284
Nicolás Avellaneda, Argentine president, 92
Nicolas Durand de Villegagnon, 18, 19, 430
Nicolau Pereira de Campos Vergueiro, 69, 106
Night of Agony, 59, 433
Nippon Amazon Aluminium Company (NAAC), 326
noble emulation, Baron of Rio Branco, 152, 447
Noel Rosa, 222, 223, 289, 291
Noite das garrafadas, 67, 435
O Cortiço (1891), 101, 135, 177

O Guarani (1870), 103, 227
O Mulato (1881), 101, 109, 227
O Naturalismo no Brasil (1965), 291
O Pagador de Promessas (film, 1962), 280
O Petróleo é Nosso (campaign), 234
Olavo Bilac, 101
Olga Benário Prestes, 203, 218, 450
Olympio Mourão Filho, 203, 273, 307
Operação Bandeirante (OBAN), 310-12, 315, 318, 357, 404
Operação Brother Sam, 275
Operação Condor (Condor Operation), 319
Operation Pan America (Kubitschek), 250
Organização Revolucionária Marxista Política Operária (POLOP), 299
Orlando Silva (singer), 289
Orpheonic Singing, 215-17
Os Sertões (1902), 125, 177, 444
Oscar Niemeyer, 254
Oscarito (actor), 228
Osvaldo Aranha, 174, 207, 210, 238, 258, 450
Oswald de Andrade, 181, 182, 184, 359, 449
Ouro Fino Pact (1913), 149, 167, 171-73
padroado, 95
Palestine Liberation Organization (PLO), 349
Panther Cruiser Case, 141
Paraguayan War, 25, 64, 73, 75, 85, 87, 92, 95, 96, 104, 132, 145, 195, 296, 306
Partido dos Trabalhadores (PT), 372, 394
Partido Social Democrático (PSD), 213, 230
Partido Trabalhista Brasileiro (PTB), 213, 230, 238
Passeata dos Cem Mil (1968), 308

Patrícia Galvão (modernist author), 359
patrimonialism, 13, 104, 227, 254, , 370
Pau-Brasil Manifesto (1924), 182
pau-de-arara, 311, 321
Paul Vidal de la Blache, 130
Paulicéia Desvairada (Hallucinated City), 181
Paulino José Soares de Sousa, Viscount of Uruguay, 79, 80, 82, 436
Paulo Cesar Farias, 379, 380, 463
Paulo Freire, 278, 279, 352, 354, 358, 451, 455
Paulo Moura (saxophonist), 361
Paulo Salim Maluf, 322, 347, 349, 372, 373, 378, 460
Peasant Leagues, 252, 259, 269, 285, 453
Pedagogy of Liberation (Paulo Freire), 279
Pedro Álvares Cabral, 9, 15
Pedro de Alcântara, Pedro I, 2, 51, 54, 56, 58, 59, 61, 62, 64, 65-70.
Pedro de Alcântara, Pedro II, 72, 74-80, 84, 85, 87, 89-98, 103, 109, 112, 114, 123, 130, 214, 436
Pedro de Araújo Lima, 72, 73, 79
Percival Farquhar, 147, 326
Percy Sydney Smythe, 6th Viscount Strangford, 42, 62
Pereira Passos (Urban Reforms), 134, 140, 162, 176, 177, 179, 237, 444
Período Joanino, 40
Pernambucan Revolution of 1817, 39, 433
Pero Vaz de Caminha, 10, 429
Petrobras, 236, 245, 272, 334, 349, 398, 420, 421, 422
petrodollar recycling, 334
Phillip II of Spain, 20
Pica-paus, 163

Pinheiro Machado (Politician). *See* José Gomes Pinheiro Machado
Pinheiro Machado (Street in Rio de Janeiro), 209
Pinheiro Machado, City in Rio Grande do Sul, 447
Plano de Integração Nacional (PIN), 315
Plano de Metas (Kubitschek), 248, 250-52
Plano Real (1994), 381, 384, 385, 388, 391, 392, 396
Plano Trienal (Celso Furtado), 262, 265, 267, 302
Platine Immobility, 80
Platine Questions, 64, 79, 434, 437
Platine War, 64, 82, 83, 437
Plínio Salgado, 181, 182, 201, 204, 209
Política das Salvações (Politics of Salvations, 1910-1914), 145, 146, 157
Política do café com leite (Coffee with Milk Politics), 144
Política Externa Independente (PEI), 258, 259, 264
Popeye Operation, 273
pornochanchada (cinema), 356, 461
Positivist philosophy, 84
Potreiro das Almas, 120
Pra Frente Brasil (film, 1982), 357
Priest Antônio Vieira, 36, 42
Primeiro Comando da Capital (PCC), 400
Prinetti Decree, 140
Programa de Ação Econômica do Governo (PAEG), 296, 301-03, 307, 313, 385, 456
Programa de Aceleração do Crescimento (PAC), 402, 420, 466
Programa de Desenvolvimento do Cerrado (PRODECER), 329, 330
Projeto Mariani (Education), 277

Prudente de Morais, 120, 122-24, 126-28, 131, 140
Putsch Integralista, 209
Questão Christie, 87
Quilombo dos Palmares, 23, 24, 431
Quintino Bocaiuva, 92, 121, 131
Rachel de Queiroz, 217, 281
Radamés Gnattali, 225
Raízes do Brasil (1936), 226, 286
Raúl Alfonsín, Argentine President, 376
Raul de Souza (trombonist), 361, 362
Raymundo Faoro, 13, 146, 429, 446
Realist Regionalism (literature), 179
Rede Globo (media conglomerate), 396-98, 401, 413, 414, 419, 466, 467
Reforma Rivadávia Corrêa, 353
Reformas de Base (João Goulart), 266, 278
Religious Question, 94, 438
República do Galeão, 242
Republican Conservative Party, Pinheiro Machado, 144, 150
Republican Manifesto, 92, 121
Republican Party of São Paulo, 92, 93, 150, 156
Republicans of May 14, 97, 110
Revolt of the Whip, 271, 446
Revolução Praieira, 70, 79
Revolutions of 1820, 47
Roberto Campos, 263, 301, 302
Roberto Simonsen, 170
Roda Viva (play), 359, 360
Rodrigo de Sousa Coutinho, 42, 432
Roque Sáenz Peña, Argentine President, 196, 197
Rothschild Bank, 151
rubber boom (1900-1913), 83, 129, 132, 133, 148, 149
Rubem Fonseca (author), 363, 411, 415, 440
Rubens Paiva, 320, 322

Rui Barbosa, 109, 115, 116, 128, 136, 137, 145, 150, 156, 157, 167, 180, 402, 448
Rural Workers' Statute (1963), 267
Ruth Escobar Theatre, 358
Ruy Guerra (filmmaker), 268, 287, 288, 409, 416
Saavedra Lamas Anti-War and Non-Aggression Pact, 197
Sabinada, 73, 436
Salvador Allende, Chilean President, 312, 331
Salvador de Mendonça, 121, 142
samba, 221-26, 256, 289-94, 360, 451, 155
Samba da legalidade (song), 294
samba de partido-alto, 289
samba de raiado, 289
samba de roda, 289
samba-canção, 289-92, 361, 455
samba-exaltação, 226
San Tiago Dantas, 264, 265, 267
Santa Elmira Massacre, 389
São Paulo Forum, 374, 395, 396, 400, 404, 466
Saquarema Trinity, 79, 93
saquaremas, 76
Sebastião José de Carvalho e Melo, Marquis of Pombal, 28, 33, 431
Seibi Group (visual arts), 184
Semana de Arte Moderna (Modern Art Week of 1922), 161, 180, 449
Sena Madureira, 96
Sepé Tiaraju, 31
Sérgio Buarque de Holanda, 226, 227, 434, 437, 438
Sérgio Paranhos Fleury, 310, 338, 404
Serviço Nacional de Informações (SNI), 299
Servile Question, 94
sesmaria, 14, 56, 57, 430
Setembrada, 70
slavery, 23, 29, 35, 38, 39, 55, 56, 68, 96-98, 103, 105, 107-09, 116, 139, 241, 269, 431, 432, 435, 436, 438, 439, 441, 442, 452, 465
slaves, 14, 17, 23, 24, 56, 69, 71, 73, 81, 93, 96, 100, 107-09, 116, 134, 140, 146, 226, 241, 274, 441, 442
Sociedade Pro-Arte Moderna (SPAM), 184
Sor Joana Angélica, 52, 53
South American Dreadnought Race, 154
Stan Getz, 293
Stuart Edgart Angel Jones, 321
sugar cane, 13, 20, 21, 28, 39, 218
Superintendência do Desenvolvimento do Nordeste (SUDENE), 250
Sylvio Frota, 307, 332
Tamoios, 18, 19, 102
Tampico Affair, 153, 154
Tancredo Neves, 265, 344, 347, 366, 367, 371
Tarsila do Amaral, 183
Taubaté Accord, 135-38, 148, 171, 445
Teatro Brasileiro de Comédia (TBC), 358, 461
Teatro de Arena (São Paulo), 358, 461
Tenentista Movement, 158-62, 164, 168, 173-75, 200, 447, 449
Teresa Cristina of Bourbon, 78
Theatre of the Oppressed (Augusto Boal), 358
Theodore Roosevelt, United States President, 132, 169
Thomas Cochrane, 53, 61
Tito de Alencar Lima, Frei Tito, 310, 312, 457
Tizuka Yamazaki (filmmaker), 357
Tomé de Sousa, 14-17, 101
Tomie Ohtake, 185
Trans-Amazonian Highway, 315, 325

Treaties of 1810, 42, 54, 55, 74, 78, 81, 82, 127
Treaty of Ayacucho (1867), 132, 133
Treaty of Fontainebleau, 41
Treaty of Madrid, 30, 32, 431
Treaty of Methuen, 29, 30, 41
Treaty of Petropolis (1903), 133, 139, 195, 196
Treaty of Tilsit, 41
Treaty on the Non-Proliferation of Nuclear Weapons (NTP), 266
Triste Fim de Policarpo Quaresma (1911), 178
Truman Doctrine, 231
Tupi language, 32, 182, 184, 355, 431
Tupinambá, 15, 18, 455
Tupiniquim, 9, 10, 181
Turma do Estácio, 222
Typhis Pernambucano, 60
Ultramontanism, 94
UNASUL, 395
União Democrática Nacional (UDN), 213, 231, 239
União Democrática Ruralista (UDR), 370
União Nacional dos Estudantes (UNE), 278, 285, 454
United Nations Conference on Trade and Development (UNCTAD), 317
United Nations Economic Commission for Latin America (UNECLA), 235
United Provinces of the River Plate, 43, 56, 61, 63
unwritten alliance, 142, 152, 169
Uruguayan War of Independence, 63
uti possidetis, 31, 133, 148

Vaccine Revolt (1904), 134-36
Vala de Perus, 322, 323, 458
Vale do Rio Doce (mining company), 297, 326
Vanguarda Popular Revolucionária (VPR), 299, 308, 320
Venancio Flores, 88
Venceslau Brás, 144, 145, 148, 150, 154-56
Vernon A. Walters, 270, 331
Vicente Celestino (singer), 289
Victor Assis Brasil (saxophonist), 361, 362, 462
Victor Meirelles, 10, 22, 104, 429, 437
Vidas secas (1938), 218, 268, 281, 286
Vila Rica Revolt, 28, 125
Vinicius de Moraes, 221, 292
Viscount of Rio Branco, 94
Vittorio Capellaro (filmmaker), 227
Vladimir Herzog, 336, 337, 456
Walter Hugo Khouri (filmmaker), 356
Walter Salles Jr. (filmmaker), 411
War of the Cabanos, 70
War of the Mascates, 16, 60, 430
Washington Consensus, 373, 378
Washington Luís, 155, 167, 168, 172, 175, 191, 192, 458
William Dougal Christie, 86
William McKinley, United States President, 132
William Sidney Smith, 62
Woodrow Wilson, United States President, 153
Yanomami, 383, 384, 464, 465
Zacarias de Góis e Vasconcelos, 86, 87, 89
Zélia Cardoso de Mello, 378